THE FERNS
OF
SOUTHERN INDIA

THE FERNS

OF

SOUTHERN INDIA.

Being Descriptions and Plates of the Ferns

OF

THE MADRAS PRESIDENCY.

BY

MAJOR R. H. BEDDOME

GYAN

Published by

Gyan Publishing House
5, Ansari Road
Daryaganj, New Delhi-110002
Phone: 011-47034999, 9811692060
E-mail: books@gyanbooks.com

Distribution Network
gyanbooks.com
India, USA, Canada, UK, Australia, France

ISBN: 978-81-212-8294-9 (PB)
First Published, 1863

2nd Impression 2023

Printed at: Gyan Press, Delhi.

THE FERNS OF SOUTHERN INDIA
Author: R. H. BEDDOME

THE FERNS

OF

SOUTHERN INDIA.

Being Descriptions and Plates of the Ferns

OF

THE MADRAS PRESIDENCY.

BY

MAJOR R. H. BEDDOME,

INSPECTOR OF FORESTS, MADRAS.

SECOND EDITION.

MADRAS:

HIGGINBOTHAM AND CO.

1873.

Synopsis

OF

THE GENERA OF FERNS

OF SOUTHERN INDIA.

Classification, (after Moore.)

FILICALES.—Acrogenous plants, with dorsal or marginal one-celled spore-cases.

* *Spore-cases furnished with a jointed ring, which is usually nearly complete, sometimes rudimentary.* — Order. POLYPODIACEÆ.

† Spore-cases not valvate.

|| Ring vertical, nearly complete, Spore-cases usually stalked, gibbous, bursting transversely. — Tribe I. POLYPODINEÆ.

[A] Receptacles universal, *i. e.,* occupying almost or quite the entire disk of the fertile fronds, both veins and parenchyma. — § I. Acrosticheæ.

[B] Receptacles Local, circumscribed, *i. e.,* confined to determinate parts of the veins, definite in form.

(1) Sori transverse to the veins (when distinct veins are present); parallel or sub-parallel with the midrib or margin; more or less elongated, usually linear, occasionally oblong or lunately curved; rarely punctiform (then marginal with transverse indusia.)

[a 1] Receptacles seated on or approximate to the midrib, therefore costal or sub-costal (often at the same time marginal by the contraction of the frond); linear or oblong.

(a) Sori linear superficial indusiate. — § 2. Lomarieæ.

(β) Sori linear or oblong, superficial or immersed, non-indusiate. — § 3. Pleurogrammeæ.

[a 2] Receptacles marginal or sub-marginal, (rarely medial) always remote from the midrib, usually linear; sometimes oblong or punctiform.

(a) Sori non-indusiate, (mostly occupying a groove or furrow, sometimes superficial), linear.

(a) Sub-marginal (often seated in a shallow dorsal furrow.) — § 4. Taenitideæ.

(β) Marginal (always in an extorse marginal furrow.) — § 5. Vittarieæ.

(b) Sori indusiate, superficial, (linear, oblong or rotundate.)

(a) Indusium bursting along its outward margin, attached interiorly. — § 6. Lindsæeæ.

(β) Indusium bursting along its outward margin, attached exteriorly.

Receptacles resupinate, *i. e.,* the Spore-cases attached on the under-surface of the indusium. — § 7. Adianteæ.

Receptacles normal, *i. e.*, the Spore-cases attached to the surface of the frond.

— punctiform. § 8. Cheilantheæ.

— linear, transverse. § 9. Pterideæ.

[*a* 3] Receptacles short, transverse or arcuate on the venules, sub-parallel with the midrib or margin.

— Sori non-indusiate. § 10. Menisciеæ.

(2) Sori parallel with the venation, oblique (rarely sub-parallel) to the midrib, oblong linear or more or less elongated, sometimes compound.

(*a*) Sori indusiate, lateral or sub-lateral on the veins. § 11. Asplenieæ.

(*b*) Sori naked or spuriously indusiate, dorsal on the veins.

(*α*) Receptacles linear, variously reticulato-anastomosed. § 12. Hemionitideæ.

(*β*) Receptacles linear, simple or forked, (sometimes short linear) *i. e.*, oblong. § 13. Gymnogrammeæ.

(*c*) Receptacles oblong, contiguous, parallel, the Spore-cases becoming confluent and simulating a broad marginal sorus (spuriously indusiate.) § 14. Platylomeæ.

(3) Sori punctiform, (rarely in § 15, sub-oblong, or by confluence more or less elongate.)

(*a*) Sori naked, *i.e.*, without true indusia; (fertile fronds sometimes contracted with involute margins—spuriously indusiate.) § 15. Polypodieæ.

(*b*) Sori indusiate, *i. e.*, with superior indusia.

(*α*) Indusium reniform or peltate, attached by the sinus or centre, free at the margins, (fertile fronds sometimes involutely contracted.) § 16. Aspidieæ.

(*β*) Indusium rotundate, attached transversely to the vein by its base, the margins free. § 17. Cystopterideæ.

(*c*) Indusium roundish or oblong, adherent at the base and margins, opening in front, *i. e.*, exteriorly. § 18. Davallieæ.

(*c*) Sori involucrate, *i. e.*, with inferior indusia.

(*a*) Indusium or involucre distinctly within the margin of the frond, forming an entire lobed or fimbriated cup; Sori therefore within a dorsal cup. § 19. Peranemeæ.

|| || *Ring more or less obliquely vertical, nearly complete, narrow, spore-cases crowded, sessile or sub-sessile, oblique-laterally compressed, or sub-compressed, bursting horizontally.* Tribe 2. CYATHEINEÆ.

[A] Sori involucrate, *i. e.*, indusia inferior, (receptacles elevated.)

(1) Fructifications dorsal. § 1. Cyatheæ.

[B] Sori naked, *i. e.*, without indusia; (receptacles elevated.) § 2. Alsophileæ.

|| || || *Ring horizontally or rarely obliquely transverse complete, spore-cases sessile or sub-sessile, usually vertically compressed, bursting longitudinally, i. e., vertically.*

[A] Ring zonal, *i. e.*, spore-cases girt by the ring.

(1) Sori-dorsal; (fronds rigid opaque with oligocarpus Sori, and globose-pyriform, spore-cases.) Tribe 3. GLEICHENINEÆ.

(2) Sori extrose-marginal (fronds usually pellucid membranaceous, with polycarpous sori and lenticular spore-cases.) Tribe 4. TRICHOMANINEÆ.

[B] Ring apical, *i. e.*, spore-cases crowned by the convergent Striæ of the ring—radiate striate at the Apex. Tribe 5. SCHIZÆINEÆ.

(1) Striæ united at the Apex, without any vacant space, (spore-cases attached laterally;) scandent plants. § 1. Lygodieæ.

(2) Striæ disjoined, forming an orbicular apical vacuity, (spore-cases attached basally;) dwarf herbaceous plants. § 2. Schizæeæ.

|| || || || *Ring rudimentary or incomplete (wanting one-third or more;) very broad, flat obliquely vertical; spore-cases sessile or sub-sessile, globose.*

	(Aquatic Annual proliferous ferns, with contracted fertile fronds.)	Tribe 6. CERATOPTERIDINEÆ.
† †	Spore-cases two valved, bursting vertically at the apex. Ring rudimentary, obliquely transverse near the apex.	Tribe 7. OSMUNDINEÆ.
* *	Spore-cases without a jointed ring.	
[A]	Fructifications dorsal on normal fronds, (vernation circinate or incurved.)	Order. MARATTIACEÆ.
(1)	Sori-oblong distinct, longitudinally bi-valved.	Tribe 1. MARATTINEÆ.
	(*a*) Spore-cases free, crowded in two opposite linear series.	§ 1. Angiopterideæ.
	(B) Spore-cases concrete, in two opposite linear series.	§ 2. Marattieæ.
[B]	Fructifications marginal, on rachiform fronds or branches, (vernation straight.)	Order. OPHIOGLOSSACEÆ.

LYCOPODALES.—Acrogenous plants with axillary radical or petiolar one-four or many-celled spore-cases.

*	Spore-cases one-three-celled, in the axils of the Stem-leaves or bracts.	Order. LYCOPODIACEÆ.
	—Stems leafy ; Spore-cases one-three-celled.	LYCOPODIEÆ.

ANALYTICAL TABLE OF GENERA

WITH THEIR SYNONYMS.

Order POLYPODIACEÆ. *Tribe* POLYPODINEÆ.

§ 1. ACROSTICHEÆ.

(*a*) *Fronds wholly fertile.*

* *Veins free, i. e., disunited at the apices of their branches.*

† *Veins simple forked or pinnate.*

1 POLYBOTRYA. *Humb. et Bonpl.* 1810.

Egenolfia, Schott, 1834.	Granulina, Bory ; Fée, 1844.
Lacaussadea, Gaudichaud, 1836-37.	Botryothallus, Kl. M. S. 1846.
Ectoneura, Fée, 1844.	Psomiocarpa, Presl. 1849.
	Microstaphyla, Presl. 1849.

† † *Veins parallel forked.*

‡ *Fronds simple.*

2 ELAPHOGLOSSUM, *Schott*, 1834.

? Phyllitis, Necker, 1790.

Acrostichum Fée, 1844.

* * *Veins transversely combined in a single series.*

† *Veins united to form narrow costal Areoles.*

3 STENOCHLÆNA, *J. Sm.* 1841.

Cafraria, Presl. 1849.

Lomariobotrys, Fée, 1851.

* * * *Veins reticulated, i. e., forming a net work.*

† *Venules arcuato-Angularly united between the pinnate veins, with excurrent veinlets.*

4 PÆCILOPTERIS, *Presl.* (Esch. 1827 emend) 1836.

Bolbitis, Schott, 1834.	Cyrtogonium, J. Sm. 1841.
Campium, Presl. 1836.	Heteroneuron, Fée, 1844.

(*b*) *Fronds fertile on the upper pinnæ only.*

* *Veins uniformly reticulated.*

5 ACROSTICHUM, *L.* 1737, (emend) Presl. 1836.

Chrysodium, Fée, 1844.

§ 2 LOMARIEÆ.

(a) *Veins free, or not uniting at their apices.*

* *Sori marginal, (the fronds contracted.)*

6 LOMARIA, *Willd.* 1809.

Onoclea, Lin. (Pt.) 1751.
Stegania, Brown, 1810.
Lomaridium, Presl. 1849.
Polygramma, Presl. 1849.
Parablechnum, Presl. (pt.) 1849.
Paralomaria, Fée, 1851.

** *Sori distinctly within the margin.*

7 BLECHNUM, *Lin.* 1754.

Orthogramma, Presl. 1849.
Spicanta, Presl. 1849.
Blechnopsis, Presl. 1849.
Diafnia, Presl. 1849.
Moesthema, Presl. 1849.
Distaxia, Presl. 1849.
Parablechnum, Presl. (pt.) 1849.

§ 3. PLEUROGRAMMEÆ.

(a) *Veins compoundly anastomosing.*

* *Fructification borne on the contracted apices of the fronds.*

8 HYMENOLEPIS, *Klfs.* 1824.

Belvisa Mirb. (pt.) 1803.
Macroplethus, Presl. 1849.
Hyalolepsis, Kze. 1850

** *Fructification occupying distinct contracted fronds.*

9 GYMNOPTERIS, *Bernh.* 1800, (emend.)

Leptochilus, Klfs. 1824.
Dendroglossa Presl. 1849.

§ 4. TÆNITIDEÆ.

(a) *Veins uniform, reticulated, with included free veinlets in the Areoles.*

* *Sori linear, continuous, near the margin.*

10 DRYMOGLOSSUM, *Presl.* 1836.

Pteropsis, Desv. (pt.) 1827.
Heteropteris, Fée, 1842.
Neurodium, Fée, 1842.
Paltonium, Presl. 1849.
Lemmaphyllum, Presl. 1849.

(b) *Veins straight, free, (except where combined by the marginal receptacles.)*

11 TÆNIOPSIS, *J. Sm.* 1841.

Chilogramma, Bl. (pt.) 1828.
Cuspidaria, Fée (pt.) 1851.
Tærniopteris, Hook. 1841.
Ampelopteris, Kl. 1847.

§ 5. VITTARIEÆ.

12 VITTARIA, *Sm.* 1793.

Runcinaria, K. Mull. 1854.
Aristaria, K. Mull. 1854.
Parenchymaria, K. Mull. 1854.

§ 6. LINDSÆEÆ.

(a) *Veins free (except where combined by the receptacles.)*

13 LINDSÆA, *Dryand, MS.—Smith*, 1793.

Lindsaya, Klfs. 1824.	Isoloma, J. Sm. 1841.
Hymenotomia, Gaud. 1826.	Lindsaynium, Fée, 1851.

(b) *Veins reticulated, without free included veinlets.*

14 SCHIZOLOMA, Gaud, MS.—Bory, 1824; Gaud. 1826.

Pericoptis, Wall, Hb. 1823.	Diellia, Brackenridge, 1854.
Synaplebium, J. Sm. 1841.	

§ 7. ADIANTEÆ.

(a) *Veins free.*

15 ADIANTUM, *Lin.* 1737.

Adiantellum, Presl. 1836.	Synechia, Fée, 1851.
Apotomia, Fée, 1851.	Mesopleura, Moore MS. 1853.

§ 8. CHEILANTHEÆ.

(a) *Sori marginal, terminal on the veins.*

* *Rhizome tufted or short creeping; Sori dispersed along the margins of the segments; fronds usually small membranaceous or sub-coriaceous.*

† *Indusia roundish, or by confluence more or less elongate (often Pteroid.)*

16 CHEILANTHES, *Sw.* 1806.

Gymnia, Hamilton MS. Don. 1825.	Myriopteris, Fée, 1851.
	Aleuritopteris, Fée, 1851.
Othonoloma, Lk. "Olim."	Cheiloplecton, Fée, 1857.
Physapteris, Presl. 1836.	Synochlamys, Fée, 1857.

** *Rhizome creeping extensively; Sori usually at the axil of the segments; fronds large herbaceous.*

17 HYPOLEPIS, *Bernh.* 1806.

§ 9. PTERIDEÆ.

(a) *Veins free.*

* *Sori oppositely marginal and connivent on the narrow segments.*

18 ONYCHIUM, *Klfs.* 1820.

Cænopheris, Thunb. 1793 (reduct): Presl. 1849.

Leptostegia, D. Don. 1825.

** *Sori linear continuous marginal.*

† *Indusium membranaceous.*

19 PTERIS, *Lin.* 1737 (emend.)

Thelypteris, Adanson, 1763.	Lytoneuron, Kl. 1847.
Cincinalis Gleditsch, 1764.	Nymphopteris, Webb. et. Berth. 1847.
Oetosis, Necker, 1790.	
Monogonia, Presl. 1836.	Macropteris, Webb. et. Berth. 1847.

Eupteris, Agardh, 1839.
Ornithopteris, Agardh, 1839.
Pteridopsis, Link. 1841.
Eupteris, Newm. 1845.
Pycnodoria, Presl. 1849.
Lonchitidium, Fée, 1851.

(*b*) *Costal veins only arcuately anastomosing.*

20 CAMPTERIA, *Presl.* 1836.

§ 10. MENISCIEÆ.

(*a*) *Venules regularly anastomosing arcuato-transversely between the pinnate parallel veins.*

21 MENISCIUM, *Schreb*, 1791.

Ampelopteris—Kunze.

§ 11. ASPLENIEÆ.

(*a*) *Indusia simple, distinct.*

* *Veins free.*

† *Sori linear, elongate, marginal on the contracted rachiform segments ; fronds, flabelliform.*

22 ACTINOPTERIS, *Link*, 1841.

Belvisia, Mirbel, (pt.) 1803.

† † *Sori linear or oblong, oblique.*

23 ASPLENIUM, *Lin.* 1737.

Caenopteris, Bergins, 1782.
Darea, Jussieu, 1789.
Onopteris, Neck. 1790.
Phyllitis, Moench, 1794.
Allantodia, R. Br. (pt.) 1810.
Acropteris, Link, 1833.
Amesium, Newm. 1844.
Homaloneuron, Kl. 1847.
Tarachia, Presl. 1849.
Brachysorus, Presl. 1849.
Hypochlamys, Fée, 1851.
Darœastrum, Fée, 1851.

† † † *Sori lunate or more or less hippocrepiform.*

24 ATHYRIUM, *Roth.* 1788, (reduct.)

Solenopteris, Zenker, MS. 1835. Kze. 1851.

* * *Veins parallel, transversely combined at the margin.*

25 THAMNOPTERIS, *Presl.* (1836) ; 1849.

Neottopteris, J. Sm. 1841.

* * * *Veins reticulated, the marginal veinlets free.*

† *Indusia vaulted ; fronds membranaceous, naked.*

26 ALLANTODIA, R. Br. 1810, (reduct) ; id. 1830.

(*b*) *Indusia connate in pairs back to back.*

* *Veins free.*

27 DIPLAZIUM, *Sw.* 1800.

Lotzea Kl. et. Karst, 1847.

* * *Veins conniventy anastomosing.*

28 CALLIPTERIS, *Bory*, 1804.

Digrammaria, Hook. (non. Pr.) 1840. | Anisogonium, Presl. 1836.
Microstegia, Presl. (pt.) 1849.

§ 12. HEMIONITIDÆ.

(*a*) *Veins uniform reticulated.*

* *Sori continuous.*

† *Sori partially reticulated usually immersed.*

29 ANTROPHYUM, *Klfs.* 1824.

Solenopteris, Wall, Herb. 1823.

† † *Sori universally reticulated, superficial.*

30 HEMIONITIS, *Lin.* 1742.

§ 13. GYMNOGRAMMEÆ.

(*a*) *Veins free.*

* *Sori linear oblong, simple.*

31 GRAMMITIS, *Sw.* 1800.

Chilopteris, Presl. 1836.
Pleurogramma, R. Br. 1838.
Leptogramma, J. Sm. 1841.
Trichothemelium, Kze. 1851.
Trichocalymma, Zenker, 1851.
Mecosorus, Kl. (pt.) 1847.

(*b*) *Veins uniform reticulated, with free included veinlets in the Areoles.*

32 LOXOGRAMMA, (*Bl.* 1828) *Presl.* 1836.

§ 14. PLATYLOMEÆ.

(*a*) *Fertile divisions plane conformable with the sterile.*

33 PLATYLOMA, *J. Sm.* 1841

Pellaea, Link, 1841. | Crypteris, Nutt, MS. Hook. 1857.

§ 15. POLYPODIEÆ.

(*a*) *Margins of the fronds not indusioid.*

* *Veins free.*

† *Sori globose, rarely sub-elongated, distinct.*

34 POLYPODIUM, *Lin.* 1737 (reduct.)

Psidopodium, Necker, 1790.
Adenophorus, Gaud. MS. Bory, 1824, Gaud. 1826.
Marginaria, Bory, (pt.) 1824 :1826.
Gymnocarpium, Newm. 1851.
Ctenopteris, Newm. 1851.
Gymnodium, A. Br. 1852.
Arthropteris, J. Sm. 1854.

Lastrea, Bory, (pt.) 1824.
Amphoradenium, Desv. 1827.
Ctenopteris, Bl. 1828. Presl. 1836, Kunze, 1846.
Dicranopteris, Bl.
Phegopteris, Presl. 1836, Fée, 1851.
Lepicystis, J. Sm. (pt.) 1841.
Cryptosorus, Fée, 1843.
Glaphyropteris, Presl. 1847.
Monachosorum, Kze. 1848.
Pseudathyrium, Newm. 1851.
Catenularia, Zipp. MS. Metten, 1856.
Cœlopteris, A. Br. MS. Metten, 1856.
Peptostegia, Zipp. MS. Metten, 1856.

Thylacopteris, Kunze, MS. Metten, 1856.
Anopodium, J. Sm. 1857.
Catopodium, J. Sm. 1857.
Cyslidium, J. Sm. MS.
Dryopteris, J. Sm. MS.
Desmopodium, J. Sm. MS.

* * *Veins conniventl y anastomosing.*

35 GONIOPTERIS, *Presl.* 1836.

Glyphotænium, J. Sm. 1854.

* * * *Veins reticulated, with free included veinlets in the areoles.*

† *Free veinlets divaricate, i. e. variously directed.*

‡ *Fronds clothed usually densely beneath (with stellate hair-scales.)*

36 NIPHOBOLUS, *Klfs.* 1824.

Pyrrosia, Mirbel, 1803.
Candollea, Mirb. (pt.) 1803.
Cyclophorus, Desv. 1811, Presl. 1849.

Scytopteris, Presl. 1836 : 1849.
Craspedaria, Link. (pt.) 1841.
Galeoglossa, Presl. 1849.
Sphaerostichum, Presl. 1849.
Polycampium, Presl. 1849.
Apalophlehia, Presl. 1849.
Gyrosorium, Presl. 1849.
Niphopsis, J. Sm. 1856.

‡ ‡ *Fronds naked, or bearing scattered peltate scales.*

|| *Sori globose (rarely short oblong, or by confluence elongated,) poly-carpous ; fronds articulated with the rhizome.*

¶ *Fronds simple pinatifid or pinnate, monomorphous, or the fertile somewhat narrowed.*

37 PLEOPELTIS, *H. et. B.* 1810 (extens.)

Marginaria, Bory, (pt.) 1824.
Atactosia, Bl. 1828.
Microsorium, Link, 1833.
Anaxetum, Schott, 1834.
Microgramma, Presl. 1836
Pleuridium, Presl. 1836.
Phymatodes, Presl. 1836.
Drynaria, Presl. (pt.) 1836.
Chrysopteris, Link. pt. 1841.
Phyllitidis, J. Sm. 1841.
Lepisorus, J. Sm. 1841.
Anapeltis, J. Sm. 1846.
Microterus, Presl. 1849.
Symplecium, Kze. 1846.
Phytogenia, J. Sm. MS. Olim.
Melanopteris, J. Sm. MS.

¶ ¶ *Fronds dimorphous, the Sterile dwarfed, Sessile, querciform.*

(*a*) *Fertile and Sterile Segments of the normal fronds uniform.*

38 DRYNARIA, (*Bory.* 1825,) *J. Sm.* 1841.

§ 16. ASPIDIEÆ.

[A] *Indusia orbicular, peltately affixed.*

* *Veins reticulated, with free included veinlets.*

† *Veins compoundly anastomosing, with included divaricate free veinlets.*

39 ASPIDIUM, *Sw.* 1800, (reduct) : *Schott*, 1834.

Bathmium, Presl. 1836 : Link, 1841.
Proferea, Presl. 1849.
Podopeltis, Fée, 1851.

† † *Veins angularly anastomosing, with 1-3 excurrent veinlets in the areoles, (sometimes the upper venules only anastomosing.)*

40 CYRTOMIUM, *Presl.* 1836.

Phanerophlebia, Presl. 1836.
Amblia, Presl. 1836.

* * *Veins free.*

41 POLYSTICHUM, *Roth*, 1788, (reduct), *Schott*, 1834.

Aspidium, Sw. (pt.) 1800.
Sectaria, Cav. (pt.) 1802.
Hypopeltis, Rich. 1803.
Rumohra, Raddi, 1825.
Hemigonium, J. Sm. 1841.
Cyclopeltis, J. Sm. 1846.
Peltochlaena, Fée, 1851.
Hemicardion, Fée, 1851.

[B] *Indusium reniform, affixed at the sinus.*

* *Veins reticulated.*

† *Fronds monomorphous, or conformable.*

‡ *Veins compoundly anastomosing, often with free included divaricate veinlets in the areoles.*

42 SAGENIA, *Presl.* 1863.

Polydictyum, Presl. 1849.
Microbrochis, Presl. 1849.
Cardiochlaena, Fée, 1851.
Lobochlaena, Fée, 1851.
Phlebiogonium, Fée, 1851.

‡ ‡ *Veins arcuately anastomosing, forming elongated costal areoles, the marginal ones free.*

43 PLEOCNEMIA, *Presl.* 1836.

Haplodictyum, 1849.

* * *Veins conniventy anastomosing.*

44 NEPHRODIUM, *Rich.* 1803 (restrict) : *Schott* 1834.

Aspidium, Sw. (pt.) 1800.
Cyclosorus, Link, 1841.
Abacopteris, Fée, 1843.
Pronephrium, Presl. 1849.
Arsenopteris, Webb et Berth, (pt.) 1847.
Plectochlaena, Fée, 1851.

* * * *Veins free.*

† *Veins simple or pinnate, the lower anterior venule (sometimes more) soriferous.*

45 LASTREA, (*Bory.*, 1824, (mutat) *Presl.* 1836.

Dryopteris, Adamson, 1763 : Schott, 1834.	Arsenopteris, Webb et B. (pt.) 1847.
Gleichenia, Necker, 1790.	Gymnothalamium, Zenker : MS. Kze. 1851.
Aspidium, Sw. (pt.) 1800.	Hemestheum, Newm. 1851.
Nephrodium, Rich. (pt.) 1803.	Lophodium, Newm. 1851.
Arthrobotrys, Wall. 1828.	Camptodium, Fée, 1851.
Thelypteris, Schott, 1884.	Oochlamys, Fée, 1851.
Hypodematium, Kze. 1837.	Pachyderris, J. Sm. MS. (1854).
Amauropelta, Kze. 1840.	Pycnopteris, Moore, 1854.
Dichasium, A. Br. 1841.	
Lastreastrum, Presl. 1849.	

† † *Veins parallel forked, soriferous at or near the base ; fronds simple, articulated.*

46 OLEANDRA, *Cav.* 1802.

Neuronia, Don. 1825.

Ophiopteris, Reinw. 1825.

‡ ‡ ‡ *Veins pinnately forked, soriferous at their apices ; fronds pinnate, the pinnæ articulated.*

47 NEPROLEPIS, *Schott*, 1834.

Nephrodium, Link, 1841.

Lepidoneuron, Fée, 1851.

§ 17. CYSTOPTERIDEÆ.

(a) *Sori terminal, rarely axillary in the forks of the venules ; fronds membranaceous or herbaceous.*

48 ACROPHORUS, *Presl.* 1836.

Lencostegia, Presl. 1836.

Odontoloma, J. Sm. 1842.

(b) *Sori terminal vertical, rarely subterminal and oblique, fronds small, coriaceous.*

49 HUMATA, *Cau.* 1801.

Pachypleuria, Presl. 1836.

Pteroneuron, Fée, 1851.

§ 18. DAVALLIEÆ.

(a) *Sori intramarginal ; indusium semi-orbicular, or half cup shaped membranaceous.*

50 MICROLEPIA, *Presl.* 1836.

Scyphofilix, Aub. du Petit. Thouars, 1811.	Neuropteris, Desv. 1827.
Saccoloma, Klfs. 1820.	Selenidium, Kze. 1837.
	Tapeinidium, Presl. 1849.

(b) *Sori marginal.*

* *Indusium tubulose, or cup shaped membranaceous.*

51 DAVALLIA, *Smith*, 1793.

Wibelia, Bernh. 1800.	Parestia, Presl. 1849.
Stenolobus, Presl. 1836.	Stenoloma, Fée, 1851.
Colposoria, Presl. 1836.	Seyphularia, Fée, 1851.
Odontosoria, Presl. 1836. Fée 1851.	

(*a*) *Sori immersed in a short marginal cyst, the indusium sub-coriaceous, continuous with and scarcely different from the substance of the frond.*

52 PROSAPTIA, Presl. 1836.

§ 19. PERANEMEÆ.

(*a*) Veins free.

* *Involucres stalked.*

PERANEMA, Don. 1825.

Sphaeropteris, Wall. MS. 1828. R. Br. 1830.	Podielema, R. Br. MS. (1830.)
	Nematopera, Kze. 1845.

Order POLYPODIACEÆ. *Tribe* CYATHEINEÆ.

§ 1. CYATHEÆ.

(*a*) *Involucres complete cup shaped.*

53 CYATHEA, *Smith*, 1793.

Sphaeropteris, Bernh. 1800.	Notocarpia, Presl. 1836.
Disphenia, Presl. 1836.	Schizocaena, J. Sm. 1838.

§ 2. ALSOPHILEÆ.

(*a*) Veins always uni-soriferous.

54 ALSOPHILA, *R. Br.* 1810.

Trichopteris, Presl. 1822.	Hymenostegia, J. Sm. pt. 1842.
Chnoophora, Klfs. 1824.	Trichostegia, J. Sm. 1842.
Gymnosphaera, Bl. 1828.	Dichorexia, Presl. 1847.
Dicranophlebia, Mart. 1828-34.	Lophosoria, Presl. 1847.
Haplophlebia, Mart. 1828-34.	Trichosorus, Liebm. 1848.

Order POLYPODIACEÆ. *Tribe* GLEICHENINEÆ.

(*a*) *Fronds dichotomously branched, (rarely unbranched,) the branches pinnatifid.*

55 GLEICHENIA, *Smith*, 1723.

Mertensia, Willd. 1804.	Sticherus, Presl. 1836.
Decranopteris, Bernh. 1806.	Hicriopteris, Presl. 1849.
Calymella, Presl. 1836.	Gleicheniastrum, Presl. 1847.

Order POLYPODIACEÆ. *Tribe* TRICHOMANINEÆ.

(*a*) *Involucres urn-Shaped or tubular.*

Veins free.

† *Receptacles exerted, bearing Sessile leuticular Spore-cases at their base ; fronds pellucid.*

‡ *Fronds monomorphous.*

56 TRICHOMANES, *Lin.* 1742.

Achomanes, Necker, 1790.	Microgonium, Presl. 1843.
Didymoglossum, Dev. 1827.	Abiodictyum, Presl. 1843.
Lecanium, Presl. 1843.	Homœotes, Presl. 1847.
Cardiomanes, Presl. 1843.	Macroglena, Presl. 1847.

Cephalomanes, Presl. 1843.
Ragatelus, Presl. 1843.
Pachychaetum, Presl. 1843.
Chilodium, Presl. 1843.
Crepidium, Presl. 1843.
Meringium, Presl. 1843.
Neurophyllium, Presl. 1843.
Hemiphlebium, Presl. 1843.
Taschneria, Presl. 1849.
Leucomanes, Presl. 1849.
Pleuromanes, Presl. 1849.
Pseudachomanes, Presl. 1849.
Crepidomanes, Presl. 1849.
Odontomanes, Presl. 1849.
Amphipterum, Presl. 1849.
Bergera, Schaffu. MS. Fée, 1857.

(b) *Involucres two-valved.*

57 HYMENOPHYLLUM, *Sm.* 1793.

Ptychomanes, Hedw. 1789.
Hymenoglossum, Presl. 1843.
Leptocionium, Presl. 1843.
Sphaerodium, Presl. 1843.
Myrmecostylum, Presl. 1843.
Cycloglossum, Presl. 1843.
Craspedophyllum, Presl. 1843.
Ptychophyllum, Presl. 1843.
Sphaerocionium, Presl. 1843.
Mecodium, Presl. 1849.
Dermatophlebium, Presl. 1849.

Order POLYPODIACEÆ. *Tribe* SCHIZÆINEÆ.

§ 1. LYGODIEÆ.

(a) *Veins free.*

58 LYGODIUM, *Sw.* 1800.

Gisopteris, Bernh. 1800.
Odontopteris, Bernh. 1800.
Ramondia, Mirbel, 1801.
Hydroglossum, Willd. (pt.)? 1802.
Ugena, Cav. 1801.
Cteisium, Rich. Mich. 1803.
Vallifilix, Aub. du Petit. Thouars, 1811.
Arthiolygodes, Presl. 1845.

§ 2. SCHIZÆEÆ.

(a) *Fructifications seated on special contracted converging pinnæform appendages.*

59 SCHIZÆA, *Sm.* 1793.

Ripidium, Bernh. 1800.
Lophidium, Rich. 1792.
Belvisia, Mirb. (pt.) 1803.
Actinostachys, Wall. 1828.

(b) *Fructification paniculate on distinct fronds or lateral branches.*

* Veins free.

60 ANEMIA, *Sw.* 1806.

Ornithopteris, Bernh. 1806.
Anemirhiza, J. Sm. 1855.
Coptophyllum, Gardn. 1842.
Spathepteris, Presl. 1845.

Order POLYPOD. *Tribe* CERATOPTERIDINEÆ.

61 CERATOPTERIS, *Brongn.* 1821.

Belvisia, Mirb. (pt.) 1803.
Chladostachys, Wallich. MS. Hb. 1823.
Cryptogenis, Richard. MS. Brongn. 1823.
Teleozoma, R. Br. 1823.
Ellobocarpus, Klfs. 1824.
Parkeria, Hook. 1825.
Furcaria, Desv. 1827.

Order POLYPODIACEÆ. *Tribe* OSMUNDINEÆ.

(a) *Fructifications paniculate, or contracted rachiform fronds or segments.*

62 OSMUNDA, *Lin.* 1737.

Struthiopteris, Bernh. 1800.	Plenasium, Presl. 1836.
Aphyllocalpa, Cav. 1802.	Osmundastrum, Presl. (1845) 1847.
Reidlea, Mirb. (pt.) 1803.	

Order MARATTIACEÆ. *Tribe* MARATTINEÆ.

§ 1. ANGIOPTERIDEÆ.

63 ANGIOPTERIS, *Hoffm.* 1793.

Clementea, Cav. 1802.	Psilodochea, Presl. 1845.

§ 2. MARATTIEÆ.

(a) *Sori sessile on the veins.*

* *Sori involucrate, i. e., Seated in an involucre.*

64 MARATTIA, *Sm.* 1793.

Celanthera, Thouin. 1786.	Discostegia, Presl. 1845.
Myriotheca, Comm. Juss. 1789.	

Order OPHIOGLOSSACEÆ.

(a) *Fructifications paniculate, on a contracted rachiform branch.*

65 BOTRYCHIUM, *Sw.* 1800.

Osmunda, Bernh. 1800.

Botrypus, Rich. Mich. 1803.

(b) *Fructifications Spicate, the Spore-cases arranged in crowded glomerate tufts, forming distichous Spikes.*

66 HELMINTHOSTACHYS, *Klfs.* 1824.

Botryopteris, Presl. 1825.

Ophiala, Desv. 1827.

(c) *Fructifications Spicate, the Spore-cases arranged in a Single marginal Series.*

67 OPHIOGLOSSUM, *Lin.* 1737.

Ophioderma, (Bl. 1828): Endl. 1836.	Cheiroglossa, Presl. 1845.
Rhizoglossum, Presl. 1845.	Cassiopteris, Karst. MS., KL. 1847.

Order LYCOPODIACEÆ.

§ 1. LYCOPODIEÆ.

(a) *Fructifications consisting of Antheridia only.*

* *Spore-cases one-celled.*

68 LYCOPODIUM, *Lin.* 1737.

Selago, Dill. 1741.	Plananthus, Pal. de B. 1805.
Huperzia, Bernh. 1800.	Chamæclinis, Mart. 1829.
Lepidotis, Pal. de B. 1805.	Diphasium, Presl. 1847.

* * *Spore-cases three-celled.*

69 PSILOTUM, *Sw.* 1800.

Bernhardia, Willd. 1802.	Garsaultia, Commerson, MS. Spring, 1848.
Hoffmannia, Willd.	
Ipphia, Noronha, 1811.	Buchosia, Commerson, MS. Spring, 1848.
Tristeca, P. de Beauv. MS. Desv. 1827.	

(b) *Fructifications comprising both Antheridia and Oophoridia.*

70 SELAGINELLA, *P. B.* 1805. *Spring*, 1838.

Mirmau, Adans. 1763.	Gymnogynum, Pal. de B. 1805.
Acopodium, Necker. 1790.	Didiclis, Pal. de B. 1803.
Diplostachyum, Pal. de B. 1805.	Stachygynandrium, P. B. 1805.

CHARACTERS OF GENERA AND SPECIES.

TRIBE I. (§ 7) ADIANTEÆ.

ADIANTUM, *Linnæus Gen. Pl.* 782.

(Adiantellum, *Presl ;* Apotomia, *Fée ;* Synechia, *Fée ;* Mesopleuria, *Moore*, MS.)

Sori indusiate, transverse marginal, reniform oblong or linear, continuous or interrupted ; the *receptacles* seated on the under surface of the indusium, and proceeding from the apices of two or more converging venules. Indusium (inverted membranaceous marginal lobe) venulose, sporangiferous beneath on the venules ; the receptacles therefore resupinate. *Veins* flabellately forked or forked from a medial costa, the furcations repeated, *venules* parallel, free, continued in the fertile parts into the indusium.

Fronds coriaceous or herbaceous, simple, pinnately or pedately divided, or supradecompound ; pinnæ often articulated, usually dimidiate with the costa wanting. Stipes and rachis ebeneous. Rhizome tufted or short creeping—(Moore.)

1. *Adiantum lunulatum* (Burm.)—Frond oblong pinnate, pinnæ alternate rather long-petiolate membranaceous oblong—lunate dimidiate below, upper margin lobed, truncate at the base, uppermost pinnæ cuneate, sori linear approximate, and often confluent, stipes and rachis ebeneous glabrous, the latter often extended beyond the pinnæ and proliferous.—*Hook. Sp. Fil.* ii. 11. *Burm. Fl. Ind. p.* 235. *Pteris lunata Retz Obs.* 11, *p.* 28. *Adiantum arcuatum Sw. Syn. Fil. p.* 22. *A. lunatum. cav. Præl.* 1801, *n.* 676. *Rheede Malab.* xii. *p.* 72, *t.* 40.

Very common throughout the Presidency, low mountainous tracts on the Eastern side, and from the sea level up to about 4,000 feet on the Western side.

PLATE No. I.

2. *Adiantum caudatum* (L.)—Fronds linear oblong elongated, attenuated, often rooting at the apex and there bare of pinnæ, pinnæ nearly sessile, alternate, rather thick membranaceous, dimidiato oblong, the upper base truncated and parallel with the rachis, the upper margin more or less deeply lobed, the lobes often bifid soriferous villous in every part, with rufous hairs or more or less glabrous, veins generally prominent, involucres nearly orbicular or subquadrate, hairy or glabrous, stipes generally short, stout, and as well as the rachis more or less clothed with fulvous chaffy hairs.—*Hook. Sp. Fil.* ii. 13. *Linn. Maut. p.* 308. *A. incisum Forst. Ægypt. Arab. p.* 187. *A. vestitum Wall. Cat. n.* 75. *A. flagelliferum Wall. Cat. n.* 76. *A. hirsutum Bory It.* i. *p.* 198. *A. capillis Gorgonis Webb. in Hook. Niger Flora, p.* 192.

One of the commonest ferns in the Presidency, in similar localities with the last.

PLATE No. II.

3. *Adiantum hispidulum* (Sw.)—Frond narrow, flabelliform, bipartito-pedately divided tripinnate, secondary pinnæ linear-lanceolate acuminate falcate, pinnules chartaceous rigid close dimidiate oblongo-cuneate, olive brown when dry glaucous beneath striated pubescenti-hirsute especially beneath (often glabrous) subspinuloso serrate, superior base truncate, apex obtuse, sori copious, small on the upper margin and reaching to the apex (on almost every pinnule) 7-11 on each pinnule, in the sinus of the serratures, involucres orbicular, cordate, hispid or glabrous convex, stipes triquetrous, ebeneous scabrous, rachis ebeneous hispid or pubescenti-scabrous. *Hook. Sp. Fil.*

ii. 31. *Sw. Syn. Fil. p.* 124 *and* 321. *A. pubescens Schkr. Fil.* 108 *t.* 116. *A. pedatum Forst. Prod. p.* 83 *n.* 458 *(not Linn.) A. nervosum Sw. Syn. Fil. p.* 123. *A. plicatum Kaulf En. Fil. p.* 201. *A. scabrum Wall. Cat. n.* 79. *A. flabellulatum Wall. Cat. n.* 2177 (not Linn.)

Pulney Hills, Anamallays and Nilgiris, up to about 3,000 feet—rather rare.

PLATE No. III.

4. *A. Capillus Veneris* (L.)—Frond ovate tri-quadri-pinnate, pinnules delicate membranaceous glabrous obliquely broad cuneate (sometimes approaching to rhomboid) tapering into a rather long slender petiolule, the superior margin deeply and irregularly inciso lobate lobes very obtuse or truncate soriferous (sterile one subinciso dentate) sori as broad as the lobe, oblong or sub-reniform, stipes and slender rachis everywhere ebeneous, glossy and quite glabrous. *Hook. Sp. Fil.* ii, 36. *Linn. Sp. Pl. p.* 1558. *A. Moritzianum. Klotzsch. A. dependens. Chapman's* Mst. (ex Torrey.)

Nilgiris, rare—Coimbatore plains, (banks of a river.)

PLATE No. IV.

5. *A. Æthiopicum* (Linn).—Frond oblong, ovate triquadri-pinnate, pinnules sub-or quite membranaceous, glabrous sub-orbicular suddenly and obliquely cuneate at the base into a rather or very slender petiolule, superior margin more or less lobed, lobes shallow emarginate, the sinus or notch of the lobe soriferous, sori rather large 2-6 on a pinnule, involucres oblong-lunulate, stipes and slender rachis every where ebeneous shining and glabrous. *Hook. Sp. Fil.* ii. 37. *Linn. Sp. Pl. p.* 1560. *A. thalictroides Willd. A. pellucidum Mart et Galeot Fil. Mex. p.* 272. *A. cyclodes Zenker.*

Nilgiris—Fair lawns near Ootacamund. Dodabetta, Nediwattam. Pulnies, by no means a common fern.

PLATE No. V.

TRIBE 4, TRICHOMANINEÆ.

(a.) Involucres urn shaped or tubular.)

TRICHOMANES, *Linnæus, Gen. pl. ed.* ii., 947.

(Achomanes, Necker, Didymoglossum, Desvaux, Lecanium, Presl.; Cardiomanes, Presl.; Cephalomanes, Presl.; Ragatelus, Presl.; Pachychœtum, Presl.; Chilodium, Presl.; Crepidum, Presl; Meringium, Presl.; Hemiphlebium, Presl.; Microgonium; Presl.; Abrodictyum; Presl.; Neurophyllum Presl.; Magroglena; Presl.; Taschneria; Presl.; Leucomanes), Presl.; Pleuromanes, Presl.; Pseudachomanes, Presl.; Amphipterum, Presl.; Crepidomanes, Presl.; Odontomanes, Presl.; Homœotes, Presl.;

Sori involucrate seated in extrorse-marginal (rarely recurved) cysts, sunk in or free on the margins of the fronds; the veins continued into filiform exserted sometimes capitate *receptacles*, which are free within the cysts, and bear sessile lenticular spore cases at their base. *Involucres* funnel-pitcher-shaped or shortly bell shaped, truncate and entire at the mouth or two lipped; *veins* simple forked or pinnate from a central costa or simple costa-like in the ultimate segments, or flabellato-dichotomous, *veinlets* free sometimes excurrent in the marginal teeth.

Fronds simple pinnate or decompound, pellucid membranaceous, rarely coriaceous—Rhizome creeping (sometimes filiform) or cœspitose—Delicate semi-transparent Ferns. *(Moore.)*

1. *Trichomanes Neilgherrense* (Beddome)—Caudex creeping more or less tomentose, fronds glabrous; very small stipitate entire ovate to elliptic lanceolate or linear thin membranaceous, margins often furnished with peltate scales—stipes 3 to 6 lines long, glabrous or tomentose, involucres terminal 1·2 sunk in the frond, mouth obscurely 2 lipped, receptacles more or less exserted.

A very small species—fronds 4 to 8 lines long—the curious peltate scales with their tufted appendage are found on both sterile and fertile fronds and are all round the margin of some fronds, whilst others are quite destitute of them. I at first thought them to be some parasite, but something similar is found on T. membranaceum (Linn.) a West Indian species; they are well represented in the magnified figure. Abundant about Walaghat on the Western slopes of the Nilgiris. I have not found it elsewhere.

PLATE No. VI.

2. *Trichomanes filicula* (Bory.) Caudex creeping cloathed with dense black down, fronds rather small opaque ovate-lanceolate bipinnatifid, the segments linear rather acute entire compactly cellular, involucres solitary supra axillary cylindrical tapering at the base wholly sunk or winged at the sides, the mouth with 2 large narrow ovate or subtriangular acute lips nearly as long as the tube, stipes

broad compressed winged above—*Hook. Sp. Fil.* i, 124. *Bory. in Daperry's Voy. Bot.* i, *p.* 283. Trichbilabiatum, *Nees.* Hymenophyllum filicula, *Bory. in Willd. Sp., Pl. V,* 528. Didymoglossum decipiens, *Deso.*

Common on trees on the higher parts of the Nilgiris, Anamallays and Pulnies.

PLATE No. VII.

3. *Trichomanes rigidum,* (Sw.)—Tufted erect, fronds ovate acuminate harsh rigid dark green almost black when dry, bipinnate, the pinnules lanceolate or linear lanceolate cuneate sub-bipinnatifid, more or less deeply, the ultimate segments various in length, subacute simple or bifid, rachis terete wingless or as well as the secondary rachis with a very narrow wing or margin sometimes setose, involucres supra axillary on the inner margin of the lower segments, on the upper side of the ultimate divisions suburceolate-cylindrical free, the mouth entire and scarcely spreading, not 2 lipped. *Hook. Sp. Fil.* i, 133. Trich. pyramidale, *Wall. Cat. n.* 162. Trich. Achillæifolium, *Willd. Sp., Pl. V, P.* 512. Trich. obscurum, *Bl. Fil. Jar., P.* 227.

In very moist dark localities on the Nilgiris and Anamallays, 3,000 to 4,000 feet elevation—abundant about Walaghat (down the Sisparah ghat.)

PLATE No. VIII.

(b) *Involucres two valved.*

HYMENOPHYLLUM, *Smith Mem. Acad. Turin, V,* 418.

(Ptychomanes, *Hedwig*; Hymenoglossum, *Presl.*; Leptocionium, *Presl.*; Sphærodium, *Presl.*; Myrmecostylum, *Presl.*; Cycloglossum, *Presl.*; Craspedophyllum, *Presl.*; Ptychophyllum, *Presl.*; Sphærocionium, *Presl.*; Mecodium, *Presl.*; Dermatophlebium, *Presl.*)

Sori involucrate, *i. e.* seated with an extrorse-marginal oblong or sub orbicular, two valved *involucre;* the veins continued into the *receptacle,* which is free, included cylindrical or globose at the apex and bears sessile or subsessile lenticular or turbinate spore cases.

Veins dichotomously branched, simple and costa-like in the ultimate segments, or simple parallel from a central costa in undivided fronds; *venules* free.

Fronds simple or decompoundly divided, pellucid membranaceous. Rhizome creeping, usually filiform. Well distinguished from the last genus in the involucres consisting of 2 valves, instead of being blended into a cup. (Moore.)

1. *Hymenophyllum exsertum,* (Wall.)—Flexile pendent, fronds oblong, elongate, acuminate, pinnated, pinnæ rather distant, lanceolate acuminate decurrent, especially the upper ones pinnatifid but not deeply, segments short linear-oblong, obtuse, entire simple or bifid, involucres on the upper side of the pinnæ solitary or 2-3 sessile or terminating short segments, ovate 2 valved almost to the base, compressed, the valves eroso-serrate or nearly entire, rachis, stipes and costa more or less crinite with long scattered rufous hairs. *Hook. Sp. Fil.* i, 109. *Wall. Cat. n.* 171. *Hymenophyllum densum, Wall. Cat. n.* 170.

Common on trees and moist rocks on the higher ranges of the Nilgiris, Anamallays and Pulnies.

PLATE No. IX.

I have another species of Hymenophyllum (H. badium ?) and also another species of Trichomanes (T. Schmidianum ?) which I shall have figured in a future number of this work.

TRIBE I. (§ 17) CYSTOPTERIDÆ.

ACROPHORUS, *Presl. Tent. Pterid.,* 93.

(Leucostegia, *Presl.*; Odontoloma, *J. Sm.?* Monachosorum, *Kunze.*

Sori indusiate, globose, superficial or immersed; *the receptacles* terminal (or rarely axillary in the forks of the venules,) indusium sub orbicular, affixed by its posterior margin or base, rarely two or three becoming confluent. *Veins* pinnato furcate from a costa or more rarely repeatedly dichotomous, *venules* free.

Fronds membranaceo-herbaceous or sub coriaceous, pinnate or more frequently decompound, the divisions isomerous or dimidiate —Rhizome creeping. (This group is separated from Davallieæ by having its indusium fixed only by its base). [Moore.]

Acrophorus pulcher, (Moore)—Caudex creeping, stout clothed with compact imbricated very broad and obtuse scales, fronds rather small (1—2 feet), ovate acuminate membranaceous flaccid generally pale green 3—4 pinnate, rachides winged, primary pinnæ oblong ovate acuminate, secondary and tertiary ones ovate obtuse, pinnules lanceolate, deeply pinnatifid with linear lanceolate falcate segments entire or with an inner tooth, involucres on the middle of the segment below the sinus of the tooth and at the axil of a pair of veinlets, reniform rather large, stipes a little scaly below and rising from a very scaly gemma, all the scales oval obtuse. *Hook. Sp. Fil.* i, 157. *Davallia chœrophylla, Wall. Cat. n.* 259. *Davallia ligulata, Wall. M. S. Leucostegia ligulata, J. Sm. Davallia pulchra, Don. Cystopteris squamata, Dcne. Jacq. Voy.* 178.

Neddiwattam, on the Nilgiris. Common in the Teak forests of the Anamallays growing on trees. Wynaad, Coimbatore hills.

PLATE No. X.

2. *Acrophorus immersus,* (Moore)—Caudex creeping downy and fibrous, with slender roots (not scaly), frond stipitate, ovate in circumscription, membranaceous opaque, tripinnate, pinnæ pinnatifid ovato-lanceolate segments subovate or obovate obliquely cuneate at the base, paler and slightly concave on the upper side, sori close to the margin, involucres large, reniform close pressed, slightly convex. *Hook. Sp. Fil.* i, 156. *Leucostegia immersa, Pr. Tent. Pter. Davallia immersa, Wall. Cat. n.* 256. *Cystopteris dimidiata, Dcne. Jacq. Voy.* 177, *Humata immersa, Metten.*

Anamallays—Wynaad, 3,000 to 4,000 feet elevation, rather rare.

PLATE No. XI.

HUMATA, *Cavanilles Prælect,* 272.

(Pachypleuria, *Presl.;* Pteroneuron, *Fée.*)

Sori indusiate rotundate; the receptacles terminal and vertical or rarely subterminal and oblique on the venules. *Indusium* suborbicular reniform or transversely oblong reniform, plane, broadly affixed at the posterior margin. Veins stout, often thickened upwards, simple forked or pinnate, from a central costa, *venules* free.

Fronds small rigid, coriaceous, simple lobed pinnatifid or pedately pinnatifid or subternate; sori usually vertical, rarely subterminal and oblique or sublateral to the veins. Rhizome creeping hirsutely, scaly or tufted.

1. *Humata pedata,* (J. Sm.)—Caudex creeping paleaceous, fronds stipitate very coriaceous small deltoideo-cordate somewhat 5 angled tripartito-pinnatifid, the segments patent but inclining upwards, oblong, obtuse, fertile ones crenato-dentate the two lower primary divisions obliquely ovate, acuminate, involucres small, semi-orbicular or nearly orbicular, alternating with the teeth of the serratures placed close to the margin and pointing to it; stipes elongated chaffy below. *Hook. Sp. Fil.* i, 154. *Davallia cordifolia, Reinw. Davallia pedata, Sw. D. subimbricata, Blume.*

The western slopes of the Nilgiris—rare.

PLATE No. XII.

TRIBE I. (§ 18) DAVALLIEÆ.

MICROLEPIA, *Presl. Tent. Pterid.*, 124.

(Saccoloma, *Kaulfuss;* Scyphofilix, *Thonars;* Neuropteris, *Desvaux;* Selenidium, *Kunze;* Tapeinidium, *Presl.;* Davalliæ, *Sp. Auctorum.)*

Sori indusiate, rotundate or transversely oblong, intra-marginal or sub-marginal; the *receptacles* terminal or axillary on the veins or venules. *Indusium* semi-orbicular, attached by the base and sides, thus half-cup-shaped; the anterior margin free, truncate or rounded. *Veins* simple forked or pinnate from a central costa; *venules* direct free.

Fronds herbaceous or sub-coriaceous, pinnate, bi-pinnate or decompound, the margin sometimes attenuated, sub-membranaceous and indistinctly crenated, simulating accessory indusia. Rhizome creeping or tufted—a genus of large growing herbaceous ferns distinguished from *Davallia* by the short half-cup-shaped fructifications and intra-marginal sori. *(Moore.)*

1. *Microlepia platyphylla,* (Moore)—Caudex creeping thick, fronds ample tall tripinnate (primary and secondary pinnules much petiolated), every where glabrous coriaceo-membranaceous, pinnæ large spreading ovato-lanceolate much and narrow-acuminated deeply pinnatifid, often pinnated at the base, segments patent lanceolate (often very broad) acuminated lobato-dentate rachis and costa flexuose, veins pinnated, sori solitary generally in the axils of the teeth near the margin, involucres small half-cup-shaped. *(Hooker Sp. Fil.* i, 173); (Davallia lonchitidea, *Wallich Cat. n.* 240); (Davallia platyphylla, *Don. Prod. Nep., p.* 10).

Up ravines on the Coonoor Ghat,—Anamallays,—Pulnies,— but not common.

PLATE No. XIII.

2. *Microlepia pinnata,* (J. Sm.)—Caudex creeping scaly, fronds lanceolate pinnate glabrous, pinnæ remote shortly petiolate sub-coriaceous opaque linear-lanceolate gradually acuminate, obliquely cuneate at the base, the upper one sessile and decurrent, sori a little distant from each other, but forming a continued series one at the base of each tooth or serrature, veins sunk obsolete (inconspicuous), generally forked, the upper veinlet bearing the sorus, involucres small half-cup-shaped, stipes and subtrigonal rachis glossy. *(Hook. Sp. Fil.* i, 174; (Davallia pinnata, *Sw. Syn. Fil., p.* 131); (Davallia flagellifera, *Wall. Cat. n.* 243); (Saccoloma pinnatum, *Pr.)*

Anamallay Hills—rare.

PLATE No. XIV.

3. *Microlepia polypodioides,* (Presl.)—Caudex creeping, frond large ovate or deltoid acuminate, tripinnate flaccid more or less hairy or downy, especially on the veins and costæ beneath, primary pinnæ and lower secondary ones distant and acuminate, pinnules oblong or rhombeo-lanceolate, obtuse deeply pinnatifid, the lobes ovate or obovate, entire or irregularly inciso-lobate or again pinnatifid, suboblique very obtuse, sori rather large (when perfect), usually solitary on the entire lobes, several on the pinnatifid ones and in the sinuses within the margin, sometimes on a small tooth, more numerous on the superior margin, involucres small half-cup-shaped glabrous or hispid, rachis downy or hispid on the underside. *(Hooker Sp. Fil.* i, 181); Dicksonia polypodioides, *Sw. Syn. Fil., p.* 137); Davallia polypodioides, *(Don. Prod. Fl. Nep., p.* 10); (Davallia flaccida, *Br.)*; (Davallia virens, *Wall. Cat.,* 264); (Davallia Roxburghii, *Wall. Cat. n.* 2218); (Dav. puberula, *Wall. Cat.,* 262—5); (Davallia pyramidata, *Wall. Cat.,* 261); Dav. pilosula, *Wall. Cat.,* 263); (Dav. rhomboidea, *Wall. Cat.,* 257.)

A very variable species.

Nilgiris, common—Davie Shola, and in ravines on Dodabett—Coonoor, ravines on the Ghat—Anamallays—Pulnies—Travancore Hills, &c.

PLATE No. XV. *Fig. A is a frond of a very juvenile state.*

DAVALLIA, *Smith Mem. Acad. Turin,* V, 414.

(Wibelia, *Bernhardi;* Stenolobus, *Presl.;* Odontosoria, *Presl., Fée.;* Colposoria, *Presl. in part;* Parestia, *Presl.;* Scyphularia, *Fée;* Stenoloma, *Fée.)*

Sori indusiate, roundish oblong or elongate-oblong, marginal or submarginal; the *receptacles* terminal. *Indusium* membranaceous, cup-shaped or tubulose, affixed at the sides and base, thus forming a vertical oblong semi-cylindrical tubulose cyst or cup, which is truncate and open at top, *i. e.,* towards the margin. *Veins* forked or pinnate from a costa; *venules* free.

Fronds herbaceous or coriaceous, pinnate or pinnately decompound—Rhizome creeping. *(Moore.)*

1. *Davallia tenuifolia,* (Sw. Syn. Fil., p. 133)—Caudex creeping, woolly with subulate ferruginous scales, stipes long, frond erect ovato-lanceolate generally elongate, glabrous subcoriaceous brown, when dry, bi-tri-pinnate with the rachis compressed and winged (in other words bi-tri-pinnatifid) the segments or ultimate divisions approximate forked linear-cuneate truncate, the apex slightly erose, involucres terminal and solitary or in pairs short (transversely)-oblong slightly erose. (*Hook. Sp. Fil.* i, 186); (Davallia remota, *Kaulf.*)

Coonoor, very common—Coimbatore hills, at an elevation of 3,000 *feet only—Anamallays—Coorg, &c.*

PLATE No. XVI.

2. *Davallia bullata,* (Wallich Cat. n. 258)—Caudex creeping, clothed with copious subsquarrose ferruginous subulate crinite scales, frond deltoideo-ovate, submembranaceous tripinnate, fertile specimens copiously bullate on the upper surface, lower primary pinnæ subopposite ovate acuminate, pinnules lanceolate deeply pinnatifid, segments entire or again inciso-pinnatifid, segments falcato-incurved linear acute, involucres oblong cup-shaped, truncate from the inside of the falcate segment arising from the sinus of a small inner tooth. (*Hook. Sp. Fil.* i, 169.)

Anamallays, on rocks and trees 3,000 *to* 4,000 *feet elevation—Wynaad—a rare fern.*

PLATE No. XVII.

3. *Davallia elegans,* (Sw. Syn. Fil., p. 132.)—Caudex stout creeping, scaly and woolly, fronds tall subcoriaceous, ovato-acuminate, tri-quadri-pinnate, pinnules lanceolate, pinnatifid acuminate striated with pseudo-veins between the true veins, ultimate pinnules lobato-crenate, lobules entire or more usually one or two toothed, involucres half-cup-shaped, a little elongated sunk inserted upon the lobe, compressed truncate at the mouth. (*Hook. Sp. Fil.* i, 164.)

Mysore—Malabar—not common.

PLATE No. XVIII.

PROSAPTIA, *Presl. Tent. Pt.*, 165.

(Davallia, *Auctorum;* Humatæ sp., *Desvaux.*)

Sori indusiate oblongo-rotundate, immersed in a short marginal cyst open externally; the *receptacles* terminal at the apex of the costa. *Indusium* sub-coriaceous, continuous with and scarcely differing from the under surface of the frond, forming an extrorse cavity in, as it were the substance of the frond itself. Veins simple from a central costa or costæform vein; the latter usually, and one or two of the upper veins (branches) sometimes soriferous.

Fronds pinnatifid, rigid, subcoriaceous. Rhizome tufted decurrent. This genus differs from Davallia in the texture of the indusium, being homogeneous with that of the frond. (*Moore.*)

1. *Prosaptia contigua,* (Presl.)—Tufted or with a very short somewhat creeping caudex, fronds aggregate, lanceolate attenuate at both extremities on a short stipes pinnatifid throughout from the margin almost to the costa glabrous, segments linear entire or sub-pinnatifid with one or more lobules towards the extremity, sori solitary terminal upon a segment or lobule. (*Hook. Sp. Fil.* i, 161); (Davallia contigua, *Sw. Syn. Fil.*, p. 130); (Polypodium, *J. Sm.*); (Trichomanes contiguum, *Forst. Prodr. n.* 463.)

Anamallay Hills, on trees and rocks, banks of the Toracadoo river, at an elevation of 4,500 *feet—a rare fern.*

PLATE No. XIX.

2. *Prosaptia Emersonii,* (Presl.)—Tufted, fronds aggregate, sessile lanceolate, pinnatifid from the margin half way down to the costa, attenuated and entire at the apex, the lobes oblong, obtuse entire, bearing 1—6 sori at the apices. (*Hook. Sp. Fil.* i, 161); (Davallia Emersonii, *Hook. et. Grev., Ic. Fil., t.* 105.)

Anamallays, with the preceding. Palghat Hills—a rare fern.

PLATE No. XX.

TRIBE I. (§ 5) VITTARIEÆ.

VITTARIA, *Smith Mem. Acad. Turin, V,* 413.

(Runcinaria, *Müller;* Aristaria, *Müller;* Parenchymaria, *Müller.*)

Sori non-induciate, linear, continuous; *the receptacles* lying in an extrorse marginal furrow, *i. e.*, a groove open exteriorly in the extreme margin of the frond. *Veins* obscure, simple, combined at their apices by the receptacle.

Fronds simple and coriaceous, narrow elongate and grass-like. Rhizome short creeping or tufted. *(Moore.)*

1. *Vittaria elongata* (Sw.)—Caudex creeping, and with the base of the stipes clothed with longish black hairs, fronds simple, long linear, grass-like, 8 to 30 in. long, 2 lines broad glabrous, with a long acumination and gradually attenuated into the stipe.

Anamallay hills, on trunks of trees in the Teak forests, from 2,000 *to* 3,000 *feet elevation—Nilgiris slopes below Neddiwattan and Coonoor—a common fern.*

PLATE No. XXI.

TRIBE I. (§ 14) PLATYLOMEÆ.

PLATYLOMA, *J. Sm. Hook. Journ. Bot.* IV. 160.

(Pellæa, *Link.;* Pteridis Sp. *Auctorum.*)

Sori spuriously indusiate, marginal, oblong; the *receptacles* oblong at the apices of the veins, contiguous, the spore cases laterally confluent and forming a broadish marginal band. *Indusium* (spurious) formed of a narrow continuous attenuated inflexed portion of the margin. *Veins* simple or forked, from a central costa; *venules* parallel, free soriferous along a portion of their length at the upper end.

Fronds pinnate or bi-pinnate, coriaceous or sub-coriaceous, often glaucescent, the pinnæ sometimes articulated. Stipes often ebeneous. Rhizome short, decumbent or creeping (*Moore.*)

1. *Platyloma falcatum, var. β. setosum* (J. Sm.)—Caudex creeping, fronds linear, oblong pinnate, pinnæ (16—30) on very short petioles, upper ones sessile, oblong lanceolate, generally subfalcate, truncate or obliquely cordate, acute or often mucronate, glabrous above except on the costa, setose beneath, stipes and rachis setose with copious spreading ferruginous hairs, indusium spurious, involute when young, at length obsolete—(Pellæa falcata, *Fée, Hook. Sp. Fil.* ii. 135); (Pteris falcata, *Br. Prod.*); (Allosorus falcatus, *Kunze*); (Pteris seticaulis, *Hook Tc. pl. rar.* iii. 209); (Pteris alternifolia, *Wall. Cat. n.* 2182.)

Anamallays—in moist woods, elevation 3,000 *to* 4,000 *feet—Pulney Hills—Nilgiris—Droog hill, and ravines on the Coonoor Ghat.—Lampen's Peak near Coimbatore.*

PLATE No. XXII.

TRIBE I. (§ 6) LINDSÆEÆ.

LINDSÆA, *Dryander Trans. Lin. Soc. Lond.* iii. 40.

(Isoloma, *J. Smith;* Lindsaynium, *Fée.*; Lindsaya, *Kaulfuss.*)

Sori indusiate, linear or oblong, continuous or interrupted; the *receptacle* sub-marginal. *Indusium* membranaceous, equalling or shorter than the margin of the frond, opening on the exterior side. Veins ecostate and flabellately forked, or forked from a central costa; venules straight, combined at their apices by the receptacle, otherwise free; sometimes thickened at their apices.

Fronds herbaceous or subcoriaceous, simple pinnate or bi-tri-pinnate; the pinnæ (or pinnules) sometimes articulate, dimidiate or equal sided; fertile only on the upper margin or on both margins. Rhizome creeping (*Moore.*)

1. *Lindsœa cultrata* (Sw. Syn. Fil. p. 119)—Caudex creeping, fronds pinnate, long lanceolate, pinnæ sub-membranaceous, horizontal, ovate, costa marginal, the upper base truncate, rather acute, slightly arcuate at the upper margins, the apex usually directed upwards, shortly and retusely lobed, the lobes bearing the oblong sori, stipes and rachis generally pale brown, the former occasionally black. (*Hook. Sp. Fil.* i, 203); (Adiantum Cultratum, *Wild.*)

Nilgiris, very common on the banks of streams—common in most hilly tracks on the western side of our Presidency.

PLATE No. XXIII.

2. *Lindsœa tenera* (Dryander in Lin. Trans. iii. p. 42). Caudex creeping scaly, stipites tufted, fronds deltoid-ovate, 3—4 pinnate, pinnules all petiolate, cuneate or obliquely cuneate, costa obsolete, membranaceous, variously cut and lobed, the lobes soriferous at the apices (*Hook. Sp. Fil.* i, 211); (Lindsæa interrupta, *Wall. Cat. n.* 2195); Vittaria interrupta, *Roxb. Crypt. pl. Ind. p.* 49).

Travancore hills—a rare fern.

PLATE No. XXIV.

TRIBE I. (§ 6) LINDSÆEÆ.—*(Continued.)*

(b) **Veins reticulated without free included veinlets.**

SCHIZOLOMA, ***Gaudichaud Freycinets, Voy.*** **378.**

(Pericoptis, *Wall.;* Synaphebium, *J. Smith;* (Synaphebium Fée) Diellia, *Brackenridge.*)

Sori indusiate, linear or oblong, continuous or interrupted; *Receptacles* sub-marginal. *Indusium* membranaceous equalling or shorter than the margin of the frond, opening on the exterior side. *Veins* ecostate, or forked from a central costa; *Venules* anastomosing in elongated oblique areoles, without free included veinlets, the marginal ones combined by the transverse receptacles.

Fronds herbaceous, simple lobed or pinnate, or sometimes bi-pinnate; pinnæ or pinnules equal sided or dimidiate, fertile on the upper margin only or on both margins. Rhizome creeping.—*This genus differs from Lindsœa in its reticulated venation.* (Moore.)

1. *Schizoloma ensifolium,* J. Sm. Caudex very short creeping, stipes and rachis glabrous, stipe as long or longer than the pinnated frond; pinnæ 3-13 linear-ensiform or lanceolate erecto-patent, sub-membranaceous, sori continuous round the whole margin except at the apex and base, sterile apex serrated—*Lindsœa ensifolia, Sw. Syn. Fil., p.* 118, *t.* 137; *Lindsœa lanceolata, Labill. pl. Nov. Holl.,* 98; *L. membranacea, Kunze; L. attenuata, Wall; L. longipinna, Wall.*

Foot of the Sisparah and Carcoor ghats in Malabar.

PLATE No. XXV.

2. *Schizoloma heterophyllum,* J. Sm. in Hook. Journ. Bot. III, 414. Fronds lanceolate or deltoid, pinnate with the pinnules pinnatifid or bi-pinnate, pinnæ or pinnules lanceolate or rhomboid-cuneate, or nearly orbicular, petiolate or sessile sub-coriaceous membranaceous opaque sori continuous. (*Hook. Sp. Fil.,* 1, 223;) *Lindsœa heterophylla, Dryander. Linn. Trans. v.* iii, *p.* 41; *Lindsœa variabilis, Hook. et Arn. Bot. of Beech. voy.*

Bolampatty valley (Coimbatore hills)—Canara.

PLATE No. XXVI.

3. *Schizoloma recurvatum,* (Moore.) Caudex creeping stipes and rachis pinkish colored longer than the frond tetragonous fronds simply pinnate or with 2-3 pinnate branches, pinnæ oblongo-lanceolate recurved, pinnules oblong very obtuse sub-falcate the lower margin formed by the costa; sori along the upper margin interrupted—*Lindsœa recurvata, Wall.; Lindsœa nitens, Blume.; Lindsœa serpens, Wall.*

Bolampatty valley Coimbatore hills—rare. The pink colored stipes and rachis give this fern a very pretty appearance. (*I am not sure whether I should not have referred* this *fern to the S. obtusum* (*Synaphebium obtusum of J. Sm.*) *rather than to S. recurvatum.*)

PLATE No. XXVII.

TRIBE I. (§ 2) LOMARIEÆ.

LOMARIA, *Willdenow Mag. Nat. Ber.* 1809, 160.

(Stegania, *Brown;* Lomaridium, *Presl.;* Polygramma, *Presl.;* Paralomaria, *Fée.*)

Sori indusiate, linear, continuous, on a broadish linear *receptacle,* occupying nearly the whole under-surface of the contracted fertile fronds. *Indusium* attached at the margin, linear, continuous, scarious, opening along the inward side. *Veins* (sterile) simple or forked from a central costa, the *venules* direct free; or (fertile) obsolete.

Fronds simple pinnatifid pinnate or bi-pinnatifid; the fertile contracted. Rhizome short thick erect or decumbent, rarely creeping or arborescent. (Moore.)

1. *Lomaria elongata,* Blume. En. Fil. Jav. 11, p. 201. Caudex short subrepent, frond long stipitate coriaceous glabrous, often reddish colored when young, 1-2 feet and more long ovato-lanceolate pinnatifid (young sterile fronds often undivided lanceolate) segments few or many, of the sterile frond oblong-lanceolate acuminate sub-falcate patent, more or less approximate entire, except sometimes at the point, which is often slightly serrated, lowest segments often reduced to mere lobes. Veins simple forked, not reaching the margin but each furcation terminating in a large dot within the margin, fertile segments linear contracted, indusium fugacious. *Hook. Sp. Fil.* III, 3; Lomaria punctata, Bl.

The normal form has all the segments of the fertile fronds contracted and fructified, some fronds however have only some of the upper or some of the lower segments fructified and the rest are sterile and leafy, and in some fronds portions of each segments only are fructified and portions sterile, this latter is represented in the Plate XXVIII A.

Very abundant in most of the sholas on the Koondah mountains, and in the shola behind the Avalanche bungalow on the Nilgiris.—Sisparah ghat all the ravines above 4,000 feet elevation.—Anamallay mountains.

PLATE No. XXVIII AND XXVIII A.

BLECHNUM, *Linnœus Gen. Pl. ed.* 5, 1,039.

(Orthogramma, *Presl.;* Spicanta, *Presl.;* Blechnopsis, *Presl.;* Diafnia, *Presl.;* Mesothema, *Presl.;* Distaxia, *Presl.*)

Sori indusiate linear, continuous or rarely interrupted on a transverse *receptacle,* approximate to the costa; central or sometimes sub-marginal by the contraction of the fronds. *Indusium* linear opening along the inward side. *Veins* (sterile) simple or forked from a central costa; venules direct free thickened at the apex; in the fertile fronds combined near the base or within the margin by the receptacle.

Fronds simple pinnatifid or pinnate; the fertile sometimes more or less contracted. Rhizome short, erect, or producing elongated creeping Stolones. (Moore.)—*This genus is very intelligibly distinct from Lomaria in those species where the indusium is costal as in the only South Indian species, but where by the contraction of the frond the indusium becomes marginal it is hardly distinguishable from Lomaria.*

1. *Blechnum orientale,* Linn. Caudex erect stout at the extremity and as well as the short stipites clothed with long falcato-subulato-setaceous glossy scales, fronds 1-8 feet long ovato-lanceolate acuminate firm coriaceous pinnated, pinnæ numerous approximate horizontal straight or decurved 6 inches to a foot long 3-4 lines broad linear-lanceolate gradually acuminate sessile entire, the base bluntly and obliquely cuneate or truncated, several of the inferior pairs are suddenly abbreviated or abortive and squamiform, those at the extremity are decurrent and coadunate at the base, terminal one more or less elongated, veins simple rarely forked very close paralelled horizontal, sori continuous close to the costa, involucre in age firm rigid and almost black. *Hook. Sp. Fil.* iii, 52; Blechnopsis latifolia, *Presl.;* Blechnum salicifolium, *Kaulf.;* Blech. pyrophyllum, *Blume. En. Fil. Jav., p.* 160.

Common on the Nilgiris—Coonoor ghat—Sisparah ghat—Anamallays—Pulneys and Coimbatore hills. Beypore and Calicut (Malabar plains).

PLATE No. XXIX.

TRIBE I. (§ 9) PTERIDEÆ.

(*a*) *Veins free.*

ONYCHIUM, *Kaulfuss Berl. Jahrb. Pharm.*, 45.

(Leptostegia, *D. Don.;* Pteridis sp., *auctorum;* Allosori sp., *Presl.*)

Sori indusiate, linear (or oblong) transverse marginal or sub-marginal; the *receptacles* continuous. *Indusium* linear (or oblong) membranaceous usually opposite, and while young connivent over the narrow ultimate segments. Veins (sterile) simple and costæform in the ultimate segments; or (fertile) pinnate from a central costa, the few branches united near the margin by the transverse receptacle.

Fronds bi-pinnately or decompoundly pinnatisected, sometimes sub-membranaceous, usually with small narrow segments. Rhizome creeping. (Moore.)

I. *Onychium auratum,* Kaulf. Roots of densely tufted fibres, stipes cæspitose, a span to a foot and more long, hispid with a few narrow scales only at the base, and as well as the rachis everywhere pale brown or straw colored, glabrous and glossy, frond a span to a foot and a half long ovato-lanceolate acuminate sub-membranaceous but firm and glossy very compound four or more times pinnatisected (primary and secondary divisions pinnated) segments all narrow linear subcuneate short (in the sterile portions) ultimate ones acute entire or incisodentate, segments all pointing upwards 1 nerved, fertile segments elongated siliquiform especially the terminal ones and mucronate, sori linear-elongated occupying the whole back of the fertile segments, involucres golden colored meeting at their edges. *Hooker Sp. Fil.* ii, 121; Lomaria aurea, *Wall. Cat. n.* 38; L. caruifolia, *Wall. Cat. n.* 39; L. decomposita, *Don. Prod. Fil. Nep., p.* 14; Pteris chrysocarpa, *Hook. et Grev. Ic. Fil., t.* 107; Pteris siliculosa, *Desv.;* Allosorus auratus, *Presl.*

Paulghaut mountains—rare.

PLATE No. XXX.

PTERIS, *Linnæus Gen. Pl.* 780.

(Thelypteris *Adanson ;* Oetosis *Necker ;* Cincinalis Gleditsch ; Monogonia *Presl.* ; Eupteris *Agardh ;* Ornithopteris *Agardh ;* Pteridopsis *Link ;* Lytoneuron *Klotzeb ;* Pycnodoria *Presl. ;* Lonchitideum *Fée ;* Pellœæ sp. *Hooker.*)

Sori indusiate, marginal, linear, continuous or interrupted ; the receptacles linear transverse, uniting the apices of the veins. *Indusium* of the same form membranaceous Veins simple or forked from a central costa. Venules free.

Fronds varying from pedate to decompound, often very large herbaceous or coriaceous, Rhizome short erect or creeping some times much elongated (Moore.)

1. *Pteris quadriaurita* Retz. *obs. VI. p.* 38. Caudex short erect, fronds glabrous or with a few hairs very variable as to size ovato or cordato-ovate acuminate coriaceo-membranaceous, pinnate pinnæ 4 to many, generally opposite, more or less pinnatifid generally deeply, segments oblong obtuse entire or serrated, pinnæ sometimes pinnatifid to the apex, sometimes ending in a long tail like entire or serrated termination, lowest pair of pinnæ (or rarely 2 lowest pair) bi-partite (or rarely bearing several pinnæ on the lower side) veins free, forked, basal ones terminating at or above the sinus indusium occupying nearly the whole length of the margin of the segments—stipes elongated smooth or scabrous.—Pteris nemoralis. *Hook. Gen. Fil. t.* 54 ;—Pteris biaurita var. *Sw. Syn. Fil. p.* 98 ; Pt. calcarata, *Bory in Bel. voy. p.* 42.

Var. B. Argentea fronds white mottled.

Var. γ. rubro-nerva. Stipes glabrous or scabrous and together with the rachis and veins deep carmine colored costa above covered with pinkish hairs, indusium only occupying a small portion of the margin of the segments. Pteris rubro-nerva *of hot houses in England* Pteris aspericaulis *Wallich ? (This is perhaps a distinct species from Pteris quadriaurita.*

The normal form is very common everywhere in the Western side of the Presidency from the sea level to the highest elevations.

Var. B. argentea—is much rarer (and is never met with in the plains) Nilgiris, Nediwattan, Avalanche, Sisparah ghat.

Var. γ. rubro-nerva—rare—Anamallays. Mr. Ouchterlony's ghat below Nediwattan or the Nilgiris.

PLATE No. XXXI. (Normal form.)

2. *Pteris pellucens.* Agardh ; Fronds membranaceous furnished above wih a few subulate scales on the rachis of the pinnæ and with hairs on the rachis of the segments, ternately divided, lateral divisions multipinnate, pinnæ short petiolate or subsessile lanceolate acuminate deeply pinnatifid to the apex or with the apex long caudate, segments oblong obtuse subtruncate, serrated at the sterile portion at their apices, sori lateral on the segments never extending to the apex or base, veins rather remote all forked—basal ones arising from the axil of the costula and extending to the margin much above the sinus, stipes and rachis pale brown. *Ag. sp. Gen. Pt. p.* 43 ; *Hook. Sp. Fil.* ii. 191 ; Pteris intermedia. *Bl. En. Fil. Jav. p.* 211 ?

Anamallays 2500 to 4000. Coimbatore hills—Carcoor ghat—by no means common.

PLATE No. XXXII.

3. *Pteris longifolia* Linn. *Sp. Pl. p.* 1531.

Caudex short stout knotty, fronds 1-2 feet long lanceolate attenuated below, pinnate, pinnules numerous approximate linear-lanceolate elongated, gradually acuminated, terminal one sometimes the largest and petiolate, the base truncate or cordate auriculate, or even hastate, lower pinnules gradually smaller—Stipes more or less chaffy. *Hook. Sp. Fil.* ii. 157 ;—Pt. costata. *Bory in Belang Voy.* Pt. vittata, *Willd. ;*—Pt. obliqua, *Forsk ;*—Pt. lanceolata, *Desf. ;*—Pt. ensifolia, *Sw. ;*—Pt. Alpinü, *Deso. ;*—Pt. semihirta, *Lk. ;*—Pt. acuminatissima, *Bl. ;*—Pt. amplectens, *Wall. ;*—Pt. diversifolia, *Sw. ;*—Pt. trapezoides, *Burm. ;*—Pt. microdonta, *Gaud. ;*—Pt. tenuifolia, *Brock.*

Banks of a river close to Coimbatore.

PLATE No. XXXIII.

4. *Pteris semipinnata* Linn ; *Sp. Pl. p.* 1534. 1-3 feet high, caudex stout creeping villoso-squamose fibrous rooted, fronds broad-lanceolate acuminate sub-membranaceous pellucid pinnate, superior pinnæ approximate linear-oblong sessile at the base adnate and decurrenti-confluent, lateral ones distant sub-petiolate semi-ovate superior margin entire, inferior sub-pectinato-pinnatifid

(lowest pair sometimes bi-partite) the extremity long-caudate, the segments oblong, all-spinuloso-serrated in the sterile fronds, linear and entire, except at the sterile apex, in the fertile ones, veins simple and forked, involucres sub-intramarginal membranaceous often continued round the apex, stipes rather stout castaneous or purple-ebeneous very glossy. *Hook. Sp. Fil.* ii. 169 ;—Pt. flabellata *Schkh ;* —Pt. dimidiata. *Bl. Fil. Jav. p.* 210. *(not Willd).*

Travancore hills—Tranquebar—rare.

PLATE No. XXXIV.

5. *Pteris crenata,* Sw. *Syn. Fil. p.* 96. 1½ to 2 feet and more high, caudex creeping scaly with long subulate rigid curved scales, fronds 6-8 inches to a foot and more long ovate or (fertile) lanceolate sub-membranaceous firm bi-pinnate, terminal pinnæ much elongated often exceedingly long and caudate generally auriculate on each side at the base ; sterile pinnules oblong or obovate obtuse half an inch long coarsely serrated sessile very often confluent and more or less decurrent sharply serrated, veinlets simple or forked thickened at the apex, fertile pinnules linear more or less elongate often much acuminated, serrated at the sterile apex, indusium intramarginal occupying nearly the whole length of the pinnules : stipites slender smooth, stramineous short, in the sterile fronds much elongated. *Hook. Sp. Fil.* ii. 163. Pt. ensiformis—*Wall. Cat. n.* 2481 ; and Pt. multiden, *n.* tata, 2681 ;—Pt. caudata *Loureiro Cochin p.* 835—Pt. heterodactyla. *Reinw.*

Cochin—Malabar Coast. Tranquebar.

PLATE No. XXXV. (A fertile frond. A. the upper portion of a sterile one).

6. *Pteris Boivini,* Moore, Cæspitose, a span to 2 feet high caudex nodose with copious wooly fibres fronds subtriangular-ovate bi-tripinnate glabrous, pinnæ generally pinnate below and entire towards the apex, pinnules sessile or short petiolate elliptical or ovate with an unequal cordate base, very coriaceous opaque ; fertile ones entire except at the crenated sterile apex, sterile ones crenated. Veins internal quite obsolete forked and free—indusium sub-intramarginal membranaceous continuous round the margin except at the very apex and base —stipes subflexnose stout and as well as the rachises jet black and furnished with tawny down—Pellæa Boivini. *Hook. Sp. Fil.* ii. 147.

Anamallays, dry rocky places 4000 feet elevation. Nilgiris—abundant on the Sisparah ghat, dry places 3000 to 5000 feet elevation. *(This fern has not been before recorded from the East Indies).*

PLATE No. XXXVI.

PTERIS, *(Continued.)*

7. *Pteris geraniifolia.* (Raddi.) Small glabrous, root cæspitose, fronds cordiform ternate and pedate, subcoriaceous opaque primary lobes broad-lanceolate pinnatifid or usually bi-pinnatifid terminal segments ovato-lanceolate entire, and as well as the sinuses, acute, stipites elongated and as well as the main rachises ebeneous. *Hook. Sp. Fil.* ii, 132. *Raddi. Fil. Brasil, n.* 110—*Pellœa geraniæfolia, Fée. Gen. Fil. p.* 130—*Pteris Pohliana, Presl. Tent. p.* 145—*Pteris pedata. Kze. in Linnœa* X. *p.* 522 *(not Linn.)*—*Pt. pedatoides, Desv.*—*Pt. Mysorensis Heyne in Wall. Cat. n.* 87—*Pteris Concolor. Langsd. et Fisch.*

Very common on the western side of the presidency up to an elevation of 5000 feet.

PLATE No. XXXVII.

8. *Pteris pellucida,* (Presl.) $1\frac{1}{2}$ to 3 feet high—Caudex, short, thick scarcely creeping, frond, a foot and more long, sometimes quite simple, broad-lanceolate, generally ternate or pinnate, ovate in circumscription, coriaceo-membranaceous, bright green, lucid, pinnæ 3 to 11 or more, generally broad (1 to $1\frac{1}{2}$ inch) 6-10 inches long, entire or subserrated at the very acuminated apex, the margin often crisped sessile or the upper ones sometimes decurrent generally all entire or lowest pair bipartite, veins simple or forked, close, almost horizontal, involucres quite marginal, narrow, stipes very variable in length, stramineous or tawny, smooth or subscabrous. *Hooker. Sp. Fil.* ii. *p.* 161.—*Presl. Reliq. Hœnk. p.* 55.—*Pt. nervosa? Wall. Cat. n.* 96 *(not Thunb.)*—*Pt. crispata, Wall. MS. Pt. serrata. Wall. MS.*

Anamallay forests 2000 to 4000 feet elevation.

(Perhaps a variety of Pteris Cretica).

PLATE No. XXXVIII.

9. *Pteris Cretica* (Linn) a foot and a half high, caudex short, thick, subrepent, frond often a foot long broad-ovate more or less acuminate, firm, coriaceo-membranaceous, bright green, glossy, pinnæ 3 or 14 on each side, rather remote, a finger's length to a span long, sterile ones lanceolate, fertile ones linear-lanceolate, acuminate sometimes very much so, sessile or the upper ones more or less decurrent lowest pair and often 2 or 3 or more pairs above them bi-tri-(or more) partite, or pinnated, the segments mostly on the lower half, sterile portions strongly spinuloso-serrated, (rarely obtusely serrated or subentire) veins simple or forked, close, almost horizontal, involucres quite marginal, narrow, stipes generally longer than the frond, and the rachises stramineous or pale brown smooth or minutely rough upon the surface. *Hook. Sp. Fil.* ii. 159.—*Linn. Mant. p.* 130.—*Pt. semiserrata. Forsk.*—*Pt. lœta. Wall. Cat.* 95.—*Pt. heterophyllus-Poir.*—*Pt. serraria Sw. Syn. Fil. p.* 96.—*Pt. pentaphylla. Willd.*—*Pt. nervosa, Thunb.*—*Pt. vittata. Bory in Bélany. Voy.*—*Pt. multiaurita. Ag. Pter. p.* 12 *(taller form and more numerous pinnæ)*—*Pt. triphylla Mart. et. Gal. p.* 51.

Very common on the higher ranges of the Anamallays, Pulnies and Nilgiris.

PLATE No. XXXIX.

10. *Pt. Hookeriana.* (Agardh)? Up to 3 feet high, stipe nearly 2 feet smooth, trisulcate, frond pinnate, broad-ovate to subrotund in circumscription, firm, coriaceo-membranaceous, pinnæ alternate, 5—6 on each side, upper ones sessile and simple, lower ones petiolulate pinnatid, or pinnatifid, sterile portions serrated, fertile pinnæ generally fructified to nearly the apex, but in some pinnæ only the lower portion is fructified and contracted.

Malabar and Cochin—rare.

(I do not known whether I am correct in referring this fern to P. Hookeriana of Agardh. It is scarcely a form of Pt. Cretica. I have a specimen of the same species, but much larger than the one here figured, from Mr. Thwaites from Ceylon, marked C. P. 1329.)

PLATE No. XL.

11. *Pteris Otaria* (Beddome) Caudex short, erect, frond oblong, coriaceo-membranaceous, below glabrous, above furnished with a few hairs on the costa, pinnate, pinnæ 5—6 pair, the upper pair generally undivided, the others irregularly pinnatifid about the centre, the apex prolonged into a long tail-like acumination, undivided at the base, but there furnished with a long tail-like segment which is obsolete in the upper pinnæ and gradually larger in the lower ones, and pinnatifid in the lowest pair, sterile apex of the pinnæ and pinnules serrated.

Slopes below Puntaloor Wynad (Malabar).

PLATE No. XLI.

12. *Pteris aquilina* (Linn.) Caudex running long and deep underground, stipites erect, remote, stramineous or tawny, fronds ample subdeltoid, coriaceous, tri-pinnate, glabrous or hairy beneath, primary divisions long petiolate, ultimate pinnæ sessile, pinnules spreading linear more or less approximate, entire or hastate or below deeply pinnatifid, sometimes to the apex, segments ovate or oblong or linear upper ones decurrent at the base, the confluent portion sometimes forming a lobe or auricle, ultimate segments often elongated; the margins closely reflexed more or less crenulated, veins approximate simple or forked, involucre double continuous, membranaceous more or less villous or ciliated (inner one generally obsolete)—*Hook. Sp. Fil.* ii. 196—*Allosorus aquilinus. Pr.—Pteris caudata. Schkuhr—Fil. t.* 95—*Pt. recurvata. Wall. Cat. n.* 113—*Pt. firma. Wall. Cat. n.* 100—*Pt. excelsa Bl. En. fil. Jav. p.* 213—*Pt. latiuscula Desv.—Pt. lanuginosa Bory—Pt. decomposita. Gaud.*

Var. B. lanuginosa; fronds evidently pubescent or silky—tomentose beneath.

Variety B is the common Indian form and is to be met with all over the hilly portions of the Western side of the Presidency.

PLATE No. XLII.

13. *Pteris longipinnula* (Wall.) Fall, frond ample oblongo-ovate, coriaceo-membranaceous, shining pinnæ large (often a span long) broad lanceolate pectinato-pinnatifid rarely bi-partite, segments spreading nearly horizontally linear-oblong subacute entire, terminal one more or less elongated, lowest pair unequal short decurrent into a short petiole, involucres very narrow extending from the sinus nearly to the apex, veins prominent, forked from their base, stipes elongated (2-3 feet long) and as well as the rachis and costa usually of the same color as the frond (rarely brown) glossy—*Hook. Sp. Fil.* ii. 179—*Wall. Cat. n.* 108.

Forests on the Travancore hills—Courtallum.

Since the above was in the press I have found a 14*th species of Pteris (P. patens. Hooker) it will be figured in a future number.*

PLATE No. XLIII.

(b) *Lower veins only arcuately anastomosing.*

CAMPTERIA *Presl. Tent. Pterid* 146.

(Pteridis. sp. *auct.* Litobrochiæ. sp. *auct.*)

Sori indusiate, marginal, linear, continuous; the receptacles linear transverse, uniting the apices of the veins. *Inducium* of the same form membranaceous,—*veins* simple or forked from a central costa, the lowest pair only arcuately anastomosing, forming a series of elongated areoles, *venules* free.

Fronds herbaceous, large pedately-branched or bi-pinnate. Rhizome short erect—(Moore).

1. *Campteria bi-aurita.* (Linn). Fronds generally ample sub-coriaceo-membranaceous pedately ovate pinnate, pinnæ sub-sessile, lanceolate, acuminate, lowest or sometimes two lowest pair bi-tri-pinnate, or again pinnate mostly downwards, all the pinnæ deeply pinnatifid (leaving however a broad wing on each side the costa) segments oblong, or linear-oblong obtuse, entire, scarcely falcate, basal veins uniting in pairs into an arch below the sinus and there bearing 4 to 8 simple veinlets which extend to the margin at or above the sinus, stipes and rachises stramineous smooth.—*Hook. Sp. Fil. p.* 203—*Pteris biaurita Linn. Sp. Fil. p.* 1534—*Campteria Rottleriana. Presl. Tent. Pter. t.* 5 *p.* 26—*Pteris geminata. Ag. Sp. Gen. Pt. p.* 31—*Pt. Kleiniana. Presl. Tent. Pter. t.* 5 *f.* 19.

(Without examining the venation this fern is hardly distinguishable from Pteris quadri-aurita).

Nilgiris, North slopes—Walghat below Sisparah—Wynad.

PLATE No. XLIV.

2. *Campteria Anamallayensis* (Beddome) 4-6 feet high, fronds very large sub-membranaceous, pedately ovate, pinnate, pinnæ sub-sessile lanceolate with a long acumination, lowest pair tri-pinnate, all the pinnæ deeply pinnatifid (leaving however a broad wing on each side of the costa) segments falcately oblong sterile ones serrated and fertile ones serrated at their sterile apices; basal veins uniting in pairs into an arch below the sinus (one generally proceeding from the midrib and the other from the costa) and bearing 3-4 free veinlets, other veins forked terminating in dots within the margin, indusium never reaching the base or apex of the segments.

Anamallay hills—banks of a stream on the hills over Colungode 5000 feet—Bolampatty hills, near Coimbatore a very large species.

PLATE No. XLV.

TRIBE I. (§ 3) PLEUROGRAMMEÆ.

(*a*) *Veins compoundly anastomosing.*

HYMENOLEPIS, *Kaulf. Enum. Fil.*, 146.

(Hyalolepis, *Kunze ;* Macroplethus, *Presl.*)

Sori superficial, linear-elongate or linear oblong, on the contracted apex of the fronds ; the *receptacles* contiguous to and coalescent with the costa, sometimes covered while young by the revolute margin ; *Veins* indistinctly pinnate from a central costa or nearly uniform, *venules* compoundly anastomosing, forming crowded irregular areoles, from which proceed variably directed, included free *veinlets.*

Fronds simple opaque, linear lanceolate the apex fertile contracted or curved—Rhizome creeping. (Moore.)

1. *Hymenolepis spicata*, (Presl.) Rhizome creeping fronds simple opaque linear lanceolate, the apex contracted and soriferous on the under side, much curved veins obscure.

Paulghaut Mountains.

PLATE No. XLVI.

GYMNOPTERIS, *Bernhardi Schrader's of Bot.* 1800, *II*, 121.

(Leptochilus, *Kaulfuss ;* Dendroglossa, *Presl.*)

Sori superficial, non-indusiate, linear continuous, at length effuse ; the *receptacles* contiguous to the costa of the contracted fronds, often occupying nearly the whole under-surface, sometimes double on each side the costa. *Veins* pinnate from a central costa, the *venules* compoundly anastomosing, forming irregular areoles, from which proceed free divaricate *veinlets*, those of the fertile fronds much less developed.

Fronds, simple, pinnatifid, or pinnate, dimorphous ; the fertile much contracted. Rhizome short creeping. (Moore.)

1. *Gymnopteris quercifolia*, (Bernh.) Caudex creeping, fronds ternate, sterile ones membranaceous, subciliate, the lateral ones small subcordato-lobate, sessile, unequal sided, the middle one much larger, petiolate, oblongo-ovate sinnately lobed, fertile fronds, on a long slender stipe which is squamose below, pinnæ small narrow linear. *Bernh., Presl., Tent., Pter., p.* 244*; Acrostichum quercifolium, Retz. obs. Bot.* 6, *p.* 39*; Osmunda trifida, Jacq.; Coll.* 3, *p.* 281*; Leptochilus quercifolius Fée mem sur la Fam des Fougères, p.* 88.

Anamallays—Travancore hills, rare.

PLATE No. XLVII.

2. *Gymnopteris Féei*, (Moore.) Caudex creeping, fronds on long stipes, dark green glabrous shining subcoriaceo-membranaceous, lanceolate acuminated, fertile ones much contracted, sori contiguous to the costa forming a broad line of each side of it or often from the greater contraction of the frond occupying the whole under surface. *Leptochilus lanceolatus, Fée.*

Very common in all alpine and subalpine forests on the western side of the presidency, growing on rocks and trunks of trees.

PLATE No. XLVIII.

TRIBE I. (§ 13) GYMNOGRAMMEÆ.

a. Veins free.

GRAMMITIS, *Swartz, Schrad. Journ.* 1800. II. 3, 17.

(Chilopteris, *Presl.*; Pleurogramma, *R. Brown*; Leptogramma, *J. Smith*; Trichothemelium, *Kunze*; Trichocalymma, *Zenker*; Gymnogrammatis, Sp. *Auct.*)

Sori non-indusiate, oblong or elliptic, oblique ; the *receptacles* medial or sub-terminal. *Veins* simple or forked from a central costa—*Venules* free.

Fronds simple pinnate or bi-pinnate, herbaceous or sub-coriaceous, the rachis sometimes proliferous, Rhizome short, erect, sometimes short or elongate creeping—(Moore).

1. *Grammitis totta* (Presl.) caudex short, stout, erect, stipites tufted copiously scaly below, clothed with soft white hairs above, more or less angled : frond elliptic-lanceolate a span to 3 feet in length, membranaceous pinnate, with the pinnæ pinnatifid ½ way down to the rachis, hairy on both sides and ciliate, venules pinnate from a central vein simple or forked—sori copious, turning quite black when ripe, occupying the whole of the lower venules and the centre of the upper ones, spore-cases hairy. *Gymnogramma totta. Schlech.*

Very common about Ootacamund on the Nilgiris—Pulney hills at the same elevation.

PLATE No. XLIX.

B. Veins uniform reticulated with free included veinlets.

LOXOGRAMMA, *Blume, Flora, Java* 73.

Sori non-indusiate, oblong or linear, oblique, the elongate *receptacles* medial at intervals between the costa and margin. *Veins* uniform, reticulated from a central costa, the *venules* forming unequal oblique hexagonal elongated areoles, with (rarely without) included free *veinlets.*

Fronds simple coriaceous or sub-coriaceous. Rhizome creeping—The veins are often indistinct, being immersed in the substance of the thickish fronds.—The uniformly reticulated venation distinguishes this genus from Selliguea, in which the veins are pinnate and prominent. (Moore.)

1. *Loxogramma involuta* (Presl.) ; Rhizome creeping furnished with numerous scales and wiry hairy roots—fronds coriaceous lanceolate 10-14 inch long, about 1 inch broad, acuminated at the apex and gradually attenuated at the base into the stipe, margins more or less involute sori linear, oblique from the costa, all situated on the upper half of the frond—free included veinlets numerous. *Grammitis involuta. Don—Selliguea involuta. Kunze.*

Very abundant on the higher ranges of the Nilgiris and other mountains on the western side of the Presidency, on rocks and trunks of trees.

PLATE No. L.

2. *Loxogramma lanceolata (Presl.)* Rhizome creeping, scaly furnished with wiry hairy roots—fronds sub-coriaceous 4 to 7 inches long, about ½ an inch broad, acuminate at the apex, attenuated at the base ; sori oblong, slightly oblique or nearly parallel with the costa, often continued to nearly the base of the frond—*Grammitis lanceolata, Sw.*

Nilgiris—Neddiwattan on trees—much rarer than the last species.

PLATE No. LI.

TRIBE I (§ 12) HEMIONITIDEÆ.

Veins uniform reticulated.

ANTROPHYUM, *Kaulfuss. Enum., Fil.,* 197.

Sori non-indusiate, usually immersed, sometimes superficial, narrow-linear, occupying the anastomosed veins which form the sides of the areoles, mostly united ; the *receptacles* therefore partially, though generally reticulated. *Veins* uniformly reticulated from a costa, or ecostate, forming sub-hexagonal areoles.

Fronds simple, coriaceous or membranaceous. Sori continuously or interruptedly reticulated. Rhizome tufted erect—Distinguished technically from Hemionitis only by the partial though frequent reticulation of the Sori. The habit and aspect are however quite dissimilar. (Moore).

1. *Antrophyum reticulatum* (Kaulf.) Rhizome tufted, erect, fronds coriaceous, 3 to 14 inches long, 1 to 2½ broad, oblongo-lanceolate, often more or less falcate, attenuated at the base and with a long acumination at the apex, ecostate, sori immersed in the frond, more or less reticulated—*Hemionitis reticulata. Forst.*

Ravines on the Coonoor ghat and Sisparah ghat and other localities on the Nilgiris, up to 5,000 feet—Anamallays 3,000 feet—a rather rare fern.

PLATE No. LII.

HEMIONITIS, *Linnæus, Gen. Pl.* 2 *Ed.* 944 *(reduct.)*

Sori non-indusiate, superficial, narrow-linear, occupying all the anastomosing veins, the *receptacles* therefore reticulated. Veins uniform, from a costa, everywhere anastomosing and forming unequal hexagonal, more or less elongated areoles.

Fronds cordate, sagittate, palmate, or pinnate, herbaceous or coriaceous, proliferous, the fertile taller. Rhizome short, erect, or creeping. Sori continuously reticulated, often becoming confluent. (Moore).

1. *Hemionitis cordata* (Roxb.) stipes long, black, more or less hairy, fronds coriaceous, slightly hairy on the costa, sterile ones cordate to triangular, fertile hastate and generally on longer stipes, sori covering all the anastomosing veins, at length confluent, i. e., the entire under-surface of the frond becoming one mass of fructification.

A common fern in dry localities in the plains and low mountainous tracts ; it is seldom found at any great elevation.

PLATE No. LIII.

TRIBE I. (§ 4) TÆNITIDEÆ.

(*a*) *Veins straight, combined (where fertile) by the marginal receptacle.*

TÆNIOPSIS, *J. Smith., Hooker., Journal, Bot.* iv. 67.

(Tæniopteris, *Hooker.* Ampelopteris, *Klotszch.*)

Sori non-indusiate, linear, continuous ; the *receptacles* sub-marginal, immersed or superficial. *Veins* simple or forked from a central costa ; *venules* parallel, combined at or near their apices (only where fertile) by the transverse, i. e., the longitudinal receptacle otherwise free.

Fronds simple or lobate, coriaceous ; the veins obscure. Rhizome short, creeping, or tufted.—(Moore).

1. *Tæniopsis lineata* (J. Smith). Fronds linear, grasslike 10 to 14 inches long, 3 lines broad, sub-coriaceous, sori sunk in a furrow within the margin of the frond, margins more or less revolute over the fructification.—*Vittaria lineata, Sw.—Pteris lineata, Linn.*

Very much the appearance of the Vittaria (Plate No. XXI) but the sori are situated within the margin and not in an extrose marginal furrow, the fronds are of a thicker texture than those of Vittaria elongata.

Nilgiris slopes, below Coonoor and Neddiwattan.

PLATE No. LIV.

B. Veins uniform, reticulated, with free veinlets.

DRYMOGLOSSUM, *Presl., Tent., Pter.*, 227.

(Heteropteris, *Fée.;* Neurodium, *Fée.;* Paltonium, *Presl.;* Lemmaphyllum, *Presl.*)

Sori non-indusiate, linear, continuous ; the *receptacles* marginal or sub-marginal, superficial or slightly immersed. *Veins* uniform, reticulated, obscure ; the *venules* anastomosing in roundish or oblong hexagonal areoles, from which proceed free included simple or hamnate obtuse *veinlets.*

Fronds simple, dimorphous or contracted at the fertile apex, usually coriaceous. Rhizome creeping. (Moore.)

1. *Drymoglossum piloselloides* (Presl.) Rhizome creeping, covered with close pressed peltate scales, sterile fronds glabrous fleshy, oblong, obovate, to rotundate, unequal sided ½ to 1 inch long by about the same breadth—fertile ones linear attenuated at the base 3 to 4½ inches long, 3 lines broad, sori linear marginal continuous—*Presl.; Tent.; Pter.* 227, *t.* 10, *fig.* 5-6—D. rotundifolium et D. spathulatum, *Presl.*—Acrostichum heterophyllum, *Linn. sp. Pl.* 1523—Nothochlæna piloselloides. *Kaulfs. Bl. Fl. Jav.* 67—Pteris piloselloides. *Linn. Sp. Pl.* 1530—Pteris piloselloides. *Desv.*—Tænitis piloselloides. *R. Br.*

Nilgiris—Anamallays—Malabār—Courtallum—on trees.

PLATE No. LV.

TRIBE I. (§ 10) MENISCIEÆ.

Veins regularly anastomosing transversely between the pinnate parallel veins.

MENISCIUM, *Schreber. Lin. Gen. Pl. Ed.* 8, ii. 757.

Sori non-indusiate, linear-oblong, curved, often becoming confluent; the *receptacles* seated on the transverse parallel-curved venules, between the primary veins. Veins pinnate from a central costa, prominent; *venules* angularly or arcuately anastomosing between the veins, producing an excurrent free sterile *veinlet* from the apex of the arc or angle.

Fronds herbaceous or sub-coriaceous, simple or pinnate. Rhizome creeping (only differs from Goniopteris in Polypodieæ in the shape of the sori). (Moore.)

1. *Meniscium triphyllum* (Sw.) caudex creeping, furnished with scales—stipe 10 to 15 inches long,—fronds pinnate, fertile more or less contracted, pinnæ 1 pair with an odd one, oblong-lanceolate, acuminate repand, cuneate and unequal at the base, slightly hairy on the costa and veins, lower pinnæ sub-opposite or alternate.

Bolumputty valley in the Coimbatore hills.

PLATE No. LVI.

TRIBE 2. CYATHEINEÆ.

§ 1. CYATHEÆ.

CYATHEA, *Smith, Mem. Acad, Turin.* v. 416.

(Sphæropteris, *Bernhardi;* Disphenia, *Presl.*, Notocarpia, *Presl.*, Schizocæna, *J. Smith.*)

Sori involucrate, globose; the receptacles columnar or globose axillary at the forking of a vein, or medial; *Involucre* membranaceous, cup shaped at first globose and covering the sorus opening in a circumscissile manner near the apex, the cup remaining entire; or the cup bursting unequally; or sometimes opening vertically in 4—6 nearly equal spreading divisions. *Veins* (in the ultimate divisions) simple forked, parallel-forked or pinnate, from a central costa; *venules* free.

Fronds large, herbaceous, simple, pinnate, bi-pinnate or decompound. Trunk or caudex arborescent—(Moore.)

1. *Cyathea spinulosa* (Wall.) stipes and lower part of the rachis much and strongly aculeated, fronds bi-pinnate, flaccid and membranaceous, pinnules sessile, lanceolate, acuminate, pinnatifid, segments oblong acute, serrulate, glabrous, with a few minute scattered deciduous scales sometimes on the costa beneath (especially on the barren frond) sori close to the costa, copious, involucres globose membranaceous, fragile, glossy, soon breaking down into a jagged irregular cup—*Hook. Sp. Fil.* 1. 25—*Wall. in Herb.* 1823 *Cat. n.* 178.

Shevagherry hills—Mr. Moore gives the Nilgiris as a locality, but I have never yet met with it on those hills.

PLATE No. LVII.

§ 2. ALSOPHILEÆ.

ALSOPHILA, *R. Brown, Prod. Fl. Holl.* 158.

(Dicranophlebia, *Martins;* Haplophlebia, *Martins;* Trichopteris, *Presl.;* Chnoophora, *Kaulfuss;* Gymnosphœra, *Blume;* Trichostegia, *J. Smith;* Hymenostegia, *J. Smith* (in part); Dichorexia, *Presl.;* Lophosoria, *Presl.;* Trichosorus, *Kunze;* Polypodii, Sp. *auctorum*).

1. *Alsophila latebrosa* (Wall.) Stipes and main rachis muricated with short elevated points, fronds bi-pinnate, pinnæ lanceolate, pinnules narrow-lanceolate, acuminate, pinnatifid, almost to the rachis, segments narrow-oblong, acute falcate, sub-coriaceous, serrated, rachis and costa with small bullate scales, and one generally at the base of the sorus, veins all once forked, sori much elevated, cylindrical, copious, occupying nearly the whole segment—*Hook. Sp. Fil.* i, 37. *Polypodium latebrosum. Wallich.*

Nilgiris—Pulnies—Anamallays—Coorg—Shevaroys.

This is the common tree fern.

PLATE No. LVIII.

2. *Alsophila crinita* (Hooker.) Stipes and main flexuose rachis pale colored, rough with minute points and muricated with very short blunt black spines, fronds bi-pinnate, coriaceous, rachis everywhere hairy above, beneath clothed as well as the costa with ciliated scales, some short and minute, the majority very long slender appressed resembling coarse shaggy hair, pinnules sessile, narrow-lanceolate gradually tapering into a very slender point deeply pinnatifid almost to the rachis, segments narrow, ovate, oblong, rather obtuse, falcate, the margin (when dry) strongly recurved, pale beneath where the costa and even the veins are often hairy, veins forked, sori occupying nearly the whole length and breadth of the segments, and in a measure covered by the crinite scales—*Hook. Sp. Fil.* 1. 54.

Nilgiris—a ravine on the road from Ootacamund to the Davie Shola—Sisparah ghat, common—Higher ranges of the Anamallays.

PLATE No. LIX.

3. *Alsophila glabra* (Hook.) unarmed, fronds bi-pinnate, pinnæ ovato-lanceolate, nearly sessile acuminate, pinnatifid about one-third down to the rachis segments, ovate, slightly falcate, serrated, tufts of hairs in the axils of the pinnæ, rachis and costa more or less strigose and scaly,—sori situated on the middle of each veinlet, therefore in a double line on each segment—*Hooker, Sp. Fil.* 1, 51. Gymnosphæra glabra, *Blume*—Alsophila gigantea *Hook. Sp. Fil.* 1, 53, Gymnosphæra gigantea. *J. Sm. Gen. Fil.* Alsophila venulosa. *Wall. Cat. p.* 63. *A. umbrosa, Wall. Cat. p.* 64. Polypodium altissimum. *Wall. Hb.* Polypodium giganteum. *Wall. Cat.* 321. Polypodium sexpedale. *Buchan, MS. Hb. Mus. Brit.* P. umbrosum. *Wall. Cat.* 336. Dichorexia gigantea. *Presl.*

Wynad—Anamallays—Coorg—up to 4,000 feet elevation. I have never found this species growing to nearly the size of either of the other two Alsophilas.

PLATE No. LX.

TRIBE 5. SCHIZÆEÆ.

(§ 1) LYGODIEÆ.

LYGODIUM, *Swartz, Schrad, Journ.* 1800. II. 7. 106.

(Ugena, *Cavanilles;* Hydroglossum, *Willdenow in part;* Gisopteris, *Bernhardi;* Odontopteris, *Bernhardi;* Cteisium, *Michaux;* Anthrolygodes, *Presl;* Ramondia, *Mirbel;* Vallifilix, *Thonars;* Ophioglossi, Sp.; *Auctorum*).

Fructifications forming compressed distichous spikelets, exserted on the marginal teeth. *Spore*-cases included beneath ovate cucullate, imbricated, persistent, scariose, bractiform indusia, solitary on the anterior side of the venules, attached sideways, oval, resupinate, sessile, or very shortly pedicellate, having a many-rayed apical ring. *Veins* forked, often repeatedly, from a central costa; *venules* free; in the fertile spikelets pinnate, *the veinlets* sporangiferous on the anterior side.

Fronds branched, the rachis scandent; the branches usually conjugate, variously digitato—or palmato-partite or pinnatifid, or pinnate, the pinnæ sometimes articulated and deciduous,—Rhizome cæspitose or creeping.—Scandent ferns (Moore.)

1. *Lygodium Scandens* (Sw.) Stems rather slender, climbing to a considerable extent, glabrous, or slightly pubescent, pair of fronds petiolate, each pair pinnate, pinnules 8-10 from ovate-cordate to oblong-lanceolate or hastate, ½ to 1½ inch long, often shortly lobed at the base, articulate on a slight thickening of the apex of the petiole, sori short, protruding from the margin of segments usually shorter and broader than the barren ones. (Bentham), Lygodium Salicifolium, *Presl.;*—Lygodium microphyllum. *Br. prod.* 1, 162.

Wynad—very abundant.

PLATE No. LXI.

2. *Lygodium dichotomum* (Sw.) Stems climbing and as well as the fronds, perfectly glabrous, pair of fronds stipitate, dichotomous, each pinnule 2-4 divided to near the base, segments linear from a few inches to above a foot long, ½ to 1 inch broad when barren—narrower when fertile. Sori projecting from the margin—Ugena dichotoma, *Cav.*

PLATE No. LXII.

3. *Lygodium flexuosum* (Sw.) Stems climbing, fronds glabrous, or slightly hairy, pair of fronds stipitate-pinnate with the pinnules again pinnate or variously lobed or sub-palmate, terminal segment linear lanceolate, all serrulate, sori protruding from the margin.

Common in most sub-alpine jungles on the western side of our Presidency—Malabar plains—Cuddapah and North Arcot hills—Nullay Mallays.

PLATE No. LXIII.

4. *Lygodium Japonicum* (Sw.) Stems climbing slender, glabrous or pubescent, fronds pinnate with the pinnæ again pinnate pinnules variously lobed, segments short, serrulate, the fertile ones much contracted, sori occupying the whole of the under surface or protruding from the margin.—*Presl.; Tent. Pterid. Suppl.* 109.

Malabar.

PLATE No. LXIV.

(§ 2.) SCHIZÆEÆ.

(*a*) *Fructifications paniculate on special contracted pinnæform appendages.*

SCHIZÆEÆ, *Smith, Mem. Acad. Turin, v.* 419.

(Ripidium, *Bernhardi.*—Lophidium, *Richard.*—Actinostachys, *Wallich.*—Belvisiæ, Sp. *Mirbel.*—Acrostichi, Sp. *Auctorum.*—Osmundæ, Sp. *Auct.*—)

Fructifications paniculate; the spore-cases borne on the inner face of contracted fertile crests or appendages, which are digitato-pinnate or pectinato-pinnate, erect, incurved, and more or less connivent.—*Spore-cases* bluntly ovate, having a many-rayed apical ring; sessile arranged in one or two series on each side the costa of the linear segments, or pinnæ of the appendages. *Veins* reduced to a costa or flabellato-dichotomous; the venules excurrent in the apical teeth.

Fronds simple bearing (when fertile) a pectinate or digitate crest of crowded terminal resupinate pinnæ; or flabellate, or dichotomously multi-partite, bearing the fertile crests on the apex of the segments.—Rhizome cæspitosely creeping—(Moore).

1. *Schizœa dichotoma.* (Sm.) Fronds flabellate, dichotomously multi-partite, bearing the fertile crests on the apex of the segments, segments linear, about a line broad and several inches long costate, more or less minutely tuberculate—crests pectinato-pinnate incurved and connivent, spore-cases biserial arranged in a series on each side of the costa—Lophidium dichotomum, Richard.

Palghat Hills.

PLATE No. LXV.

(*b*) *Fructifications paniculate on distinct fronds or lateral branches.*

* *Veins free.*

ANEMIA, *Swartz, Synops, Fil.* 155.

(Ornithopteris, *Bernhardi*;—Coptophyllum, *Gardner*;—Spathepteris, *Presl*; Anemirhiza, *J. Smith*;—Osmundæ Sp. Auctorum;—Mohriæ Sp.; *J. Smith.*)

Fructifications paniculate on the lower (pair of) branches of a three-branched frond, or on distinct fertile fronds; the fertile branches or fronds erect, contracted, rachiform, decompound, the segments unilaterally sporangiferous. *Spore-cases* oval or sub-globose having a many-rayed apical ring, sessile, bi-serial on the ultimate segments. *Veins* flabellately dichotomous, sometimes dimidiately so; or forked, often repeatedly, from an evident or indistinct costa; or simple in the narrow ultimate segments; *venules* free.

Fronds pinnate or bi-tri-pinnate; dimorphous, the fertile and sterile distinct; or monomorphous, the fertile ones then always ternately branched, the two lateral branches distinct, erect, stipitate, fertile, the terminal one spreading sterile—Pinnæ sometimes dimidiate. Rhizome short, erect, or slowly or cæspitosely creeping—A genus recognized by the distinct branches of its fronds which, respectively resemble the foliage and inflorescence of a phænogamous plant—(Moore).

1. *Anemia Wightiana* (Gard.) Stipes rachises and fronds densely tomentose with long yellowish brown or golden hairy scales, fronds monomorphous, ternately divided, the two lateral branches fertile, the terminal one spreading sterile, bi-pinnate, with the pinnules variously lobed, or pinnatifid.

Sisparah ghat—dry places 3,000 to 4,500 feet elevation—Anamallays—dry rocky places—on the hills over Colengode at 4,000 feet elevation.

PLATE No. LXVI.

Order OPHIOGLOSSACEÆ.

(*a*) *Fructifications on a branched panicle.*

BOTRYCHIUM, *Swartz. Schrad. Journ.* 1800, II. 8, 110.

(Osmunda *Bernhardi*;—Botrypus, *Michaux*).

Fructifications paniculate, formed of numerous secund spikelets, on a distinct branch of the frond. *Spore-cases* erect, sessile free bi-serial, globose, fleshy-coriaceous, bursting vertically in two equal hemispherical valves. *Veins* flabellato-dichotomous or dichotomo-furcate, from a central costa; venules free.

Fronds herbaceous or sub-carnose, pinnatifid or ternately decompound; the sterile and fertile branches distinct—Rhizome short, erect, fleshy. (Moore).

1. *Botrychium virginicum var lanuginosum* (Moore.) Fronds sub-carnose, bi-pinnate with the pinnules, very variously lobed and decompound, the fertile branch from the centre of the frond, main and partial rachises more or less hairy. Botrychium, lanuginosum. Wall. Cat. 48.

On most mountainous tracts on the western side of the Presidency.

PLATE No. LXVII.

2. *Botrychium sub-carnosum* (Wall.) Fronds sub-carnose, bi-pinnate, pinnules variously lobed and pinnatifid, more or less sharply serrated; the fertile branch from below the sterile portion of the frond; main and partial rachises slightly hairy or glabrous. Botrychium daucifolium. *Hook. et Grev. Icon. Fil. t*, 161 (not in Wall. Cat.)—Botrychium speciosum, *Wall. Hb.*—Osmunda lavigera, *Wall. Hb.*

Nilgiris—Anamallays—Bolampatty valley—3,000 feet elevation.

PLATE No. LXVIII.

(*b*) *Fructifications Spicate, the spore-cases in glomerate tufts.*

HELMINTHOSTACHYS, *Kaulfus. Enum. Fil.* 28 *t.* 1.

(Botryopteris, *Presl.*;—Ophiala, *Desvaux*;—Botrichü, Sp. *Auctorum*;—Ophioglossü Sp. *Auct*;—Osmundæ, Sp. Auct.—)

Fructifications consisting of glomerate, verticillate, pedicillate tufts of spore-cases, the whorls terminated by a crest-like appendage and arranged in distichous spiked panicles on a distinct branch of the frond. Spore-cases, fleshy-coriaceous, globose, sessile, inverse bursting on the outer side, from the base upwards, in two equal or sub-equal hemispherical valves. Veins forked from a central costa; *venules* parallel, free.

Fronds herbaceous or coriaceous, trifoliately digitato-pedate, the fertile and sterile branches distinct. Rhizome stout, horizontal with coarse roots. (Moore.)

1. *Helminthostachys Zeylanica* (Hook). Rhizome stout, tuberous, with coarse roots. Fronds glabrous, shining trifoliately digitato-pinnate, each of the pinnæ with 2-5 lanceolate entire or crenated segments—fertile branch proceeding from the base of the sterile frond erect. Helminthostachys dulcis *Kaulfuss*;—Ophioglossum laciniatum, *Rumph*;—Osmunda Ceylanica, *Linn.*;—Botrychium Ceylanicum, *Sw.*

Anamallays,—moist bamboo clumps in the Teak forests, 2,000 to 3,000 feet elevation—Malabar plains—foot of the Carcoor pass very abundant.

PLATE No. LXIX.

(*c*) *Fructification Spicate, the spore-cases in a single marginal series.*

OPHIOGLOSSUM, *Linnæus, Gen. Pl.* 779.

(*Ophioderma* Endlicher;—Cheiroglossa, *Presl.*;—Rhizoglossum, *Presl.*;—Cassiopteris, *Karsten*, MS. (Klotzsch).

Fructifications on a distichous spike, terminating a distinct branch of the frond, or on distinct fronds. *Spore-cases* uniseria, along each margin of the compressed spike, with which they are connate, horizontal globose, bursting in two equal hemispherical valves. *Veins* uniformly reticulated in roundish or elongated areoles, sometimes from an indistinct costa, occasionally obscure; the ultimate areoles with or without included free *veinlets.*

Fronds sub-carnose two-or-many-branched, the sterile branch simple dichotomously-parted or palmato-lobate, the fertile simple; sometimes the fronds simple, the fertile and sterile distinct and dissimilar. Rhizome fleshy, sub-globose or short cylindrical-ovate.

1. *Ophioglossum reticulatum* (Linn.) Rhizome tuberous cylindrical, stipe long, bearing a single cordato-ovate, acute or obtuse sterile frond and the lengthened fertile spike (contracted frond)—fronds 1½ to 2 inches long 1 inch broad,—stipe 3 inches long.

Anamallays—Teak forests—Nilgiris.

PLATE No. LXX.

2. *Ophioglossum parvifolium* (Linn.) Rhizome small, tuberous, stipe bearing a single linear to lanceolate acute frond and the lengthened fertile spike.—Sterile frond with no evident costa ½ to ¾ inch, long by 2 to 5 lines broad.

Anamallays—in wet grassy places—2,500 feet elevation.

PLATE No. LXXI.

3. *Ophioglossum brevipes.* (Beddome) Rhizome a large round bulb with numerous fibrous roots—stipe very short, bearing a single lanceolate sterile frond close to its base and an elongated fertile spike. Sterile fronds about 2 inches long by ¾ inch broad.

Anamallays—in swampy places 2,500 feet elevation.

PLATE No. LXXII.

TRIBE 1. (§ 19) PERANEMEÆ.

PERANEMA, *Don. Prod. Fl. Nep.* 12.

(Shæropteris, *Wallich ;—R. Brown* (non-Bernhardi) ; Podeilema, *R. Brown, MS. ;* Nematoptera, *Kunze ;*——)

Sori involucrate, globose ; the *receptacles* globose, stipitate, medial on the lower anterior venules. *Involucre* coriaceous, stalked, globose, entire, at length bursting vertically into two irregular valves. *Veins* forked or pinnate, from a central costa ; *venules* free, thickened at the apex.

Fronds tri-pinnate, herbaceous, the stipes and rachis densely clothed with spreading scales.—Rhizome large globose—(Moore).

1. *Peranema cyatheoides* (Don.) Fronds 2-3 feet long tri-pinnate ; the base of the stipes densely clothed with long brown membranaceous acuminated scales ; the main and partial rachis with fewer scattered smaller ones. Pinnules oval, oblong, sessile, decurrent, so that the partial rachis is winged, obtuse, glabrous, turning brownish black in drying, nerves indistinct ; rarely more than one sorus on each pinnule, stalk of the involucre often longer than the involucre itself—*Hooker, Sp. Fil.* 1. 58. Sphæropteris barbata *Wall. in Herb.* 1823, *Cat. n.* 183 ; *Pl. Asiat. Rar. p.* 42 *t.* 18.

Western ghats—rare.

PLATE No. LXXIII.

TRIBE 4. GLEICHENINEÆ.

GLEICHENIA, *Smith, Mem. Acad. Turin. V.* 419.

(Mertensia, *Willdenow ;*—Dicranopteris, *Bernhardi ;*—Calymella, *Presl. ;*—Sticherus, *Presl. ;*—Hicriopteris, *Presl. ;*—Gleicheniastrum, *Presl. ;*—Platyzomatis Sp. *Desvaux ;*—)

Sori non-indusiate, round, superficial, or immersed, consisting of few (usually 2-4 sometimes 5-6 or even 8-12) spore-cases, which are sessile, deciduous, globoso-pyriform, sometimes concealed by the revolute margins ; the *receptacles* terminal or medial or axillary on the venules. *Veins* simple or forked, from a central costa ; *venules* free, the lower anterior one usually soriferous.

Fronds rigid, rarely simply pinnatifid, usually once or oftener dichotomously branched, the ultimate branches pinnatifid or pinnate ; the segments small, ovate, or orbicular, and sometimes remarkably revolute, or larger plane linear or oblong.—Rhizome creeping (Moore.)

1. *Gleichenia dichotoma.* (Willd.) Stipes rounded, ultimate branches with a pair of pinnæ, and a pair also at the base of the di-trichotomy, pinnæ lanceolate, acuminate, pinnatifid, segments linear, obtuse, or emarginate, glaucous beneath, glabrous or nearly so, lower external ones generally the largest, often again pinnatifid, capsules 8-12.—*Hooks. Sp. Fil.* 1. *p.* 12.—Mertensia dichotoma, *Willd.*—Mertensia discolor, *Schrad.*—M. Sieberi, *Presl.*—Polypodium dichotomum, *Thunb. Jap. t.* 37.—Gleichenia, lanigera, *Dou.*—Sticherus, laniger, *Presl.*—Gleichenia Hermanni, *Br. Prod. p.* 161.—Mertensia, Hookeri, *J. Smith.*—M. flexuosa, *Mart. Crypt. Brazil, p.* 108.—M. Pusilla, *Mart, l. c. p.* 111.—Gleichenia rigida, *J. Smith.*

A very common fern from the sea level on the western coast to the tops of the highest mountains,—ravines on the North Arcot hills.

PLATE No. LXXIV.

TRIBE 6. CERATOPTERIDINEÆ.

CERATOPTERIS, *Brougniart, Bull. Soc. Phil.* 1821, 184.

(Teleozoma, *R. Brown ;*—Cryptoyenis, *Richard, MS. ;*—Chladostachys, *Wallich, MS. ;*—Ellobocarpus, *Kaulfuss ;*—Parkeria, *Hooker ;*—Belvisia, Mirbel in part ;—Furcaria, *Desvaux ;*—Pteridis, Sp. *Auctorum ;*—Acrostichi, Sp. *Auct.*)

Sori indusiate, continuous, occupying the longitudinal veins, *spore-cases* few, loosely disposed, globose, furnished with a very broad incomplete ring, of which from one-third to three-fourths or more is wanting, (sometimes almost obsolete consisting of 3-4 striæ). *Indusium* universal, formed of the membranaceous revolute margins of the narrow siliquiform segments. Veins of the sterile fronds uniformly reticulated in oblique oblong hexagonal areoles ; of the fertile few, longitudinal, distantly anastomosing.

Fronds herbaceo-membranaceous, annual proliferous bi-tri-quadri-pinnatifid dimorphous; segments of the fertile ones linear, revolute siliquiform. Rhizome short, erect. Aquatic ferns. (Moore).

Ceratopteris thalictroides (Brougn). Fronds bi-pinnate, the fertile ones erect, 6 inches to one foot high, with linear acute segments ¾ to 1 inch long; the margins revolute and covering the fructification their whole length. Barren fronds shorter and more spreading, the segments cuneate with 2-3 oblong or lanceolate lobes, of a soft half-succulent texture. *Bentham, Hongkong flora. p.* 443—Parkeria pteridioides, *Hook. Exot. Fl. t.* 147 *and* 231;—

Common in swampy places, in the plains and sub-alpine jungles.

PLATE No. LXXV.

TRIBE 7. OSMUNDINEÆ.

OSMUNDA, *Linnæus, Gen. Plant,* 778.

(Aphyllocarpa, *Cavanilles*;—Struthiopteris, *Bernhardi*;—Plenasium, *Presl.*;—Osmundastrum, *Presl.*;—Riedlea, *Mirbel in part.*)

Fructifications paniculate, terminal or lateral on contracted rachiform portions of fronds, or occupying distinct contracted fronds. *Spore-cases* crowded on the margins or over the surface of the segments, obovate-globose, pedicillate or sessile, having an incomplete or rudimentary gibbous ring, (represented by a few parallel striæ) near the apex and bursting vertically in two equal hemispherical valves. *Veins* forked from a central costa; *venules* free.

Fronds coriaceous or herbaceous, pinnate or bi-pinnate, the pinnæ or segments often artieulate; fertile segments contracted usually rachiform, simple or compound, terminal, medial or basal on the fronds, or sometimes occupying distinct contracted fronds. Rhizome caudiciform or tufted. (Moore).

1. *Osmunda regalis* (Linn.) Fronds twice pinnate, 1 to several feet high, quite glabrous; barren segments oblong-lanceolate 1 to 2 inches long, serrulate, or nearly entire, very oblique at the base. Fertile segments linear ½ to 1 inch long, forming a terminal panicle above the barren branches. *Bentham, Hongkong fl. p.* 440.—O. Japonica, *Thunb. Fl. Jap.* 330.

Most abundant on the banks of rivers and streams on the Nilgiris and other high mountains on the western side of the presidency. (Called "The Royal Fern.")

PLATE No. LXXVI.

2. *Osmunda Javanica* (Blume) Fronds 1 to 2 feet high or more, glabrous, simply pinnate. Barren segments linear or linear-lanceolate 3 to 6 inches long, entire or more or less deeply serrate. Fertile pinnæ occupying the centre, or rarely the base or summit of the frond, each pinna pinnatifid or almost pinnate, with numerous globular or oblong segments (or clusters of spore-cases). *Bentham, Hongkonk Fl. p.* 441. O. Vachellii. *Hook. Ic. P. t.* 15.

Western ghat forests.

PLATE No. LXXVII.

Order MARATTIACEÆ.

TRIBE MARATTINEÆ.

(§ 1.) ANGIOPTERIDEÆ.

ANGIOPTERIS, *Hoffman Comm, Gött.* XII. 29, *t.* 5.

(Clementea Cavanilles;—Psilodochea, Presl.;—Polypodii, Sp. Auctorum.)

Sori dorsal, involucrate, sessile, linear-oblong or oval-elliptic, consisting of two opposite contiguous series of 5-12 free spore-cases; which are obovate retuse, sometimes marginate, affixed by the base, and bursting on the inner face by an obovate or elliptic vertical cleft. *Receptacles* linear elevated. Involucres linear scariose, fimbriate persistent. *Veins* simple or forked from a central costa; *venules* parallel, free, dorsally soriferous near the margin.

Fronds ample pinnate, or bi-pinnate, pinnules articulate. Spore-cases at first laterally connected, at length free. Rhizome fleshy, sub-globose, often becoming erect in age. (Moore).

1. *Angiopteris evecta* (Hoffm.) Stem forming an erect thick trunk, sometimes attaining 2 or 3 feet or more in height, fronds generally bi-pinnate (but the young sterile ones are often, and the fertile ones are sometimes, simply pinnate) very broad spreading up to 12 or 15 feet long, glabrous, shining green, segments linear-oblong 3 to 8 inches long, abruptly acuminate, crenate-serrate or rarely entire. Stipes more or less downy. Veins simple, forked, nearly parallel. Sori usually consisting of 8 to 12 spore-cases.— Angiopterus crassipes. *Wall. Cat.* 187.

[*Mr. Moore enumerates numerous Indian species, but they all I believe belong to one and the same plant.*]

Very common in most sub-alpine jungles on the western side of the presidency, up to 4,000 or 5,000 feet.

PLATE No. LXXVIII.

(§ 2.) MARRATTIEÆ.

MARATTIEA, *Smith. Plant. Icon. Ined. t.*—46—48.

(Myriotheca, *Commerson* ;—Celanthera, *Thouin* ;—Discostegia, *Presl.* ;—)

Sori dorsal, involucrate, sessile, oblong, horny, opaque, longitudinally divided into two opposite series of 3-11 conate spore-cases; the valves convex outside, plane within, the spore-cases of each valve bursting on their inner face by a vertical cleft or slit, *receptacles* linear or globose, medial. *Involucres* linear-elliptic, oval or orbicular, scariose, fimbriate, persistent. Veins simple or forked from a central costa; venules parallel, free dorsally soriferous near or at the margins.

Fronds ample bi-tri-pinnate; pinnules articulate. Rhizome large, globose or caudiciform, consisting of the thick squamæ—form bases of the fronds. (Moore.)

The Marattieæ are distinguished from the Angiopterideæ by having the spore-cases consolidated into bi-valved sori, along which they form two opposite lines; while in the latter, the spore-cases, which are also placed in two opposite lines, are distinct and separable.

1. *Marattia fraxinea.* (Smith.) Rhizome large globose, Fronds bi-pinnate, (pinnules rarely again pinnate,) pinnules lanceolate, serrated, with a long terminal acumination, partial rachis often winged towards the apex.

Sisparah ghat—Bolamputty valley (Coimbatore hills.)

PLATE No. LXXIX.

TRIBE I. (§ 16.) ASPIDIEÆ.

1. *Indusium reniform, affixed at the sinus.*

* *Veins reticulated.*

SAGENIA, *Presl. Tent. Pterid.* 86.

(Polydictyum, *Presl.* ;—Microbrochis, *Presl.* ;—Cardiochlæna, *Fée* ;—Lobochlæna, *Fée* ;—Phlebiogonium, *Fée* ;—Aspidii, Sp. *Auctorum* ;—Nephrodii, Sp. *Auct.* ;—Polypodii, Sp. *Auct.* ;—Bathmii, Sp. *Auct.*)

Sori indusiate, rotundate, superficial or immersed; the *receptacles* terminal on free veinlets, or medial or compital on anastomosed veinlets. *Indusium* cordato-reniform affixed at the deep sinus. Veins pinnate from a central costa, prominent, *venules* arcuately and compoundly anastomosing in about two or three series of irregular unequal variously-shaped areoles, from the sides of which are often produced free included divaricate (sometimes fertile) *veinlets.*

Fronds simply or often pedately pinnate or bi-tri-pinnate, herbaceous, usually ample. Rhizome short, erect or decumbent or somewhat creeping. (Moore.)

1. *Sagenia gigantea* (Blume) Caudex stout ascending. Stipites 1-2 feet long, brown as well as the rachises generally glossy, fronds ample 1-2 or more feet long, sub-membranaceous, dark greenish-brown when dry, pinnate with 4-5 pair of pinnæ below, bi-pinnate, pinnæ numerous 4-5 pairs 6-12 inches and more long, broad-lanceolate, deeply pinnatifid, the uppermost ones gradually smaller and

confluent into a pinnatifid apex, superior pinnæ generally having the basal segment decurrent upon the rachis, lowest pair of pinnæ (and base of the next pair) often very long a foot or more, and again more or less pinnated, segments more or less acute or acuminated, serrato-dentate or lobato-pinnatifid, veinlets forming oblong areoles near the costa and costales then variously anastomosing in the pinnæ and partially in the segments, the veinlets in the segments nearly all free, flexuose, more or less divaricating and once or twice forked, areoles including free simple or forked fertile veinlets (rarely any sterile veinlets) and generally with a terminal sorus, within the segments, the lowest veinlet on the superior side bears a terminal sorus, sori sub-marginal, involucres reniform. *Hook. Sp. Fil.* iv. 50;—Aspidium giganteum, *Blume, En. Fil. Jav. p.* 159;—Polydictyum, *Presl.*;—Aspidium intermedium. *J. Smith in Hook. Journ. of Bot.* iii. 410;—

Anamallays—Malabar.

PLATE No. LXXX.

2. *Sagenia coadunata* (Moore) Caudex stout ascending clothed at the apex with black subulate falcate scales, stipites more or less tufted from 1-2 inches to a foot and half long, stramineous or castaneous or ebeneous, scaly, scales lanceolato-subulate, spreading deciduous, fronds 4-6 inches to 2-3 feet long, oblong or ovate, membranaceous, pinnate, (young plants three-foliate,) or below bi-pinnate, the apex variously pinnatifid, pinnæ generally opposite oblong sub-sessile obtuse or acuminate variously lobed and pinnatifid, often unequally, lowest pair petiolate, semi-ovate, with the lower segments very long and pinnatifid—primary veins nearly straight, the rest variously anastomosing inappendiculate, sori in two series one on each side the costal vein of each segment compital (on the net work of the veins) or terminating a veinlet within a large costal areole, involucres reniform. Aspidium cicutarium. *Hook. Sp. Fil.* iv. 48 *in part* —Aspidium coadunatum, *Wall. Cat. n.* 337.

Very abundant in most sub-alpine jungles on the western side of the presidency.

PLATE No. LXXXI.

3. *Sagenia pteropus* (Moore) Caudex stout erect, stipites tufted short, stout partially scaly at the base, fronds 2-3 feet or more long, firm, membranaceous, sub-coriaceous, broad-oblong, deeply pinnatifid with 3-4 or 6 pair of long (6 inches to 1 foot, 1 inch and more broad,) oblong or oblong-lanceolate, more or less acuminated segments, lowest pair bi-tri-partite at the inferior margin, terminal lobe often trifid, the margin entire or more or less sinuate or pinnatifido-lobate, primary veins distinct, parallel, flexuose, secondary ones transverse with these forming arched areoles which are occupied by anastomosing veins, including copious free veinlets and two sori on short free veinlets, these sori form two lines or series between the primary veins, involucre on a large oblong receptacle rotundato-cordate persistent—*Hook. Sp. Fil.* iv. 47—Aspidium pteropus, *Kunze, Bot. Zeit.* iv. *p.* 462;—Aspidium decurrens. *J. Smith, Journ. of Botany*, iii. *p.* 410.—Asp. platynotus, *Kunze*;—Cordiochlæna alata, *Fée, Gen. Fil. p.* 315—Asp. macrophyllum, *Bl. En. Fil. Jav. p.* 144 (exd. syn.)

Bolampatty valley (Coimbatore hills.)

PLATE No. LXXXII.

Pleocnemia, *Presl. Tent. Pter.* 183.

(Haplodictyum, *Presl.*;—Polypodii, Sp. *Auct.*;—Aspidii, Sp. *Auct.*;—Nephrodii, Sp. *Auct.*;—Cyclodii, Sp. *(Moore.)*

Sori indusiate, globose; the *receptacles* medial on the free or anastomosed venules. *Indusium* reniform, affixed at the sinus. Veins (of segments, *i. e.*, venules) simple or forked from a costæ form mid-vein, the lower opposite ones arcuately anastomosing, forming elongated, angulate, costal areoles; the upper free; the intermediate usually forming one series of unequal hexagonal areoles next the costæ form vein; margin veinlets free.

Fronds herbaceous, ample, bi-pinnato-pinnatifid, the lower pinnæ bi-partite, or small and pinnatifid. Rhizome short, creeping or sub-arborescent.—(Moore.)

Pleocnemia aristata (Hooker) Caudex creeping, stipites close-placed a span to a foot long, fronds of the same length as the stipites (fertile ones, often longer than the sterile) ovate sub-membranaceous pinnate, pinnæ 7-13 spreading all petiolate 3-6 inches long $\frac{3}{4}$ to $1\frac{1}{2}$ inches broad oblongo-lanceolate falcate, finely acuminate, lobato-pinnatifid obliquely cuneate at the base rarely with 2 or 3 obovate auricles or distinct pinnules, their lobes triangular-ovate acute and as well as the apices of the pinnæ sub-aristato-serrate, primary veins (or costules of the lobes) pinnated with obliquely patent veinlets of which 1-3 pairs of the lower ones unite and form a very acute angle, sori dorsal on free or united veinlets, involucres subreniform, or oblong or lunate (as in Athyrium) sometimes ciliate. *Hook. Sp.*

Fil. iv. 62. *Nephrodium aristatum Hook.* ;—Goniopteris aristata, *Fée* ;—Anisocampium Cumingianum, *Pr. Epimel. Bot. p.* 58 ;—Cyclodium Cumingianum, *Moore* ;—Aspidium Otaria, *Kunze, Herb. Metten. Aspid. p.* 34.

A fern of doubtful genus, the involucres are more like those of Athyrium, in the Asplenieæ, than of the Aspidieæ.

Anamallays—abundant in the Teak forests 2,000 to 4,000 feet elevation. Yeddicarrah and the plains of Malabar, about the foot of the Carcoor pass.

PLATE No. LXXXIII.

* * *Veins conniventaly anastomosing.*

NEPRODIUM, *Richard, Mich. Fl. Bor. Amer.* II—266 *(reduct.)*

(Aspidium, *Swartz in part* ; *Auctorum* ;—Cyclosorus, *Link* ;—Abacopteris, *Fée* ;—Plectochlæna, *Fée* ;—Pronephrium, *Presl.* ; —Arsenopteris, *Webb. et Berthelot in part* ;—Polypodii Sp. *Auctorum* ;—Lastrea, Sp. *Auct.* ;—Cyclodii, Sp. *Auct.* ;—)

Sori indusiate, globose ; the receptacles medial on the venules. *Indusium* reniform, affixed at the sinus— *Veins* (of pinnæ) pinnate from a central costa, prominent ; *venules* simple, the lower pair or more, sometimes all, angularly connivent—anastomosing, producing from the angle an excurrent veinlet, which (in deeply pinnatifid pinnæ) is free or (in less divided pinnæ) joins the next anastomosed angle.

Fronds simple, pinnatifid, pinnate or pinnato-pinnatifid, herbaceous or sub-coriaceous. Spore-cases sometimes echinate Rhizome short, erectish, or slowly creeping—(Moore).

1. *Nephrodium molle.* (Desvaux.) Caudex stout, horizontal, short, densely rooting, stipites a span to a foot and more long, fronds rather soft-membranaceous 1-2 feet long, more or less pubescent ; oblong-lanceolate, abrupt at the base (or sometimes much attenuated there with distant dwarfed pinnæ) pinnated, pinnatifid at the apex, pinnæ numerous, horizontal, sessile, oblong, and generally broadest at the base, or lanceolate, more or less acuminate 3-5 inches long, pinnatifid more or less deeply, the segments semi-ovate, obtuse or oblong a little falcate, lowest pair of veinlets, uniting and sending out a veinlet which is prolonged to the sinus of the segments the rest free, simple rarely forked, sori in two rows situated near the middle of the free veinlets or at the junction of the two basal ones involucres reniform more or less villous—*Hooker, Sp. Fil.* iv. 67.—Aspidium appendiculatum, *Wall. in part.*—Asp. parasiticum, *Wall. Cat. n.* 2239—Polypodium nemorale, *Wall. Cat. n.* 1317—Polyp. mollusculum, *Wall. Cat.* 332—Asp. Canescens, *Wall. Cat.* 354—Asp. nymphale, *Forst. prod. p.* 81—Nephrodium Helsinbergii, *Pr.*—Polypodium diversifrons, *Kl. and Kunze*—Asp. patens, *Link.*

One of the commonest ferns in India.

PLATE No. LXXXIV.

Nephrodium (*Continued*)

2. *Nephrodium extensum* (Blume) Stipes 1-1½ foot long slightly scaly at the base—fronds 1½ to 3 feet or more long 1-1½, broad oblongo-lanceolate, acuminate sub-membranaceous, copiously pinnate, pinnatifid at the apex, pinnæ numerous approximate, sub-horizontal 8-12 inches long, in the broadest part ½-¾ of an inch broad, from a broad sessile base linear oblong, finely acuminated, glabrous, pinnatifid, about half way down to the rachis, the acumen entire, segments narrow, ovate or oblong, or oblong linear sub-falcate, entire, sub-acute, lowest pairs of veinlets angularly uniting, the rest free, sori copious but solitary on the veinlets between the costule and the margin strictly confined to the segments, or extending to the lowest veinlets, so that the disk is soriferous, involucres, small reniform glabrous. *Hook. Sp. Fil.* iv. 72 ;—Aspidium multijugum. *Wall. Cat. No.* 348 ;—Nephrodium caudiculatum. *Sieb. Syn. Fil. n.* 47.

Nilgiris—Anamallays and other mountainous tracts.

PLATE No. LXXXV.

3. *Nephrodium abruptum* (Presl.) Caudex stout, stipes very stout, 2 feet and more long, fronds ample 2-3 feet long, 1 to 1½ feet broad, firm coriaceo-chartaceous, glabrous, pinnated, pinnæ large 6 inches to 1 foot long, ¾ to 1¼ inches broad, sub-sessile from a truncated or short cuneated broad base, oblong, finely acuminated, shortly lobato-pinnatifid at the margin, lobes rounded, obtuse and sub-erose-truncate, or acute sub-falcate, (inclined towards the apex of the pinnæ,) lowest pinnæ often dwarfed, costules slightly elevated, numerous, veinlets 6, 8 or 10 pairs (according to the space between the costa and the sinus of the lobes) united and then forming a spurious intermediate costule, 3 or 4 only of the veinlets free within the short lobes, sori copious each on the middle of the veinlets in 2 distinct lines, or series between each pair of costules never extending to the lobes, involucres rotundato-cordate, sub-ciliate or glabrous, soon deciduous.—*Hook. Sp. Fil.* iv. 78 (the fertile fronds are sometimes considerably contracted, and sometimes as broad as the sterile ones).—Aspidium multilineatum. *Wall. Cat. n.* 353 ;—Aspidium prionophyllum. *Wall. Cat. n.* 355. A variety only.—A. pennigerum. *Bl. En. Fil. Jav. p.* 153 (but not of other authors)—Asp. truncatum. *Gaud. in Freyc. Voy. Cryp. p.* 333 *t.* 10.

Sisparah and Carcoor ghats—Nilgiris—Anamallays—a very large species.

PLATE No. LXXXVI.

4. *Nephrodium Arbuscula* (Desv.) Caudex creeping, stipites approximate, a span to a foot or more long, fronds firm-membranaceous, scarcely sub-coriaceous, pubescent 1-2 feet long, a span broad, oblong-lanceolate, acuminate a good deal yet abruptly attenuated at the base, pinnated, pinnæ approximate sub-petiolate from a dilated base, frequently auricled above, and rotundate below, narrow-oblong gradually and finely acuminated, coarsely crenato-serrate, lower ones (several pairs) dwarfed, remote sub-deltoid and sub-trilobed, three or four pairs of the veinlets anastomosing, a few free veinlets only in the teeth, sori solitary near the middle of each veinlet except on the teeth, indusium small reniform.—*Hook. Sp. Fil.* iv. 74.—Aspidium Hookeri. *Wall. Cat. n.* 338.—Asp. puberulum. *Wall. Cat. n.* 338.—Nephrodium Hookeri. *Moore.*

Anamallays and Pulneys—beds of rivers at 3 to 4,000 feet.

PLATE No. LXXXVII.

5. *Nephrodium unitum* (Sieb.) Root long creeping underground, densely rooting, stipites a span to a foot and more long, stout glossy brown ; fronds 1-2 feet long, rigid-coriaceous oblong acuminate, suddenly contracted and attenuated at the base (by the dwarfing of the pinnæ there) glabrous above, cano-tomentose beneath, especially on the rachis costæ and veins, pinnated, pinnæ numerous approximate 4-6 inches long erecto-patent from a truncated sessile sub-hastate base, linear-oblong gradually acuminated 3-6 lines wide, the margin pinnatifid, lobes short, traingular, ovate, acute, rigid, the margins a little reflexed, veinlets very prominent beneath 3 or 4 of the lowest pair uniting, and at their junction excurrent and forming as it were a false or intermediate vein reaching to the sinus, sori copious on all the veins crowded, at length confluent, involucres small reniform at length glabrous—*Hook. Sp. Fil.* iv. *p.* 81 ;—*Sieber Syn. Fil. n.* 43 ;—Aspidium callosum, *Blume* ;—Aspidium lanuginosum, *Bory in Hb. Hook.* (but not of Willd) ;—Asp. aridum, *Don.* ;—Asp. venulosum, *Wall. Cat. n.* 352 ;—Polypodium scabridum, *Wall. n.* 302 ;—Asp. cucullatum, *Bl. En. Fil. Jav. p.* 151 ;—Nephrodium canescens, *J. Sm. in Hook. Journ. of Bot.* iii. *p.* 411 (not Wallich) ;—Asp. pteroides, *Bl.* (not Sw.) ;—Nephrodium mucronatum, *J. Sm.* ;—N. Smithianum, *Presl.*

Nilgiris and Anamallays—not very common.

PLATE No. LXXXVIII.

6. *Nephrodium propinquum* (Br.) Caudex very long, creeping sometimes copiously, and luxuriantly rooting, stipites varying much in length from 1-2 feet, fronds sub-coriaceous 1-2 feet long, glabrous, or often more or less pubescent, resinoso glandulose, especially beneath, reddish-brown when dry, rather glossy, pinnated, pinnæ numerous, shortly petiolate, 3-5 inches long, ¼ to ½ an inch or more wide, linear-lanceolate, acute rather than acuminate, sometimes broader and cuneate at the base, sometimes contracted, pinnatifid ⅓rd or ½ down to the costa, the segments rounded or ovate, obtuse or acute, veinlets curved, one or two of the lowest opposite pair united, sori near the middle of the veins, or sub-marginal, sometimes confined to the lobes, sometimes extending to the disk, and not unfrequently forming a continuous intramarginal line following the course of the sinuses, the whole length of the pinnæ, involucres reniform, setose. *Hook. Sp. Fil.* iv. *p.* 79 ;—Aspidium unitum, *Sw. Syn. Fil. p.* 47 ;—Asp. gongylodes, *Schk. Fil. p.* 193 ;—Asp. Pohlianum, *Pr. and Kze.* ;—A. obtusatum, *Willd. Sp. Pl.* v. *p.* 241 ;—Nephrodium unitum, *Br. Prod. Fil. Nov. Holl. p.* 148 ;—Polypodium secundum, *Wall. Cat. n.* 301 ;—Neph. paludosum, *Liebm—Fil. Mex. p.* 123 ;—Filix Zeylan, denticul, non ramosa. *Burm. Zeyl. p.* 98 *t.* 44 *f.* 1.

Anamallays—3,000 feet in the Karambe-Vile (a large swamp) Elev. 2,500—Malabar, in wells.

PLATE No. LXXXIX.

7. *Nephrodium terminans* (J. Smith) Caudex creeping scaly, stipes 1-2 feet long, a little scaly at the base, frond about the same length, sub-membranaceous, oblong or ovato-oblong, acuminate, pinnate, terminal pinnæ, generally free but often deeply pinnatifid, lateral pinnæ 4-8 inches long patent, scarcely petiolate from a broad (or sometimes contracted) base linear oblong finely acuminated, pinnatifid about halfway down towards the costa, with numerous subovate rather acute slightly falcate segments, lowest pair of veinlets united below the sinuses, sori confined to the segments, involucres reniform. *Hook. Sp. Fil.* iv. 73 ;—Asp. terminans, *Wall. Cat. n.* 386 ;—Nephrodium Cumingii. *J. Smith. Hooker journ. Bot.* iii. *p.* 411 ;—Neph. conioneuron. *Fée. Gen. Fil.* 308 ;—Lastrea Malaccensis, *Pr. Epim. Bot. p.* 35 ;—Asp. Schwenkii *β. Bl. in Hb. Hook.* ;—Aspidium unitum, *Hook. et Arnt. Bot. of Beech. Voy.*

Anamallays—In moist forests and outskirts of Sholas 2,000 to 4,000 feet elevation.

PLATE No. XC.

* * * *Veins free.*

OLEANDRA, *Cavanilles Prœlect* (1801) 252.

(Neuronia, *Don.* ;—Ophiopteris, *Reinwardt* ;—Aspidü sp. *Auct* ;—Hypopeltidis sp. *Bory* ;—Polypodü sp. *Auct*).

Sori indusiate, globose, approximate to the costa, the *receptacles* therefore sub-basal on the veins or venules. *Indusium* reniform, affixed at the sinus. *Veins* simple or forked from a central costa ; *venules* parallel, unisoriferous dorsally near their base, their apices curved forwards, and connivent with the thickened margin.

Fronds simple, sub-membranaceous or sub-coriaceous, stipes nodoso-articulate. Rhizome creeping or erect and frutescent.—(Moore).

1. *Oleandra neriiformis.* (Cav.) Caudices sub-erect or scandent, stout, woody, knotted, copiously rooting below, densely clothed with appressed imbricate subulate scales, at first ferruginous then diaphanous at length deciduous, or leaving only small black spots, the remains of the persistent scales ; fronds 6 inches to 1½ foot long, scattered or often in terminal whorls, lanceolate, acuminate, generally attenuated at the base, 1 to 2 inches broad, coriaceous and glossy, or firm-membranaceous, glabrous or partially villous or pubescent on the veins and costa and ciliated on the margin ; petiole 2 lines to 1 inch long, jointed very near the base, glabrous or setose or scaly, sori in a continuous but flexuose line near the costa—*Hook. sp. Fil.* iv. 156 ;—Aspidium neriiforme, *Sw. Syn. Fil. p. p.* 42 ;—Asp. Wallichianum. *Belanger et. Bory Fl. Ind. Or Crypt. p.* 51. *t.* 9 ;—Asp. articulatum, *Sw. Syn. Fil. p. p.* 42 ;—Oleandra mollis. *Presl.* ;—Oleandra hirtella, *Miq. in Schk. Fil. Suppl. t.* 129.

Anamallays rare—Western slopes of Nilgiris—Ravines in Mr. Ouchterlony's valley, 5,000 feet elevation.

PLATE No. XCI.

NEPHROLEPIS, *Schott. Gen. Fil.* (*t.* 3.)

(Nephrodium, *Link* ;—Lepidoneuron, *Fée.*—Aspidii sp. *Auct.* ;—Nephrodii sp. *Auct.* ;—Hypopeltidis sp. *Bory* ;—Polypodii sp. *Auct.* ;—Davalliæ sp. *Auct.* ;—Tectariæ sp. *Cavanilles* ;—Polystichi sp. *Auct.* ;—Anthropteridis sp. *J. Smith.*

Sori indusiate, rotundate ; the *receptacles* terminal on the lower anterior venules, *Indusium* rotundato-cordato-reniform, affixed at the sinus or sub-reniform affixed oblique-transversely by the arcuate posterior margin. *Veins* pinnato-furcate from a central costa ; *venules* direct free, thickened at the apices.

Fronds pinnate, narrow elongate, herbaceous or sub-coriaceous, the pinnæ articulated. Rhizome short erect, producing elongated slender stolones which bear fasciculate crowns at intervals ; or elongately creeping ; sometimes tuber bearing. (Moore.)

1. *Nephrolepis tuberosa* (Presl.) Caudex indistinct, apparently wiry root-fibres, frequently bear large oval scaly tubers, stipites 1-4 inches and more long, deciduously paleaceous, from 1-3 feet long linear-lanceolate, coriaceo-sub-membranaceous acuminate, pinnate, pinnæ numerous approximate ½-1 inch long glabrous, horizontal from a truncate or cordate base, more or less auricled above, oblong obtuse, or especially the fertile ones crenated, rarely acuminate, often subfalcate, lower and sterile ones shorter and more obtuse, auricle acute, sori transverse about equidistant from the margin and the costa, involucres firm, coriaceous reniform or nearly half-moon-shaped, brown, opening towards the apex of the pinnæ, the base and point of insertion broad and generally black. *Hook. Sp. Fil.* iv. 151 ;—Aspidium sublanosum, *Wall. Cat. n.* 365 (*in part*) ;—Aspidium pendulum, *Raddi, Fil. Bras., p.* 30 *t.* 45 ;—Nephrodium delicatulum, *Dcne. in-Jacqem. Voy. Bot., p.* 178 *t.* 179 ;—Aspidium Tavoyanum, *Wall. Cat. n.* 1032.

Common in subalpine jungles on the Western side of the Presidency.

PLATE No. XCII.

2. *Nephrolepis exaltata* (Schott) stipes 1 foot and more long, and as well as the rachis and costa more or less villoso-paleaceous, often quite glabrous, fronds sub-coriaceous 1½-2 feet long oblong-lanceolate pinnated, pinnæ 1-3 inches long ; oblong more or less acuminated with a broad truncated or sub-cordate base, parallel with the rachis, with a sharp auricle above and sometimes below the margin entire or crenato-serrate, sori almost quite marginal, involucres coriaceous reniform with a very broad sinus. *Hook. Sp. Fil.* iv. 152 ;—Nephrolepis hirsutula, *Presl.* ;—Aspidium pilosulum, *Langsd. and Fisch., p.* 14 *t.* 16 ;—A. Schkuhrii, *Bl. En. Fil. Jav., p.* 147.

Wynad—Anamallays—Nilgiris.

PLATE No. XCIII.

3. *Nephrolepis acuta* (Presl.) Stipites 1-2 feet long, sub-paleaceous with subulate long ciliated scales mixed with longer ones, terete, very smooth olivaceous, fronds 2-4 and more feet long 8-12 inches broad oblong-lanceolate, membranaceous, more or less firm ; pinnæ horizontal ½ to 1 inch broad 5-8 inches long, oblongo-lanceolate, distant, more or less acute or acuminate, obliquely truncato-cuneate at the base, entire or serrated or irregularly and coarsely crenate, rarely sub-auriculate lower ones oblong-elliptical obtuse, sori distant from the margin, but nearer to it than to the costa, involucres cordate.—*Hook. Sp. Fil.* iv. *p.* 153 ;—Aspidium acutum, *Schk. Fil. p.* 32 *t.* 31 ;—Asp. splendens, *Willd. Sp. Pl. V, p.* 220 ;—Asp. paludosum, *Raddi. Fil. Bras., p.* 29 ;—Nephrolepis biserrata, *J. Smith. in. Hook. Journ. Bot. III, p.* 413 ;—Arana-panna, *Rheed Hort. Malab.* XII, *p.* 61 *to* 31.

Ravines near Kirkumbaddy, (North Arcot Hills.)

PLATE No. XCIV. *Fig. A is a portion of a hairy sterile form of frond which grows often on the same plant with the fertile fronds.*

LASTREA, *Bory. Dict., class d' Hist. Nat.* v 588.

Dryopteris, *Adanson* ;—Gleichenia, *Necker* ;—Aspidium, *Swartz in part* ;—Nephrodium, *Richard* in part ;—other authors ;—Thelypteris, *Schott* ;—Arthrobotrys, *Wallich* ;—Hypodematium, *Kunze* ;—Amauropelta, *Kunze* ;—Arsenopteris, *Webb et Berthelot* in part ;—Hemistheum, *Newman* ;—Lophodium, *Newman* ;—Gymnothalamium, *Zenker m. s.* ;—Dichasium, *A. Braun* ;—Camptodium, *Fée* ;—Oochlamys, *Fée* ;—Pachyderris, *J. Smith m. s* ;—Lastreastrum, *Presl.* ;—Pycnopteris, *Moore* ;—Polypodii sp. *Auct* ;—Tectariæ p. *Cavanilles* ;—Phegopteridis sp. *Auct.* ;—Arthropteridis sp. *J. Smith* ;—Cystopteridis sp. *Auct.* ;—Polystichi sp. *Auct.*

Sori indusiate globose ; the *receptacles* medial, or rarely terminal or sub-terminal on the venules. *Indusium* roundish, reniform or sometimes small and irregularly reniform, plane or fornicate fugacious or persistent ; the basal sinus at which it is affixed, variously deep, narrow broad or shallow. *Veins* simple, forked or pinnate from a central costa ; *venules* free, the anterior usually (sometimes more) fertile.

Fronds herbaceous or coriaceous, pedate, pinnate or bi-tri-pinnate, the fertile ones sometimes contracted—Rhizome-short thick erect or decumbent or elongately creeping. (Moore.)

1. *Lastrea eriocarpa* (Descaisne) Caudex ascending, stout, clothed with a very dense cushion-like mass, 1-3 inches thick of aureous subulate scales from ½ to 1 inch long, not extending to the stipes, stipites a span to 1 foot long, pale-brown, glossy, quite

glabrous and scaleless as are the main rachises ; fronds firm-membranaceous, pale-green, 3 inches to 1½ foot long, sub-quinquefidly deltoid, acuminate, very pilose on all the costæ and costules on both sides, and on the veins beneath with white hairs, tripinnate, primary pinnæ oblong or ovate acuminate 3 inches to a span long, petiolate lowest pair especially on petioles or branches 2-3 inches long semi-ovate, the lowest basal secondary pinnæ the longest, pinnules oblong-ovate ¼ to 1 inch long obtuse deeply pinnatifid, decurrent at the base, the segments oblong-ovate toothed or subinciso-pinnatifid, veinlets forked, sori most copious, involucres large pale-colored membranaceous reniform convex very villous.—*Hook. Sp. Fil.* iv. 141 ;—Nephrodium hirsutum, *Don. Prod. Nep., p.* 6 ;—Hypodematium onustum, *Kunze. in Flor.* 1833, *p.* 689 ;—Aspidium pilosulum, *Wall. Cat. n.* 337 (*not Kunze*) ;—Asp. subdiaphanum, *Wall. Cat. n.* 343 ;—Hypodematium Ruppellianum, *Kunze. in Schk. Fil. Suppl. t.* 21 ;—Cystopteris odorata, *Pr. Tent. Pterid p.* 93.

Anamallays, on the Peringoonda Hill 5,000 feet elevation.

PLATE No. XCV. *The plant figured is rather a dwarf form of this species.*

2. *Lastrea hirtipes* (Moore) Caudex short thick erect and as well as the stout tufted stipites and rachis densely crinite with large long subulate intensely black flexuose scales (more or less deciduous) fronds 2-3 feet long, sub-coriaceous ovato-lanceolate pinnate confluently pinnatifid at the apex, pinnæ 3-6-8 inches long more or less remote, horizontally patent from a truncated or subcordate and nearly sessile inauriculated base oblong, long-acuminated variously lobed or pinnatifid or crenated or even serrated at the margin, lobes obtuse or acute, veins pinnated sori dorsal upon the veinlets remote from the margin, involucres, small reniform sub-coriaceous—*Hooker sp. Fil.* iv. 115—Nephrodium hirtipes, *Hooker*—Aspidium atratum, *Wall. Cat. n.* 380.

Nilgiris—very abundant 4,000 feet and upwards. Anamallays—Pulneys.

PLATE No. XCVI.

Lastrea (*continued.*)

3. *Lastrea divisa* (Wallich.) Caudex large, fleshy creeping, furnished with numerous coarse roots, stipes 2-3 feet long, very scaly at the base, hairy and furrowed above, fronds 3 or more feet long, triangular-ovate membranaceous, bi-pinnate with the pinnules pinnatifid ⅗ down to the costa, pinnæ petioled, distant broad-oblong acuminated, varying in length from 3 inches above to 1½ foot below, rachises of the pinnæ furrowed above and covered with weak hairs on both sides, and furnished with a broad glabrous wing which gradually disappears towards the base of the rachis of the lower pinnæ, but is so prominent the whole length of the rachis of the upper pinnæ, that they may be said to be pinnatifid rather than pinnate, costa and veins furnished more or less with weak hairs on both sides, sometimes glabrous, pinnules alternate distant sub-sessile 1-4 inches long, broad lanceolate acuminate, pinnatifid nearly down to the costa, segments very obtuse, crenated, about ½ an inch long with narrow acute sinuses, veins pinnate, veinlets simple or forked, sori in 2 rows between the costa of the segments and the margin, 4 to 8 on each side (*i. e.*, 1 to each lobe or crenature) involucre much lacerated, very membranaceous and fugacious, rarely to be detected except under the microscope.—Nephrodium divisum, *Hooker*, *Sp. Fil.* iv, 133 ;—Aspidium divisum, *Wallich*, *Cat. n.* 393.

Sholas about Ootacamund on the Nilgiris 7,000 feet elevation—Anamallay Hills 3,000 feet elevation.

PLATE No. XCVII.

4. *Lastrea recedens.* (J. Smith ;) Caudex, a short thick ascending rhizome, paleaceous with subulate ferrugineous scales, stipites tufted a span to a foot long, rather slender, very scaly at the base, the rest and the rachises rather densely fusco-pubescent, fronds a foot long, and equally broad at the base, firm, membranaceous deltoid more or less pubescent beneath, often nearly quite glabrous above, below tri-pinnate, above bi-pinnate, primary pinnæ broad-oblong acuminate petiolate patent (but not horizontal) from 3 to 8 inches long, the basal ones much the largest 2½ inches broad, secondary ones oblong, sessile and decurrent at the base, so as to form a narrow wing to the rachis, oblong an inch and more long, very acute, coarsely and very acutely almost pungently serrate or pinnatifid, veinlets simple or once or twice forked, sori 1 to 5 on each lobule of the pinnule. *Hooker*, *Sp. Fil.* iv, 135.—Nephrodium recedens, *Hook.*—Lastrea elegans, *Moore. En. of cult. Ferns.*—Polypodium, *J. Smith. En. Fil. Philipp in Hook. jour. : Bot.* iii, *p.* 394.

Nilgiris—Pulney mountains—4,000 feet elevation—a rare fern.

PLATE No. XCVIII.

5. *Lastrea flaccida.* (Hooker ;) Caudex erect, furnished with numerous fibrous roots, stipites tufted stramineous, below scarcely scaly, above very glaucous, rachis with a line of hairs on the sulcated upper side, glabrous beneath ; fronds 1-3 feet and more long, broad ovato-lanceolate acuminate membranaceous, bi-pinnate with the pinnules pinnatifid nearly to the costæ, pubescenti-hirsute, with long white hairs on the costæ and costules on both sides, rachis of the pinnules furnished with a very regular line of dense hairs on the upper side, glabrous and convex below ; pinnæ rather remote, opposite or alternate, lanceolate acuminate, inferior ones 10-12 inches long, by 3 inches broad, superior, gradually smaller (so that one of the superior pinnæ is similar to a pinnule of an inferior pinnæ) pinnules up to 2 inches long, oblong, lanceolate from a broad adnate base (which is decurrent, so as to form a winged rachis particularly in the upper pinnæ) pinnatifid (in the lower pinnæ almost to the costa,) secondary pinnules pinnatifid in the lower pinnæ, entire or with the apex crenated in the upper portion of the frond : veinlets pinnate from a central vein, terminating within the margin ; sori 1-6 on each lobe of the secondary pinnules.—Nephrodium flaccidum, *Hook. Sp. Fil.* iv, 133.—*There is no trace of any involucre in the numerous specimens that I have examined. Sir W. Hooker's figure of this plant (Tab.* cclxiii, *Vol.* iv. *Sp. Fil.,) does not give a good idea of the plant as it grows on the Nilgiris ; I have a specimen from Ceglon exactly corresponding with the figure in the Sp. Fil. but my Nilgiri specimens are far more compound, the pinnules being about equal to the pinnæ of the specimen figured by Hooker. I feel certain however, that they are one and the same plant.*

Nilgiris—abundant on the Carcoor ghat—Anamallays 3,000 feet elevation.—Wynads.

PLATE No. XCIX.

(The upper portion of a large frond showing the pinnules decurrent on the rachis).

A. Magnified upper portion of one of the pinnæ showing the line of hairs on the rachis.
B. Lobes of a pinnule magnified, showing the under side.
C. A lobe of a pinnule, upper side.
D. A portion of one of the lower pinnæ of a frond.

6. *Lastrea ferruginea.* (Beddome ;) Caudex short, stout, erect, stipes densely clothed with large paleaceous scales and scabrous with rough tubercles—fronds large deltoid-ovate, tri-pinnate or in large fronds below quadri-pinnate, generally one or two pair of pinnules

wanting at the inferior base of the lowest pair of pinnæ, pinnules (*i. e.*, pinnules in the upper portion of the fronds and secondary pinnules below) divided one-third to three-fourths down to the costa, apices of the segments very broad, obtuse, crenated, each of the upper segments generally bearing one sorus at the apex of the superior veinlet, the lower segments of the pinnules being generally barren—rachises, costa and costules densely clothed (especially above) with reddish brown ferruginous pubescence, veins above covered with long ferruginous hairs, below slightly pubescent or glabrous—indusium, reniform, large glabrous, generally persistent.

Nilgiris, in Sholas on the Koondahs on the road between Avalanche and Sisparah.

PLATE No. C.

7. *Lastrea aristata.* (Moore ;) Caudex long, stout, creeping densely crinite with long subulate ferruginous scales, stipites distant a span to a foot and 2 feet long, the base copiously crinite (as in the caudex below) the rest and the rachises partially and sparsely setoso-paleaceous, fronds a span to 2 feet long, deltoideo-ovate, suddenly acuminate 3-4 pinnate, more or less coriaceo-membranaceous glossy ; primary pinnæ all petiolate, lanceolate finely acuminate, lowest primary ones with the basal secondary pinnæ very much elongated (hence the frond is pedate) and again once or twice pinnated, sub-falcate, sub-auriculate, mostly mucronato-serrate ; sori generally in 2 rows on each pinnule, involucres rather small, reniform. *Hook., Sp. Fil.* iv, 27.—Polypodium aristatum, *Forst.*—Aspidium aristatum, *Sw. Syn. Fil., pp.* 53—var *β.* coniifoiia—fronds larger below 4 pinnate, pinnules generally larger and more lax.—Aspidium coniifolium, *Wall. Cat. n.* 341.—Aspidium palmipes, *Kunze in Linnæa.* xxiv, *p.* 287.—Aspidium carnuifolium, *Kunze in Linnæa, p.* 292.

Nilgiris—Pulneys—Anamallays and all mountainous tracts on the Western side of the presidency—very common.

PLATE No. CI. *(Figure A. is the upper portion of one of the pinnæ of a frond of variety, β. coniifolia, a more compound and larger variety.)*

8. *Lastrea membranifolia,* (Presl. ;) Caudex a thick, erect rhizome with black subulate scales, stipites tufted a span to a foot or more long, firm, membranaceous, dark-green, deltoid ovate somewhat 5-angled, acuminate, primary pinnæ 3-6 inches long, 1½-2 inches broad, middle ones sessile deeply pinnatifid, uppermost ones coadunate into a deeply pinnatfid apex with more or less entire segments, lower ones more compound and petiolate, lowest pair the largest half-ovate acuminate, the lowest basal pinnæ the longest and deflexed, secondary pinnæ and pinnules resembling the middle pinnæ similarly pinnatifid with oblong sub-acute and slightly falcate, large spreading lobes often an inch long and ¼ of an inch wide, veins pinnated all free, veinlets simple or forked, sori in general forming a single series close to and chiefly upon the lobes or segments rarely on the disk and then scattered, involucres rather small reniform.—*Hook. Sp. Fil.* iv, 131.—Nephrodium membranifolium, *Hook.*—Lastrea paradoxa, *Moore.*—Aspidium fuscipes, *Wall. Cat. n.* 361.—Aspidium sagenioides, *Metten. Aspid., p.* 269.

Nilgiris—Sisparah and Carcoor ghats—Wynaad—Anamallays.

PLATE No. CII.

9. *Lastrea sparsa.* (Moore ;) Caudex short, erect, stout, densely rooting below, paleaceous with copious ovate acuminate scales above ; stipites tufted a span to 1-2 feet long, more or less scaly as is the rachis, fronds 1-1½ foot long, sub-coriaceous ovate acuminate, bi-tri-pinnate, primary pinnæ 3-5-6 inches long, distant much petiolate, ovate or oblong-acuminate, secondary ones ovate or ovato-oblong, obtuse, petiolate, those above the middle of the frond sub-obliquely rhomboid cuneate, at the base all more or less pinnatifid especially in the lower half with rounded obtuse entire lobes, superior basal segment generally tbe largest, hence sub-auriculate, ultimate pinnules (when tri-pinnate) of the same character, veinlets simple or mostly forked, sori rather irregular nearer the costule than the margin, involucres rather large, persistent, reniform. *Hook., Sp. Fil.* iv, 132.—Nephrodium purpurescens, *Hooker.*—Aspidium sparsum, *Spr.*—Aspidium densum, *Wall. Cat. n.* 290.—Aspidium purpurescens, *Bl. En. Fil. Jav., p.* 169.—Aspid. nitidulum, *Wall. Cat. n.* 392.—Asp. Weiglianum, *Kze. in Linnæa* xxiv, *p.* 284.—Asp. catophoron, *Kze. Bot. Zeit.* vi, *p.* 262.

A common fern in most mountainous tracts on the Western side of the presidency.

PLATE No. CIII.

10. *Lastrea deparioides* (Hook. ;) Stipes slender, 1-1½ foot long, very paleaceous below with large lanceolato-subulate brown scales, fronds 2 feet long, ovato-acuminate, membranaceous glabrous, bi-pinnate, primary pinnæ 4-5 inches long, broad-lanceolate, petiolate,

acuminate, pinnules about an inch long, rather distant, obliquely rhombeo-ovate, acuminate, laciniato-pinnatifid, unequally cuneate at the base and there sub-auricled above, the segments or teeth each bearing a solitary sorus at the very extremity terminating a veinlet, involucre generally larger than the tooth which bears it, convex cordiform with a deep sinus. *Hook. Sp. Fil.* iv. 139—*Hooker, Fil. Exot. t.* 3.—Diclisodon deparioides, *Moore. Index. Fil., p.* xcv *and* 316.

Anamallay Hills—Rare.

PLATE No. CIV.

11. *Lastrea falciloba.* (Hooker ;) Caudex short, thick, tufted, copiously rooting, stipites tufted a span to a foot long, free from scales ; fronds 1 to 1½ foot long, more or less slightly hairy on both sides, firm, rigid, coriaceo-membranaceous, ovato-lanceolate, finely acuminate, pinnate, main and partial rachises hairy, pinnæ 2-4 inches long, numerous rather distant, sessile linear lanceolate, deeply nearly down to the costa pinnatifid, the apex long tail-like entire or serrated, segments oblong, linear, falcate ; the superior basal segments of each of the pinnæ generally much longer than the others, involucres reniform very hairy—Aspidium falcilobum, *Benth. Hong Kong. Flora, p.* 455.—Nephrodium (Lastrea.) calcaratum, *Hook. Sp. Fil.* iv, 93.—Aspidium ciliatum, *Wall. Cat. n.* 351.—Aspidium Reinwardtianum, *Kze. Bot. Zeit.* vi, *p.* 261 ?—Lastrea viscosa, *J. Smith in Hooker. Journ of Bot.* iii, *p.* 412.

Nilgiris—common in ravines about half way down the Sisparah ghat—Anamallays, beds of rivers 2,000 to 4,000 feet elevation.

PLATE No. CV.

12. *Lastrea ochthodes.* (Kunze ;) Rhizome short, stipites crowded, moderately long flexuose, fusco-paleaceous towards the base, rachis and costa hispidulous above, and glabrous below, or hispidulous on both sides, frond sub-coriaceous, firm, glabrous, the margin sparingly canescently hispidulous, olivaceous above, paler beneath, lanceolate acuminate, at the base gradually and long attenuated, pinnate, pinnæ deeply pinnatifid, sessile with a callous gland at the base beneath, patent or divergenti-patent from a broad sub-equal base linear-attenuated, the lower ones gradually abbreviated and dwarfed, the lowest abortive segments falcato-oblong, or linear rather acute, margin more or less reflexed in fructification, the lowest segments on each side longer, distinctly but slenderly pinnatedly veined, sori either in a continuous line near the costule, one at the base of each vein, or near the centre of the veins. *Hook. Sp. Fil.* iv, 109.—Aspidium glanduliferum, *Wall.*

Var : *a.* Aspidium ochthodes, *Kunze in Linnæa.* xxiv, *p.* 282—rachis costæ and costules canescently hispidulous on both sides, sometimes nearly glabrous below, except a glandular pubescence on the veins ; pinnæ gradually attenuated, sori at or above the centre of the veins, involucre often hairy when young, margin of frond often much reflexed in fructification.

A very common fern.

PLATE No. CVI.

13. Var. *β.* Aspidium tylodes, *Kunze in Linnæa,* xxiv, *p.* 281—rachis costæ and costules glabrous below, lower pinnæ suddenly abortive, reduced to tuberculated glands—sori at the base of the veins close to the costule.

Nilgiris—rather rare.

PLATE No. CVII.

14. *Lastrea spectabilis,* (J. Smith ;) Caudex erect, ½ an inch in diameter and together with the base of the stipes, clothed with long brown ovate acuminate scales, stipites 1 foot and more long and with the rachis and primary costa elongated, stramineous glabrous, fronds 1½-2-3 feet long, 1-1½ foot broad, membranaceous, firm, broad-oblong or ovate acuminated, pinnate, pinnæ patent 1-2 inches broad, from a truncate or sub-cuneate base, oblong acuminated, deeply pinnatifid three-quarters or four-fifths of the way to the costæ, segments oblong or broad-oblong, rather obtuse, sub-falcate rather sharply serrated, the sinuses rounded at the base and there furnished with a short ligulate but very distinct tooth or gland, veinlets conspicuous, flexuose forked, sori small on a superior branch, rather near the margin than the costule, involucres small reniform.—*Kze. Hook. Sp. Fil.* iv, 115.—Aspidium spectabile, *Blume, En. Fil., p.* 158—Lastrea, *J. Smith in Hook. Journ. Bot.* iii, *p.* 412.

Carcoor ghat. (Wynad)—Anamallays—rare—Ravines in the North Arcot hills near Kirkumbaddy.

PLATE No. CVIII.

15. *Lastrea amabilis.* (Moore ;) Caudex, decidedly creeping, thick as a swan's quill, paleaceous with ferruginous scales, stipes solitary, a span to a foot long, slender, sub-flexuose, paleaceous below, fronds 6-12 inches long, sub-deltoideo-ovate, acuminate, bi-pinnate, sub-

membranaceous, primary pinnæ 5-12 rather distant, terminal one as large as or larger than the rest, all long petiolate, lowest pair often bipartite, so as to form a pedate frond, pinnules petiolulate $\frac{1}{2}$-$\frac{3}{4}$ of an inch long, obliquely rhombeo-ovate, sub-falcate, acute, sub-auriculate at the superior truncated base and coarsely spinuloso-serrated, except at the inferior base, sori in a single series at the sinuses of the serratures close to the superior margin and apex of the pinnules, indusium reniform.—*Hook. Sp. Fil.* iv, 25.—Polystichum amabile, *Hook.*—Aspidium amabile, *Blume. En. Fil. Jav., p.* 165.—Aspidium rhomboideum, *Wall Cat. n.* 364.—*(I have always found the involucre in young state quite reniform and not peltate as described by Sir W. Hooker).*

Pulney Hills—Anamallays. Not common.

PLATE No. CIX.

16. *Lastrea gracilescens.* (Hook ;) Caudex rather short, thick, horizontal creeping on the surfaces of the ground, scaleless, copiously rooting beneath, stipites very numerous and crowded on the upper surface of the caudex, slender a span to a foot long, stramineous-brown, fronds a span to $1\frac{1}{2}$ foot and more long, membranaceous, oblong-ovate or sub-lanceolate acuminate pinnated, pinnatifid at the apex, pinnæ sessile, 2-3-4 inches long, nearly $\frac{1}{2}$ an inch wide, oblong acuminate deeply pinnatifid, segments oblong, obtuse, plane quite entire, veins distant, all simple, sori small nearer the margin of the segments than the costules, involucres small, reniform, glabrous soon obsolete. *Hooker. Sp. Fil.* iv, 93 ;—Aspidium, *Bl. En. Fil. Jav., p.* 155 ;—Aspidium Thelypteris, *Benth. Fl. Hong Kong (vix. Swartz)* ;—A. glandiligerum, *Kze. Analicta Pteridoge, p.* 44—*Metten Asp., p.* 86.

Travancore Hills—Rather rare.

PLATE No. CX.

LASTREA—(*continued.*)

The Filix-Mas group.

17. *Lastrea patentissima.* (Presl. ;) Caudex short, stout, erect, densely paleaceous with broad-lanceolate scales varying much in colour, stipites short, copiously scaly, rachis densely clothed with long subulate tawny or golden scales : fronds very large, pinnate 14-16 inches broad ; pinnæ patent, deeply almost to the partial rachis pinnatifid, segments very close and compact, oblong-parallelogram more or less sharply toothed towards the apex, margins ciliated, partial rachis and costa more or less scaly below, nearly glabrous above, sori in 2 rows, one on each side of the costa of the segments, situated on the centre of the superior veinlet, indusium reniform—Nephrodium (Lastrea) Filix-mas variety *β.* parallegrammum, *Hooker. Sp. Fil.* iv. 116 ;—Lastrea Filix-mas variety *γ. Moore* ;—Aspidium patentissimum, *Wall. Cat. n.* 340 ;—Aspidium Donianum, *Spr.* iv., *p.* 321 ;—Aspidium Wallichianum, *Spr.* iv., *p.* 104 ;—Aspidium paleaceum, *Don. fl. Nep., p.* 4 (not Swartz) ;—Lastrea patentissima, *Presl. Tent. Pterid* ;—Dichasium patentissimum, *Al. Braun. Flora.* 1841, *p.* 710.

Nilgiris, common in ravines and sholas about Ootacamund.

PLATE No. CXI.

18. *Lastrea elongata.* (Swartz ;) Caudex short, stout, erect, paleaceous, stipe and rachis more or less scaly, or nearly quite glabrous, fronds large, very broadly ovate, bi-pinnate with the lower portions often tri-pinnate, partial rachis more or less scaly, pinnules glabrous, segments more or less deep, obtusely rounded, crenated ; sori generally one to each segment on the centre of the superior veinlet, indusium very large (as in L. Cochleata, but the frond is not contracted as in that species).—Aspidium marginatum, *Wall. Cat. n.* 391 ;—Aspidium elongatum, *Swartz. Syn. Fil., p.* 55 ;—Lastrea elongata et marginata, *Moore* ;—Aspidium Filix-mas var. *γ.* elongatum, *Hook. Sp. Fil.* iv. 117 ;—Asp. depastum, *Schk. Fil., p.* 50 *t.* 51 ;—A. erosum, *Schk. t. c., p.* 46 *t.* 45 ;—Aspid. Canariense, *Al. Braun. Flora.* 1841, *p.* 708—(*Kze. Linnœa* xxiv, *p.* 285) ;—A. Ludovicianum, *Kze. in Sillim Journ. 2nd Series.* vi., *p.* 84 ;—Nephrodium Floridanum, *Hook. Fil. Exot. t.* 99 ;—Asp. Schimperianum, *Hochst and A. Braun. Flora.* 1841, *p.* 708.

Anamallays—Nilgiris rocky hills—5,000 feet and upwards.

PLATE No. CXII.

19. *Lastrea intermedia.* (Beddome ;) Caudex short, erect, paleaceous, stipe short scaly ; fronds pinnate, ovato-lanceolate, 6-10 inches long, 3-4 inches broad, pinnæ distant, short ovate to broad lanceolate, pinnatifid more or less deeply, (but not pinnated) segments broad, obtusely rounded, glabrous—sori very large, reniform, irregularly placed.

This small pinnate species seems a very distant variety of the Filix-mas group, it has the very large involucres of cochleata, but it seeds on all its fronds, and they are never contracted, or very slightly so—it is intermediate between the next species and cochleata.

Nilgiris—near Malee Mand.—Anamallays 5,000 feet.

PLATE No. CXIII.

20. *Lastrea odontoloma.* (Moore ;) Caudex short, erect, densely paleaceous, stipes and rachis more or less densely covered with golden, or tawny scales, fronds lanceolate, pinnate, with the lower pinnæ again pinnated (hence bi-pinnate below) partial rachis scaly, pinnæ narrow, lanceolate to linear-lanceolate, pinnules more or less sharply toothed (sometimes with very long sharp teeth at the apex) often lobed at the base, sori reniform small, in a nearly regular row on each side of the flexuose costa of the pinnules.

Nilgiris—Anamallays—above 5,000 feet.

PLATE No. CXIV.

21. *Lastrea cochleata.* (Moore ;) Caudex stout, erect, paleaceous, stipes and rachis scaly, or often quite glabrous, fronds 1½ to 3 feet long, broad ovate-lanceolate, pinnate with the pinnæ pinnatifid to nearly the base, pinnules incised with sharp teeth on the lobes below the serratures ; fertile fronds contracted, lower pinnæ again pinnated, upper ones pinnatifid, sori very large, closely packed and perfectly covering the under-surface of the fronds. Nephrodium (Lastrea) Filix-mas, var. *δ.* Cochleata, *Hook. Sp. Fil.* iv. 117 ;—Nephrodium cochleatum, *Don. Prod. Fl. Nep.* ;—Arthrobotrys avara, *Wall. Cat. n.* 1034 ;—Arthrobotrys macrocarpa, *Wall. Cat. n.* 395.

This very curious species is only to be found in fructification in the cold weather, the fertile fronds, when they first appear in October or November, are quite contracted and covered with one mass of fructification; they die off again in January or February. I have never detected any appearance of fructification on the broader sterile leaves which are growing all the year round, and it is quite an error I think to suppose, that the enlarged sorus is the effect of a disease.

Wynad, Anamallays and other localities, very abundant from 2,500 to 4,000 feet elevation—Nilgiris 5,000 to 6,000 feet rare.

PLATE No. CXV.

The above 5 species belong to the Filix-Mas group of Lastrea, and probably few Botanists would agree as to what are distinct species, and what varieties only. Sir William Hooker considers them all (even the last) as only varieties of the European " Lastrea Filix-Mas." Mr. Moore looks upon them as different species, and Dr. Wallich founded a new genus for the last curious species under the name of " Arthrobotrys." I have had most of them growing under cultivation, and have found them constant; whether they are distinct species, or only varieties, I have thought it less puzzling to figure them each under a distinct name, than to give them two names such as " Lastrea Filix-Mas, patentissima," &c.

(*b*) *Indusia orbicular, peltately affixed.*

* *Veins reticulated, with free included veinlets.*

ASPIDIUM—*Swartz Schrad, Journ.* 1,800. ii 4. 29 *(reduct).*

(Bathmium, Presl ;—Proferea, Presl ;—Podopeltis, Fée ;—Polypodii. sp. Auct. ;—Tectarieæ sp. Cavanilles ;—Phymatodis sp. Presl ;—Drynariæ. sp. Fée :—)

Sori indusiate, rotundate, the receptacles compital, *i.e.* produced on the points where several veins join, or medial, more rarely terminal. *Indusium* orbicular peltate. *Veins* pinnate from a central costa, prominent ; or rarely uniform ; *venules* and *veinlets* compoundly anastomosing in (about two or three series of) irregular or nearly equal sided areoles, from the ultimate of which proceed free divaricate veinlets.

Fronds simple, pinnate or tri-pinnate, herbaceous. Rhizome short, erect, or decumbent. (Moore.)

1. *Aspidium polymorphum.* (Wallich) Caudex creeping, stipites from a few inches to 1-2 feet long, fuscous a little scaly at the base, fronds very variable in size, from 3-6 inches (when they are geneally cordate or 3-lobed, or tri-foliate) to 2 feet or more long, adult coriaceo-membranaceous, pinnated with 4-8 pairs of pinnæ and terminated by an odd one, as large as or larger than the rest, (sometimes confluent with the two below it) basal ones very large and long, and generally unequal, bi-fid or bi-partite, or more frequently bi-foliate, the segments curved upwards, intermediate ones 5-6, or 8 inches long, oblong, acute or acuminate, sub-opposite, in distant pairs sub-petiolate, inferior base unequal, the lowest often dilated, primary or costal veins horizontally patent, slightly arcuate, these are connected by arched veins transversely, the meshes or areoles are occupied by copiously anastomosing veinlets, and their areoles with free sterile simple or forked veinlets, sori copious, generally small, all compital; involucres peltate, rarely present or very fugacious—*Hooker. Sp. Fil.* iv. 54.—*Wall. Cat. n.* 382.—Aspid. rostratum, *Wall. Cat. n.* 383.—Aspid. repandum, *Willd. Sp. Pl.* v., *p.* 216.—Bathmium, *Fée.*

Nilgiris—very common in ravines on the Coonoor ghat, and other localities—Pulney Hills.

PLATE No. CXVI.—*(Fig A. a juveline simple frond).*

PLATE No. CXVII, is a figure of a fern common on the Anamallay Hills, 3,000 feet elevation. It is, I believe, only a variety of *A. polymorphum*, and I have called it *polymorphum β. contractum;* it differs from the normal form in having contracted fertile fronds and very large sori. I have never been able to trace any sign of an indusium even on the youngest specimens, but that is very seldom traceable on the normal form—the sterile fronds do not seem to differ in any way from *polymorphum.*

2. *Aspidium?* pl. No. CXVIII.—This is a sterile frond of a species of Aspidium or Sagenia, it is probably an undescribed species. I procured it on the Anamallays, and was not fortunate enough to find it in fructification, the fronds are perfectly glabrous and shining on both sides.

CYRTOMIUM, *Presl. Tent. Pterid.* 86.

(Phanerophlebia, Presl. ;—Aspidii Sp. Auct. ;—Polypodii Sp. Auct.)

Sori indusiate, globose in several series parallel to the costæ ; the *receptacles* medial on the excurrent, free or anastomosed venules or veinlets, rarely terminal near the margin. *Indusium* orbicular peltate. *Veins* pinnato-furcate, from a central costæ ; the lower anterior *venules* free, the rest angularly and irregularly anastomosing, forming unequal sub-hexagonal areoles, within which are produced 1-3 excurrent *veinlets ;* or the upper venules only angularly anastomosing.

Fronds robust coriaceous pinnate. Rhizome short, thick, erect. (Moore).

1. *Cyrtomium caryotideum* (Presl. ;) Caudex short, thick, erect, densely paleaceous with large erect scales, stipites tufted 10-12 inches long, very scaly below, fronds ½ a foot to 2 feet long, oblong sub-coriaceo-carnose, (when recent) of a pale yellowish green colour, opaque (not glossy) pinnated, pinnæ 3-4-6 inches long, petiolate ovate much acuminated (sometimes repando-lobate) falcate sharply serrated, superior base much broader than the inferior, generally extended into a long sharp acuminated appendage or ear, the lowest pair and terminal pinnæ often with one on each side, veins anastomosing, pinnate flexuose, costal areoles with a solitary soriferous free veinlet, superior ones with two or three veinlets clavate at their apex, sori scattered or sub-seriate, indusium orbicular, peltate entire or laciniated at the margin, rachis and rather short petioles setaceo-paleaceous. *Hook. Sp. Fil.* iv, 40 ;—*Presl. Tent. Pterid., p.* 86 *t.* 2, *f.* 26 ;—Aspidium caryotideum, *Wall. Cat. n.* 376 ;—Aspidium anomophyllum *(Zenker Plantæ Indicæ)* var. macroptera et microptera, *Kunze ;*—Cyrtonium falcatum, *Pappe et Raws. Syn. Fil. Afr. Austr., p.* 15 *(not of Swartz).*

Nilgiris—Sholas about Ootacamund—rather rare.

(The variety "microptera" of Kunze has more numerous and smaller pinnæ than the plant here figured, which is "macroptera" of Kunze, there are however intermediate forms, and they cannot even be considered as varieties.)

PLATE No. CXIX.

POLYSTICHUM, *Roth. Tent. Fl. Germ.* iii. 69 *(reduct).*

(Hypopeltis, *Richard ;* Aspidium, *Auct. ;* Rumohra, *Raddi ;* Hemigonium, *J. Smith ;* Peltochlæna, *Fée ;* Cyclopeltis, *J. Smith ;* Hemicardion, *Fée ;* Teetariæ Sp. *cavanilles ;* Nephrodii Sp. *Presl. ;* Lastrea Sp. *Auct. ;* Polypodii Sp. *Auct. ;)*

Sori indusiate, globose ; the *receptacles* medial, or rarely terminal on the venules. *Indusium* orbicular peltate. Veins pinnato-furcate, or simply forked from a central costa, *veinlets* free ; the lower anterior one usually, sometimes more fertile.

Fronds simple pinnate, or bi-tri-pinnate, rigid, coriaceous, the margins usually mucronate-serrate—Rhizome short, thick, erect. (Moore).

1. *Polystichum auriculatum.* (Swartz ;) Caudex stout, thick, erect or oblique, more or less copiously scaly, stipites brown or stramineous, 4 inches to a span long, more or less paleaceous, as is the rachis, fronds ½ a foot to 2 feet long oblong—or broad-lanceolate, pinnated sub-membranaceous, or coriaceous, pinnæ horizontal, varying much in size and form 1-3 inches in length, sessile or nearly so, in the normal state from a broad cuneate base ; truncated and sharply auricled above ; excised beneath, falcato-lanceolate, acuminate, subentire or serrated especially on the upper margin and towards the apex unarmed, or varying extremely in length and breadth, and becoming more or less pinnatifid with the segments or lobes or teeth variously spinulose, often deeply pinnatifid, and even again pinnate at their base, sori in two rows nearer the margin than the costa, involucres membranaceous, very fugacious, (only to be detected in very young fronds)—*Hooker. Sp. Fil.* iv, 11 ;—*Sw. Syn. Fil., p.* 44 ? Polypodium, *Linn. Sp. Pl., p.* 1548.

(The normal form which is the only one found in Southern India has simply pinnated fronds, in some of the forms found in Northern India, the fronds are bi-pinnate).

Very common on the higher ranges of the Nilgiris and other lofty mountains on the Western side of the Presidency.

PLATE No. CXX.

2. *Polystichum aculeatum* (Sw. ;) Caudex short, sub-erect, stipites tufted and rachises more or less clothed with ferruginous scales of two forms, one slender and resembling hairs on the stipes especially, mixed with large ovate or lanceolate ones, sometimes two

colored, fronds 1-3 feet long, oblong-lanceolate acuminate, sometimes proliferous, bi-rarely tri-pinnate, sub-coriaceous, primary pinnæ approximate from a broadish sub-petiolate, base long—or linear-lanceolate, sub-falcate, pinnules close, sub-rhombeo-ovate or lanceolate free, sub-petiolate or decurrent at the very base with the adjacent ones, spinosely or setosely serrated or lobate, the superior base more or less auricled, sori generally in 2 rows on each pinnule, and usually nearer the costa than the margin, costæ and costules more or less villoso-paleaceous beneath—*Hook. Sp. Fil.* iv, 18;—Polypodium, *Linn*;—Aspidium aculeatum, *Sw.*;—Aspidium rufo-barbatum, *Wall. Cat., p.* 369 *and* 370;—Asp. squarrosum, *Don. Prod. Nep., p.* 1;—Aspidium setosum, *Wall. Cat. n.* 371;—Polystichum Wallichianum, *Presl*;—Aspidium brachypterum, *Kze. in* xxiv, *Linnœa, p.* 288;—Asp. sub-inerme, *Kze. l. c., p.* 200;—Polystichum tacticopterum et mucronifolium, *Kze. l. c.*

Very common about Ootacamund and the higher elevations of the Pulneys and Anamallays—a very variable species, and there are numerous forms which have received different names, but they all run one into another. *Polystichum rufo-barbatum* (Wallich) is a very beautiful form, common about Ootacamund; it is densely clothed with reddish hairs. Plate cxxii is the *Polystichum angulare* (Willd. Sp. Pl. v., p. 257) considered a distinct species by most botanists, but united with P. aculeatum by Sir W. Hooker—it is a very common form at Ootacamund—fronds much more membranaceous, pinnules small, orbicular, rhomboid, mostly auriculate, the serratures setiferous rather than spinulose.

PLATE No. CXXI. *Polystichum aculeatum* (Sw.)

PLATE No. CXXII. *Polystichum angulare* (Willd.)

TRIBE 1. (§ 11) ASPLENIEÆ.

(*a*). Indusium simple distinct.

* Veins parallel transversely combined by a marginal vein.

THAMNOPTERIS, *Presl. Tent. Pterid.* 105.

(Neottopteris, *J. Smith*;—Asplenii Sp. Auct.)

Sori indusiate, linear-elongate, parallel oblique, the *receptacles* lateral, anterior. *Indusium* narrow-linear, membranaceous, plane. Veins simple or forked from a central costa; *venules* approximate, parallel united at their apices by a continuous slightly arcuate marginal vein.

Fronds simple, coriaceous often robust. Rhizome short, thick, erect. (Moore).

1. *Thamnopteris Phyllitidis* (Don.) Fronds tufted about 1½ foot long 2-3 inches broad, lanceolate sub-coriaceous, tapering at the base, sessile or decurrent into a more or less elongated stipes, costa at the back below sub-acute, veins approximate spreading. *Don. Prod. Nep., p.* 7—*Hooker. Sp. Fil.,* iii. 80;—Neottopteris stipitata, *J. Sm.*;—Neottopteris Phyllitidis, *J. Sm.*; *in Hook. Journ. of Botany,* iii. 400;—Asplenium simplex, *Blume. En., p.* 174.

Moist woods on the Anamallays 3,000 to 4,000 feet elevation, very abundant—(only differs from *T. Nidus* in being much smaller).

PLATE No. CXXIII.

ASPLENIEÆ *(continued.)*

* * *Veins free.*

ACTINIOPTERIS, *Link. Fil. Sp.* 73, 79.

(Belvisiæ sp. *Mirbel* ;—Asplenii sp. *Auct* ;—Blechni sp. *Presl* ;—Acrostichi sp. *Auct* ;—Pteridis sp. *Auct* ;—Acropteridis sp. *Fée*).

Sori indusiate, linear, elongate ; the *receptacles* marginal in the contracted rachiform segments, lateral on the veins (which are few and longitudinal). *Indusium* plane, membranaceous, opening on the inner side. *Veins* few simple, nearly parallel from an indistinct costa ; the basal and external ones sub-marginal, soriferous.

Fronds flabellately-partite, the segments rachiform, hardly foliaceous with few veins and marginal sori. Rhizome sub-globose. A curious little palm-like fern, the sori though marginal and apparently pteroid, are really parallel with and lateral on the veins, it must therefore be placed amongst Asplenieæ. (Moore).

1. *Actiniopteris radiata.* (Link). *Link. Fil. Sp. Hort. Berol. p.* 80—*Hooker Sp. Fil.* iii, 276. Asplenium radiatum, *Konig* ;—Acrostichum australe, *Vahl Symbol* i, *p.* 84. t. 25 ;—Acropteris radiata, *Fée Gen. Fil. p.* 76 ;—Pteris, *Metten. Fil. Hort. Lips. p.* 53 ;—Blechnum flabellatum, *Presl. Tent. Pterid. p.* 103.

Found all over the presidency in dry rocky places from the sea level up to 3,500 or 4,000 feet.

PLATE No. CXXIV.

ASPLENIUM, *Linnæus Gen. Pl.* 783.

(Phyllitis, *Mœnch* ; Onopteris, *Necker* ; Cœnopteris, *Bergius* ; Daræa, *Jussieu* ; Acropteris, *Link* ; Amesium, *Newman* ; Homaloneuron, *Klotszch* ; Tarachia, *Presl* ; Brachysorus, *Presl* ; Hypochlamys, *Fée* ; Daræastrum, *Fée* ; Allantodieæ sp., *R. Brown* ; Athyrii sp. *Auct* ; Polypodii sp. *Auct* ; Aspidii sp. *Auct* ; Scolopendrii sp. *Roth* ; Diplazii sp. *Auct.* ; Acrostichii sp. *Linn* ; Blechni sp. *Auct.*)

Sori indusiate, linear short, or elongate oblique ; the *receptacles* lateral on the anterior side of the veins. *Indusium* linear membranaceous, plane, or fornicate. *Veins* simple or forked from a central costa (sometimes single and costæform in the ultimate narrowly cut segments) or forked from the base of the segments, the costa being evanescent or wanting, *venules parallel*, direct free.

Fronds coriaceous, herbaceous or membranaceous ; rarely rachiform, simple lobed pinnate or variously decompound ; the rachis or veins not rarely proliferous. Sori usually on the anterior side of the venules, but often inverse in the basal auricles, sometimes diplazioid. Rhizome short, erect, or decumbent, sometimes stoloniferous. (Moore).

1. *Asplenium ensiforme.* (Wallich). Caudex short, thick, scarcely repent bearing dark-brown subulate scales at its summit, and at the base of the stipes—fronds cœspitose a span to 1 and 1½ foot long, ½ to ¾ inch broad, linear lanceolate, elongate firm, coriaceo-carnose, brownish green entire, gradually acuminated, and gradually and finely attenuated at the base into a petiole 2 or more inches long, veins sunken, erecto-patent usually once sorked, sori linear, broad in age, neither extending to the costa nor to the margin, about half an inch long. *Hook. Sp. Fil.* iv, 89—*Wall. Cat. n.* 200.

Anamallays—banks of the Toracadoo river, 4,500 feet elevation—rare.—Sholas on the Kudrà Mukh (5,550 feet) near Manglore.

PLATE No. CXXV.

2. *Asplenium Wightianum.* (Wallich.) Caudex small, sub-repent rooting scaly above, stipites tufted a span or more high, fronds a foot and a half to two feet long, ovato-lanceolate coriaceous, pinnæ distant, petiolate, erecto-patent 4-6 inches and more long, elongato-lanceolate, subglossy rather coarsely, but not deeply serrated, (or occasionally in some sterile fronds deeply and irregularly pinnatifid with the segments serrated) rather longly acuminated and entire at the apex, attenuated at the base and gradually decurrent into the petiole, veins simple, rarely forked approximate, sori erecto-patent linear extending from the costa but not to the margin, indusium firm, white, and the same white color and texture extends to the vein, or as much of it as is occupied by the indusium, rachis compressed, scarcely winged. *Hook Sp. Fil.* iii, 105.—*Wall Cat. n.* 2215.—A. coriaceum, *Bory in Bel. Crypt. p.* 46.—A. longipes, *Fée.*—A. Walkeræ, *Hook. Sp. Fil.* iii, 108.

Anamallays—Bolamputty valley in the Coimbatore hills.—Pulney mountains—on rocks and trees in moist forests on the banks of rivers 2,000 to 4,00 feet elevation.

PLATE No. CXXVI.

3. *Var. β. A. Wightianum microphyllum* (R. H. B.) pinnæ much smaller with an unequal cuneate base—scarcely acuminated the apex—serratures obtusely rounded, superior basal serrature generally deeper than the others and bifid.

Anamallays.

PLATE No. CXXVII.

4. *Asplenium persicifolium.* (J. Smith). Stipes and rachis livid, slightly scaly, fronds 2 feet and more long, sub-coriaceous, ovato-lanceolate, very opaque, dark-green, impari-pinnate, or terminated by a viviparous scaly bud, pinnæ numerous, yet distant. (20-30) patent 4-6 inches long, petiolate narrow-oblong lanceolate, finely acuminate, sometimes sub-falcate, more or less serrated at the apex, deeply inciso-serrate, the base obliquely cuneate, superior rounded or sub-truncate, inferior sub-excised, veins sunk obscure, usually forked, sori linear, remote rather short, patent often irregular not reaching to the costa nor the margin, involucre linear, firm, sub-coriaceous. —*Hook. Sp. Fill.* iii, 108.—Aspl. Zenkerianum, *Kze. in Linnœa*, xxiv, *p.* 259.

Nilgiris—Sholas on Dodabett and behind the Avalanche bungalow.—Anamallays.

PLATE No. CXXVIII.

5. *Asplenium varians.* (Hook. and Grev.) Caudex small, erect, densely rooting, stipites tufted slender, 1-2 inches long, slightly paleaceous above, fronds 2-4 inches long, membranaceous, lanceolate bi-pinnate, primary pinnæ ½ an inch long on short petioles, distant, patent obtuse, pinnules few on each pinna 1-1½ line long, cuneate and irregularly incised, sometimes all the pinnules are confluent, and then the pinnæ are pinnatifid, veins variously forked, sori few, 2-3 on each pinnule at length confluent, involucres pale brown, membranaceous, entire sub-athyroid. *Hook. Sp. Fil.* iii, *p.* 192 ;—Aspidium varians, *Wall in Herb.—Hook.* ;—Asplen. plebeium, *R. Br* ;—Aspl. fimbriatum, *Kze. in Linnœa*, xviii, *p.* 117.

Nilgiris—Common about Ootacamund.

PLATE No. CXXIX.

6. *Asplenium tennifolium.* (Don.) Caudex horizontal stout, when old, scarcely paleaceous, stipites tufted 3-4 inches to a span long, castaneous at the base, fronds oblong-ovate, acuminate pale green, membranaceous 6-12 inches long, tri-sub-quadri-pinnate, pinnæ and pinnules all petiolate, primary pinnæ patent 2-3 inches long, broad-lanceolate, ultimate pinnules obovato—or linear-cuneate tapering into the petiole, bifid or pinnatifid or laciniated, the segments very acute, almost mucronate, apices of the fronds and primary pinnæ pinnatifid with linear segments, veins solitary, central terminating much short of the apices, sori rarely more than 2 on the disc or pinnule, oblong, generally on a forked nerve, and the membranaceous involucres open towards each other.—*Hook. Sp. Fil.* iii, 193.—*Don. Prodr. Fl. Nep. p.* 8.—Asplenium Concinuum, *Wallich.*

Nilgiris—Common in Sholas on the banks of streams at Ootacamund, and at the Avalanche—Anamallays.

PLATE No. CXXX.

7. *Asplenium heterocarpum.* (Wallich). Caudex long, creeping horizontally, young frond-buds clothed with small black subulate scales, fronds sparse but approximate, stipites 4 inches to a span long, scaly at the base, and as well as the slender rachis purple-ebeneous glossy, fronds oblong or linear, lanceolate 6-14 inches long, and acuminate, membranaceous dark-green sub-translucent pinnated, pinnæ very numerous, approximate horizontally patent 1-1½ inch long, petiolate (ultimate ones very small and decurrent into a pinnatifid acumen) oblongo-lanceolate generally obtuse, dimidiate (the lower half as it were cut off parallel with the rachis in a straight line nearly to the apex) superior base truncate parallel with the rachis not auricled, superior margin and apex only deeply inciso-serrate, segments bi-dentate monosorus, veins forked, sori solitary (rarely 2) confined to the marginal serratures or segments, small oval-oblong, involucre brown, membranaceous entire. *Hook Sp. Fil.* iii, 132—*Wall. Cat.* 218.—Asplenium cheilosorum, *Kze. in Metten. Asplen. p.* 133 *t.* 5. *f.* 12, 13.

Travancore Hills—Mercara—Nilgiris (Avalanche and Neddiwattan).

PLATE No. CXXXI.

8. *Asplenium resectum.* (Sm.) Caudex long, creeping, branched about as thick as a goose quill, stipites scattered distant generally (as well as the slender rachis) ebeneous-purple and very glossy, sometimes herbaceous and opaque, 5 inches to a span long, fronds membranaceous, dark-green 4-5 inches to a foot and a half long, from deltoid-ovate to narrow-oblong acuminate, pinnate, pinnæ varying much in number, size and shape (terminal ones very small or more or less confluent) sub-rhombeo-ovate or lanceolate often falcate, especially towards the apex, acute or even acuminate, generally approximate from ½ an inch to 3 inches long, more or less inciso-serrate, superior base truncated and parallel with the rachis not auricled, inferior base, and sometimes the whole inferior half-excised, cut off as it were in a straight line or deeply lunate form, so that the costa is in part, or nearly wholly close to the inferior margin, veins forked at the superior base two or three times, sori (rarely sub-diplazioid) rather numerous, small oblong in the superior half, in the inferior few and those towards the apex, or none ; indusium membranaceous. *Hook. Sp. Fil. III,* 130 ;—Asplenium eroso-dentatum, *Bl. En. Fil. Jav., p.* 183 ;—A. decurrens, *Wall.* ;—Asp. unilaterale, *Lam. Encycl. II,* 305 ;—A. cristatum, *Wall. Cat* ;—A. serræforme, *Metten. Asplen. p.* 119. *t.* 4, *fig.* 13 ;—A. emarginato-dentatum, *Zenkes M. S. Kunze in Linnœa XXIV, p.* 263 ;—A. amœnum, *Presl.* ;—A fraternum, *Presl.* ;—A. abscissum, *Bl. En. Fil. Jav., p.* 182 ;—A. porphyrocanlon et erythrocanlon, *Bl. l. c. p.* 182 *and* 3 ;—A. lætum, *Wall. Cat. n.* 209 *(not Sw.)* ; —A. excissum, *Presl.*

Nilgiris, Anamallays, Pulnies, &c., very common at an elevation of 3,000 to 5,000 feet.

PLATE No. CXXXII.

9. *A. multijugum.* (Wallich.) Caudex erect, stout, with densely fibrous roots, stipites very numerous, cœspitose 4-6 inches long ebeneous, black glossy as well as the rachis, fronds erect or flexuose, or sub-decumbent, 8 inches to a foot long, elongated linear-oblong, moderately acuminated, sometimes proliferous at the apex, rather firm-membranaceous in texture, dark opaque green, pinnated, pinnæ 12-30 and more pairs horizontally approximate, gradually smaller at the apex, 4-8 lines long, falcato-oblong, obtuse, obliquely cuneate at the apex, 4-6-8 inches long, falcato-oblong, obtuse obliquely cuneate at the base sessile, superior base truncate prolonged into a sharp auricle parallel with and contiguous to the rachis, inferior base cut with a horizontal line which extends nearly the length of the inferior margin of the pinnæ, the rest superior, and the apex crenato-dentate, costa slender, reniform parallel with and very near the lower margin, veins distant, superior ones oblique, simple or forked, inferior ones few and almost parallel with the costa and margin, sori oblong, rather large, those above the costa 2-5 rarely more oblique, inferior ones 1-3, involucres broad. *Hook. Sp. Fil. III,* 140—*Wallich Cat. n.* 207 ;—Aspl. normale, *Don. Prod. fl. Nep., p.* 7 ;—Asp. multicaule, *Wall. Cat. n.* 208 ;—Aspl. opacum, *Kunze in Linnœa XXIV, p.* 261.

Nilgiris—Anamallays. Common on the higher elevations.

PLATE No. CXXXIII.

10. *Asplenium trapeziforme?* (Roxb.) Rhizome erect, rachis flattened above, fronds 14 inches to nearly 2 feet long, 3 to 3½ inches broad, membranaceous glabrous, lanceolate, pinnated, the lower pinnæ the largest, and gradually smaller upwards, pinnæ 16-20 pair, shortly petiolate, the lower ones from 1½ to nearly 2 inches long, 6 lines broad, trapezoid-lanceolate, acuminate, crenated with the crenatures obtusely or acutely bifid, superior base generally more or less auricled, inferior exciso cuneate, costa flexuose, all the veins forked, except 1 or 2 near the apex, which are simple ; sori 5-7 on each side of the costa, involucres membranaceous—*Roxb. Crypt., p.* 497 ?

Nilgiris and Anamallays—Common.

PLATE No. CXXXIV.

11. *Asplenium Brasiliense.* (Raddi.) Rhizome erect, stipes glabrous, grooved and winged above, convex beneath, fronds 10 inches to 1½ foot long, about an inch and a half broad, elliptic linear-lanceolate, rigidly membranaceous, glabrous, dark-green, pinnated with the upper and lower pinnæ gradually smaller, pinnæ numerous very shortly petiolate, ½ to ¾ of an inch long, 3-4 lines broad, trapezoid-lanceolate obtuse, crenated with the crenatures obtuse, entire or obtusely bifid, superior base auricled, inferior base exciso-cuneate, costa of the pinnæ flexuose, superior basal veins forked, the upper ones simple, inferior veins all entire, or the basal one only forked, sori 2-4 on each side of the costa, but none on the auricle, involucre membranaceous thin, at length reflexed. *Raddi. Fil. Bras. p.* 36, *t.* 51, *f.* 1.—Aspl. lunulatum, *Swartz.*—A. lunulatum var. sphenolobium, *Kze. in Linnœa* xxiv, p. 264.—A. pulchrum, *Wall. Cat. n.* 2211.—A. brachyotus, *Kunze in Linnœa* xxiv, 261.

Nilgiris—Common about Ootacamund.

PLATE No. CXXXV.

12. *Asplenium formosum.* (Willd.) Caudex short, stout, densely radiculose, stipites very numerous, cœspitose scarcely an inch long, and as well as the rachis ebeneous, with a narrow wing on each side, fronds a span and more long, elongato-lanceolate acuminate rigid, sub-coriacio-membranaceous blackish-green, pinnated, pinnæ an inch long, numerous approximate horizontal, semi-ovate sub-sessile rather obtuse, superior base dilated, truncate and parallel with the rachis scarcely auricled, inferior base cut off horizontally, the rest of the margin deeply and pinnatifidly incised, lobes oblong, obtuse, those nearest the base bifid, inferior pinnæ distant, smaller sub-triangular, veins simple or forked, sori broad, oblique 2-3 on the lower side of the costa, none or rarely one on the upper side. *Hook. Sp. Fil.*, iii, 143 ;—*Willd. Sp. Pl. v. p.* 329 ;—Asp. subalatum, *Hooker et. Arn. Bot. Beech. Voy. p.* 312. *t.* 71 ;—Asp. odontophyllum, *Wall. Cat n.* 2216.

Nilgiris—very abundant in moist woods at the higher elevations.

PLATE No. CXXXVI.

ASPLENIUM *(continued.)*

13. *Asplenium auritum.* (Swartz.) Caudex short, ascending, crowned with paleaceous ovate acuminate scales, stipites cœspitose 4-6 inches long, slightly winged above, lurid greenish-brown, fronds oblong or broad ovato-lanceolate, acuminate pale green, coriaceous truncated not contracted at the base, pinnate pinnatifid at the acuminate apex, pinnæ often numerous, horizontal sub-petiolate 2-3 inches long, straight lanceolate or linear-lanceolate, acute or acuminate, or oblong and obtuse, the margin entire or variously toothed or serrate pinnatifid, superior base generally auricled, auricle often free or truncate with a sub-triangular auricle, sometimes the pinnæ are deeply pinnatifid in a regular manner, or the pinnæ are in part or wholly again pinnated with the pinnules various in shape, entire or serrated, veins oblique, once or twice forked, sori oblong, generally copious, arranged in 2 series between the costa and margin, often confluent, indusium rigid-membranaceous of the same color as the frond, rachis compressed green, more or less sulcate and winged. *Hook. Sp. Fil.* iii, 178 ;—*Swartz, Fl. In. Occ., p.* 1616 ;—Asplenium sulcatum, *Moore.*

Nilgiris, Coonoor on rocks rare—Anamallays rocks in the bed of the Toracaddoo river 4,500 feet elevation.

PLATE No. CXXXVII.

14. *Asplenium prolongatum.* (Hooker.) Caudex small woody inclined, rooting scarcely scaly, stipites 2-4 inches long, tufted stramineous sub-compressed, fronds 4-5 inches to a foot long at the utmost, coriaceous or sub-chartaceous, oblong or narrow linear-oblong falcate, suddenly terminated in a caudate, naked extension of the rachis 1-2 inches long, rooting at the very apex, bi-scarcely tri-pinnate, primary pinnæ 1-1½ inch long, horizontally patent, generally approximate, or crowded, semi-ovate obtuse, petiolate semi-pinnate (pinnules more numerous on the superior than the inferior side) pinnules 3-4 lines long, mostly simple, entire rarely forked, still more rarely, and only in the lowest superior pinnule bi or tri-partite, pinnules and segments narrow linear often curved, obtuse monosorous, veins single, sori oblong or linear, very narrow, marginal, involucres firm-membranaceous of the same pale green color as the frond.—*Hooker, Sp. Fil.* iii, 209.—*Hook. 2nd Cent. of Ferns*—42.

Shevagherry Hills—rare.

PLATE No. CXXXVIII.

15. *Asplenium planicaule.* (Wallich.) Caudex small, thick, erect, densely rooting, crowned with black subulate scales, stipites 3-5 inches long, tufted, and as well as the rachis compressed sparsely and deciduously villoso-paleaceous, fronds a span rarely to a foot long, sub-coriaceous, firm oblong acuminate (apex pinnatifid) petiolate, sub-horizontal dimidiato-ovate, acuminate venoso-striate from 1 to (rarely) 1½ inch long, superior base obliquely truncate, sub-auriculate, inferior base excised for half or more of the length from the base, the rest of the margin irregularly and often deeply inciso-pinnatifid, segments narrow, sometimes pungent, veins erecto-patent, conspicuous approximate, once or more forked, sori linear-elongated, those towards the apex of the pinnæ and those below the costa parallel with the costa, those in the auricle more patent, involucre pale-brown, firm. *Hook. Sp. Fil.* iii, 163 ;—*Wall. Cat. n.* 189 ;—Asplenium falcatum var. c. abbreviatum, *Kze. in Linnœa.* xxiv, *p.* 260 ;—A. semihastatum, *Wall. M. S. (not Kze.)* ;—Tarochia truncata, *Br.*

Very common in most mountainous tracts on the western side of the presidency.—Myhendra hill near Berhampore.

PLATE No. CXXXIX.

16. *Asplenium contiguum.* (Klfs.) Fronds pinnate, pinnæ linear-lanceolate attenuate, inciso-serrate, serratures toothed, the superior base rotundato-cuneate sub-auriculate, inferior abscisso-attenuate, sori contiguous, parallel with the costa, caudex repent, stipes 6 inches long, frond equally long, pinnæ an inch and a half to 3 inches. *Hook. Sp. Fil.* iii, 156 ;—*Kaulf. En. Fil., p.* 175.

Anamallay Hills, 3,000 feet elevation ; Nilgiris 7,000 feet—Wynad.

PLATE No. CXL. (Fig. A is one of the pinnæ of a more cut variety, common in the Wynad.)

17. *Asplenium falcatum.* (Lam.) Caudex repent, stout, more or less clothed with dark-bown sphagnoid scales, stipites 6-10 inches long, lurid-brown, and as well as the rachis deciduously villoso-paleaceous, fronds 8-10 inches to 2 feet long, sub-coriaceous ovato-lanceolate, pinnate, pinnæ horizontal rather long-petiolate 4-6 inches and more long from a broad obliquely cuneate base, ½-¾ of an inch broad, lanceolate, much and often finely caudato-acuminate, lobato-pinnatifid, the segments pointing upwards, the superior

base the broadest, sub-auricled generally acute, and as well as other of the inferior lobes serrated, inferior base excised, towards the apex the lobes are reduced to rather large remote serratures, veins approximate, erecto-patent with forked branches, sori long-linear, numerous diverging from near the costa in the direction of the veins to near the margin, giving a striated appearance to the pinnæ, involucres narrow, firm-membranaceous. *Hook. Sp. Fil.* iii, 160;—*Lam. Encycl.* ii, *p.* 306;—Asplenium polyodon, *Forst. Prod., p.* 80;—Aspl. zamiæfolium, *Pr. Relig. Hænk.* i, *p.* 43?;—Tarachia Hænkeana, *Pr. Epim. Bot., p.* 76;—Asp. cultratum, *Gaud in Freyc. Voy. Bot., p.* 317.

Anamallay forests on rocks 3,500 feet—Courtallum and Travancore. (Wight.) (The scales of the caudex are hair-like, and the plant here figured is perhaps rather a variety of A. longissimum, Blume—if so I have not found the true falcatum.)

PLATE No. CXLI.

18. *Asplenium macrophyllum.* (Swartz.) Caudex repent, stout, paleaceous with subulate sphagnoid, dark-brown scales stipites 4-5 inches to a foot long, lurid or greenish brown, deciduously paleaceous, fronds 8-10 inches to a foot and more long, broad-ovate coriaceous firm-reddish-brown, when dry, pinnate, pinnæ 3-5 to 24-25 petiolate, horizontal from a broad cuneate base, trapezio-ovate or broad-lanceolate, gradually tapering into a more or less elongated acumen 3-5-6 inches long, undivided or with one or two sharp lobes, especially the superior ones, from 1 to 3 inches broad in the broadest part, superior base rounded, inferior excised in a straight line, unequally and slightly or deeply inciso-serrate, straight or falcate, striated with venation, terminal pinnæ often much larger than the rest bifid or trifid, veins numerous, crowded parallelo-radiate several times forked, sori very long in the large pinnæ as long as the veins 2-3 inches, involucres very narrow, firm. *Hook. Sp. Fil.* iii, 158;—*Sw. in Schrad. Journ.* 1800 ii, *p.* 52;—A. intermedium, *Kaulf. in Sieb. Syn. n.* 68;—A. Kaulfussii, *Pr. Tent. Pterid, p.* 106;—A. canaliculatum, *Bl. En. Fil. Jav., p.* 180;—A. coriaceum, *Rox. Crypt. Fil., p.* 497;—A. Finlaysonianum, *Wall. Cat., p.* 101;—A. megalophyllum, *Desv. in Mem. Soc. Linn.* vi, 275;—A. platyphyllum, *J. Sm., Hook. Journ. Bot.* iii, 408;—A. oxyphyllum, *J. Sm. l. c.*, 408.

Var. β urophyllum—pinnæ broad-lanceolate long caudate;—A. urophyllum, *Wallich Cat. n.* 192;—A. Tavoyanum, *Wall. Cat. n.*, 1035;—Anamallay forests on rocks and trees 2,000 to 4,000 feet elevation.—Nilgiris.

PLATE No. CXLII.

19. *Asplenium caudatum.* (Forst.) Caudex nearly as thick as a swan's quill, terete clothed especially towards the apex, with broad-subulate brown sphagnoid imbricated falcate scales, stipites (rachis and the whole frond when young) villoso-squamose, sub-aggregate a span or more long, dull-lurid-brown, fronds 1-1½ foot long, coriaceo-chartaceous broad lanceolate, pinnated acuminated, the apex pinnatifid, pinnæ numerous rather remote, 2-3-4 inches long, petiolate sub-falcate from a more or less elongated and obliquely cuneated sub-rhomboid base, lanceolate, gradually and very long acuminated (caudate) superior base rounded or sub-auricled, scarcely truncate, the inferior more or less excised, the margins very coarsely serrato-pinnatifid, superior serratures entire sharp, the rest bifid or inciso-serrate, veins erecto-patent mostly forked, sori-linear, elongated almost parallel with and near the costa, often imbricating in age, frequently confluent, involucres firm-membranaceous. *Hook. Sp. Fil.* iii, 152.—*Forst. Prod., p.* 80;—Aspl. aureum, *Bl. En. Fil. Jav., p.* 184;—Aspl. truncatilobum, *Fée*;—A. cyatheæfolium, *Bory in Rich. Voy. Astrolab. Bot., p.* 19;—Diplazium cyatheæfolium, *Pr. Epim. Bot., p.* 88;—A. multisectum, *Bl. En. Fil. Jav., p.* 185.

Cochin—(I have not myself met with this species, and the drawing is taken from a specimen kindly sent me from Ceylon by Mr. Thwaites.)

PLATE No. CXLIII.

NOTE.—*The above 5 species of the (simply pinnate) furcatum group, viz., planicaule—contigum—falcatum—macrophyllum, and caudatum are very closely allied, and Botanists do not agree as to the limits of the species.*

20. *Asplenium furcatum.* (Thunb.) Caudex oblique, scarcely repent, stout, clothed above with copious very slender glossy brown silky hair-like ciliated scales, stipites copious, tufted 4 inches to a span long, more or less clothed as is the rachis with ferrugineous ciliated hair-like scales or glabrous, fronds a span to a foot and more long, ovato-lanceolate, acuminate coriaceous rigid, mostly bi-rarely tri-pinnate dark-green and glabrous above, pale and often villous beneath, pinnæ and pinnules more or less patent, primary ones petiolate, secondary ones more or less decurrent generally narrow, cuneate or sub-spathulate or rhomboidal, truncated or rounded or acuminated, at the apex bi-trifid or bi-tripartite, the apices dentate, or variously and often very irregularly incised; veins conspicuous, compact, once or more forked erect (giving a striated appearance to the pinnæ) linear elongate parallel with the central vein (there is no distinct costa)

chiefly on the lower half of the pinnule, involucre membranaceous very narrow. *Hook. Sp. Fil.* iii, 165 ;—*Thunb. Prodr. Fl. Cap. p.* 172 ;—Asp. fragrans, *Schk. Fil. p.* 199 *t.* 130 *b.* (not Swartz) ;—Asp. falsum, *Retz. obs.* vi. *p.* 83 ;—A. adiantoides, *Lam.* (non alior) ;—A. præmorsum, *Sw. Fl. In. Occ.* iii, 1620 ;—A. Camriense, *Willd. Sp. Pl.* v, *p.* 339 ;—A. geminaria. *Bory* ;—A. strictum, *Bory* ;—A. Mascariense, *Desv.* ;—Asp. nigricans, *Kze.* ;—A. tripartitum, *Bl.* ;—A. falcatum var. abbreviatum, *Blume* ;—A. cuneatum, *Hook. et. Grev. t.* 189 (not Lam.) ;—A. laceratum, *Desv. Mem. Linn. Soc.* vi, 278 ;—A. hirsutum, *Heyne in Wall. Cat. n.* 212 ;—A. Mysureuse, *Roth. in Wall. Cat. n.* 213 ;—A. cicutarium, *Roxb. Crypt Pl. p.* 38 ;—Tarachia Browniana, *Presl. Epimel. Bot. p.* 260.

Very abundant about Ootacamund in the Nilgiris and on the higher ranges of other lofty mountains on the western side of the presidency.

A very variable species as to the shape of the pinnules and the amount of pubescence.

PLATE No. CXLIV.

A—is one of the pinnæ of a much cut and hairy variety, very common at Ootacamund (A. præmorsum var. β. furcatum, *Moore.*)

B—pinnules of a broader-leaved hairy variety.

21. *Asplenium laciniatum.* (Don.) Caudex thick, short, ascending, densely clothed with blackish falcate imbricated subulate rigid scales, stipites cæspitose 4-6 inches, brown, and as well as the stramineous rachis partially and deciduously scaly compressed, fronds erect a span to a foot long, oblong-acuminate, subcoriaceous tawny, brown when dry, very opaque, pinnate, the apex narrow, pinnatifid, pinnæ distinctly petiolate 20-50 horizontal, ½ an inch to 1 inch long, semiovate or semiovato—lanceolate, subfalcate auricled at the superior base, excised at the inferior, far more than half the length of the pinnæ lobed and inciso-serrate, or again pinnate especially in the lower half, the rest laciniato—pinnatifid, pinnules cuneate bi-trifid, superior basal one (corresponding to the auricle in the more entire pinnæ) large broad flabelliform cristato-laciniate, veins distant forked, sori oblong 3-4 radiating in the auricle (or ultimate pinnule) towards the apex arranged nearly parallel with the costa. *Hook. Sp. Fil.* iii, 164 ;—*Don. Prodr. Nep., p.* 8 ;—Aspl. cæspitosum, *Wall. Cat. n.* 217 ;—A. falcatum v. β. laceratum, *Kunze in Linnæa* xxiv, 260 ;—Aspl. dapauperatum, *Wall. Cat., p.* 234.

Nilgiris—(Schmidt.)

I have never met with this fern, and the figure here represented is taken from Sir William Hooker's Species Filicum.

PLATE No. CXLV. (*Fig A. variations of the pinnæ.*)

22. *Asplenium exiguum.* (Beddome.) Caudex, a small erect rhizome with copious fibrous radicles and clothed above with numerous subulate black scales, stipites numerous, 3-12 lines long blackish purple more or less furnished with long black subulate scales, fronds 1½ inch (often copiously in seed) to 6 in. long, 2½ to 8 lines broad, rachis sulcated above, convex beneath, slightly flexuose, more or less extended at the apex into a naked tail and often bearing a young plant, pinnæ numerous, subsessile from a broad base, when young more or less hairy (under the microscope) at length glabrous, membranaceous, in the smaller fronds sub-orbicular and simply crenate, in the larger ones oblong-lanceolate pinnatifid, below cuneato-excised, the superior and inferior basal auricles 3-4 dentate or crenate, the other lobes bi-denate or entire, superior piunæ gradually smaller, uppermost ones often very minute, distinct or spathulate but fertile, (bearing 1-2 sori) inferior pinnæ gradually smaller, subrotund or flabelliform (always fertile) sori of the larger pinnæ arranged in a double row, 1 row of 4-5 on each side of the costa and approximate to it, superior auricle generally bearing 1 diverging sorus, rarely two, sometimes none, lower auricle generally barren, rarely bearing 1 or very rarely 2 sori—veins obscure, terminating in a thickened point with the magin.

Nilgiris rare. I have only found it on the banks of the river in the shola above the Kalhatty water-fall, growing on rocks. It would be difficult to give a correct idea of this variable little species from description only, the figures however are very characteristic. It is nearly allied to Asp. camptorachis, Kunze, Linn. XXIV, 262, and I should have referred it to that species, except for the character, " soris in parte pinnæ inferioris nullis," which could not apply to any of the fronds that I have gathered to this species.

PLATE No. CXLVI.

23. *Asplenium Trichomanes.* (L.) Caudex short, thick, densely fibrous, stipites, 1-4 or 5 inches long, numerous tufted dark, castaneous or black ebeneous glossy marginal, fronds 4-6-12 inches long, linear-lanceolate coriaceo-membranaceous, dark dull-green paler beneath pinnated, pinnæ numerous horizontal, scarcely petiolate, lower ones distant and smaller, oval or obovate or oval-oblong, obliquely cuneate at the base, superior base rounded, sometimes truncated or even auriculate, sometimes excised at the inferior base, the margin

entire or irregularly crenato-serrate, costa subcentral, veins few, distant oblique, generally forked above the middle, sori oblique in two equal series, involucres pale-brown, membranaceous entire or jagged. *Hook. Sp. Fil.* iii, 136 ;—*Linn. Sp. Pl., p.* 1540, *in part* ;—A. Trichomanoides, (*Cav. Dem.* 257, *n.* 635 (*not Mich.*) ;—A. melanocaulon, *Willd. Sp. Pl.* v, 332 ;—A. Harovii, *Godr.* ;—A. microphyllum, *Tineo* (*fide Metten*) ;—A. saxatile, *Salisb. Prod., p.* 403 ;—A. densum, *Brack, fil. U. S. Expl. Exp., p.* 151 *t.* 20 ;—A. dichroum, *Kze.* (*Moore*) ;—A. heterochroum, *Kze. in Linn.* ix, 139 ;—A. anceps, *Sol. M. S. Hook. et Grev. Ic. Fil. t.* 195 ;—A. castaneum, *Schl. in* v, *p.* 611, *Linn.*

Kalhutty on the Nilgiris between 5,000 and 6,000 feet elevation.

PLATE No. CXLVII.

24. *Asplenium nitidum.* (Sw.) 2-3 feet high, stipes a foot and more high, terete glabrous, blackish-brown, frond deltoid a foot broad, bi-pinnate rachis, terete furrowed, pinnæ alternate, horizontally patent, pinnules distinct, petiolate rhombeo-ovate, angled at the base above and below, rounded at the apex, serrato-dentate above lineato-striate beneath radiato-venose, lowest pinnules pinnatifid at the base or furnished with a cuneato-obovate auricle, superior ones gibbous above, all quite glabrous, glossy above, paler beneath, sori contiguous, straight and oblique near the costa not extending to the margin, involucres whitish membranaceous. *Sw. Syn. Fil., pp.* 84 *and* 280 ;—A. insigue, *Blume. En. Fil. Jav., p.* 188 ;—A. pulchellum, *Wall Cat. n.* 214.

Sisparah ghat on the Nilgiris 4,000 feet elevation.

PLATE No. CXLVIII.

25. *Var. β obtusum*, pinnules obtuse—veins more prominent.

Bolampatty Valley—Coimbatore Hills—Travancore Hills.

PLATE No. CXLIX.

(Note variety β. has the pinnules shaped more like those of A. spathulinum, (J. Sm.) a Ceylon species, the sori of spathulinum, however are longer and extend to the margin. The following 5 *species—Aspl. nitidum, Sw.; Aspl. cuneatum, Lam.; Aspl. affine. Sw.; Aspl. spathulinum, J. Sm.; and Aspl. laserpitiifolium, Lam. are all very closely allied, and it is no easy point to decide to which species any fern of the cuneatum group should be referred).*

ATHYRIUM, *Roth. Tent. Fl. Germ.* iii. 58. *reduct.*

(Solenopteris, *Zenker*; Asplenii sp. *Auct*; Aspidii sp. *Auct.*; Diplazii sp. *Auct*; Polypodii sp. *Auct*; Nephrodii sp. *Auct*; Dareæ sp. *Auct.* ; Tectarieæ sp. *Cavanilles*; Lastrea sp. *J. Smith* ; Allantodieæ sp. *Auct.* ; Cystopteridis sp. *Auct.*)

Sori indusiate, short-oblong-lunate, or unequally or sometimes equally hippocrepiform ; the receptacles on the anterior or sometimes also crossing and returning along the posterior side of the veins. *Indusium* of the same form, often lacerato-fimbriate. *Veins* simple or forked from a central costa ; *venules* free, sometimes pinnate.

Fronds herbaceous, bi-tri-pinnate. Sori more or less generally, the basal ones usually rarely nearly all arcuate. Rhizome short, erect or creeping—although some or a greater portion of the sori are similar to those of Asplenium, the occurrence of hippocrepiform sori, more or less numerous, sufficiently distinguishes this genus. (*Moore*).

1. *Athyrium Hohenackerianum.* (*Kze.*) Rhizome short, horizontal cæspitose, densely ferrugineo-paleaceous, partial rachises, margined glabrous, primary short or shortish, and the stipes angled loosely squamoso-paleaceous, rhizome short, horizontal cæspitose, densely ferrugineo-paleaceous ; fronds membranaceous flaccid, nearly glabrous, opaque olivaceous, paler beneath, lanceolate long-acuminate, slightly flexuose, pinnato-pinnatifid or sub-bi-pinnate, pinnæ decurrent into a short petiole, divergenti-patent rather remote, obliquely oblong, auricled above, attenuate at the apex more or less obtuse, lower ones divaricated, abbreviated, superior ones confluent, pinnules or segments ovato-elliptic, sub-falcate, rotundate or truncate, decurrently cuneate at the base more or less confluent, involucres bullate, pale brown. *Hook Sp. Fil.* iii, 220 ;—Allantodia Hohenackeriana, *Kze. in Schk. Fil. Supp.* 11—*p.* 63—*t.* 26 ;—Asplenium, *Metten. Aspl., p.* 193.

Nilgiris, Anamallays and Wynad, not uncommon—Jungles about Palghat,—Coorg and South Canara, very abundant from the plains up to 4,000 feet.

PLATE No. CL.

ATHYRIUM *(continued.)*

2. *Athyrium falcatum* (R. H. B.) Rhizome short cæspitose densely covered with golden scales—stipes short more or less covered with linear golden scales, fronds 6 to 12-14 inch long with the rachis above dilated or winged, pinnate, linear-lanceolate acuminate pinnæ numerous sessile alternate, smaller towards the base of the frond, and confluent or pinnatifid at the apex, 8-12 lines long, falcato-ovate deflexed, obtuse or acuminated, generally furnished with a large obtuse auricle at both the superior and inferior base, above pinnatifid about ½ down to the costa, segments obtuse crenated, sori numerous in a line on each side of the costa, and on each side of the vein of the auricles, at length confluent and nearly covering the under surface of the pinnæ.

Anamallays, elevation 5,000 feet, dry grassy places.—The Myhendra hill near Berhampore, 4,500 feet—Mahableshwar hills.

PLATE No. CLI.

3. *Athyrium macrocarpum.* (Blume.) Fronds sub-coriaceous glabrous pinnate with the pinnules pinnatifid or pinnated (*i. e.*, bi-pinnate) pinnæ petiolate, pinnules sessile trapezoideo-oblong obtuse, obtusely crenated at the apex, superior ones confluent, superior basal one larger, repando-crenulate at its upper base sub-rotundo-auriculate, sori very large, involucres more or less lacerato-fimbriate, asplenioid, lunate or hippocrepiform, rachises sub-marginate, glabrous or slightly furfuraceous stipes paleaceous below. *Blume in Herb. Hooker ;*—Aspidium, *Blume En. Fil. Jav., p.* 162 ;—Athyrium foliolosum, *Moore Ind. Fil., p.* 143 *(vix Wallich) ;*—Lastrea macrocarpa, *Moore Ind. Fil., p.* 95 ;—Aspl. fallax, *Metten Asplen., p.* 194, *t.* 6 *f.* 7-8.

Nilgiris—Anamallays.

PLATE No. CLII.

4. *Athyrium macrocarpum var. β.* (R. H. B.) Fronds much larger and bi-pinnate, lower pinnæ with their pinnules petioled with their petioles dilated so as to form a broad wing to the partial rachis, or sessile with a dilated base, sori not so large as in the normal form (at least for the size of the plant).

Nilgiris—abundant near Neddiwattam.

PLATE No. CLIII.

5. *Athyrium Filix-fœmina.* (Bernh.) Caudex ascending paleaceous with broad ferruginous scales, stipites tufted a span to a foot and more long, stramineous-brown fronds 1½-3 feet long, oblong rather suddenly acuminate, sub-membranaceous bi-rarely tri-pinnate, primary pinnæ numerous patent from a moderately broad sessile base oblong-lanceolate acuminate 4-6 inches long, pinnules numerous, approximate horizontally patent sessile ½-¾ inch long, oblong rather obtuse, lower ones deeply pinnatifid, the segments ovate with 2 or 3 strong and sharp serratures, superior ones more entire coarsely serrated, uppermost ones confluent into a pinnatifid or serrated acumen, sori copious, one to each segment of the pinnule near the rachis oblong, involucre very convex, straight or variously curved or hippocrepiform membranaceous more or less fringed or erose at the margin. *Hook. Sp. Fil.*, iii, 218 ;—*Bernh. Schrad N. Journ. Bot.* 1806, 1 *pt.* 2, *p.* 26 *t.* 2 *f.* 7 ;—Allantodia tenella, *Wall. M. S. in Herb. Hook. ;*—Athyrium tennifrons, *Wall. Cat. n. p.* 206 ?

Forests on the north bank of the Godavery—Camptee.

PLATE No. CLIV. A. A magnified portion of one of the pinnæ shewing the spiculæ on the rachis.

6. *Athyrium pectinatum.* (Wallich.) Stipes scaly below, rachis glossy furrowed, sometimes furnished with a few deciduous scales ; fronds membranaceous very variable in size, 6 inches to 3 feet long bi-pinnate with the pinnules of the lower pinnæ pinnatifid almost to the rachis—(*i. e.* sub-tri-pinnate) pinnæ distant 3 to 8 inches long, short petioled ovato-lanceolate acuminate rachis of pinnæ often dilated or winged, pinnules ½ to 1 inch long (the superior basal one generally longer and larger), sub-sessile from a dilated base, more or less deeply pinnatifid (as shewn in figures A and B) segments crenated often sharply so, the superior basal one generally larger, veins pinnate, veinlets simple or forked, sori near the costa, 2-3 on the larger basal segment and 1 on each of the other segments, involucres membranaceous straight curved or hippocrepiform—spore cases very black when ripe.

Nilgiris—very abundant about Ootacamund, banks of streams by road-sides (a dwarf form with incurved pinnules) and in all Sholas.

PLATE No. CLV.

A very variable species, the figure represents nearly ⅔rds of a frond (the apex and stipe wanting). *Athyrium aspidioides* (Schlecht) is, I believe, only one of the more compound and finely cut varieties of this species, there are numerous intermediate forms—*Athyrium gymnogrammoides* (Kl.), specimens of which I have received from Ceylon through Mr. Thwaites (C. P. 1344) seems to differ in its much larger pinnæ, (14 inches long) and in its more regular asplenioid sori—Plate No. CLVI is a drawing from Mr. Thwaites' specimen, it is recorded by Sir W. Hooker as from the Nilgiris, but I have never myself met with it.

8. *Athyrium nigripes.* (Metten). Frond bi-pinnate, membranaceous nearly glabrous, pinnæ petiolate oblongo-lanceolate, acute, pinnules sub-decurrent cuneato-oblong rather obtuse, lowest ones sub-petiolate more or less pinnatifid, superior ones inciso-serrate confluent sori near the costules rachis, glabrous very flexuose.

Nilgiris—in Sholas Neddiwattan and Sisparah.

PLATE No. CLVII.

9. *Athyrium australe.* (Brack). Fronds bi-pinnate, deltoid membranaceous, pinnules pinnatifid attenuated at the apex, lobes oblong-obtuse, inciso-serrate involucres quite terete, (sausage like), lower ones often double bursting irregularly. *Brack. Fil. U. St. Expl. Exp.* 173 ;—Allantodia australis and tenera, *Br. Prod. Fl. Nov. Holl., p.* 149 ;—Aspl. Brownii, *J. Smith, Hook. Fil. N. Zeal.*, ii, *p.* 149 ; —A. assimile, *End. Prod. Fl. Norf., p.* 30 ;—A. spectabile, *Wall. Cat. n.* 237 ;—Aspl. multicaudatum, *Wall. Cat.* 229 ;—Allantodia sylvatica, *Bl. En. Fil. Jav.*, 173 ;—Diplazium brachysorum, *Metten* ;—Aspl. physosorum, *Sieb. Fl. Mixta n.* 268.

The indusium is like that of Allantodia, the lower ones are often double as in Diplazium, it has hardly a right to a place in Asplenium, Athyrium, or Diplazium, and would be better placed next to Allantodia in a genus distinguished by free venation.

Nilgiris—about Ootacamund and Neddiwattan.

PLATE No. CLVIII.

A. Magnified portion of a pinnule upper side showing the winged costa.

B. C. Under side showing the fructification and the cordate acuminate scales present on the costa.

D. A magnified sorus.

(Athyrium Selenopteris, (Metten), said to be found on the Nilgiris, is quite unknown to me, it is perhaps a form of A. Hohenackerianum).

* * * Veins reticulated, the marginal veinlets free.

ALLANTODIA, *R. Brown. Prod. Fl. Nov. Holl.* 149. (reduct).

(Asplenii Sp. *Mettenius* ;—Hemidictyi Sp. *Presl.*)

Sori indusiate, oblong-cylindrical ; the *receptacles* sub-lateral, anterior on the basal part of the veins. *Indusium* membranaceous fornicate at first involving the sorus at length reflexed, *veins* simple, parallel at the base and there soriferous, becoming forked and reticulated in elongated areoles towards the margin ; the ultimate veinlets free clavate terminating within the margin.

Fronds pinnate tender herbaceous, Rhizome decumbent. (Moore.)

1. *Allantodia Brunoniana.* (Wall). Fronds ample pinnated herbaceo-membranaceous, pinnæ large, numerous oblong-lanceolate, sessile, finely acuminated, veins free and forked near the base, and there only soriferous, anastomosing into sub-hexagonal areoles towards the margin. *Wall. Pl. Asiat. Rar., p.* 44. *t.* 52 ;—Hemidictyum ? Brunonis, *Presl. Tent. Pter., p.* iii. *t.* 3 *and* 25-26 ;—Asplenium Brunonianum, *Metten Fil. Hort. Lips., p.* 71 ;—Asplen. reticulatum, *Wall. Cat. n.* 188 ;—A. Javanicum, *Bl. En. Fil. Jav., p.* 175.

Ghats in Canara, rare.

PLATE No. CLIX.

(*b*) *Indusia connate in pairs back to back.*

* Veins free.

DIPLAZIUM, *Swartz Schrad. Journ.* 1800. ii. 4. 61.

(Lotzea, *Klotzsch and Karsten* ;—Asplenii sp. *Auct* ;—Scolopendrii sp. ;—Allantodeæ. sp. *Auct* ;—Callipteridis sp. *Bory* ;—Hemionitidis sp. *Swartz* ;—Anisogonii sp. *Hooker* ;—Microstegiæ sp. *Presl* ;—Hypochlamydis sp. *Fée* ;—Athyrii sp. *Auct.*)

Sori indusiate, linear all or the lowermost only double, *i. e.*, the *receptacles* occupy both sides of the veins. *Indusium* narrow, membranaceous, plane or fornicate ; in the double sori affixed in pairs back to back on opposite sides of the same venule, one opening anteriorly, the other posteriorly ; in the simple sori, as in Asplenium. *Veins* simple or forked from a central costa ; venules direct free.

Fronds herbaceous or coriaceous, simple pinnate or variously compound. Rhizome short, erect, rarely sub-arborescent. (The limit between Asplenium and the present genus is not very definite, in consequence of some species having but few of the double sori, notwithstanding which Diplazium has been almost universally admitted since the time of Swartz, by whom it was founded). (Moore.)

1. *Diplazium lasiopteris.* (Kunze.) Caudex creeping with wiry roots compactly scaly at the apices of the branches, stipites a span and more long, brown scaly and hispid, fronds 8 to 12 inches long ovato-lanceolate acuminate membranaceous pinnate, pinnatifid at the apex pinnæ 2-5 inches long, ½ to ¾ inch wide, sessile from an obliquely truncated auriculate base linear-lanceolate acuminate more or less deeply pinnatifid, segments falcate more or less serrated and generally with an incurved acumen, hairy above, glabrous below, except on the costa, veins pinnated in each segment, veinlets simple or rarely forked, nearly all soriferous, lower ones double. *Kunze Fil. Hort. Lips. Bot. Zeit.* 1-456.—*Linnæa* xviii, 568 *and* xxiv, 270.—Diplazium decussatum, *Moore and Houlst Gard. Mag. Bot.* iii, 231.—Asplenium tomentosum, *Mett. Asp. p.* 182.—Asplenium Schkuhrii, *Hooker Sp. Fil.* iii. 251 ?

(Asplenium Thwaitesii (C. P. 1343) a specimen of which has been forwarded me by Mr. Thwaites from Ceylon seems hardly distinct—the large bi-pinnate species (C. P. 3100) is quite distinct from this).

Pulney Hills—very abundant about Poombarry.—Nilgiris, near Ootacamund rare.

PLATE No. CLX.

2. *Diplazium sylvaticum.* (Presl.) Caudex stout erect woody sending down very stout unbranched vermiculate fibres, paleaceous at the summit with rather large almost black subulate scales; stipes a span to a foot long stout scaly only at the base, fronds 1½-2 feet long ovato-lanceolate sub-membranaceous, pinnated, pinnatifid at the apex, pinnæ below petiolate horizontally patent from a generally truncated base elongate oblongo-lanceolate acuminate sub-falcate entire or sub-sinuate or sub-pinnatifido-lobate rarely sub-auriculate at the superior base, lobes rounded entire or serrated, veins fasciculato-pinnate in the lobed pinnæ each fascicle corresponding to a lobe, sori very slender, lower ones or more double. *Hooker Sp. Fil.* iii. 248.—*Presl. Rel. Hænk.* i, *p.* 42.

Nilgiris—abundant down the Sisparah ghat.

PLATE No. CLXI.

3. *Diplazium dilatatum.* (Blume.) Caudex stout woody erect, stipes stout 2 feet and more long below paleaceous with lanceolate acuminate scales, fronds glabrous very large membranaceous or coriaceo-membranaceous tri-pinnate below with the pinnules often deeply pinnatifid (hence sub-tri-pinnate) pinnate above, and pinnatifid at the apex ; pinnæ more or less petiolate, again pinnated or pinnatifid with the pinnules or segments from simply crenated or even entire to deeply pinnatifid, very variable in size, veins pinnate simple or forked never uniting, sori narrow linear not extending to the margin, lower ones double. *Blume En. Pl. p.* 194 ;—Asplenium diversifolium, *Wall. Cat. n.* 203 *(not Bl.)* !—Diplazium extensum, *J. Sm. Hook. Journ. Bot.* iii, 408 ;—Dipl. affine, *J. Sm. l. c.* 407 ;—Asplenium dilatatum, *Hook. Sp. Fil.* iii, 258 ;—D. acuminatum, *J. Sm. Cat. Cult. Ferns ?*—Dipl. elatum, *Mett. p.* 180 ?—D. latifolium, *Moore.*

(This and the last species are both very variable, it is doubtful if the two are really distinct.)

Nilgiris—Sisparah ghat and elsewhere.—Wynad—Anamallays—Coorg, &c.

PLATE No. CLXII.

DIPLAZIUM *(continued.)*

4. *Diplazium polypodioides.* (Metten.) Caudex erect, often a trunk, stipes and rachis more or less prickly and scaly, fronds very large, coriaceo-membranaceous, bi-pinnate with the pinnules more or less deeply pinnatifid, often nearly down to the rachis, primary pinnæ (at least the lower ones) petiolate, ovato-lanceolate, acuminate 8 inches to nearly 2 feet long, pinnules sessile or sub-sessile, 3-5 inches long, ½ to 1 inch broad, oblong broader at the base and gradually attenuate to the acuminated apex, segments oblong-parallelogram, or slightly falcate obtuse, crenated or serrated; veins simple or forked, extending to the margin, sori one to each vein, on each side of the costa touching the costa, but not extending to the margin, generally only one of the lowest ones double. *Metten. Fil. Hort. Lips., p.* 78;—Diplazium frondosum, *Wallich*;—Aspl. ambiguum, *Hook. et Arnt. Bot. of Beech—Voy., p.* 107;—Diplaz. nigro-paleaceum, *Kze. in Linnœa* xxiv, *p.* 270;—Asplen. Fieldingiana, *Kze. in Linnœa* xxiv, *p.* 268;—Diplaz. asperum, *Metten and Blume.*

Very abundant in most mountainous parts of the western side of the presidency. In some parts of the Anamallays, it is quite a tree fern.

PLATE No. CLXIII.

* *Veins conniventl y anastomosing.*

CALLIPTERIS, *Bory. Voy.* i. 282.

(Anisogonium, *Presl.*; Digrammaria, *Hook.* (not *Presl.*); Microstegia, *Presl.*; Asplenii sp. *Auct*; Diplazii sp. *Auct*; Oxygoni sp. *J. Smith*).

Sori indusiate linear, all or the lowest only double, *i.e.*, the *receptacles* occupying both sides of the veins. Indusium narrow membranaceous plane or fornicate, in the double sori affixed in pairs back to back on opposite sides of the same venule, one opening, anteriorly, the other posteriorly; in the simple sori as in Asplenium. *Veins* forked or pinnate from a central costa; *venules* anastomosing irregularly at an acute angle, or each opposite pair uniting between the primary veins in superposed acute sub-triangular areoles, the marginal or superior *veinlets* free.

Fronds herbaceous or coriaceous, pinnatifid, pinnate, or bi-tri-pinnate, sometimes proliferous. Rhizome short, erect. Large growing ferns only distinguished from Diplazium by the conniventl y anastomosing veins which are analagous to those of Nephrodium (in Aspidieœ) and Goniopteris (in Polypodieæ.) (Moore).

1. *Callipteris esculenta.* (Houlst. et Moore.) Caudex stout, erect, very scaly at the summit, stipites tufted, stramineous-brown, angled; fronds ample broad, oblong acuminate bi-pinnate, below pinnatifid, in the middle simply pinnate, terminal pinnæ large, pinnatifid at the base, primary lateral pinnæ 1½-2 feet long, petiolate horizontal oblong acuminate, pinnules distant horizontal sessile, or shortly petiolate from a broad truncate frequently hastate base oblong gradually acuminated 4-6 inches long, varying in breadth entire or serrated, or variously and regularly lobed or pinnatifid at the margin, most so at the base, the lobes obtuse, serrated, veins very patent, fasciculate pinnate, the branches uniting with those of the opposite fascicle, sori copious on the veinlets rather short, linear decussate often diplazioid, and at length confluent, involucres narrow, brown membranous, costæ beneath often squamuloso-furfuraceous. *Hook. Sp. Fil.* iii, 268;—*Houlst. et Moore, Gard. Mag. Bot.*, iii, 265;—Callipteris ambigua, *Moore*;—Callipteris Malabarica, *J. Sm. Hook. Journ. of Bot.*, iii, 409;—C. Serampureuse, *Fée Gen. Fil.* 219;—C. Wallichii, *J. Sm.*;—Asplenium ambiguum, *Sw.*;—A. esculentum, *Presl.*;—A. bi-pinnatum, *Roxb. Cal. Journ. Nat. His.*, iv, 499;—A. Moritzii, *Metten*;—Anisogonium esculentum, *Presl.*;—Digrammaria esculenta, *Fée*;—Diplazium Malabaricum, *Spreng*;—Hemionitis esculenta, *Konig. M. S. Herb. Brit. Mus.*;—Microstegia ambigua esculenta et pubescens, *Presl. Epim. Bot.* 91-91-260.

Very common in moist places and banks of streams in the plains throughout the western side of the presidency—Nilgiris and Anamallays—banks of streams, &c., at no great elevation.

PLATE No. CLXIV.

(TRIBE 1, § 15,) POLYPODIEÆ.

POLYPODIUM, *Linnœus, Gen. Pl.* 784, *(reduct).*

(Psidopodium, *Necker*;—Marginaria, *Bory*;—Cryptosorus, *Fée*;—Cenopteris, *Blume*;—Dicranopteris, *Bl.*;—Adenophorus, *Gaudichaud*;—Amphoradenium, *Desvaux*;—Phegopteris, *Presl.*;—Pseudathyrium, *Newman*;—Gymnocarpium, *Newman*;—Gymnodium,

A. Braun ;—Arthropteris, *J. Smith in part* ;—Glaphyropteris, *Presl.* ;—Catenularia, *Zippell M. S.* ;—Cælopteris, *A. Braun M. S.* ;—Leptostegia, *Zippell M. S.* ;—Phylacopteris, *Kunze M. S.* ;—Hypolepidis sp. *Auct.* ;—Lepicystidis sp., *J. Smith.*

Sori non-indusiate, globose or ovoid, superficial or immersed ; the *receptacles* terminal or medial on the free veins. *Veins* simple or forked from a central costa, or simple costæform in the ultimate segments, *venules* free.

Fronds coriaceous, herbaceous, or membranaceous simple, pinnatifid pinnate or bi-tri-pinnate, articulated or continuous with the rhizome, the pinnæ sometimes articulated with the rachis—Rhizome creeping, or short, erect, or decumbent, or caudiciform.

1. *Polypodium parasiticum.* (Metten.) Caudex ascending, furnished with ovate peltate scrobiculate scales, stipes 2-4 lines long, very hairy, fronds coriaceous, sparingly clothed with black hairs beneath 1½-2½ inches long, linear lanceolate, ciliated rather obtuse entire ; veins forked, lower veinlet generally extending to the margin, superior veinlet terminating with the sorus, sori short, oblong or subrotund on a rather prominent receptacle furnished with long black setæ. *Metten, Polyp., p.* 36 ;—Grammitis attenuata, *Kunze in Linnæa* xxiv, *p.* 251.

Anamallays—Common on trees at 5,000 feet elevation—Nilgiris—at Neddiwattam, and on rocks and trees down the Sisparah ghat.

PLATE No. CLXV.

2. *Polypodium parvulum.* (Bory.) Caudex creeping, clothed with ferruginous narrow lanceolate scales, stipites 3-4 lines long margined, fronds rigidly membranaceous, glabrous 3-4 inches long, lanceolate deeply almost to the costa pinnatifid, segments 3-4 lines long, 1½ line wide, at the inferior base coadunate and continuous, oblong or ovate-oblong rather obtuse, rarely oblong-lanceolate entire, lower ones abbreviated and long decurrent, veins evident, incrassated below the apex, rarely soriferous in the middle of the back, sori 3-6 on each side. *Metten, Polyp., p.* 43.—*Bory in Willd. Sp. Pl.* v, *p.* 182 ;—P. inconspicuum, *Bl. Fil. Jav., p.* 130.

Anamallays on rocks, banks of the Toracadu river 4,500 feet elevation—Nilgiris, Lamb's rock (near Coonoor).

PLATE No. CLXVI.

3. *Polypodium obliquatum.* (Blume.) Caudex short, creeping, rather stout ferrugineo-paleaceous, stipites approximate 2-3 lines to 1½ inch long glabrous, fronds firm-membranaceous, scarcely sub-coriaceous 6-12-14 inches long, 1½-2 inches broad, lanceolate acuminate and sub-caudate tapering below, deeply pectinato-pinnatifid nearly to the base, segments approximate from a broad base, lineari-acuminate often acute entire, lower ones gradually shorter, the lowest triangular much abbreviated, costule and simple oblique veins evident not extending to the margin, sori several in 2 rows, one on each side, the costa oblique, sunk in an oval cavity (which is protuberant on the upper side of the frond) surrounded by an elevated border. *Hook. Sp. Fil.* iv, 190 ;—*Blume, Fil. Jav., p.* 181., *t.* 58, *B.* ;—Cryptosorus Blumei, *Fée Gen., p.* 231 ;—Ctenopteris rufescens, *Kze. Bot. Zeib.* iv, *p.* 425.

(The fructification of this species which belongs to the genus "Cryptosorus," Fée is very peculiar, it is sunk into oval cavities on the lower side of the frond ; the fructification of Prosaptia is somewhat similar, but in that genus the cyst is marginal, the general appearance of this species is very similar to the Prosaptias ; it would be better if it was removed from Polypodium and placed in the genus proposed by Fée, viz., "Cryptosorus.")

Shevagherry mountains.

PLATE No. CLXVII.

4. *Polypodium paludosum.* (Blume.) Caudex short, erect, covered with scales at the apex, furnished with numerous black wiry roots ; stipes elongated 1½ foot and more, long fusco-stramineous, scaly only at the very base, fronds 1½-3 feet long, 6-12 inches wide, firm sub-coriaceo-membranaceous broad-oblong-lanceolate acuminate, sometimes bi-pinnate below, above pinnate, pinnatifid at the apex, pinnæ distant, sub-petiolate alternate 3 to 10 inches long, 1-2 inches broad, in some cases sub-erecto-patent elongato-oblong acuminate, those that are again pinnated have distant patent pinnules ½-1 inch long from a broad always adnate, but not decurrent base, oblong obtusely acuminated, always more or less deeply pinnatifid at the margin, basal pair often more elongated, superior pinnæ deeply pinnatifid with long obtuse pinnatifid or entire segments, veinlets rather distant, simple or forked, sori rather large not numerous, intermediate between the costule or primary vein, and the margin, rachis, costæ, costules and principal veins often hirsute. *Hook. Sp. Fil.* iv, 244 ;—*Blume Fil.*

Jav., p. 192 *t.* 90 ;—Polyp. brunneum, *Wall. Cat. n.* 333 ;—P. longipes, *Wall. Cat. n.* 316 ;—P. adnatum, *Wall. Cat. No.* 328 ;—Phegopteris, *Metten Phegopt., p.* 29.

Very common about Ootacamund on the Nilgiris.

PLATE No. CLXVIII.

Polypodium nigro-carpum. (Beddome.) Caudex stout, sub-oblique densely paleaceous, stipes 1-2-3 feet long, densely paleaceous towards the base, scabrous above, fronds membranaceous, semi-transparent, deltoid-ovate acuminate, tri-pinnate below, bi-pinnate above and pinnatifid at the apex, pinnæ alternate, distant petioled deltoid ovate 6-12 inches long, in the basal pair the inferior basal pinnule is wanting, and the other inferior pinnules are larger than the superior ones, pinnules shortly petiolate in the inferior pinnæ, sessile in the superior ones, oblongo-ovate, secondary pinnules sessile from a broad base or the lower pairs shortly petiolate, obtuse at the apex more or less pinnatifid, segments obtuse, veins prominent not extending to the margin, but terminating within it in a pellucid dot, costa and veins furnished with weak whitish hairs on both sides, sori medial on the veins, 1 to 8 on each of the secondary pinnules becoming quite black when ripe.

Nilgiris—Very common in the Sholas on the higher ranges.

PLATE No. CLXIX.

6. *Polypodium rugulosum.* (Labill.) Caudex long, creeping, rufo-villous, whole plant more or less hairy and glanduloso-viscid, especially beneath, stipes 1-2 feet and more long, varying in size from a crow's to a swan's quill, and as well as the main rachises glossy and rough with elevated points, bright castaneous or stramineous, frond varying from 6-8 inches in length, very slender (perfect and fertile) to 5 feet in length, from 4 inches to 3 feet wide at the base, deltoid-ovate sub-coriaceous (rarely sub-membranaceous and flaccid) tri-pinnate, primary pinnæ generally in distant petiolated pairs, lowest primary pinnæ oblong-ovate acuminate ; secondary pinnæ sessile from a broad base, oblong acuminate pinnules ½ to ¾ inch long, oblong or linear-oblong obtuse lobato-pinnatifid with small rounded lobes, rarely angulato-dentate at the margin, margins often much reflexed, the veins of the lobes very flexuose, veinlets pinnate, simple or forked, the lower veinlet extending to the margin of the sinus of the lobes, and there bearing a solitary sorus (10-14 on each pinnule) but so copious that they frequently cover the whole under surface of the frond, secondary rachises terete, not winged. *Labill. Fil. Nov. Holl.* ii, *p.* 92 *t.* 241 ;—*Hook. Sp. Fil.* iv, *p.* 272 ;—Polypodium Pæppigii, *Kze. in Lin.* ix, *p.* 50 ;—Pol. fulvescens, *Hook. et Grev. Bot. Mix.* ii, *p.* 239 ;—Pol. viscidum, *Spr. ;*—P. viscosum, *Roxb. ;*—Pol. viscoso-viscidum, *Thouars Fl. Trist. d'Acunha, p.* 33 ;—Cheilanthes ambigua, *A. Rich. Fl. n. Zeal. ;*—Cheilanthes Dicksonioides, *Endl. and Kze. in Schk. Fil. Supp. t.* 8 ;—Hypolepis Dicksonioides, *Hook. Sp. Fil.* ii, *p.* 61 ;—Hyp. Pæppigiana, *Metten Fil. Lechl., p.* 18.

Nilgiris, most abundant about Coonoor and Ootacamund.

This fern when growing has much the general aspect of " Pteris aquilina"—the fructification is of course quite different.

PLATE No. CLXX.

7. *Polypodium ornatum.* (Wallich.) Caudex erect, clothed with copious long subulate scales, stipites stramineous, 1-3 feet long and up to about an inch in diameter, paleaceous at the base, smooth and polished or setaceo-paleaceous above, fronds generally very large, 1 to 6 feet long, broad ovate acuminate, firm-membranaceous quadri-pinnate, costæ, costules and veins furnished with long white soft silky spreading hairs, rachis of the pinnæ muricated beneath with hard aculii and furnished with setaceous scales, pinnæ opposite, petiolate or sessile 1-2 feet long, 8-14 inches broad, broad-oblong acuminate, pinnules sessile, oblong acuminate 4-7 inches long, rachis furnished with a very regular broad wing, tertiary pinnules 6 to 10, 1-1½ lines long, entire or slightly crenated, veinlets simple, forked, or pinnate terminating within the margin, apex thickened—sori 1 on the lower vein of each tertiary pinnule (*i. e.*, in two lines, on each side of the costa of the secondary pinnules). *Wall. Cat., p.* 327.

Wynad—Carcoor ghât abundant, one of the handsomest ferns in the presidency.

PLATE No. CLXXI.

*** Veins connivently anastomosing.*

GONIOPTERIS, *Presl. Tent. Pterid.* 181.

(Glyphotænium, *J. Smith* ;—Polypodii sp. *Auct.* ;—Meniscii sp. *Auct.* ;—Gymnogrammatis sp. *Auct.* ;—Aspidii sp. *Auct.* ;—Ct enopteridis sp. *J. Smith* ;—Phegopteridis sp. *Auct.*)

Sori non-indusiate, globose; the receptacles medial or terminal. *Veins* pinnate, prominent, *venules* (the lower pair or more) connivently anastomosing at an acute angle, from the apex is produced an excurrent veinlet, which is either short and free or lengthened to reach and unite with the next pair of the venules.

Fronds herbaceous or sub-coriaceous, pinnatifid, pinnate, or pinnato-pinnatifid. Spore cases often echinate. Rhizome short, decumbent. (Moore).

This genus bears the same relation to Polypodium in Polypodieæ, as Nephrodium does to Lastrea in Aspidieæ.

1. *Goniopteris prolifera.* (Presl). Caudex thickish, sub-repaud, stipites clustered, erect, varying in length, fronds glabrous or pilosulous, 1-2 feet and more long, sub-coriaceous pinnated, and at the apices and the axils of the pinnæ repeatedly proliferous and widely extended, pinnæ 3-6 inches long, sessile oblong-lanceolate acuminate, sometimes auricled at the base, venules 4 to 5 pairs or 8-10 in the larger pinnæ connivent at an acute angle, from the apex of which are produced excurrent veinlets, which are generally all united, so as to form a continued spurious vein or costule ; these veinlets however are sometimes short and free, and sometimes some are altogether wanting ; sori oval, rather than sub-rotund in the middle of the veinlet, sometimes near the point of junction, and then confluent and menisciod. *Hook. Sp. Fil.* iv. 13 ;—Polypodium proliferum, *Roxb. in Wall. Cat. n.* 312, *(not Kaulf.)* ;—Meniscium, *Sw. Syn. Fil., p.* 19 *and* 207 ;—*Hook. 2nd Cent. of Ferns, t.* 15 ;—*Willd. Sp. Pl.* v, *p.* 135 ;—P. luxurians, *Kze.* ;—Phegopteris, *Metten* ;—Ampelopteris elegans, *Kze. in Bot. Zeit.* vi, *p.* 114 ;—A. firma, *Kze. in Lin.* xxiv, *p.* 133.

Hills near Kamptee and Jubbulpore, very common—Nilgiris, (Zenker).

PLATE No. CLXXII.

**** Veins reticulated with free included veinlets.*

Free veinlets, divaricate.

PLEOPELTIS, *Humboldt and Bouplaud. Willd. Sp. Pl.* v, 211. *(extens).*

(Atactosia, *Blume* ;—Anapeltis, *J. Smith* ;—Chryopteris, *Link in part* ;—Microgramma, *Presl.* ;—Microsorium, *Link* ;—Anaxetum, *Schott* ;—Pleuridium, *Presl.* ;—Phymatodes, *Presl.* ;—Lepisorus, *J. Smith* ;—Phyllitidis, *J. Sm.* ;—Symplecium, *Kunze* ;—Microterus, *Presl.* ;—Dryomenis, *J. Sm.* ;—Colysidis sp., *Presl.* ;—Mecosori sp., *Klotzsch.* ;—Polypodii sp., *Auct.* ;—Tectariæ sp., *Cavanilles* ;—Drynariæ sp., *Auct.* ;—Craspedaria sp., *Auct.* ;—Phebodii sp., *Auct.* ;—Dryostachyi sp., *Auct.* ;—Dipteridis sp., *J. Sm.* ;—Niphoboli sp., *Auct.* ;—Sellignea sp., *Presl.* ;—Marginariæ sp., *Bory.*

Sori non-indusiate, sometimes covered while young by peltate scales, rotundate or elliptic (sometimes with the receptacles diffuso-confluent in lines) superficial or immersed ; the *receptacles* compital, *i. e.*, produced on the points whence several reticulated veins radiate, rarely medial. *Veins* pinnate or pinnato-furcate, from a central costa, parallel or flexuose, sometimes evanescent, the *venules* much branched, reticulated in (usually) several series of irregular or hexagonal areoles, within the ultimate of which are produced variously directed straight curved or hamate, often numerous, free sterile *veinlets* which are generally distinctly clavate at their apices.

Fronds membranaceous, or more or less coriaceous, often opaque, simple pinnatifid or pinnate, sometimes furnished with scattered peltate scales. Sori serial or irregular, rhizome creeping, the fronds articulated. (Moore).

1. *Pleopeltis phymatodes.* (Linn). Caudex long, creeping, more or less clothed with dark-brown deciduous subulato-setaceous scales or bristles, in age the caudex is covered with a chalky-white coat, stipites 2-3 inches to 1 foot and more long, fronds very polymorphous, carnoso-coriaceous from a few inches to 2-3 feet long, often simple (undivided) and lanceolate, and then rarely exceeding 10 inches long, or trifid or tripartie, or more or less deeply pinnatifid, and then appearing to attain the largest size and a diameter of 10-12 inches deltoideo-ovate, the segments as many as 17-23 to 3-8 inches long, 1-1½ wide, lanceolate oblong or linear, acute or obtuse, the margin thickened entire, venation internal, generally obscure, sometimes when the frond is translucent the veins are apparent, but veniform soon diverging and anastomosing, and forming a series of large costular areoles with often lessor but unequally-sized ones, secondary veins

numerous, united into smaller areoles, but varying in size and form and including numerous free divaricating veinlets more or less impressed, and forming pustules at the back, sori often very large, oval or globose, compital either forming a single or double series between the costa and the margin, or irregularly scattered over the frond. *Hook. Sp. Fil.* v, *p.* 83 ;—Polypodium phymatodes, *Linn. Maut., p.* 360 ;—Drynaria, *Fée* ;—Chrysopteris peltideum, longipes *and* terminalis, *Link. (fide Metten)*;—Polypodium ensiforme, *Kze. in Schk. Fil. t.* 54, *f. a* ;—Polyp. alternifolium, *Lk.* ;—Polyp. grossum, *Langsd. and Fisch., p.* 9 *t.* 8 ;—Drynaria vulgaris, *J. Sm.* ;—Phymatodes, *Presl.*

Malabar, at no great elevation.

PLATE No. CLXXIII.

2. *Pleopeltis leiorhiza.* (Wallich.) Caudex very thick, creeping, paleaceous with ovate oppressed deciduous peltate scales, stipites $1\frac{1}{2}$ and more feet long, stout, fronds ample, subcoriaceo-membranaceous glabrous, 2-3 feet long oblong or oblong-ovate pinnated, pinnæ 10-12-30, erecto-patent 8-12 inches and more long, oblongo-lanceolate much and very finely acuminated, cuneate and slightly petioled, superior ones sessile and sub-decurrent, terminal one very long, the margins entire, venation manifest uniform, costules scarcely distinct from the veins, but they do anastomose, so as to form large costal soriferous areoles, and a less imperfect series near the margin, the rest of the frond is occupied by a net-work of small areoles, including free veinlets, sori large in a single series nearer the costa than the margin, moderately sunk, so as to form slightly elevated corresponding pustules on the back of the frond. *Hook. Sp. Fil.* v, *p.* 91 ;—Polypodium leiorhizon, *Wall. Cat. n.* 303.

Anamallays, on the Kooch Mallay 4,300 feet elevation.

PLATE No. CLXXIV.

PLEOPELTIS, *(continued.)*

3. *Pleopeltis oxyloba.* (Wall.) Caudex creeping, stout, paleaceous with dense subulato-falcate ferruginous scales 2-5 inches long, fronds coriaceous, or coriaceo-membranaceous 6-12 inches and more long, deltoideo-ovate acuminate trifid, or deeply pinnatifid to within ½ an inch of the rachis with 5-11 segments, which are 3-6 inches long, ½ to 1 inch wide, very patent from a broad base oblongo lanceolate, very finely acuminated entire, thickened at the margin, the lowest ones cuneato-decurrent, terminal segment often the longest and most narrowly acuminated, venation conspicuous, costules often prominent beneath distant, united by transverse veins forming 3-4 series of primary areoles, which are filled up by lesser ones including free veinlets, sori large not sunk, arranged in a single series nearer the costa than the margin. *Hook. Sp. Fil.* v, 77 ;—Polipodium oxylobum, *Wall. Cat.* 294, *Mett. Polyp., p.* 106 ;—*Phymatodes,* Pr.

Nilgiris—On trees about Neddiwattan—rocks near Makurty peak—Sisparah ghât, and many other localities—Anamallays 4,000 feet and upwards, and other localities on the Western ghâts.

PLATE No. CLXXV.

4. *Pleopeltis longissima.* (Blume.) Caudex creeping, fleshy, partially paleaceous with rather large ovate appressed brownish scales, stipites 1-1½ foot or more long, fronds sub-coriaceous, 1½-4 feet and more long, 6-10 inches wide, narrow-oblong, scarcely acuminated, deeply pinnatifid, nearly if not quite to the rachis, generally leaving only a narrow wing, segments very numerous, 22-40, and probably many more, 4-6-8 or 10 inches long, rarely exceeding ½ an inch wide from a broad decurrent base, elongato-oblong acute or obtusely acuminate, the margin slightly thickened, venation evident, often slightly prominent and distinct (except the veinlets) on the under side, costules or rather primary veins horizontal, flexuose forming a series of large costal soriferous areoles and a second lesser series, secondary veins forming a net-work of small areoles including free veinlets, sori large, copious sub-oval, sunk into a hemispherical cavity (forming a pustule or pouch on the upper side, the mouth with a distinct elevated rim) arranged in a single series on nearly the whole length of every segment and close to the costa. *Hook. Sp. Fil.* v, *p.* 80 ;—Drynaria rubida, *J. Sm.* ;—Polypodium longissimum, *Metten, Fil. Hort. Lips., p.* 37. *t.* 25. *f.* 18, *Polyp. p.* 102 *(in part only ?)* Mettenius unites this with P. nigrescens of *Blume.* Sir Will. Hooker thinks them distinct and refers the Ceylon specimens to "nigrescens."

Bolamputty valley in the Coimbatore hills, banks of the Pámbár—Foot of Carcoor ghât, Wynad.

PLATE No. CLXXVI.

5. *Pleopeltis membranacea.* (Don.) Caudex creeping, stout, the younger portion paleaceous with blackish-green ovate acuminate scales, stipites distant or sub-aggregated 1-5 inches long, if longer winged above with the decurrent base of the frond, fronds 6 inches to 2-3 feet long by less than an inch to 6 inches broad, thin membranaceous and translucent or firm-membranaceous and opaque, lanceolate or oblongo-lanceolate, or oblanceolate, acuminate, the base long attenuated and much gradually decurrent upon the stipes glabrous, the margin entire (or rarely more or less deeply sinuato-lobate or pinnatifid, and even fimbricated throughout the whole length with long narrow unequal segments), venation very distinct, costules horizontal or nearly so slender, usually remote, connected by transverse veins which form the primary areoles, and these are filled up with irregular net-work, of which the areoles are very unequal and include copious free veinlets ; sori compital, rather small, usually in two series between the costules, more or less numerous according to the width of the frond, rarely reduced to one sorus near the costa, where a single series parallel with the costa is formed, not unfrequently there are 3-4-5 series (not very regular) between the costa, (in one instance a single series only appears between the costules and those of a very large size and abnormal in form, often oval or oblong and lying parallel with the costules.) *Hooker Sp. Fil.* v, 70 ;—Polypodium membranaceum, *Don. Prod. Fil. Nep., p.* 2 ;—Polyp. grandifolium, *Wall. Cat. n.* 282 ;—P. heterocarpum, *Bl. Fil. Jav., p.* 167 *t.* 75.

Nilgiris on trees near Neddiwattan—Anamallays from 2,000 feet upwards—Wynad, Coorg, South Canara ghâts and other mountainous tracts.

PLATE No. CLXXVII.

6. *Pleopeltis irioides.* (Lam.) Caudex creeping, clothed with brown-black ovate obtuse scales, fronds 1-3 feet long, coriaceo-carnose very glabrous, sessile or shortly stipitate, elongato-lanceolate towards the base, gradually attenuated and decurrent as far as the very base of the stipes entire, the margin revolute, acuminate or obtuse at the apex, undivided or irregularly dichotomous, fertile in the upper portion, costa manifest, venation that of "Drynaria" immersed (visible in the dried state) areoles with numerous incurved appendices, free veinlets incrassated at the apex, costal areoles sterile, the rest 4-6 seriate fertile, bearing numerous sori (14-20) irregularly scattered,

sori semi-immersed minute, inserted on a manifest receptacle on the bank of the veinlets or on the angle of the lesser areoles. *Metten* ;—Polypodium irioides, *Hook. Sp. Fil.* v, 67 ;—Phymatodes, *Presl.* ;—Drynaria, *J. Sm.* ;—P. sessile, *Kaulf.* ;—Microsorium, *Link* ;—M. irregulare, *Link Fée Gen. t.* 20, *B. f.* 3 ;—Phymatodes polycephala, *Pr. Tent.*, *p.* 198. *t.* 8, *f.* 19 ;—Aspidium microcarpum, *Bl. En. Fil. Jav.*, *p.* 142 ;—Polypodium glabrum, *Roxb. in Wall. Cat. n.* 281 ;—P. polycephalum, *Wall. Cat. n.* 273.

On trees in moist woods—Anamallays, Coimbatore hills, Nilgiris, &c., at no great elevation.

PLATE No. CLXXVIII.

7. *Pleopeltis tridactyla.* (Wall.) Aquatic, caudex creeping, branched, the young apices only paleaceous with blackish lanceolato-subulate scales, stipites more or less apart, 1-3-4 inches to 1 foot long, winged upwards, and as well as the back of the costa and costules furfuraceo-squamose, fronds 2-3-9 inches long, ¾-1½ and 2 inches wide, firm membranaceous very dark, dirty green (when dry often black) lanceolate acuminate entire, (rarely sub-hastato, tri-lobate or tri-partite, or 5 fido-pinnatifid) below long-tapering into a gradually decurrent wing upon the petiole, glabrous above, margin entire, venation very conspicuous, costules prominent beneath, rather wide apart, extending about two-thirds of the way to the margin, then uniting and forming large costal areoles, within which the sori have their origin, a second series of smaller areoles is formed nearer the margin, and these and the rest of the frond are filled up with a net-work of smaller irregular areoles including free simple or forked veinlets which have clavate apices, sori small not very numerous, 1-3 in each, large areole compital upon the secondary veins of the primary areole, often confluent into transverse, oblong or linear (grammitoid) sori. *Hook. Sp. Fil.* v. 75 ;—Polypodium tridactylon, *Wall. Cat. n.* 315 ;—*Hook. et Grev. Ic. Fil. t.* 209 ;—Phymatodes, *Presl.* ;—Drynaria dubia, *J. Sm. in Hook.* ; *Journ. of Bot.* iii, *p.* 397 ;—Polypodium pteropus, *Bl. Fil. Jav.*, *p.* 168 *t.* 76.

(I have never seen the fronds tri-partite or pinnatifid in any of the Southern Indian or Ceylon specimens).

Anamallays—very abundant in rivers : 3,000 to 4,000 feet elevation, growing on rocks under water—Rivers in the Bolamputty valley (Coimbatore hills).

PLATE No. CLXXIX.

8. *Pleopeltis Wightiana.* (Wallich.) Caudex creeping, blackish, paleaceous with rather dirty-brown ovato-lanceolate scales, stipites sub-aggregated a few lines to 1-2 inches long, fronds extremely variable in size and texture, from 3-4 inches to 1½ foot, and from ¼ of an inch to nearly 2 inches wide, lanceolate or linear-lanceolate coriaceous and opaque, or coriaceo-membranaceous or quite membranaceous, bluntly or sharply acuminated, much and gradually attenuated, at the sometimes quite sessile base, the margin entire or subsinuate : venation reticulated with free included veinlets, but there are primary veins which form large costal areoles including the lesser ones and numerous forked free veinlets and the compital sori, sori often much sunk (with protuberances at the back) forming a single series nearer the costa than the margin varying much in size, when young wholly or partially covered with very compact peltate long-stalked scales which are soon deciduous, then the sori becomes very large and pulvinate. *Hook. Sp. Fil.* v, 57 ;—*Wall. Cat. n.* 2,222 ;—Polypodium loriforme, *Hook. l. c.* ;—*Wall. Cat. n.* 271 ;—P. leiopteris, *Kze. in Linn.* xxiii, *p.* 319 ;—Pleopeltis nuda, *Hook. E. Fil.*, *p.* 63, *and Gen. Fil. f.* 18, (*not* P. nudum, *Metten*) ;—Lepisorus, *J Smith* ;—Drynaria, *Fée Gen. Fil.*, *p.* 270 ;—Polyp. nudiusculum, *Kze. in Linn.* xxiv, *p.* 253 ;—P. sesquipedale, *Wall. Cat.*, *p.* 275 ;—P. excavatum, *Willd. Sp. Pl.* v, 158 ;—P. gladiatum, *Wall. Cat. n.* 279 ;—P. phlebodes, *Kze. Mett. Polyp.*, *p.* 92 ;—P. atro-punctatum, *Hook. and Arnt. Bot. Beech Voy.*, *p.* 103 ;—P. lineare, *Th. Jap.*, *p.* 335, *Ic. t.* 19 ;—Pleopeltis elongata, *Klfs.* ;—Polyp. Gueintzii, *Metten Polyp*, *p.* 91.

Common in all hilly regions on the Western side of the presidency.

A very variable species—Pleopeltis sesquipedalis, (Wallich) is the larger and more membranaceous variety, but there are intermediate forms.

PLATE No. CLXXX.

9. *Pleopeltis lepidota.* (Willd.) Caudex long-creeping, paleaceous with lanceolate ferruginous scales, stipites remote, 1-2-4 inches long, fronds coriaceo-carnose, 3-9 inches long, ¼ to ¾ inch wide, lanceolate more or less acuminate, long and gradually attenuated at the base above, sparingly beneath, copiously furnished with orbicular ovate, small appressed peltate scales dark in the centre, pale in the circumference and denticulate veins immersed indistinct, the primary veins form large obliquely elongated areoles, which include very irregular and different sized areoles and a few free veinlets which are rarely forked, sori generally very large and often exceedingly prominent, pulvinate globose or oval, stalked scales mixed with the spore cases. *Hook. Sp. Fil.* v, 56 ;—*Willd. in Schlecht Adunbr.*, *p.* 17,

t. 8 ;—P. macrocarpum, *Willd. Sp. Pl.* v, *p.* 147 ;—Pleopeltis linearis, *Klfs.* ;—Pleopeltis ensifolia, *Hook. Ex. Fil. t.* 62 ;—Polypodium marginale, *Willd. Sp. Pl.* v, *p.* 149 ;—Grammitis revoluta, *Willd. Sp. Pl.* v, 139 ;—Pleopeltis Kaulfussiana, *Presl.* ;—Polyp. leucosporum, *Kl. in Linn.* xx, 404.

Nilgiris common in woods about Ootacamund.

Very similar to the last species in outward appearance, the venation however is different, and the under-surface of the frond is always clothed with orbicular peltate scales. The venation is only to be detected by soaking the frond, it is then much more prominent than that of P. Wightiana. The venation is more that of Phlebodium than of Pleopeltis, and there is sometimes a narrow areole formed near the costa within the large elongated areole ; this areole, however, is not always formed, the connecting veinlet being sometimes absent. (Vide magnified figure of venation) the receptacles are situated on the converging apices of several veinlets.

PLATE No. CLXXXI.

10. *Pleopeltis hemionitidea.* (Wall.) Caudex creeping, scaly, furnished with wiry scaly fibrous roots, stipites very short (3-6 lines long) scaly winged upwards, fronds 6 inches to 1½ foot long, 1-2 inches broad, membranaceous sub-chartaceous, sub-transparent very dark shining green, broad lanceolate, gradually acuminated into a fine point at the apex and gradually attenuated at the base, entire glabrous, main costa slightly scaly beneath near the base—venation very prominent, costules and veins blackish, the former pinnate nearly horizontal, the latter forming about 5 series of sub-quadrate areoles, in which are inconspicuous free veinlets which are either simple or forked, but without clavate apices. Sori compital rather large, forming one series between the costules, and these very irregular in shape and size, sub-globose or oblong, or even (by confluence) linear lying transversely with regard to the costa, parallel with the costules. *Wall. Cat., p.* 284 ;—Polypodium hemionitideum, *Hook. Sp. Fil.*, v, 73 ;—*Metten Polyp., p.* 112 ;—Drynaria, *J. Sm.* ;—Selliguca, *Pr. Tent. Pt. p.* 216. *t.* 9, *f.*17 ;—Colysis, *Pr. Epim., p.* 147.

My specimens have only a single sorus between each of the costules situated in the 2nd areole from the costa, they are not probably in full seed. It is allied to " P. membranacea," but differs in having much darker green, more crisp fronds ; the veins form more regular areoles than in that species, and both costules and veins are dark and prominent, the venules are very inconspicuous and are not as recurved nor are their apices as thickened as in " membranacea."

Sampajee ghât, (Coorg) 4 miles down from Mercara in ravines growing on rocks—Nilgiris, (MacIvor, in Herb. Hook.)

PLATE No. CLXXXII.

Niphobolus, *Kaulf. Enum. Fil.* 124.

Cyclophorus, *Desvaux* ;—Pyrrosia, *Mirbel* ;—Candollea, *Mirbel in part* ;—Scytopteris, *Presl.* ;—Spharostichum, *Presl.* ;—Polycampium, *Presl.* ;—Apalophlebia, *Presl* ;—Gyrosorium, *Presl.* ;—Galeoglossa, *Presl.* ;—Gynosorum, *Presl.* ;—Craspedaria, *Link in part* ;—Niphopsis, *J. Smith* ;—Polypodii sp., *Auct.*

Sori non-indusiate, globose, cyclose or elliptic, superficial or immersed, buried amongst dense stellate pubescence ; the *receptacles* terminal or medial on the excurrent free or irregularly anastomosing veinlets. *Veins* internal obscure, pinnate prominent or uniform, from a central costa *venules* anastomosing, sometimes transversely parallel, forming parallelogrammoid areoles with excurrent free or occasionally connivent or anstomosed veinlets, sometimes uniting in roundish or oblong hexagonal unequal oblique areoles with variously directed simple or divaricately forked *veinlets*, the veins of the fertile fronds when contracted less developed.

Fronds simple or lobed, rigid coriaceous opaque, clothed especially beneath with stellate hair-scales or sometimes even lanate ; the fertile often contracted, sometimes also more elongated, occasionally fertile at the apex only, and then there contracted, clothed especially beneath with dense stellate pubescence. Sori uni-multi-serial, often crowded and confluent. Rhizome creeping often elongated, or sometimes short, decumbent. The species of Niphobolus may be known by having polypodioid sori buried amongst stellate hairs. (Moore).

The venation of Niphobolus is very variable in different species. Presl. has formed 8 *genera out of it.*

1. *Niphobolus porosus.* (Wallich.) Caudex creeping, subulato-paleaceous with ferruginous scales, stipites aggregated short scarcely any or 3-5 inches long, and then winged or margined to the base, fronds carnoso-coriaceous 6 inches to a foot and more long, ½ an inch to 1-1½ inch wide, lanceolate or linear-lanceolate or even linear often finely acuminated, the margin quite entire (or rarely spuriously and very unequally pinnatifid with remote long and narrow segments) from near the middle gradually attenuated downwards to the caudex, at

first wholly tomentose with deep ferruginous stellated hairs, at length glabrous on the upper side and depresso-punctate the dots corresponding with the sori, venation quite sunk, veins pinnate but not prominent, venules transversely parallel and forming with the veins parallelogrammoid areoles, with two sometimes only one excurrent free clavate veinlet in each areole, sori copious and at first quite sunk among the tomentum appearing in the form of small tubercles, at length a circular opening appears, but the sori scarcely rise above the surface of the tomentum arranged indeed in series, but it is impossible to say how far these series are confined within certain areoles. *Hook. Sp. Fil.* v, 48 ;—Polypodium porosum, *Wall. Cat. n.* 266 ;—Polypodium sticticum, *Metten Polyp., p.* 128.—Niphobolus sticticus, *Kze.* ;—Niph. Schmidianus, *Kze. Bot. Zeit.* vi, *p.* 121 ;—Cyclophorus, *Presl* ;—Niph. fissus, *Bl. Fil. Jav., p.* 58. *t.* 24 ;—Polyp. Mysurense, *Heyne, Wall. Cat.* 269 ;—P. lanatum, *Wall. M. S.*

(The venation which is quite that of the genus "Campyloneurum" is evident in the young sterile fronds, but in the older fronds it can only be detected by rubbing off the tomentum and soaking the frond in water).

All mountainous tracts on the Western side of the presidency, from 1,000 feet up to 8,000.

PLATE No. CLXXXIII.

Fig. A, a magnified portion of a frond showing the venation.

Fig. B, a portion of a frond showing the dots on the upper surface, which correspond with the receptacles on the thickened apices of the veinlets.

2. *Niphobolus adnascens.* (Sw.) Caudex creeping, paleaceous with lanceolato-setaceous scales, stipites distant 1-2 inches long, fronds dimorphous carnoso-coriaceous dark-green above, but hoary with sparse stellated pubescence beneath and paler and even white with more copious compact hairs ; sterile fronds 2-4 inches long, spathulate or elliptical-lanceolate obtuse : fertile ones 6-8 inches long, linear or oblong obtuse or acute, both kinds tapering below into the stipes, costa sub-carinate, costules sunk obscure, their areoles including 4 (sometimes only 3 or 2) veinlets which are generally free with clavate apices, though they sometimes anastomose ; sori deep sunk in the tomentum and in the substance of the frond on each side of the costa, arranged 5-6 in obliquely transverse series, capsules long stalked, mixed with long stalked stellated scales. *Hooker, Sp. Fil.* v, 47 ;—Polypodium adnascens, *Sw. Syn. Fil., pp.* 25 *and* 228 ;—Cyclophorus, *Desv.* ;—Polyp. pertusum, *Roxb. Hook. Ex. Fil. t.* 162 ;—Niph. elongatus, *Bl. Fil. Jav., p.* 52 *t.* 20 ;—N. varius, *Klfs. En. Fil., p.* 125 ;—Polyp. verrucosum, *Wall. Cat. n.* 267 ;—P. caudatum, *Mett. Poly., p.* 126 ;—P. vittarioides, *Wall. Cat., p.* 270 ;—Niph. Chamissoanus, *Presl.* (fide *Metten.*)

(The venation is only to be detected by thoroughly soaking the frond).

Common in all the Western Coast forests from the plains up to 5,000 feet.

PLATE No. CLXXXIV.

3. *Niphobolus angustatus.* (Sw). Caudex long, creeping, branched paleaceous with falcate subulato-setaceous scales, stipites remote 1½-4 inches long, fronds 5 inches to a span or more long, ¾-2 inches wide, tapering below into a petiole, glabrous above hoary, sub-ferruginous with dense stellated pubescence, coriaceo-carnose sterile fronds usually the smallest and broadest and with shorter petioles broad or oblongo-lanceolate ; fertile ones longer and generally narrower in proportion, venation sunk obscure, costular areoles with free or branched and more or less connected veinlets, sori very large, sub-globose oval partially sunk in the frond, very convex forming a single series on each side between the costa and margin, sometimes longitudinally confluent. *Hook. Sp. Fil.* v, 43 ;—*Sw. Syn. Fil., pp.* 27 *and* 224 ;—Niphopsis, *J. Sm.* ;—Pleopeltis macrosora, *Presl.* ;—Polypodium sphærocephalus, *Wall. Cat. n.* 272 ;—Niphobolus, *Hook. et Grev. Jc. Fil. t.* 94 ;—N. macrocarpus, *Hook. et Arnt. Bot. of Beech Voy., p.* 74 *t.* 18.

Nilgiris, very rare—(the specimen here figured was found by the late General Johnston, I have not myself found it) Tranquebar, (Rottler).

PLATE No. CLXXXV.

4. *Niphobolus nummularifolius.* (Metten.) Caudex very long filiform, copiously rooting, paleaceous with appressed setaceous ferruginous scales, fronds dimorphous carnoso-coriaceous sub-glabrous above, beneath densely clothed with ochraceous or sub-ferruginous stellated tomentum, sterile fronds (on petioles 1-3 lines long) ½ to 1 inch long orbicular or elliptic, or sub-cordate ; fertile ones (on stipites 1-1½ inch long), 1½-2 inches long, ½ inch wide, linear or linear oblong obtuse, venation immersed in the fleshy fronds (though promi-

nent in the younger fronds when dry)—2-3 series of very irregular-shaped areoles on each side of the costa, which are empty or contain one or two clavate simple or forked free veinlets, sori generally covering the whole back of the linear fronds without order, the elliptic (generally sterile) fronds are sometimes slightly contracted and fructified at the apex. *Metten. Polyp., p.* 123, *t.* 3 *and* 9-10;—*Hook. Sp. Fil.* v, 54;—Acrostichum, *Sw. Syn. Fil., pp.* 191-419: *Tab.* ii. 1;—*Willd. Sp. Pl.* v, *p.* 100;—Galeoglossa, *Presl.*

(It is very doubtful if this fern should be retained in this genus).

Common in the lower forests of the Anamallays, Wynad, Coorg, &c., parasitic on trees.

PLATE No. CLXXXVI.

DRYNARIA. *Bory. Ann. Sc. Nat.* v, 464. *t.* 12-14.

(Polypodii Sp., *Auct.*—Phymatodis Sp., *Presl*).

Sori non-indusiate, large rotundate, or by confluence elongated, sometimes immersed: the *receptacles* produced on the points where several reticulated veins join, *i. e.*, compital. *Veins* pinnate prominent from a central costa; *venules* compoundly anastomosing in two or three series of irregular quadrate areoles, within the ultimate of which are produced free divaricate sterile *veinlets.*

Fronds pinnatifid or pinnate, dimorphous, the sterile short sessile, querciform, strongly veined; the fertile many times larger, with the segments articulated. Rhizome creeping.

1. *Drynaria quercifolia.* (L.) Caudex creeping, short, stout, densely clothed with red-brown satiny lanceolato-subulate soft scales, fronds coriaceous or sub-coriaceous of two kinds; sterile ones varying in size from 3-12 inches and more long and 7-8 inches wide, green when very young, but soon turning dark-brown, glossy, cordato-ovate variously lobato-pinnatifid, sometimes half way down to the costa; fertile ones 2-3 feet long, long-petiolate broad-ovate deeply, nearly to the rachis, pinnatifid, segments 5-9 inches long, 1-1½ wide oblong acuminate entire, venation manifest, costules distinct rather distant, united by transverse veins forming 4-6 primary soriferous areoles filled up with a network of small quadrangular areoles with or without free veins, sori compital small, numerous, two in each primary areole, consequently in two series between and parallel with the costules. *Hooker Sp. Fil.* v, *p.* 96;—Polypodium quercifolium, *Lin. Sp. Pl., p.* 1547;—Phymatodes, *Presl.*;—Polyp. Linnæi, *Bory. An. Sc. Nat. Ser.* i, v, *p.* 464, *t.* 12;—P. sparsisorum, *Desv.*;—P. Schkuhrii, *Bory. b. c.*

Very common on the Western side of the Presidency from the plains up to 4,000 feet—growing on trees or rocks.

PLATE No. CLXXXVII.

TRIBE I. (§ 8) CHEILANTHEÆ.

Sori marginal, terminal on the veins.

CHEILANTHES, *Swartz. Synop. Fil.* v, 126.

(Gymnia, *Hamilton M. S. (Don.)*;—Othonoloma, *Link.*;—Physapteris, *Presl.*;—Myriopteris, *Fée*;—Aleuritopteris, *Fée*;—Adianti sp., *Auct.*;—Allosori sp., *Auct.*;—Pteridis sp., *Auct.*;—Cassebeeræ sp., *J. Sm.*;—Nothochlænæ sp., *Auct.*;—Hypolepidis sp., *Auct.*;—Acrostichi sp., *Auct.*;—Pelleæ sp., *Auct.*;—Adiantopsidis, *Fée*).

Sori indusiate, transverse marginal, generally on a reflexed tooth or lobule; normally sub-orbicular, small distinct, sometimes contiguous and by lateral confluence elongate, the *receptacles* punctiform at the apex of the veins. *Indusium* membranaceous or formed of revolute portions of the slightly altered margin of the same form as the sorus. *Veins* simple or forked from a central costa; venules free.

Fronds usually small, pinnate variously pinnatifid or bi-tri-pinnate; membranaceous or sub-coriaceous, sometimes pulverulent or densely hairy or scaly beneath. Stipes and rachis generally ebeneous. Rhizome tufted or creeping—(Moore).

This genus differs from Pteris in the receptacle being punctiform instead of linear elongated.

1. *Cheilanthes tenuifolia.* (Sw). Caudex short, creeping scaly, stipes elongated rarely scaly, frond sub-membranaceous glabrous 3-4 inches to a span and more long, ovate acuminate or more or less deltoid sub-tri-pinnate, ultimate lobes of the primary and secondary divisions the largest more or less pinnatifid, pinnules elliptic, oblong or oblongo-lanceolate sub-pinnatifid or crenate with broad blunt teeth, involucres mostly elongated more or less confluent, more or less crenated or denticulate, sometimes transversely wrinkled, stipes and rachis purple-black, main rachis winged above, secondary and tertiary rachises all with a narrow wing. *Hook. Sp. Fil.* ii. 82 ;—*Sw. Syn. Fil., pp.* 129 *and* 332 ;—C. rupestris, *Wall. Cat. n.* 67 ;—C. micrantha, *Wall. Cat. n.* 68 ;—Aspidium tenue, *Retz. Obs.* vi, *p.* 39 ;—Pteris humilis, *Forst. Prod. n.* 421 ;—Trichomanes tenuifolia, *Burn. Ind., p.* 237 ;—Dryopteris Campestris, *Rumph. Amb.* v, 77, *t.* 34 *and* 2.

A common fern in dry localities all over the Presidency, it is not found at any great elevation.

PLATE No. CLXXXVIII.

CHEILANTHES *(continued.)*

2. *Cheilanthes varians,* (Hooker.) Root tufted, stipites 4-6 inches long, slender, ebeneous glossy, plane and margined on the upper side, obsoletely setoso-paleaceous, fronds sub-membranaceous glabrous about a span long, the pinnatifid apex acuminated, pinnated above, bi-pinnate below ; primary pinnæ distant, spreading or a little curved upwards sessile, superior ones lanceolate, acuminate sinuato-pinnatifid at their base, and somewhat auricled at the upper base, lower ones deltoid, acuminate pinnate at their base, pinnatifid acuminated (caudate) in the upper half, pinnules lanceolate acuminate or acute pinnatifid below, the lowest inferior pinnæ the longest. *Hooker Sp. Fil.* ii, 89 ;—Pteris varians, *Wall. Cat. n.* 86 ;—Pteris cæspitosa, *Ejusd. Cat. n.* 90 ;—Cheilanthes tenuifolia, *J. Smith in Hook. Lond. Journ. Bot.* iii, *p.* 404 ;—Ch. laxa, *Moore.*

Anamallays—rare.

PLATE No. CLXXXIX.

3. *Cheilanthes Mysorensis,* (Wallich.) Roots densely cæspitose, the fibres very woolly, stipites slightly scaly below, short 1-2 inches, and as well as the main rachises, deep glossy ebeneous rigid, frond a span or more long, in outline narrow oblong, acute, tapering below by the diminishing of the pinnæ, glabrous membranaceous but firm, bi-pinnate lower pinnæ very small, all of them oblong-ovate sessile, frequently opposite pinnate below, the upper half pinnatifid, pinnules or segments linear-oblong plane, (much incurved if dried without pressure) toothed or lobato-pinnatifid, each tooth or lobe bearing one or two sub-confluent small whitish sub-orbicular sori. *Hook. Sp. Fil.* ii, *p.* 94 ;—*Wall. Cat. n.* 66 ;—Cheil. fragrans, *Swartz Syn. Fil., p.* 127. *et* 325, *t.* 3, *f.* 6 ;—Cheil. Swartzii, *Webb. et Bert Phytogr. Canar., p.* 454 *in note ;*—Ch. opposita, *Kaulf. En. Fil., p.* 211 ;—Asplenium Mysorense, *Heyne in Roth. Nov. Sp. Ind. Or., p.* 395 ?

Common in dry rocky places on hill sides up to 3,000 or 4,000 feet.

PLATE No. CXC.

4. *Cheilanthes farinosa,* (Kaulf.) Roots tufted, stipites more or less elongated, ebeneous glossy deciduously scaly, fronds sub-coriaceous from a span to a foot long, deltoidly lanceolate, or lanceolate glabrous, white and powdery beneath, pinnate, the apex pinnatifid, acuminate, pinnæ mostly lanceolate pinnatifid, the one or two lower most pair more or less half deltoid bi-pinnatifid below, involucres brown, scariose rounded, sometimes confluent and then waved or lobed, the margin entire or toothed and jagged. *Hook. Sp. Fil.* ii, 77 ;—*Kaulf En. Fil., p.* 212 ;—Pteris farinosa, *Forst. Fl. Ægypt. Arab, p.* 187 ;—Cheilanthes dealbata, *Don. Prod. Fl. Nep., p.* 16 ; Pteris argyrophylla, *Sw. Syn. Fil., p.* 105 ;—Pt. argentea, *Bory ;*—Pt. decursiva, *Forst et. Sw. ;*—Cassebeera, *J. Sm. ;*—Allosorus, *Presl.*

Nilgiris and other mountainous tracts in the Presidency very common ; called "the silver fern,"—there is a variety with the powder of a pale sulphur colour.

PLATE No. CXCI.

5. *Cheilanthes bullosa,* (Kunze.) Rhizome short, thick, obliquely descending, stipites 6-8 inches long, terete, asperous at the base, and as well as the rachis, and stout prominent partial rachis beneath, which extends to the apex of the pinnæ, deep glossy ebeneous ; frond rigid, coriaceous glabrous (dark olive-brown when dry) oblong-lanceolate, opaque above, and there under the microscope as it were minutely granulated, pinnato-pinnatifid, 6-8 inches long, pinnæ rather distant nearly opposite, the lower ones sometimes sub-bi-pinnate, ovato-oblong, patent, deeply pinnatifid, the lobes linear crenate on the lowest inferior ones, often again pinnatifid, singularly bullate on the upper side, in consequence of the sunken costa, and veins (the spaces between them thus being convex) the primary lobes of the pinnæ are rather distant, so that the pinnæ may almost be said to be pinnate with a winged rachis, the margins of the lobes and teeth of the crenatures are much reflexed and form semi-orbicular involucres pale at the edge, which become united and more or less continuous and slightly erose at the margin, in age becoming more membranous. *Hook. Sp. Fil.* ii, 88 ;—*Kunze in Lin.* xxiv, *p.* 274.

I have no doubt that the plant here figured is the "Cheilanthes bullosa" of Kunze, but I believe it to be only a mountain variety of "Ch. farinosa," it is always more or less white and powdery beneath.

Nilgiris—very common,

PLATE No. CXCII.

6. *Cheilanthes Dalhousiæ*, (Hook.) Roots tufted, stipites rather short, ebeneous glossy, deciduously scaly, fronds about a span long, deltoidly lanceolate, glabrous on both sides, and perfectly free from powdery substance beneath, pinnate, the apex deeply pinnatifid and acuminate; pinnæ, upper ones lanceolate pinnatifid, the rest broader and bi-pinnatifid, lowest pair very broad at the base with their lowest inferior segments (or pinnules) much longer than the rest, the margin crenated, sometimes in the barren portions ciliated, involucres brown scariose reniform close, but generally distinct, sometimes confluent and then less ciliated, but lobed and jagged. *Hook. Sp. Fil.* ii, 80.

Very nearly allied to *Cheilanthes farinosa*, but always destitute of powdery substance—its fronds are larger and more membranaceous.

Nilgiris, in woods near Makoorty.

PLATE No. CXCIII.

TRIBE 1. (§ 1) ACROSTICHEÆ.

(*a*) *Fronds wholly fertile.*

* *Veins free.*

POLYBOTRYA, *Humboldt and Bonplaud; Willd, Sp. Pl. V*, 99.

(Egenolfia, *Schott.;* Lacaussadea, *Gaudichand;*—Ectoneura, *Fée;*—Granulina, *Bory;*—Botryothallus, *Klotzsch. M. S;*—Psomiocarpa, *Presl.;*—Microstaphyla, *Presl.;*—Acrostichii sp., *Auct.;*—Olfersiæ sp., *Presl.;*—Anogrammatis sp., *Fée;*—Gymnogrammatis sp., *Auct;*—Osmundæ sp., *Jacquin.*)

Sori superficial, non-indusiate, the *receptacles* occupying the whole under-surface, or both upper and under-surface of the rachiform fertile fronds. Veins simple or forked, or pinnate from a central costa; venules simple or forked, free.

Fronds dimorphous, pinnate, or bi-tri-pinnate, the fertile with linear contracted segments. Rhizome creeping or scandent. In this genus occurs the highest degree of development of which Ferns seem susceptible. The whole of the under-surface (and in some species the whole surface both above and below) is sporangiferous, (Moore.)

1. *Polybotrya appendiculata*, (J. Sm.) Rhizome thick, short creeping, stipes and rachis scaly; fronds pinnate glabrous, the sterile ones viviparous at the apex, pinnæ 25 to 50 pair, sub-opposite or alternate oblong lanceolate obtuse, 2 to 3 inches long, ½ an inch broad, rather deeply crenated with a setaceous bristle between each crenature, superior basal crenature the largest, inferior base cuneate and slightly unequal, veins pinnate free, fertile fronds much contracted, pinnæ much shorter than the sterile ones.

Moist forests at no great elevation. Anamallays, Nilgiris, &c.

PLATE No. CXCIV.

2. *Polybotrya aspleniifolia*, (Bory.) Rhizome thick, short creeping, stipes and rachis very scaly, fronds pinnate glabrous, sometimes viviparous at the apex; pinnæ 25 to 50 pair opposite or alternate, oblong obtuse very unequal sided (the inferior basal portion being, as it were, cut away) pinnatifid nearly ½ way to the costa, with a setaceous bristle between each segment, upper basal segment the largest and crenate or serrate, others entire or crenulate, veins pinnate free, fertile fronds much contracted, pinnæ much shorter than the sterile ones.

Closely allied to the preceding species, but easily distinguished.

Moist Forests at no great elevation. Nilgiris—Anamallays, &c.

PLATE No. CXCV.

ELAPHOGLOSSUM, *Schott. Gen. Fil. (under t.* 15*)* (Acrostichum, *Fée and Auct.;*—Phyllitis, *Necker;*—Olfersiæ sp., *Presl.)*

Sori superficial, non-indusiate, the *receptacle* occupying the whole under-surface of the fertile, sometimes contracted fronds. *Veins* simple or parallelo-furcate from a central costa; *venules* free; clavate at the apex, terminating within the margin.

Fronds simple, entire, the fertile often somewhat narrower, naked or clothed with scales. Rhizome short erect, or decumbent or elongately creeping ; rarely humifuse and ramose. (Moore.)

1. *Elaphoglossum viscosum*, (Schott.) Rhizome short creeping, densely tufted with shining brown linear acuminate scales, sterile fronds linear lanceolate acuminate gradually attenuated at the base 10-16 inches long (of which the scaly stipe is often 4-5 inches) and $\frac{3}{4}$ of an inch broad, clothed on both sides as is the stipe with stellate pubescence, fertile fronds much contracted, $\frac{1}{4}$ to $\frac{3}{8}$ of an inch broad. *Schott. Gen. Fil. (Sub. t.* 15*);—J. Sm., Hook. Journ.* iv, 148 ;—Elaphoglossum Blumeanum, *J. Sm., Hook. Journ. Bot.* iii, 400 ;—Acrostichum augustatum, *Bojer M. S.* ;—A. Brentelianum, *Kze. Schkr. Supp.* ii, 3 *t.* 102 ;—A. Gardnerianum, *Lowe* vii, *t.* 58 ;—A. lancifolium, *Desv. Berl. Mag.* v, 310 ;—A. neriifolium, *Wall. Cat.* 16 ;—A. petiolatum, *Sw. Fl. Ind. Occ.* iii, 1588 ;—A. Plumeri, *Desr. Prod.* 209 ;—A. salicifolium, *Willd.* ;—A. viscosum, *Sw. Syn. Fil.* 10-193 ;—Olfersiæ neriifolia, salicifolia et viscosa, *Presl. Tent. Pter.* 234-5.

Anamallay forests, rocks in the bed of the Toracadoo river, 4,000 feet elevation, rare.

PLATE No. CXCVI.

2. *Elaphoglossum squamosum*, (J. Sm). Rhizome short creeping, scaly, furnished with numerous wiry roots, stipes 1-2 inches long, very scaly, fronds linear-lanceolate obtuse, gradually attenuated at the base, 4-14 inches long, $\frac{1}{2}$ to $\frac{3}{4}$ inch broad, densely covered on both sides with velvetty ciliated scales, fertile fronds not contracted. *J. Sm. Hook. Journ. Bot.* iv, 148 ;—E. vestitum, *Brack. M. S. Expl. Exp.* xvi, 69 ;—Acrostichum hirtum, *Sw. Syn. Fil.*, 194-419 ;—A. Loweanum, *Kze. Hb.* ;—A. Lowei, *Fée* ;—A. paleaceum, *Hook. et Grev. Icones Fil. t.* 235 ;—A. squamosum, *Sw. Schrad. Journ.* 1,800 ii, 11 ;—Olfersiæ paleacea, *Presl. Tent. Pter.* 234.

Nilgiris, on trees about Nediwattan and on the Sisparah ghât, abundant.

PLATE No. CXCVII.

3. *Elaphoglossum conforme*, (Schott). Rhizome long creeping, scaly, furnished with hairy fibrous roots, stipes 2-3-4 inches long, (those of the fertile fronds often longest) black at the base, furnished with peltate or sheathing scales, fronds narrow lanceolate acuminate furnished with diaphanous margin which is revolute in age ; 3 to 5 inches long, and $\frac{7}{8}$ of an inch broad, glabrous, but furnished with deciduous scales on both sides : fertile frond more or less contracted. *Schott. Gen. Fil.* (*Sub. t.* 15) ;—Acrostichum conforme, *Sw. Syn. Fil.* 10-192. *t.* 1—*Fig.* 1 ;—A. marginatum, *Wall. Cat.* 17.

Nilgiris—very common on trees on the higher ranges.

PLATE No. CXCVIII.

4. *Elaphoglossum stigmatolepis* ? (Fée). Rhizome creeping, very scaly, and furnished with densely hairy wiry roots ; stipes scaly, of the sterile fronds 1-2 inches long, of the fertile 4 to 5 inches, sterile fronds glabrous, often furnished with deciduous scales beneath, lanceolate acuminate very gradually attenuated at the base and decurrent on the stipe, 8-15 inches long, 1 to $1\frac{1}{4}$ inch broad, furnished with a diaphanous margin, fertile fronds more or less contracted and much smaller than the sterile ones. *Fée Acrost.* 62 *t.* 24—*Fig.* 2 ? *Kze. Linn.* xxiv, 248.

Nilgiris and Anamallays—common in ravines at no great elevation, on rocks and trees.

PLATE No. CXCIX.

5. *Elaphoglossum laurifolium.* (Thouars). Rhizome creeping, scaly, furnished with hairy wire-like roots, stipes scaly often as long as the frond, fronds very coriaceous lanceolate acuminate, sometimes angled at the margin, 4-6 inches long, $1\frac{3}{4}$ to 2 inches broad, furnished with a very conspicuous diaphanous margin, fertile fronds more or less contracted. *Pet. Thouars Fl. Tristam D'Acunha*, 31 ;—Elaphoglossum angulatum, *Bl. En.* 201 ;—*Id. Fl. Jav.* 25, *t.* 6 ;—Olfersiæ angulata et laurifolia, *Presl. Tent. Pter.* 234.

Anamallays higher ranges on trees—Nilgiris (Honamund.)

PLATE No. CC.

* * *Veins transversely combined in a single series.*

STENOCHLÆNA.—*J. Smith, Hook. Journ. Bot.* iii, 401.

(Cafraria, *Presl.* ;—Lomariobotrys, *Fée* ;—Osmundæ sp., *Auct.* ;—Onodeæ sp., *Auct.* ;—Anemiæ sp., *Auct.* ;—Lomariæ sp., *Auct.* ;—Polybotryæ sp., *Mettenius.*)

Sori superficial, non-indusiate, the *receptacles* occupying the under-surface of the contracted fertile fronds. *Veins* arcuate at the base forming narrow costal areoles ; *venules* parallelo-furcate, connivent with the thickened cartilagineo-serrate margin.

Fronds dimorphous, the barren pinnate, the fertile contracted pinnate or bi-pinnate having slightly revolute margins. Pinnæ with a marginal gland near the base on the upper edge ; sometimes articulated. Rhizome scandent, (Moore.)

1. *Stenochlæna scandens.* (J. Smith). Rhizome scandent, (often reaching the tops of the highest trees,) fronds glabrous, pinnate, 1 to 4 feet long, pinnæ articulated numerous, alternate, lanceolate, acuminate, pungently serrate towards the apex, oblique at the base and furnished with a marginal gland on the upper edge, 5-10 inches long, 1 to 1½ inch broad. Veins forming narrow costal areoles, conspicuous towards the apex of the pinnæ, obsolete below ; fertile fronds very much contracted. *J. Smith, Hook. Journ. of Bot.* iii, 401 ;—Lomaria scandens, *Willd.*

Anamallays, moist forests up to 4,000 feet elevation—Carcoor ghât (Wynad)—Sampagee ghât (Coorg)—South Canara, &c.

PLATE No. CCI.

* * *Veins reticulated.*

PÆCILOPTERIS. *Presl. Tent. Pter.* 241. (Eschw. Emend.)

(Poikilopteris, *Eschweiler* ;—Bolbitis, *Schott.* ;—Campium, *Presl.* ;—Cyrtogonium, *J. Smith* ;—Heteroneuron, *Fée* ;—Acrostichi sp., *Auct.*)

Sori superficial, non-indusiate, the *receptacles* occupying the under-surface of the contracted fertile fronds. *Veins* pinnate from a central costa, prominent. *Venules* arcuately, angularly or irregularly anastomosing, sometimes producing exterior free or irregularly anastomosing veinlets.

Fronds dimorphous, pinnate often viviparous, rhizome creeping. (Moore.)

1. *Pæcilopteris repanda,* (J. Sm.) Rhizome thick, shortly creeping, fronds glabrous, pinnate 1-2 feet high, of which the stipe is about ⅓, stipe and rachis more or less scaly—rachis more or less winged, sometimes very conspicuously ; sterile fronds, pinnæ 11-30, alternate sessile or very shortly petiolate, lanceolate from nearly entire or slightly crenated to pinnatifid with the segments serrated, the terminal one longest and often viviparous—primary veins pinnate, veinlets anastomosing and forming irregular areoles, from which proceed veinlets which are generally free with a clavate apex—fertile fronds conform to sterile but much contracted, sori when ripe very black, *J. Sm. in Seem. Bot. Her.* 426 ;—Acrostichum rependum, *Blume En. Pl. Jav.* 104 ;—Heteroneuron proliferum, *Fée, Hook. in Kew. Jour. Bot.* ix, 359 ;—Acrost. heteroclitum, *Presl. Rel. Hænk.* 1-15 *t.* 2, *Fig.* 2.—Pœcilopteris heteroclita, *Presl.* ;—Acrostichum contaminans, *Wall.* ;—Pœcilopteris contaminans, *Moore Ind. Fil., p.* 8 ;—Cyrtogonium repandum, *J. Sm., Hook. Journ. of Bot.* iii, 403.

Very common on the western side of the Presidency in moist forests at no great elevation. Anamallays and Sisparah ghât, abundant.

PLATE No. CCII.

Pæcilopteris terminans, (Wall.) Rhizome thick, fronds glabrous pinnate, 1-4 feet of which the stipe is sometimes nearly ½ stipes and rachis furnished with a few scales. Sterile fronds, pinnæ 4-12 alternate or sub-opposite petiolate, broad lanceolate sinuate or waved with a longish serrated acumination, terminal pinnæ much the longest, (sometimes 2 feet long) proliferous at the apex, primary veins pinnate, veinlets anastomosing pretty regularly at right angles, from which proceed one or two generally free veinlets with clavate apices, fertile fronds conform to sterile, but much contracted. Pœcilopteris Hookeriana, *Thw. En. Zey. Pl.* Moist forests on the western side of the Presidency at no great elevation—Bolamputty valley near Coimbatore. Lower part of the Sisparah ghât—South Canara plains. Very abundant throughout Coorg.

PLATE No. CCIII.

(b.) Fronds fertile on the upper pinnæ.

ACROSTICHUM ; *Linnæus, Gen. Fil.*, 785. (Emend.) *Presl. Tent. Pter.* 240.

Sori superficial, non-indusiate ; the *receptacles* occupying the whole under-surface of the upper pinnæ. *Veins* uniformly reticulated in small regular hexagonal meshes, without free veinlets.

Fronds pinnate, thick coriaceous, the upper fertile pinnæ usually somewhat narrower. Rhizome thick, sub-globose decumbent, (Moore.)

1. *Acrostichum aureum.* (Linn.) Fronds firm, 1 to 3 or 4 feet high, pinnate. Barren segments linear-oblong, about 4 to 8 inches long, very obtuse, oblique at the base and petiolulate, the midrib prominent, the very numerous equally reticulated veinlets covering the under-surface, fertile segments usually occupying the upper part of the frond, and rather smaller than the barren ones. *Linn. Sp. Pl.* 1525 ;—*Benth. Hong-Kong Fl., p.* 443 ;—A. emarginatum, *Roxb. Crypt. Pl. Cal. Journ. Nat. Hist.* iv, 480 ;—Chrysodium vulgare, *Fée. Acrost.* 97 ;—A. inæquale, *Willd. Sp. Pl.* v, 117 ;—A. speciosum, *Willd. Sp. Pl.* v, 117.

Banks of rivers and backwaters on the Western Coast—very abundant.

PLATE No. CCIV.

ADDENDA.

14. *Pteris patens.* (Hook.) Caudex erect, stipes numerous, stout scaly at their base, rachis stout glabrous, frond ample, erect, strict, membranaceous, pinnate, lower pinnæ bi-tri-partite, pinnæ 8-16 inches long, strict horizontally patent, numerous approximate, elongato-oblong, acuminate, rarely sub-caudate, sessile or lower ones shortly petiolate, deeply (almost to the rachis) pinnatifid, segments horizontal, very uniform, linear, scarcely acuminate, serrulate where sterile, the base dilated decurrenti-confluent on both sides, especially at the lower base, sometimes apart, veins all free, simple or once or twice forked ; sori continuous nearly to the apex. *Hook. Sp. Fil.* ii, 177 ;—Pteris excelsa, var., *J. Sm. Herb.* ;—Pt. decussata, *J. Smith in Hook. Journ. of Bot.* iii., *p.* 405.

New Carcoor ghât, (Wynad) abundant—a very large handsome species. I have not met with it elsewhere in the Presidency.

PLATE No. CCV.

NOTE.—*Sir W. Hooker informs me that " Campteria Anamallayensis," (Pl.* xlv) *of this Work is " Campteria geminata" of Agardh, which species is referred by Sir W. Hooker as a synonym to " Campteria biaurita." (L.) I feel quite certain that the two species " C. Anamallayensis" and " bi-aurita" are quite distinct, the venation and whole habit are different ; if my plant is the same as Agardh's, the name " Anamallayensis" will however have to be changed to " geminata."*

Campteria nemoralis, (Willd.) or what I take to be that species is not uncommon in this Presidency. In outline and general appearance it is in no way different from Pteris quadri-aurita, (Retz.) but whilst some entire fronds have quite the venation of Pteris and are consequently not distinguishable from " P. quadri-aurita," other fronds or some of their pinnæ have the venation of Campteria, but with smaller costal areoles and fewer free veins than in " C. bi-aurita." I have always found this fern growing in localities where both

"Pteris quadri-aurita" and "Campteria bi-aurita" were also to be found, and suspect that it must be a hybrid between the two. Mr. Bentham in his Hong-Kong Flora joins the two species "nemoralis" and "quadri-aurita." In "P. quadri-aurita," "C. nemoralis" and "bi aurita," the veins always reach the margin, in "C. Anamallayensis" never.

3. *Lindsæa heterophylla,* (Bedd.) Glabrous fronds 10-15 inches high, deltoid, bi-pinnate, and in the lower portion sometimes tri-pinnate, simply pinnate at the apex, lower pinnæ 4-6 inches long, upper ones gradually smaller and less compound, pinnules numerous, (as many as 20) very various in form, sub-rotund, rhomboidal, or lanceolate, viens simple or forked, all free, sori continuous round the whole margin except at the base.

Shevaroy Hills, (ravines on the green hills.)

This fern is quite distinct from "*Schizoloma heterophyllum,*" J. Smith, (Plate xxvi of this Work) the veins are always free and never anastomosing. I am not sure, however, that it is not one of the forms referred by Sir William Hooker to his "*Lindsæa (Schizoloma) heterophylla," Sp. Fil., p.* 223.

PLATE No. CCVI.

2. *Hymenophyllum crispatum.* (Wall.) Erect, fronds ovato-acuminate tri-pinnatifid, the segments linear obtuse generally plane, sometimes waved entire, involucres terminal, sometimes on lateral segments copious ovate, sessile free entire, 2 valved to the very base, the valves convex, receptacles wholly included, stipes with broad crisped wings almost to the base, wing of the rachis also crisped. *Wall. Cat. n.* 169 ;—*Hook. Sp. Fil.,* 1-105 ;—H. atrovirens, *Colenso in Tasm. Phil. Journ.* ?

Common in moist forests on the Nilgiris, Anamallays, Wynad, &c., up to 4,000 feet elevation.

PLATE No. CCVII.

4. *Trichomanes intramarginale.* (Hook. et Grev.) Caudex creeping, somewhat tomentose, fronds small erect pinnatifid, tapering into a short stipes, the segments few, linear-oblong obtuse erecto-patent, slightly waved opaque with a slender intramarginal vein, the apices retuse, involucres sub-cylindrical tapering at the base, sunk entirely in the apex of the segments, the mouth spreading of 2 short lips, receptacles protruding. *Hook. et Grev. Ic. Fil. t.* 211 ; *Hook. Sp. Fil.* 1-120.

Shevagherry Hills.

PLATE No. CCVIII. *(Fig. A. at the corner of the plate is a single frond of a species of Trichomanes, lately detected on trees near Neddiwattan on the Nilgiris. It is probably undescribed, but as my specimen consists of only a single frond and no root, I do not attempt a description of it.)*

NOTE.—*Trichomanes proliferum, (Blume) about to be figured in one of the supplementary numbers of this Work as a Ceylon fern, has just been detected abundant on the Western slopes of the Nilgiris at an elevation of* 3,000 *feet growing with T. Neilgherrense.*

NOTE.—Nos. 17 to 20 of this work are four Supplementary Numbers to "*The Ferns of Southern India*," and contain all the Ceylon ferns not as yet detected in Southern India. Since the first portion of this work has been in the Press, three of these ferns have been found on the hills near Courtallum in the Tinnevelly district, and one has been detected on the Nilgiris, many more will doubtless still be found in Southern India, as most of them are also natives of Northern India, Burmah, or the Straits, so that this work would hardly be complete if they were not figured, all the other ferns found in Ceylon have already appeared in the former numbers of this work, so the entire work of 20 numbers will contain figures of all the ferns of Southern India and Ceylon.

ACROSTICHEÆ.

Fronds wholly fertile.—Veins free.

* ELAPHOGLOSSUM. See page 68.

1. *Elaphoglossum spathulatum.* (Sw.) Rhizome short, creeping or sub-erect, densely scaly, furnished with numerous wiry roots. Stipes 2-4 inches long, densely covered with reddish setaceous scales, fronds linear-lanceolate to rhomboid-lanceolate 1 to 2 inches long, covered on both sides with numerous hair-like scales, fertile fronds, broad ovate, smaller than the sterile ones. Acrostichum piloseloides var. δ spathulatum. *Hook. Sp. Fil.* v, 228.

Ceylon 5,000 to 6,000 feet elevation, rare.

PLATE No. CCIX.

PLEUROGRAMMEÆ.

* *Veins consisting of a costa only.*

MONOGRAMMA. *Schkuhr Crypt Gewäch* 82.

(Vaginularia, *Fée* ;—Cochlidii sp., *Kaulfuss* ;—Grammitidis sp., *Auct.* ;—Pteridis sp., *Auct.* ;—Pleurogrammatis sp., *Fée* ;—Asplenii sp., *Swartz* ;—Acrostichii sp., *Swartz* ;—Tænitidis sp., *Mettenius* ;—Dididopteris, *Brack.*)

Sori sub-immersed, linear elongated, the *receptacle* formed of a portion of the costa—*Veins* consisting only of a costa.

Fronds small, graminiform or rachiform, simple or forked, Rhizome creeping. (Moore.)

1. *Monogramma Junghuhnii.* (Hooker.) Rhizome creeping hairy; fronds linear filiform, grass-like, 2-3 inches long, 2 lines broad, sori in two rows within a vaginiform expansion of the costa, one side of which is larger than the other. *Hook. Sp. Fil.* v, 123. Vaginularia Junghuhnii, *Mett.*—Pleurogramme? paradoxa, *Fée Vitt. p.* 38.—Diclidopteris angustissima, *Brack Fil. U. St. Exp. p.* 135.—Monogramme linearis, *Junghuhn.*

Ceylon. (C. P. 1281.)

PLATE No. CCX.

* *Veins Compoundly anastomosing.*

GYMNOPTERIS. See page 15.

1. *Gymnopteris Feei. Var. pinnatifida.* (R. H. B.) Fronds deeply and irregularly pinnatifid. Segments of the fertile fronds very narrow.

Ceylon. (C. P. 1318.)

A curious lyrate variety of the common Gymnopteris Feei. (See page 15.) I have not found it in Southern India, though the common form occasionally has the sterile fronds forked, variously lobed, or even sub-pinnatifid, the fertile fronds seem always to remain simple. I may here also mention that I have occasionally found the broad sterile fronds of the common variety with a contracted fertile apex (as in Hymenolepis), it is, however, an abnormal state.

PLATE No. CCXI.

TÆNITIDEÆ.

TÆNIOPSIS. See page 18.

1. *Tæniopsis scolopendrina.* (J. Smith.) Caudex creeping, paleaceous with subulate scales, fronds linear, lanceolate membranaceous; gradually attenuated at both ends, 16 to 28 inches long by 1 inch broad—glabrous on both sides, scarcely stipitate. Sori sunk in a furrow within the margin of the upper portion of the fronds, inner margin of the furrow winged, margin of the frond revolute over the fructification diaphanous or sub-indusiate. Haplopteris scolopendrina, *Pr. Tent. Pter. p.* 141;—Tæniopteris Forbesii, *Gen. Fil. t.* 76;—Pteris scolopendrina, *Bory*;—Vittaria Zeylanica, *Fée.*

Ceylon. (C. P. 1304.)

PLATE No. CCXII.

LINDSÆEÆ.

LINDSÆA. See page 7.

* *Fronds pinnate.*

† *Costa excentric or marginal or obsolete. Sori on the superior margin.*

1. *Lindsæa repens.* (Thw.) Caudex creeping, scaly. Stipes short, fronds rigid membranaceous linear-lanceolate, 10-18 inches long, ½ inch broad, pinnate attenuated at the base, pinnæ very numerous, 40 or more pair, half deltoid-ovate obtuse or sub-acute, base nearly parallel with the rachis, and with the lower margin quite entire, upon margin lobulato-crenate, costa parallel with and close to the margin, veins simple or forked, free, sori short, oblong, one near the margin of each lobule. Lindsæa oblongifolia, *Reinw.*;—*Hook. Sp. Fil.* i, 206;—Davallia Boryana, *Presl. Reliq. Hænk.* i, *p.* 66;—*Hook. Sp. Fil.* i, 175;—Acrophorus repens, *Moore. Ind. Fil.*;—Dicksonia repens, *Bory Voy.* ii, *p.* 323;—Davallia Macræana, *Hook. et. Arnt. Bot. of Beechy. Voy. p.* 108.

Ceylon. (C. P. 3389.)

PLATE No. CCXIII.

2. *Lindsæa repens Var minor.* (Thw.) A smaller form with the pinnæ more membranaceous, and pinnatifid or serrate, sori much shorter.—Odontoloma Boryanum, *J. Sm. ?*

Ceylon. (C. P. 1389.)

PLATE No. CCXIV.

† † *Costa central. Sori on both margins.*

3. *Lindsæa Walkeræ.* (Hook.) Caudex creeping, thicker than a crow's quill, ferruginous with scale like hairs. Stipes very long, often 1 foot, and as well as the rachis dark-purple glossy, fronds lanceolate, pinnate 6 inches to 1 foot long, pinnæ 6-9 pairs with a terminal one which is sometimes confluent with one or both of the upper pair, coriaceous, sub-opposite remote lanceolate or linear-lanceolate equal, costa central, veins copious, almost parallel with the costa. Sorus marginal, continuous on both sides. *Hook. Sp. Fil.* i, 209.

Ceylon. (C. P. 1379.)

PLATE No. CCXV.

* *Fronds bi-tri-pinnate or decompound.*

† *Costa excentric or marginal, or obsolete. Sori on the superior margin.*

4. *Lindsæa flabellulata.* (Dry.) Caudex creeping, stipites tufted, generally elongated, fronds linear-lanceolate and pinnate or

deltoid and bi-pinnate, pinnules approximate, shortly petiolate, rather rigid flabellate and approaching to lunate or sub-rhomboid with the sides unequal, the base obliquely cuneate, sometimes the upper ones are confluent, the superior margin crenulate or soriferous. Sori continuous or interrupted, involucres toothed. *Hook. Sp. Fil.* i, 211.—*Dry. in Linn. Trans.* v, iii, *p.* 41, *t.* 8. *f.* 2;—L. polymorpha, *Wall. Cat. n.* 14.

A very valuable species. Sir W. Hooker enumerates 3 varieties.

Ceylon. (C. P. 3311.)

PLATE No. CCXVI.

5. *Lindsœa caudata.* (Hook). Stipes terete and as well as the rachis deep brown glossy, fronds bi-pinnate, pinnæ narrow, numerous, (11-17), lanceolate, the apex long, attenuate caudate, pinnules half ovate, lunulato-falcate decurved, membranaceous close, superior base truncate, upper margin forming almost the segment of a circle quite entire, terminal ones gradually smaller on the caudex or tail-like point, sori at the very margin and continuous to the obtuse apex. *Hook. Sp. Fil.* i, 215.

Ceylon. (Adam's Peak.) (C. P. 1380.)

PLATE No. CCXVII.

ADIANTUM. See page 1.

1. *Adiantum flabellulatum.* (Linn.) Frond flabellate, bipartito-pedately divided, tri-pinnate, secondary pinnæ lanceolate acuminated, pinnules glabrous, sub-coriaceo-chartaceous, obliquely cuneate or semi-orbicular-cuneate, superior base truncate, superior margin 2-4 lobed and serrato-dentate in the sterile one, lobes soriferous, involucres large, the breadth of the lobe oblong, straight, rarely a little curved, hard coriaceous, stipes elongated, ebeneous scabrous below, the rest as well as the slender rachis glossy and glabrous. *Hook. Sp. Fil.* ii, 30; —*Linn. Sp. Pl., p.* 1,558;—A. fuscum, *Retz. Obs.*, ii, *p.* 28. *t.* 5;—A. amænum, *Wall. Cat. n.* 78.

Ceylon. (C. P. 3390.)

NOTE.—Adiantum rhizophorum (C. P. 3102), appears to be only a glabrous variety of Adiantum caudatum.

PLATE No. CCXVIII.

PETERIDEÆ.

PTERIS. See page 11.

PLATE No. CCXIX. Is a curious *Pteris* forwarded from Ceylon by Mr. T. W. Beckett. It is, I believe, a variety of my Pt. Otaria, and seems intermediate between *Pteris otaria* and *Pt. crenata*—it is, I believe *Pt. quadri—aurita var. ludens* of Mr. Thwaites' enumeration (C. P. 1351 and 3060) and Mr. Thwaites suggests that it may be a hybrid.

C. *Veins uniformly reticulated, without free included veinlets.*

LITOBROCHIA. *Presl. Tent. Pter.* 148.

(Histiopteris, *Agardh.*;—Doryopteris, *J. Sm.*;—Hetero phlebium, *Fée*;—Pteridis sp., *Auct.*;—Polypodii sp., *Auct.*;—Acrostichii sp., *Auct.*;—Cheilanthes sp., *Auct.*;—Lonchitidis sp., *Linn.*)

Sori indusiate, marginal linear continuous, the *receptacles* linear transverse, uniting the apices of the veins. *Indusium* of the same form, membranaceous. *Veins* simple or forked from a central costa, uniformly reticulated, evident or obscure, the hexagonal simple, areoles universal, or rarely the basal portion of the veins parallel.

Fronds herbacious or coriaceous, simple, pedate, palmate, pinnate or bi-tri-pinnate. Rhizome short, erect or creeping (Moore.)

1. *Litobrochia tripartita.* (Sw.) Stipes elongated, stout, and with the rachis sub-castaneous, fronds ample, tripartite lateral branches, pinnate spreading long, petiolate sub-membranaceous glabrous, pinnules 4-6 inches or more long, linear-oblong or linear, lanceolate sub-sessile, acuminate rather deeply pinnatifid, segments approximate, linear-oblong falcate (upwards) obtuse or acute, entire or scarcely serrated and only at the apex, nearly half an inch long, sinuses obtuse, basal veins forming a single arc parallel with the costa, veins forming a series of 2 or more areoles (parallel with the costule), from which proceed free veinlets which do not extend to the margin but termi-

nate with a thickened apex just within it, involucres continuous on the lower ⅗ of the margin of the pinnules not extending to the apex. *Hook. Sp. Fil.* ii, 225 ;—Pteris tripartita, *Sw. Syn. Fil., pp.* 100 *and* 293 ;—Pteris semiovata, *Poir. Encycl. v, p.* 723 ;—Pt. revolvens, *Ag. lc., p.* 73 ;—Pt. intermedia, *Bl. En. Fil. Jav., p.* 211 ;—Pt. longipes, *Don. Prod. Fl. Nep., p.* 15 ?—Pt. uniserita, *Poir. Encycl. Bot. Sup.* iv, *p.* 608 ;—Pt. linearis, *Poir. l. c. v, p.* 273 ;—*Wall. Cat. n.* 105 ;—Pt. marginata, *Bory. Voy.* 2, *p.* 192 ;—*Willd. Sp. Pl.* v, 399 ;—Pt. connexa, *J. Sm. Fil. Philip in Hook. Journ. Bot.* iii, 405 ;—Pt. sub-pedata, *Wall. Cat. n*, 10 *juvenile.*

Ceylon. (C. P. 1327.)

PLATE No. CCXX.

2. *Litobrochia aurita.* (Blume.) Caudex long creeping, subterraneous, stipes and rachis castaneous, glossy fronds, ample sub-membranaceous, distant ovate, long stipitate, glaucous beneath, tripinnate, pinnæ all sessile, subadnate mostly opposite horizontal, pinnules opposite sessile, lanceolate obtuse, more or less deeply lobed and pinnatifid. Segments ovate or oblong, (sterile ones subsinuate) or triangular, lowest one often remote and forming auricles on the rachis, superior ones confluent, veins all anastomosing, areoles next the costa and costules the largest and most elongated, involucres continuous or interrupted membranaceous entire at the edge. *Hook. Sp. Fil.* ii, 231 ;—*Bl. En. Fil. Jav., p.* 113 ;—Pt. Brunoniana, *Endl. Prod. Fl. Norfolk, p.* 12.

This species only differs from L. vespertilionis *Labill, (L. incisa,* Thunb.) by the anastomosing of the veins being always constant. Sir W. Hooker keeps them distinct, but Dr. Hooker unites the two in his "Floræ Novæ Zelandiæ."

Ceylon. (C. P. 1326.)

PLATE No. CCXXI.

[a 3]. *Receptacles short, transverse, or arcuate on the venules, sub-parallel with the midrib or margin.*

Sori indusiate—Woodwardieæ.

Doodia. *(R. Brown.)*

(Woodwardia, *Metten.*)

Sori oblong or sub-lunulate, in one or more series, arranged transversely with the veins forming areoles which are superficial, not sunk. *Involucres* membranaceous, of the same form as the sori, opening towards the costa and lying parallel with it. *Veins* uniform, the lower ones arcuately anastomosing, forming elongated costal areoles (one or more series), the marginal venules free.

Fronds pinnate or pinnatifid. Segments or pinnæ sharply serrated, rhizome sub-globose.

1. *Doodia dives.* (Kunze). Rhizome obliquely ascending, paleaceous, radicoses clothed with black fibre, stipes angled brown, very paleaceous near the base, fronds coriaceous, glabrous ovato-oblong, long caudate at the apex pinnate, at the base with some of the lower pinnæ auricled, pinnatifid above, pinnæ and segments patently divergent, oblong margins pungently serrated, pinnæ or segments of the fertile fronds often distant, sori in 1 or 2 series on each side of the costa of the pinnæ and segments, and also on the wings of the rachis, lunate often more or less confluent. *Hook. Sp. Fil.*, iii, 73.

Ceylon. (C. P. 976).

PLATE No. CCXXII.

MENISCIEÆ.

Meniscium. See page 19.

1. *Meniscium Thwaitesii.* (Hook). Caudex creeping more or less scaly, and furnished with wiry roots, stipes angled, very long 6 inches to 1 foot, and with the rachis puberulous, fronds deltoid, 6-8 inches long, 4 inches broad at the base, pinnated, pinnatifid at the apex, pinnæ alternate or opposite, lanceolate rounded at the base, obtuse or acute or caudate at the apex, crenato-lobate, lower ones much the largest, costa and veins puberulous especially beneath ; sori linear, oblong becoming confluent.

Mr. Thwaites informs me that Sir W. Hooker thinks that this may be only a variety of Goniopteris prolifera.

Ceylon. (C. P. 3145).

PLATE No. CCXXIII.

Asplenium. (See page 43.)

1. *Asplenium elongatum.* (Sw.) Caudex a small thick rhizome sparsely scaly, stipites 6-8 inches long, cæspitose, and as well as the compressed rachis pale-brownish-green and sub-furfuraceous with small lacerated deciduous scales, fronds pale-green 8 to 12 inches long, oblong, suddenly acuminate, coriaceo-membranaceous opaque pinnate, pinnæ 1-2 inches long, petioled horizontally-patent, gradually smaller, upwards approximate (in general), oblong quite straight or sub-falcate, very obtuse, strongly serrated, the base truncato-cuneate oblique, superior base distinctly auricled, inferior sub-excised, terminal pinnæ narrow elongated, acuminate pinnatifido-serrate, sometimes twice or thrice as long as the rest, veins simple oblique, sori copious on almost every vein, short-linear intermediate between the margin and the costa, involucres narrow-linear, very firm. *Hook. Sp. Fil.* iii, 117.—*Sw. Syn. Fil., p.* 79.—*Kze. Bot. Zeit.* vi, *p.* 174.—*Metten. Asplen., p.* 112;—A. caudatum, *Cav. Demonst., p.* 265, *n.* 632;—A. productum, *Pr. Reliq. Hoenk.* i, *p.* 42, *t.* 8. *f.* 1. (excellent).—Var. *acuminatum;* segments acuminate;—A. Doreyi, *Kze. Annal Pterid., p.* 23. *Moore. Ind. Fil., p.* 126.

Ceylon. (C. P. No. 1078.)

PLATE No. CCXXIV.

2. *Asplenium laserpitiifolium.* (Lam.) Caudex rather stout, sub-repent clothed at the extremity with copious satiny ferruginous subulate scales, stipites aggregate 3-4 inches to a foot long, lurid-brown, fronds a span to 2-3 feet long, ovato-lanceolate finely acuminated, membranaceous often delicate green, 3-4 pinnate, the surface opaque, primary pinnæ 3 inches to a span long, petiolate, from a broad base, broad-lanceolate finely acuminate into an incised cauda, secondary pinnæ 1-3 inches long, ultimate pinnules and segments small for the size of the fronds, 3-5 lines long, cuneate undivided or deeply pinnatifid or 3-lobed, the lobes or segments generally narrow-cuneate, sometimes broad, incised or toothed at the apex, veins flabelliform, nearly erect parallel, sori linear, rather short, 2-4 on a pinnule or segment, often exactly opposite to each other and opening face to face, involucres membranaceous. *Hook Sp. Fil.* iii, 171.—*Lam. Encycl., p.* 310.—*Sw. Syn. Fil., p.* 65.—*Willd. Sp. Pl.* v, *p.* 347.—*Bl. Enum. Fil. Jav., p.* 188.—*Brack. Fil. U. S. Expl. Exp., p.* 166.—*Metten. Asplen., p.* 160.—*Moore, Ind. Fil., p.* 140.—Aspl. riparium, *Brack. Fil. U. S. Expl. Exp., p.* 162.—*(not Liebm.)*—A. robustum, *Bl. En. Fil. Jav., p.* 189;—*(in Herb. Hook.)*—A. tri-pinnatum, *Roxb. Crypt., p.* 300.—*(fide Moore.)* Tarachia, *Pr.* A. patens, *Klfs. Enum. Fil., p.* 175.—*Hook. et. Arn. Bot. of Beech. Voy., p.* 274.—*(not* 106.*)*—*Metten. Asplen., p.* 159.—*Moore, Ind. Fil., p.* 152.—Diplazium, *Presl. Fée.*

Ceylon. (C. P. 3801.)

Very nearly allied to A. nitidum.

PLATE No. CCXXV.

3. *Asplenium spathulinum.* (J. Sm.) Stipites 6 inches and more high, quite smooth and naked lurid-brown, fronds 1½ feet long, broad, or ovato-lanceolate, acuminate coriaceous, dark brown when dry and very opaque, quite free from scales, bi-pinnate in the perfect state, pinnate at the very apex, sometimes pinnate with pinnæ from an unequally cuneate and auricled base entire, and others deeply pinnatifid at their base or sub-pinnate, pinnæ lanceolate broad at their base, pinnules or lobes obovate, the former tapering at the more or less oblique cuneate base, so as to be spathulate always, more or less serrated towards the apex, ultimate ones more or less confluent into an acuminated serrated apex, intermediate ones frequently decurrent so as to form a winged rachis, veins erecto-patent, flabellate conspicuous and with the long linear sori giving a striated appearance to the pinnules, involucres firm-membranaceous narrow. *Hook. Sp. Fil.* iii, 170.—*J. Sm. in Hook. Journ. of Bot.* iii, *p.* 408, *(name only.) Moore, Ind. Fil., p.* 139.—A. nitidum, *Metten. Asplen., p.* 162.—Aspl. institutum, *Brack. Fil. U. S. Expl. Exp.* 161, *t.* 22. *f.* 2. *Metten. Asplen., p.* 159.

Ceylon. (C. P. 2905.)

Nearly allied to A. nitidum.

PLATE No. CCXXVI.

Diplazium. (See page 53.)

1. *Diplazium lanceum.* (Thunb.) Caudex long-repent, rooting sparingly scaly, stipites distant 4 inches to a span long, slender, thickened at the base, and paleaceous with black scales, fronds chartaceous, firm opaque longer than the stipes, rarely an inch wide, lanceolate attenuated and acuminated at each extremity entire, sometimes a little repand, costa slender prominent beneath, veins horizontal, fascicled, the superior and sometimes the inferior branch only fertile. Sori linear distant remote from the costa, often diplazioid. *Hook.*

Sp. Fil. iii, 235.—*Thunb. Fl. Jap., p.* 333.—*Ic. Plant. Jap. Dec.* II. *t.* 18.—*Sw. Syn. Fil., p.* 74.—*Willd. Sp. Pl.* v, *p.* 303.—*Hook. in Florul. Hongkong Kew. Gard. Misc.* ix, *p.* 342.—Diplazium, *Pr.* Kl.—Aspl. sub-sinuatum, *Hook. et. Grev. Ic. Fil. t.* 27.—Aspl. erosum *and* A. rigidum, *Wall. M. S. in Hook. Herb.*—Scolopendrium dubium, *Don. Prodr., p.* 9.

Ceylon. (C. P. 1335.)

PLATE No. CCXXVII.

2. *Diplazium Zeylanicum.* (Hook.) Caudex terete, repent subterraneous naked black, stipites remote solitary, 4 inches to a span long, paleaceous with lax dark subulato-lanceolate scales, fronds sub-coriaceo-membranaceous, a span to a foot long, 1-2 inches broad, lanceolate acuminate, deeply pinnatifid in the middle, pinnate at the base, serrated only towards the apex, lobes and pinnæ horizontal, oblong obtuse, veins pinnated, entire or forked, sori linear, involucres with the superior basal one principally diplazioid. *Hook .Sp. Fil.* iii, 237.—*Hook. 2nd Cent. of Ferns, t.* 16.

Ceylon. (C. P. 1249.) Elevation, 4,000 feet.

PLATE No. CCXXVIII.

3. *Diplazium decurrens.* (Bedd.) Caudex erect, fronds ample glabrous, coriaceo-membranaceous, bi-pinnate with the pinnules more or less pinnatifid, primary pinnæ distant, petiolate lanceolate acuminate, 10 to 18 inches long, pinnules numerous, petioled or decurrent, 1 to 3 inches long, linear lanceolate more or less pinnatifid, segments obtuse crenated. Veins pinnate simple, rather distant. Sori curved, one double one to each segment and 1-5 single ones. *Hook. Sp. Fil.* iii, *p.* 258, *note under D. polypoidioides ;*—Diplazium polypodioides var. *β.* an. Sp. dist. ? *Thwaites En. Cey. Pl.*

Ceylon. (C. P. 3332.)

PLATE No. CCXXIX.

4. *Diplazium Schkuhrii.* (Metten.) ? Rachis and fronds glabrous, or very slightly puberulous beneath, fronds simply pinnate with the pinnules 3 inches long, and deeply pinnatifid, or ample bi-pinnate, pinnæ lanceolate acuminate 6-8 inches long, pinnules decurrent from a broad base and forming a narrow wing on the rachis, more or less pinnatifid, often half way down to the costa, segments obtuse (not falcate) entire or crenated, veins pinnate simple, sori slightly curved, one double and several single ones to each lobe. *Thw. En. Cey. Pl. (C. P.* 3100*).*—Diplazium dilatatum ;—*Hook. Sp. Fil.* iii, 259—*in part as referred to Ceylon C. P., No.* 1059.

The figure represents portions of both the pinnate and bi-pinnate forms, in the former some of the lobes of the pinnules have all the sori asplenioid.

PLATE No. CCXXX.

NOTE.—" *Diplazium Thwaitesii." (A. Br.)* (C. P. 1343), appears to be the same as "*D. Lasiopteris,"* (Kunze) *Plate CLX*, of this work, they are both always simply pinnate, and the pubescence is the same, the pinnæ in my specimens of *Thwaitesii* are more approximated than in Lasiopteris, and the pinnules are more obtuse and less falcate, but they can hardly be more than varieties.

ANTROPHYUM. (See page 17.)

PLATE No. CCXXXI, is a figure of *Antrophyum reticulatum* (Kaulf) from Ceylon, Fig. LII, of this work is the *Antrophyum plantagineum* (Cav.) and not reticulatum, and the name must be altered accordingly. The two species are nearly allied and perhaps not really distinct ; the following are the distinguishing characters.

1. *Antrophyum plantagineum.* (Cav.) Fronds broad, falcato-lanceolate receptacles deeply immersed, sub-glabrous. Plate LII. Nilgiris—Ceylon.

2. *Antrophyum reticulatum.* (Kaulf.) Fronds narrow-lanceolate, receptacles immersed hairy. Plate CCXXXI.—Ceylon. (C. P. 1305.)

GYMNOGRAMMEÆ.

(a) Veins free.

*** Sori linear forked distinct.*

GYMNOGRAMMA. *Desvaux. Berl. Mag.* v. 304.

(Gymnopteris, *Bernhardi in part* ;—Neurogramma, *Presl.* ;—Ceterach, *Presl. in part* ;—Calomelanos, *Presl.* ;—Anogramma, *Link* ;—Ceropteris, *Link* ;—Hecistopteris, *J. Smith* ;—Stenogramma, *Klotzsch.* ;—Chrysodia, *Fée* ;—Argyria, *Fée* ;—Trismeria, *Fée* ;—Comogramma, *Fée* ;—Pleurosorus, *Fée* ;—Eriosorus, *Fée* ;—Dicranodium, *Newman* ;—Asplenii sp. ;—Acrostichi sp. ;—Hemionitidis sp. ;—Grammitidis sp. ;—Scolopendrii sp. ;—Polypodii sp. ;—Osmundæ sp., *Auctorum* ;—Cryptogrammatis sp., *Hook. et. Grev.* ;—Phyllitis sp., *Necker.*)

Sori non-indusiate, linear, sometimes elongated, simple or forked, *i. e.*, bi-partite, oblique, often at length confluent ; the *receptacles* elongate above or continued below the forks of the veins. *Veins* simple or forked from a central costa, or the costa sometimes indistinct, *venules* free.

Fronds lobed pinnate or bi-pinnate, herbaceous or sub-membranaceous, often farinosely ceraceous, sometimes lanate beneath, rhizome short erect, sometimes annual.

This genus differs from Grammitis, in having forked sori. (Moore).

1. *Gymnogramma Javanica.* (Blume.) Fronds 1-2 feet high (of which the stipe is 8-10 inches) pinnate, pinnæ 2-4 pair with an odd one, lanceolate with a longish acumination pungently serrate, lower pinnæ sometimes auricled, glabrous above, puberulous beneath, veins forked, terminating with a thickened apex, just within the margin. Sori simple or forked, not reaching the margin. *Blume* ;—Gymnogramma serrulata, *Blume* ;—G. falcata, *J. Sm.* ;—Diplazium falcatum, *Don.* ;—Dipl. fraxineum, *Don.* ;—Grammitis caudata, *Wall.*

Ceylon. (C. P. 3264.)

PLATE No. CCXXXII.

**** Sori oblong, lying in the folded cucullate lobes.*

CALYMMODON. *Presl. Tent. Pter.* 203.

(Plectopteris *Fée* ;—Grammitidis sp., *Auct.* ;—Polypodii sp., *Auct.* ;—Xiphopteridis sp., *Auct.*)

Sori non-indusiate, oblong (sub-globose) solitary ; the receptacles seated at the thickened apices of the simple vein which occupies each lobe, the margin of the lobe being longitudinally folded sub-cucullately over the sorus, in the manner of a spurious involucre. Veins simple.

Fronds small, fasciculate, thin, somewhat rigid, pinnatifid, the lower barren lobes longer, the fertile folded longitudinally. Rhizome short erect. Small plants with a tendency towards polypodioid structure. (Moore).

1. *Calymmodon cucullatus.* (Presl). Caudex very small, ascending, fibroso-radicant, stipites densely cæspitose, 1-2-3 lines long, fronds membranaceous, 1-5 inches long, linear lanceolate acuminate, deeply nearly to the costa, pinnatifid segments, 1-2 lines long, ovato-oblong, recurvo-patent, obtuse entire, those of the upper half of the frond broader fertile, costa and sometimes the frond deciduously piloso-setose. *Hook. Sp. Fil.* iv, 176.—Polypodium cucullatum, *Hook. l. c. Metten. Poly., p.* 33.—*Nees. et. Bl. Nov. Acad.* ii. *p.* 121, *t.* 12, *f.* 3. —Plectopteris gracilis, *Fée Gen., p.* 230. *t.* 19. *B.*

Ceylon, Rhamboda. (C. P. 1282).

PLATE No. CCXXXIII.

(b.) Veins conniventIy anastomosing below.

STEGNOGRAMMA. *Bl. En. Fil. Jav.* 172.

(Syneuron, *J. Smith* ;—Gymnogrammatis sp., *Bl.*—)

Sori non-indusiate, linear or oblong oblique parallel, the *receptacles* simple elongated naked. *Veins* simple from a central costa ; the lower or more opposite pairs angularly anastomosing.

Fronds herbaceous, pinnate or pinnato-pinnatifid. Rhizome thickish decumbent or erect and sub-arborescent. (Moore.)

1. *Stegnogramma aspidioides.* (Hook.) Fronds hairy on both sides, especially the veins, ovato-lanceolate acuminated, pinnate firm-membranaceous, pinnæ opposite or alternate, sessile sub-truncate or adnate, at the base 3-4 inches long, rarely an inch wide, oblongo-lanceolate, lobato-pinnatifid. Veins 5 or 6 pair, 3 lower united, with an excurrent spurious vein reaching to the sinus, those in the lobes free, all soriferous, sori linear-oblong, nearly the length of the veins. *Hook. Sp. Fil.* v. 150.—*Bl. Fil. Jav., p.* 172.—Phegopteris Stegnogramme, *Metten.*

Ceylon. (Gardner No. 1292.) *I have not been able to procure a specimen of this species, it is not in Mr. Thwaites' List.*

POLYPODIEÆ.

POLYPODIUM. (See page 54).

1. *Polypodium Walkeræ.* (Hook). Stipes 1 to 1½ foot and more long, stout, densely paleaceous at the base with ovate acuminate pale brown glossy scales, mixed with slender linear setaceous ones, which latter often continue up the rachis; fronds ample, 2½ feet and more long, 6 inches to 1 foot and more broad, firm coriaceous, oblong lanceolate, pinnated with the pinnæ nearly entire (normal form) more or less deeply pinnatifid, (varieties β and γ) or pinnate with the pinnules deeply pinnatifid, (sub-bi-pinnate) (variety δ) costa of the pinnæ beneath often furnished with setaceous scales; veins copious, fasciculato-pinnate, sori dorsal upon the veinlets in 2 or more lines between the costa and margin. *Hook. Sp. Fil.* iv, 233.

Ceylon. (C. P. 1256, 3276, 3286), a very variable species.

PLATE No. CCXXXIV.—*Normal form.*

PLATE No. CCXXXV. B. *Variety β marcrocarpum.* Fronds very large, pinnate with the pinnæ pinnatifid ⅓rd to ½ of the way down to the rachis, and often furnished with a large auricle at the superior base. Sori very large.

PLATE No. CCXXXV. C. *Variety γ pinnatifidum.* Pinnæ pinnatifid almost to the rachis, leaving only a broad wing along the rachis, lower pinnæ sometimes pinnate.

PLATE No. CCXXXV. D. *Variety δ bi-pinnatum.* Pinnæ, sub-bi-pinnate. (C. P. 3286) a species dist.? Thwaites En.

2. *Polypodium rufescens.* (Blume.) Caudex creeping, furnished with appressed scales and wiry roots, stipes 8 to 16 inches long, and together with the main and partial rachises slightly asperous, fronds sub-coriaceous, puberulous beneath with minute yellow hairs, bi-tri-pinnatifid, *i. e.*, lower pair of pinnæ often bi-pinnatifid, upper ones pinnatifid pinnules oblong obtuse, spinuloso-serrate, veins pinnate, veinlets simple or forked, reaching to the margin. Sori medial on the veinlets. *Bl. Fil. Jav. p.* 194. *t.* 91.—*Hook. Sp. Fil.* iv, 257.

Ceylon. (C. P. 3143.)

PLATE No. CCXXXVI.

3. *Polypodium Zeylanicum.* (Mett.) Caudex creeping, as thick as a duck's quill, rooting, branched, clothed with sphagneous scales, stipites scattered but approximate, ½-1 inch long, black patently hispid, fronds 6-10 inches long, ⅓rd of an inch wide, sub-membranaceo-coriaceous, sub-pellucid, linear-lanceolate repando-dentate, especially in the upper half glabrous or sub-ciliate, and with the remains of hairs here and there on the surface, sharply acuminated, below gradually attenuated into the stipes, costa rather slender, slightly prominent on both sides, veins rather distant, moderately patent, once forked near or above the middle not extending to the magin, upper branch bearing the sorus chiefly in the upper half of the frond, obliquely patent in a line half way between the costa and the margin, and a little distant from each other. *Hook. Sp. Fil.* iv, 169.—*Metten. Polypod. p.* 38.—Grammitis Zeylanica, *Fée. Gen. Fil. p.* 234.

Ceylon. (C. P. 3074.)

PLATE No. CCXXXVII.

Polypodium decorum. (Brack.) Caudex short, rather thick, creeping densely ferrugineo-squamose, stipites approximate, sub-terminal on the caudex, 2-4 lines long, ½-1 inch broad, narrow-lonceolate much and almost caudato-acuminate, the base very gradually attenuated into the short stipes deeply and nearly to the rachis pinnatifid, segments horizontally patent, narrow-oblong obtuse, quite entire, below gradually becoming shorter and broader and forming shallow elongated lobed wings at the base, costa glabrous or pilosulous, costule and veins quite sunk and inconspicuous, sori oblong, 5-8-10 in two rows parallel with the costa and between the costa and the margin partially sunk in a hairy cavity (but with no raised border) at length confluent. *Hook. Sp. Fil.* iv, 179.—*Brack. Fil. U. St. Expl. Exp., p. 7. t. 2. f. 2. (excellent.)*—P. nutans, *J. Sm. in Hook. Journ. Bot.* iii, *p.* 394, *and Metten., Polyp., p.* 41, *(excl. syn. "Bl. Fil. Jav., p.* 182. *t.* 86. *A.")*—P. Serra, *Wall. Cat.* 313/2.

Ceylon. I have lately detected this species on the mountains near Courtallum (Tinnevelly.)

PLATE No. CCXXXVIII. A.

5. *Polypodium glandulosum.* (Hook.) Caudex small, indistinct, clinging to the bark of trees by copious rooting fibres, the rest of the plant all over piloso-glandulose most so beneath, stipites tufted 1-3 lines long, fronds 2-4 inches long, ¼ inch broad, linear obtuse, scarcely attenuated at either extremity, rather firm-membranaceous, sub-succulent, deeply nearly to the rachis pinnatifid, segments ovate, sub-acute, horizontally patent, decurrent at the base, lowermost ones free, all of them serrato-pinnatifid, costule, and rather distant, few and oblique simple veins indistinct, sori few globose. *Hook Sp. Fil.* iv, 193.

Ceylon. (C. P. 1289.)

PLATE No. CCXXXVIII. B.

GONIOPTERIS. (See page 57).

1. *Goniopteris urophylla.* (Wall.) Caudex? stipes 2 and more feet long, sometimes very stout, testaceous brown, paleaceous at the base with rather large dark-brown subulate scales, fronds ample firm but not thick, coriaceous rarely membranaceous, glabrous or pilosulous above, and more or less densely pubescent, and sometimes subscabrous or minutely glandulose beneath, 2-3 and more feet long, subovate pinnated, pinnæ distant, petioled below, 8 inches to 1½ foot long, ½ to 2½ inches wide from a more or less obtusely and unequally cuneated base, elliptical-oblong finely caudato-acuminate, quite entire or sub-sinuated, more or less grossly obtusely or rarely acutely serrated upwards, terminal pinnæ most so, often larger than the rest and long-petioled, veinlets numerous, 15-20 pairs all connivent, save the few in the teeth or serratures, soriferous in the middle, the sori consequently forming 2 series each between the costules, and the spurious costule, or orbicular or 2-lobed sori are borne at the point of junction of the 2 veinlets, and are then uniserial. *Hook. Sp. Fil.* v, 9.—*Wall. Cat. n.* 299 *(excl. n.* 3.*)*—Goniopteris, *Pr.*—Phegopteris, *Metten, Phegopt.*—Pol. asperum, *Pr. Reliq. Hœnk., p.* 24. *t.* 3. *f.* 4.—Goniopteris, *Pr.*—Meniscium cuspidatum, *Bl. Fil., Jav. p.* 102. *t.* 45, *(excellent, but sori too long and narrow.)*—Phegopteris, *Metten, Phegopt., p.* 25.—Nephrodium glandulosum, *J. Sm. in Hook. Bot. Journ.* iii, *p.* 411 *(according to the reference to Cuming, n.* 16 *not of Blume.)*—Aspidium repandum, *Bl. Fil. Jav., p.* 144 *in Herb. Hook. (not Willd.)*—*β. uniseriale;* sori uniserial, P. granulosum, *Benth. Fl. Hongkong, p.* 400, *(according to the specific character of the locality of Col. Urquhart,) not of Presl.*—Nephrod. glandulosum, *J. Sm. in Seem Bot. Herald, p.* 428 *?*

Ceylon. (C. P. 3063.)

PLATE No. CCXXXIX.

2. *Goniopteris lineata.* (Coleb.) Caudex? stipes 1½ feet and more long, rather stout, scaleless, glossy, and as well as the rachis reddish (rarely stramineous), fronds 1-3 feet long, broad-oblong or lanceolate, coriaceo-membranaceous, pinnated glabrous, pinnæ numerous, rather distant, patent sessile 5-8 inches long, about ½ an inch broad, (on sterile fronds sometimes exceeding 1 inch) from an obliquely cuneato-truncate sessile base, (lower ones rather more attenuated and sub-petiolate), lanceolate or elongato-oblong finely acuminated at the apex, the margin coarsely and sharply sub-mucronato serrated, serratures pointing a little forward, uniform, costa prominent beneath of the same color as the rachis, and stipes generally reddish, veinlets about 6-8 pairs, of which all are connivent except 2-3 short pairs in the teeth of the serratures, sori in 2 series on the middle of the veinlets. *Hook. Sp. Fil.* v, 12.—Polypodium lineatum, *Coleb. in Herb. Wall. and Wall. Cat n.* 300.—*Hook. l. c.*—Polyp. costatum, *Wall. Herb.* (not Goniopteris costata, *Brack*).

Ceylon.

I have not been able to obtain a specimen of this species, as it has not been found by Mr. Thwaites.

NIPHOBOLUS. (See page 61.)

1. *Niphobolus Lingua.* (Sw.) Caudex very long, creeping, rather slender, flexuose paleaceous with ferruginous subulate scales, stipites 3-6 inches and more long, remote, always arising from a short very paleaceous branch of the caudex, upper scales longest and spreading, fronds 4-8 inches long, lanceolate or ovate or oblong, obtuse or acuminated, densely and very compactly stellato, and sometimes sub-squamuloso tomentose at length glabrous above. Sori sub-elevated, copious in 4-6 close series between the primary or costular veins, and from 9-20 between the secondary veins. *Hook. Sp. Fil. v.* 49.—*Sw. Syn. Fil., p.* 29.—*Willd. Sp. Pl. v., p.* 162.—*Langsd. et Fisch. Fil.* i, *p.* 7, *f.* 5.—*Metten, Polyp., p.* 130.—Acrostichum, *Th. Fl. Jap., p.* 330, *t.* 33.—*Schk. Fil., p.* 1, *t.* 1.—Niphobolus, *Spr. Kze. Schk. Fil. Suppl., p.* 144, *t.* 63.

Ceylon. (C. P. 1294.)

PLATE No. CCXL.

2. *Niphobolus Gardneri.* (Metten.) Caudex somewhat creeping, the younger portions densely ferrugineo-paleaceous, stipites approximate arising from a scaly branch of the caudex, 2-4 inches long, fronds about a foot long, carnoso-coriaceous lanceolate, obtusely acuminate, gradually attenuated upon the stipes, densely clothed with a very compact firm sub-furfuraceous mass of whitish or ferruginous stellated tomentum, costa and primary veins or costules slightly elevated beneath, venation of *Campyloneurum*, secondary transverse veins more obscure, veinlets generally free and soriferous, sori superficial (not sunk) in about four series, parallel with the costules and 10-12 transverse series between the costa and the margin.—Var. *a subferruginea, Hook. Sp. Fil. v.,* 51.—*Metten, Polypod., p.* 129.—Niphobolus Gardneri, *Kze. J. Sm. Cat. Cult. Ferns, p.* 12.—*Hook. Fil. Exot. t.* 68.—N. acrostichoides, *J. Sm. Cat. Kew. Gard. Ferns,* p. 2.—N. costatus, *J. Sm. Cat. Kew. Ferns, p.* 6 ?—(*not* Polyp. acrostichoides, Forst.)

Ceylon. (C. P. 988.)

PLATE No. CCXLI.

NOTE.—*Pleopeltis Sp. (C. P.* 1296) *is referred by Sir W. Hooker, to Pnigrescens, (Blume.) I have a Specimen now before me, and it is certainly the same as the plant figured in Plate No. CLXXVI of this work, specimens of which are referred by Sir W. Hooker to P. longissima (Blume.) Mettenius unites the two species of Blume, and if they are distinct, I expect that Sir W. Hooker has made a mistake in referring the South Indian and Ceylon specimens to different species, as mine is certainly the same as the Ceylon plant.*

ASPIDIEÆ.

SAGENIA. (Vide page 27.)

1. *Sagenia subtriphylla.* (Hook.) Caudex creeping, and as well as the base of the stipites moderately scaly, stipites a span to 1½ foot or more long, generally brownish, fronds glabrous or pubescent, sub-coriaceo-membranaceous when young, entire or 3-lobed, cordate acuminate, in maturity 3-foliate or pinnated with 5-7 pinnæ, terminal pinna large, sub-rhomboid, variously pinnatifid, lower lobes the longest, intermediate ones sessile or petiolate, oblong more or less acuminate, lowest pair distant, large semi-ovate more or less acuminate, and pinnatifid, lowest segments (especially at the inferior base) generally very much elongated, patent or deflexed, or not unfrequently (unless I am mistaken in the limits of species), the lowest pinnæ are pinnate, and even sub-bi-pinnate, all costate, veins uniformly anastomosing with areoles, having free, simple or forked veinlets. Sori scattered, all compital (on back of the anastomosing veins), involucres cordiform. *Hook Sp. Fil.* iv, 52.—Polypodium subtriphyllum, *Hook. and Arn. Bot. of Beech. Voy., p.* 256, *t.* 50.—Aspidium trifoliatum, *Hook. in Floral Hongkong. Kew. Gard. Misc.* ix, *p.* 341.—*Benth. Fl. Hongkong, p.* 450.—*(Excl. Syn. of A.* variolosum, *Wall.) Eat. in C. Wright. Herb. of U. St. Pacif. Expl. Exp. (in Herb. Hook.)*—Drynaria latifolia, *Brack. Fil. U. St. Expl. Exped., p.* 50.

Ceylon. (C. P. 1300.)

PLATE No. CCXLII.

2. *Sagenia gigantea, var. minor.* (Hook.) This species is very similar to the normal form of *S. gigantea,* described and figured in a former number of this work, vide page 27 and Plate LXXX, it is, however, a much smaller variety, the fronds are more deeply lobed and more delicate in texture, and it may perhaps be a distinct species.

Ceylon. (C. P. 1358.)

PLATE No. CCXLIII.

3. *Sagenia Thwaitesii.* (Bedd.) Caudex stout, ascending, stipes rachis and costa beneath ebeneous glossy, fronds 2-3 feet long, oblong or ovate, firm, coriaceo-membranaceous, pinnate or below bi-tri-pinnate, the apex pinnatifid, pinnæ nearly opposite, lower ones petioled, upper ones sessile, oblong acuminated, variously lobed, and pinnatifid often unequally, segments acuminated or obtuse, entire or obtusely lobed, margins ciliated, veins and costa on the uppper side slightly rufo-pubescent, glabrous beneath, veins forming long costal areoles along the rachis of the pinnæ from which proceed several free or anastomosing veinlets, veins from the costa of the segments forming small costal areoles (from which proceed free veinlets), or free, simple, forked or pinnate, the superior veinlets terminating with a sorus far within the margin, all the veinlests terminating with a thickened apex within the margin, involucres reniform.—Sagenia cicutaria, Var. β.—an species dist. *Thwaites' En.* part V.

Nearly allied to Sagenia coadunata of this work, though very similar to that Fern in form and general aspect, the venation is more like that of S. gigantea.

Ceylon. (C. P. 3331.) Badulla, near Ondaatche ; Hinidon Pattoo, not uncommon.

PLATE No. CCXLIV.

4. *Sagenia pteropus-minor.* (Bedd.) Stipes of the sterile fronds short, clothed at the base with dark brown linear scales, more or less winged towards the apex, fronds 8-12 inches long, sub-coriaceous, tri-partite or sub-pinnatifid, lower segments 2 to 4 inches long with a large basal lobe, upper portion more or less pinnatifid and irregularly, fertile fronds on a much longer stipe very much contracted, pinnatifid with the lower segments bi-lobed, primary veins pinnate with the veinlets in between forming numerous pretty regular areoles, within which are free included re-curved forked venules. Sori in two rows between the primary veins, generally on free veinlets, or sometimes at the joining of two anastomosing veinlets.—Sagenia pteropus, variety minor. *Thwaites.*

Ceylon. (C. P. 3808.) Paradenia.

This may be only a dwarf variety of "Sagenia pteropus," but it seems rather to deserve the rank of a distinct species. Mr. Thwaites says that it grows intermixed with "Sagenia pteropus," normal form and "Gymnopteris quercifolia" and suggests that it may be a hybrid between the two.

PLATE No. CCXLV.

LASTREA. (See page 33.)

1. *Lastrea calcarata.* (Bedd.) Caudex short, tufted rooting, stipites scaleless, 3-8 inches long, fronds 8-18 inches long, coriaceo-membranaceous, rigid oblongo-lanceolate pinnate, perfectly glabrous except on the rachis, pinnæ alternate or sub-opposite—10-14 pair 1 and ½ inch long, attenuated and entire at the base, above more or less pinnatifid, but never more than ½ down to the costa, veins pinnate with thickened apices, terminating just within the margin. Sori, one on each vein a little above the centre, involucres reniform, glabrous. A. (Lastrea) falcilobum, Var. β. *Hook. Sp. Fil:* iv, *p.* 108.

Nearly allied to L. falciloba, (Plate CL. of this work) but sufficiently distinct to entitle it to the rank of a species. Sir W. Hooker's two species "L. falciloba" and "calcarata," seem to be one and the same ; in fact, the same number of the Ceylon Catalogue, (C. P. 1363), is referred to both. I have retained the name of the latter for this species.

Ceylon. (C. P. 3050.)

PLATE No. CCXLVI.

2. *Lastrea concinna.* (Thwaites.) Caudex short, stipites scaly at the base, fronds lanceolate or triangular—lanceolate glabrous, shining with the stipes about 2 feet long, pinnæ lanceolate acuminate, pinnules trapezoideo lanceolate, crenato-lobate, lobes sparingly denticulate, veins simple, forked, or pinnate, terminating with a thickened apex within the margin, superior veinlet soriferous at its apex—involucres small, reniform glabrous. *Thwaites En. Cey. Pl.*

Ceylon. Singhe Rajah Forests. (C. P. 3798.)

Nearly allied to "Lastrea deparioides," *Hook.* (Plate CIV of this work) ; and Mr. Thwaites suggests that it may be a form of that species, without intermediate forms, however it would hardly be safe to unite them.

PLATE No. CCXLVII.

3. *Lastrea deltoidea.* (Bedd.) Caudex erect, fronds about 1 foot long, glabrous, deltoid-ovate, bi-pinnate with the pinnules deeply pinnatifid, pinnæ lanceolate acuminated, the 2 or 3 lower pair 4 to 5 inches long, getting gradually smaller towards the apex, pinnules narrow lanceolate ¾ to 1½ inch long, deeply pinnatifid, segments obtuse, crenated, and spinuloso-dentate, the primary vein of the pinnules flexuose, veinlets pinnate, terminating with a thickened apex just within the margin, one to four of the veinlets soriferous at their apex involucres reniform glabrous. Lastrea sparsa var. lata. (Moore.) Certe species distincta. *Thwaites En.*

Nearly allied to Lastrea sparsa, (Plate CIII of this work,) but its very broad deltoid form seems sufficiently to distinguish it.

Ceylon. (C. P. 1368, 1369, 3383.)

PLATE No. CCXLVIII.

4. *Lastrea Blumei.* (Hook.) Stipes very shaggy with long linear rufous scales, main and partial rachises rufo-pubescent and copiously furnished with rufous scales, fronds very large, tri-pinnate with the pinnules, pinnatifid to nearly the base, pinnules obtuse, entire or inciso-serrate, sparingly hairy above and pubescent on the costa on both sides, veins pinnate, extending to the margin, soriferous about their centre, involucres fimbriated. Aspidium intermedium, *Bl. En. Fil. Jav., p.* 161, *(not of others.)*—N. (Lastrea) Blumei, *Hook. Sp. Fil.* iv, *p.* 135 *in part, (not C. P.* 3042, *which is Lastrea ferruginea.) (Mihi.)*

Ceylon. (C. P. 3059.)

PLATE No. CCXLIX.

PLATE No. CCL. Is a figure of Lastrea flaccida, Hooker, from Ceylon, (C. P. 3802.) Plate No. XCIX of this work is the Lastrea tenericaulis (Hooker), and the name should be accordingly altered ; if really distinct, the two species are very nearly allied, tenericaulis only differing from flaccida in being more compound, and I have specimens which seem to connect the two.

NOTE.—*Polystichum bi-aristatum.* (Blume.) *C. P.* 3275 is I believe only one of the numerous varieties of P. aculeatum, (Sw.) *Polystichum anomalum,* (Hook. et. Grev.) *C. P.* 3504 is very curious in having its fructification on the upper side of the frond, it does not seem otherwise to differ from some forms of P. aculeatum, and is probably an abnormal form of that species.

NEPHROLEPIS. (See page 32.)

1. *Nephrolepis obliterata.* (Hook.) Caudex very long filiform, here and there sub-squamoso-tomentose rooting with few short-fibres, stipites scattered short 1-2 inches long and as well as the rachis dark-brown sub-pubescent, fronds 3-14 inches long, oblong or linear-oblong, membranaceous, invariably black when dry, pinnated, pinnæ from ½-1½ inches long, horizontally patent, rather distant dimidiato-oblong, obtuse or acute, rarely acuminate, obliquely cuneate at the base, sessile, straight or sub-falcate, superior base truncate and parallel with the rachis, frequently with a sharp auricle, the margin entire or crenate or lobato-dentate especially on the fertile pinnæ, costa slender flexuose, veinlets forked, upper branch bearing sori at the apex, a little distance from the margin, involucre small cordato reniform, soon obliterated. *Hook. Sp. Fil.* iv, *p.* 154.—Nephrodium obliteratum, *Brown. Prodr. Fl. Nov. Holl., p.* 148.—Aspid. undulatum, *Sw. Syn. Fil., p.* 45?—*(Excl. Syn. Cav. fide Willd.) Willd. Sp. Plate V., p.* 223?—Nephrod sub-pectinatum, *Bl. En. Fil. Jav., p.* 145.—N. trichomanoides, *J. Sm. in Hook. Bot. Journ.* iii, *p.* 413, *(name only.)*—N. repens, *Brack. Fil. U. S. Expl. Exp., p.* 209.

Ceylon. (C. P. 1094 and 1376.)

PLATE No. CCLI.

CYSTOPTERIDEÆ.

ACROPHORUS. (See page 3.)

1. *Acrophorus affinis.* (Moore). Caudex creeping, thick, clothed with long narrow subulate scales, fronds ample, tall, ovato-lanceolate, membranaceous, 3-4 pinnate or supra decompound, primary pinnæ petiolate, ovato-lanceolate acuminate, secondary petiolate oblong-ovate, pinnules ovate, deeply pinnatifid, the segments ovate acute, sub-falcate, entire or generally (the fertile ones) with a tooth on the inner margin, involucres small hemispherical or sub-reniform placed near the centre of a segment below the sinus of the tooth, veins slender, black. *Hook. Sp. Fil.* i, *page* 158.—Leucostegia affinis, *J. Sm. En. Fil. Philipp. l. c. (name only).*

Ceylon. (C. P. 1384.) Very like A. pulcher (Dav. ckærophylla, Wall.) but with a very different caudex.

PLATE No. CCLII.

DAVALLIEÆ.

HUMATA. (See page 4.)

1. *Humata vestita.* (Blume.) Caudex creeping, paleaceous, stipes elongated, paleaceous with lanceolate chaffy scales, fronds coriaceous (a span or more high), bi-pinnate, pinnæ lanceolate, sub-petiolate pinnatifid, the lowermost ones at the base again pinnate, inferior segments the largest, all of them serrato-dentate, rachis and costa beneath beset with broadly ovate obtuse chaffy appressed sub-peltate scales, fructification small in the axils of the teeth, involucres sub-orbicular, rather broader than long. *Hook. Sp. Fil.* i, *page* 156.—Davallia vestita, *Bl. in En. Fil. Jav., p.* 233.

Ceylon. (C. P. 3068.)

PLATE No. CCLIII.

MICROLEPIA. (See page 5.)

1. *Microlepia proxima?* (Blume.) Caudex creeping tomentose, of the thickness of a man's finger, stipites scaleless, sub-glabrous shining ½ a foot long; fronds tri-pinnate, lanceolate, or deltoid-lanceolate, sub-glabrous, sparingly pilose on the veins beneath, 2-3 feet long, rachis slightly scabrous; pinnæ (and pinnules) approximate lanceolate caudato-acuminate, alternate; pinnules pinnatifid or at the base pinnate, lobes falcato-trapezioid, acute or obtuse, crenato dentate. Sori a little within the margin.—Involucres, cup-shaped.—*Thwaites En. Cey. Pl.—Bl. En. Plant Jav.* 2, *p.* 238.—*Hook. Sp. Fil.* i, 183?

Ceylon. (C. P. 3827.) Oova district in the Central Province.

PLATE No. CCLIV.

2. *Microlepia strigosa.* (Moore.) Fronds tall, lanceolate, bi-pinnate, stipes elongated, rachis and veins pubescenti-hispid, primary pinnæ petiolate, lanceolate acuminate, secondary (or pinnules) mostly petiolulate, sub-dimidiato-ovate, obtuse pinnatifid, chiefly on the upper edge, lower lobes obovate deep, the rest short, all of them angulato-dentate, veins pinnated, furnished with a few long scattered hairs both above and beneath (the remaining surface of the frond beneath being sometimes furnished with numerous small hairs, or sometimes glabrous as is the upper surface), involucres hairy, small half cup-shaped. *Hook.*—Dicksonia strigosa, *Sw.*—Davallia Khasiyana, *Hook. Sp. Fil.* i, 173.—Microlepia cristata, *J. Sm. En. Fil. Philipp.*

Ceylon. (C. P. 1386.)

Chokampatty Hills (Tinnevelly district) abundant, at an elevation of 5,000 feet, (only lately detected in the Madras Presidency.)

PLATE No. CCLV.

3. *Microlepia hirta.* (Kaulf.) Tall, fronds erect, rigid ovato-lanceolate, much and gradually acuminate, rather glossy, tri-pinnate, pinnules approximate, rhombeo-lanceolate, sub-dimidiate, acute decurrent, upper ones coadunate, all of them inciso-pinnatifid, segments acute, sori small on the inner margin in the sinus of a lobe, involucres half cup-shaped, veins prominent and hairy, especially beneath, rachis hispido-tomentose. *Hook.*—Davallia hirta, *Kaulf En. Fil.*, *p.* 223.—Dicksonia Kaulfussiana, *Gaud. in Freyc. Voy. Bot.*, *p.* 368.—Davallia villosa, *Don.* (*Sprengel.*)

Ceylon. (C. P. 3272.)

Malabar, Manantody, and the slopes of the Brumagherries. I have long had this fern in my herbarium, but until I received a specimen of it from Mr. Thwaites as an authentic spec. of *M. hirta*, I had always considered it only as a variety of *M. polypodioides*, (Don.,) plate XV of this work. I have given a figure of it in case it should be distinct, but I still suspect it is only a variety of *polypodioides*. I have lately collected on the Courtallum Hills (Tinnevelly), what I take to be a third variety : it is very nearly allied to the Ceylon and Malabar *M. hirta*, but is more delicate—the secondary pinnules are narrower, the involucres are quite glabrous, and the fronds nearly so.

PLATE No. CCLVI.

NOTE.—*Davallia* (*Microlepia inæqualis*, (Kunze), recorded as a Ceylon fern, is probably the same as *M. hirta*.

PERANEMEÆ.

(*d.*) *Veins free.*

* * *Involucres sessile.*

DIACALPE. *Blume. Enum. Pl. Jav.* 241.

(Aspidii sp., *Wallich*;—Physematii sp., *Kunze*;—Cystopteridis sp., *Presl.*;—Cyatheæ sp., *Mettenius.*)

Sori involucrate globose, the receptacles punctiform, medial on the anterior lower venules. *Involucre* firm, membranaceous, or sub-coriaceous, sessile attached to a small point globose, entire, at length bursting and splitting irregularly from the top. *Veins* simple, forked, or (in the secondary pinnules) pinnate, *venules* simple free.

Fronds decompound, herbaceous. Rhizome short. The chief peculiarity in this genus is the hard globose, entirely closed involucre, which at length bursts open irregularly, and is affixed by a small point of contact. (Moore).

1. *Diacalpe aspidioides.* (Bl.) 2-4 feet high, stipes long, clothed below with very large, broad opaque, brown, membranaceous scales ; fronds tri-pinnate, primary pinnæ often nearly sessile ; main and partial rachis frequently beset with copious short setose scales, especially beneath, sometimes with long crinite deciduous scales which also appear on the veins above, pinnules sub-membranaceous, oblong-cuneate, pinnatifido-lobate, more or less decurrent, so that the rachis and ultimate pinnæ are generally winged, veins dark colored, not reaching to the margin.

Ceylon. (C. P. 3282.)

PLATE No. CCLVII.

(3.) *Sori punctiform, &c., &c.*

(c.) Sori involucrate, i. e., with inferior indusia.

(b.) Special indusium, more or less adherent to, and connivant with the margin of the frond, forming an entire or 2-valved cup; sori, therefore, within a marginal cup.

(TRIBE 1, § 20,) DICKSONIEÆ.

(a.) Indusium cup-shaped, reflexed.

DENNSTÆDTIA. *Bernhardi. Schrad. Journ.* 1800, ii, 124, *t.* 1, *f.* 3.

(Dicksonia, *Kaulfuss, Presl.*;—Sitobolium, *Desvaux.*;—Patania, *Presl.*;—Sitobolium, *J. Sm.*;—Adectum, *Link.*;—Depariæ sp., *Hooker*;—Polypodii. sp., *Auct.*;—Cyatheæ sp., *Auct.*;—Trichomanes, *Auct.*;—Nephrodii sp., *Auct.*)

Sori involucrately-indusiate, globose, marginal reflexed, *the receptacles* small, punctiform terminal; *Indusium*, cupuliform or pateriform, sub-membranaceous, the special and accessory valves nearly equal, and coalescing into an almost entire, rarely sub-bilabiate reflexed cup. *Veins* pinnate from a central costa, *venules* simple or forked free.

Fronds herbaceous, bi-pinnate or decompound, the sori exerted within the cup-shaped involucriform indusia, and reflexed. Rhizome creeping. This genus differs from Dicksonia in a cup-shaped entire, instead of a 2-valved indusium. (Moore.)

1. *Dennstœdtia deltoidea.* (Moore.) Stipes 6-8 inches long, a little rough, glossy brown, fronds deltoid-ovate, 1 foot long, quadripinnate, pinnules oblong-cuneate, pinnatifid, the segments linear obtuse few on a winged rachis, sori terminal upon the shorter segments, rachises (the main one zigzag) costæ, and frond (in a slight degree) hairy. *Hook.*—Davallia deltoidea, *Hook. Sp. Fil.* i, 80.

Ceylon. (C. P. 1397.)

PLATE No. CCLVIII.

NOTE.—Mr. Moore enumerates two other species from Ceylon, viz., *D. flaccida* and *scabra.* Mr. Thwaites says he does not know them unless they are forms of the above, nor does he know anything of *Dicksonia Zeylanica*, (Sw.), unless it is also the same as *Dennstœdtia deltoidea.*

CYATHEA. (See page 19.)

Cyathea sinuata. (Hook. et Grev.) Caudex 1 inch in diameter, fronds simple, lanceolate, very much elongated, sinuate at the margin, veins pinnate, veinlets soriferous near the middle, involucre globose or slightly depressed, bursting very irregularly at the top, so as to become cup-shaped with a very uneven margin, receptacle globose. *Hook. Sp. Fil.* i, 15.

Ceylon. (C. P. 3052.)

PLATE No. CCLIX.

2. *Cyathea Hookeri.* (Thw.) Caudex elongate, about 1½ inch in diameter, stipites sparingly muricated at the base and furnished with rather rigid setosely acuminated scales, fronds 3 feet or more long, narrow, lanceolate acuminate, pinnate, pinnatifid at the apex, pinnæ lanceolate, sub-entire or crenately lobate, and broadly truncate at the base, shortly petiolate, superior sessile, inferior gradually smaller, costa beneath sparingly paleaceous, veins pinnate, indusium globose, bursting irregularly. *Thw. En. Pl. Ceylon, part V.*

Ceylon; Singhe-Rajah Forest. (C. P. 3722.)

PLATE No. CCLX.

3. *Cyathea Walkeræ.* (Hook.) Unarmed, stipes and main rachis mahogany coloured-fronds bi-pinnate, pinnules thick, firm, very coriaceous, deeply pinnatifid, pinnate below, segments and ultimate pinnules (the latter contracted at the base) oblong, very obtuse, entire or slightly crenate, often scaly, (scales deciduous) on the costa beneath, veins copious, sunk, forked at the very base, often again about half way up, sori occupying the lowest fork close to, almost upon the costa, involucres large, opaque, bursting, as it were, on the superior side, only reflexed upon the costa, and partially covering the sorus in the form of a broad bifid hood. *Hook. Sp. Fil.* i, 24.

Amphicosmia Walkeræ, *Moore.* Mr. Moore places this plant in the genus *Amphicosmia,* distinguished from *Cyathea* by the involucres being half cup-shaped ; but Mr. Thwaites, who has noticed living specimens, informs me that the involucre is very variable, and ranges between *Cyathea* and true *Alsophila.*

Ceylon. (C. P. 1398, 1399, and 3053.)

PLATE No. CCLXI.

TRICHOMANES. (See page 2.)

1. *Trichomanes proliferum.* (Blume.) Caudex creeping, downy much entangled, stipes elongated bearing fronds which are proliferous from the axils, and which are subreniform or cordate, deeply divided palmate or almost digitate, the segments linear and often again divided obtuse, involucres sub-cylindrical and quite sunk, the mouth more or less spreading, obscurely 2-lipped, receptacles exserted.

Ceylon. (C. P. 3329.)

I have lately found this species abundant on the Western slopes of the Nilgiris, 3,000 feet elevation.

PLATE No. CCLXII.

2. *Trichomanes glauco-fuscum.* (Hook.) Fronds rather tall, oblongo-lanceolate, bi-pinnatifid, glauco-fuscous when dry, primary divisions, broad lanceolate, the segments all acute, linear simple or forked, involucres superaxillary on short segments, partially sunk, short, cylindrical attenuated at the base, the mouth broad, spreading scarcely 2-lipped, stipes filiform glabrous, indistinctly winged except above. *Hook. Sp. Fil.* i, *p.* 128.

Ceylon. (C. P. 3330.)

PLATE No. CCLXIII.

3. *Trichomanes corticola.* (Hook. M. S.) Rhizome hair-like repent, and with the longish stipes hispidulous, fronds ½ to 1 inch, cuneato-orbicular palmato-incised, glabrous, segments linear retuse, costa central, sori terminal, involucres poculiform, sub-bilabiate. *Thw. En. Pl. Ceylon, part V.*

PLATE No. CCLXIV.

HYMENOPHYLLUM. (See page 3.)

1. *Hymenophyllum Tunbridgense.* (Sm.) Procumbent densely matted, fronds small, rather tender pinnated, pinnæ distichous, sub-vertical pinnatifid, segments linear simple or bifid, and as well as the superaxillary solitary sub-compressed involucres spinuloso-serrate, the valves semi-orbicular, the very short cuneate base sunk, rachis winged above. *Hook. Sp. Fil.* i, 95 ;—*Smith. Fl. Brit., p.* 1,141 ;—H. minimum, *Rich. Fl. Nov. Zeal., p.* 91 ;—H. revolutum, *Colenso in Tasm. Phil. Journ.* ;—H. asperulum, *Kze. Pl. Crypt. Pœpp., p.* 109 ;—H. Thunbergii, *Eckl. in Schied. Pl. Exsic. Cap. Un. It. n.* 92 ;—H. unilaterale ? *Willd.* ;—H. cupressiforme, *Lab. Nov. Holl., p.* 102.

Ceylon. (C. P. 2984.)

I have lately detected this species on the mountains close to Chokampatty (Tinnevelly), at an elevation of 5,000 feet.

PLATE No. CCLXV.

2. *Hymenophyllum Blumeanum ?* (Spr.) Caudex creeping, scrobiculate glabrous, stipes terete, fronds elongate, linear-lanceolate glabrous, rachis winged, pinnæ rather remote, irregular in size and shape, from narrow-cuneate to variously digitato-pinnate, veins very prominent, involucres oblong 2-valved entire.

Ceylon. (C. P. 1391.)

PLATE No. CCLXVI.

3. *Hymenophyllum polyanthos.* (Sw.) Erect or drooping, ovate or oblong, tri-pinnatifid, the segments short, entire, generally spreading, sometimes a little waved and flexuose, involucres terminal, ovate, or nearly orbicular, free, or the base slightly sunk, deeply 2-valved, the valves convex, entire or somewhat erose, stipes terete, naked or moderately winged above,—*var. a ;* fructifications mostly terminal on elongated sub-palmated segments, involucres ovate, slightly sunk in the frond. *Hook. Sp. Fil.* i, 106 ;—H. polyanthos, *Sw. Syn Fil., p.* 149 ;—*Willd. Sp. Pl. l. c., p.* 531 ;—*Hedw. Fil. cum. Ic.* ;—H. abietinum, *Kze. Pl. Crypt. Pæpp., p.* 109 ;—vix, *Hook.* H. Jalapense, *Chan et Schlecht in Linnæa* v, *p.* 619 ;—H. badium, *Wall. Cat. n.* 172, *not Hook. et. Grev.* ;—H. ricciæfolium, *Klotzch. in Herb. Reg. Berol. an Jacq.* ?

Ceylon. (C. P. 1279, 1395.)

PLATE No. CCLXVII.

SCHIZÆA. (See page 21.)

1. *Schizæa digitata.* (Sw.) Fronds long, linear, grass-like, 10-15 inches long by 2-3 lines broad, bearing, a digitate fertile crest at the apex, crest 8-14 parted to the base, segments 1 inch long by a line broad, sori in 4 series, (*i. e.,* 2 series each side of the costa.)

Ceylon. (C. P. 3105.)

PLATE No. CCLXVIII.

OPHIOGLOSSUM. (See page 23.)

1. *Ophioglossum pendulum.* (L.) Sterile fronds linear-lanceolate, longer than the fertile spike, up to 2 feet long by ½ to ¾ of an inch broad, veins reticulated in very elongated areoles without free veinlets.

Ceylon. (C. P. 1,409.)

PLATE No. CCLXIX.

ADDENDA.

GYMNOGRAMMA. (See page 77.)

1. *Gymnogramma leptophylla.* (Desv.) Root a small annual tufted mass of fibres, stipites tufted, slender, filiform, 1-3 inches long, fronds small, delicate, membranaceous very transparent, all fertile, varying from reniform crenated to variously pinnate or bi-tripinnate, those on the shorter stipes being less compound, pinnæ spathulate to obovate, decurrent, deeply crenated, lobes entire or serrulate, veins simple or forked, not reaching to the margin, sori oblong, simple or forked. *Desv. Journ. Bot.* i, *p.* 26—*Hook. Sp. Fil.* v, 136.

Sir Will. Hooker describes this species as having fertile, and sterile fronds, but, all my specimens have all the fronds fertile.

Nilgiris—Mahableshwar Hills,—Sattara Fort walls (Bombay Presidency.)

A very delicate little species only appearing during the rainy season, the specimens figured are from Sattara. I have not succeeded in finding it on the Nilgiris, though it has been found by several Collectors, and I have seen specimens collected on rocks between Ootacamund and Kotagherry.

PLATE No. CCLXX.

LASTREA. (See page 82.)

5. *Lastrea undulata.* (Thw.) Stipes paleaceous, fronds tri-pinnate deltoid, rachis geniculato-flexuose, pinnæ alternate or sub opposite deflexed deltoid-lanceolate with their rachis very flexuose, secondary pinnæ alternate lanceolate, inferior basal ones much the largest, pinnules rhomboid-oblong (the lower ones lobed or pinnatifid) more or less decurrent, crenulato-dentate, sori solitary or few medial on the veins, indusium reniform, veins terminating within the margin with a thickened apex. *Thw. M.S.*

Ceylon. (C. P. 3858.) Wattekelle, Kallibokka, elevation 5,000 feet.

This very distinct and elegant species has just been discovered by Mr. Beckett and named by Mr. Thwaites from whom I have just received the frond here figured.

PLATE No. CCLXXI.

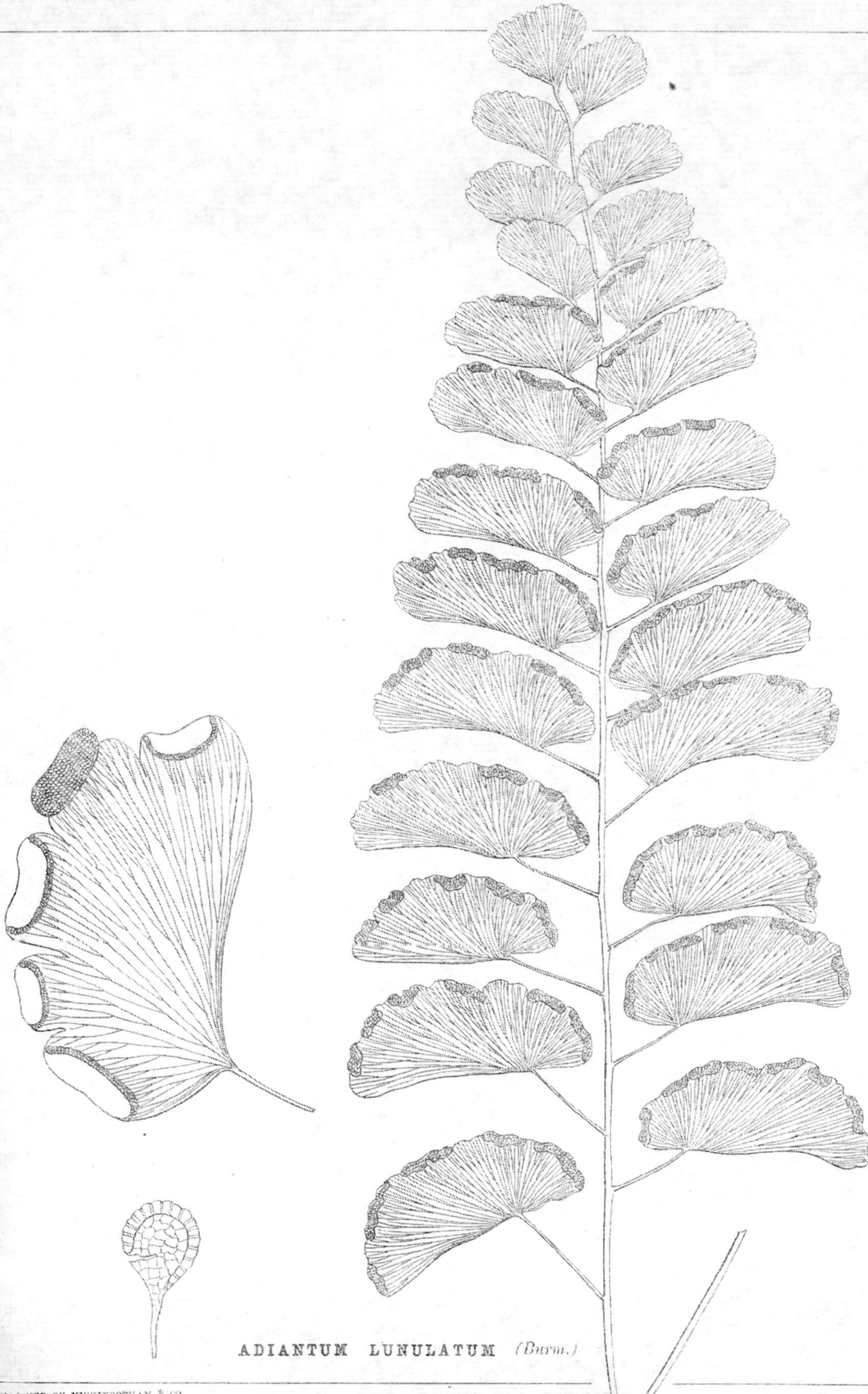

ADIANTUM LUNULATUM *(Burm.)*

PUBLISHED BY HIGGINBOTHAM & CO. ORIENTAL LITHOGRAPHIC PRESS, MADRAS 1872 LITHOGRAPHED BY ALEX : BARREN

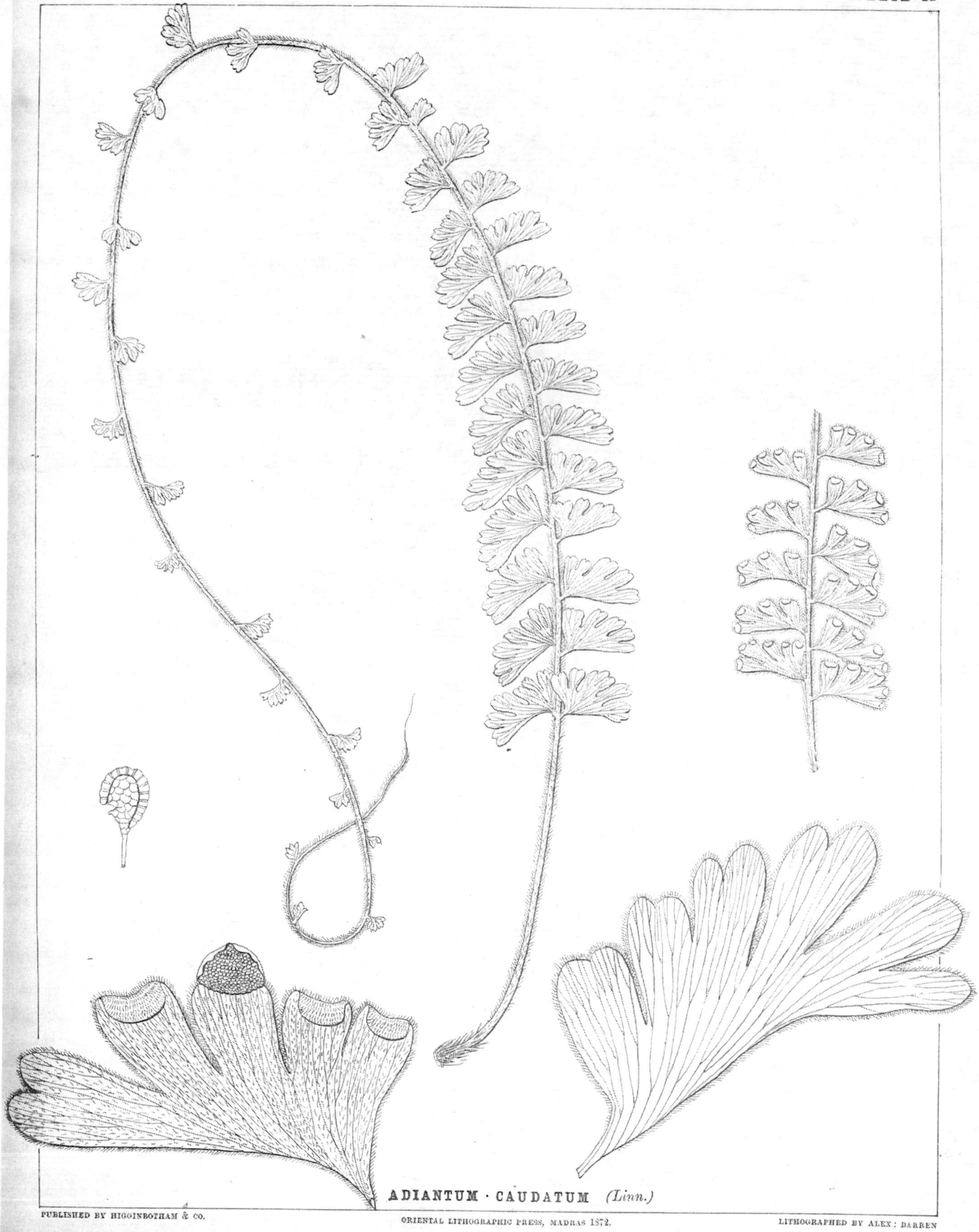

ADIANTUM · CAUDATUM (*Linn.*)

PUBLISHED BY HIGGINBOTHAM & CO. ORIENTAL LITHOGRAPHIC PRESS, MADRAS 1872. LITHOGRAPHED BY ALEX: BARREN

ADIANTUM HISPIDULUM *(Sw.)*

PUBLISHED BY HIGGINBOTHAM & CO. ORIENTAL LITHOGRAPHIC PRESS, MADRAS 1872 LITHOGRAPHED BY ALEX: BARREN

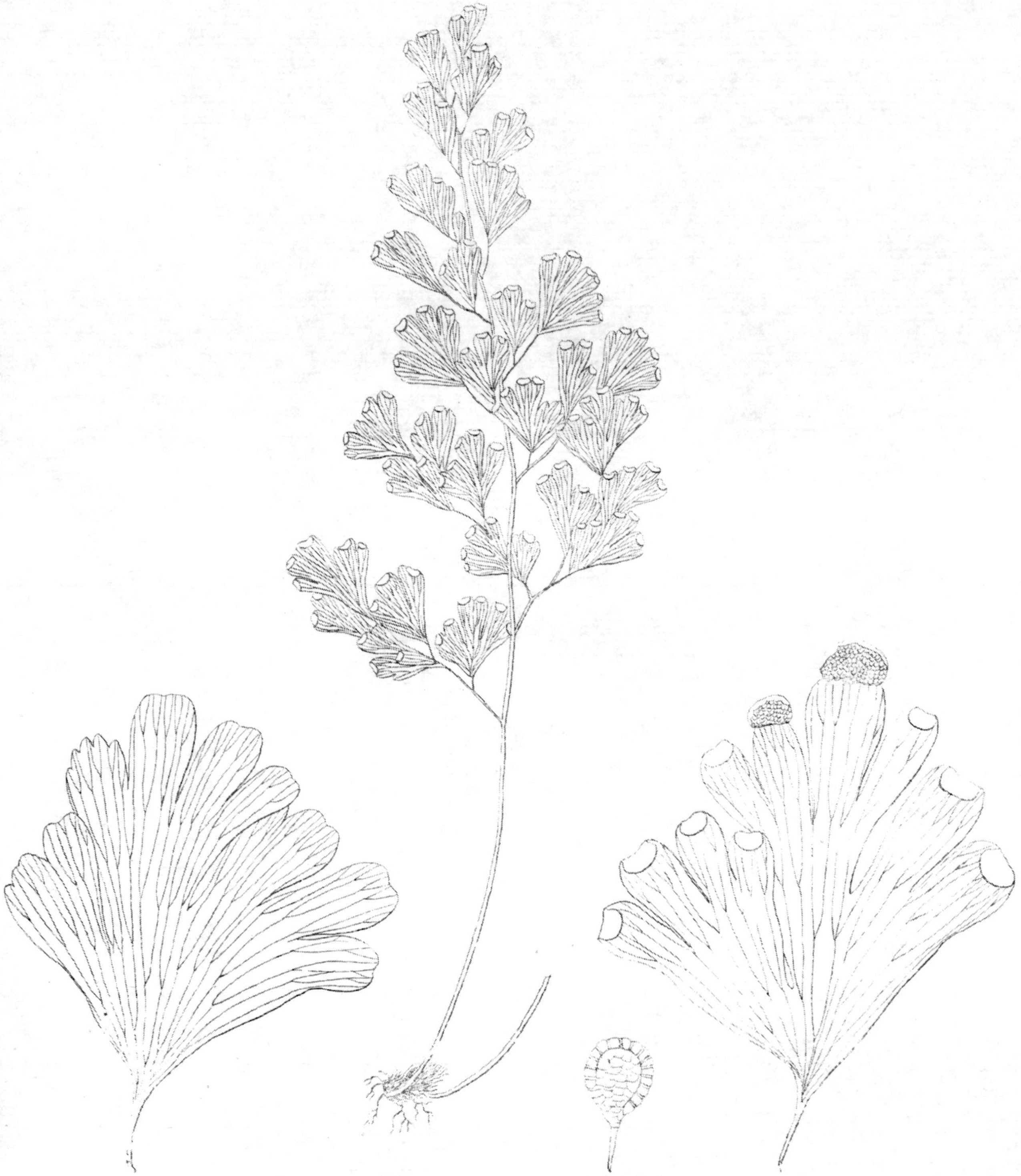

ADIANTUM CAPILLUS VENERIS *(Linn.)*

PUBLISHED BY HIGGINBOTHAM & CO. ORIENTAL LITHOGRAPHIC PRESS, MADRAS 1872. LITHOGRAPHED BY ALEX. BARREN

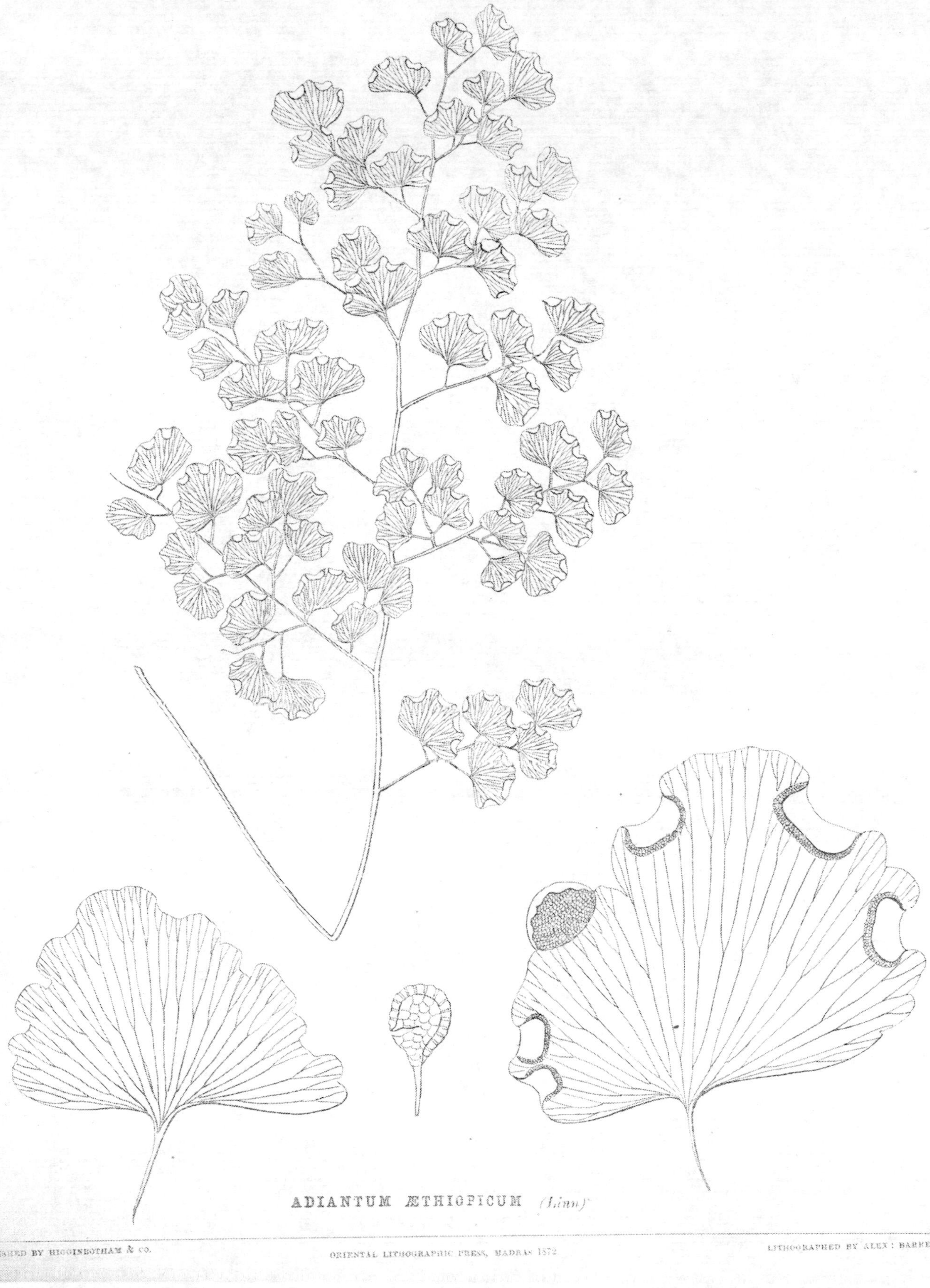

ADIANTUM ÆTHIOPICUM (Linn)

PUBLISHED BY HIGGINBOTHAM & CO. ORIENTAL LITHOGRAPHIC PRESS, MADRAS 1872 LITHOGRAPHED BY ALEX: BARREN

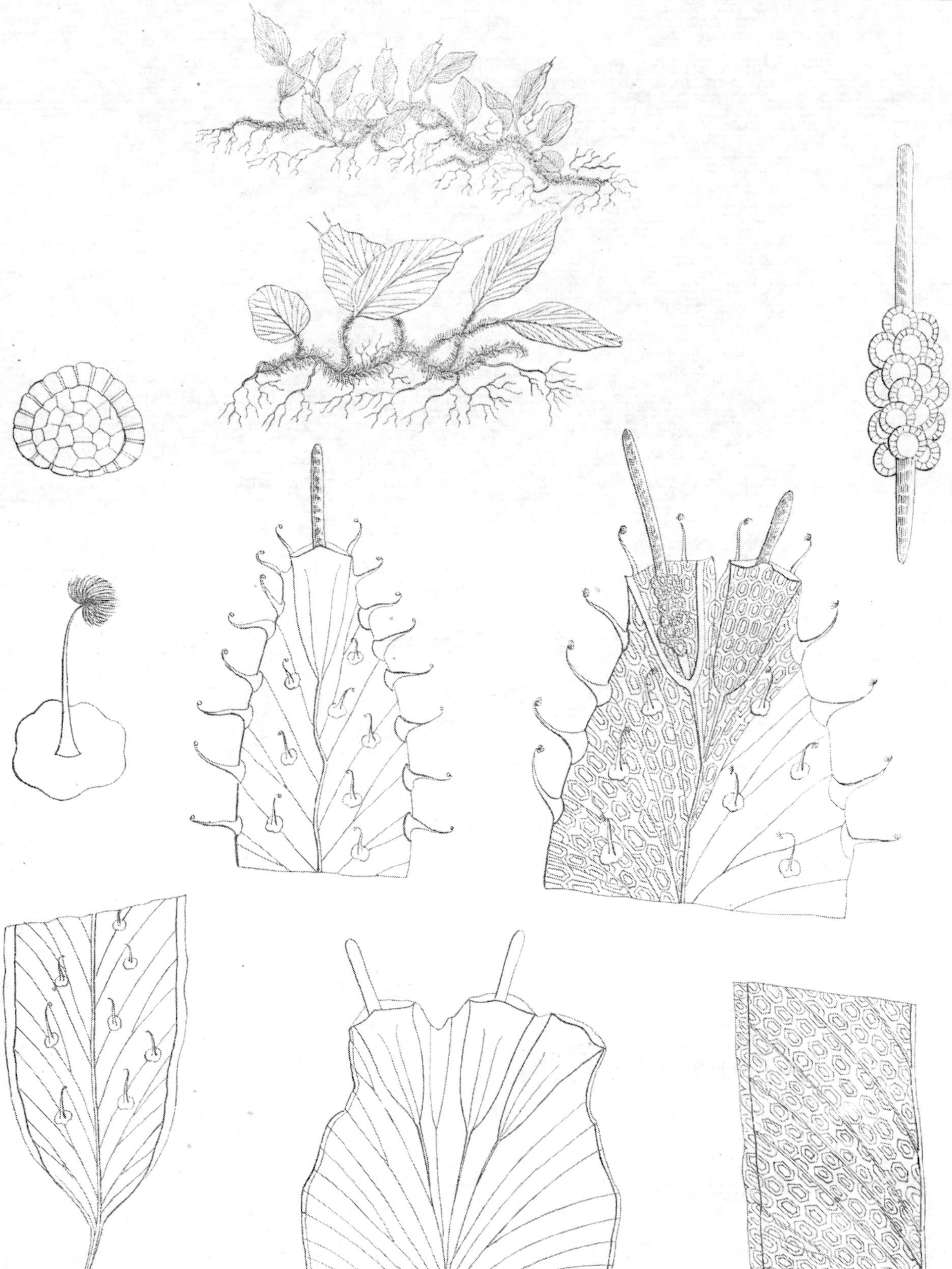

TRICHOMANES NEILGHERRENSE (Bedd)

PUBLISHED BY HIGGINBOTHAM & CO. ORIENTAL LITHOGRAPHIC PRESS, MADRAS 1872 LITHOGRAPHED BY ALEX: BARREN

TRICHOMANES FILICULA (Bory)

PUBLISHED BY HIGGINBOTHAM & CO. ORIENTAL LITHOGRAPHIC PRESS, MADRAS 1872 LITHOGRAPHED BY ALEX: BARREN

TRICHOMANES RIGIDUM (Sw)

PUBLISHED BY HIGGINBOTHAM & CO. ORIENTAL LITHOGRAPHIC PRESS, MADRAS 1872. LITHOGRAPHED BY ALEX: BARREN

HYMENOPHYLUM EXSERTUM (Wall)

J. L.

PUBLISHED BY HIGGINBOTHAM & Co. ORIENTAL LITHOGRAPHIC PRESS, MADRAS 1874. LITHOGRAPHED BY ALEX: BARREN

ACROPHORUS PULCHER *(Moore)*

PUBLISHED BY HIGGINBOTHAM & CO. ORIENTAL LITHOGRAPHIC PRESS, MADRAS 1872. LITHOGRAPHED BY ALEX: BARREN

ACROPHORUS IMMERSUS (*Moore.*)

PUBLISHED BY HIGGINBOTHAM & CO. ORIENTAL LITHOGRAPHIC PRESS, MADRAS 1879 LITHOGRAPHED BY ALEX: BARREN

HUMATA PEDATA (*J. Sm.*)

PUBLISHED BY HIGGINBOTHAM & CO. ORIENTAL LITHOGRAPHIC PRESS, MADRAS 1872 LITHOGRAPHED BY ALEX: BARREN

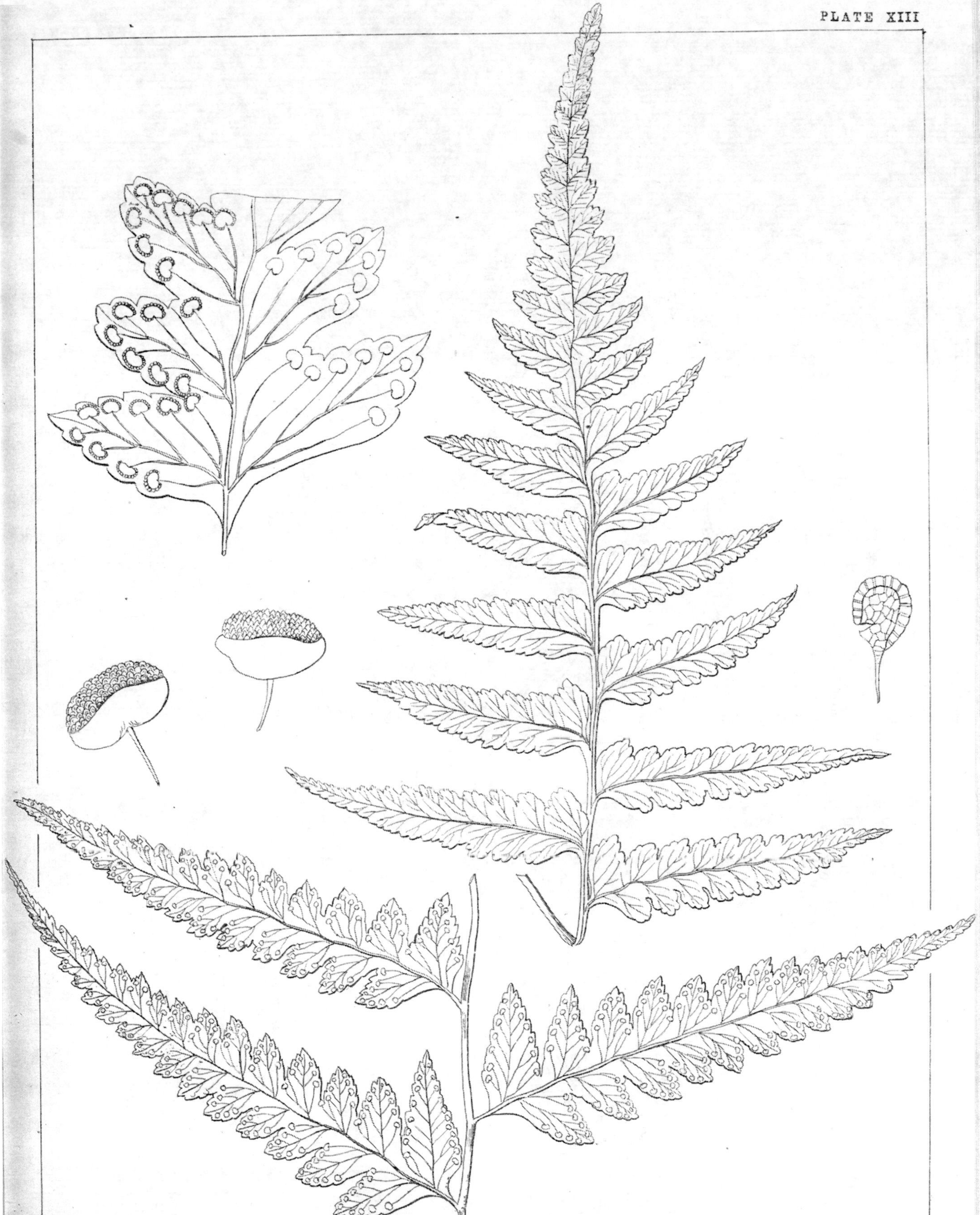

MICROLEPIA PLATYPHYLLA *(Moore.)*

PUBLISHED BY HIGGINBOTHAM & CO. ORIENTAL LITHOGRAPHIC PRESS, MADRAS 1872. LITHOGRAPHED BY ALEX: BARREN

MICROLEPIA PINNATA *(Moore.)*

PUBLISHED BY HIGGINBOTHAM & CO. ORIENTAL LITHOGRAPHIC PRESS, MADRAS 1872. LITHOGRAPHED BY ALEX: BARREN

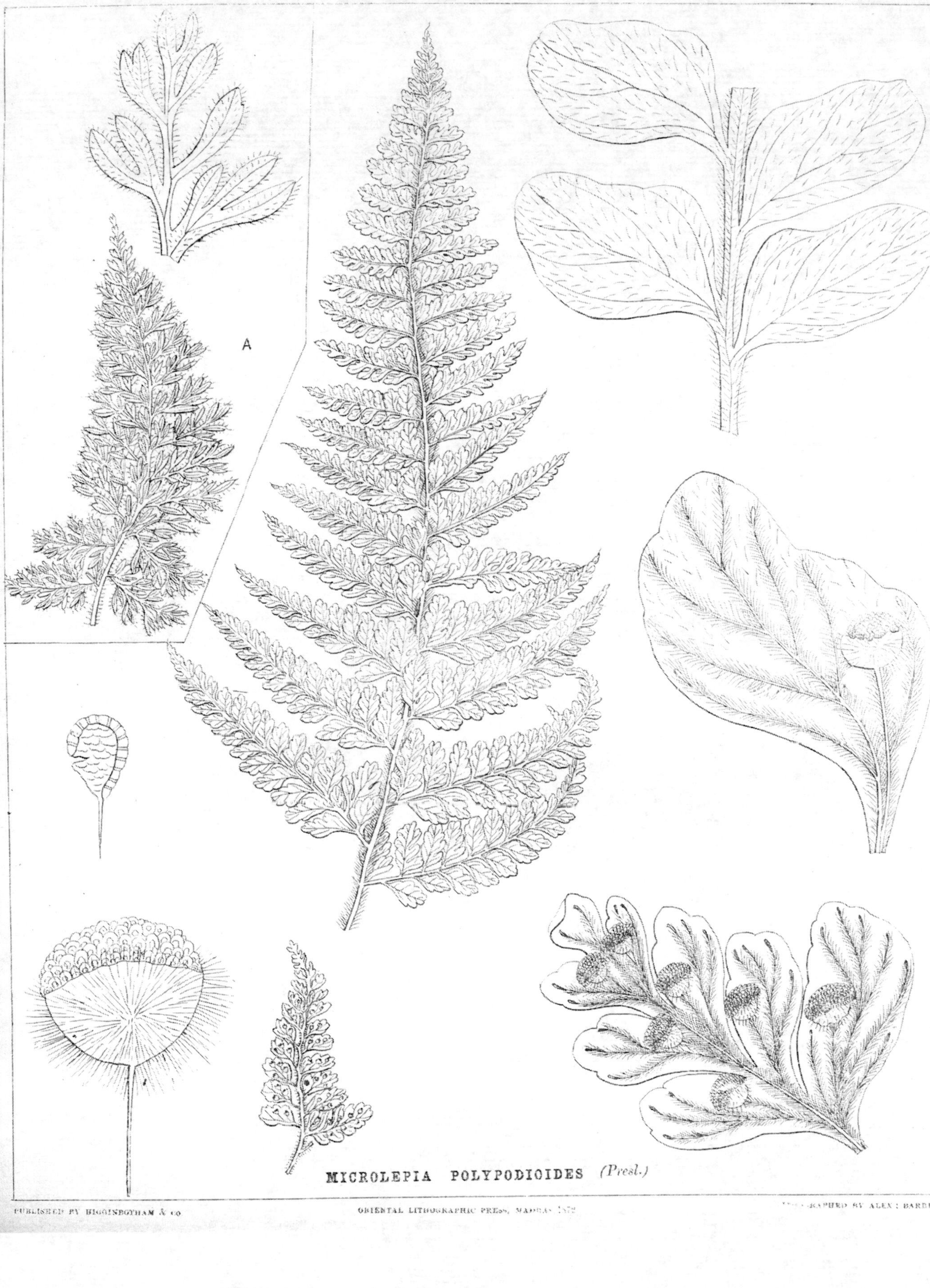

MICROLEPIA POLYPODIOIDES *(Presl.)*

PUBLISHED BY HIGGINBOTHAM & Co.   ORIENTAL LITHOGRAPHIC PRESS, MADRAS   LITHOGRAPHED BY ALEX: BARRES

PLATE XVI

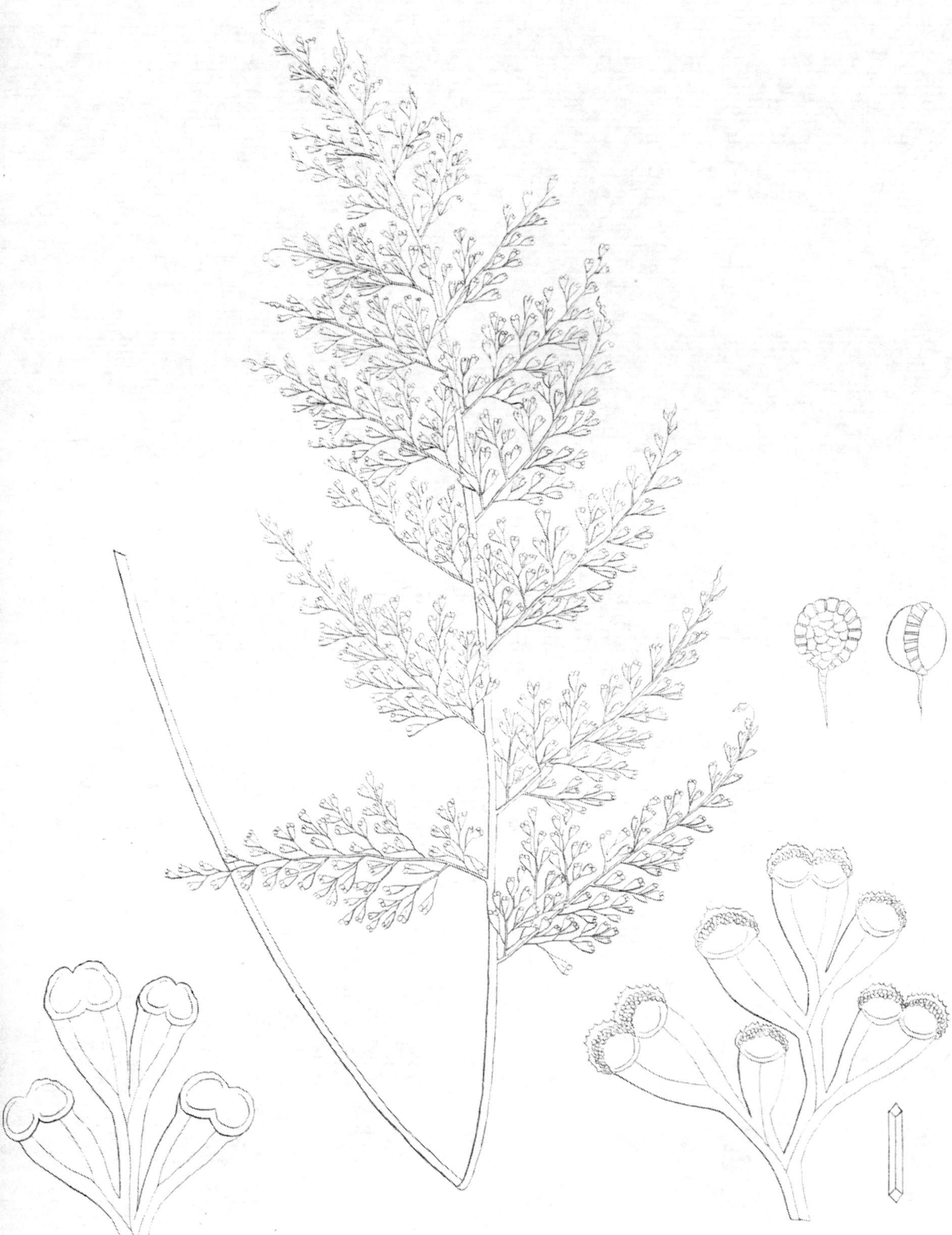

DAVALLIA TENUIFOLIA *(Sw.)*

PUBLISHED BY HIGGINBOTHAM & CO. ORIENTAL LITHOGRAPHIC PRESS, MADRAS 1872. LITHOGRAPHED BY ALEX: BARREN

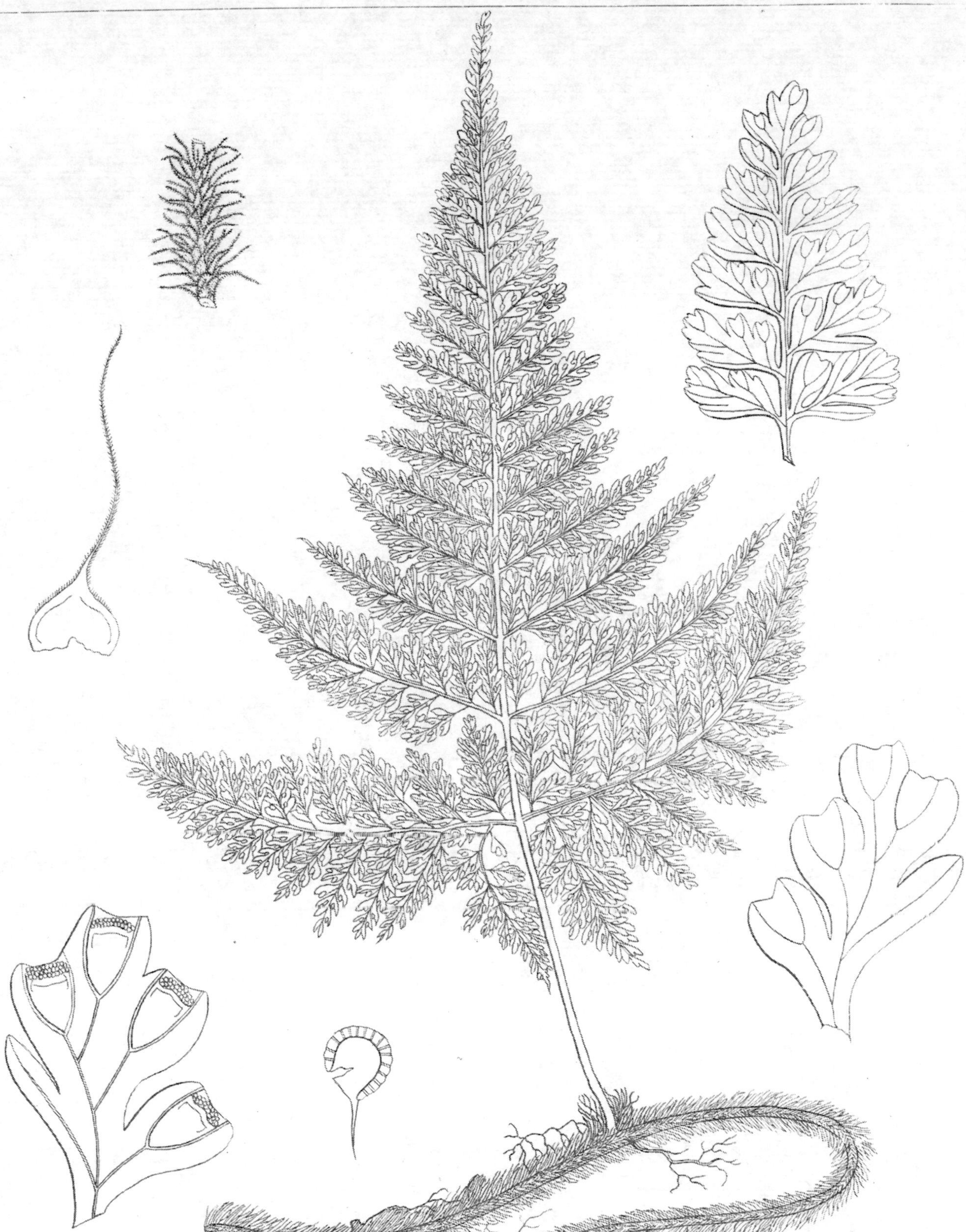

DAVALLIA BULLATA (*Wallich.*)

PUBLISHED BY HIGGINBOTHAM & CO. ORIENTAL LITHOGRAPHIC PRESS, MADRAS 1872. LITHOGRAPHED BY ALEX: BARREN

DAVALLIA ELEGANS (Sw.)

PUBLISHED BY HIGGINBOTHAM & Co

ORIENTAL LITHOGRAPHIC PRESS, MADRAS 1872

LITHOGRAPHED BY ALEX: BARREN

PROSAPTIA CONTIGUA *(Pr.)*

PUBLISHED BY HIGGINBOTHAM & CO. ORIENTAL LITHOGRAPHIC PRESS, MADRAS 1872. LITHOGRAPHED BY ALEX: BARREN

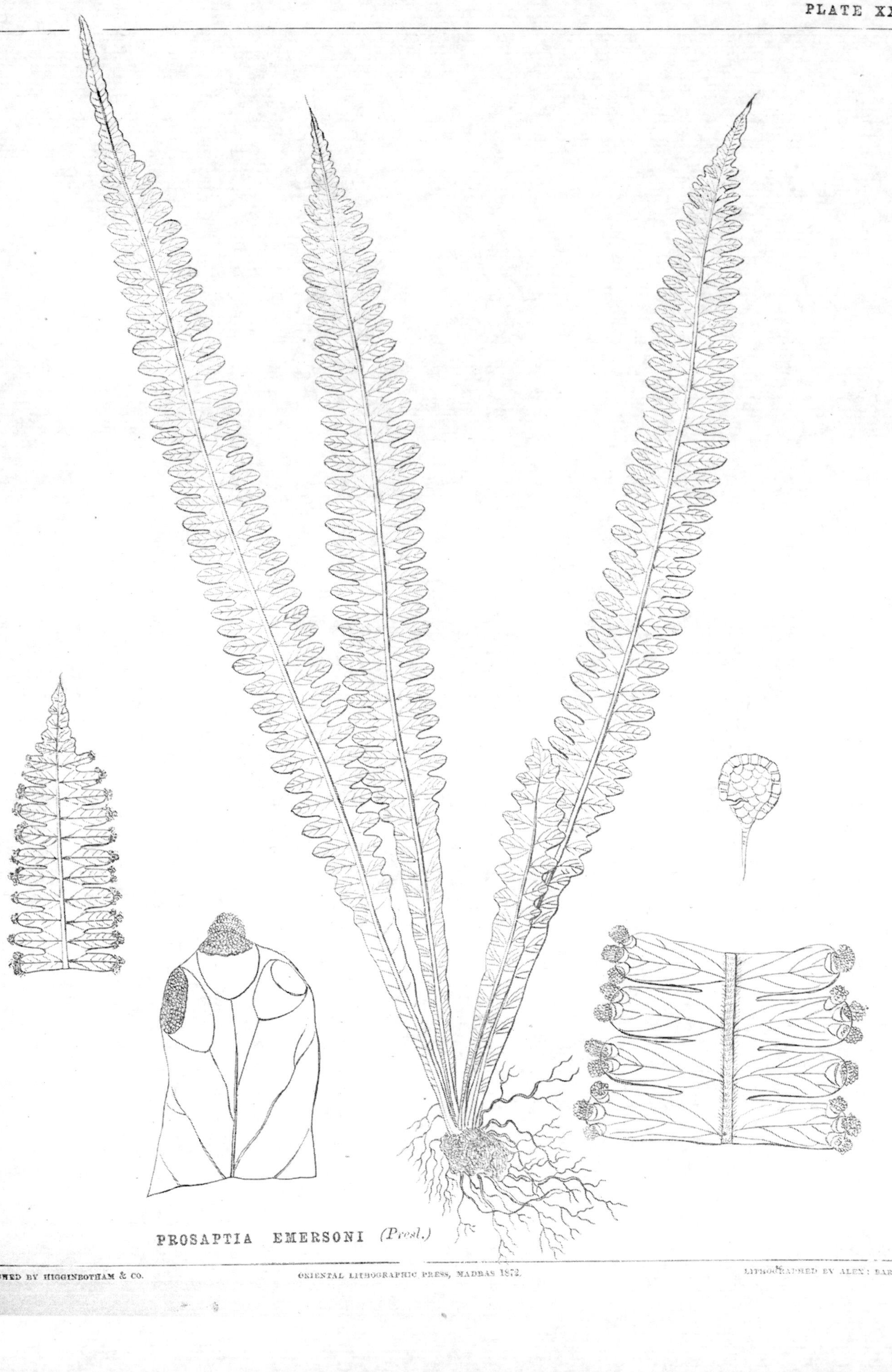

PROSAPTIA EMERSONI *(Presl.)*

PUBLISHED BY HIGGINBOTHAM & CO. ORIENTAL LITHOGRAPHIC PRESS, MADRAS 1872. LITHOGRAPHED BY ALEX: BARREN

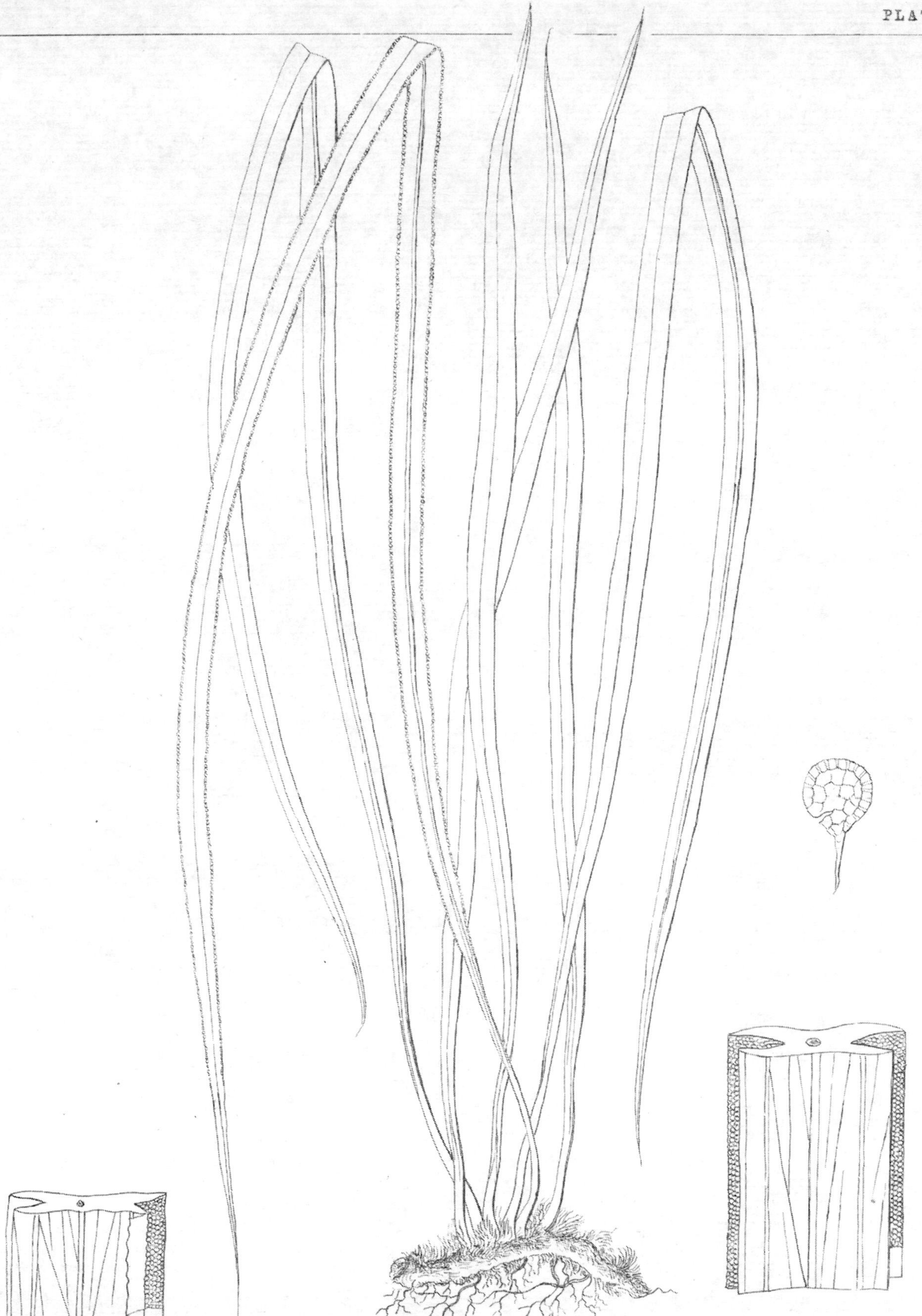

VITTARIA ELONGATA *(Sw.)*

PUBLISHED BY HIGGINBOTHAM & CO. ORIENTAL LITHOGRAPHIC PRESS, MADRAS 1872. LITHOGRAPHED BY ALEX : BARREN

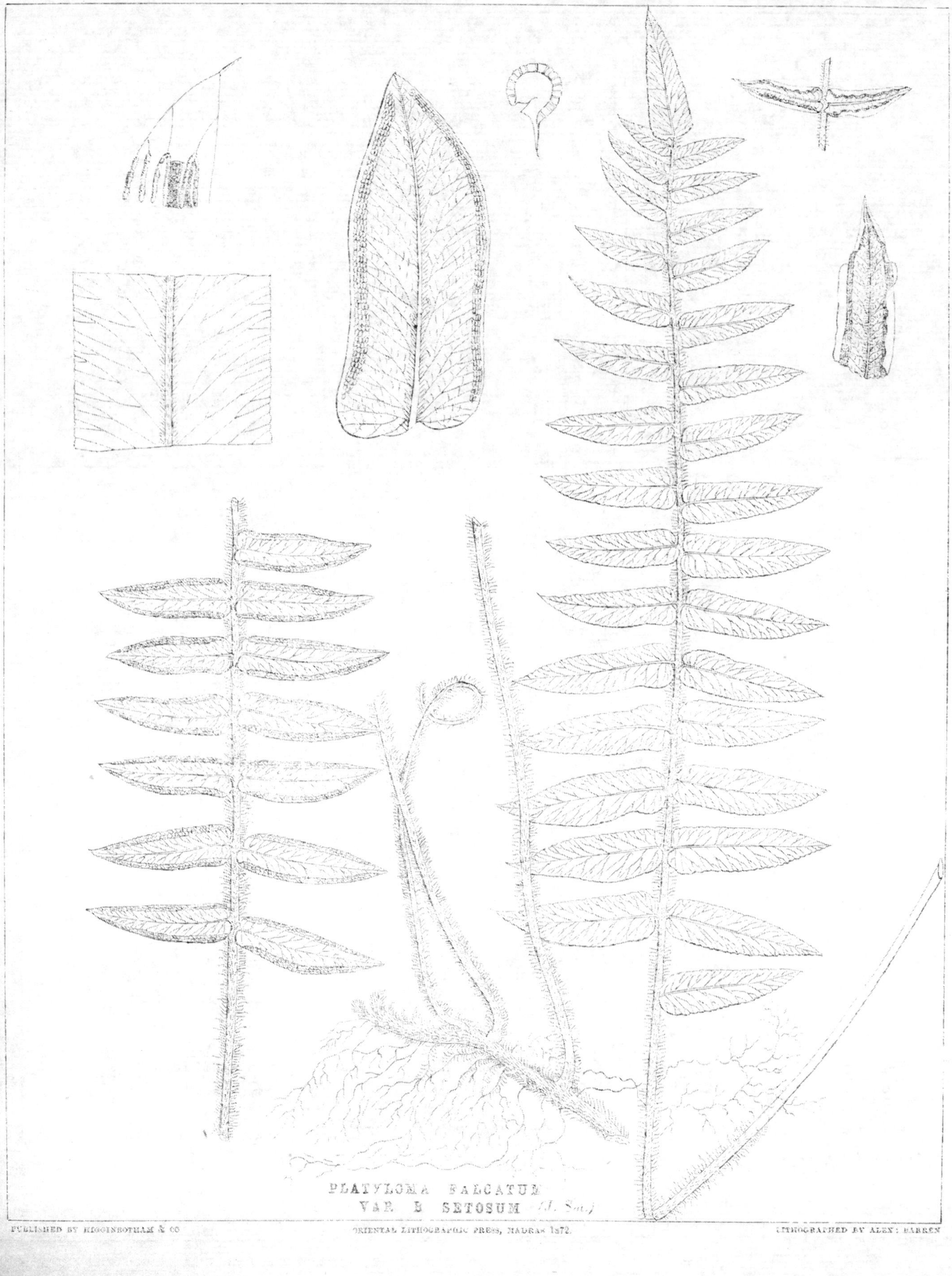

PLATYLOMA FALCATUM
VAR. B SETOSUM (J. Sm.)

PUBLISHED BY HIGGINBOTHAM & CO ORIENTAL LITHOGRAPHIC PRESS, MADRAS 1872. LITHOGRAPHED BY ALEX: BARREN

LINDSŒA CULTRATA (*Sw.*)

PUBLISHED BY HIGGINBOTHAM & CO. ORIENTAL LITHOGRA[illegible]IC PRESS, MADRAS 1872 LITHOGRAPHED BY A. EN. BARREN

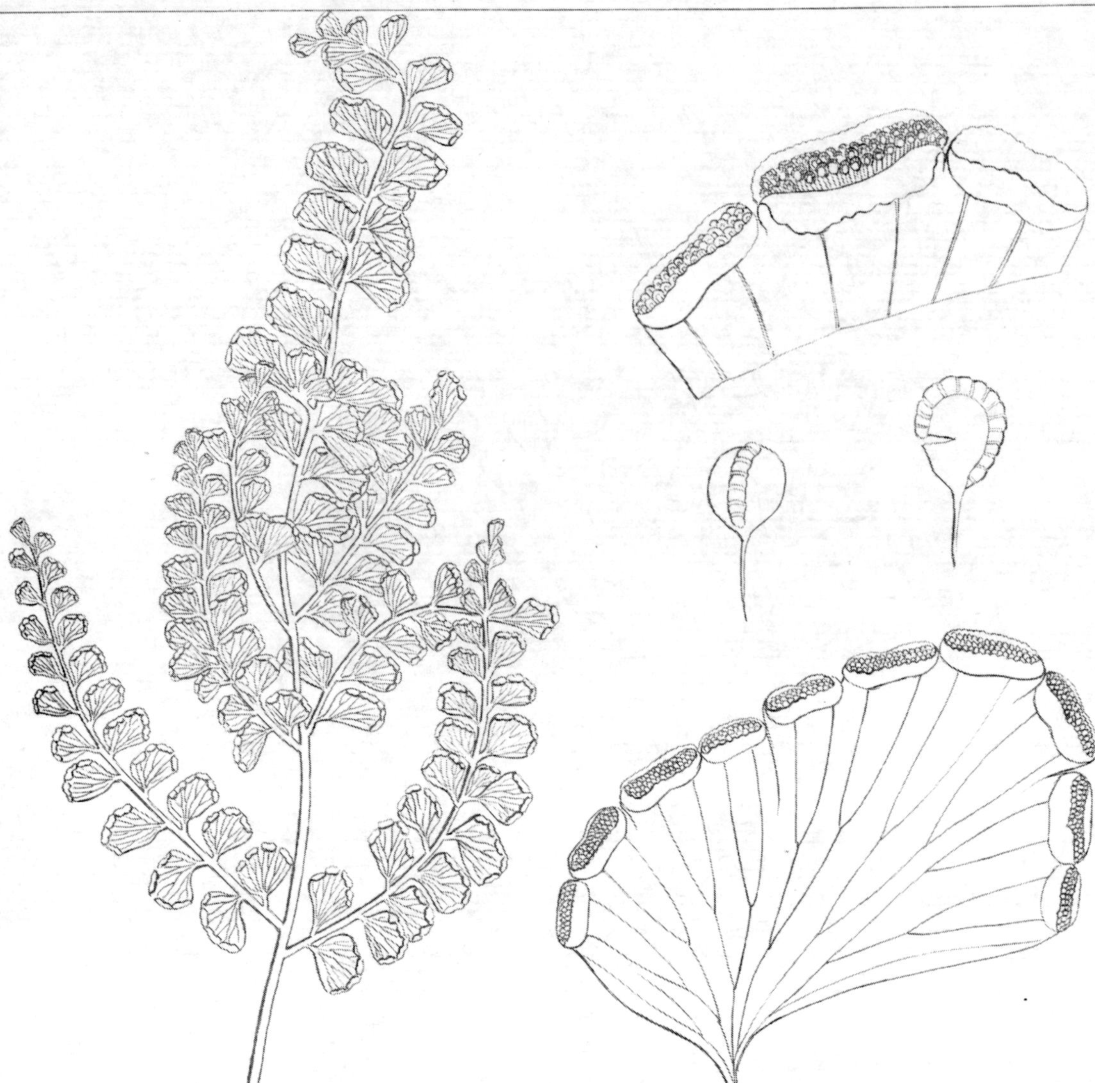

LINDSŒA TENERA *(Dryand.)*

PUBLISHED BY HIGGINBOTHAM & CO. ORIENTAL LITHOGRAPHIC PRESS, MADRAS 1872 LITHOGRAPHED BY ALEX: BARREN

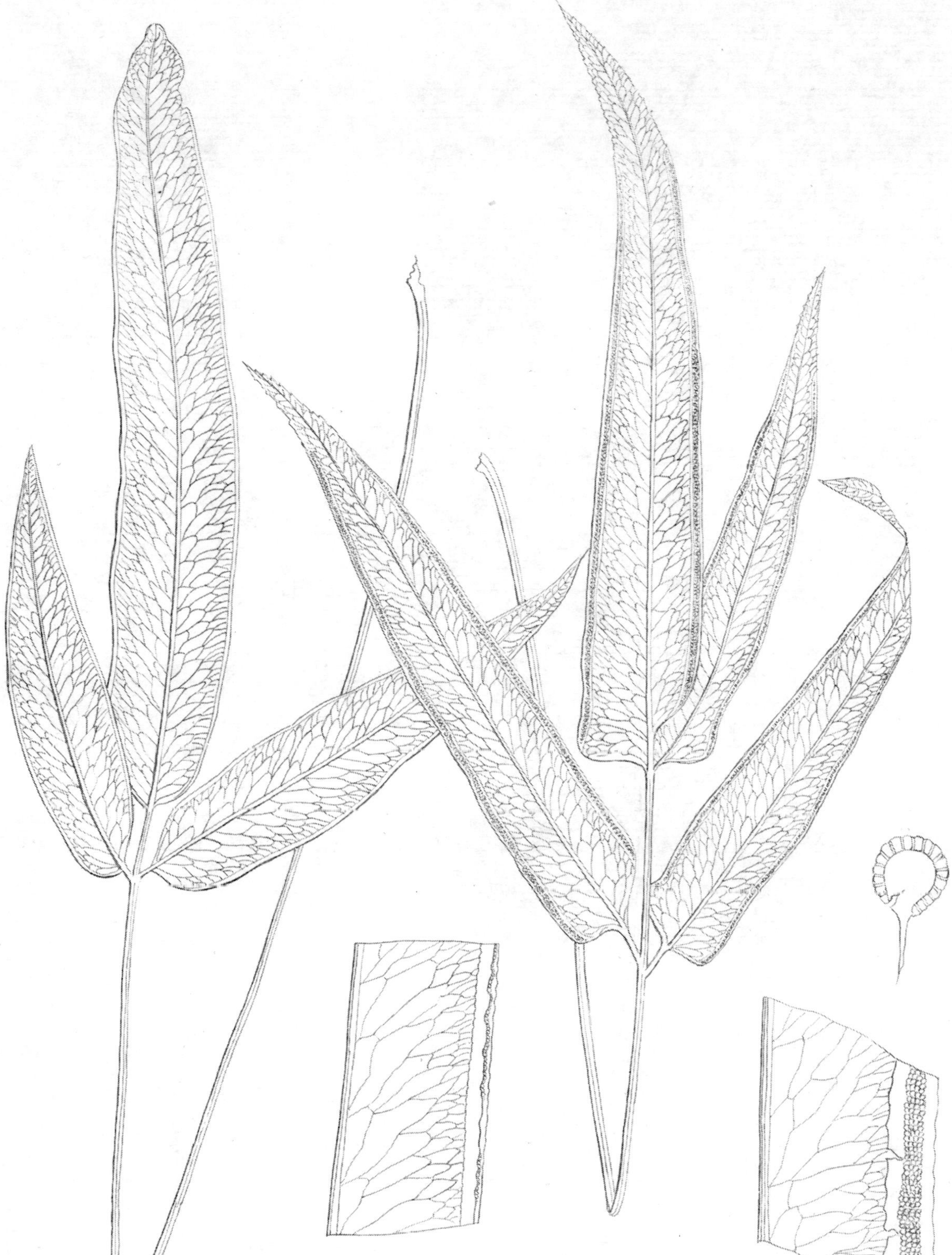

SCHIZOLOMA ENSIFOLIUM (*J. Smith.*)

PUBLISHED BY HIGGINBOTHAM & CO. ORIENTAL LITHOGRAPHIC PRESS, MADRAS 1872. LITHOGRAPHED BY ALEX: BARREN

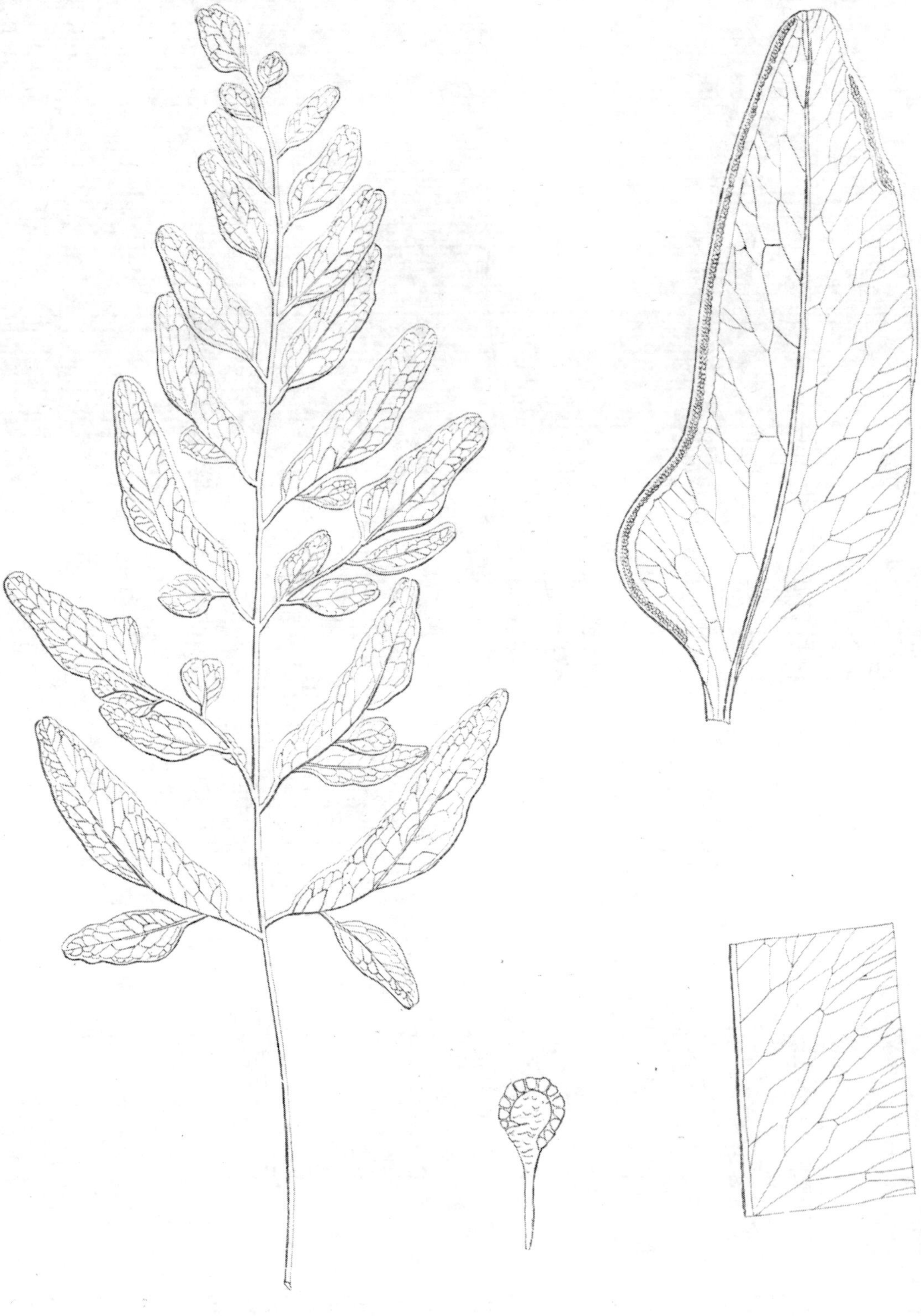

SCHIZOLOMA HETEROPHYLLUM (J. Sm.)

PUBLISHED BY HIGGINBOTHAM & C ORIENTAL LITHOGRAPHIC PRESS, MADRAS 1872. LITHOGRAPHED BY ALEX: BAR. EN

SCHIZOLOMA RECURVATUM (*Moore.*)

PUBLISHED BY HIGGINBOTHAM & CO. ORIENTAL LITHOGRAPHIC PRESS, MADRAS 1872 LITHOGRAPHED BY ALEX: BARREN

LOMARIA ELONGATA (Blume.)

PUBLIS·ED BY HIGGINBOTHAM & CO. ·RIENTAL LITHOGRAPHIC PRESS, MADRAS 1872. LITHOGRAPHED BY ALEX: BARREN

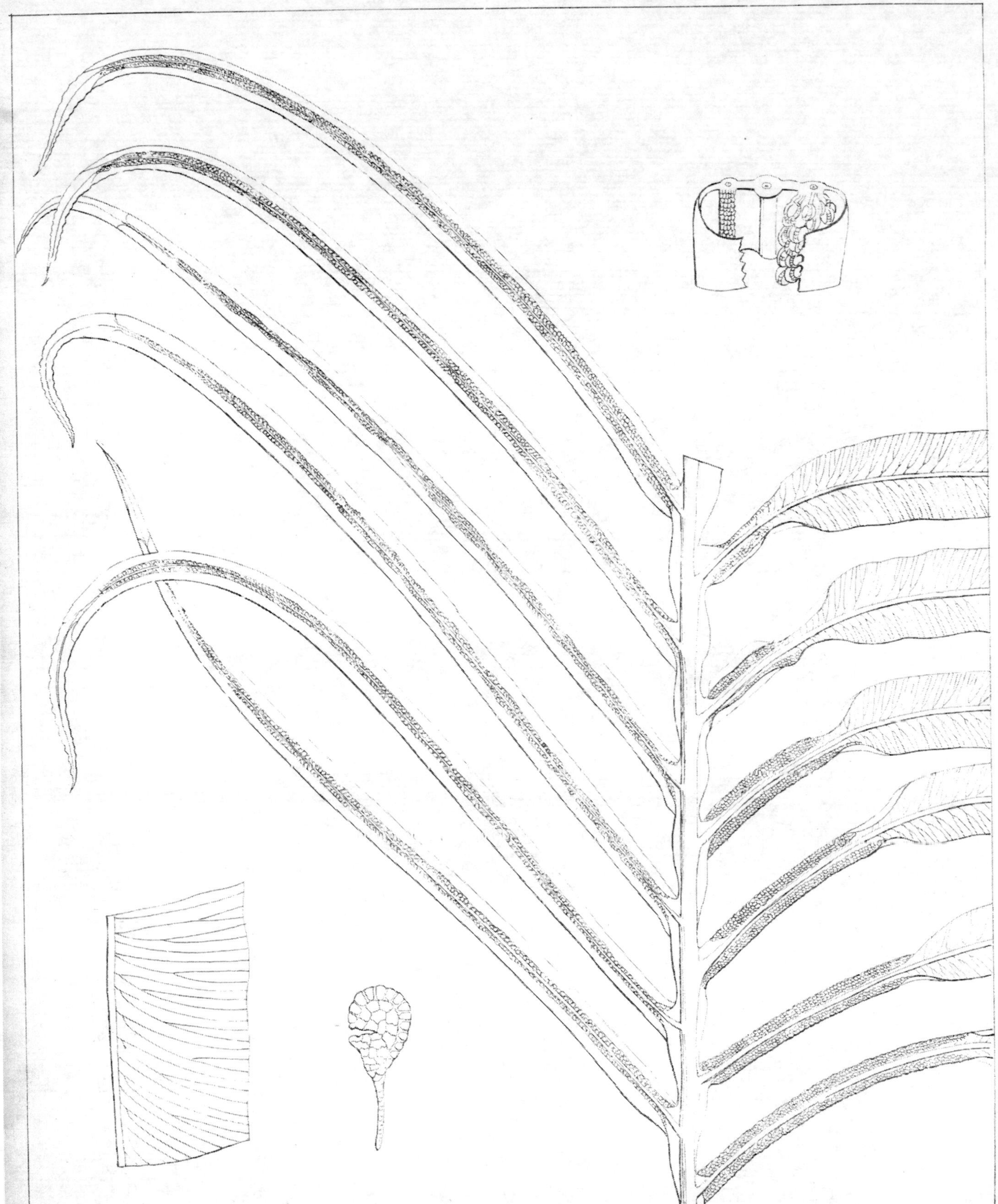

LOMARIA ELONGATA *(Blume.)*

PUBLISHED BY HIGGINBOTHAM & Co. ORIENTAL LITHOGRAPHIC PRESS, MADRAS 1872. LITHOGRAPHED BY ALEX: BARREN

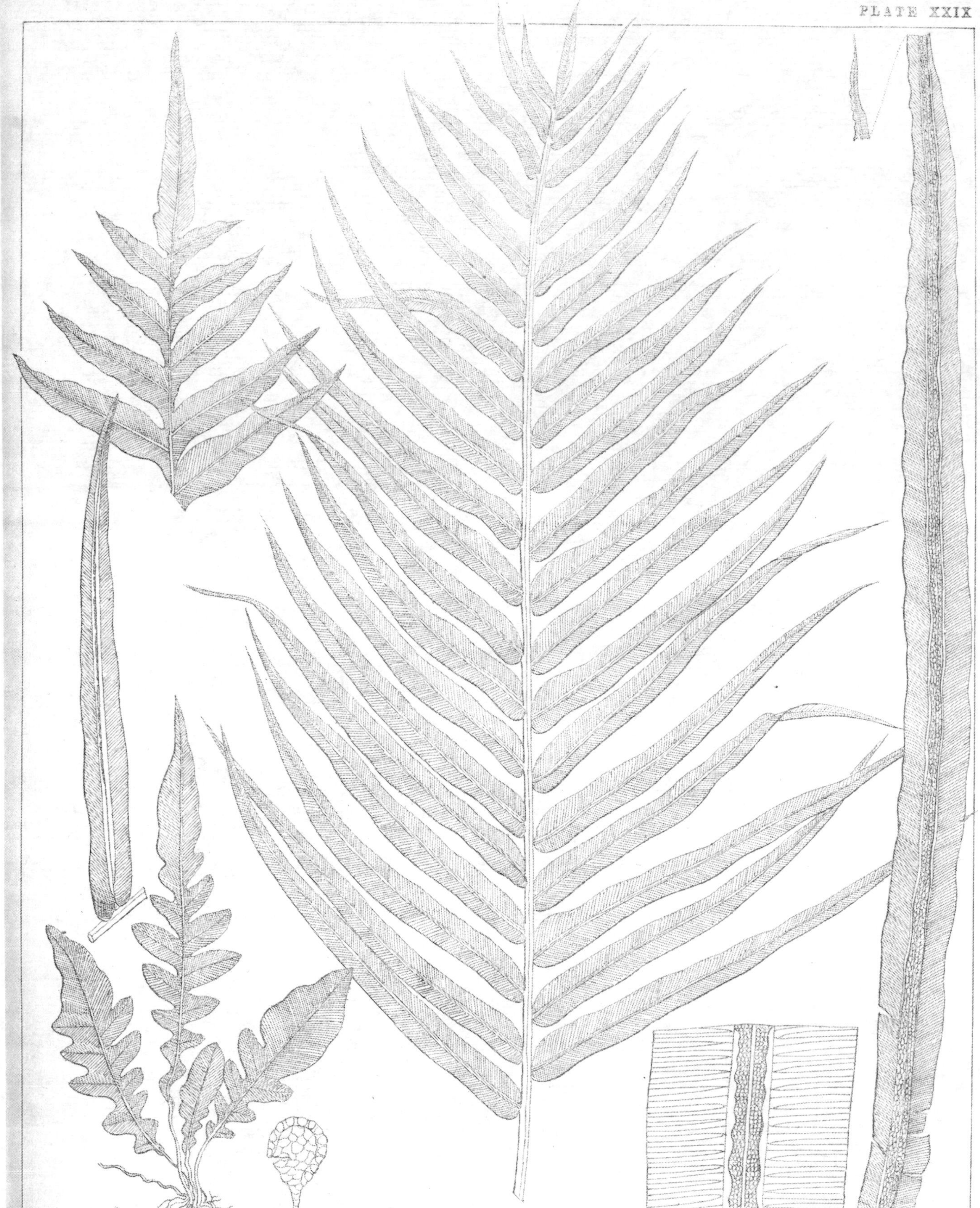

BLECHNUM ORIENTALE *(Linn.)*

PUBLISHED BY HIGGINBOTHAM & CO. ORIENTAL LITHOGRAPHIC PRESS, MADRAS 1872. LITHOGRAPHED BY ALEX: BARREN

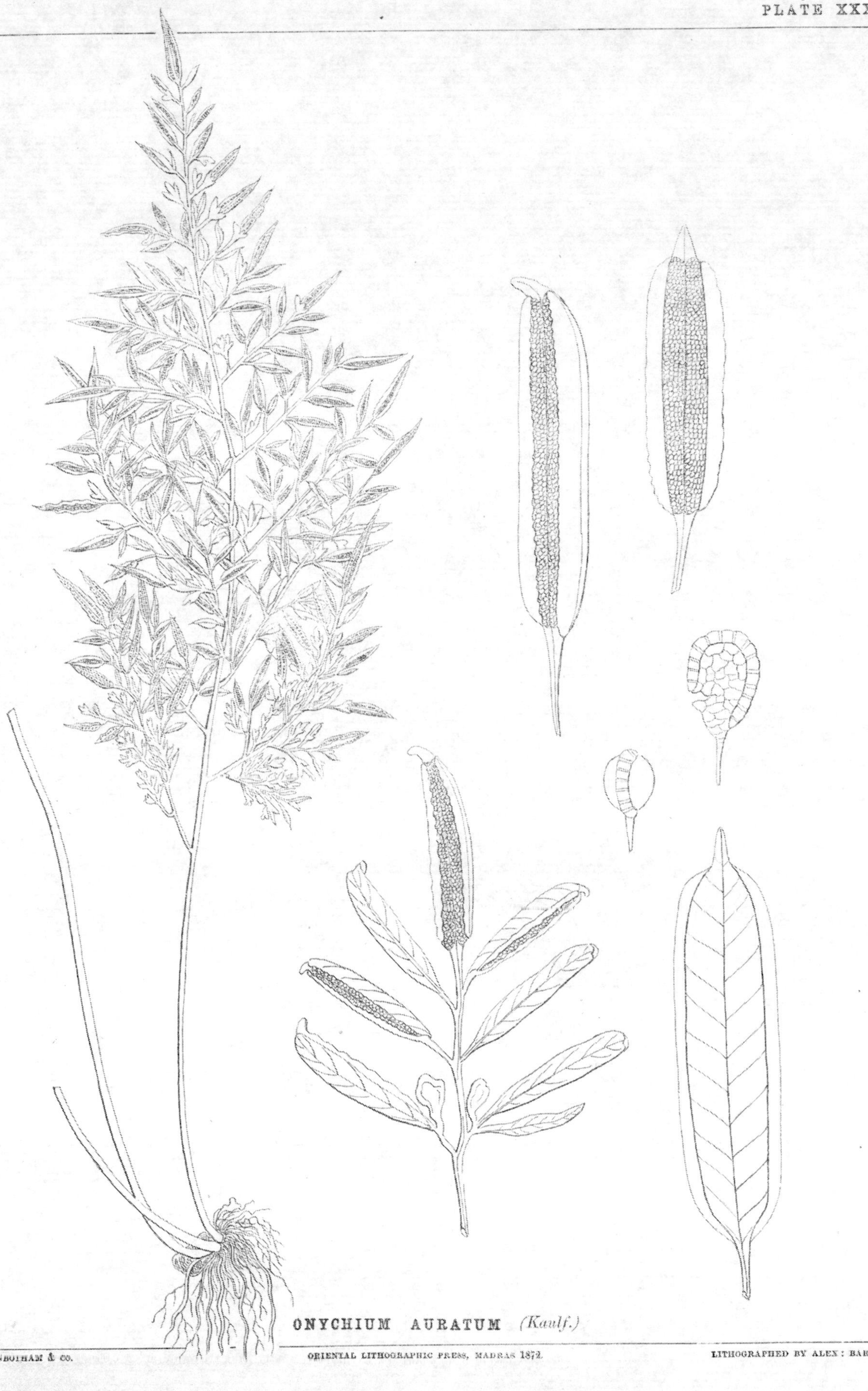

ONYCHIUM AURATUM (*Kaulf.*)

PUBLISHED BY HIGGINBOTHAM & CO. ORIENTAL LITHOGRAPHIC PRESS, MADRAS 1872. LITHOGRAPHED BY ALEX: BARREN

PTERIS QUADRIAURITA *(Retz.)*

PUBLISHED BY HIGGINBOTHAM & CO. ORIENTAL LITHOGRAPHIC PRESS, MADRAS 1872. LITHOGRAPHED BY [illegible]

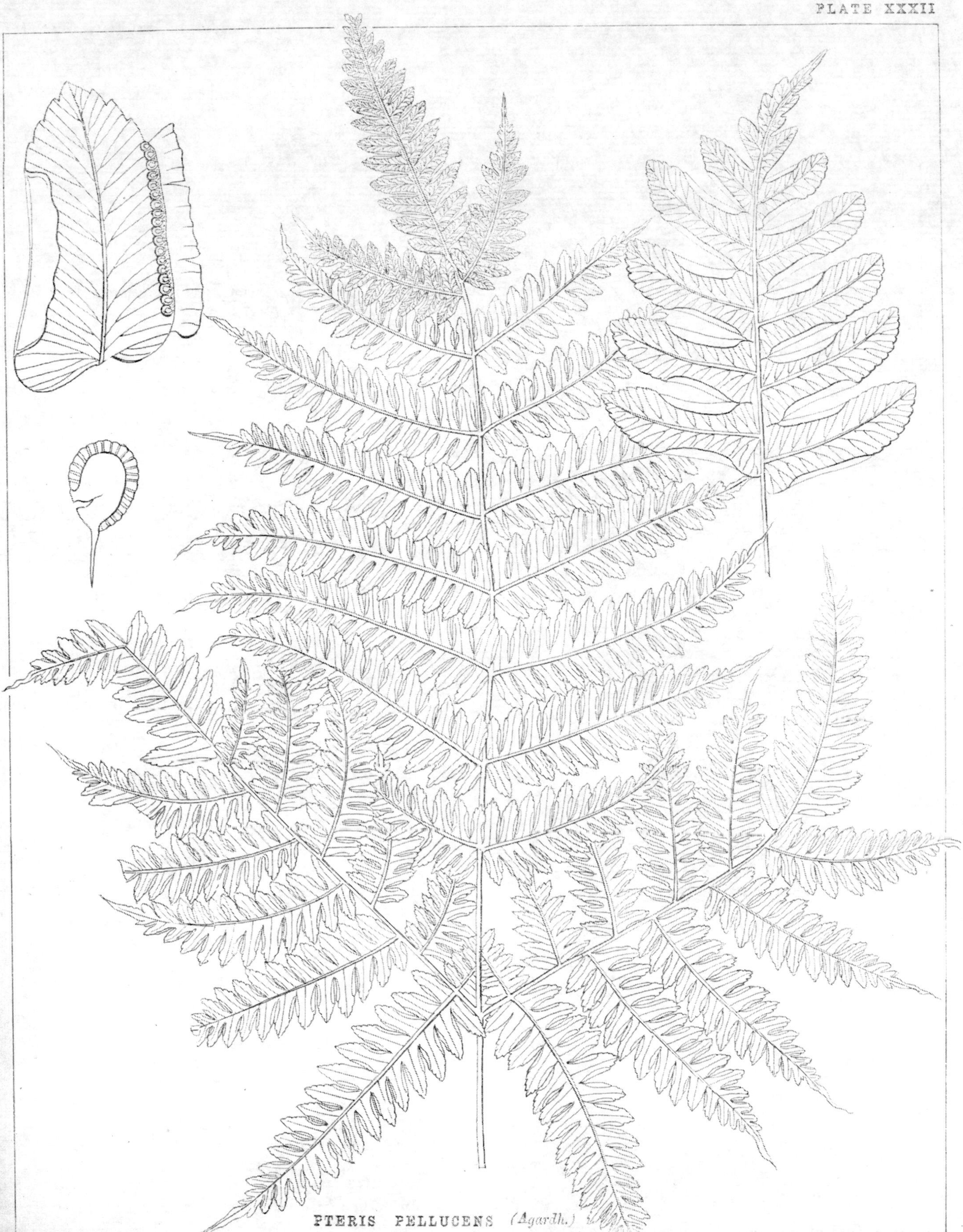

PTERIS PELLUCENS (*Agardh.*)

PUBLISHED BY HIGGINBOTHAM & Co. ORIENTAL LITHOGRAPHIC PRESS, MADRAS 1879 LITHOGRAPHED BY ALEX: DARREN

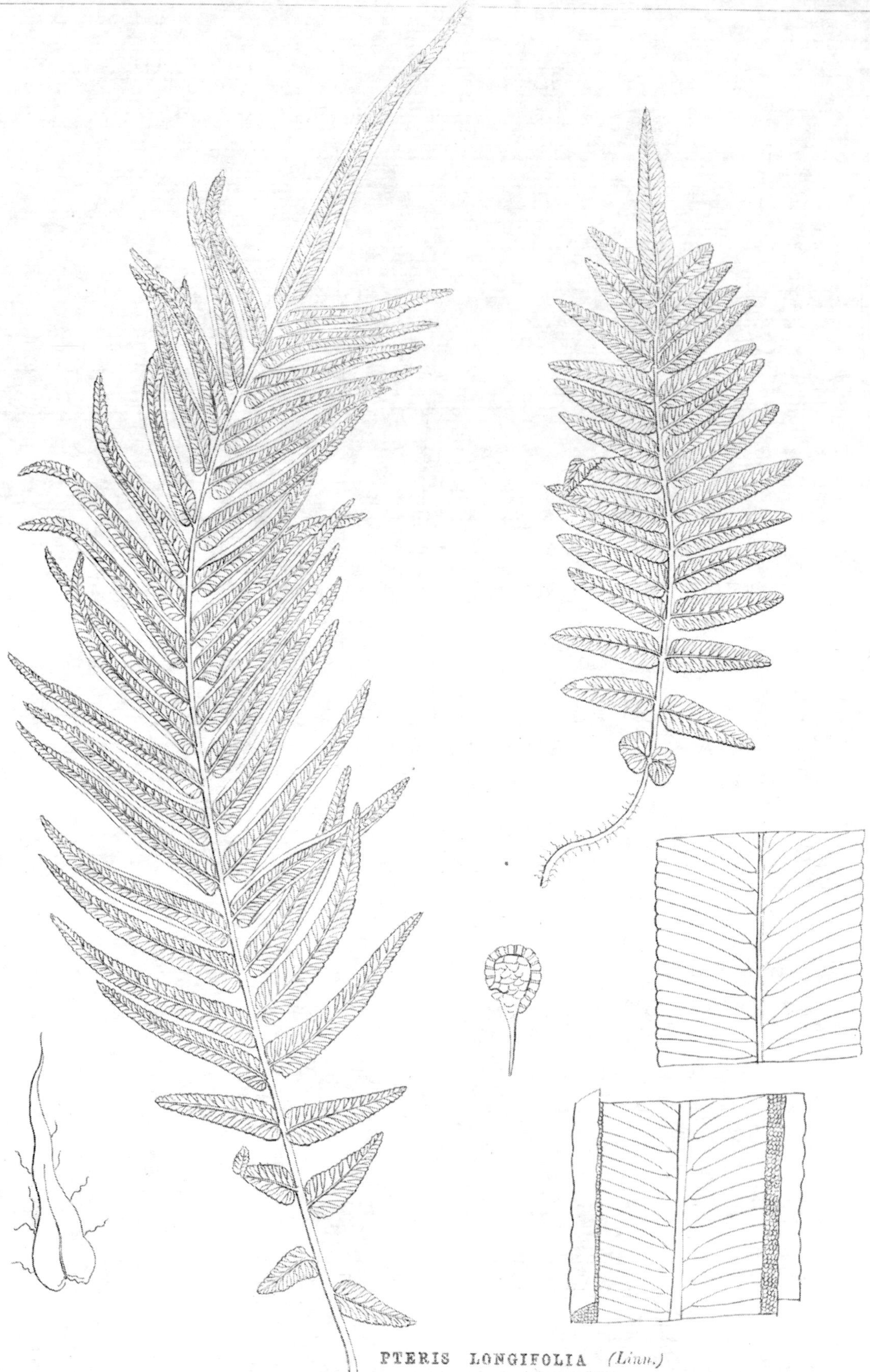

PTERIS LONGIFOLIA *(Linn.)*

PUBLISHED BY HIGGINBOTHAM & CO ORIENTAL LITHOGRAPHIC PRESS, MADRAS 1872. LITHOGRAPHED BY ALEX: BARREN

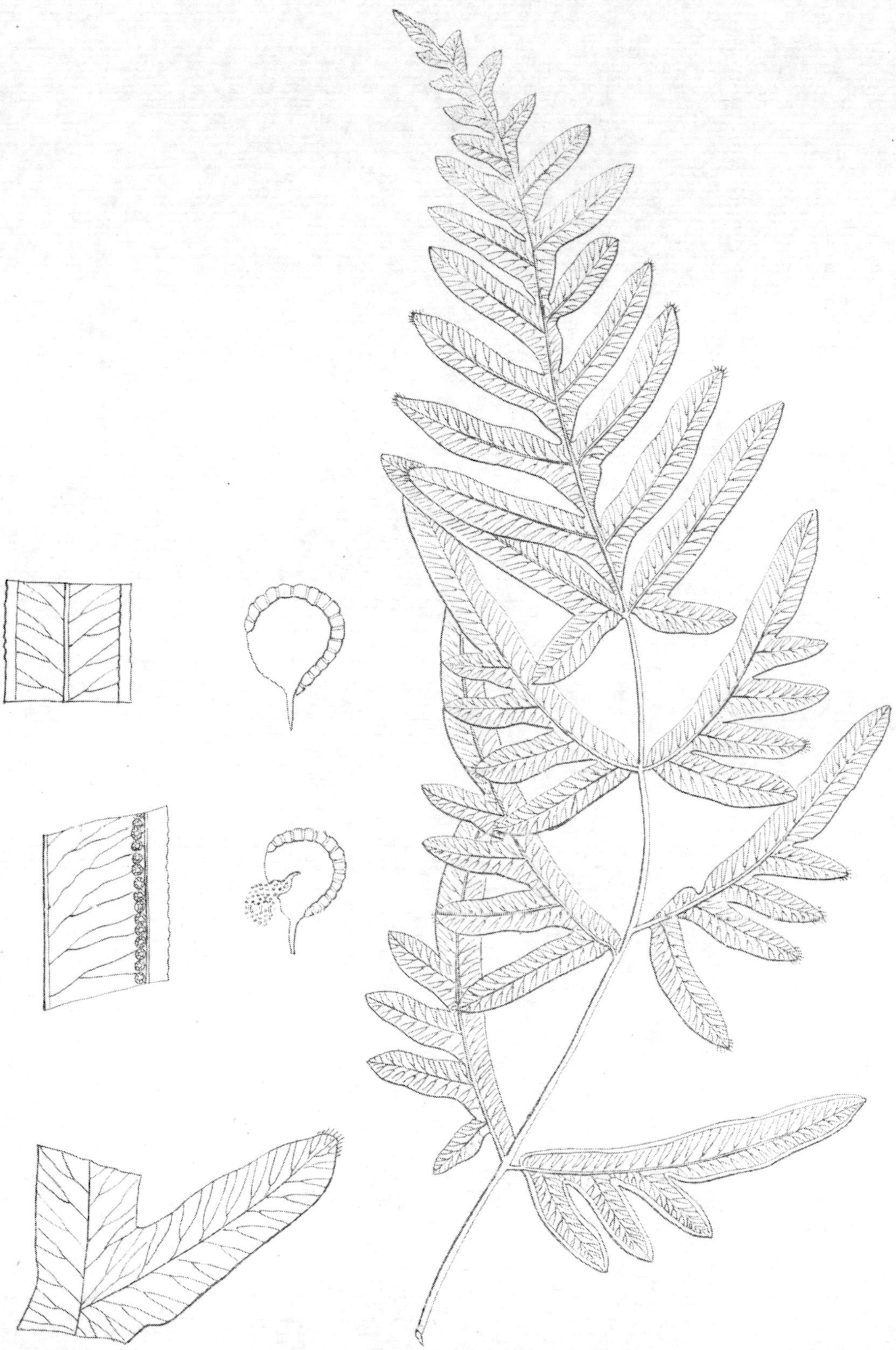

PTERIS SEMIPINNATA *(Linn.)*

PUBLISHED BY HIGGINBOTHAM & CO. ORIENTAL LITHOGRAPHIC PRESS, MADRAS 1872. LITHOGRAPHED BY ALEX: BARREN

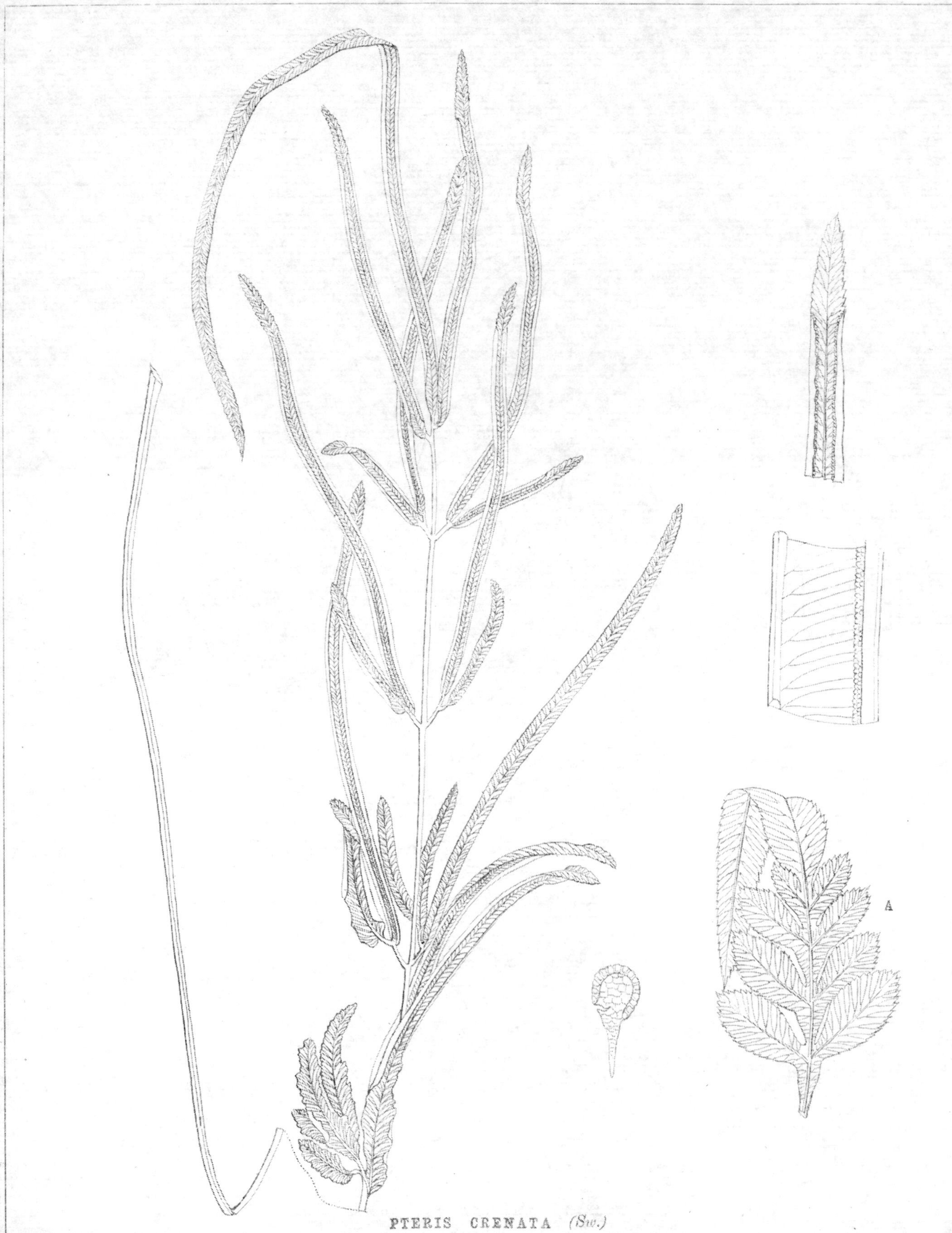

PTERIS CRENATA (*Sw.*)

PUBLISHED BY HIGGINBOTHAM & CO. ORIENTAL LITHOGRAPHIC PRESS, MADRAS 1872. LITHOGRAPHED BY ALEX : BARREN

PTERIS BOIVINI (Moore.)

PUBLISHED BY HIGGINBOTHAM & CO. ORIENTAL LITHOGRAPHIC PRESS, MADRAS 1872. LITHOGRAPHED BY ALEX: BARREN

PTERIS GERANUFOLIA (Raddi.)

PUBLISHED BY HIGGINBOTHAM & CO. ORIENTAL LITHOGRAPHIC PRESS, MADRAS 1872. LITHOGRAPHED BY ALEX: BAEREN

PTERIS PELLUCIDA *(Presl.)*

PUBLISHED BY HIGGINBOTHAM & CO. ORIENTAL LITHOGRAPHIC PRESS, MADRAS 187[illegible] LITHOGRAPHED BY ALEX : BARREN

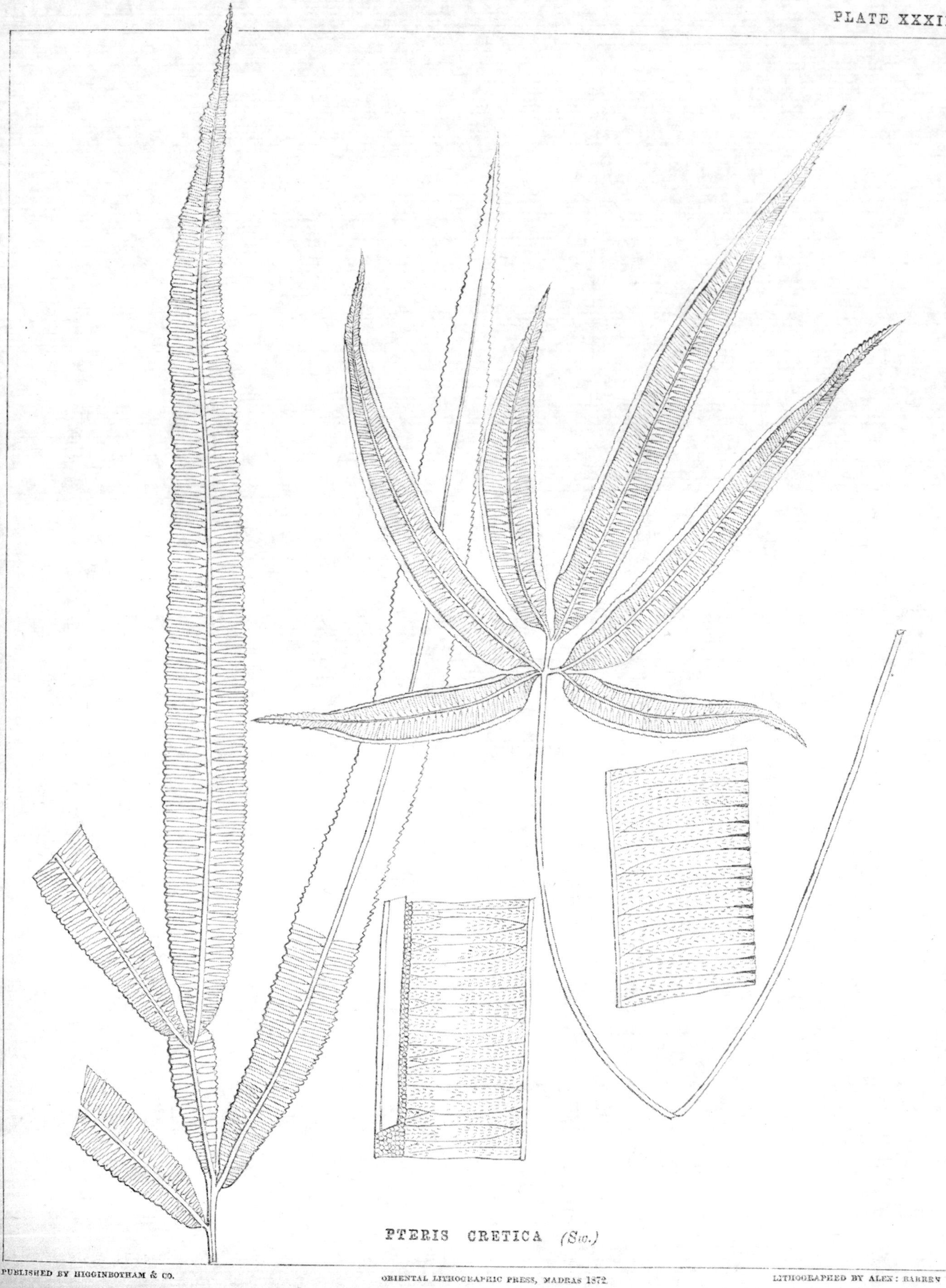

PTERIS CRETICA (Sw.)

PUBLISHED BY HIGGINBOTHAM & CO. ORIENTAL LITHOGRAPHIC PRESS, MADRAS 1872. LITHOGRAPHED BY ALEX: BARREN

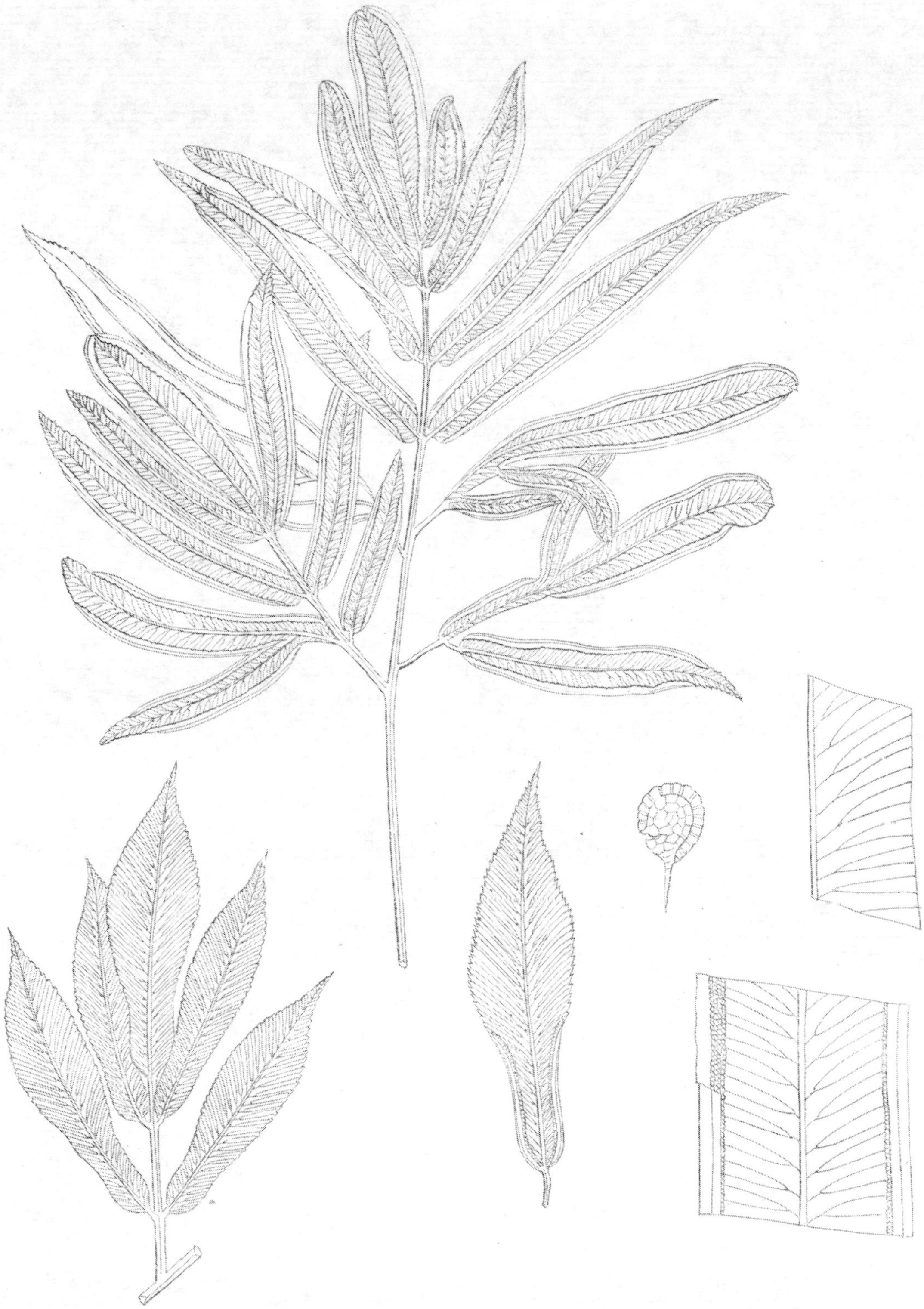

PTERIS HOOKERIANA ? *(Agardh.)*

PUBLISHED BY HIGGINBOTHAM & CO. ORIENTAL LITHOGRAPHIC PRESS, MADRAS 1872. LITHOGRAPHED BY ALEX: BARREN

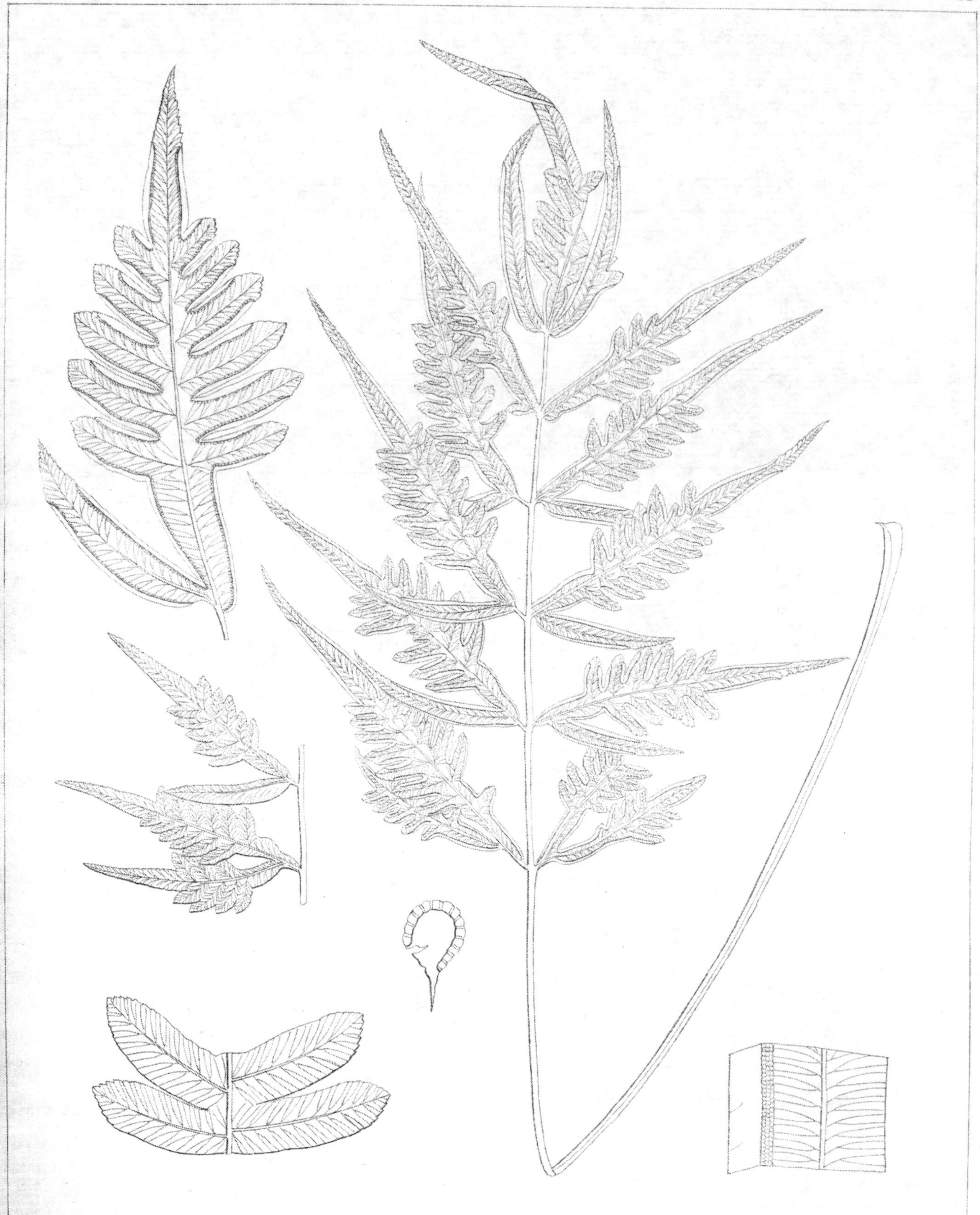

PTERIS OTARIA (Bedd.)

PUBLISHED BY HIGGINBOTHAM & CO. ORIENTAL LITHOGRAPHIC PRESS, MADRAS 1872 LITHOGRAPHED BY ALEX: BARREN

PTERIS AQUILINA *(Linn)*

VAR B. LANUGINOSA

PUBLISHED BY HIGGINBOTHAM & CO. ORIENTAL LITHOGRAPHIC PRESS, MADRAS 1872. LITHOGRAPHED BY ALEX. BARREN

PTERIS LONGIPINNULA *(Wallich)*

PUBLISHED BY HIGGINBOTHAM & CO. ORIENTAL LITHOGRAPHIC PRESS, MADRAS 1872. LITHOGRAPHED BY ALEX: BARRES

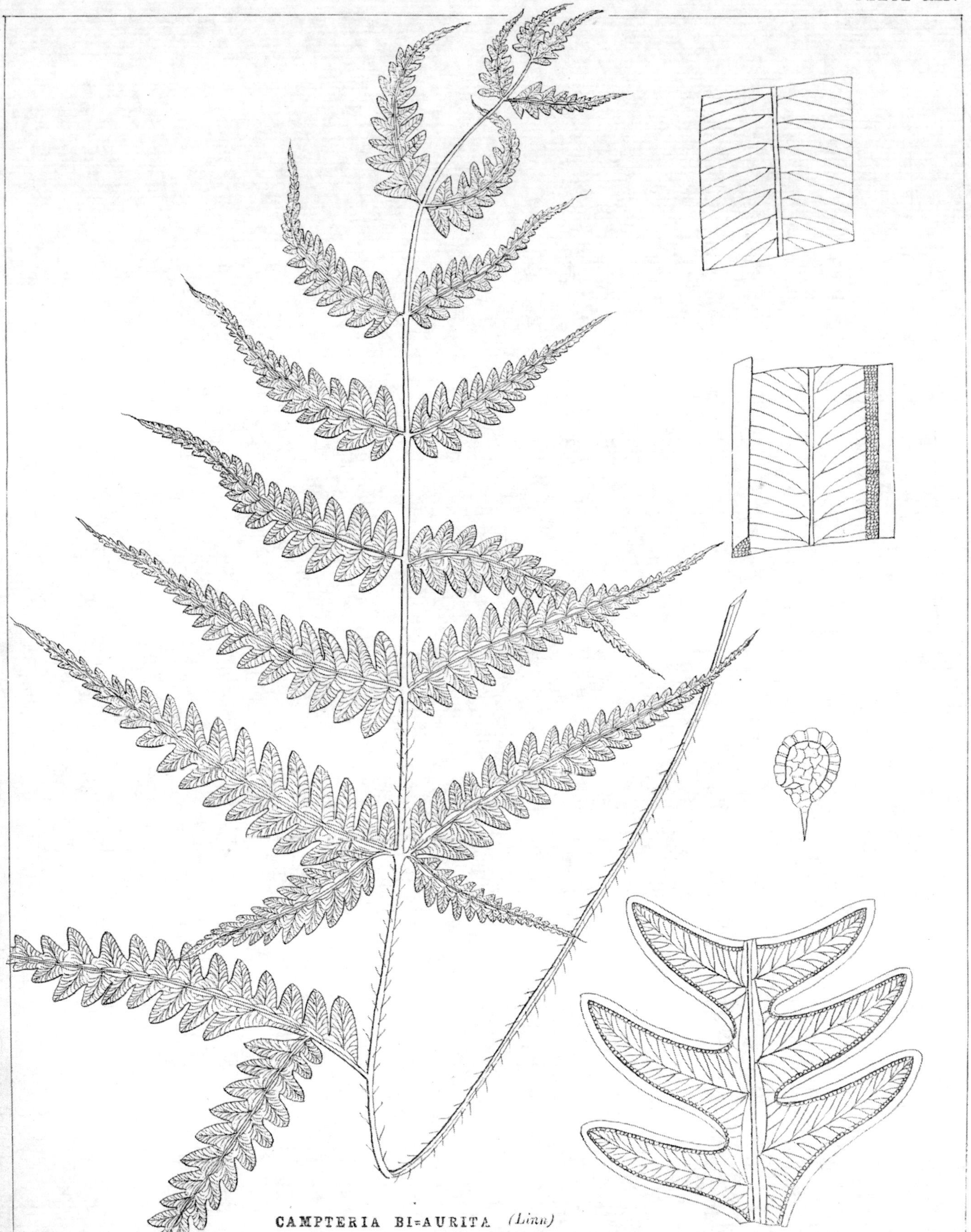

CAMPTERIA BI-AURITA (*Linn*)

PUBLISHED BY HIGGINBOTHAM & CO. ORIENTAL LITHOGRAPHIC PRESS, MADRAS 1872. LITHOGRAPHED BY ALEX: GARREN

CAMPTERIA ANNAMULLAYENSIS (Bedd)

PUBLISHED BY HIGGINBOTHAM & CO. ORIENTAL LITHOGRAPHIC PRESS, MADRAS 1872 LITHOGRAPHED BY ALEX: BARREN

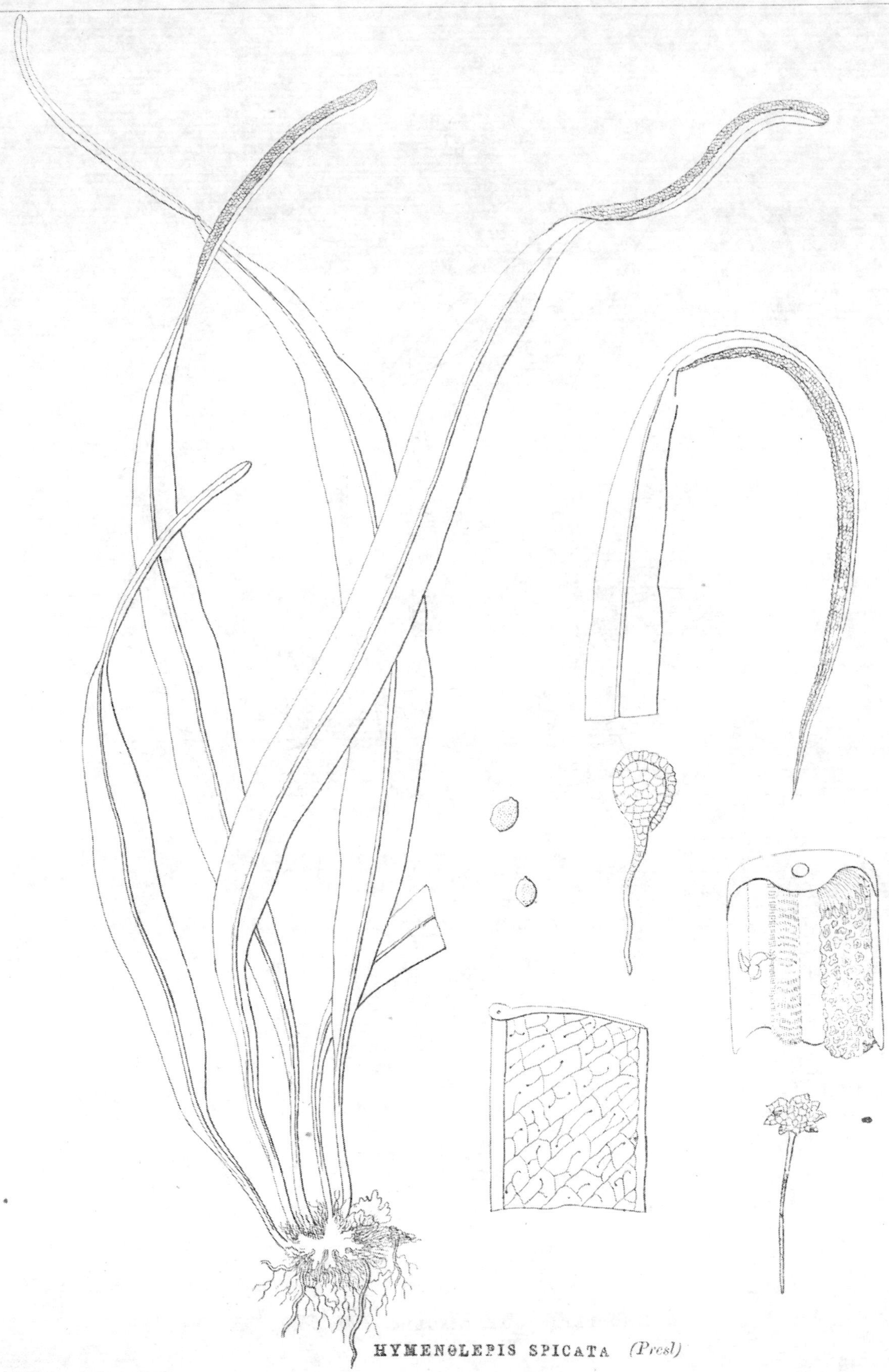

HYMENOLEPIS SPICATA (*Presl*)

PUBLISHED BY HIGGINBOTHAM & CO. ORIENTAL LITHOGRAPHIC PRESS. MADRAS 1872. LITHOGRAPHED BY ALEX : BARREN

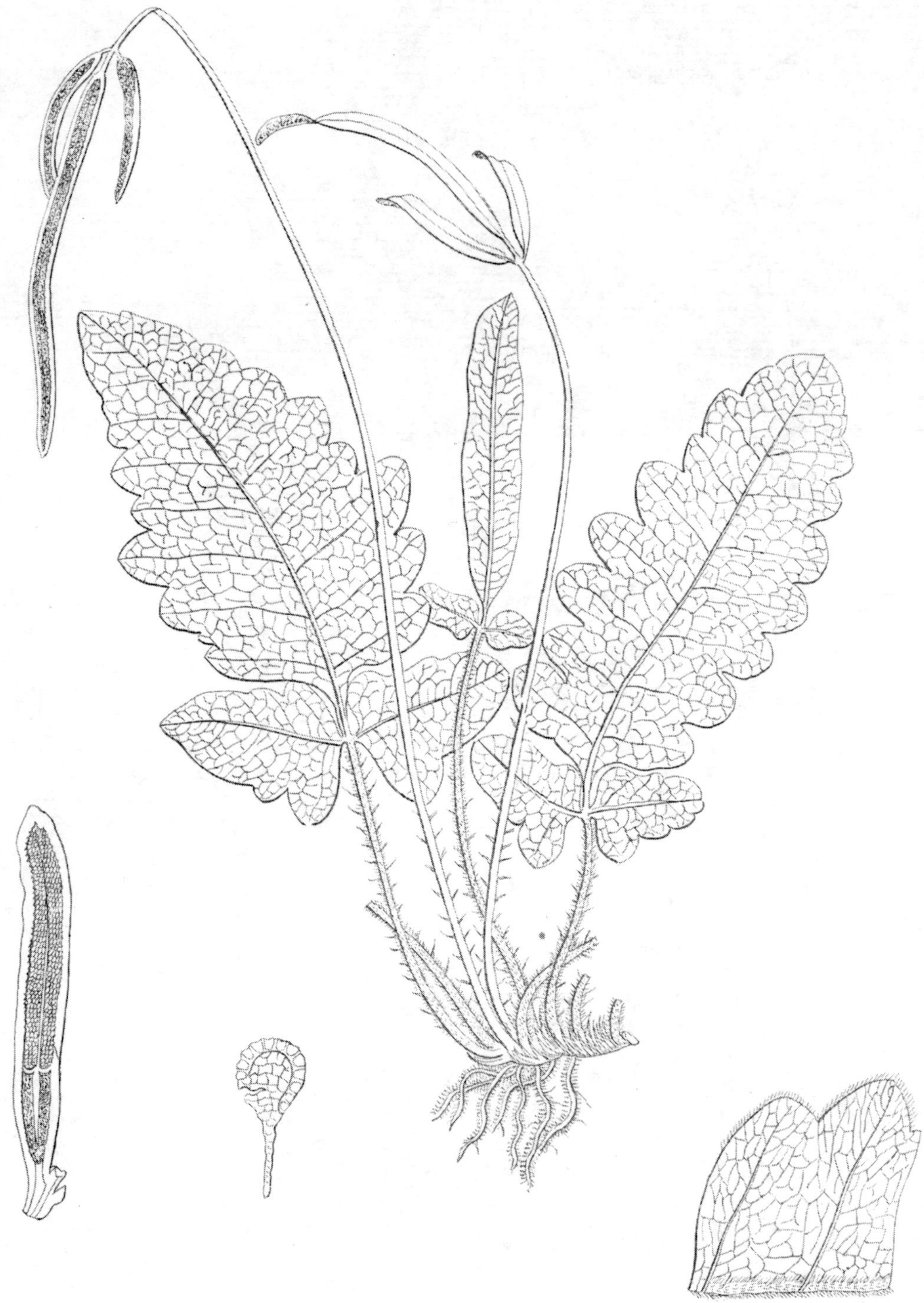

GYMNOPTERIS QUERCIFOLIA *(Bernh)*

PUBLISHED BY HIGGINBOTHAM & CO. ORIENTAL LITHOGRAPHIC PRESS, MADRAS 1872. LITHOGRAPHED BY ALEX: BARREN

PLATE XLVIII

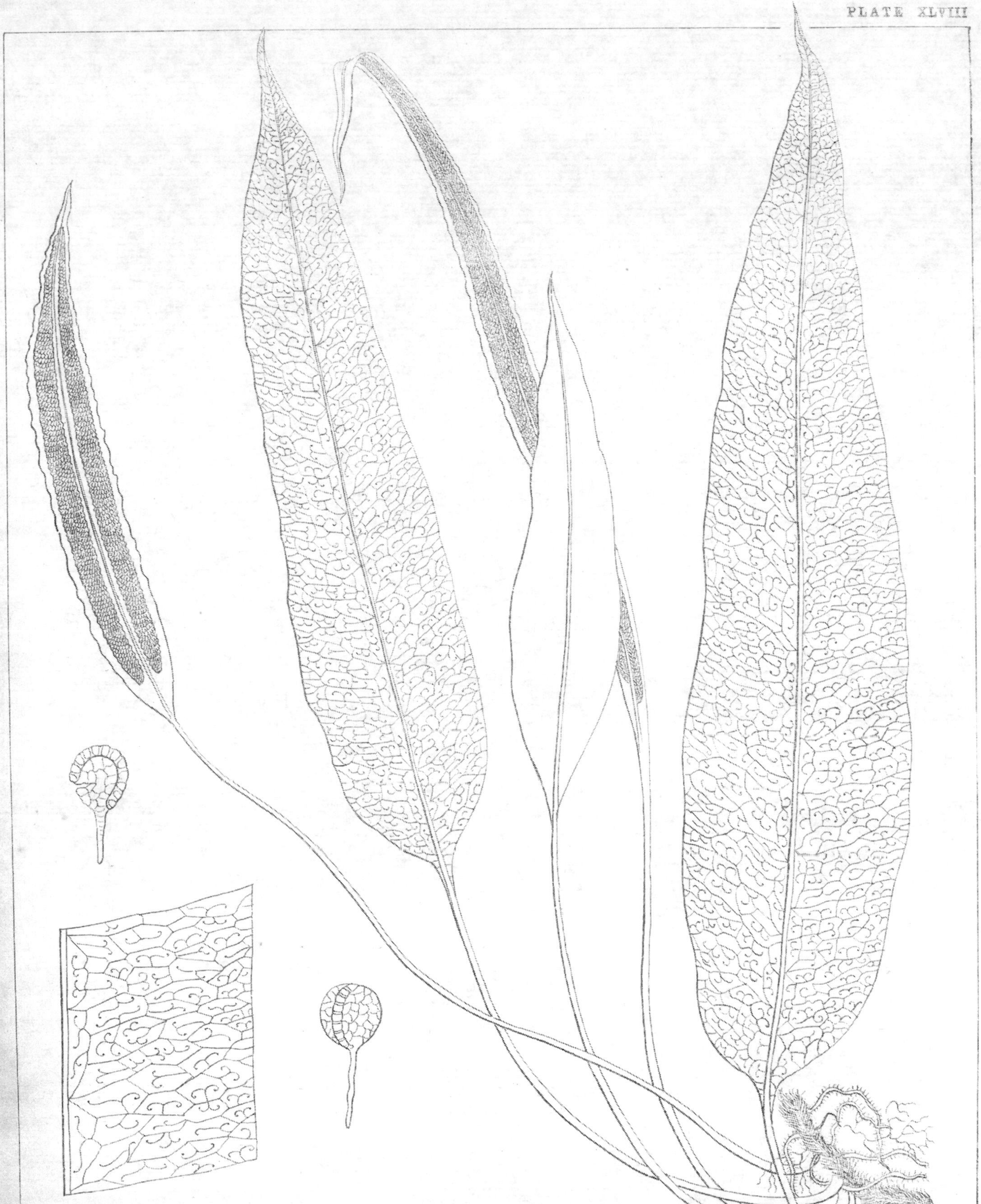

GYMNOPTERIS FEEI (*Moore*)

PUBLISHED BY HIGGINBOTHAM & CO. ORIENTAL LITHOGRAPHIC PRESS, MADRAS 1872 LITHO. BY ALEX. BARREN

GRAMMITIS TOTTA (*Prest*)

PUBLISHED BY HIGGINBOTHAM & CO. ORIENTAL LITHOGRAPHIC PRESS, MADRAS 1872. LITHOGRAPHED BY ALEX: BARREN

LOXOGRAMMA INVOLUTA *(Presl)*

PUBLISHED BY HIGGINBOTHAM & CO.   ORIENTAL LITHOGRAPHIC PRESS, MADRAS 1872.   LITHOGRAPHED BY ALEX: BARREN

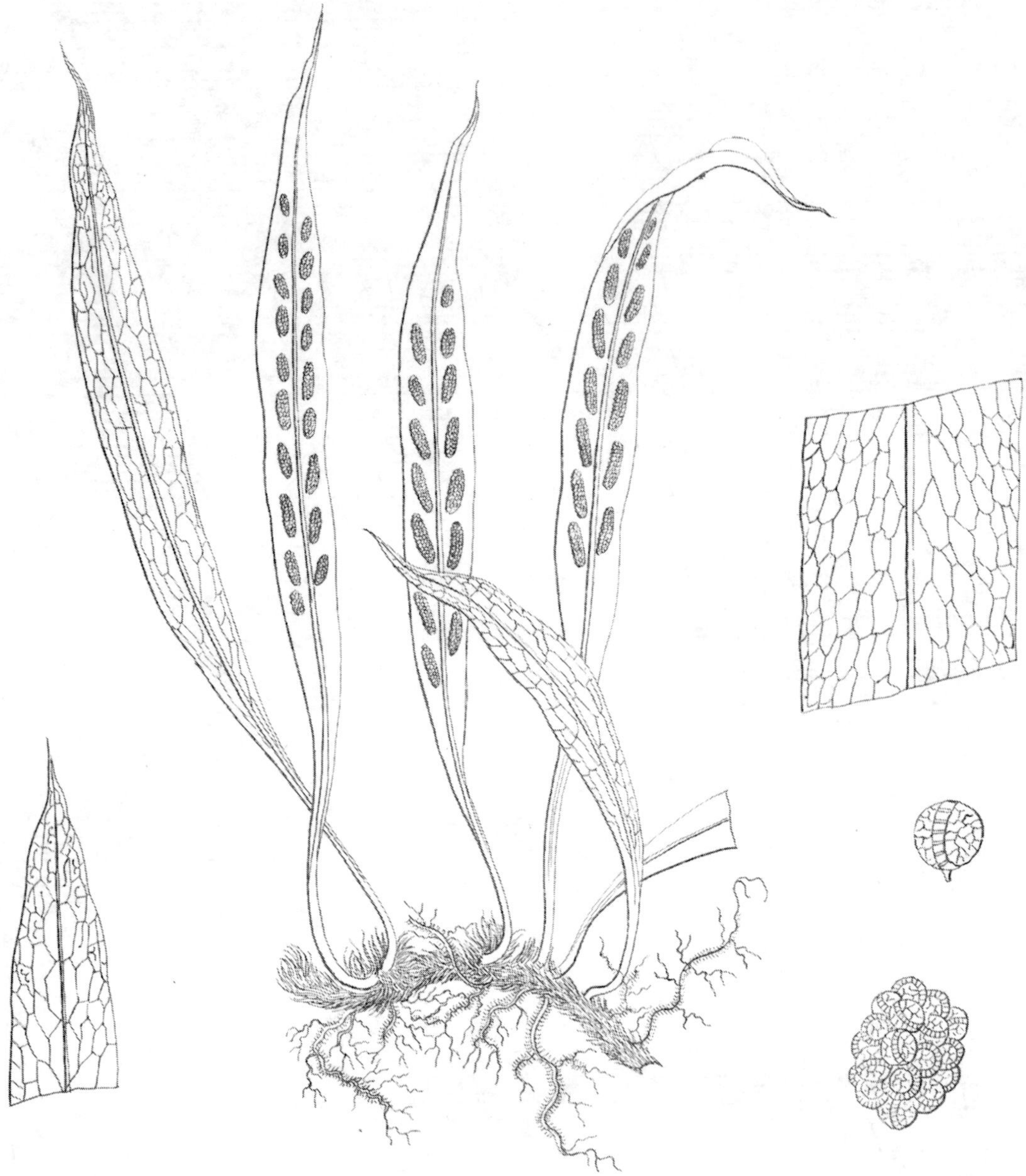

LOXOGRAMMA LANCEOLATA *(Presl)*

PUBLISHED BY HIGGINBOTHAM & CO. ORIENTAL LITHOGRAPHIC PRESS, MADRAS 1872. LITHOGRAPHED BY ALEX: BARREN

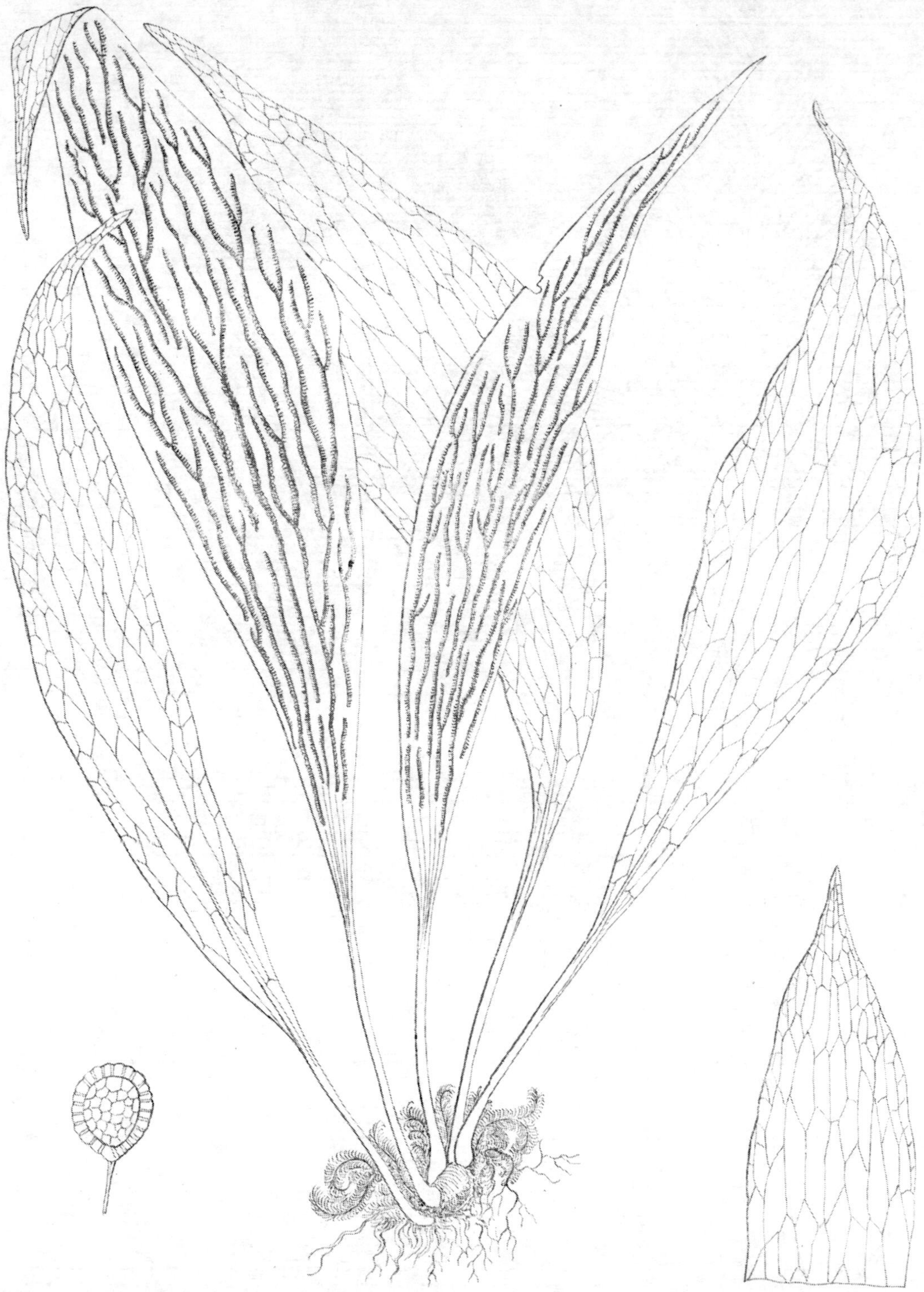

ANTROPHYUM RETICULATUM (Kaulfuss)

PUBLISHED BY HIGGINBOTHAM & CO. ORIENTAL LITHOGRAPHIC PRESS, MADRAS 1872. LITHOGRAPHED BY ALEX: BARREN

PALTE LIII

HEMIONITIS CORDATA (Roxburgh)

PUBLISHED BY HIGGINBOTHAM & CO. ORIENTAL LITHOGRAPHIC PRESS, MADRAS 1872. LITHOGRAPHED BY ALEX: BARREN

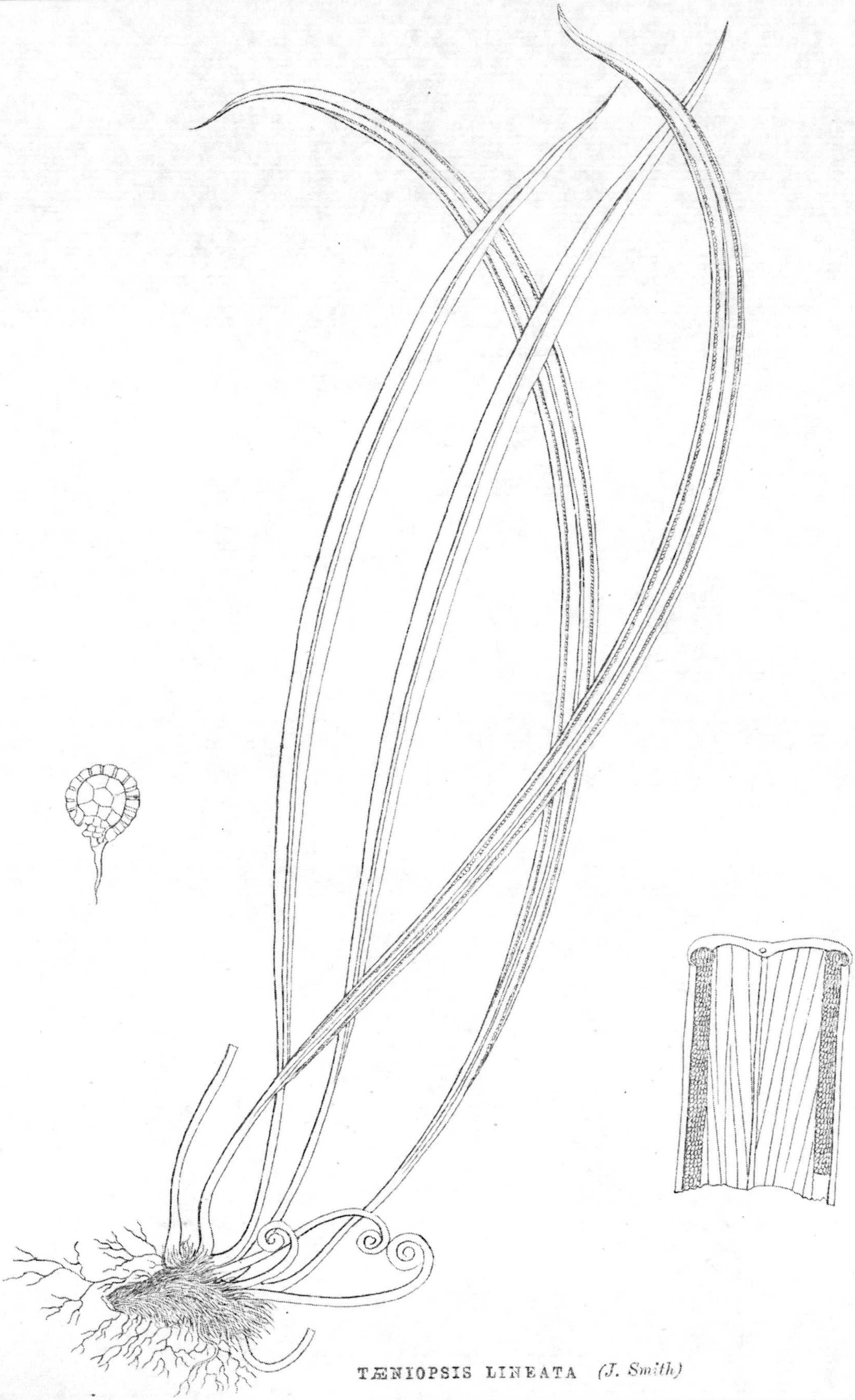

TÆNIOPSIS LINEATA (*J. Smith*)

PUBLISHED BY HIGGINBOTHAM & CO.

ORIENTAL LITHOGRAPHIC PRESS, MADRAS 1872

LITHOGRAPHED BY ALEX: BARREN

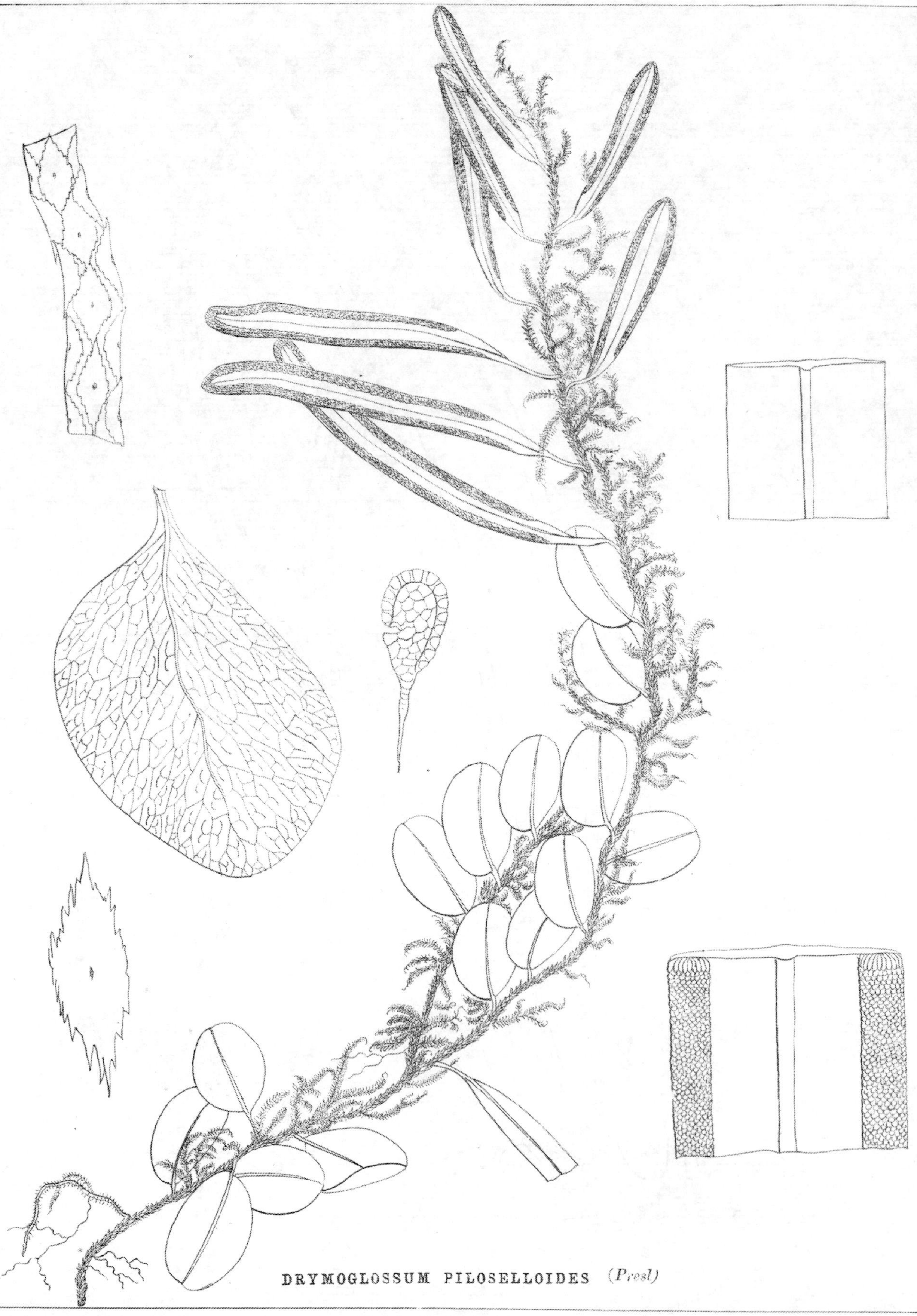

DRYMOGLOSSUM PILOSELLOIDES *(Presl)*

ORIENTAL LITHOGRAPHIC PRESS, MADRAS 1872.

LITHOGRAPHED BY ALEX. BARREN

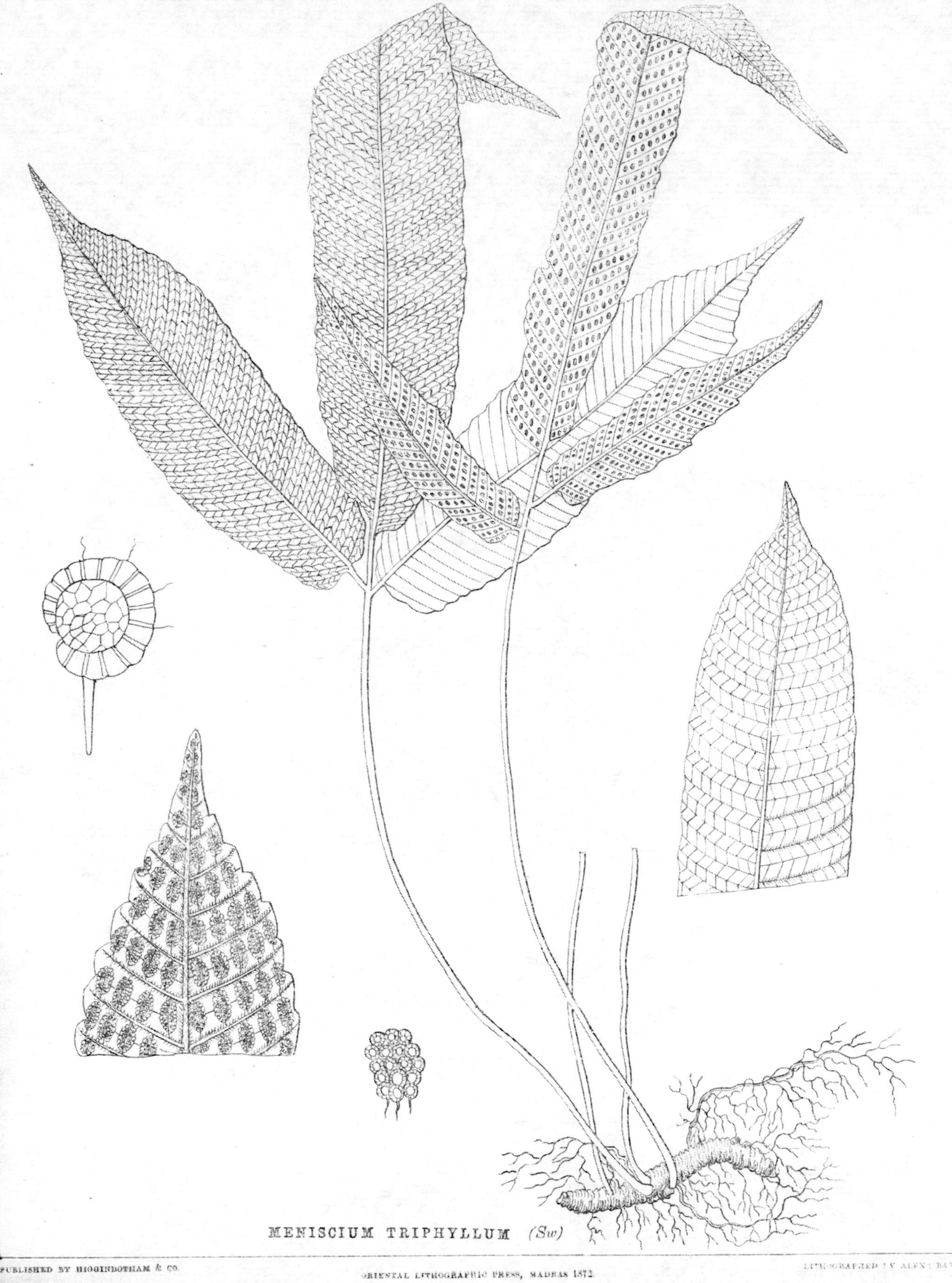

MENISCIUM TRIPHYLLUM *(Sw)*

PUBLISHED BY HIGGINBOTHAM & CO.

ORIENTAL LITHOGRAPHIC PRESS, MADRAS 1872.

LITHOGRAPHED BY ALEX: BARREN

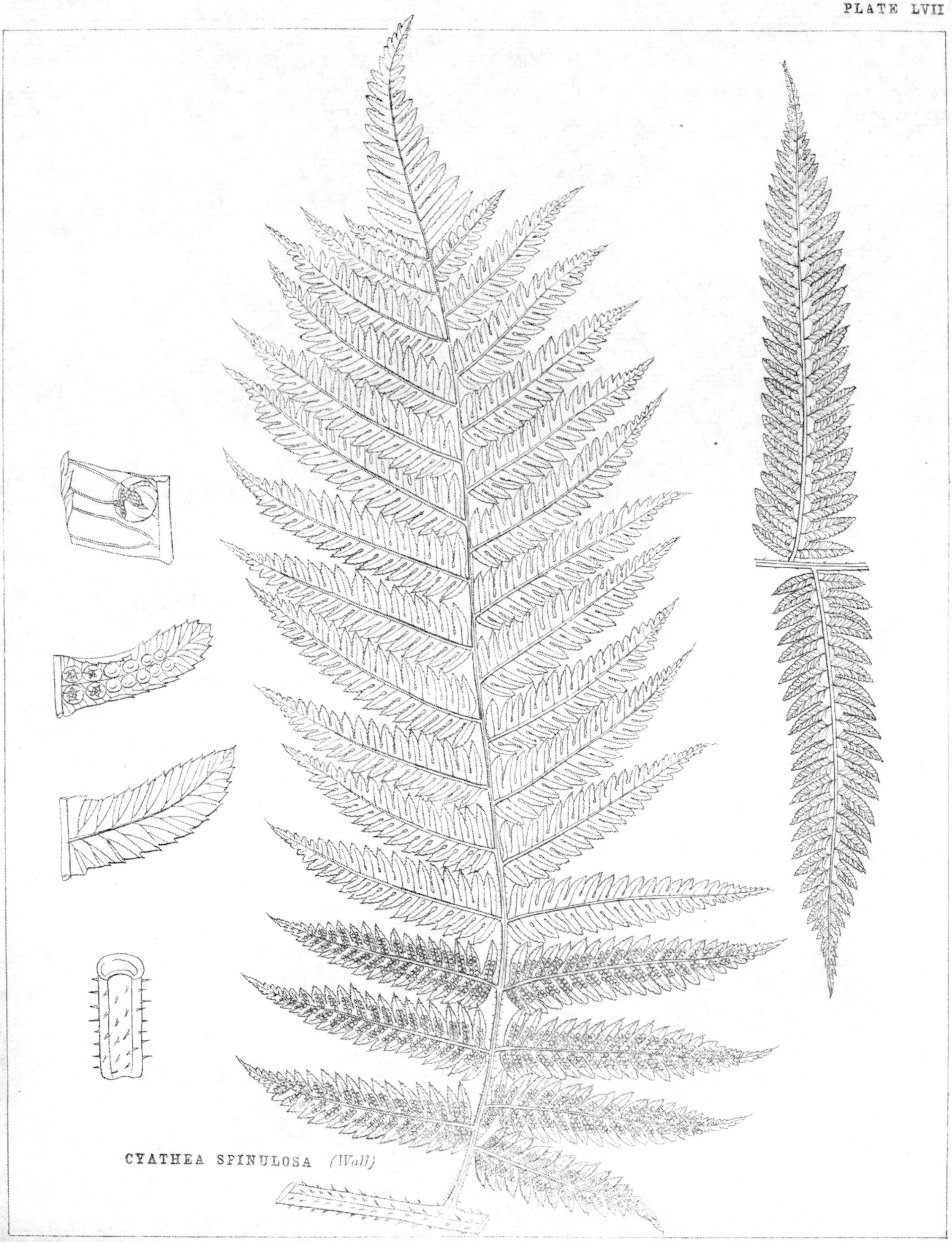

CYATHEA SPINULOSA *(Wall)*

PUBLISHED BY HIGGINBOTHAM & CO. ORIENTAL LITHOGRAPHIC PRESS, MADRAS 1872 LITHOGRAPHED BY ALEX : BARREN

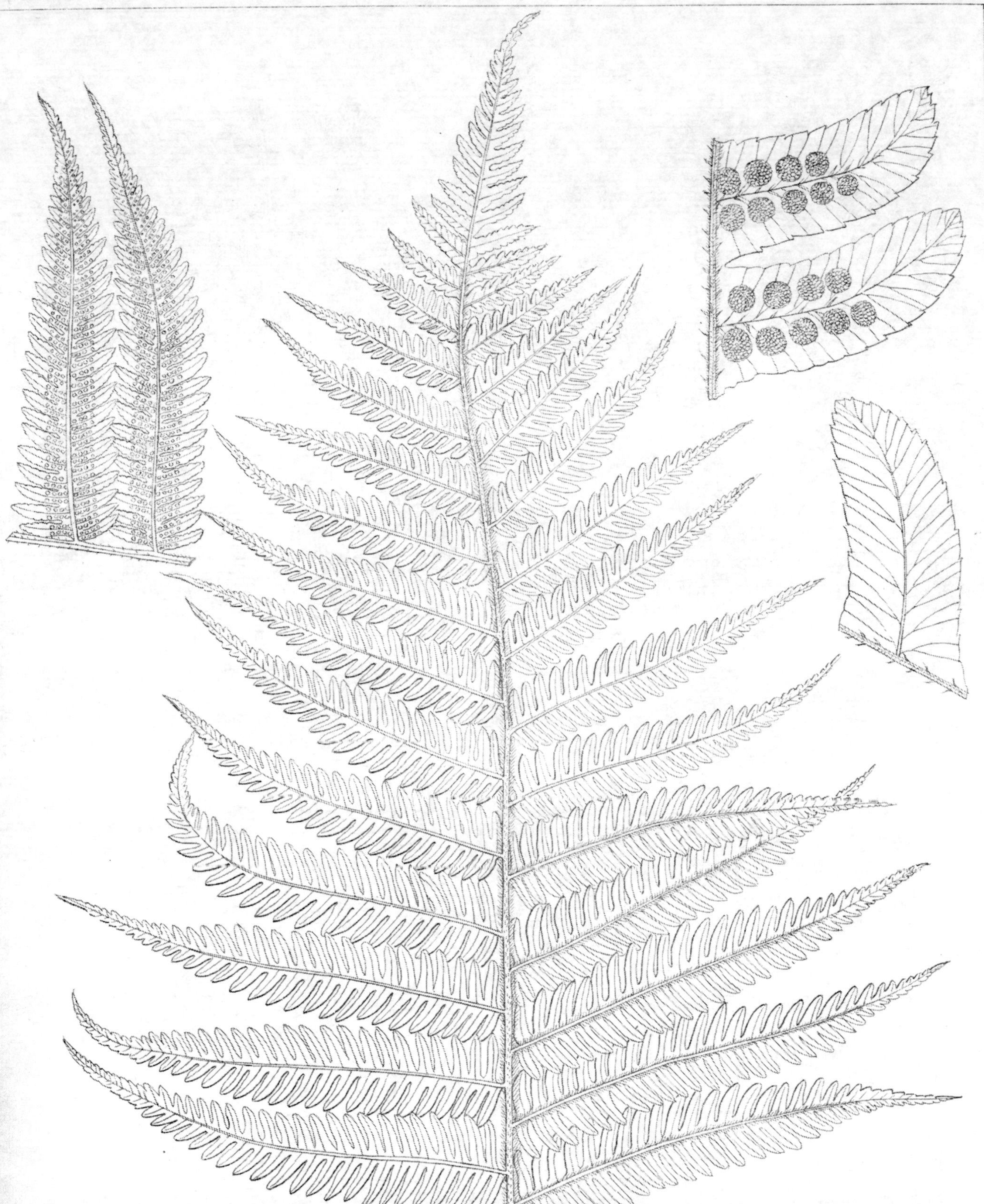

ALSOPHILA LATEBROSA *(Wallich)*

PUBLISHED BY HIGGINBOTHAM & CO. ORIENTAL LITHOGRAPHIC PRESS, MADRAS 1872. LITHOGRAPHED BY ALEX : BARREN

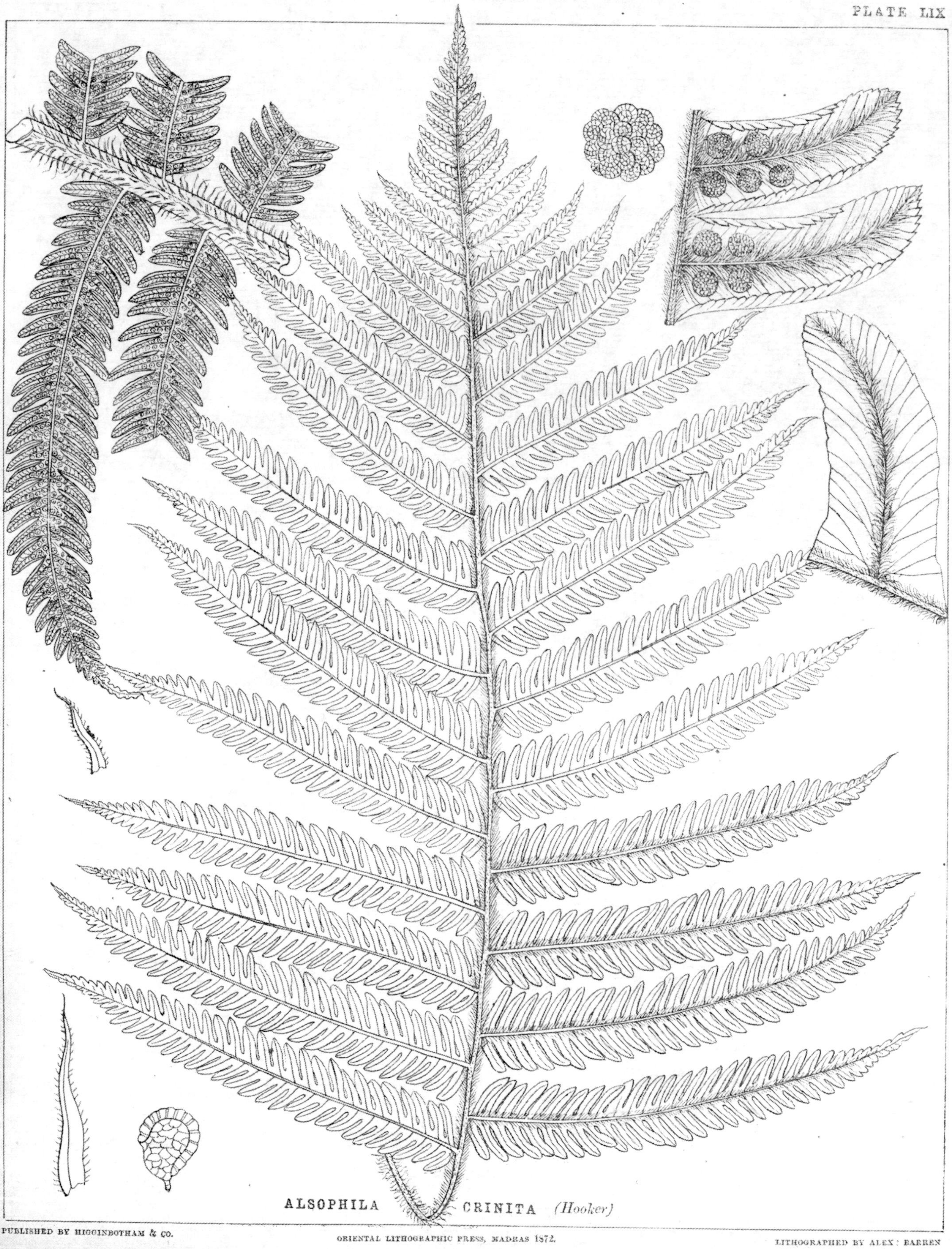

ALSOPHILA CRINITA *(Hooker)*

PUBLISHED BY HIGGINBOTHAM & CO. ORIENTAL LITHOGRAPHIC PRESS, MADRAS 1872. LITHOGRAPHED BY ALEX: BARREN

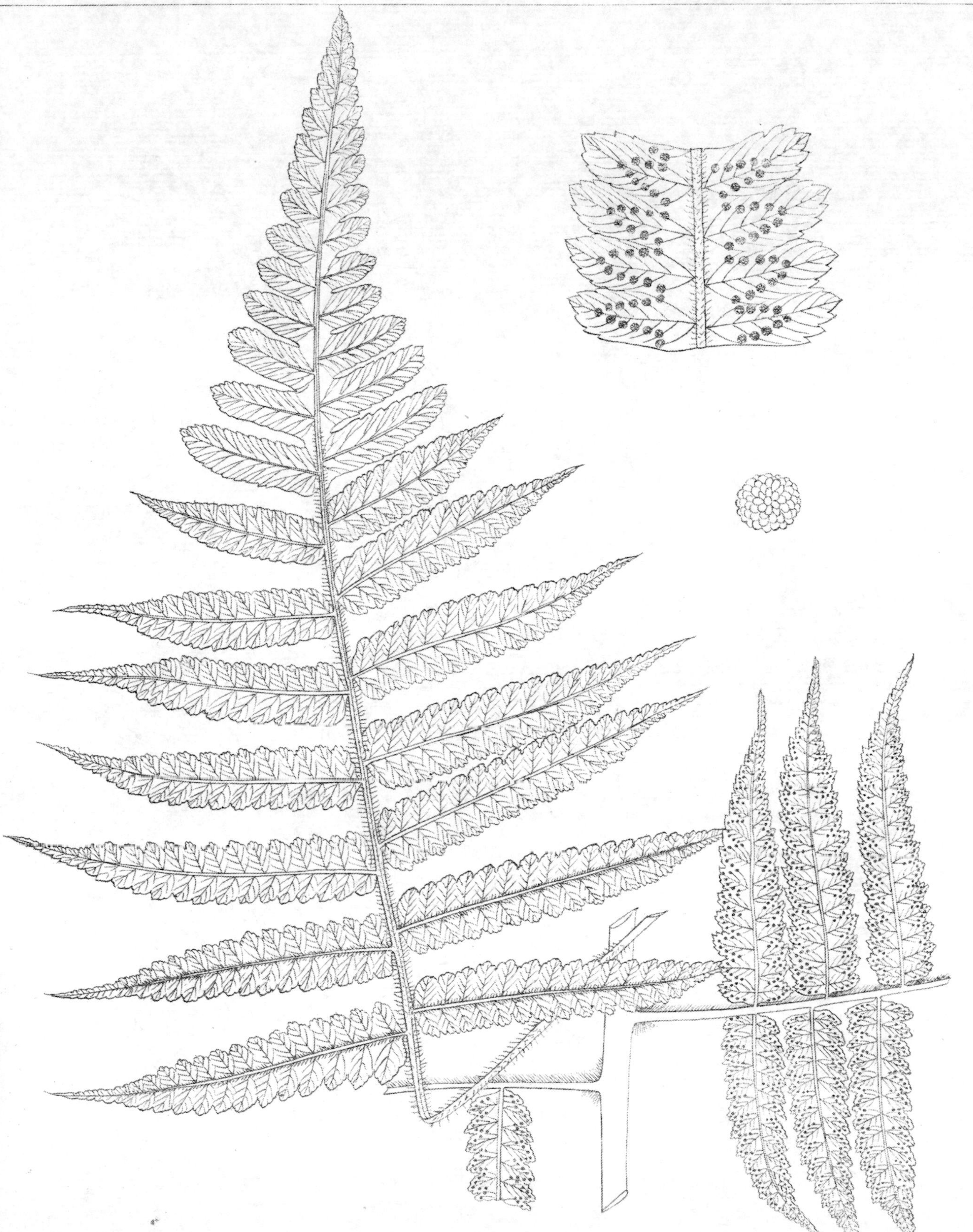

ALSOPHILA GLABRA *(Blume)*

PUBLISHED BY HIGGINBOTHAM & CO. ORIENTAL LITHOGRAPHIC PRESS, MADRAS 1872. LITHOGRAPHED BY ALEX: BARREN

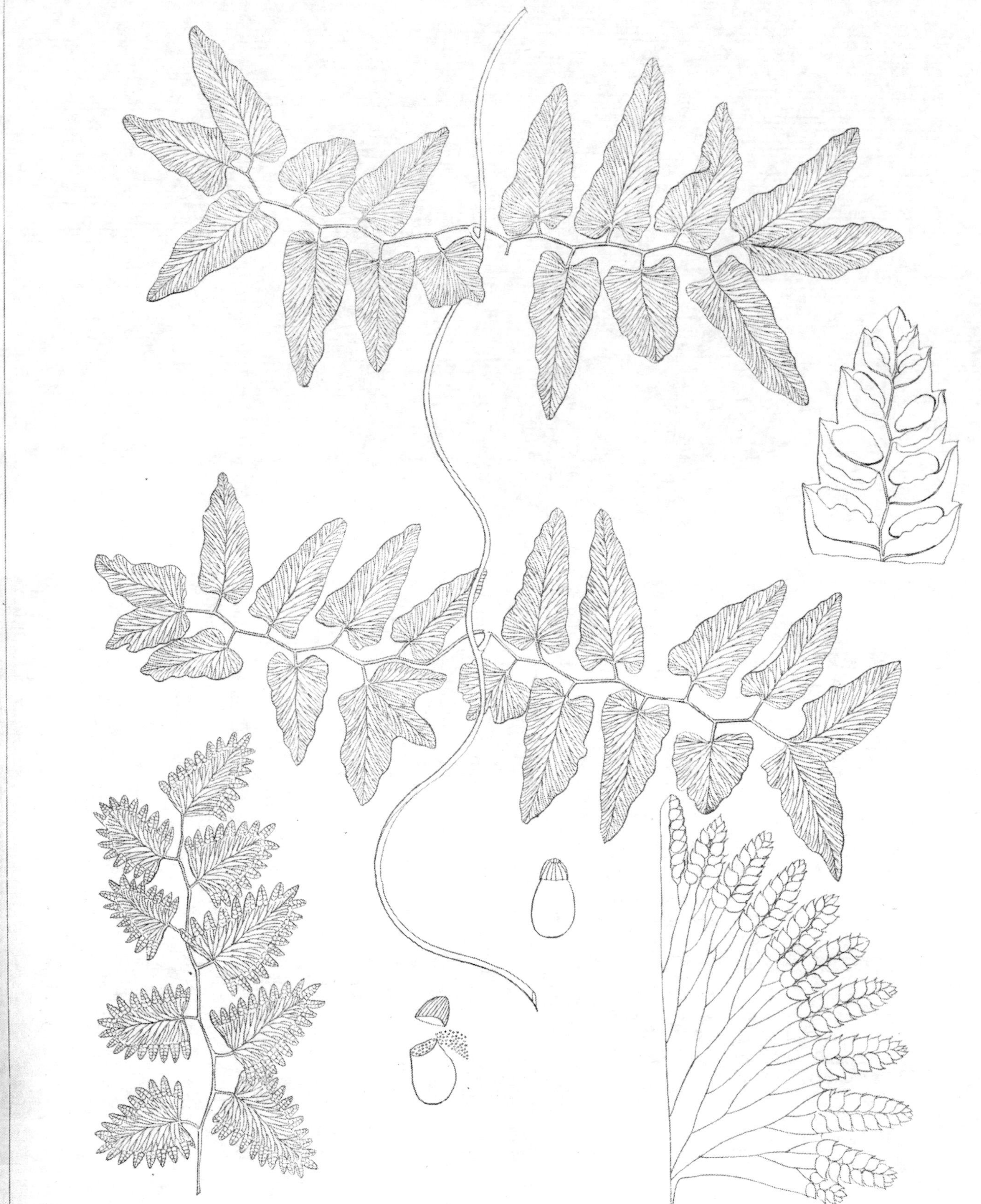

LYGODIUM SCANDENS (*Sw*)

PUBLISHED BY HIGGINBOTHAM & CO. ORIENTAL LITHOGRAPHIC PRESS, MADRAS 1872 LITHOGRAPHED BY ALEX: BARREN

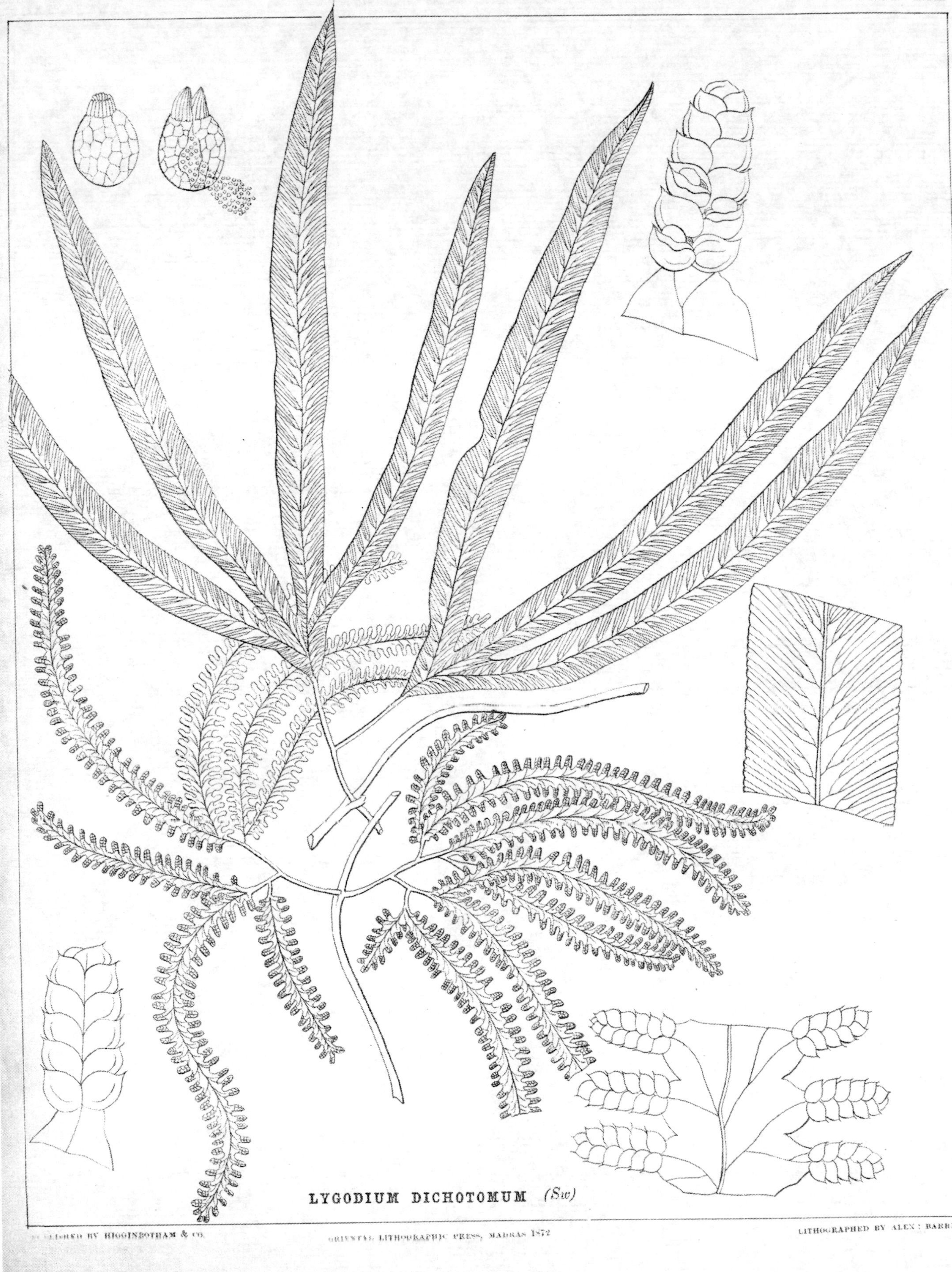

LYGODIUM DICHOTOMUM *(Sw)*

PUBLISHED BY HIGGINBOTHAM & CO. ORIENTAL LITHOGRAPHIC PRESS, MADRAS 1872 LITHOGRAPHED BY ALEX: BARREN

LYGODIUM FLEXUOSUM *(Sw)*

PUBLISHED BY HIGGINBOTHAM & CO. ORIENTAL LITHOGRAPHIC PRESS, MADRAS 1872 LITHOGRAPHED BY ALEX : FARREN

LYGODIUM JAPONICUM (Sw.)

PUBLISHED BY HIGGINBOTHAM & CO. ORIENTAL LITHOGRAPHIC PRESS, MADRAS 1872 LITHOGRAPHED BY ALEX: BARREN

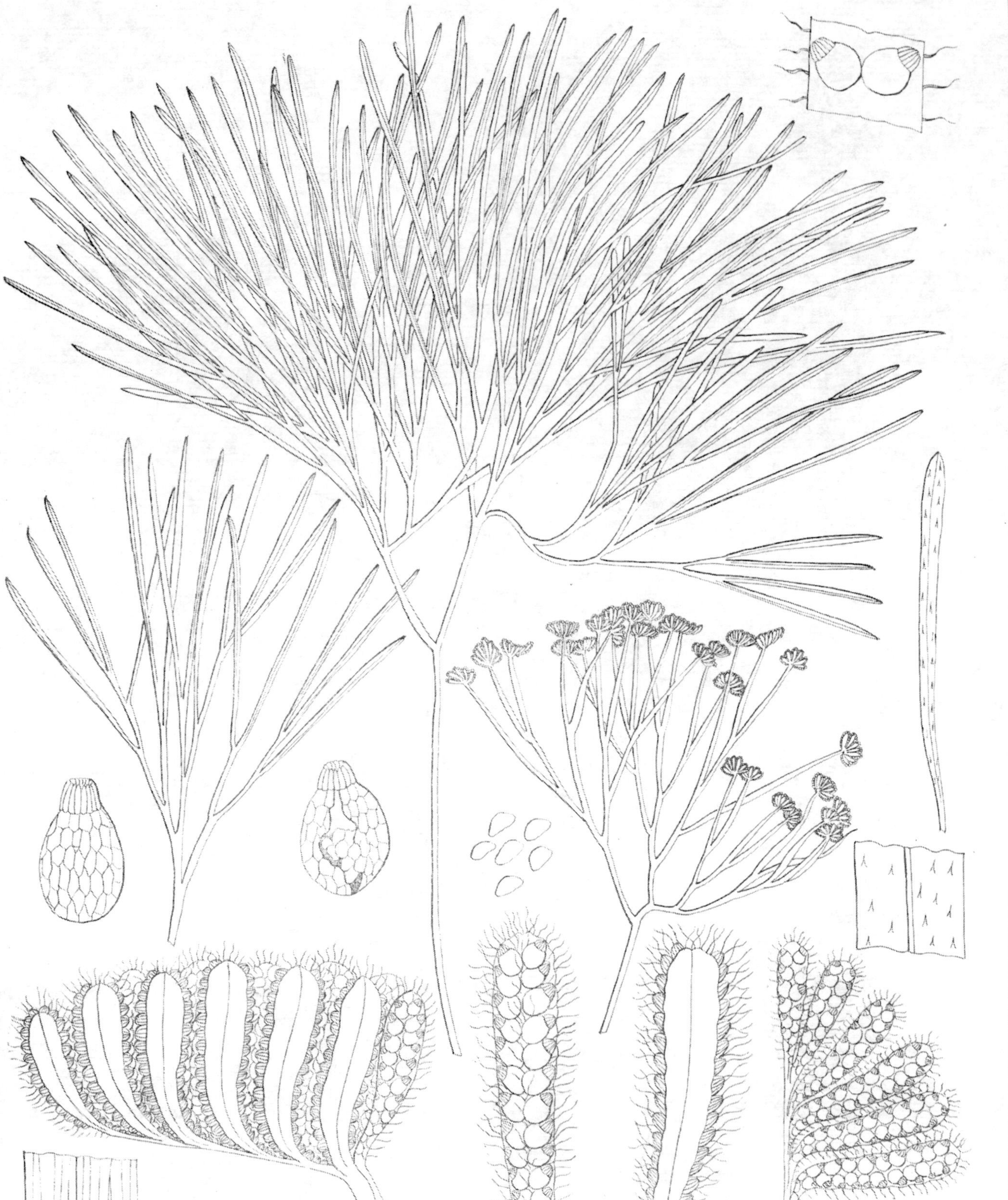

SCHIZÆA DICHOTOMA (Sm)

PUBLISHED BY HIGGINBOTHAM & CO. ORIENTAL LITHOGRAPHIC PRESS, MADRAS 1872. LITHOGRAPHED BY ALEX: BARREN

ANEMIA WIGHTIANA *(Gard)*

PUBLISHED BY HIGGINBOTHAM & CO. ORIENTAL LITHOGRAPHIC PRESS, MADRAS 1872. LITHOGRAPHED BY ALEX: BARREN

BOTRYCHIUM VIRGINICUM

VAR. LANUGINOSUM *(Moore)*

PUBLISHED BY HIGGINBOTHAM & CO.

ORIENTAL LITHOGRAPHIC PRESS, MADRAS 1872.

LITHOGRAPHED BY ALEX : BARREN

BOTRYCHIUM SUBCARNOSUM (*Wall*)

PUBLISHED BY HIGGINBOTHAM & CO. ORIENTAL LITHOGRAPHIC PRESS, MADRAS 1872. LITHOGRAPHED BY ALEX : BARREN

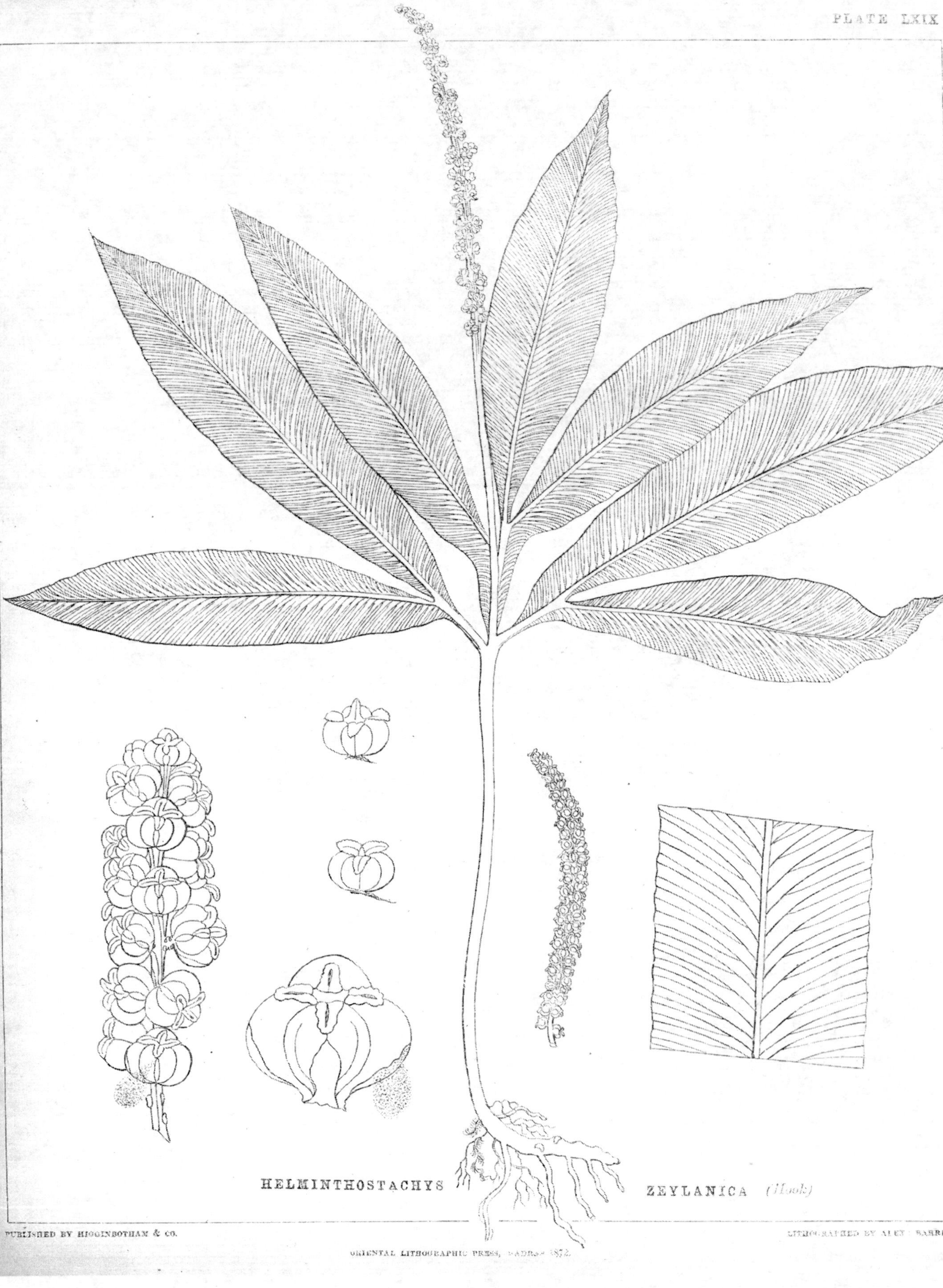

HELMINTHOSTACHYS ZEYLANICA (Hook)

PUBLISHED BY HIGGINBOTHAM & CO.

LITHOGRAPHED BY ALEXR BARREN

ORIENTAL LITHOGRAPHIC PRESS, MADRAS 1872.

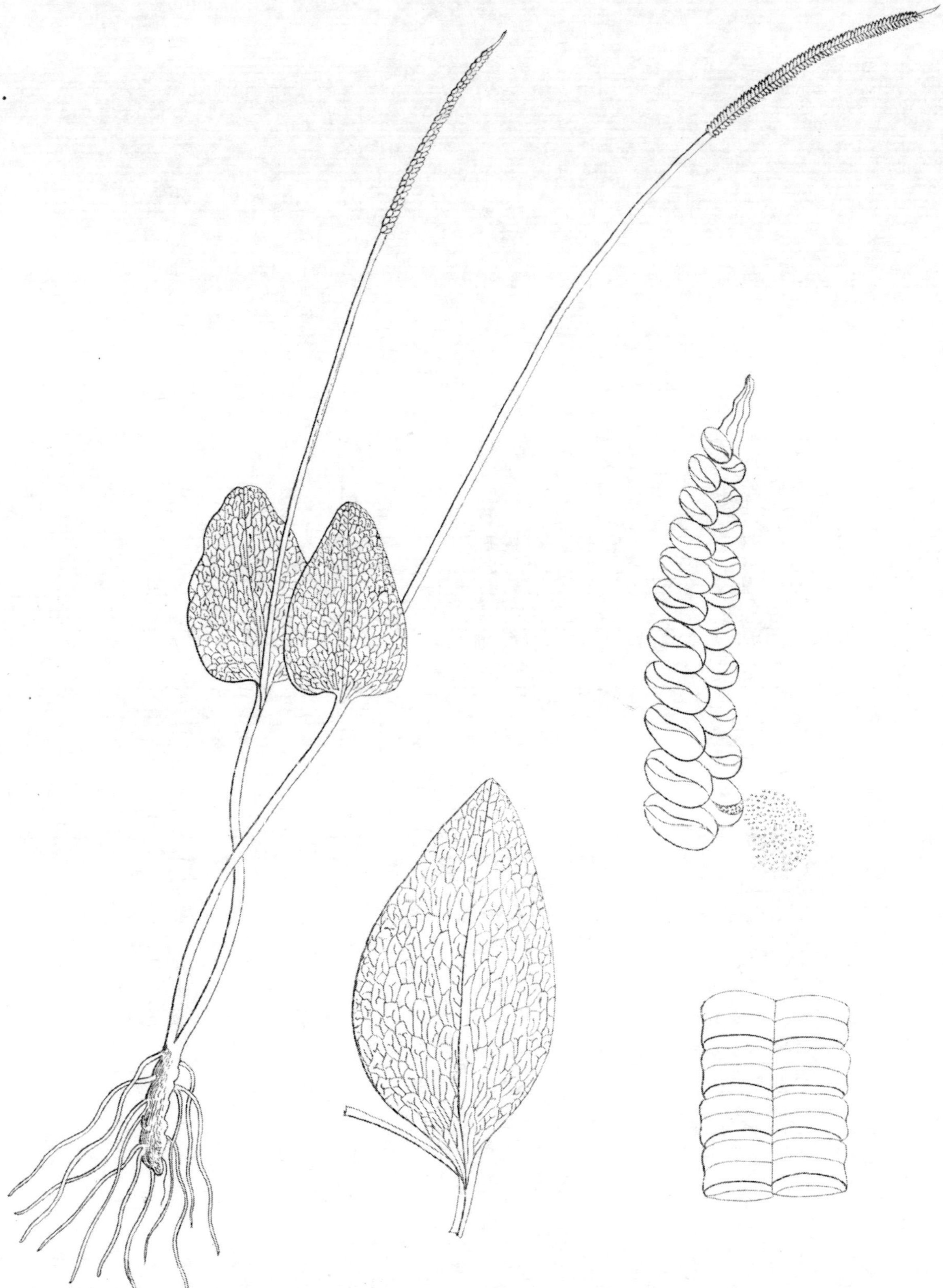

OPHIOGLOSSUM RETICULASUM *(Linn)*

LITHOGRAPHED BY ALEX: BARREN   ORIENTAL LITHOGRAPHIC PRESS, MADRAS 1872.   PUBLISHED BY HIGGINBOTHAM & CO.

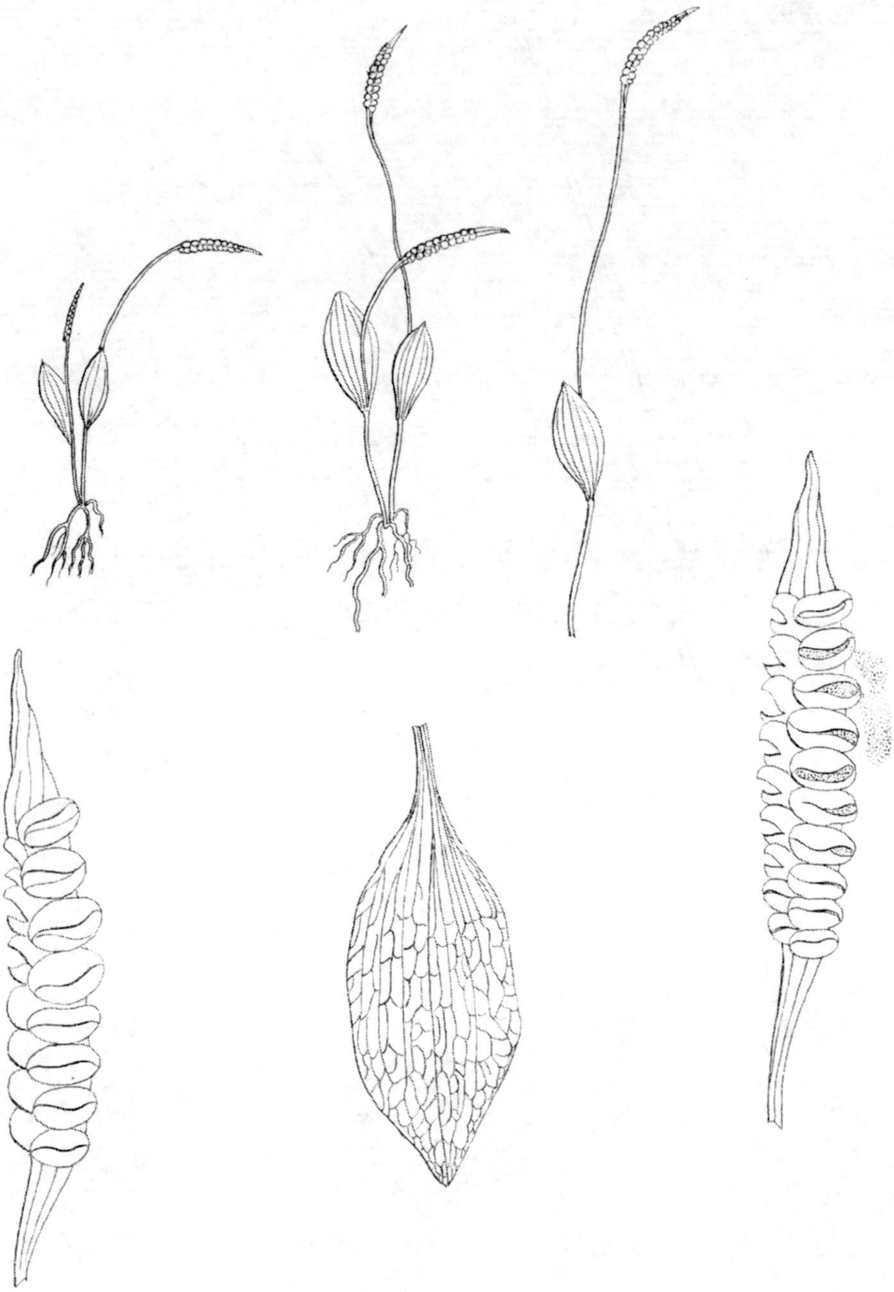

OPHIOGLOSSUM PARVIFOIUM (Linn)

PUBLISHED BY HIGGINBOTHAM & CO. ORIENTAL LITHOGRAPHIC PRESS, MADRAS 1872 LITHOGRAPHED BY ALEX: BARREN

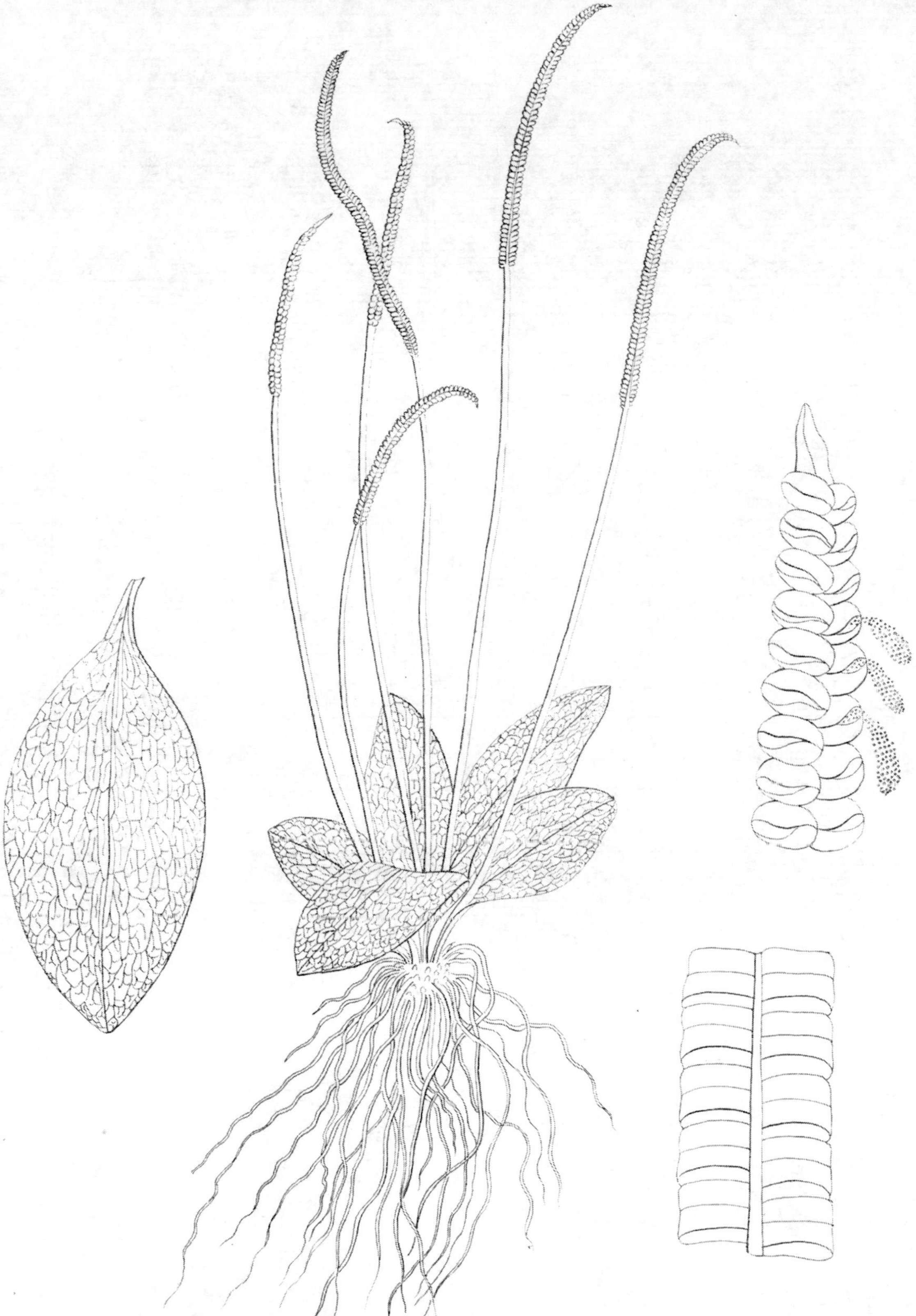

OPHIOGLOSSIUM BREVIPES *(Bedd)*

PUBLISHED BY HIGGINBOTHAM & CO. ORIENTAL LITHOGRAPHIC PRESS, MADRAS 1872 LITHOGRAPHED BY ALEX : BARREN

PERANEMA CYATHEOIDES *(Don)*

PUBLISHED BY HIGGINBOTHAM & CO. ORIENTAL LITHOGRAPHIC PRESS, MADRAS 1872 LITHOGRAPHED BY ALEX: BARREN

GLEICHENIA DICHOTOMA *(Willd)*

PUBLISHED BY HIGGINBOTHAM & CO. ORIENTAL LITHOGRAPHIC PRESS, MADRAS 1872 LITHOGRAPHED BY ALEX. BARREN

CERATOPTERIS THATICTROIDES *(Brongn)*

PUBLISHED BY HIGGINBOTHAM & CO. ORIENTAL LITHOGRAPHIC PRESS MADRAS 1872 LITHOGRAPHED BY ALEX BARREN

OSMUNDA REGALIS (*Linn*)

PUBLISHED BY HIGGINBOTHAM & CO. ORIENTAL LITHOGRAPHIC PRESS, MADRAS 1872. LITHOGRAPHED BY ALEX: BARREN

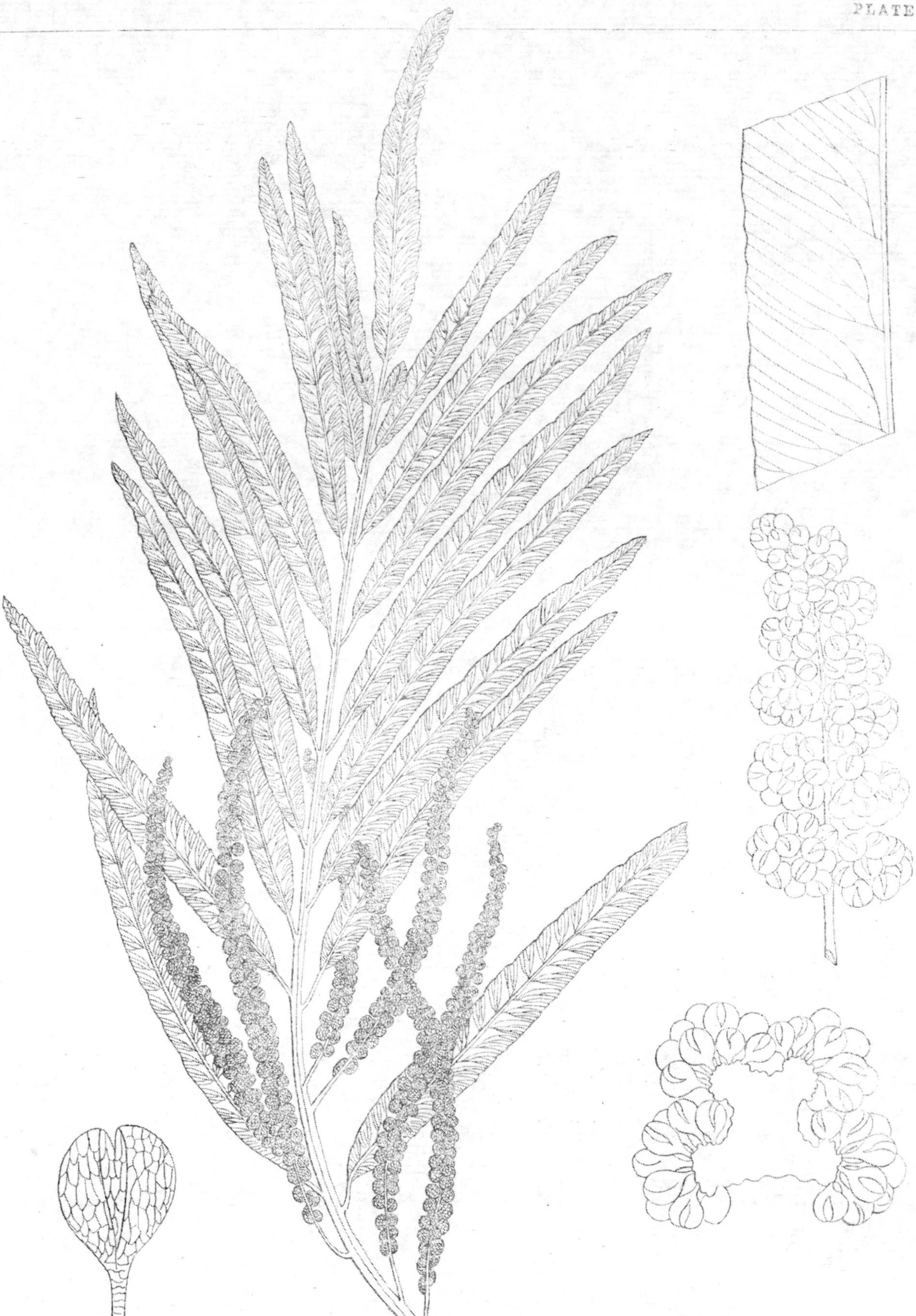

OSMUNDA JAVANICA *(Blume)*

PUBLISHED BY HIGGINBOTHAM & CO. ORIENTAL LITHOGRAPHIC PRESS, MADRAS 1874. LITHOGRAPHED BY ALEX : BARREN

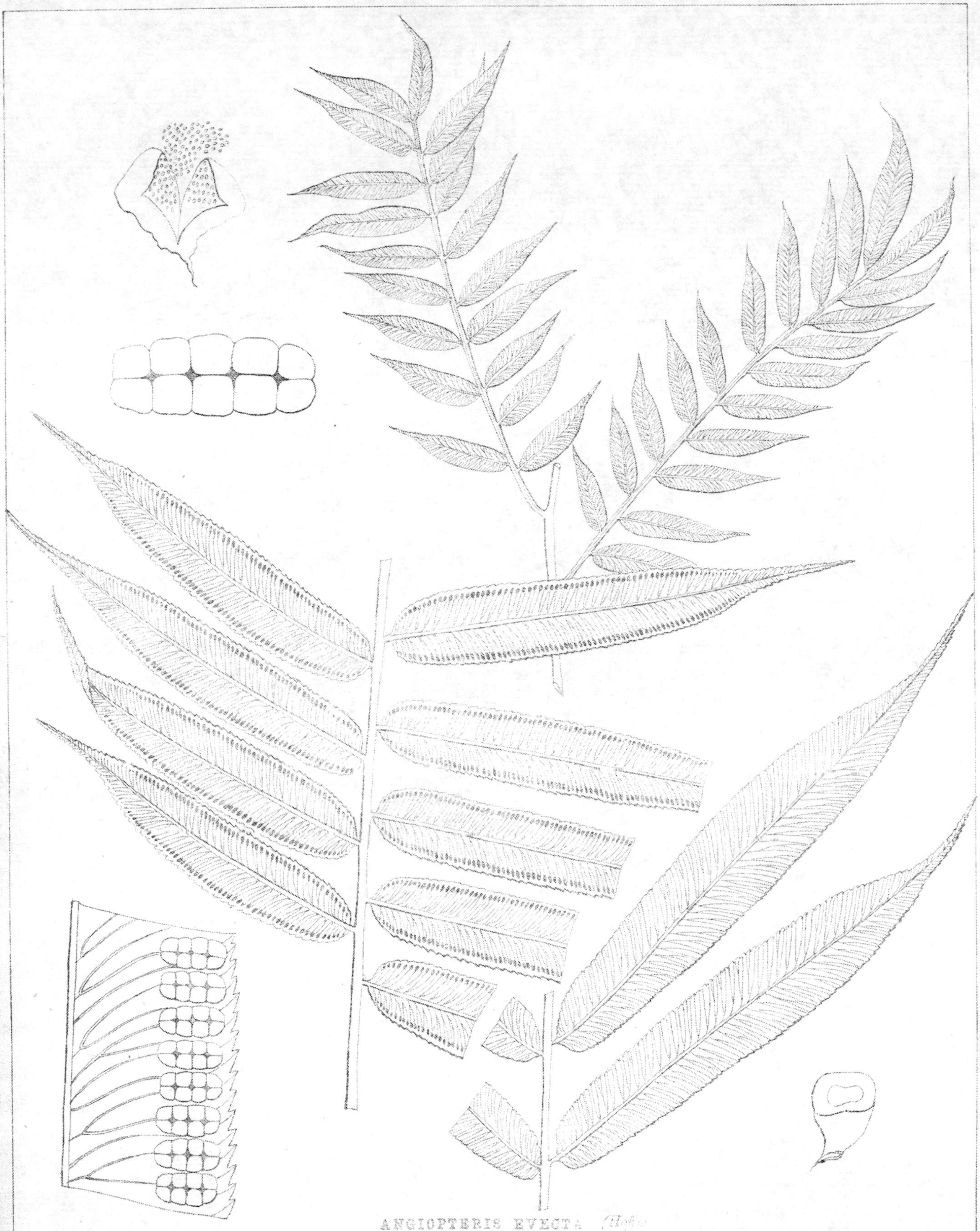

ANGIOPTERIS EVECTA (Hoffm.)

PUBLISHED BY HIGGINBOTHAM & CO. ORIENTAL LITHOGRAPHIC PRESS, MADRAS 1877. LITHOGRAPHED BY ALEX: BARRÉN

PLATE LXXIX

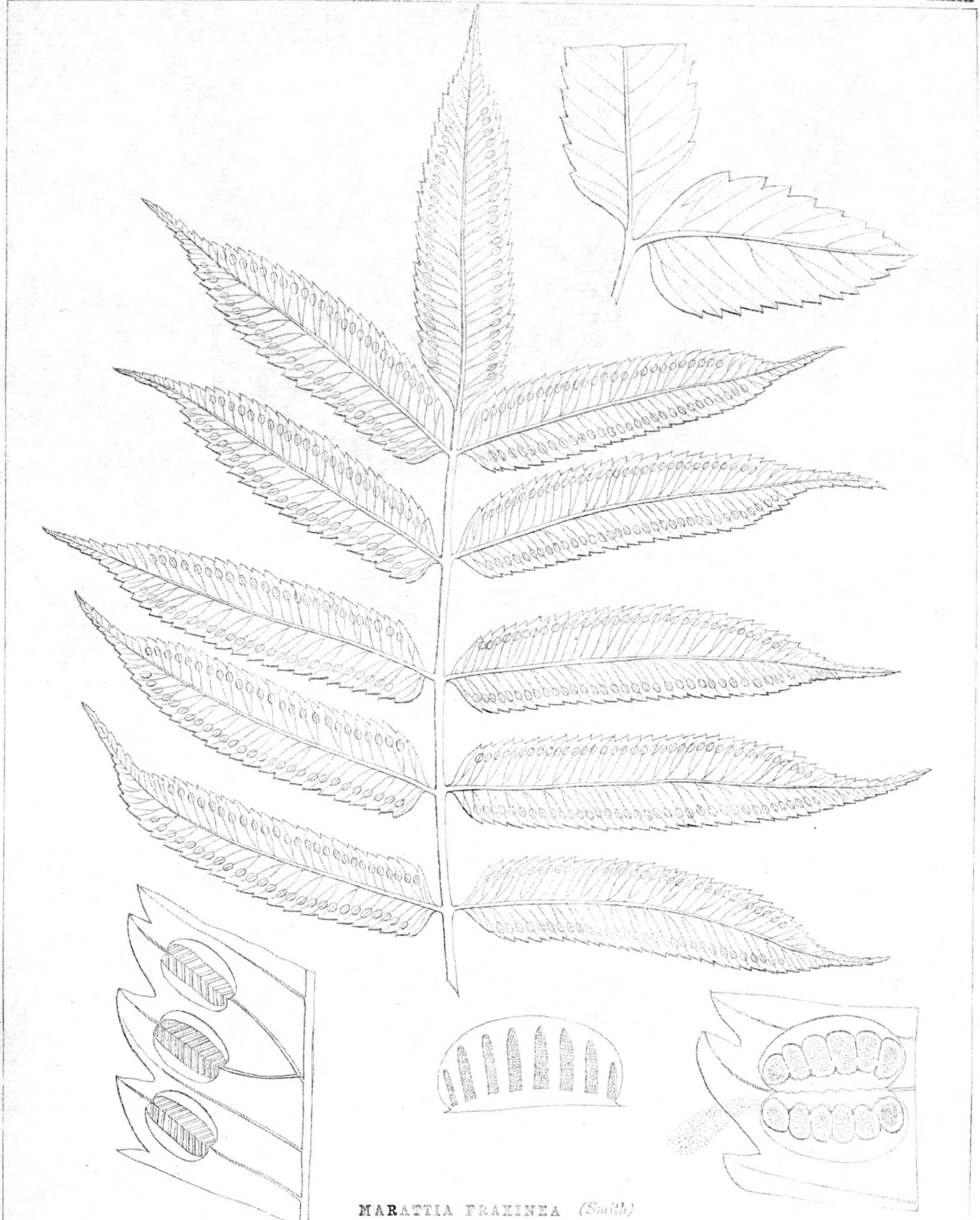

MARATTIA FRAXINEA (*Smith*)

PUBLISHED BY HIGGINBOTHAM & CO.   ORIENTAL LITHOGRAPHIC PRESS, MADRAS 1872.   LITHOGRAPHED BY ALEX. BARREN

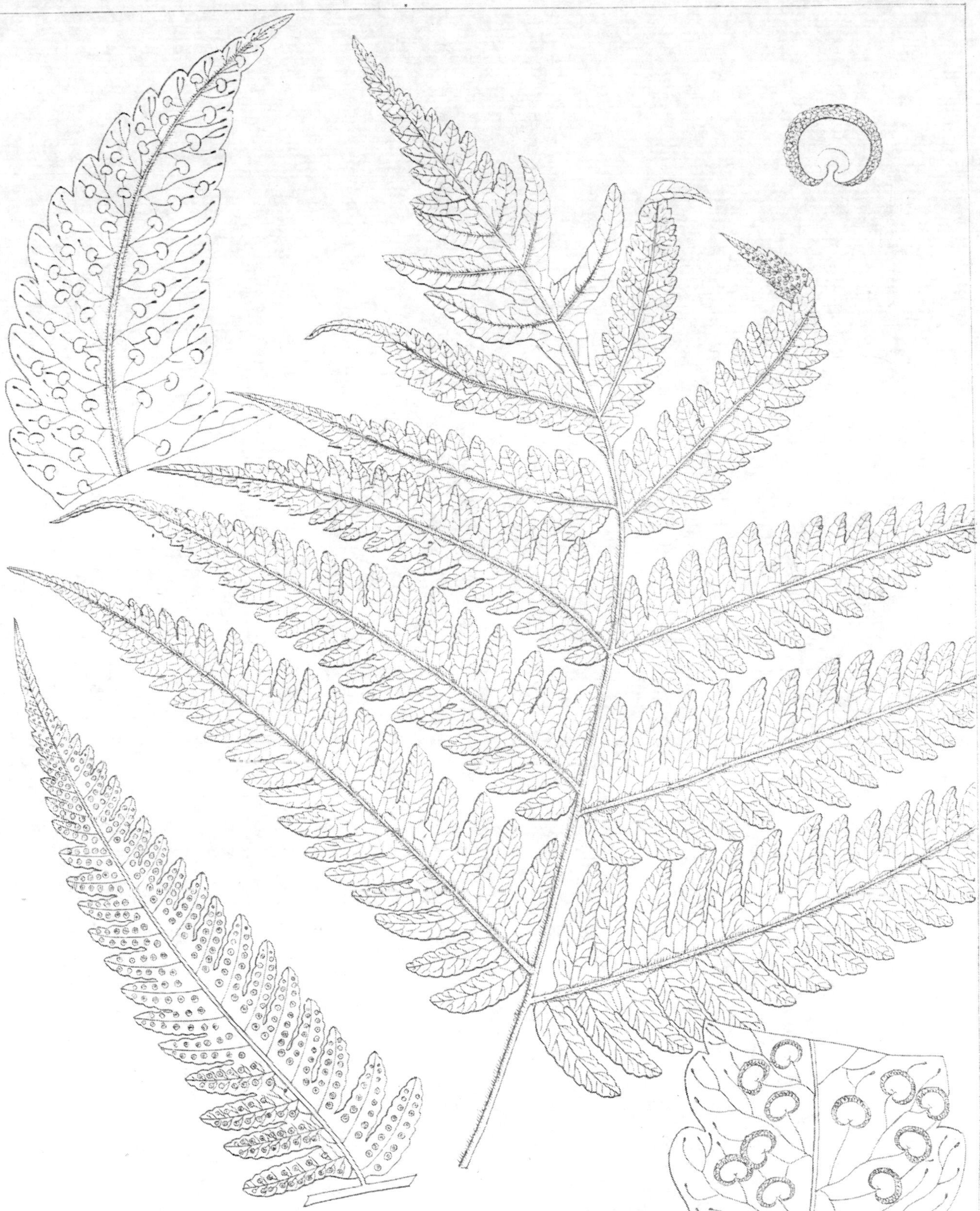

SAGENIA GIGANTEA *(Blume)*

PUBLISHED BY HIGGINBOTHAM & CO. ORIENTAL LITHOGRAPHIC PRESS, MADRAS 1872. LITHOGRAPHED BY ALEX: BARREN

SAGENIA COADUNATA (Moore)

PUBLISHED BY HIGGINBOTHAM & CO. ORIENTAL LITHOGRAPHIC PRESS. MADRAS 1872. LITHOGRAPHED BY ALEX: BARREN

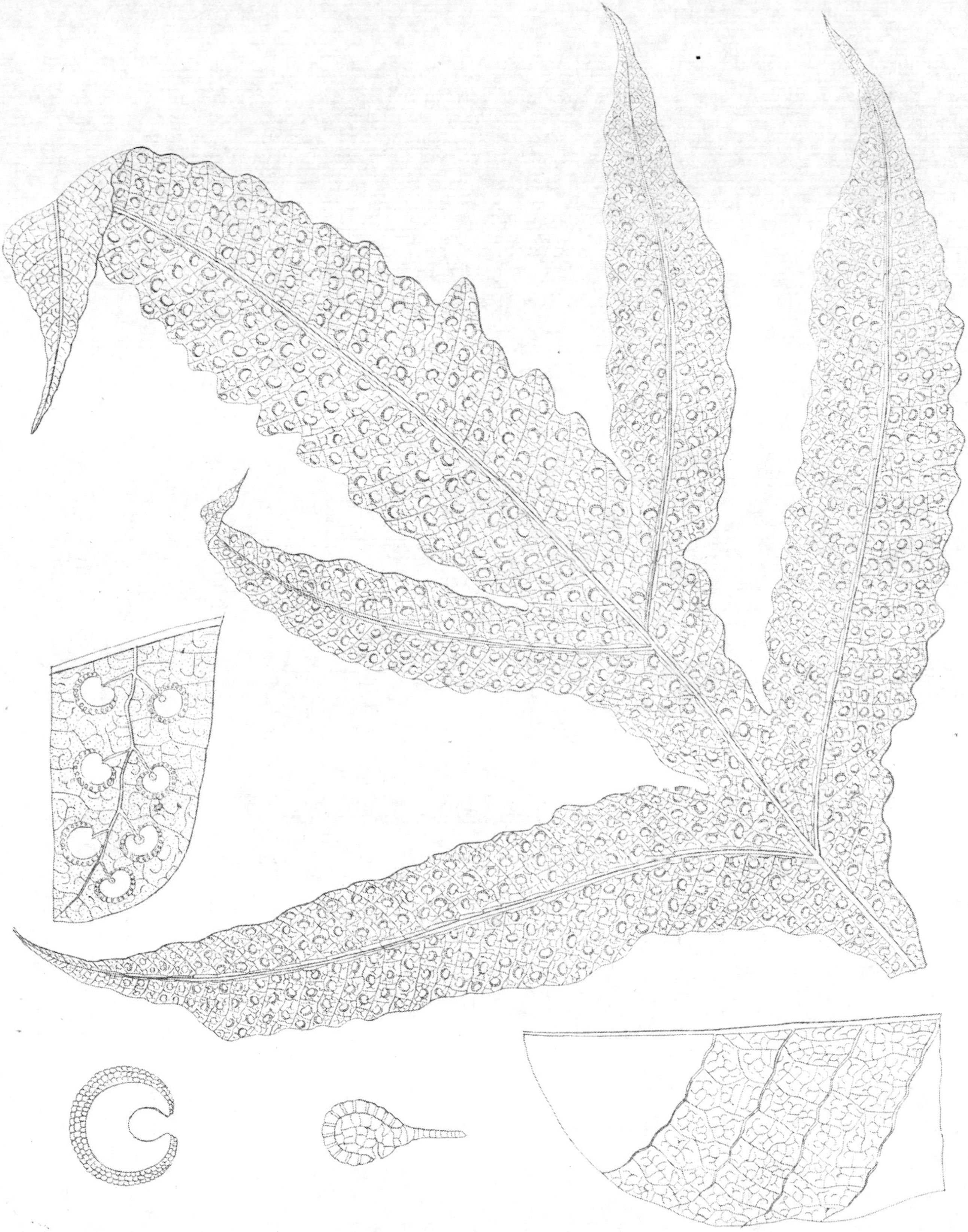

SAGENIA PTEROPUS *(Moore.)*

PUBLISHED BY HIGGINBOTHAM & CO. ORIENTAL LITHOGRAPHIC PRESS, MADRAS 1872. LITHOGRAPHED BY ALEX: BARREN

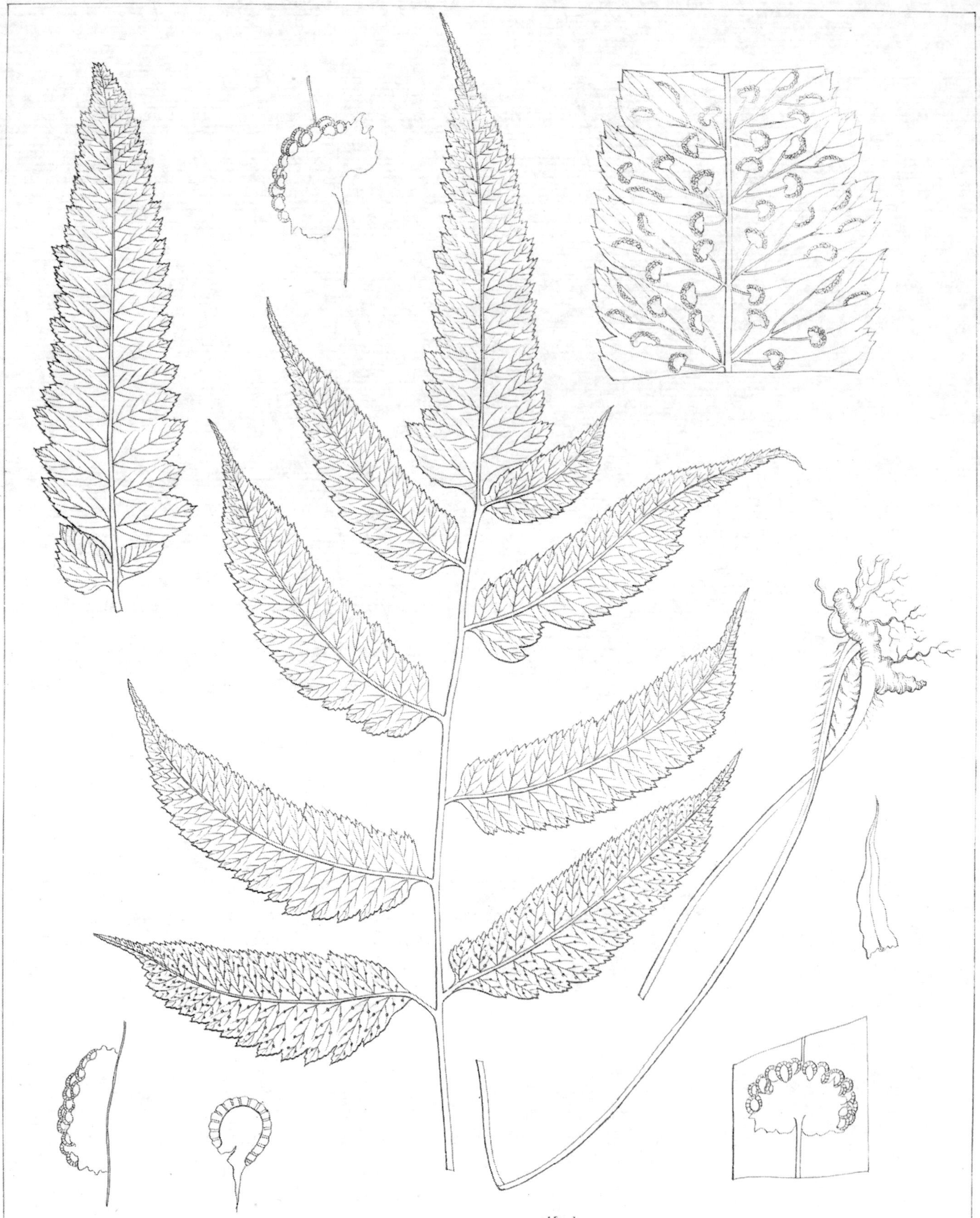

PLEOCNEMIA ARISTATA *(Hooker)*

PUBLISHED BY HIGGINBOTHAM & CO. ORIENTAL LITHOGRAPHIC PRESS, MADRAS 1872. LITHOGRAPHED BY ALEX. BARREN

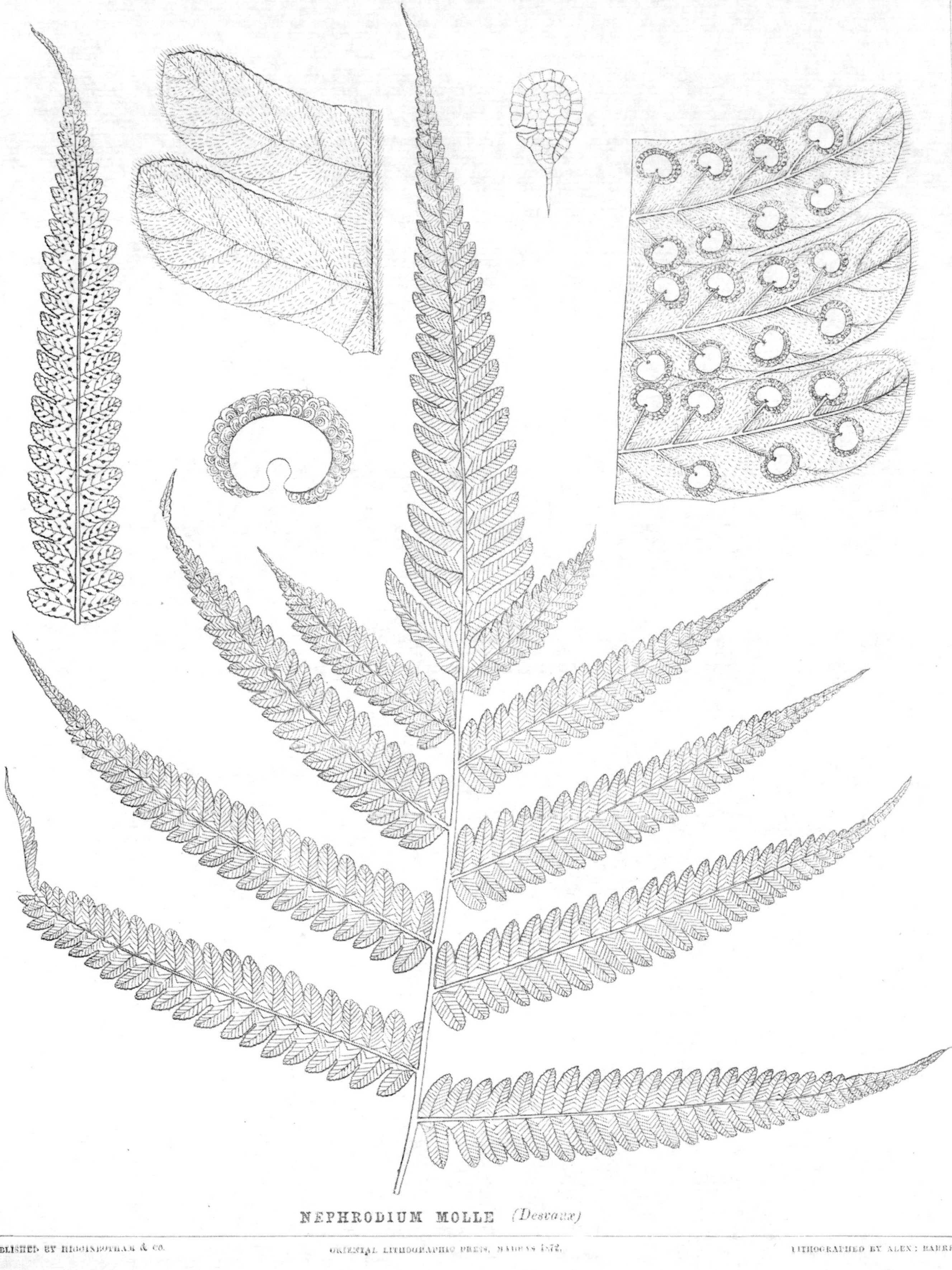

NEPHRODIUM MOLLE *(Desvaux)*

PUBLISHED BY HIGGINBOTHAM & CO. ORIENTAL LITHOGRAPHIC PRESS, MADRAS 1872. LITHOGRAPHED BY ALEX: BARREN

NEPHRODIUM EXTENSUM (*Blume*)

PUBLISHED BY HIGGINBOTHAM & CO. ORIENTAL LITHOGRAPHIC PRESS, MADRAS 1872. LITHOGRAPHED BY ALEX: BARREN

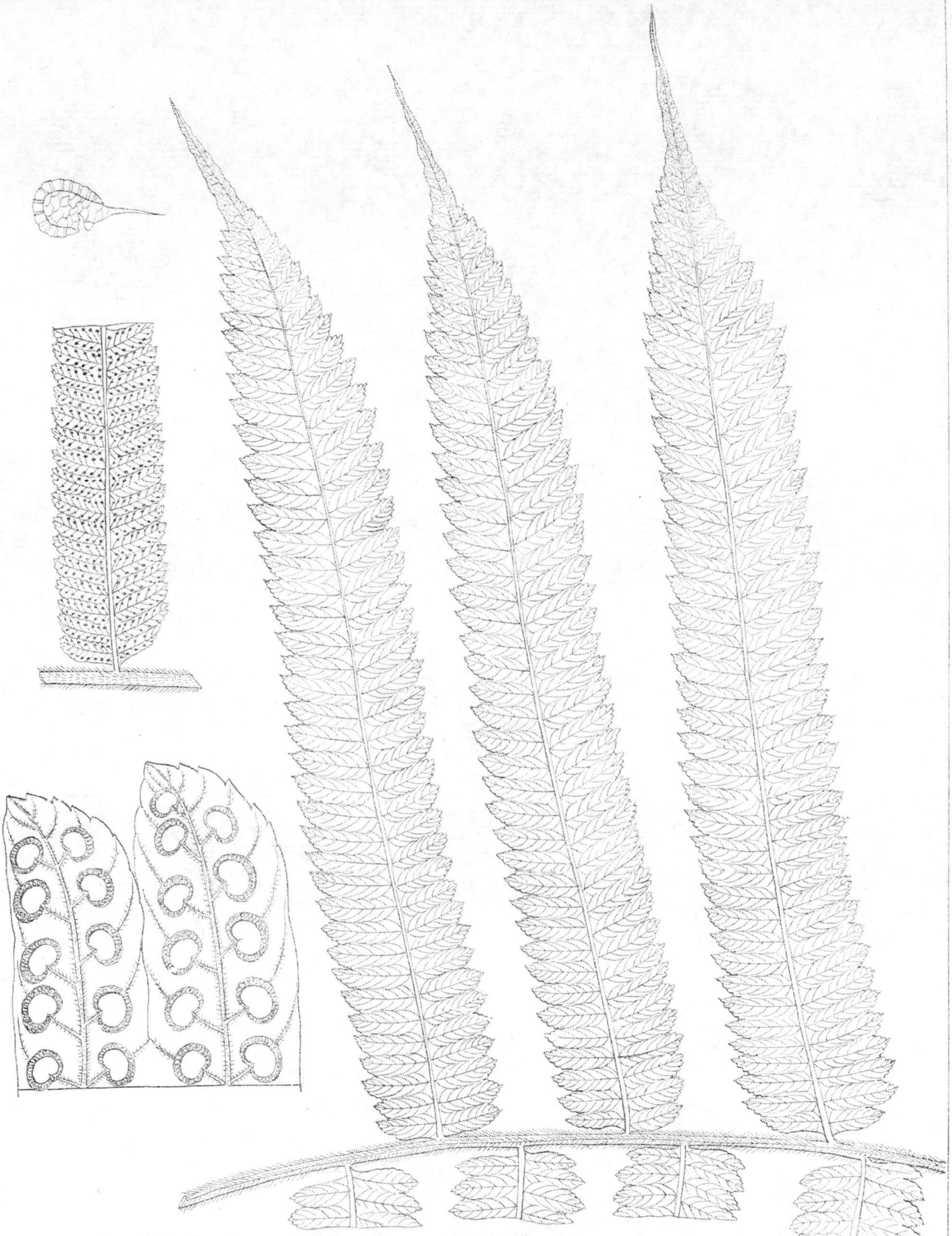

NEPHRODIUM ABRUPTUM *(Presl.)*

PUBLISHED BY HIGGINBOTHAM & CO. ORIENTAL LITHOGRAPHIC PRESS, MADRAS 1872. LITHOGRAPHED BY ALEX: BARREN

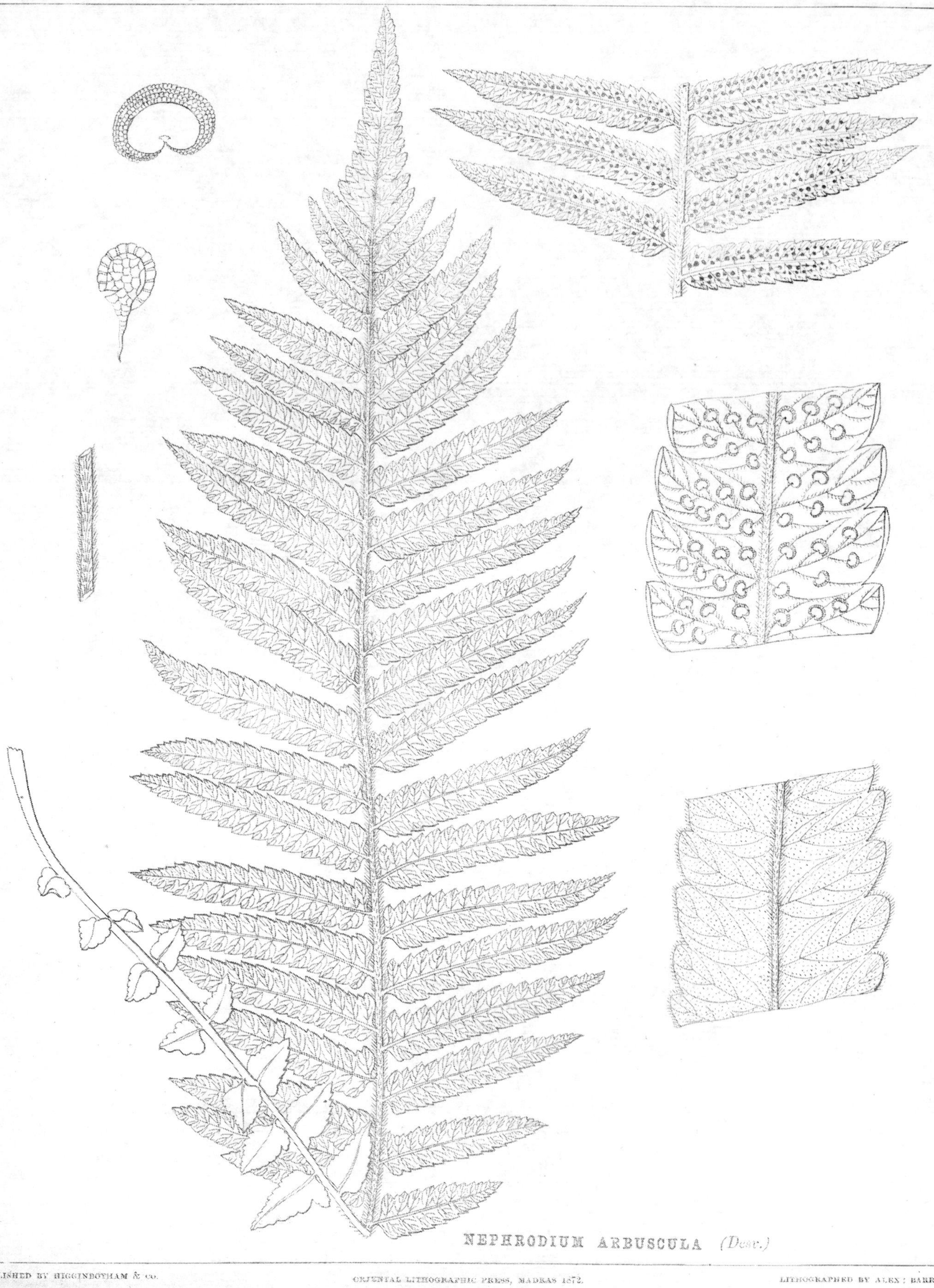

NEPHRODIUM ARBUSCULA *(Desv.)*

PUBLISHED BY HIGGINBOTHAM & CO. ORIENTAL LITHOGRAPHIC PRESS, MADRAS 1872. LITHOGRAPHED BY ALEX: BARREN

PLATE LXXXVIII

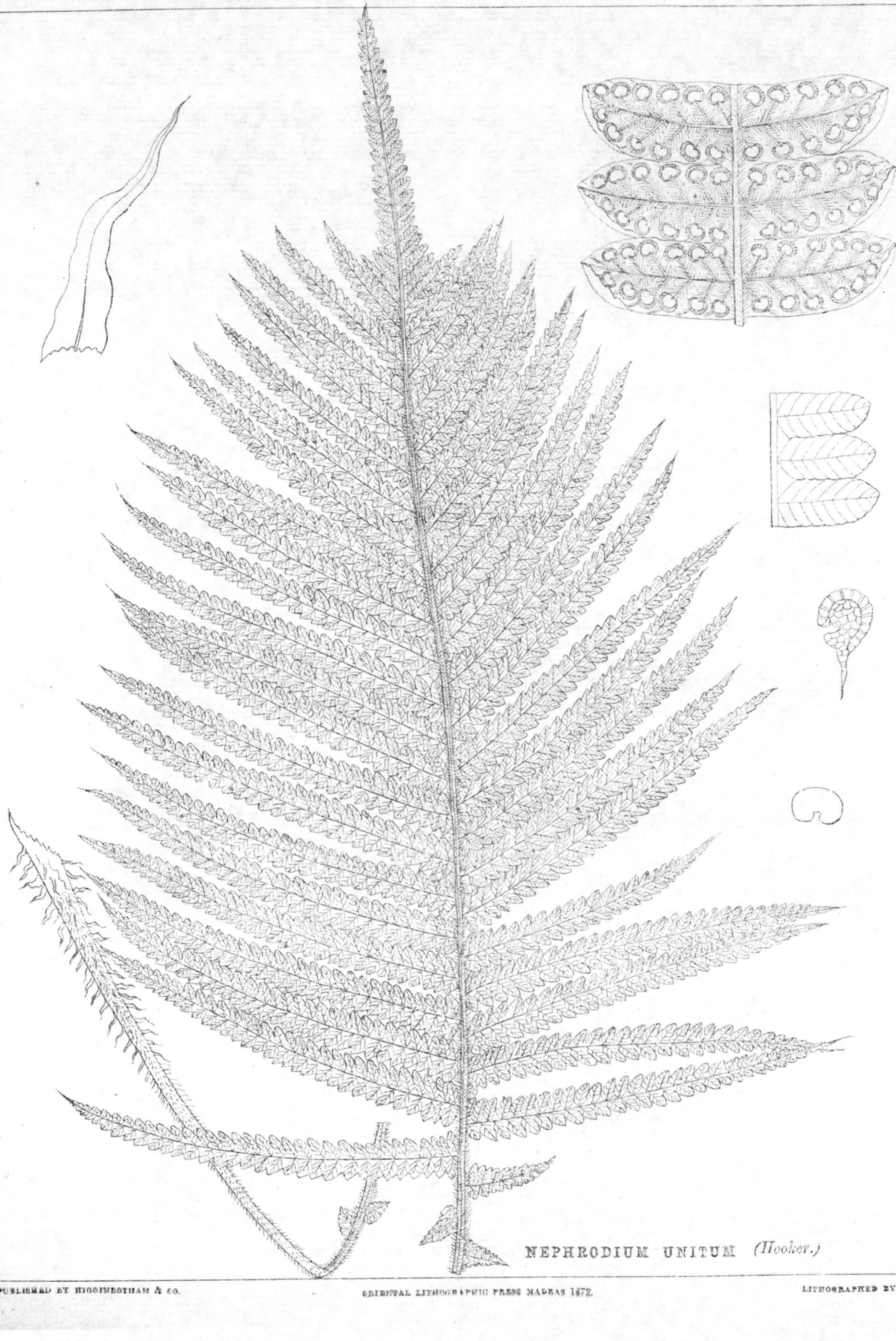

NEPHRODIUM UNITUM (*Hooker.*)

PUBLISHED BY HIGGINBOTHAM & CO. ORIENTAL LITHOGRAPHIC PRESS MADRAS 1872. LITHOGRAPHED BY ALEX: BARREN,

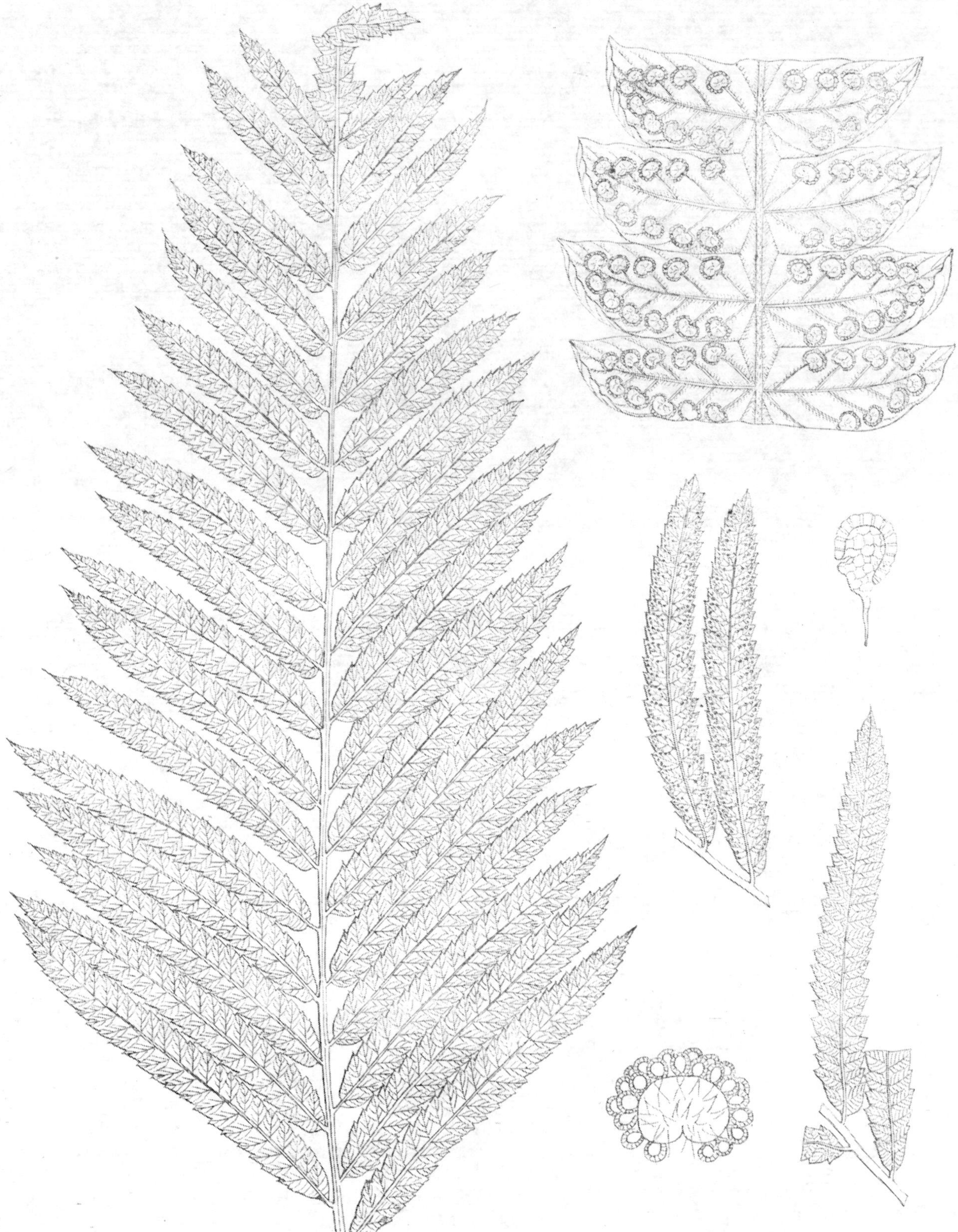

NEPHRODIUM PROPINQUUM *(Br.)*

PUBLISHED BY HIGGINBOTHAM & CO. ORIENTAL LITHOGRAPHIC PRESS MADRAS 1872. LITHOGRAPHED BY ALEX: BARREN,

PLATE XC

NEPHRODIUM TERMINANS *(J. Sm.)*

PUBLISHED BY HIGGINBOTHAM & CO. ORIENTAL LITHOGRAPHIC PRESS MADRAS 1872. LITHOGRAPHED BY ALEX: BARREN,

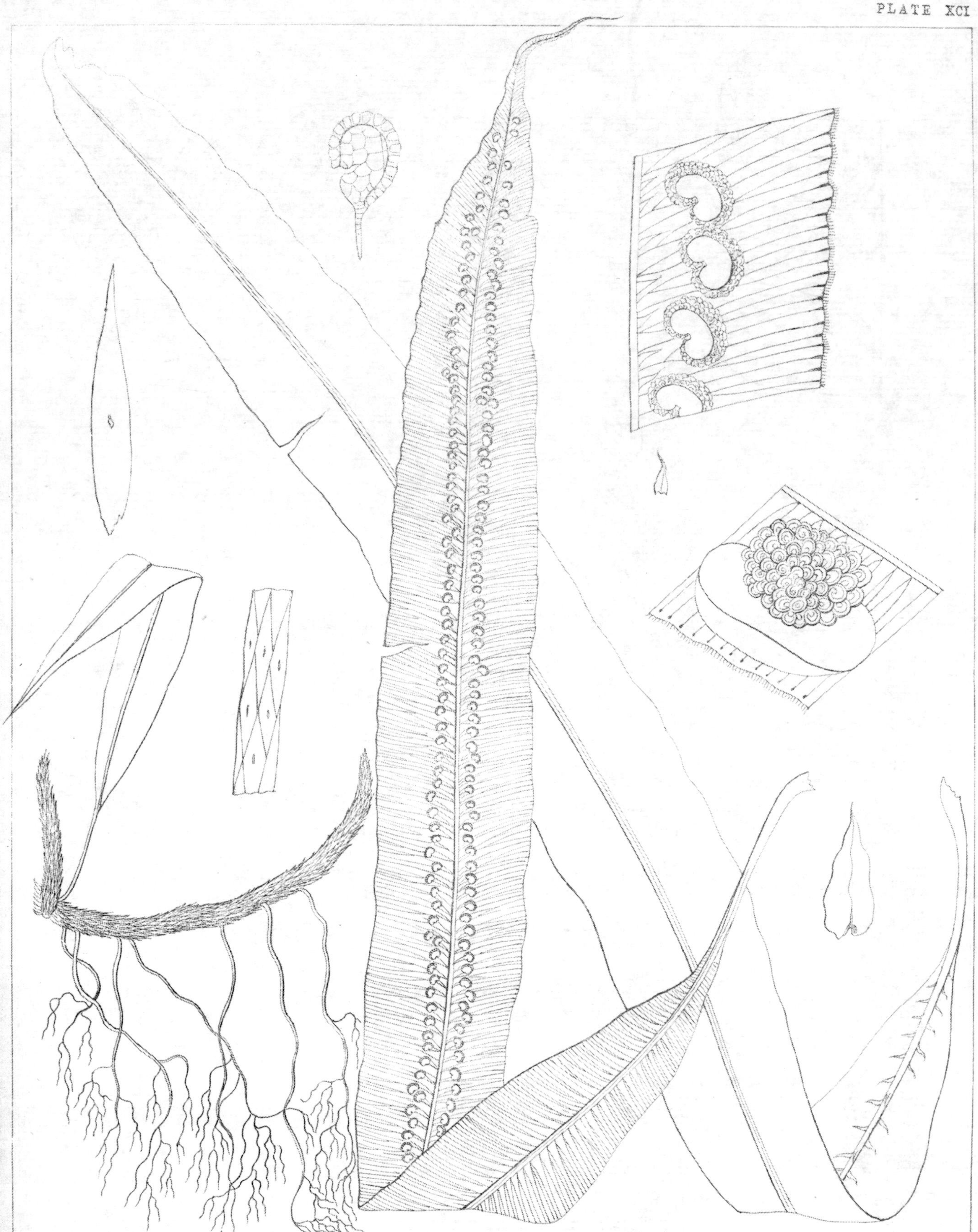

OLEANDRA NERIIFORMIS (Cav.)

PUBLISHED BY HIGGINBOTHAM & Co. ORIENTAL LITHOGRAPHIC PRESS, MADRAS 1872. LITHOGRAPHED BY ALEX: BARREN

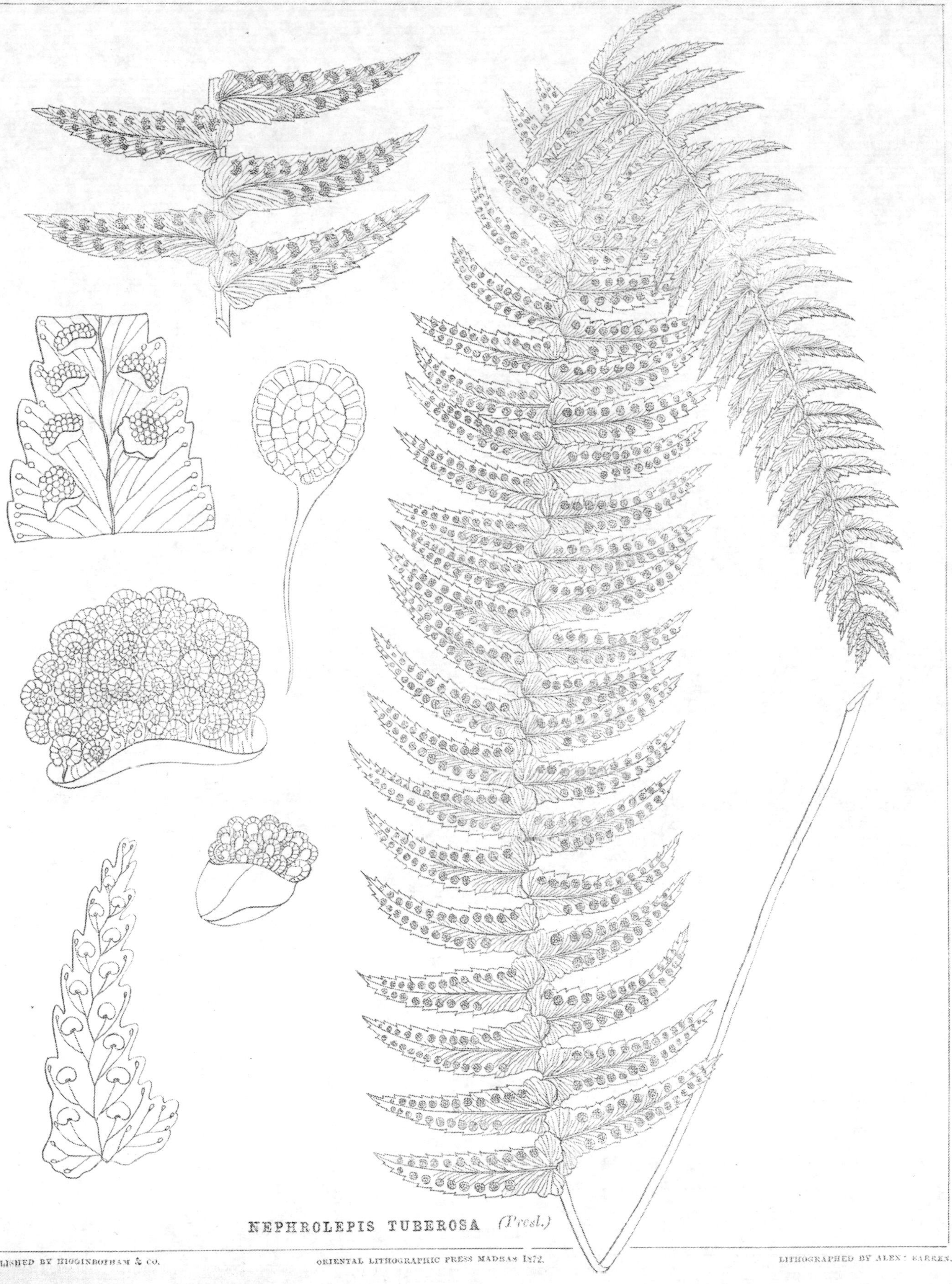

NEPHROLEPIS TUBEROSA *(Presl.)*

PUBLISHED BY HIGGINBOTHAM & CO. ORIENTAL LITHOGRAPHIC PRESS MADRAS 1872. LITHOGRAPHED BY ALEXR. BARREN.

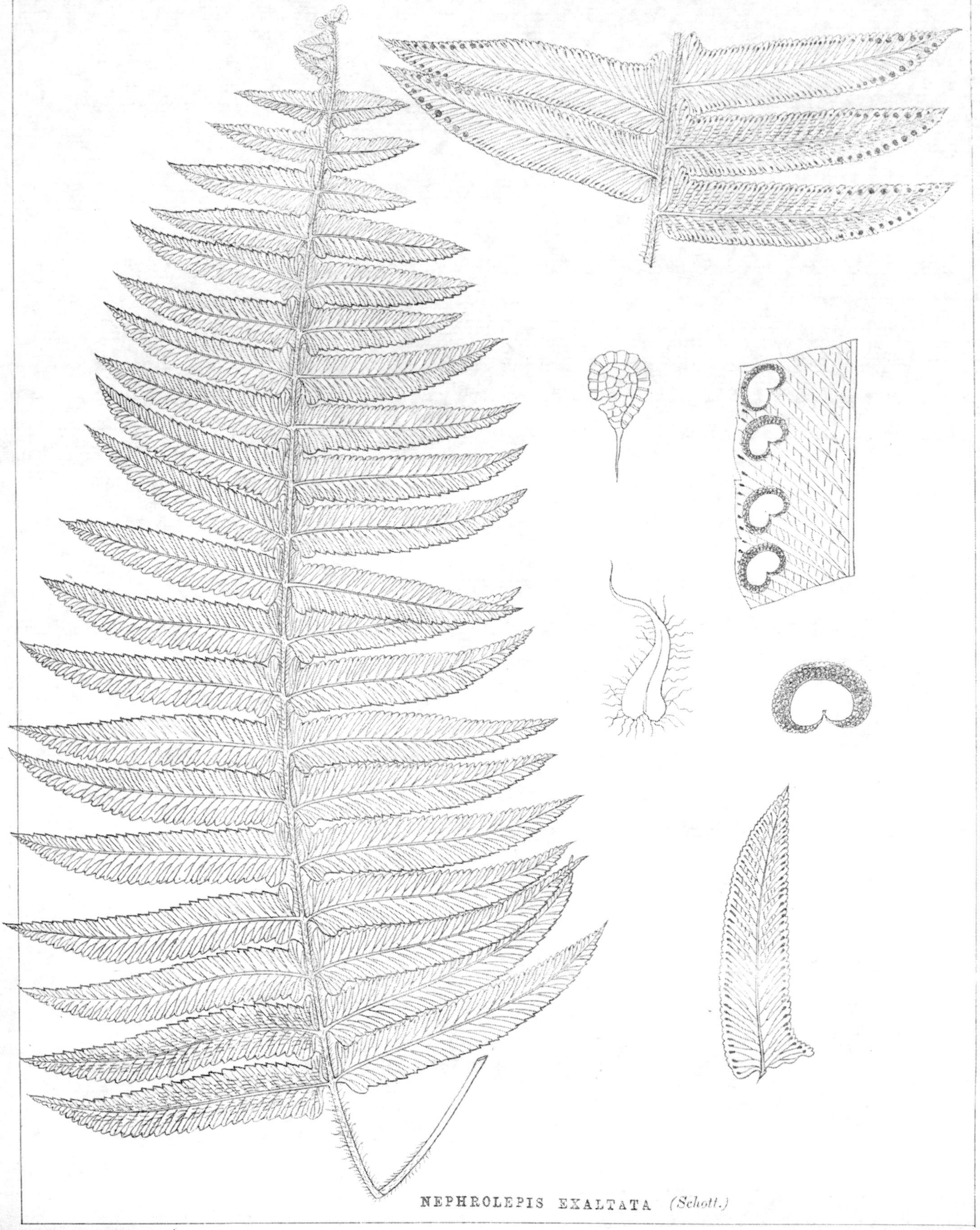

NEPHROLEPIS EXALTATA *(Schott.)*

PUBLISHED BY HIGGINBOTHAM & Co. ORIENTAL LITHOGRAPHIC PRESS, MADRAS 1872 LITHOGRAPHED BY ALEXR BARR[illegible]

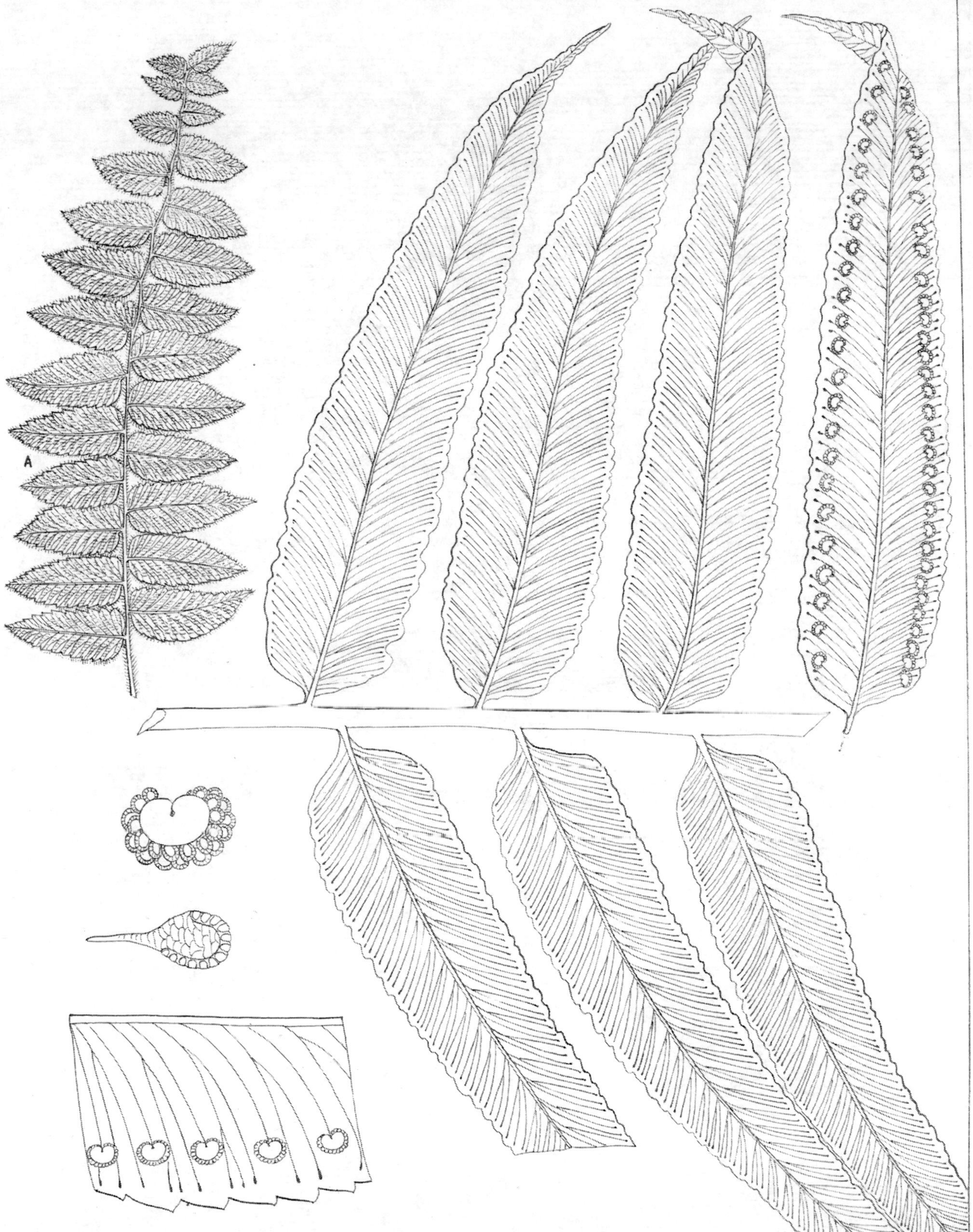

NEPHROLEPIS ACUTA *(Presl.)*

PUBLISHED BY HIGGINBOTHAM & CO. ORIENTAL LITHOGRAPHIC PRESS MADRAS 1872. LITHOGRAPHED BY ALEX: BARREN.

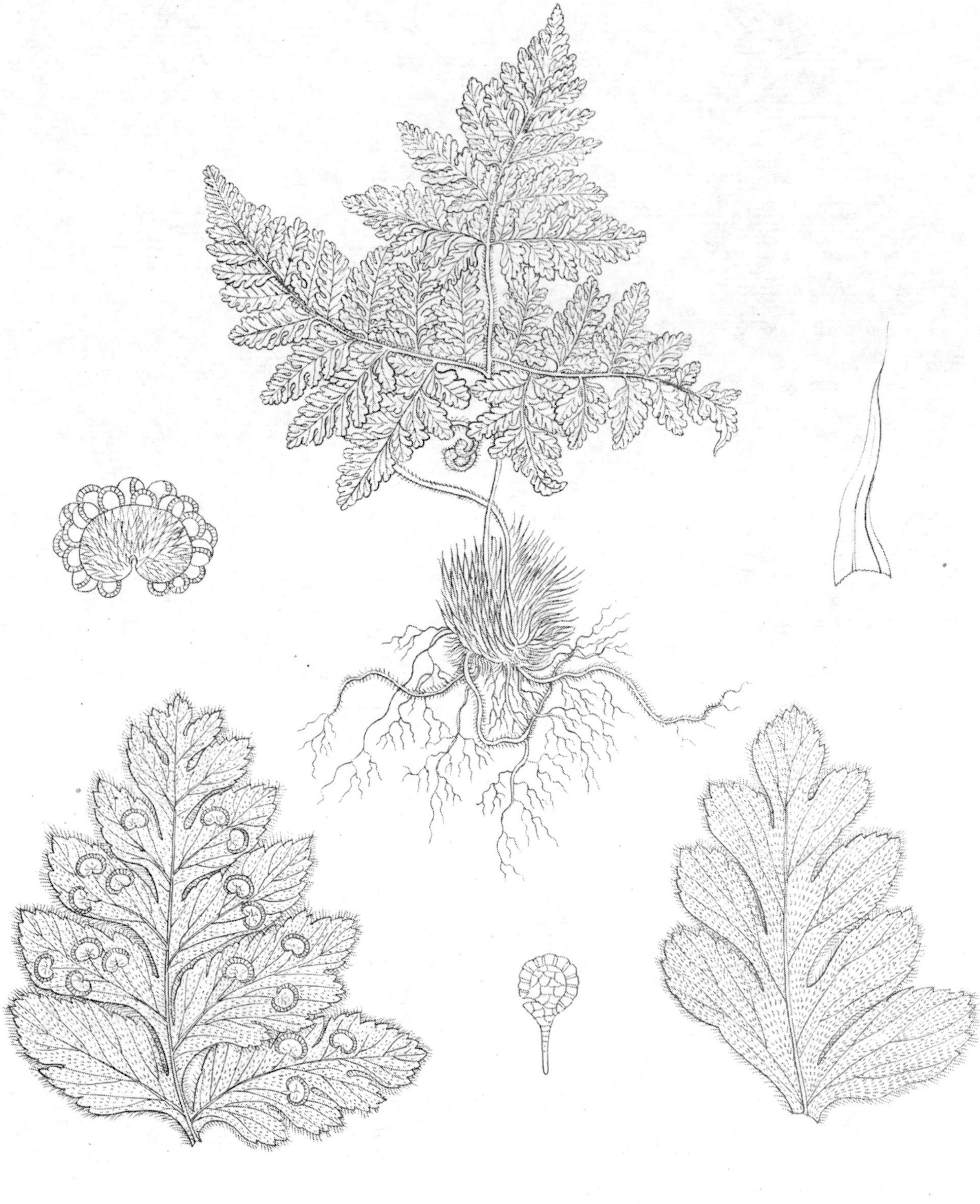

LASTREA ERIOCARPA *(Decaisne.)*

PUBLISHED BY HIGGINBOTHAM & CO.   ORIENTAL LITHOGRAPHIC PRESS MADRAS 1872.   LITHOGRAPHED BY ALEX: BARREN,

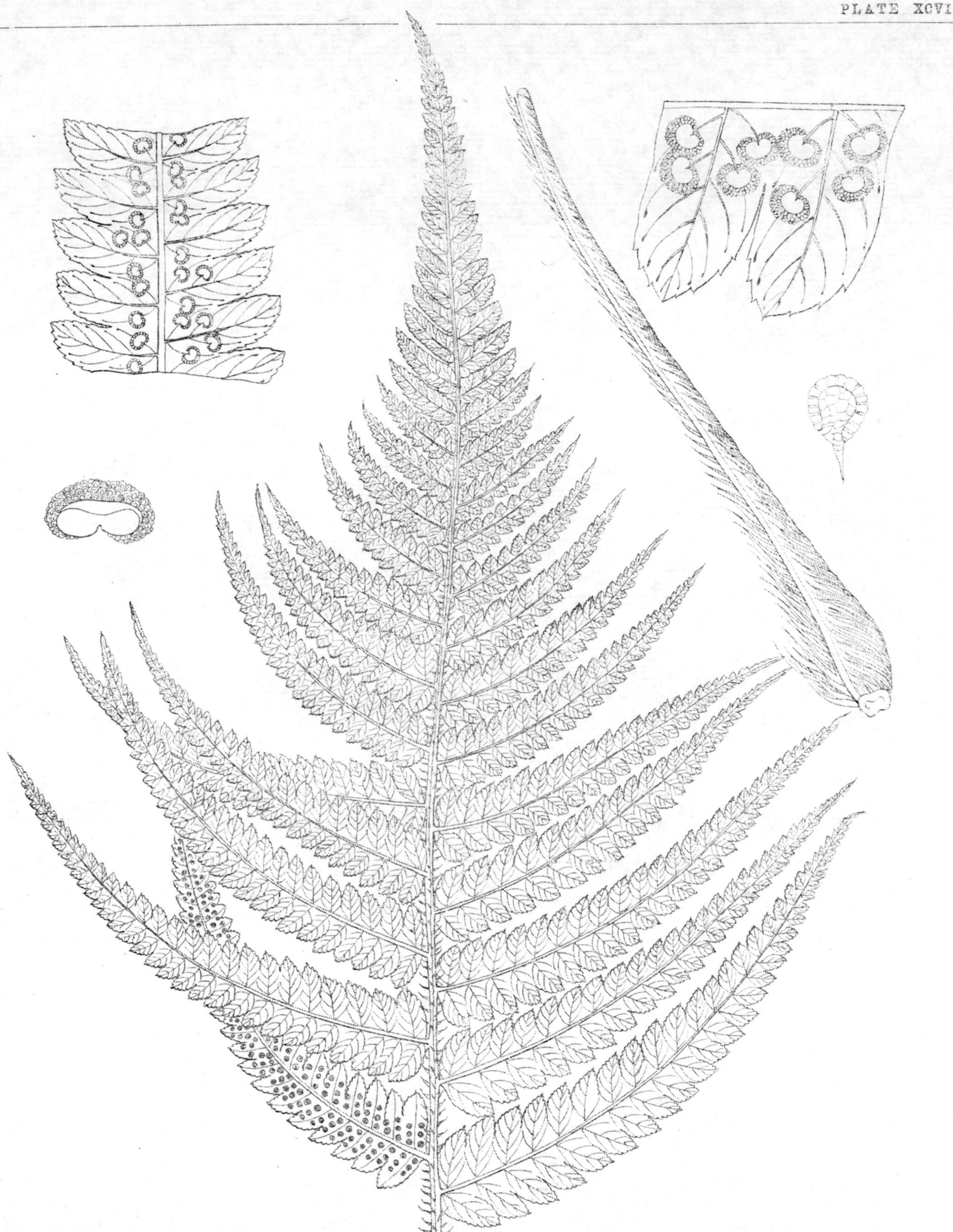

LASTREA HIRTIPES (*Hooker*)

PUBLISHED BY HIGGINBOTHAM & CO. ORIENTAL LITHOGRAPHIC PRESS MADRAS 1872. LITHOGRAPHED BY ALEX: BARREN.

LASTREA DIVISA (*Wallich*)

PUBLISHED BY HIGGINBOTHAM & CO. ORIENTAL LITHOGRAPHIC PRESS MADRAS 1872. LITHOGRAPHED BY ALEX: BARREN.

LASTREA RECEDENS (*J. Sm.*)

PUBLISHED BY HIGGINBOTHAM & CO. ORIENTAL LITHOGRAPHIC PRESS MADRAS 1872. LITHOGRAPHED BY ALEX: BARREN.

PLATE XCIX

LASTREA FLACCIDA *(Hooker.)*

PUBLISHED BY HIGGINBOTHAM & CO. ORIENTAL LITHOGRAPHIC PRESS MADRAS 1872. LITHOGRAPHED BY ALEX: BARREN.

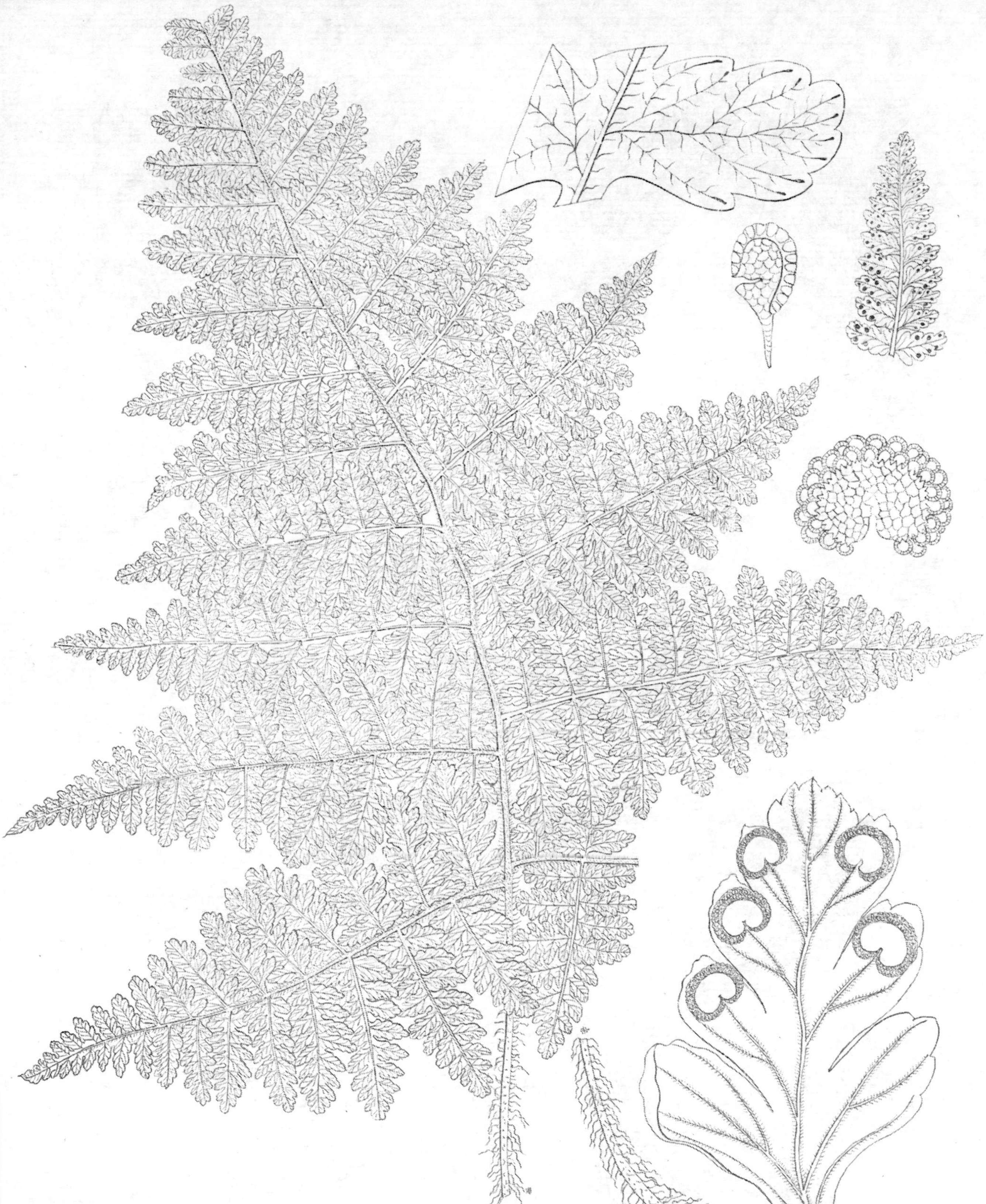

LASTREA FERRUGINEA (*Bedd.*)

PUBLISHED BY HIGGINBOTHAM & CO. ORIENTAL LITHOGRAPHIC PRESS MADRAS 1872. LITHOGRAPHED BY ALEX: BARREN.

LASTREA ARISTATA (*Moore.*)

PUBLISHED BY HIGGINBOTHAM & Co. ORIENTAL LITHOGRAPHIC PRESS MADRAS 1872 LITHOGRAPHED BY ALEXR. BARREN.

LASTREA MEMBRANIFOLIA *(Presl.)*

PUBLISHED BY HIGGINBOTHAM & CO   ORIENTAL LITHOGRAPHIC PRESS MADRAS 187?   LITHOGRAPHED BY ALEX: BARREN,

LASTREA SPARSA *(Moore.)*

PUBLISHED BY HIGGINBOTHAM & CO. ORIENTAL LITHOGRAPHIC PRESS MADRAS 1872. LITHOGRAPHED BY ALEX. BARREN.

LASTREA DEPARIOIDES *(Hooker.)*

PUBLISHED BY HIGGINBOTHAM & CO. ORIENTAL LITHOGRAPHIC PRESS MADRAS 1872 LITHOGRAPHED BY ALEX: BARREN.

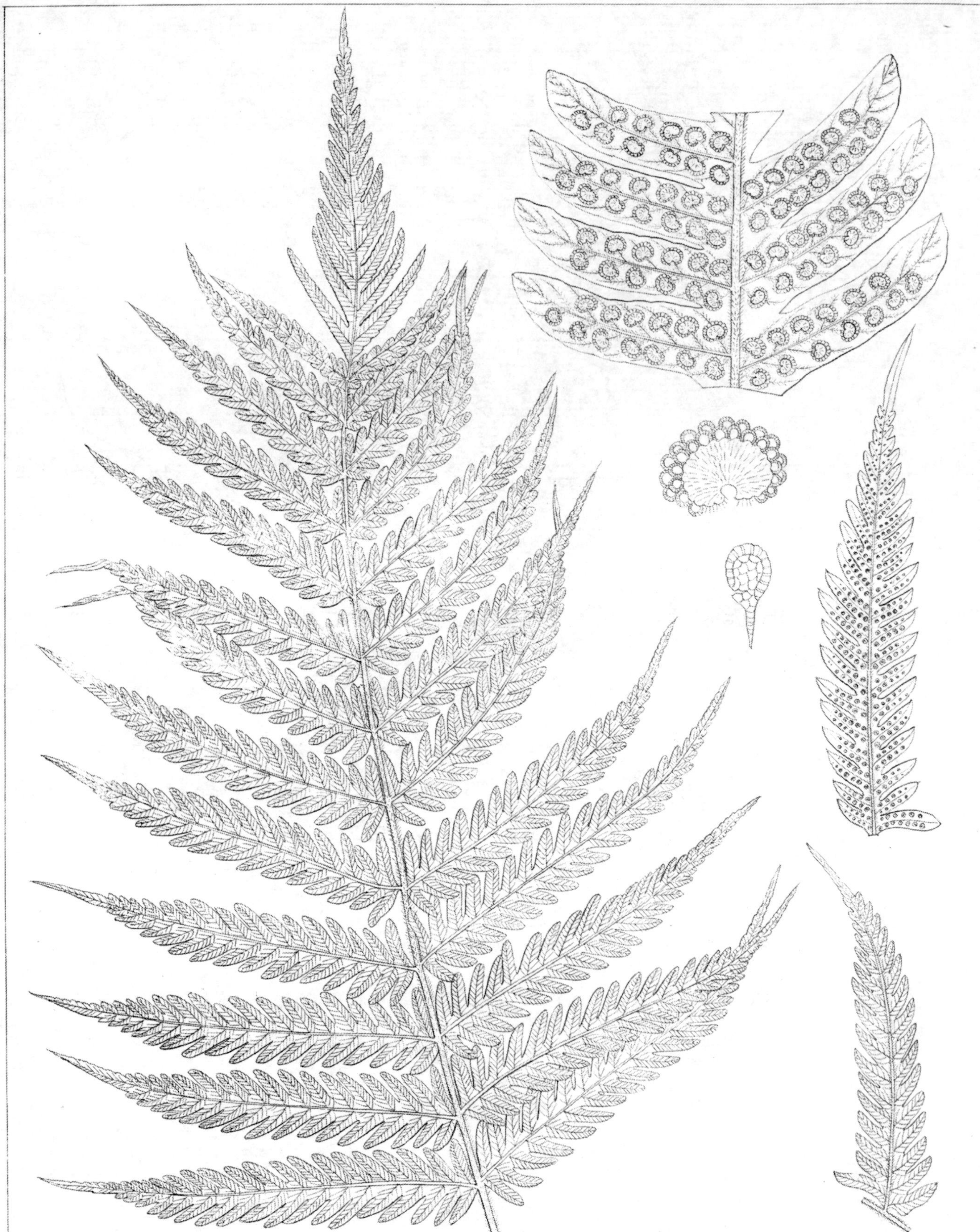

LASTREA FALCILOBA (Hooker.)

PUBLISHED BY HIGGINBOTHAM & CO. ORIENTAL LITHOGRAPHIC PRESS MADRAS 1872. LITHOGRAPHED BY ALEX: BARREN,

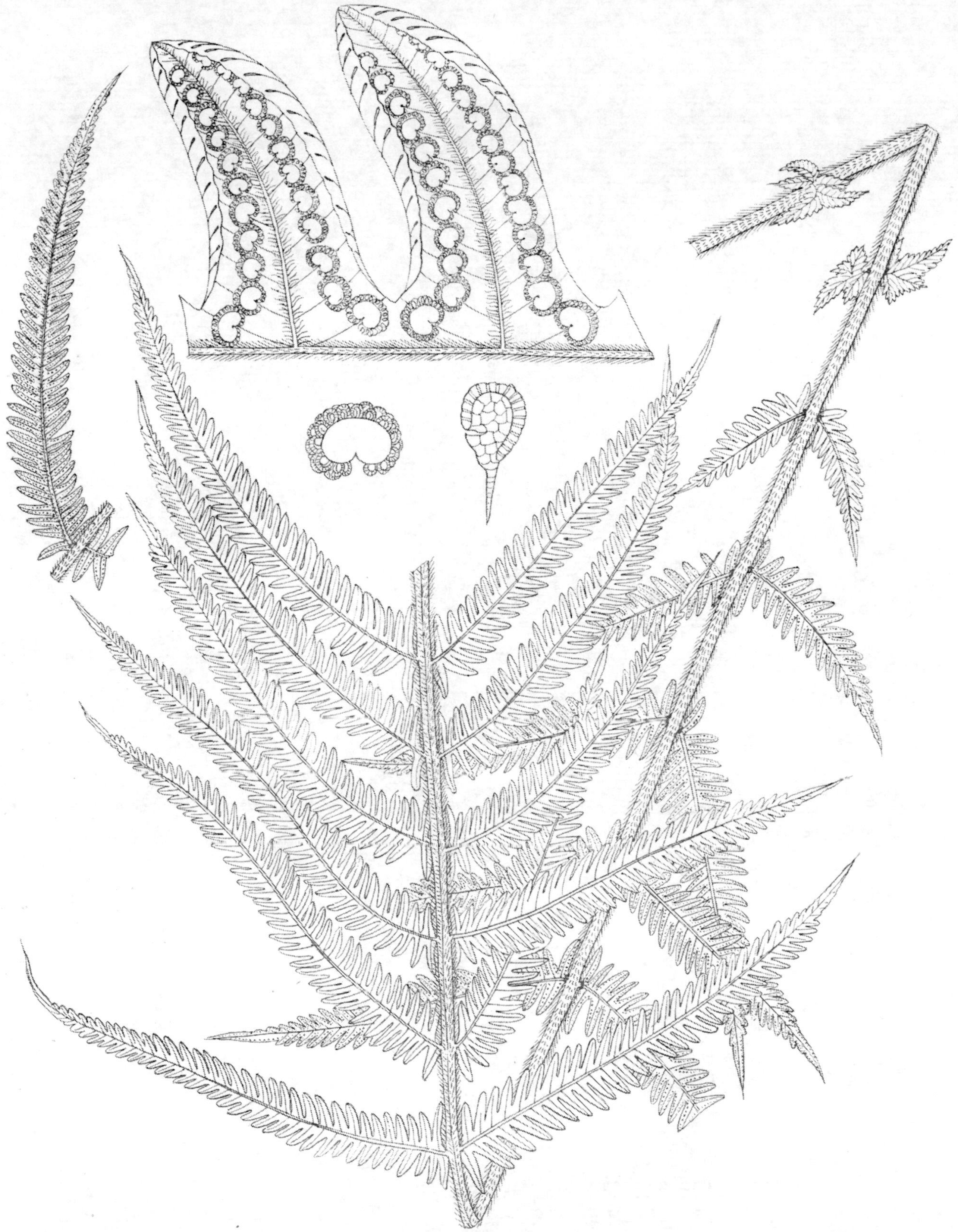

LASTREA OCHTHODES *(Kunze.)*

PUBLISHED BY HIGGINBOTHAM & CO. ORIENTAL LITHOGRAPHIC PRESS MADRAS 1872 LITHOGRAPHED BY ALEXR BARREN.

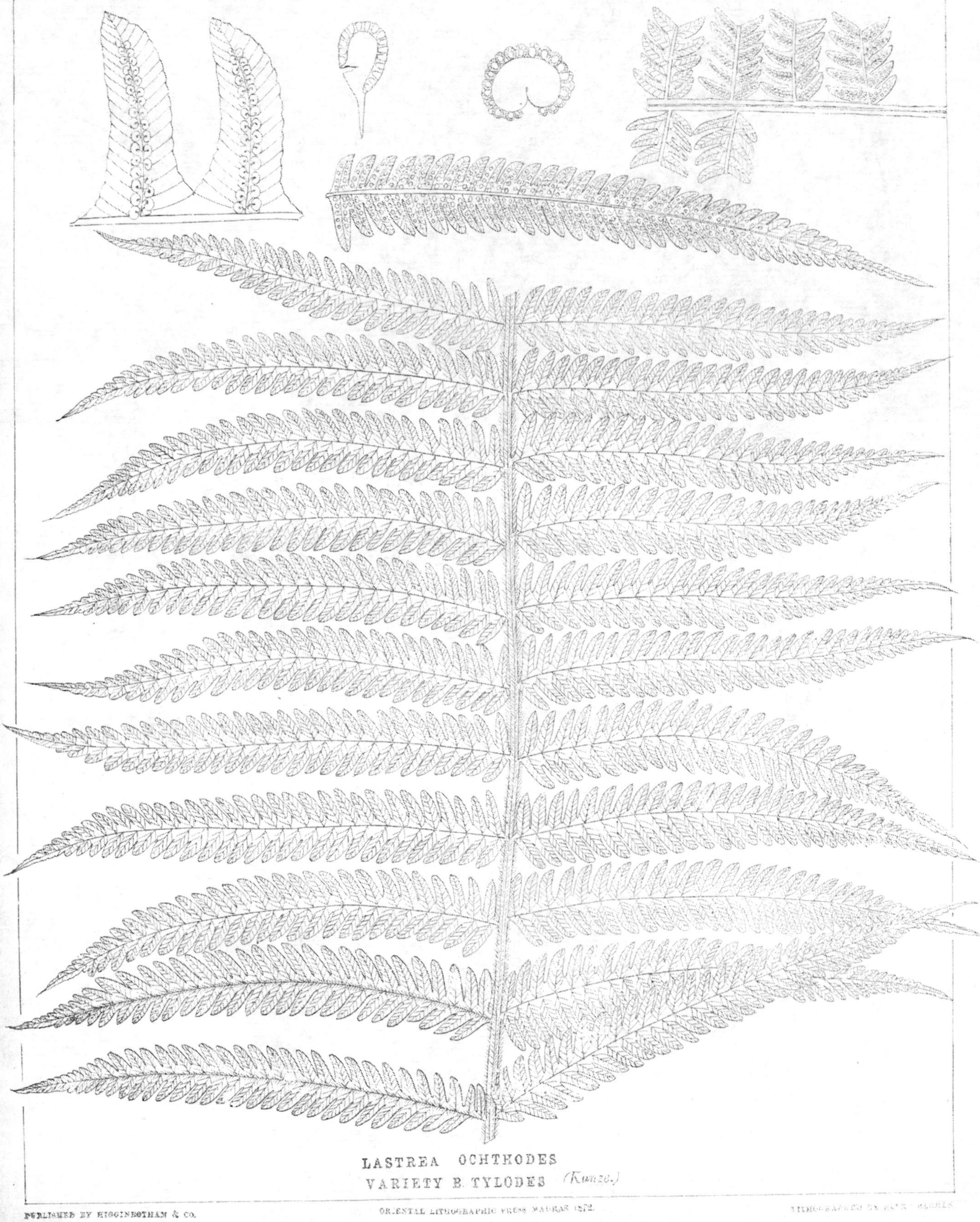

LASTREA OCHTHODES
VARIETY B. TYLODES *(Kunze.)*

PUBLISHED BY HIGGINBOTHAM & CO.   ORIENTAL LITHOGRAPHIC PRESS MADRAS 1872.

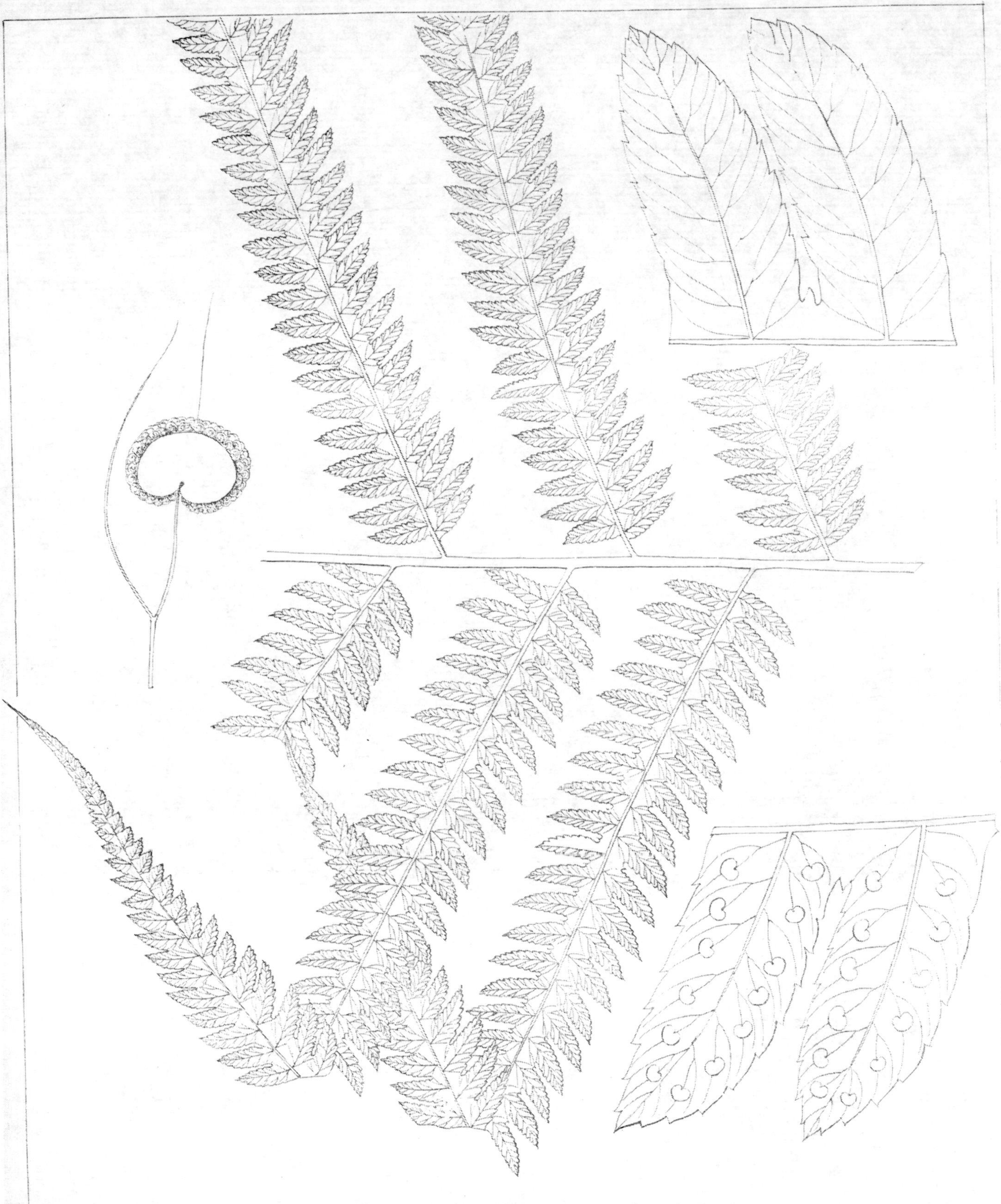

LASTREA SPECTABILIS (*J. Smith.*)

LITHOGRAPHED BY ALEX. BARREN.

PLATE CIX

LASTREA AMABILIS Moore

PUBLISHED BY HIGGINBOTHAM & CO   ORIENTAL LITHOGRAPHIC PRESS MADRAS 1872   LITHOGRAPHED BY ALEX. BAKER

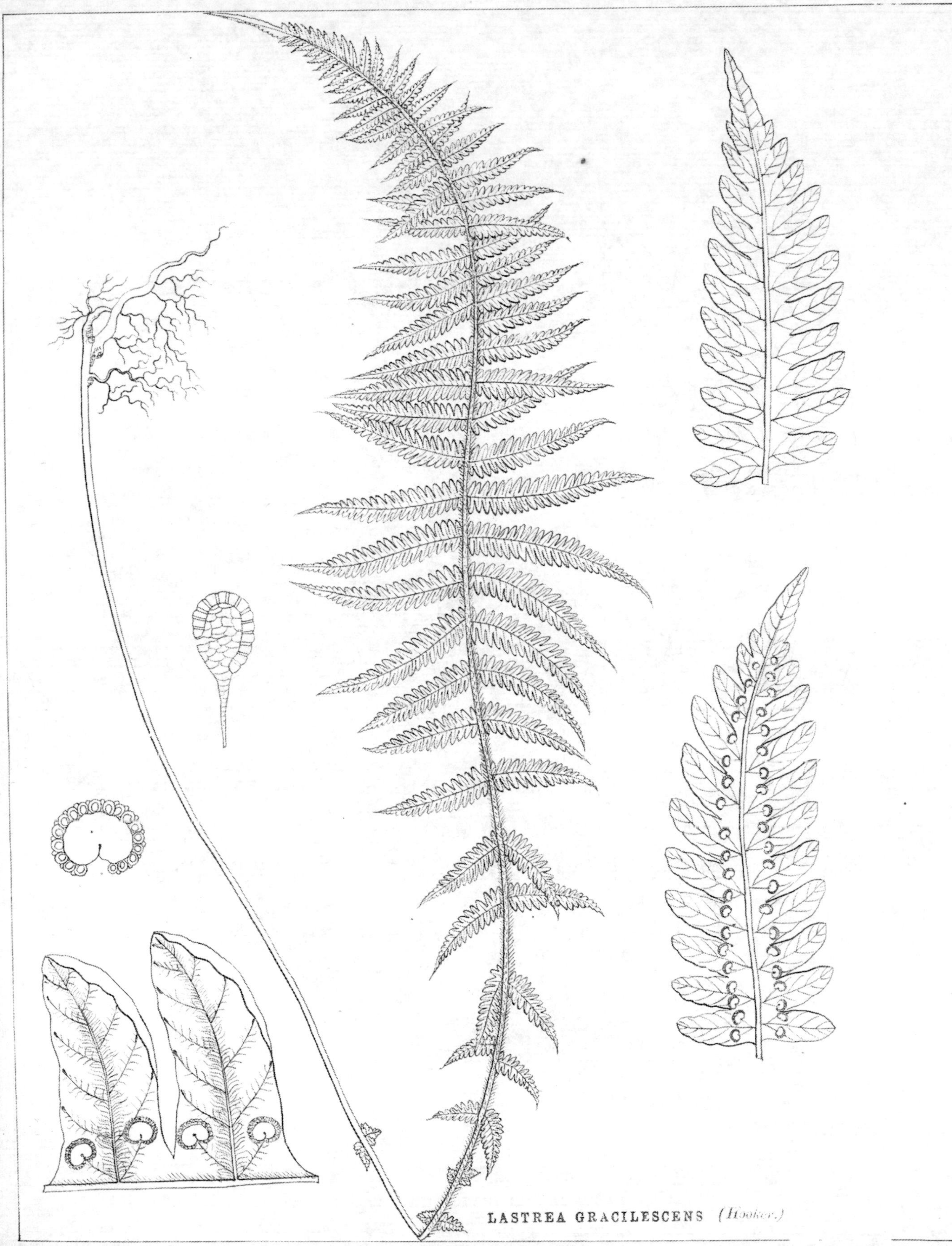

LASTREA GRACILESCENS *(Hooker.)*

PUBLISHED BY HIGGINBOTHAM & CO. ORIENTAL LITHOGRAPHIC PRESS MADRAS 1879. LEX: BARREN,

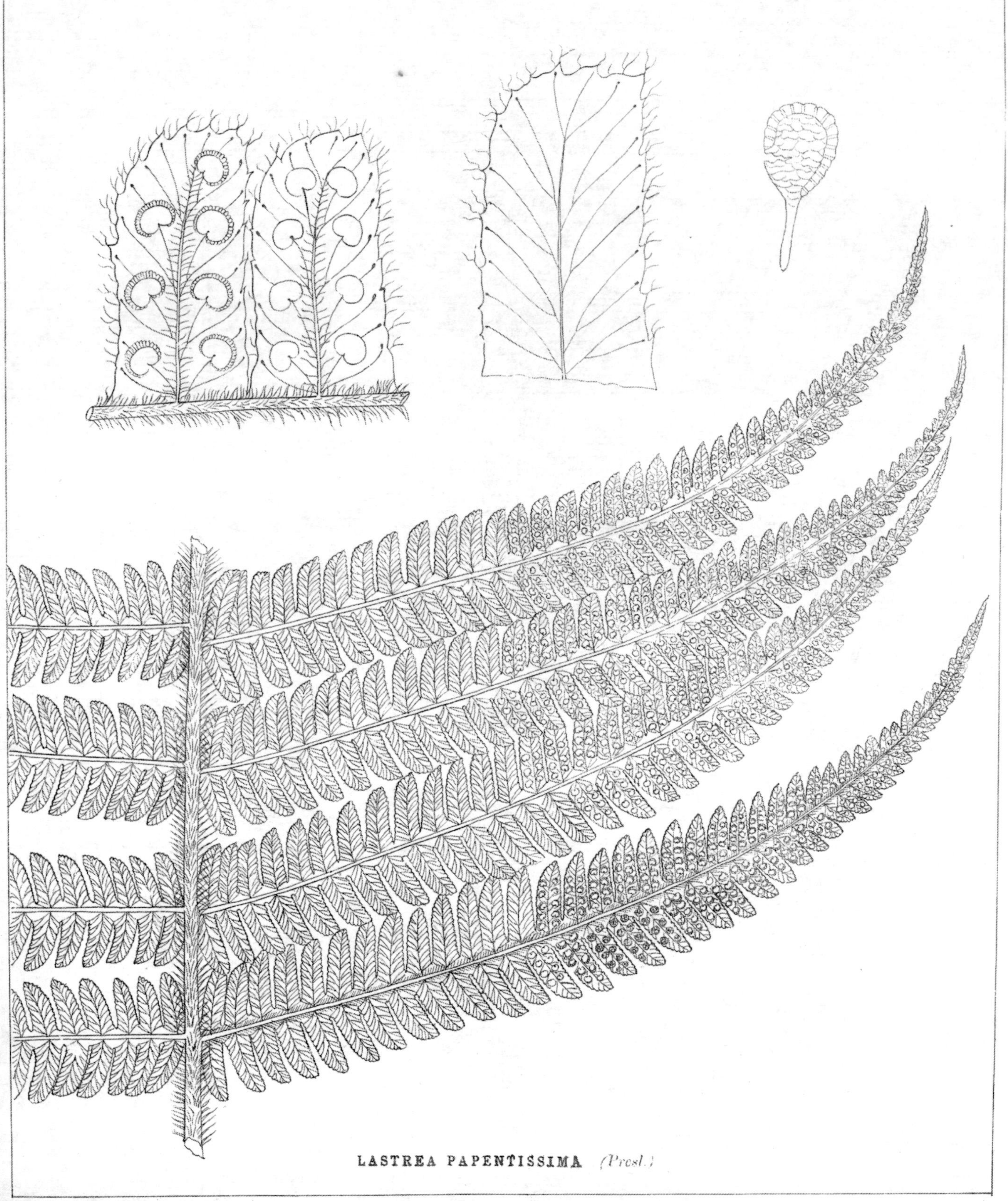

LASTREA PAPENTISSIMA *(Presl.)*

PUBLISHED BY HIGGINBOTHAM & CO. ORIENTAL LITHOGRAPHIC PRESS MADRAS 1872 LITHOGRAPHED BY ALEX. BARREN.

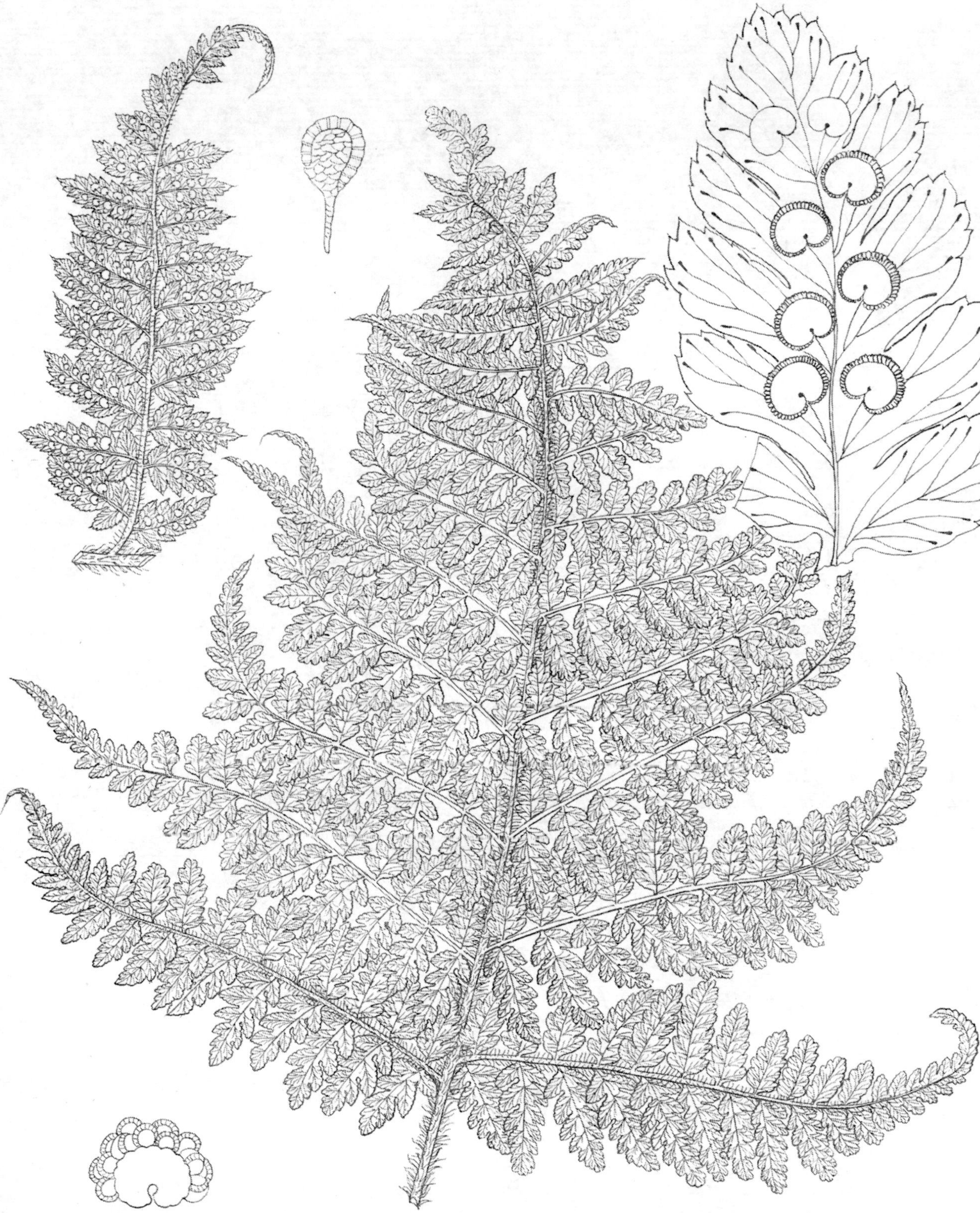

LASTREA ELONGATA *(Swartz.)*

PUBLISHED BY HIGGINBOTHAM & CO. ORIENTAL LITHOGRAPHIC PRESS MADRAS 1872. LITHOGRAPHED BY ALEX. BARREN.

LASTREA INTERMEDIA (Bedd.)

PUBLISHED BY HIGGINBOTHAM & Co. ORIENTAL LITHOGRAPHIC PRESS MADRAS 1872. LITHOGRAPHED BY ALEX. BARREN.

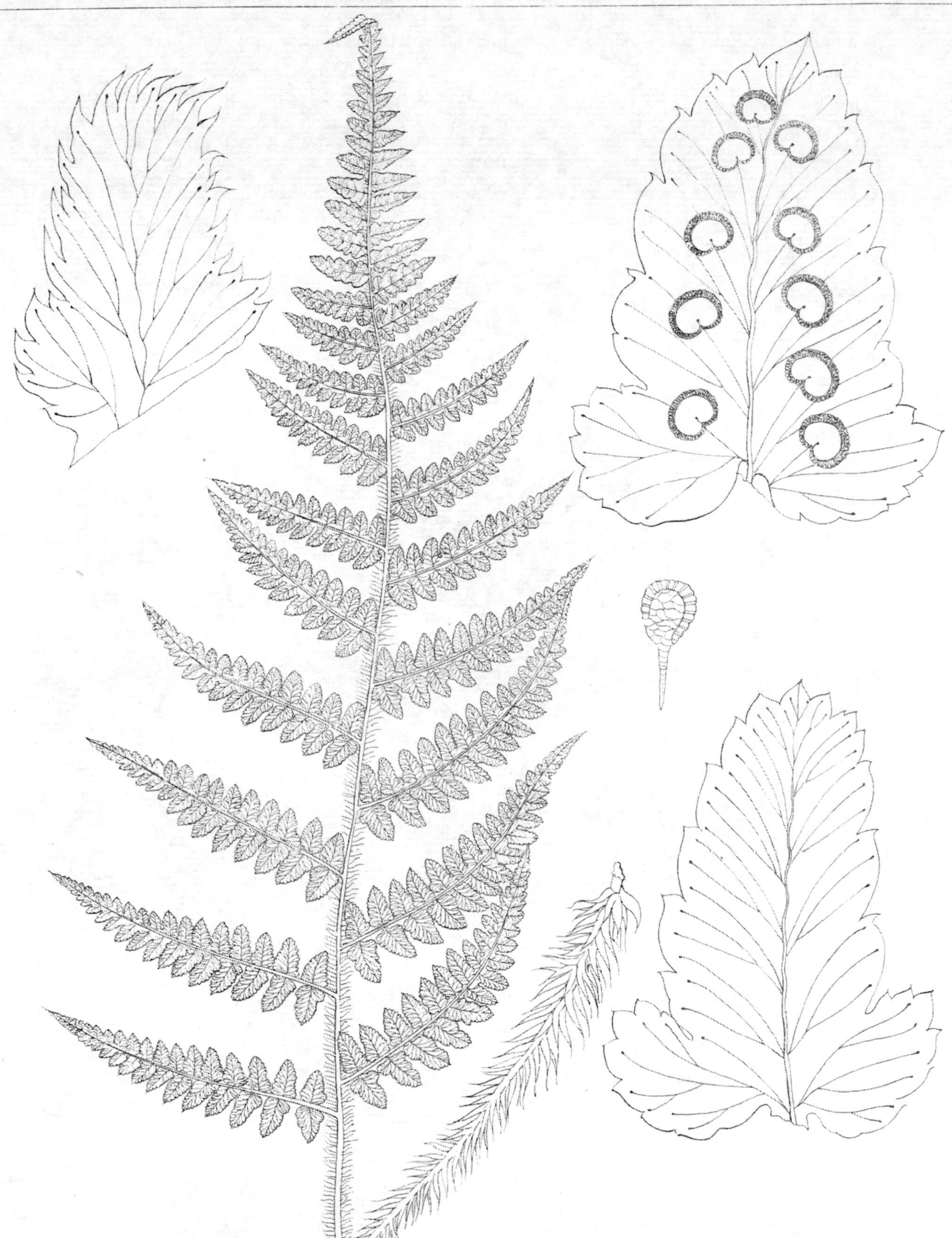

LASTREA ODONTOLOMA (Moore.)

PUBLISHED BY HIGGINBOTHAM & CO. ORIENTAL LITHOGRAPHIC PRESS MADRAS 1872. LITHOGRAPHED BY ALEX. BARKER

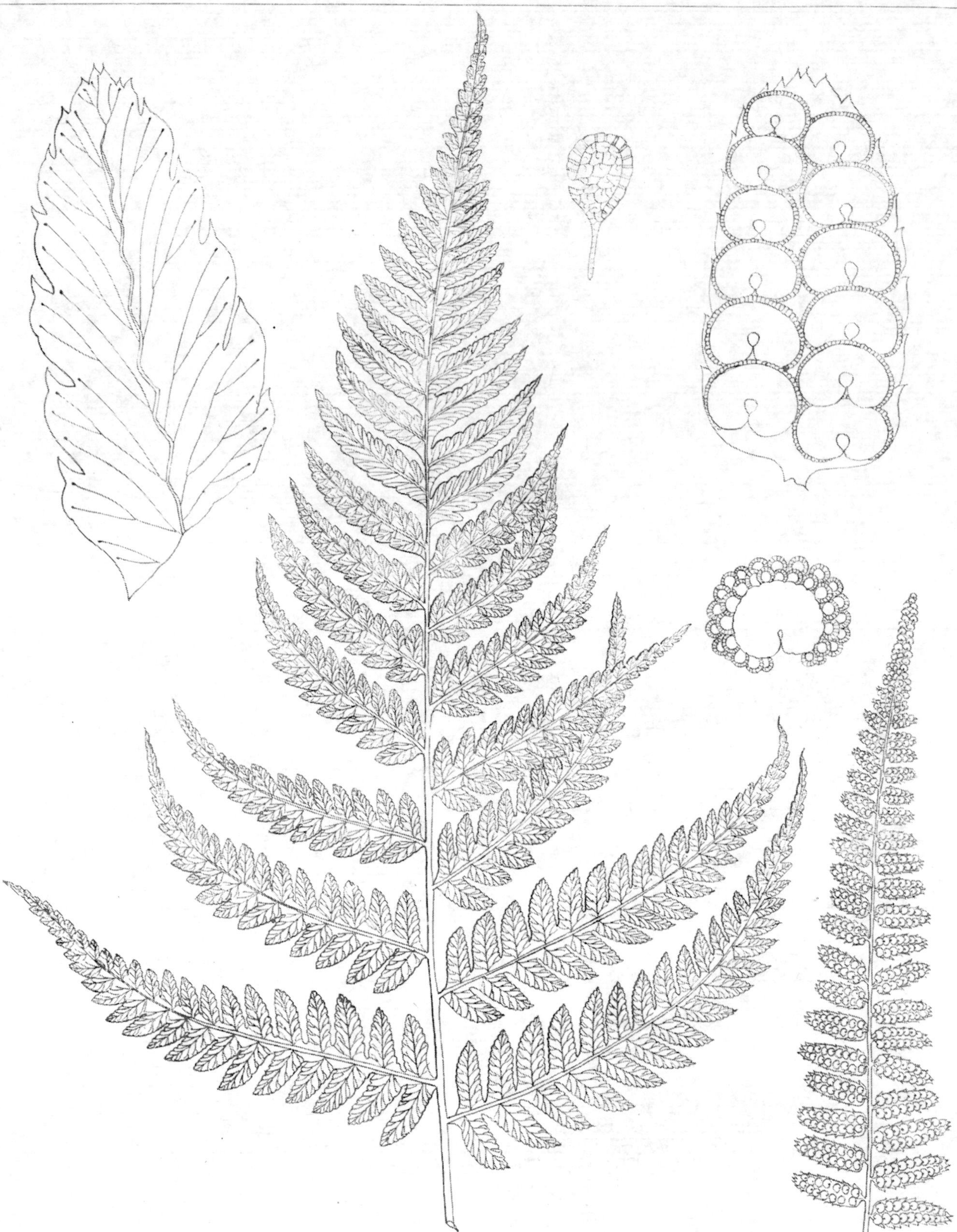

LASTREA COCKLEATA (Moore)

PUBLISHED BY HIGGINBOTHAM & CO. ORIENTAL LITHOGRAPHIC PRESS MADRAS 1872 LITHOGRAPHED BY ALEX: BARREN.

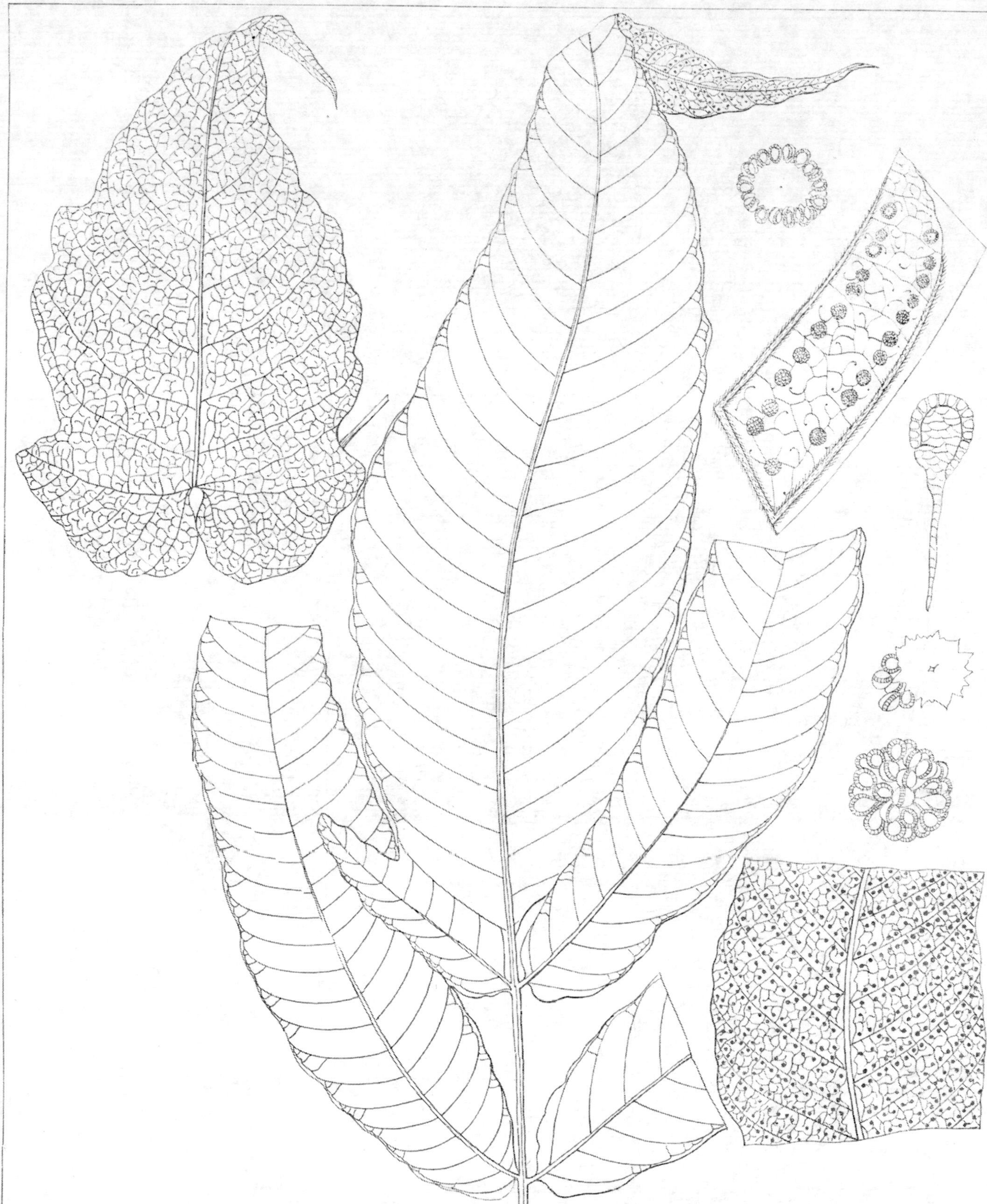

ASPIDIUM POLYMORPHUM (*Wallich*)

PUBLISHED BY HIGGINBOTHAM & CO.   ORIENTAL LITHOGRAPHIC PRESS MADRAS 1872.   LITHOGRAPHED BY ALEX: BARREN.

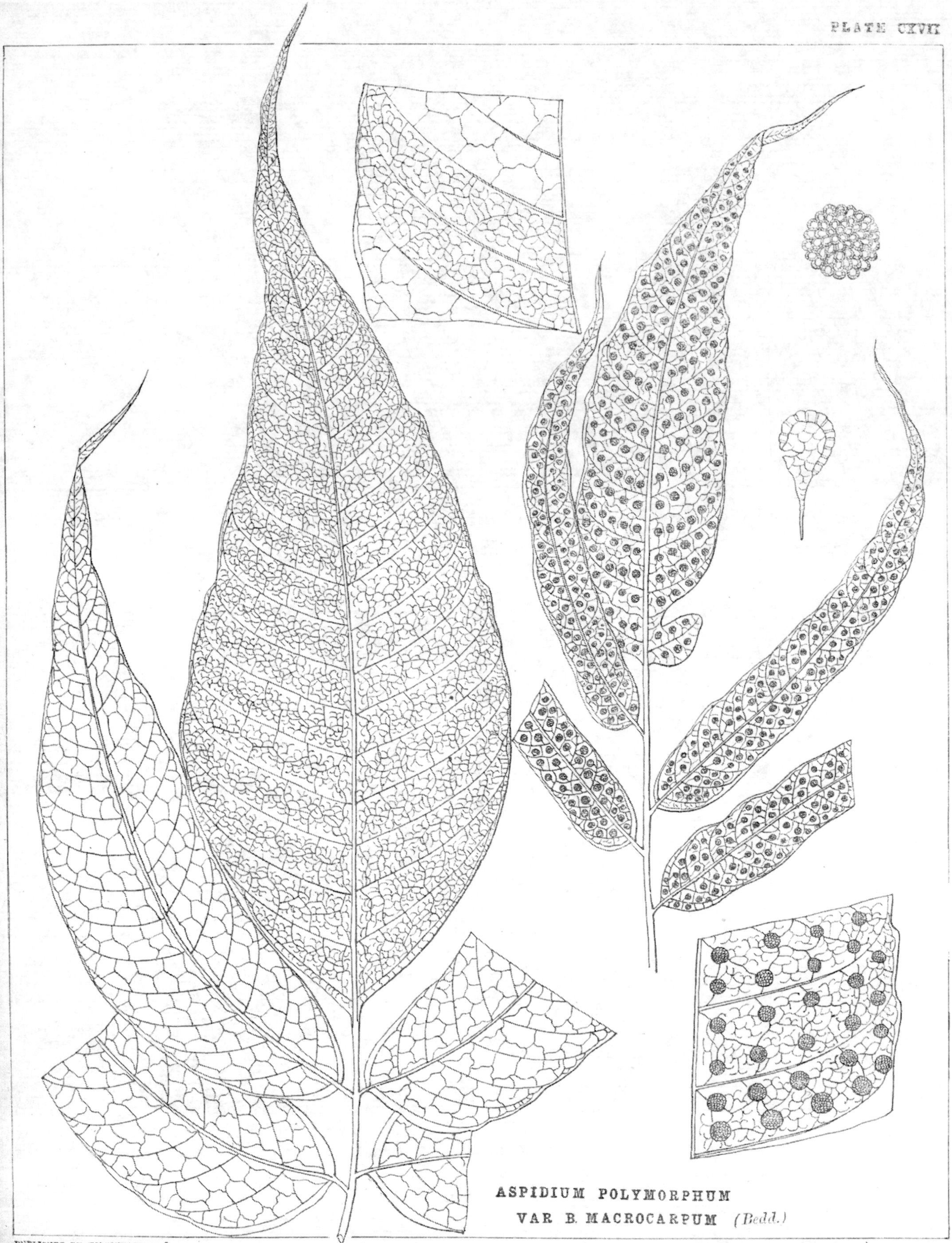

ASPIDIUM POLYMORPHUM
VAR B. MACROCARPUM (Bedd.)

PUBLISHED BY HIGGINBOTHAM & CO. ORIENTAL LITHOGRAPHIC PRESS MADRAS 1872. LITHOGRAPHED BY ALEX: BARREN,

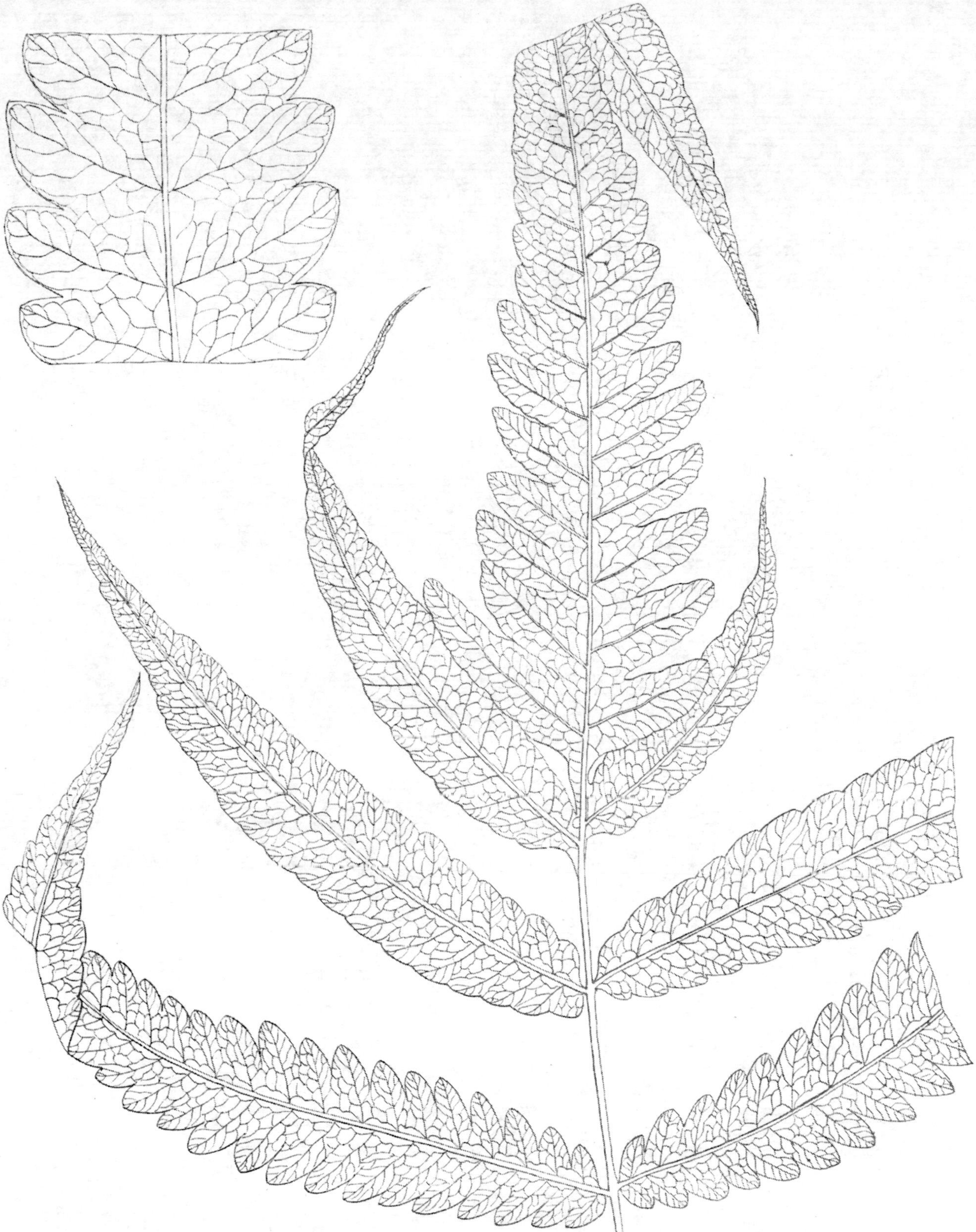

ASPIDIUM ?

PUBLISHED BY HIGGINBOTHAM & Co. ORIENTAL LITHOGRAPHIC PRESS MADRAS 1872. LITHOGRAPHED BY ALEX : BARREN.

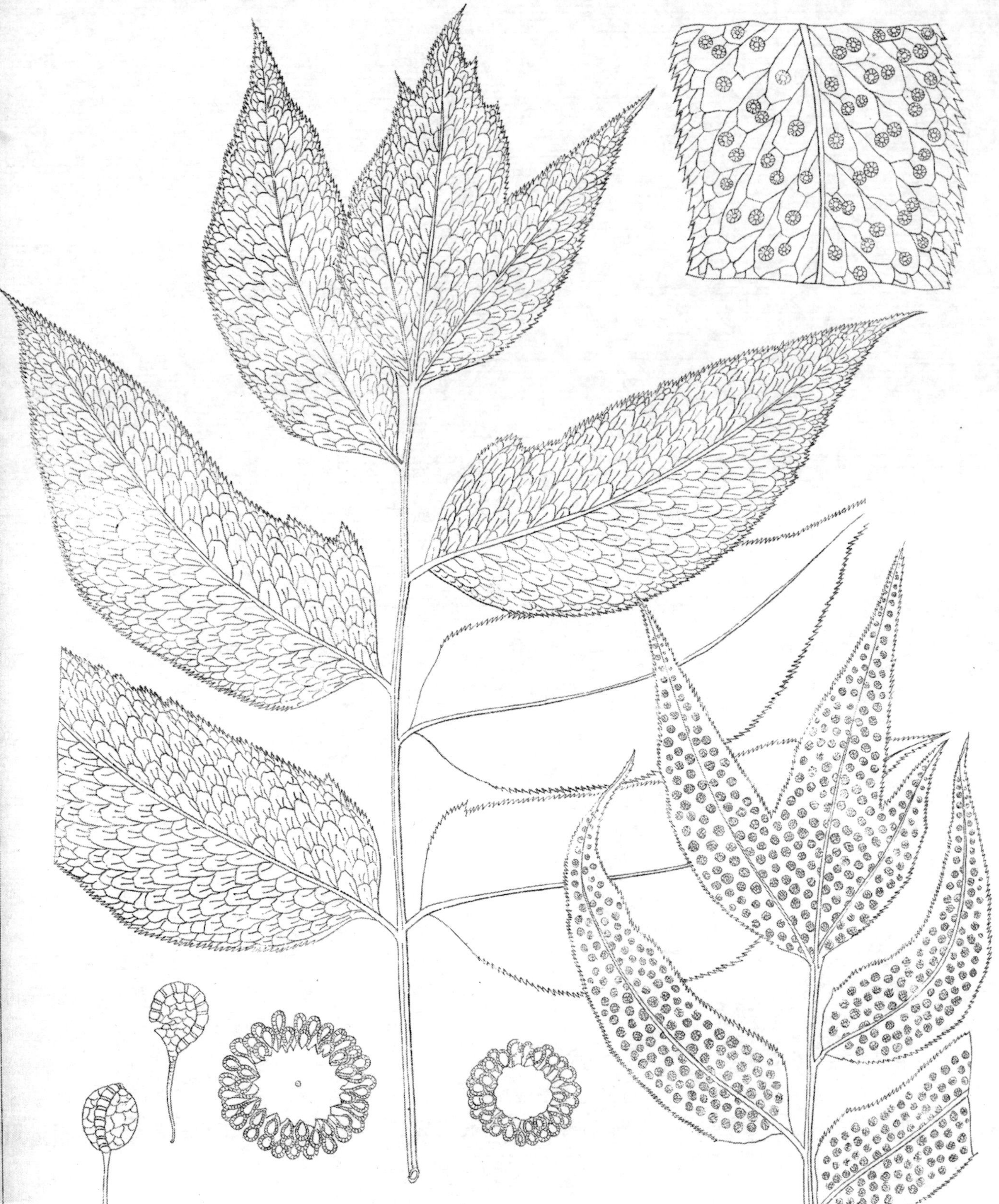

CYRTOMIUM CARYOTIDEUM (Presl.)

PUBLISHED BY HIGGINBOTHAM & CO. ORIENTAL LITHOGRAPHIC PRESS MADRAS 1872 LITHOGRAPHED BY ALEX. BARREN.

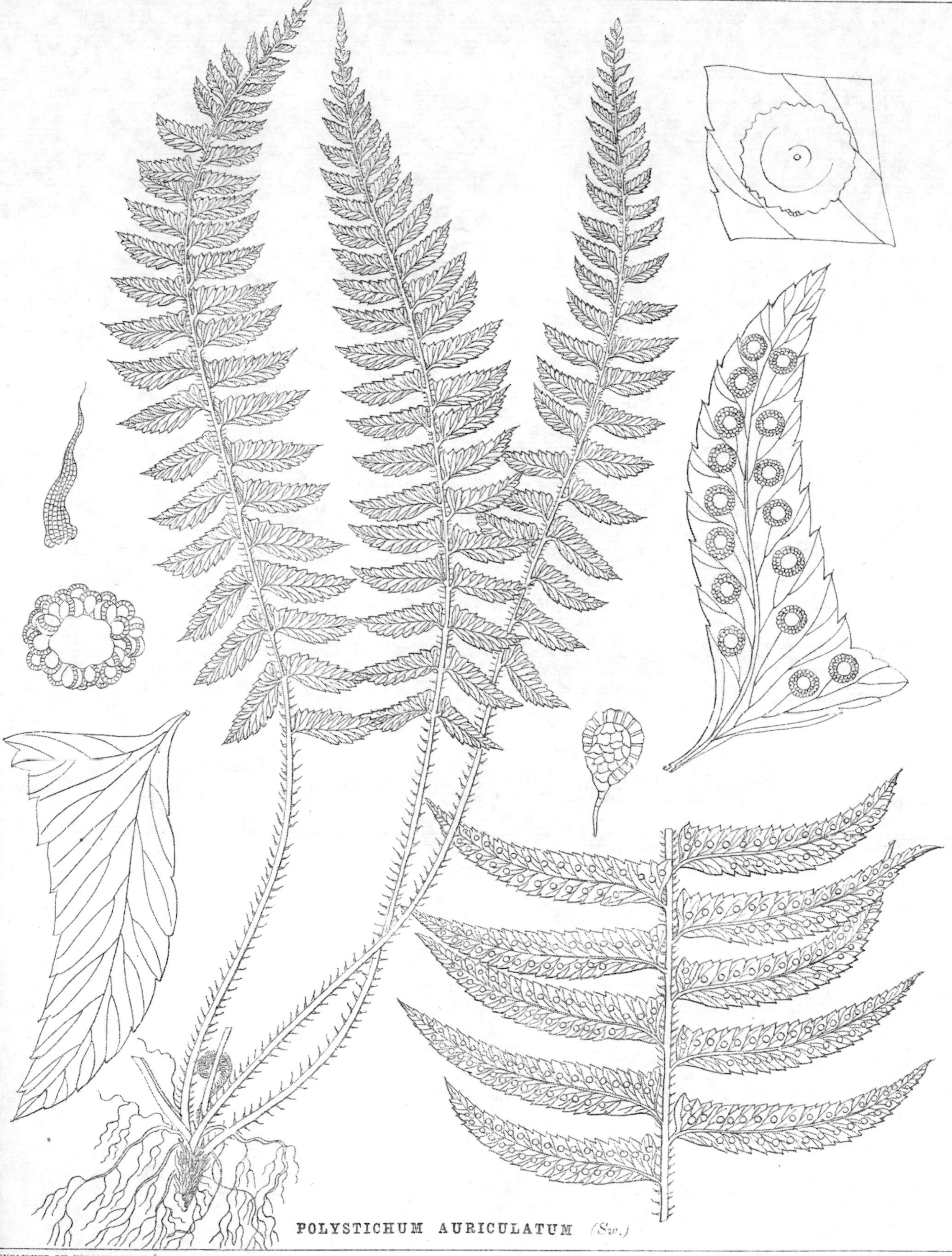

POLYSTICHUM AURICULATUM (Sw.)

PUBLISHED BY HIGGINBOTHAM & CO. ORIENTAL LITHOGRAPHIC PRESS MADRAS 1872. LITHOGRAPHED BY ALEX: BARREN.

POLYSTICHUM ACULEATUM (*Swartz.*)

PUBLISHED BY HIGGINBOTHAM & CO. ORIENTAL LITHOGRAPHIC PRESS MADRAS 1872 LITHOGRAPHED BY ALEX' BARREN.

POLYSTICHUM ANGULARE *(Presl.)*

PUBLISHED BY HIGGINBOTHAM & CO ORIENTAL LITHOGRAPHIC PRESS MADRAS 1872 LITHOGRAPHED BY ALEX. BARREN.

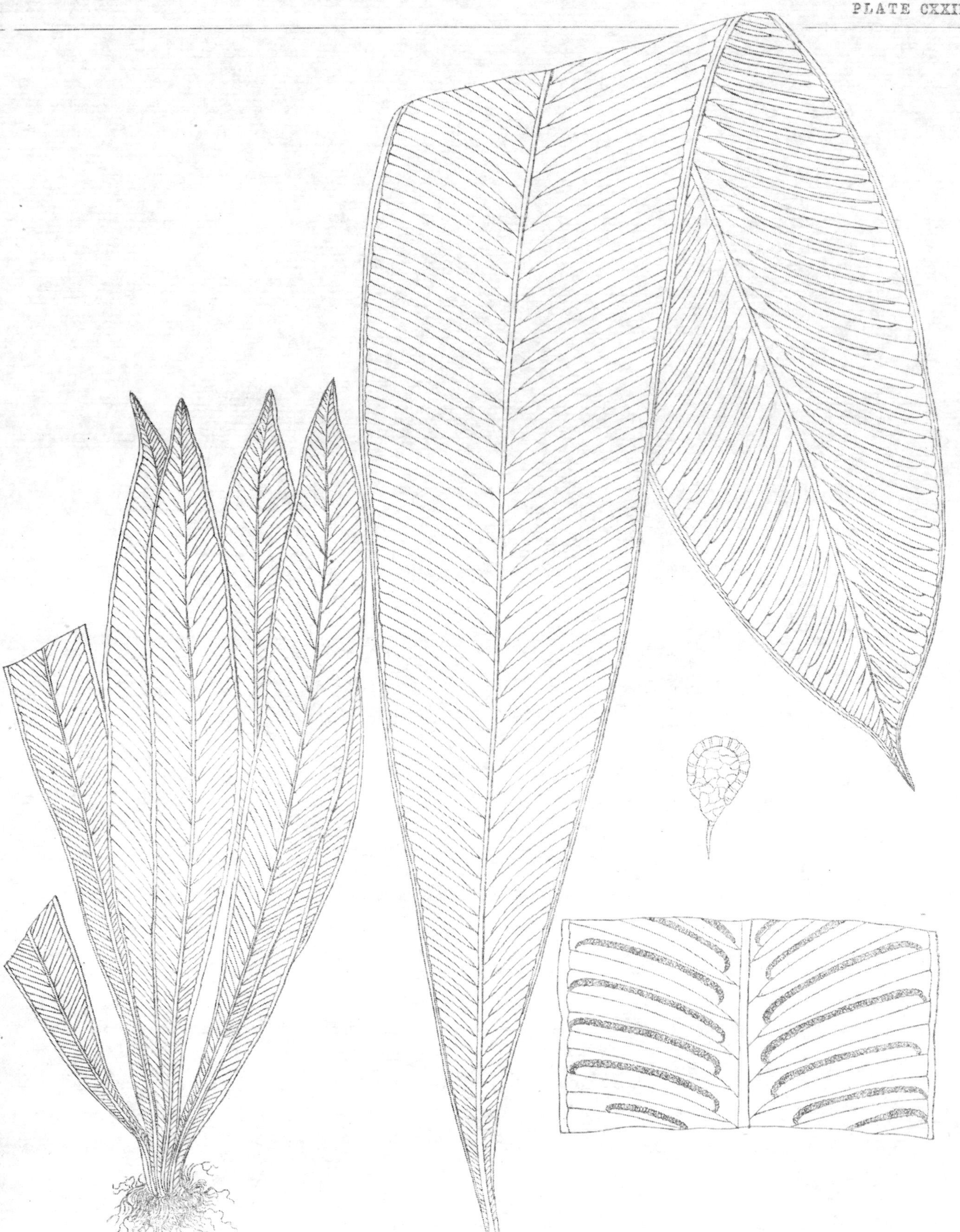

THAMNOPTERIS PHYLLITIDIS *(Don.)*

PUBLISHED BY HIGGINBOTHAM & Co. ORIENTAL LITHOGRAPHIC PRESS MADRAS 1872. LITHOGRAPHED BY ALEX: BAREEN.

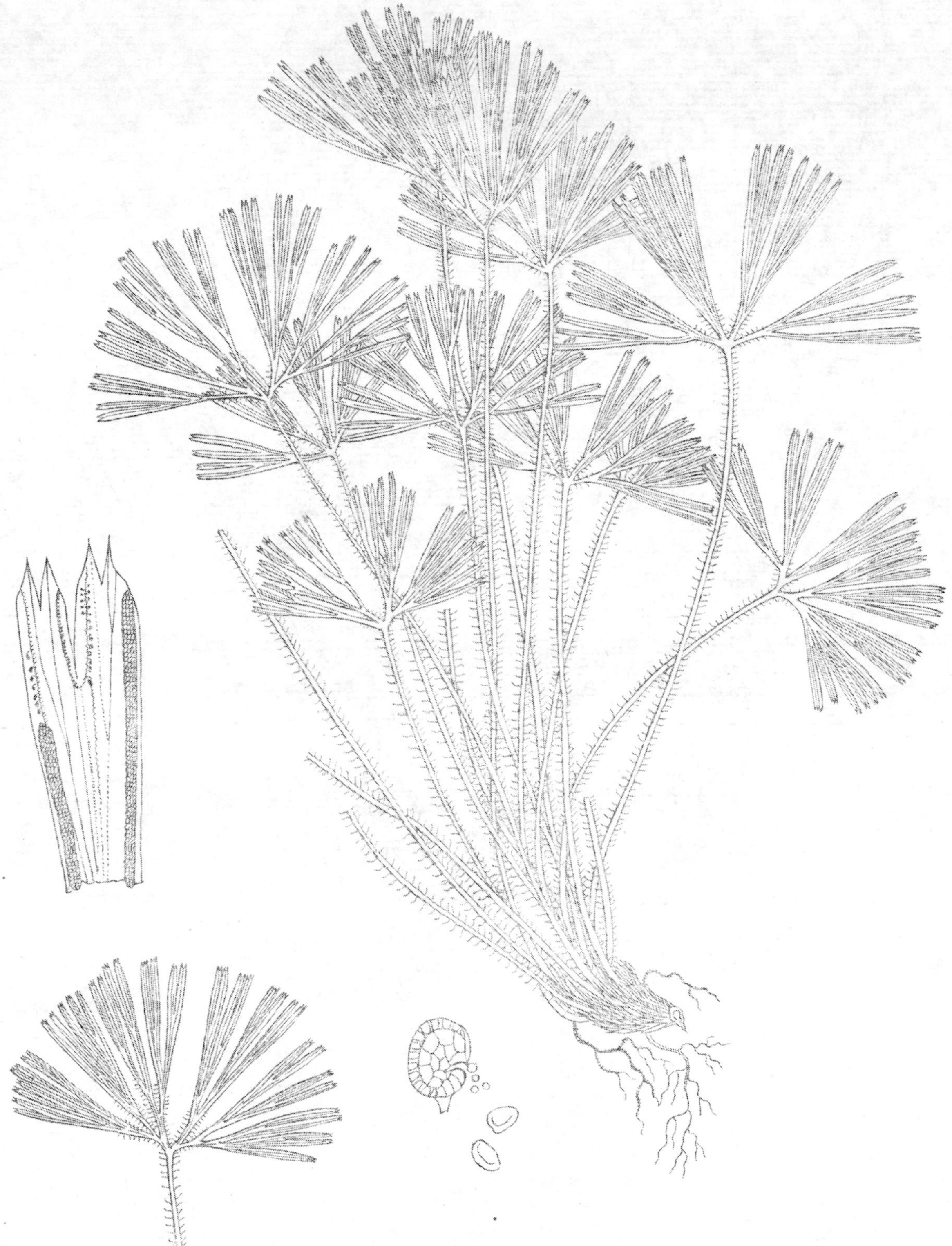

ACTINIOPTERIS RADIATA (*Link.*)

PUBLISHED BY HIGGINBOTHAM & CO. ORIENTAL LITHOGRAPHIC PRESS MADRAS 1872. LITHOGRAPHED BY ALEX: BARREN,

ASPLENIUM ENSIFORME (*Wallich.*)

PUBLISHED BY HIGGINBOTHAM & CO. ORIENTAL LITHOGRAPHIC PRESS MADRAS 1872 LITHOGRAPHED BY ALEX: BARREN.

ASPLENIUM WIGHTIANUM (*Wallich.*)

PUBLISHED BY HIGGINBOTHAM & CO   ORIENTAL LITHOGRAPHIC PRESS MADRAS 1872.   LITHOGRAPHED BY ALEX: BARREN,

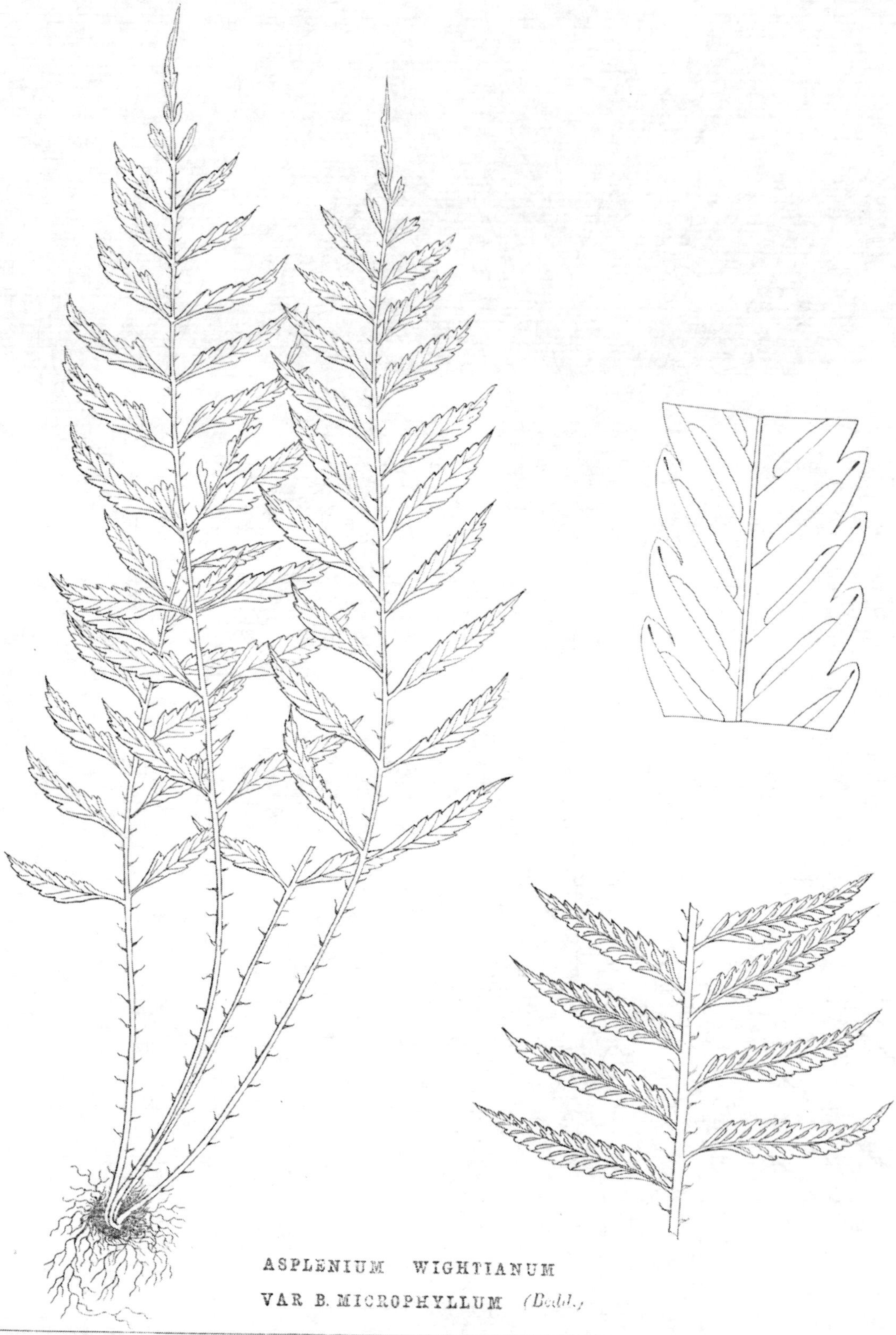

ASPLENIUM WIGHTIANUM

VAR B. MICROPHYLLUM (Bedd.)

PUBLISHED BY HIGGINBOTHAM & CO. ORIENTAL LITHOGRAPHIC PRESS MADRAS 1872 LITHOGRAPHED BY ALEX; BARREN,

PLATE CXXVIII

ASPLENIUM PERSICIFOLIUM (J. Smith)

PUBLISHED BY HIGGINBOTHAM & CO. ... ORIENTAL LITHO. ... MADRAS 1872 LITHOGRAPHED BY ... BARKER.

PLATE CXXIX

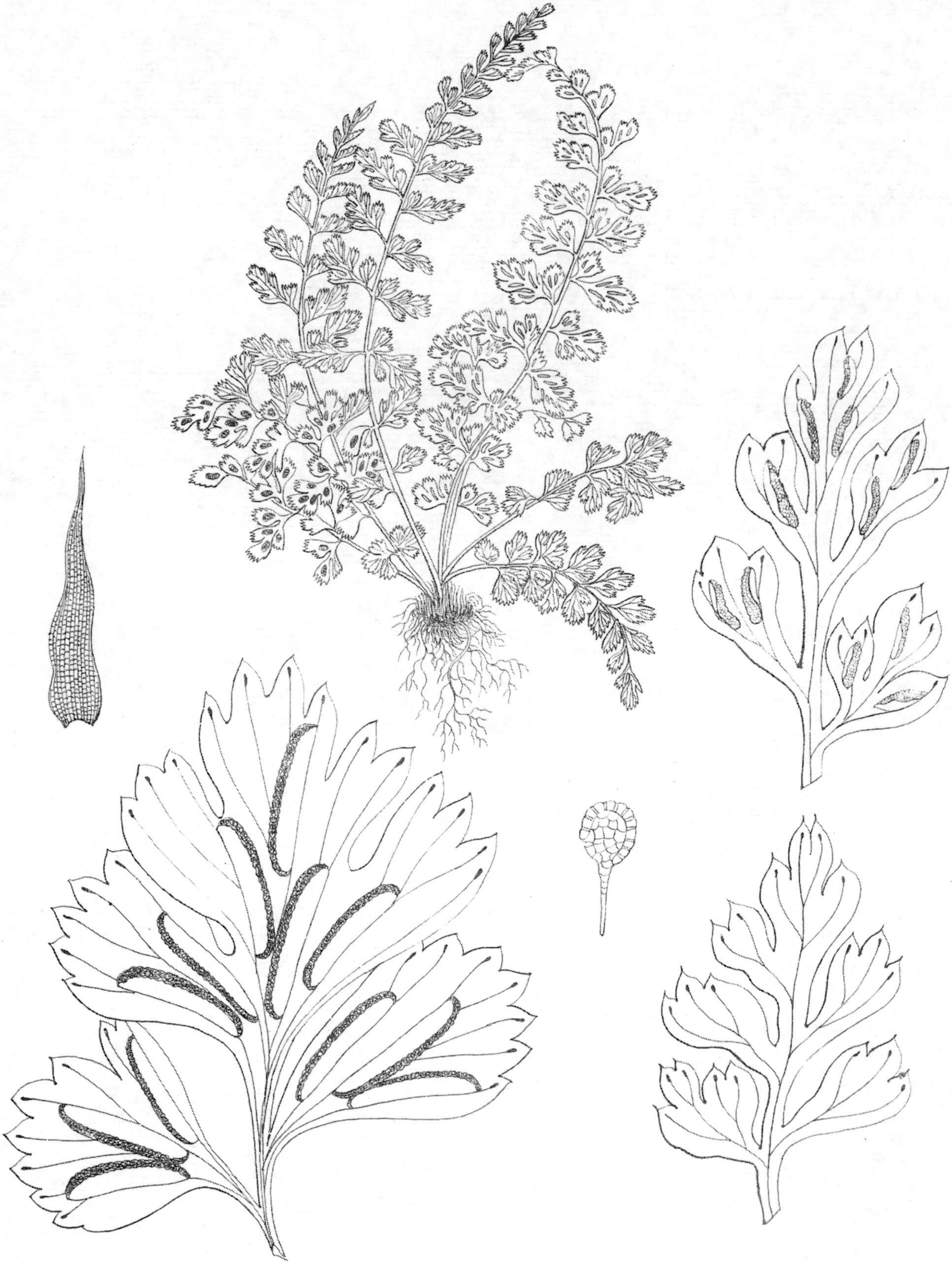

ASPLENIUM VARIANS *(Hooker et Grev.)*

PUBLISHED BY HIGGINBOTHAM & CO. ORIENTAL LITHOGRAPHIC PRESS MADRAS 1872 LITHOGRAPHED BY ALEX: BARREN.

PLATE CXXX

ASPLENIUM TENUIFOLIUM (*Don.*)

PUBLISHED BY HIGGINBOTHAM & CO.

LITHOGRAPHED BY ALEX: BARREN.

ORIENTAL LITHOGRAPHIC PRESS MADRAS 1872

ASPLENIUM HETEROCARPUM (Wallich.)

PUBLISHED HIGGINBOTHAM & CO. ORIENTAL LITHOGRAPHIC PRESS MADRAS 1872 LITHOGRAPHED BY ALEX : BARREN,

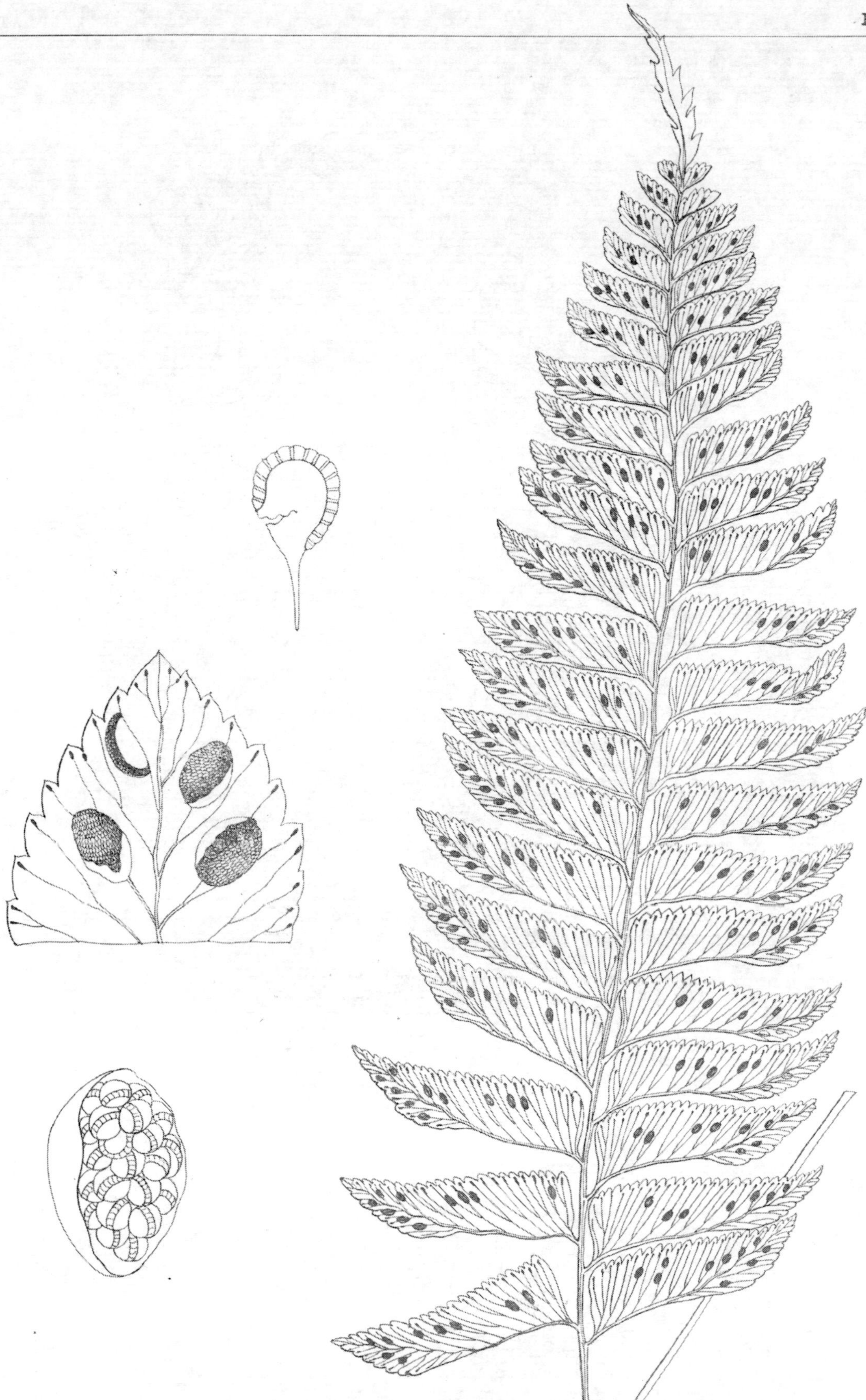

ASPLENIUM RESECTUM (*Smith.*)

PUBLISHED HIGGINBOTHAM & CO. ORIENTAL LITHOGRAPHIC PRESS MADRAS 1872. LITHOGRAPHED BY ALEX. BARREN,

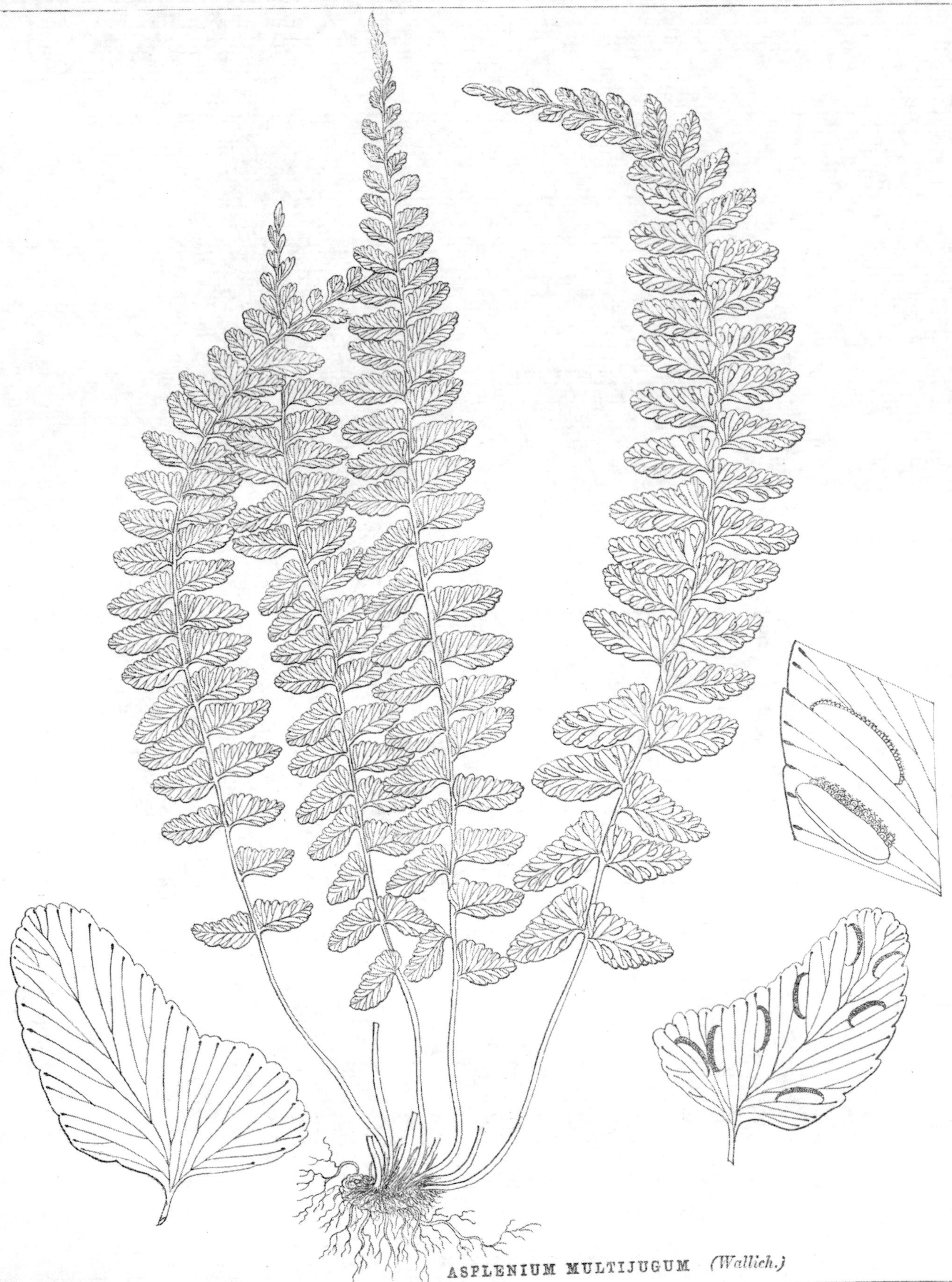

ASPLENIUM MULTIJUGUM *(Wallich.)*

PUBLISHED HIGGINBOTHAM & CO. ORIENTAL LITHOGRAPHIC PRESS MADRAS 1872. LITHOGRAPHED BY ALEX: BARREN,

ASPLENIUM TRAPEZIFORME (*Roxb?*)

PUBLISHED HIGGINBOTHAM & CO.

ORIENTAL LITHOGRAPHIC PRESS MADRAS 1872.

LITHOGRAPHED BY ALEX: DARRUN,

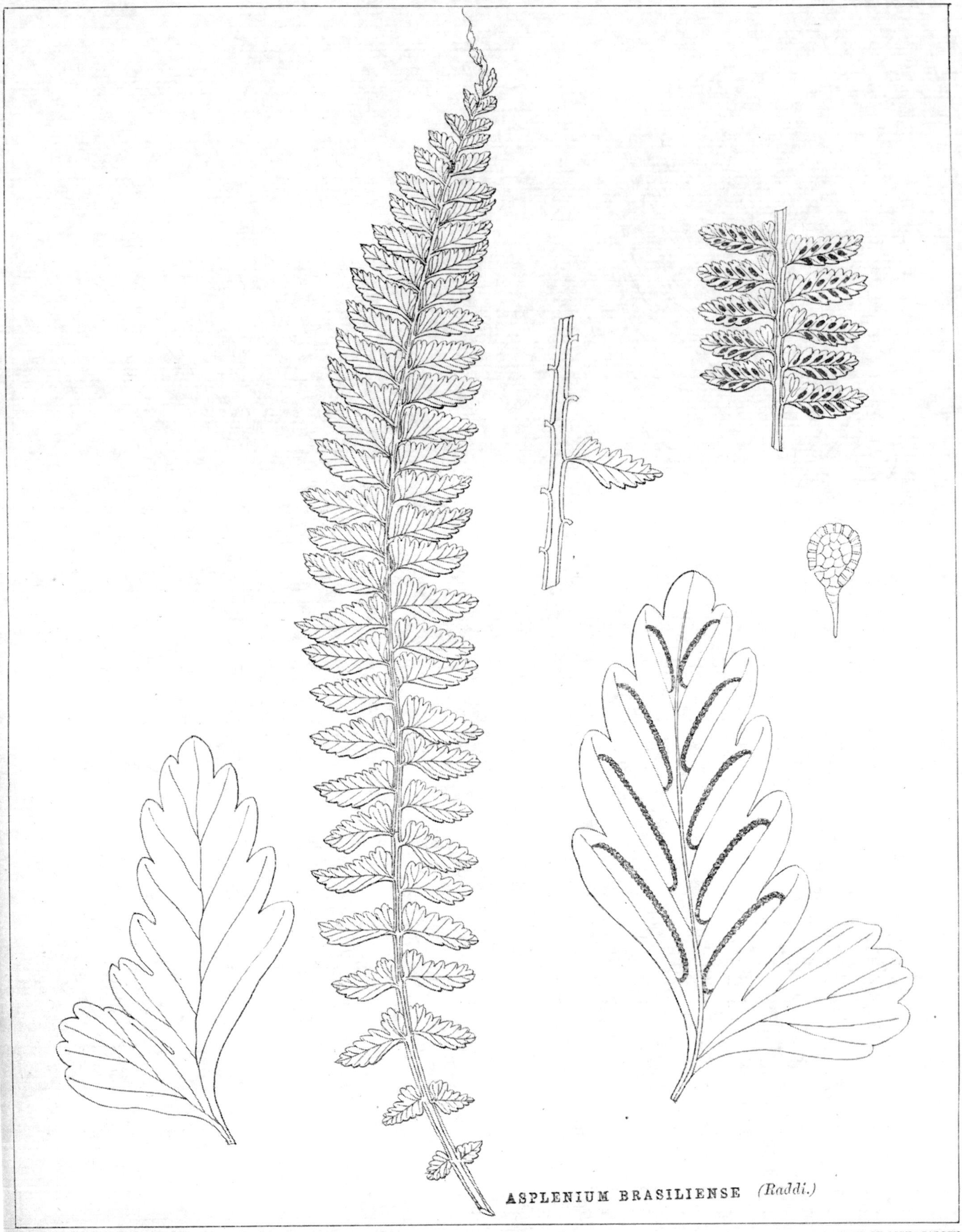

ASPLENIUM BRASILIENSE *(Raddi.)*

PUBLISHED BY HIGGINBOTHAM & CO. ORIENTAL LITHOGRAPHIC PRESS MADRAS 1872. LITHOGRAPHED BY ALEX : BARREN,

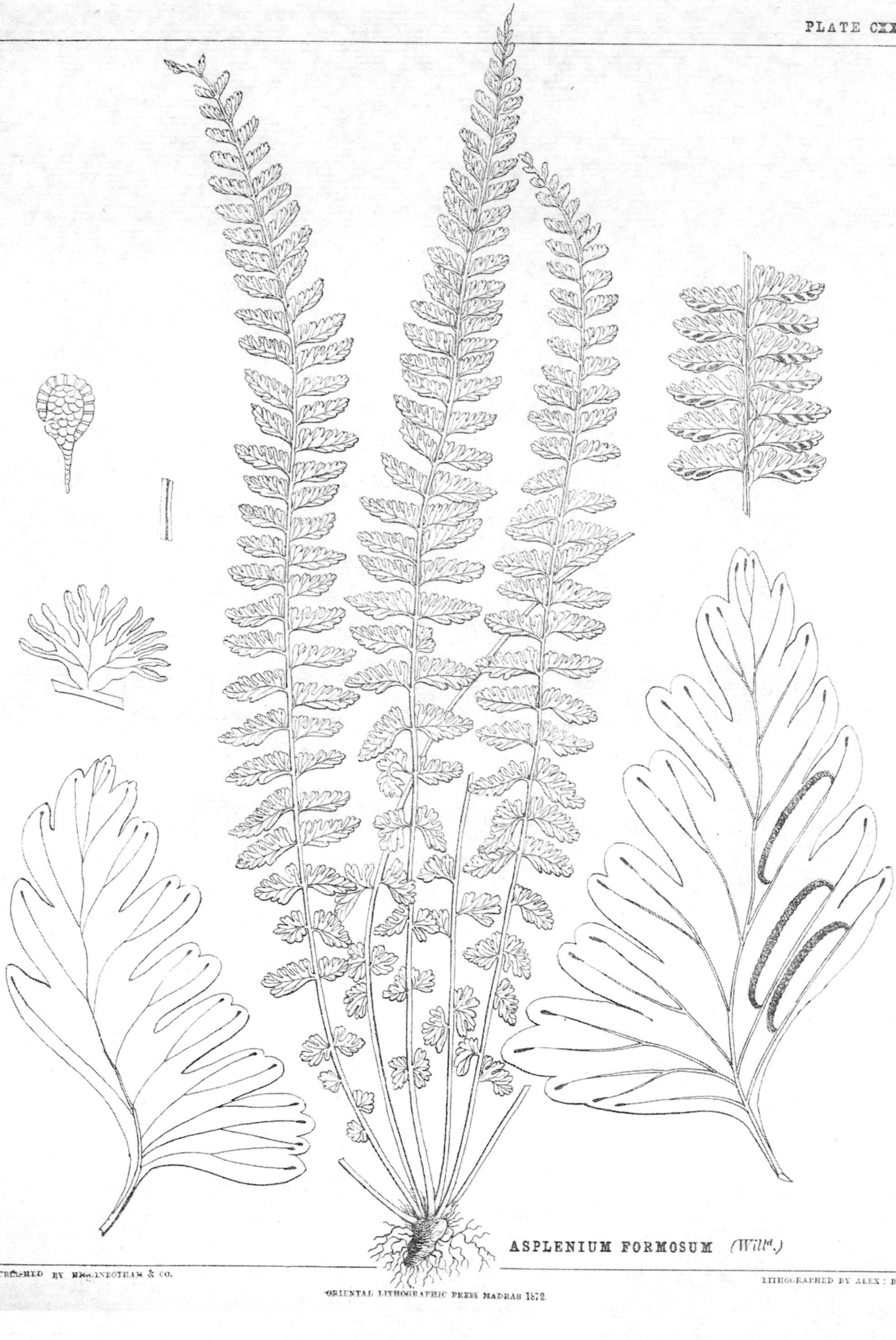

ASPLENIUM FORMOSUM *(Willd.)*

PUBLISHED BY HIGGINBOTHAM & CO.

LITHOGRAPHED BY ALEX : BARREN,

ORIENTAL LITHOGRAPHIC PRESS MADRAS 1872.

ASPLENIUM AURITUM *(Swartz.)*

PUBLISHED BY HIGGINBOTHAM & CO. ORIENTAL LITHOGRAPHIC PRESS MADRAS 1872. LITHOGRAPHED BY ALEX: BARREN,

ASPLENIUM PROLONGATUM (*Hooker.*)

PUBLISHED BY: HIGGINBOTHAM & CO. ORIENTAL LITHOGRAPHIC PRESS MADRAS 1872. LITHOGRAPHED BY ALEX: FARREN,

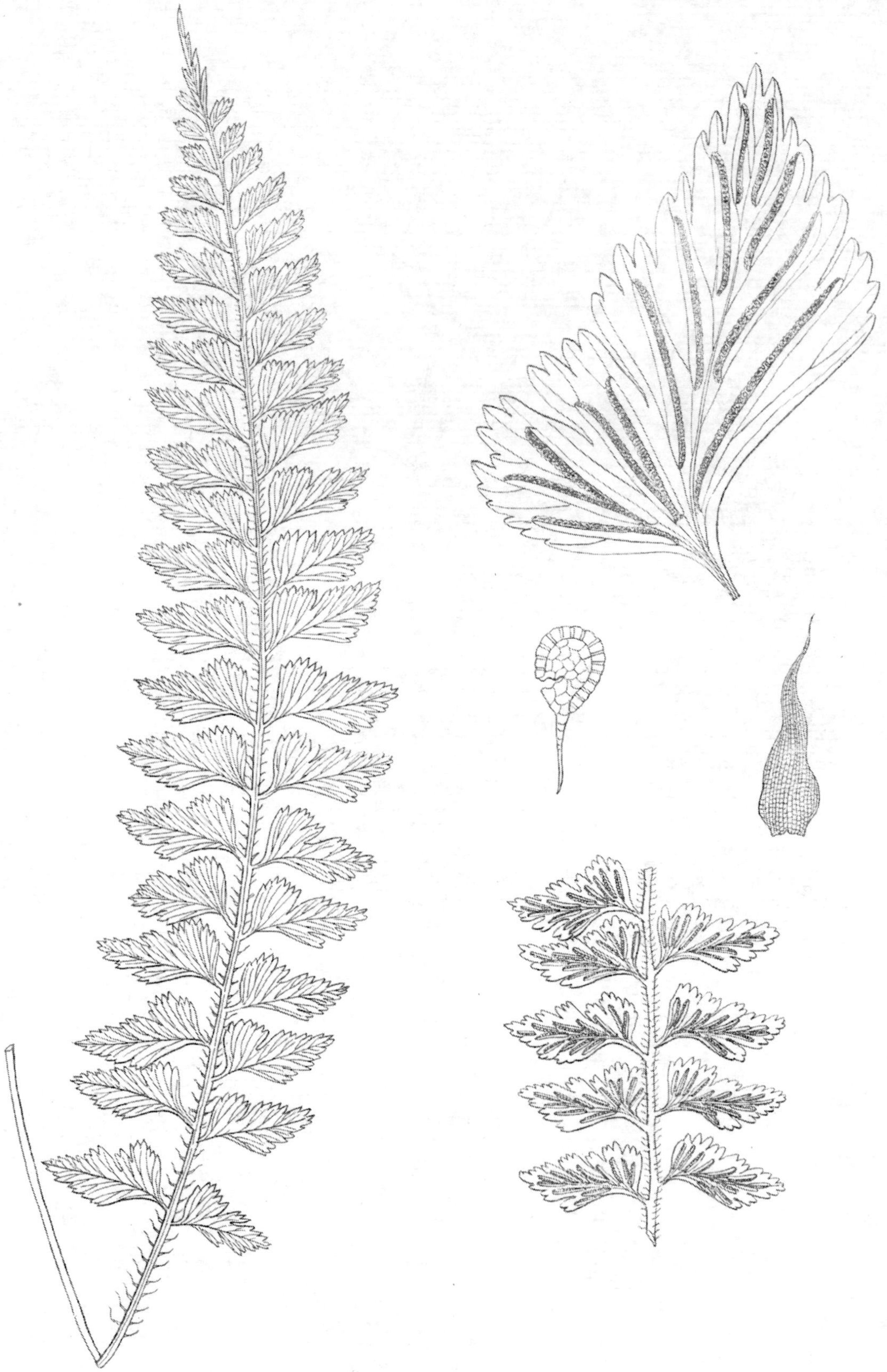

ASPLENIUM PLANICAULE *(Wallich)*

PUBLISHED BY HIGGINBOTHAM & CO. ORIENTAL LITHOGRAPHIC PRESS MADRAS 1872. LITHOGRAPHED BY ALEX: BARREN,

ASPLENIUM CONTIGUUM (*Klfs.*)

PUBLISHED BY HIGGINBOTHAM & CO.

ORIENTAL LITHOGRAPHIC PRESS MADRAS 1873.

LITHOGRAPHED BY ALEX: BARREN,

PLATE CXLI

ASPLENIUM FALCATUM (*Lam.*)

PUBLISHED BY HIGGINBOTHAM & Co. ORIENTAL LITHOGRAPHIC PRESS MADRAS 1872 LITHOGRAPHED BY ALEXR. BARREN.

ASPLENIUM MACROPHYLLUM VAR UROPHYLLUM *(Sw)*

LITHOGRAPHED BY ALEX. BARREN. ORIENTAL LITHOGRAPHIC PRESS MADRAS 1872. PUBLISHED BY HIGGINBOTHAM & CO

PLATE CXLIII

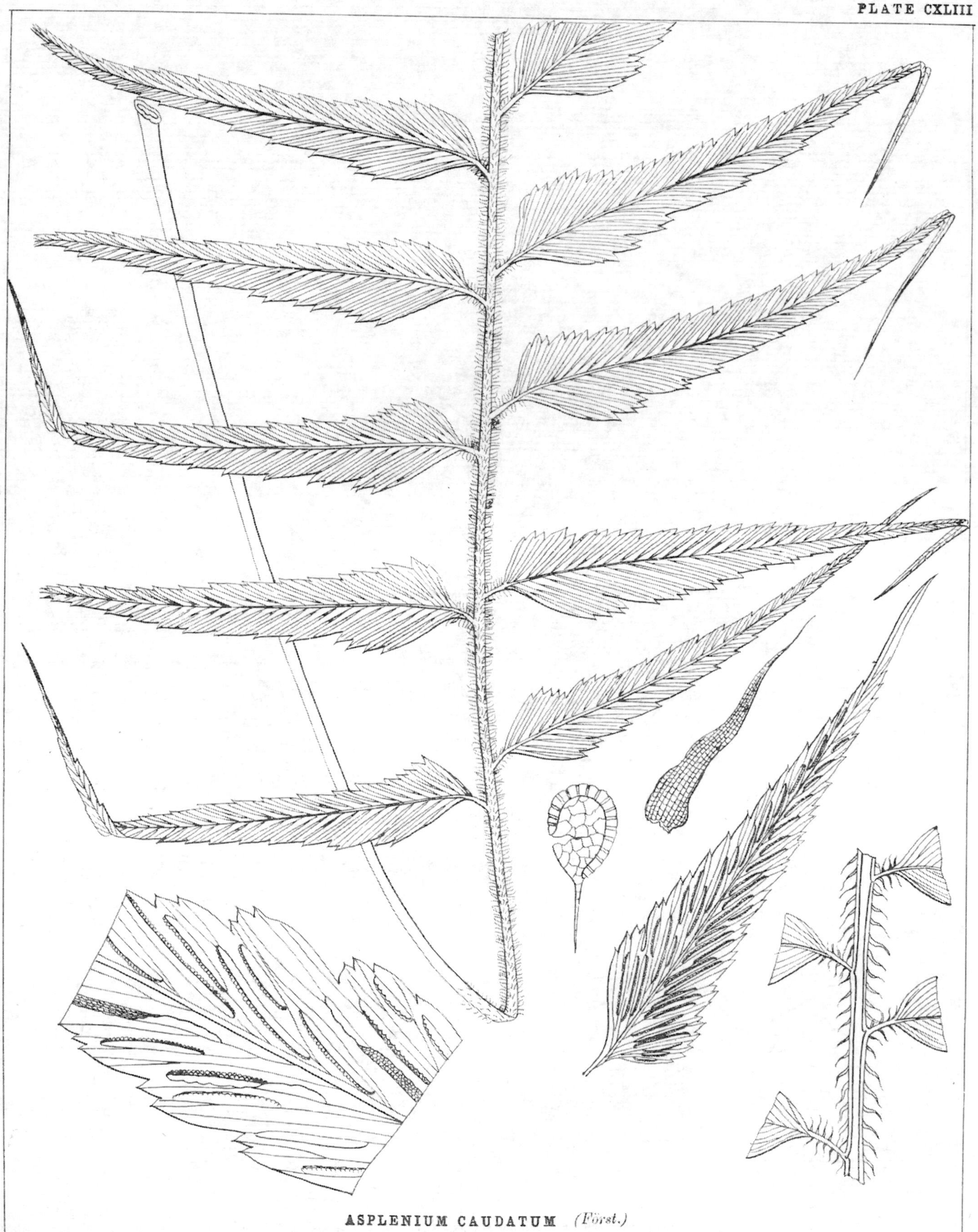

ASPLENIUM CAUDATUM *(Först.)*

PUBLISHED BY HIGGINBOTHAM & CO ORIENTAL LITHOGRAPHIC PRESS MADRAS 1872. LITHOGRAPHED BY ALEN: BARREN.

ASPLENIUM FURCATUM (*Thumb.*)

PUBLISHED BY HIGGINBOTHAM & CO. ORIENTAL LITHOGRAPHIC PRESS MADRAS 1872. LITHOGRAPHED BY ALEX. BARREN.

ASPLENIUM LACINIATUM *(Don.)*

PUBLISHED BY HIGGINBOTHAM & CO   ORIENTAL LITHOGRAPHIC PRESS MADRAS 1872   LITHOGRAPHED BY ALEX: BARREN,

ASPLENIUM EXIGUUM (*Bedd.*)

PUBLISHED BY HIGGINBOTHAM & CO · ORIENTAL LITHOGRAPHIC PRESS MADRAS 1872 · LITHOGRAPHED BY ... BARREN,

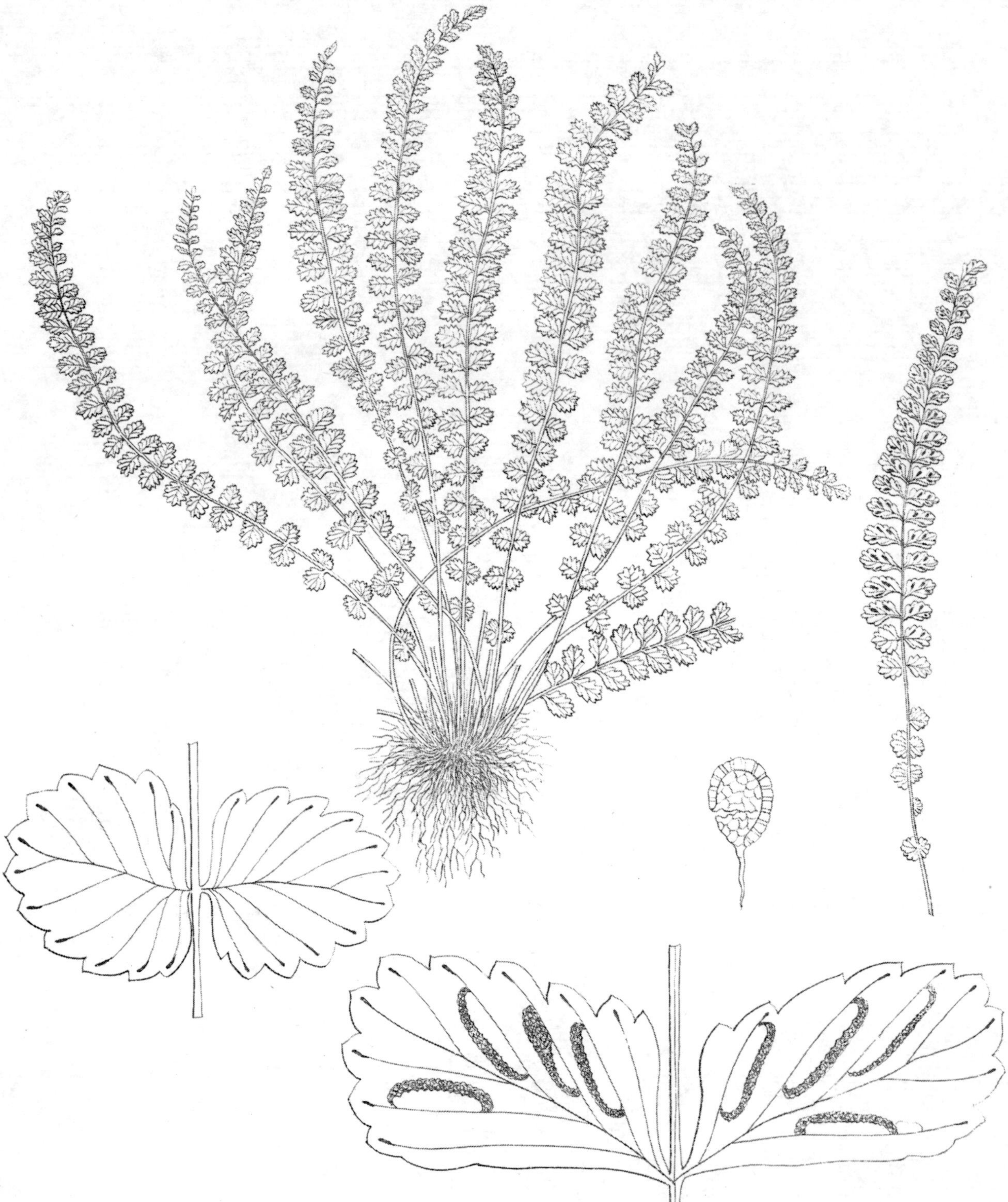

ASPLENIUM TRICHOMANES (*L.*)

PUBLISHED BY HIGGINBOTHAM & CO. ORIENTAL LITHOGRAPHIC PRESS MADRAS 1872. LITHOGRAPHED BY ALEX: BARKER.

ASPLENIUM NITIDUM (Sw.)

PUBLISHED BY HIGGINBOTHAM & CO. ORIENTAL LITHOGRAPHIC PRESS MADRAS 1872. LITHOGRAPHED BY ALEX: BARREN,

ASPLENIUM NITIDUM

VAR OBTUSUM *(Sw.)*

PUBLISHED BY HIGGINBOTHAM & CO. ORIENTAL LITHOGRAPHIC PRESS MADRAS 1872. LITHOGRAPHED BY ALEX: BARREN,

ATHYRIUM HOHENACKERIANUM (*Kunze*)

PUBLISHED BY HIGGINBOTHAM & CO. ORIENTAL LITHOGRAPHIC PRESS MADRAS 1872. LITHOGRAPHED BY ALEX: BARREN,

ATHYRIUM FALCATUM *(Bedd.)*

PUBLISHED BY HIGGINBOTHAM & CO.   ORIENTAL LITHOGRAPHIC PRESS, MADRAS 187[illegible]   LITHOGRAPHED BY ALEX: BARREN,

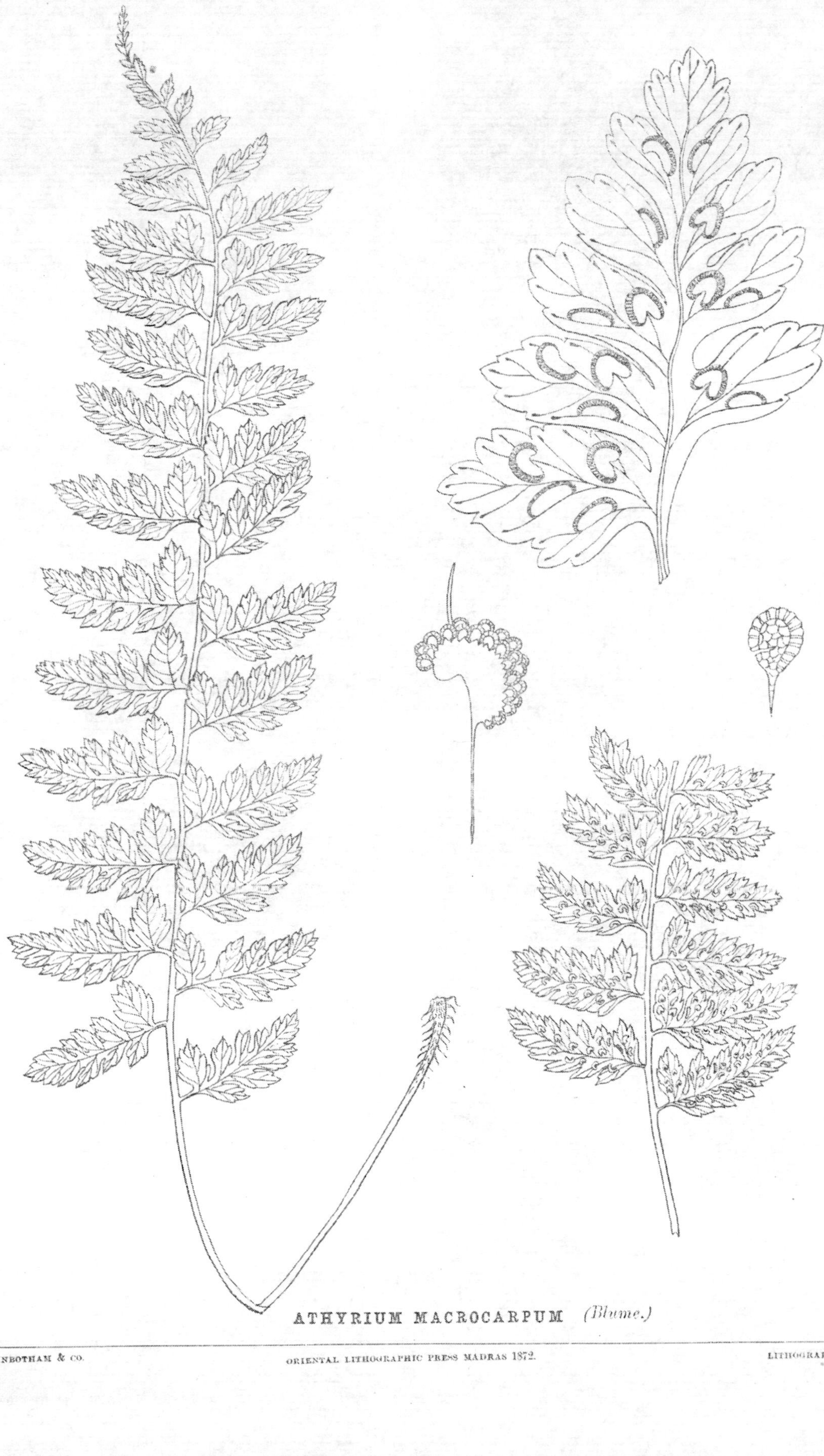

ATHYRIUM MACROCARPUM *(Blume.)*

PUBLISHED BY HIGGINBOTHAM & CO. ORIENTAL LITHOGRAPHIC PRESS MADRAS 1872. LITHOGRAPHED BY ALEX: BARREN,

ATHYRIUM MACROCARPUM
VAR. B. (Bedd.)

PUBLISHED BY HIGGINBOTHAM & CO. ORIENTAL LITHOGRAPHIC PRESS MADRAS 1872. LITHOGRAPHED BY ALEX: BARREN,

ATHYRIUM FILIX-FEMINA *(Bernh.)*

PUBLISHED BY HIGGINBOTHAM & CO. ORIENTAL LITHOGRAPHIC PRESS MADRAS 1872. LITHOGRAPHED BY ALEXR WARREN,

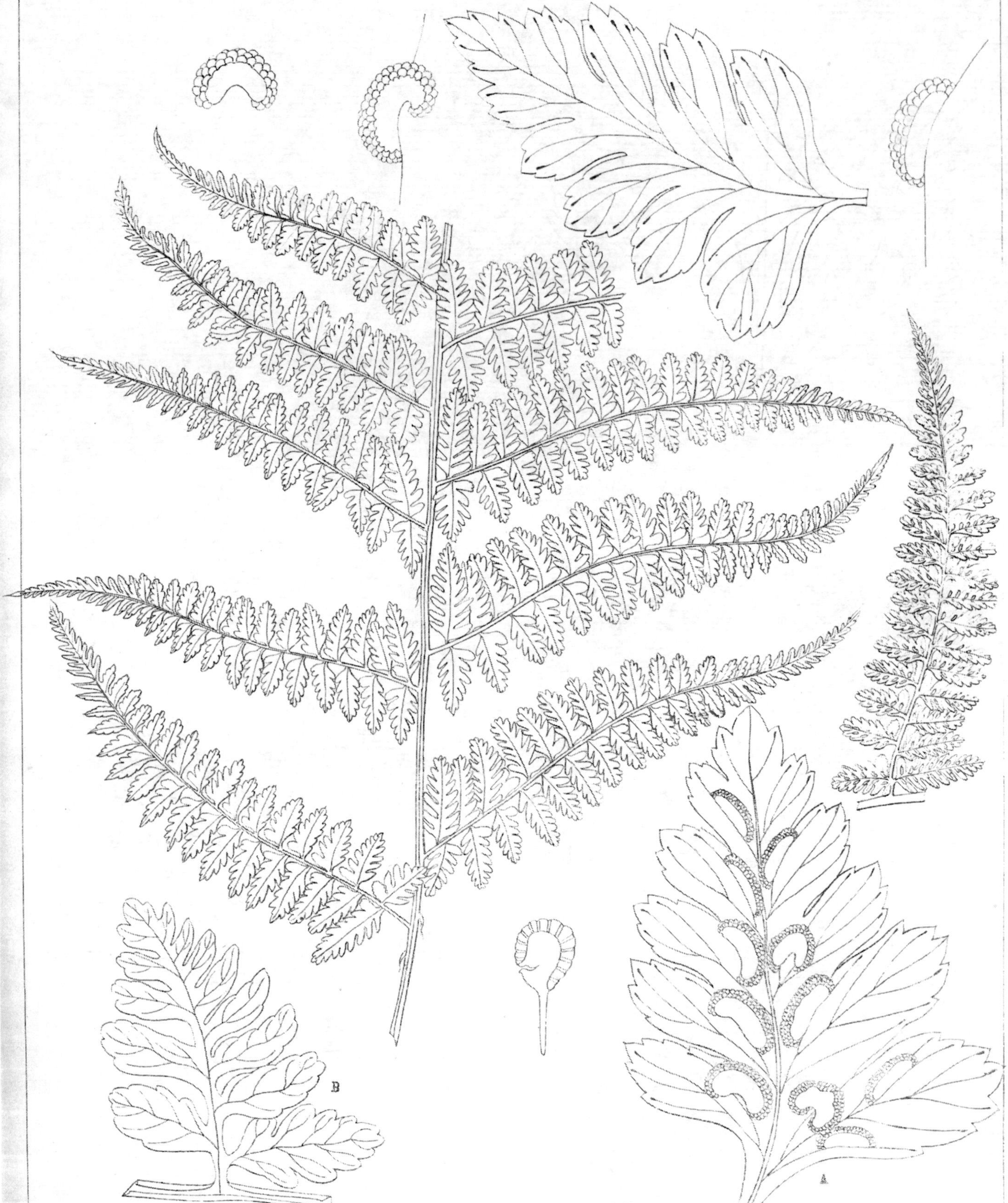

ATHYRIUM PECTINATUM (Wallich.)

PUBLISHED BY HIGGINBOTHAM & CO. ORIENTAL LITHOGRAPHIC PRESS MADRAS 1872. LITHOGRAPHED BY ALEX. BARREN.

ATHYRIUM GYMNOGRAMMIDES (*Kl.*)

PUBLISHED BY HIGGINBOTHAM & CO. ORIENTAL LITHOGRAPHIC PRESS MADRAS 1872. LITHOGRAPHED BY ALEX: BARREN,

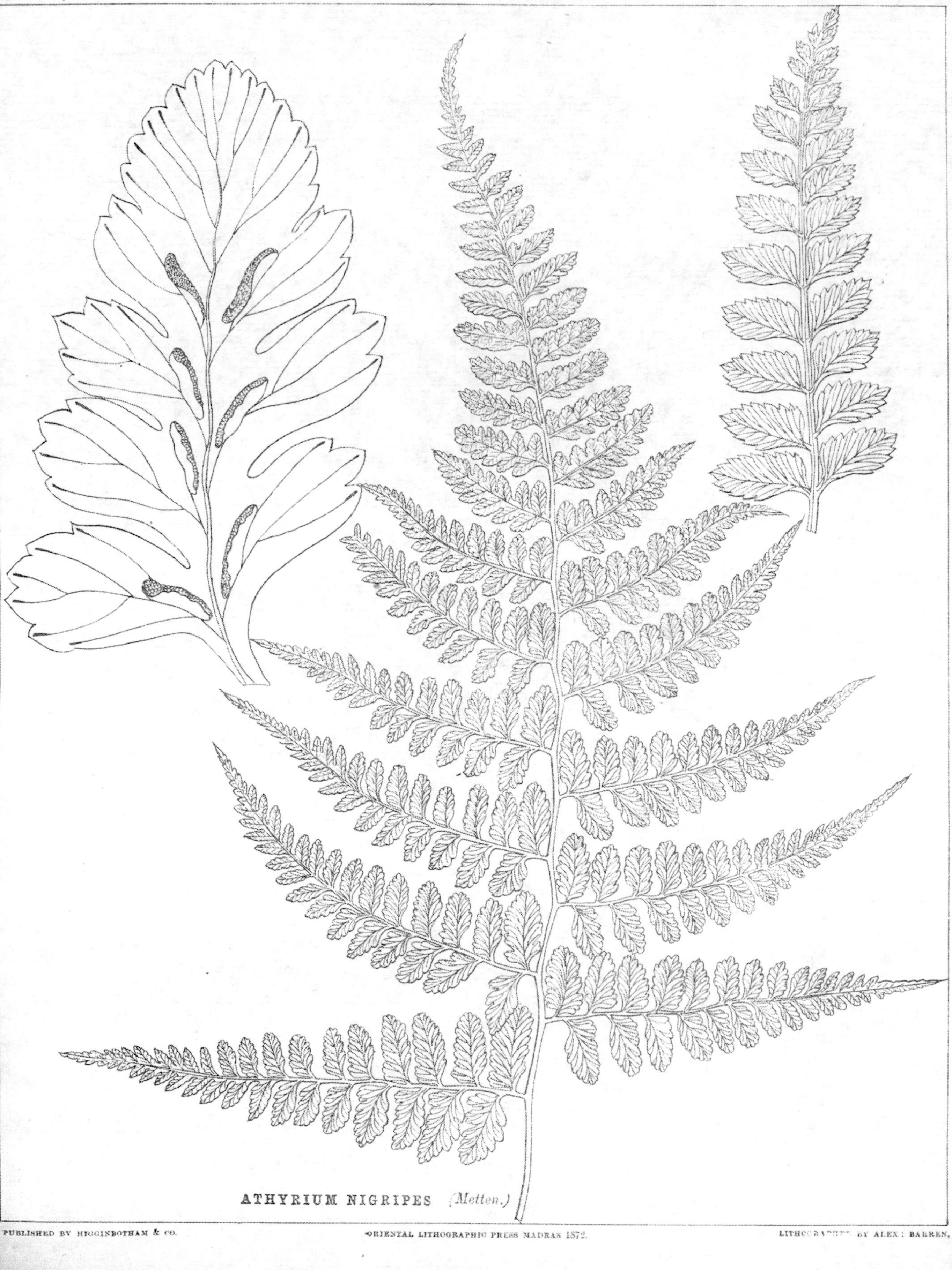

ATHYRIUM NIGRIPES *(Metten.)*

PUBLISHED BY HIGGINBOTHAM & CO. ORIENTAL LITHOGRAPHIC PRESS MADRAS 1872. LITHOGRAPHED BY ALEX: BARREN,

ATHYRIUM AUSTRALE (*Brack.*)

PUBLISHED BY HIGGINBOTHAM & CO   ORIENTAL LITHOGRAPHIC PRESS MADRAS 1872.   LITHOGRAPHED BY ALEX: BARREN,

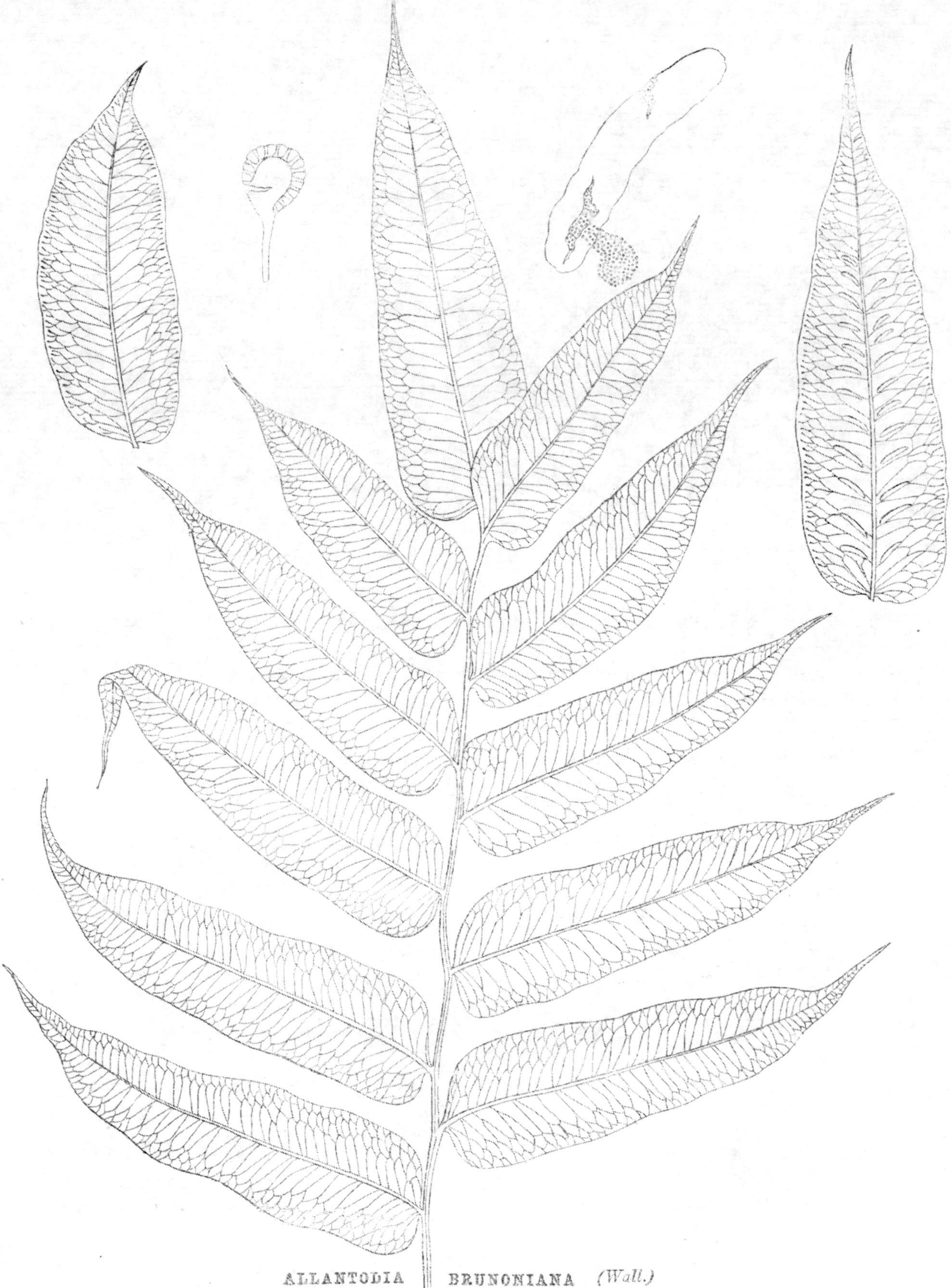

ALLANTODIA BRUNONIANA *(Wall.)*

PUBLISHED BY HIGGINBOTHAM & CO. ORIENTAL LITHOGRAPHIC PRESS MADRAS 1872. LITHOGRAPHED BY [illegible] BARREN,

DIPLAZIUM LASIOPTERIS *(Kunze.)*

PUBLISHED BY HIGGINBOTHAM & CO. ORIENTAL LITHOGRAPHIC PRESS MADRAS 1872. LITHOGRAPHED BY ALEX: BARREN.

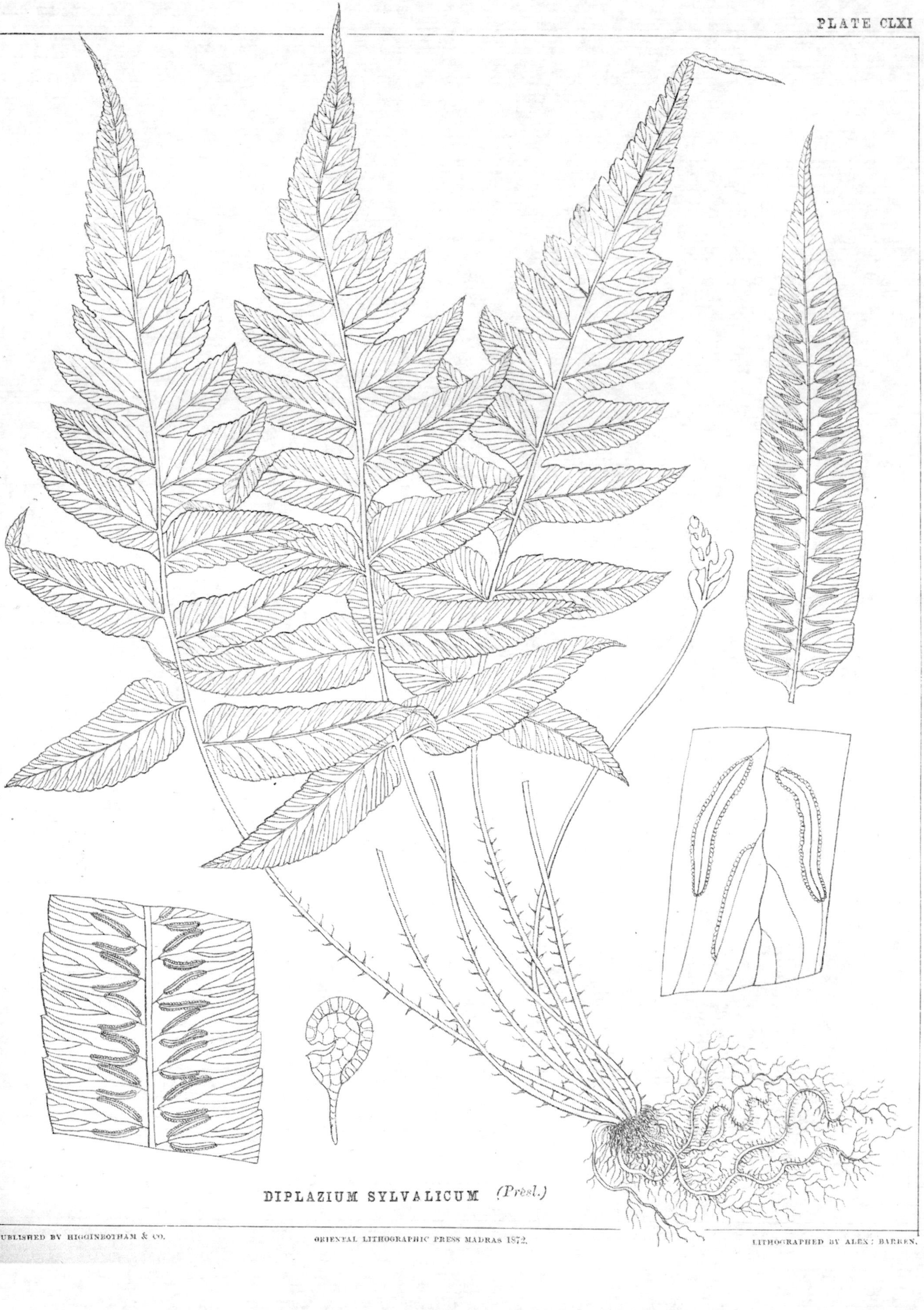

DIPLAZIUM SYLVALICUM (Presl.)

PUBLISHED BY HIGGINBOTHAM & CO. ORIENTAL LITHOGRAPHIC PRESS MADRAS 1872. LITHOGRAPHED BY ALEX: BARREN.

DIPLAZIUM DILATATUM *(Blume.)*

PUBLISHED BY HIGGINBOTHAM & CO. ORIENTAL LITHOGRAPHIC PRESS MADRAS 1872. LITHOGRAPHED BY ALEX: BARREN,

DIPLAZIUM POLYPODIOIDES *(Mett.)*

PUBLISHED BY HIGGINBOTHAM & CO.

ORIENTAL LITHOGRAPHIC PRESS MADRAS 1872.

LITHOGRAPHED BY ALEX: BARREN,

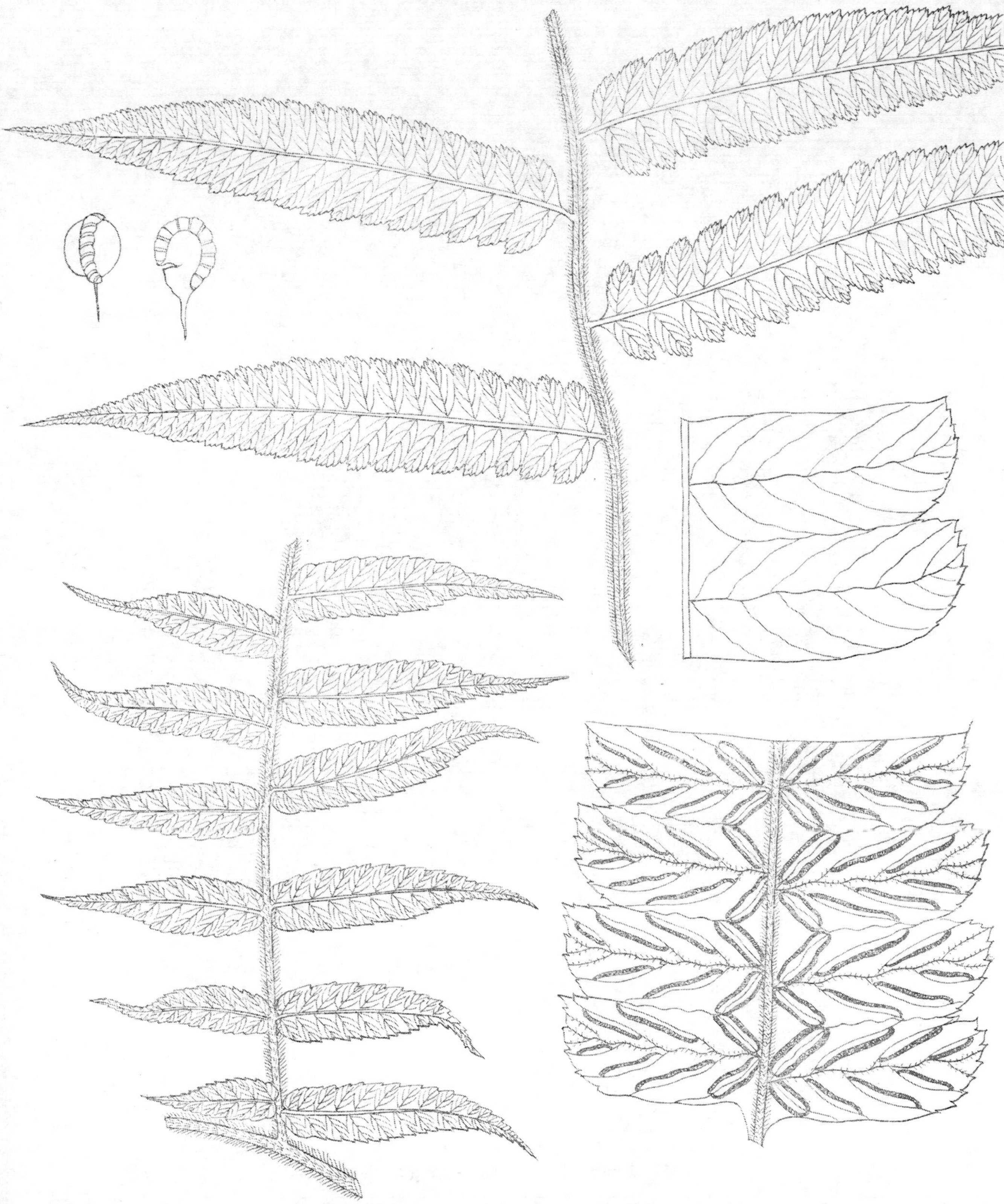

CALLIPTERIS ESCULENTA *(Houlst et Moore)*

PUBLISHED BY HIGGINBOTHAM & CO. ORIENTAL LITHOGRAPHIC PRESS MADRAS 1872. LITHOGRAPHED BY ALEX: BARREN,

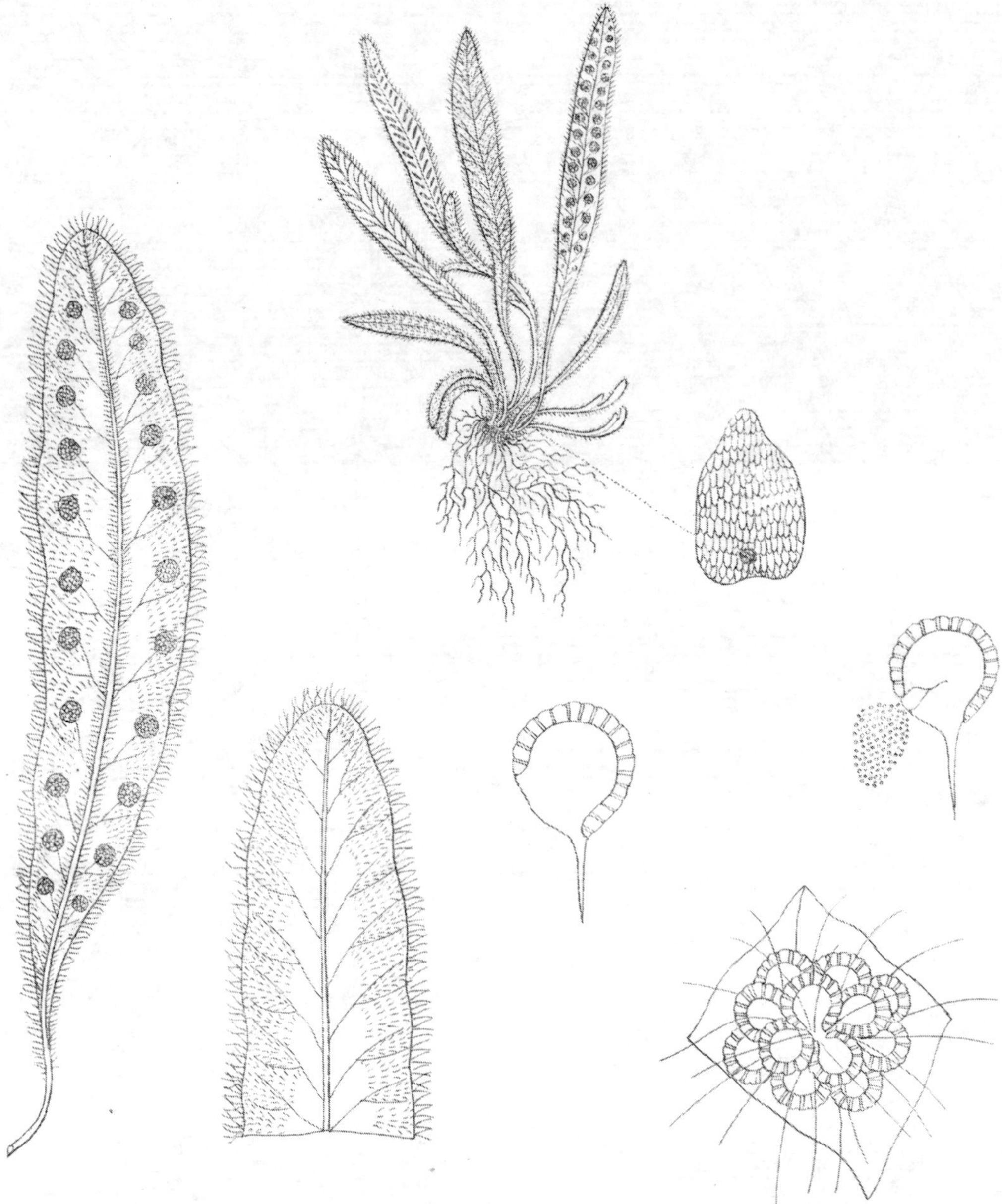

POLYPODIUM PARASITICUM *(Metten.)*

PUBLISHED BY HIGGINBOTHAM & CO. ORIENTAL LITHOGRAPHIC PRESS MADRAS 1872. LITHOGRAPHED BY ALEX: BARREN,

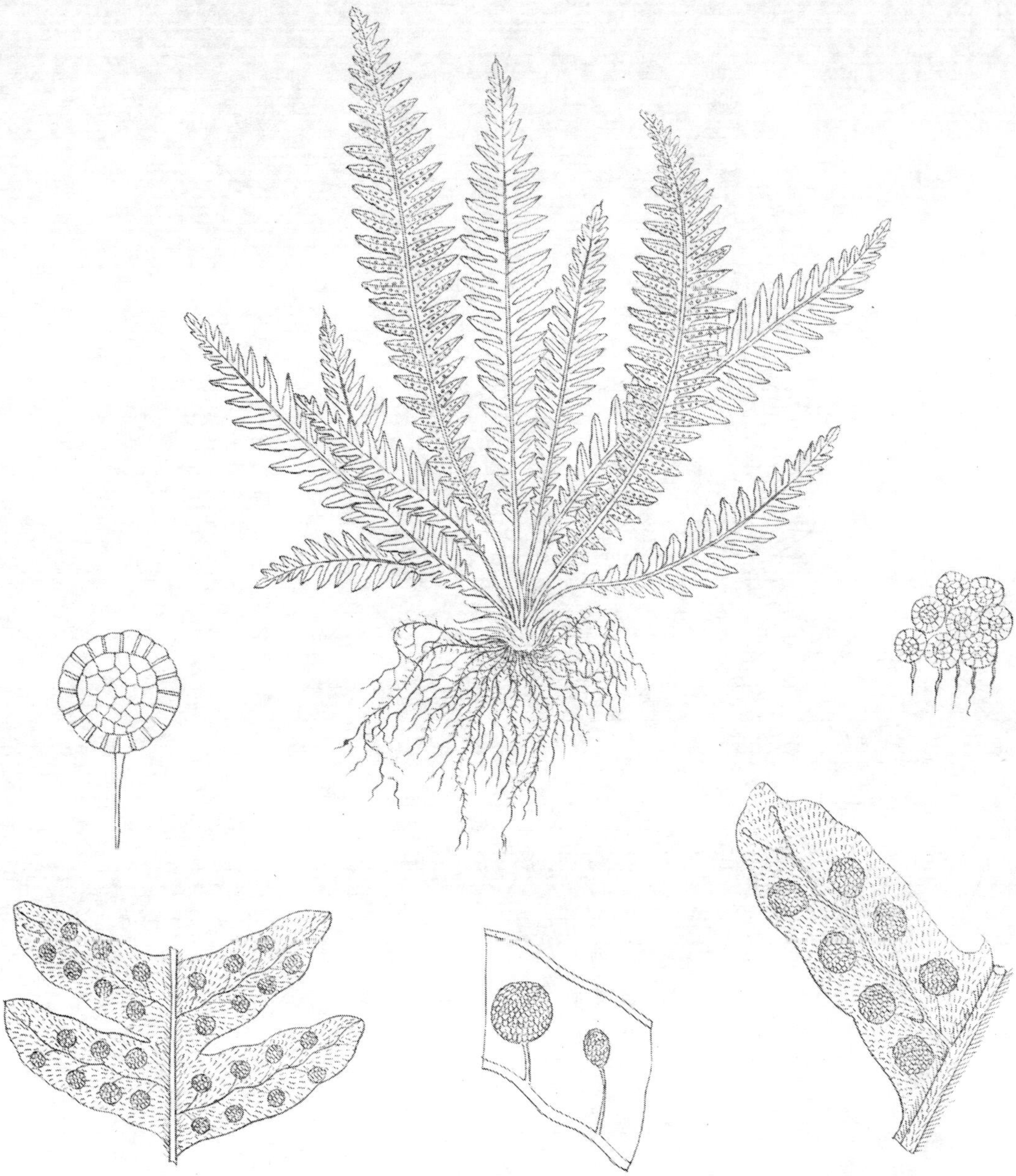

POLYPODIUM PARVULUM (Bory.)

PUBLISHED BY HIGGINBOTHAM & CO. ORIENTAL LITHOGRAPHIC PRESS MADRAS 1872. LITHOGRAPHED BY ALEX. BARREN,

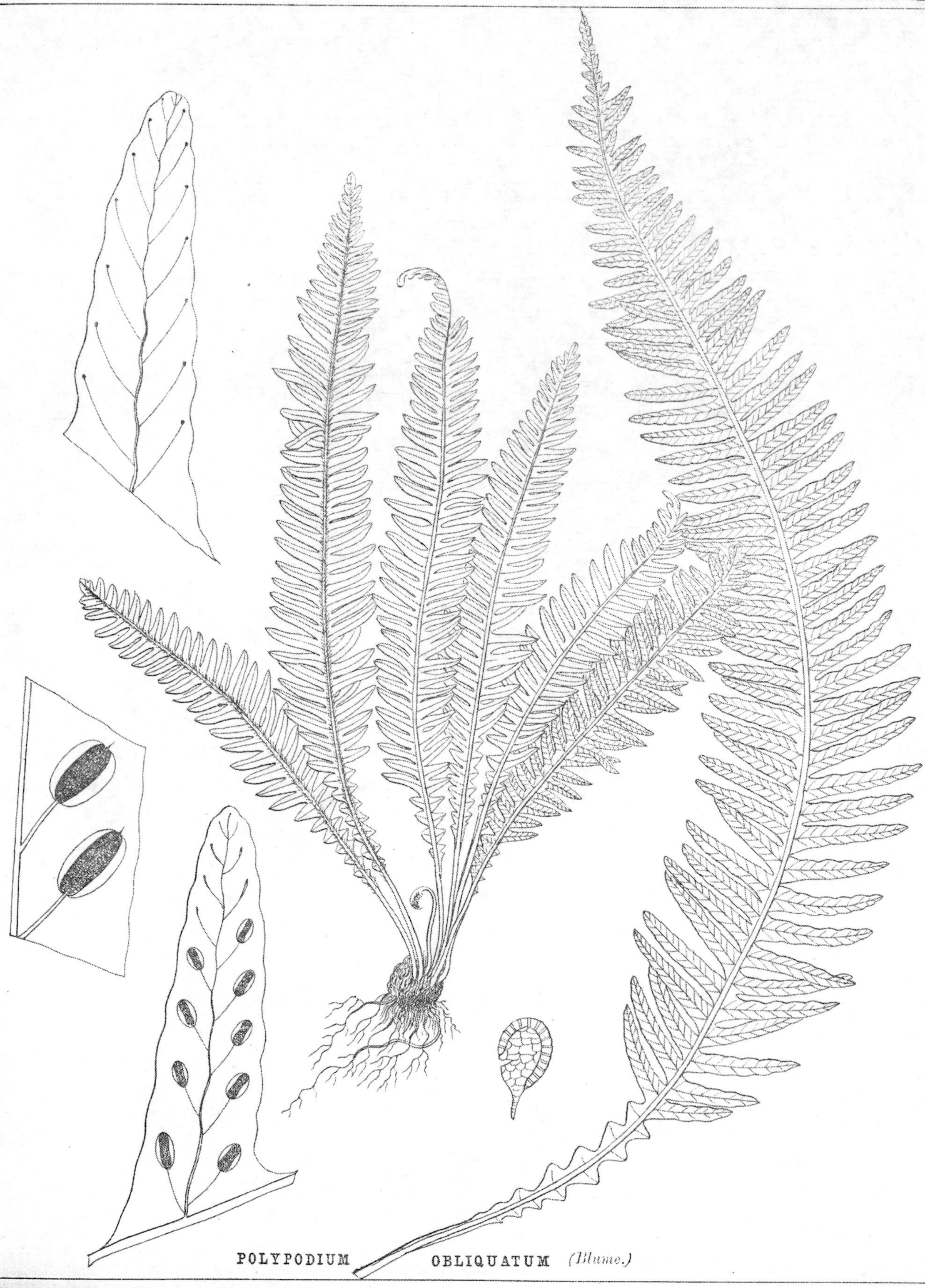

POLYPODIUM OBLIQUATUM *(Blume.)*

PUBLISHED BY HIGGINBOTHAM & CO ORIENTAL LITHOGRAPHIC PRESS MADRAS 1872. LITHOGRAPHED BY ALEX: BARREN,

POLYPODIUM PALUDOSUM *(Blume.)*

PUBLISHED BY HIGGINBOTHAM & CO. ORIENTAL LITHOGRAPHIC PRESS MADRAS 187[illegible]. LITHOGRAPHED BY ALEX: BARREN.

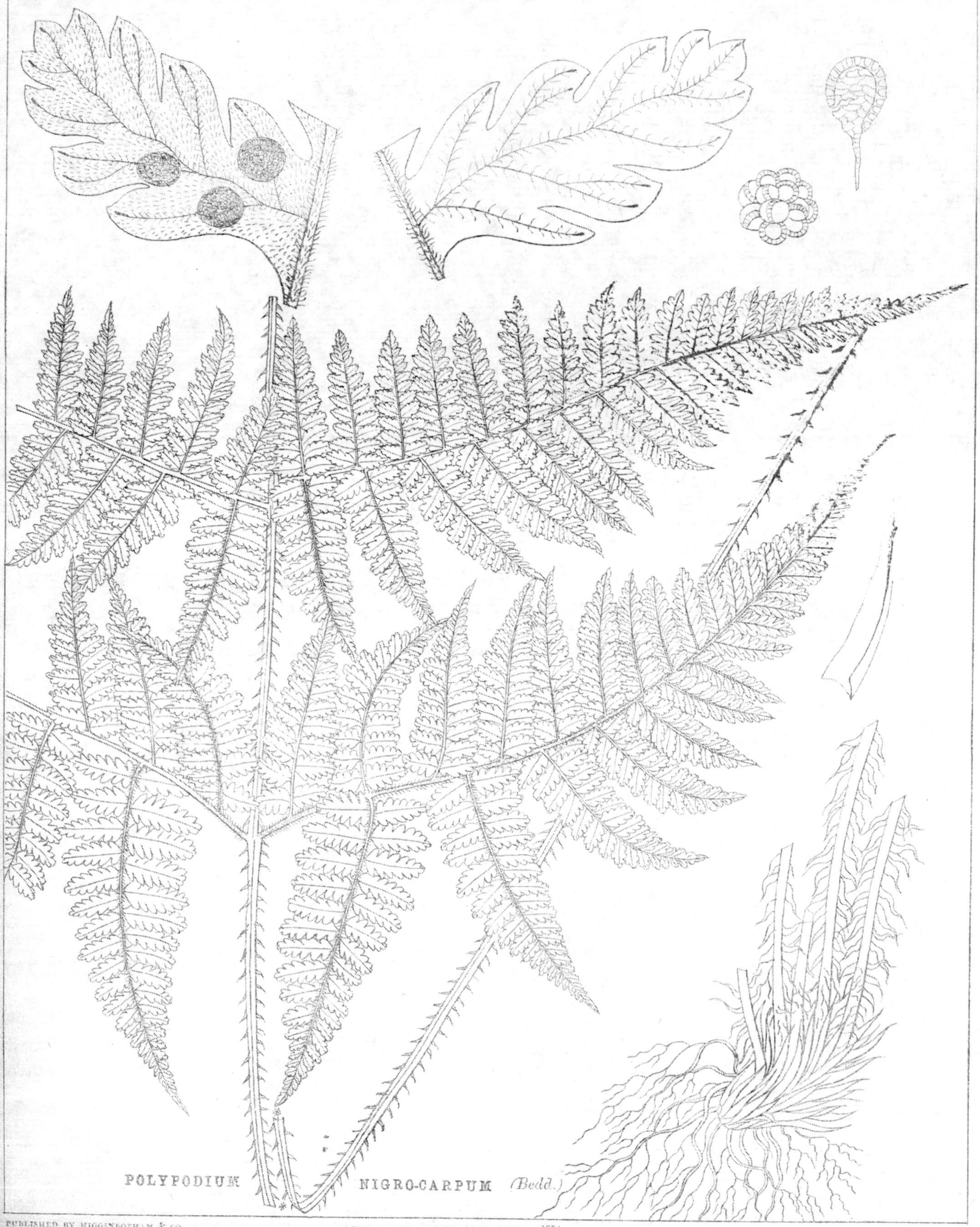

POLYPODIUM NIGRO-CARPUM (Bedd.)

PUBLISHED BY HIGGINBOTHAM & CO. ORIENTAL LITHOGRAPHIC PRESS MADRAS 1872. LITHOGRAPHED BY ALEX.^R BARREN.

POLYPODIUM RUGULOSUM (*Labill.*)

PUBLISHED BY HIGGINBOTHAM & CO. ORIENTAL LITHOGRAPHIC PRESS MADRAS 1872. LITHOGRAPHED BY ALEX: BARREN.

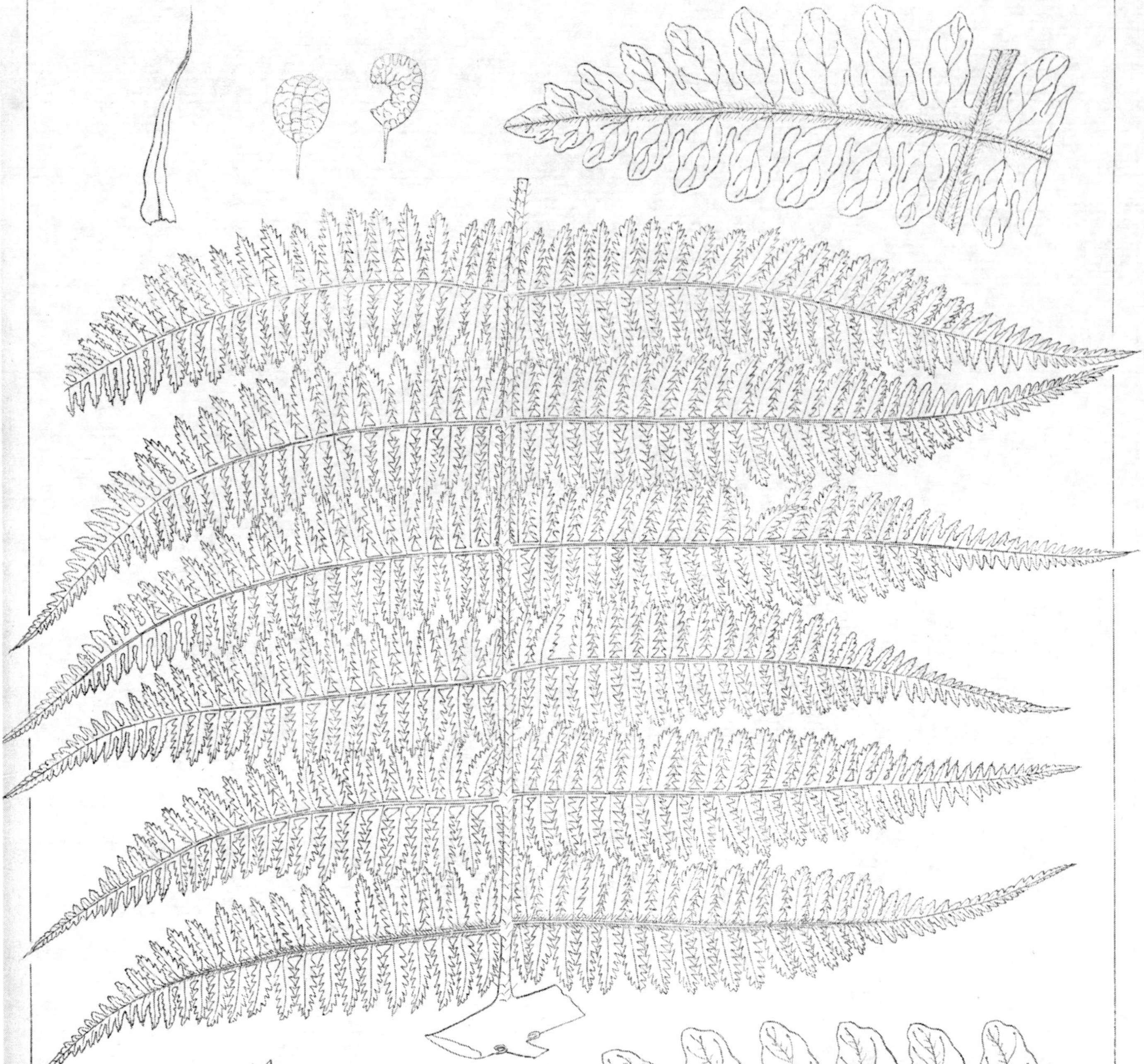

POLYPODIUM ORNATUM *(Wallich.)*

PUBLISHED BY HIGGINBOTHAM & CO. ORIENTAL LITHOGRAPHIC PRESS MADRAS 187[illegible] LITHOGRAPHED BY ALEXR. BARREN,

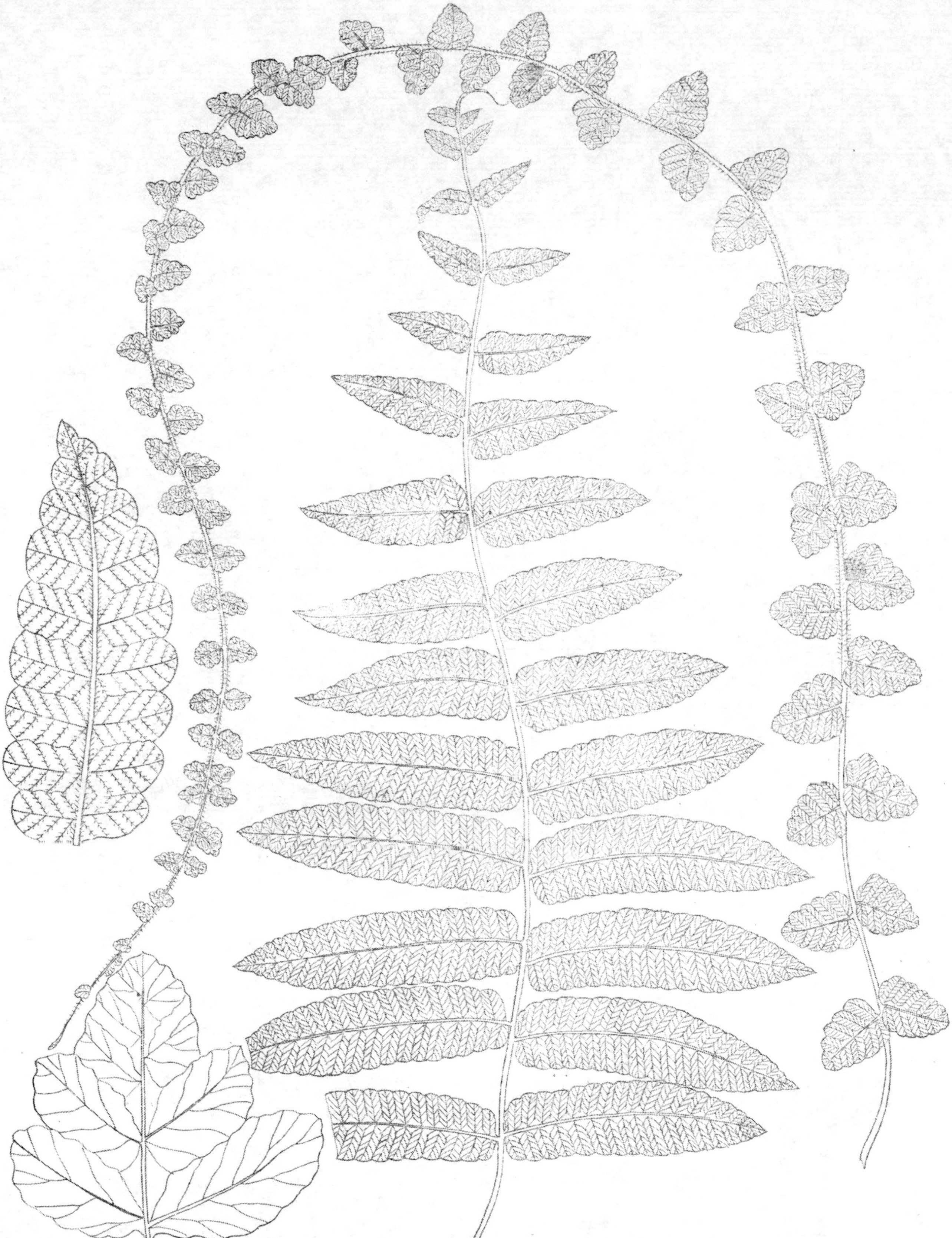

GONIOPTERIS PROLIFERA *(Presl.)*

PUBLISHED BY HIGGINBOTHAM & CO. ORIENTAL LITHOGRAPHIC PRESS MADRAS 1872 LITHOGRAPHED BY ALEX: BARREN.

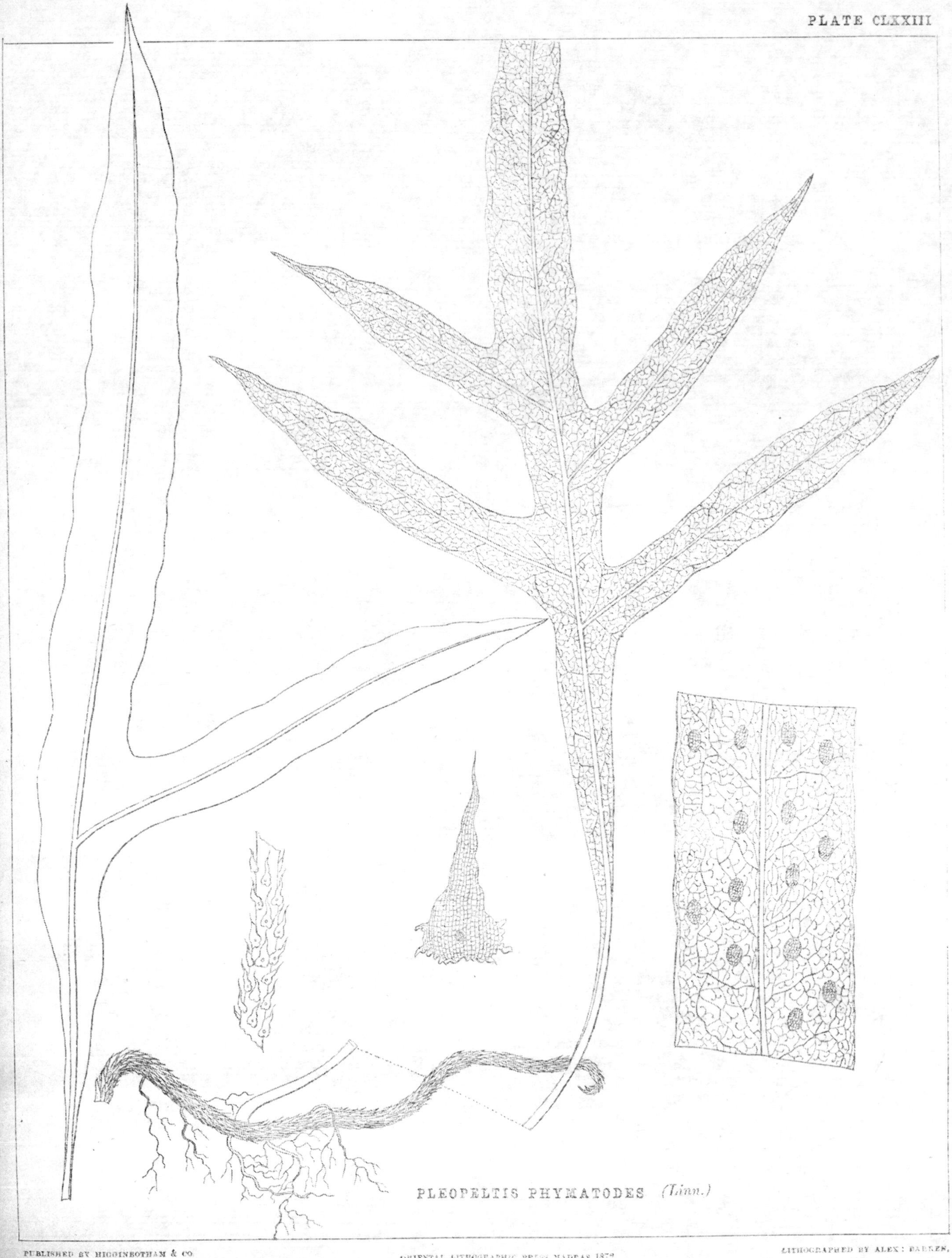

PLEOPELTIS PHYMATODES *(Linn.)*

PUBLISHED BY HIGGINBOTHAM & CO. ORIENTAL LITHOGRAPHIC PRESS MADRAS 1872. LITHOGRAPHED BY ALEX: BARREN.

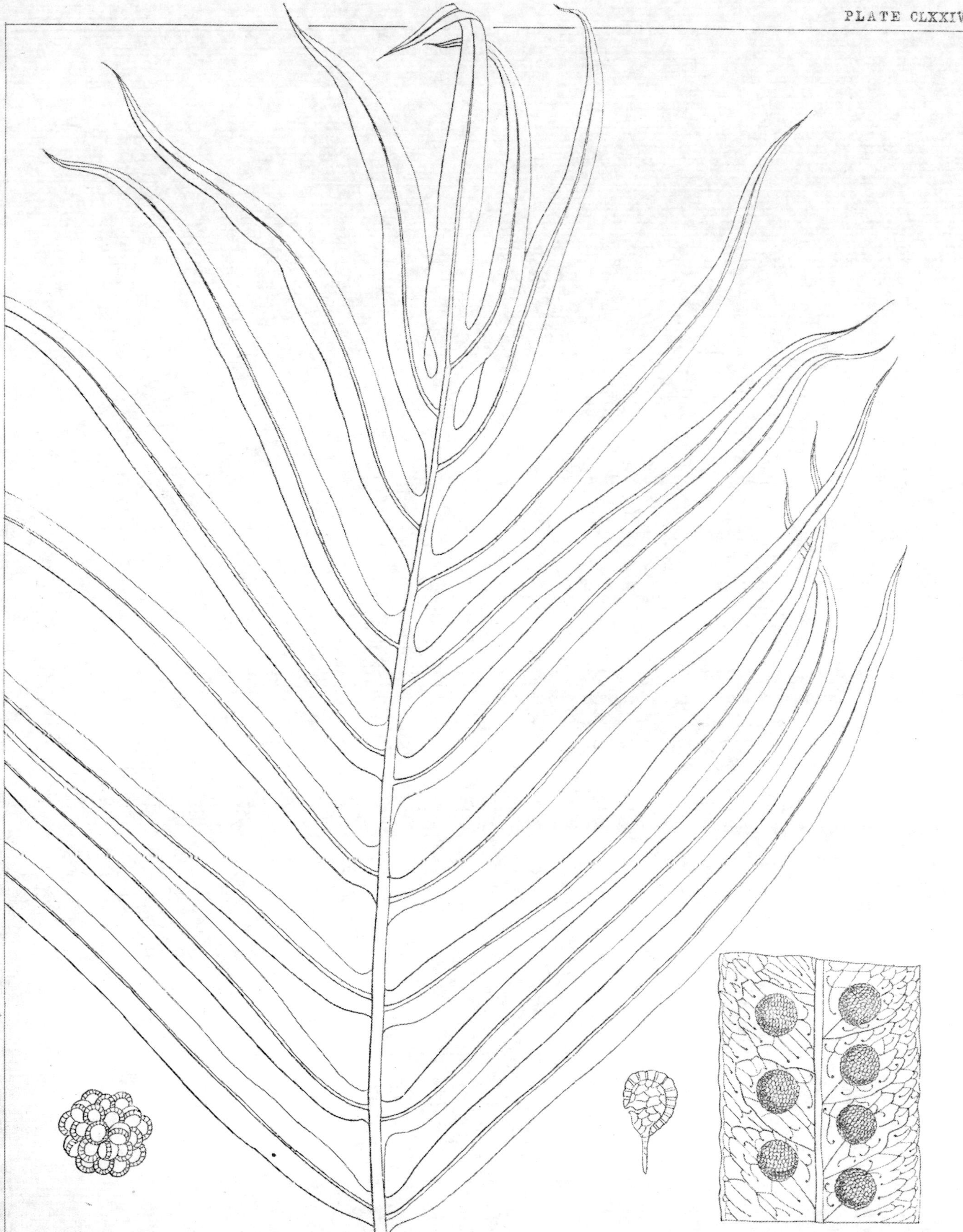

PLEOPELTIS LEIORHIZA *(Wallich.)*

PUBLISHED BY HIGGINBOTHAM & CO ORIENTAL LITHOGRAPHIC PRESS MADRAS 1872. LITHOGRAPHED BY ALEX: BARREN,

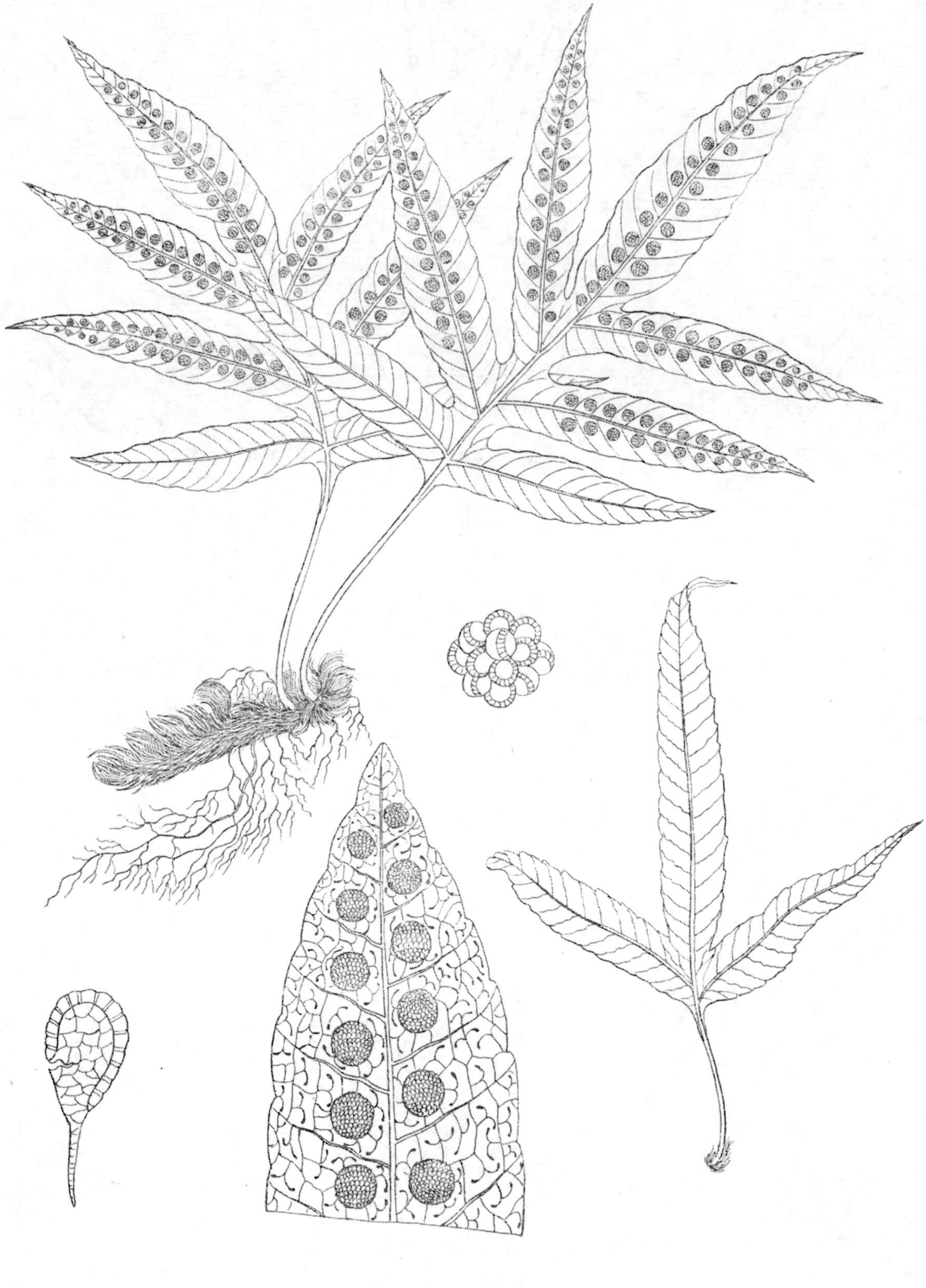

PLEOPELTIS OXYLOBA *(Wallich.)*

PUBLISHED BY HIGGINBOTHAM & CO ORIENTAL LITHOGRAPHIC PRESS MADRAS 1872. LITHOGRAPHED BY ALEX: BARREN,

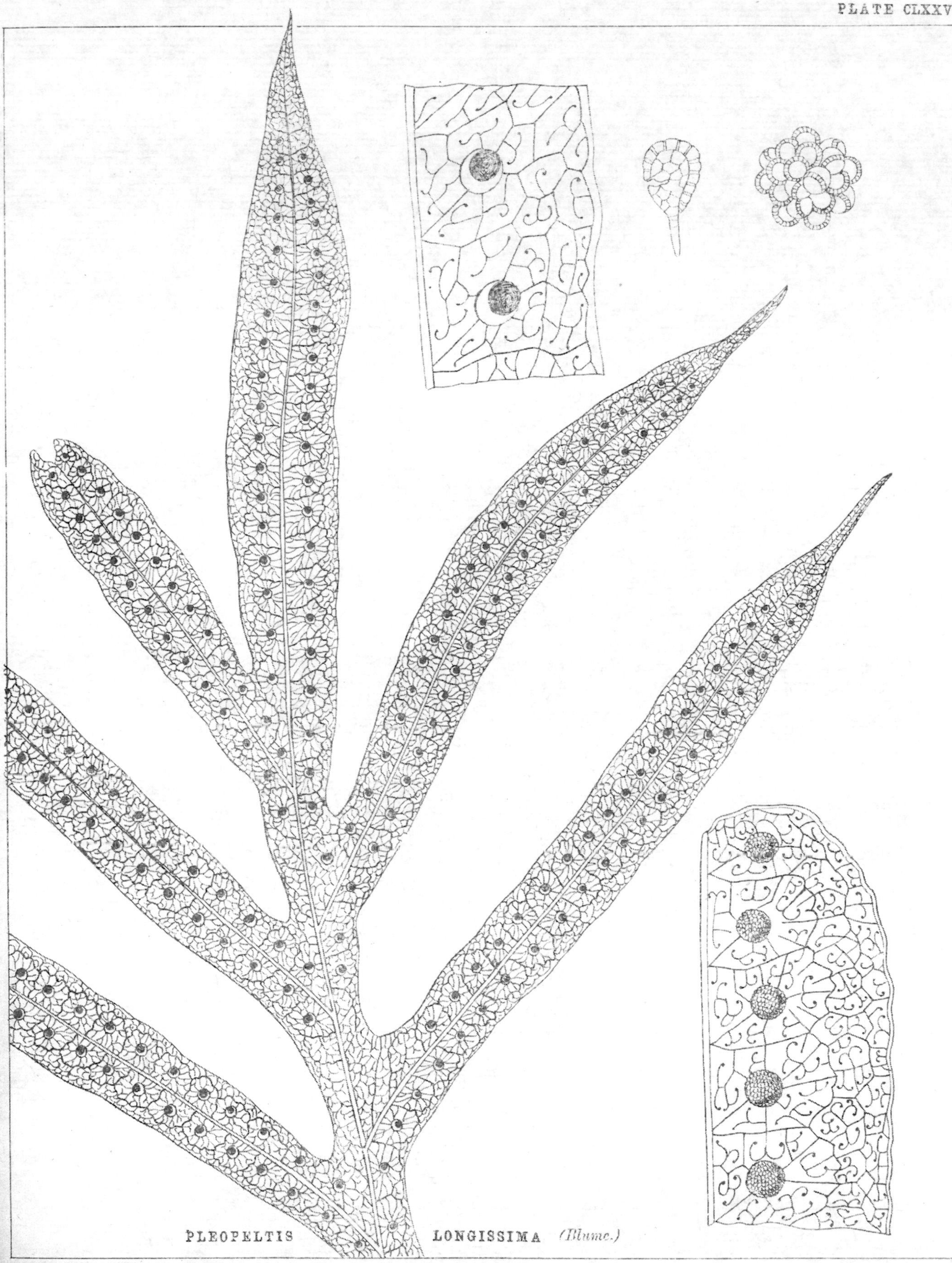

PLEOPELTIS LONGISSIMA *(Blume.)*

PUBLISHED BY HIGGINBOTHAM & CO. ORIENTAL LITHOGRAPHIC PRESS MADRAS 1872. LITHOGRAPHED BY ALEX: FARREN,

PLATE CLXXVII

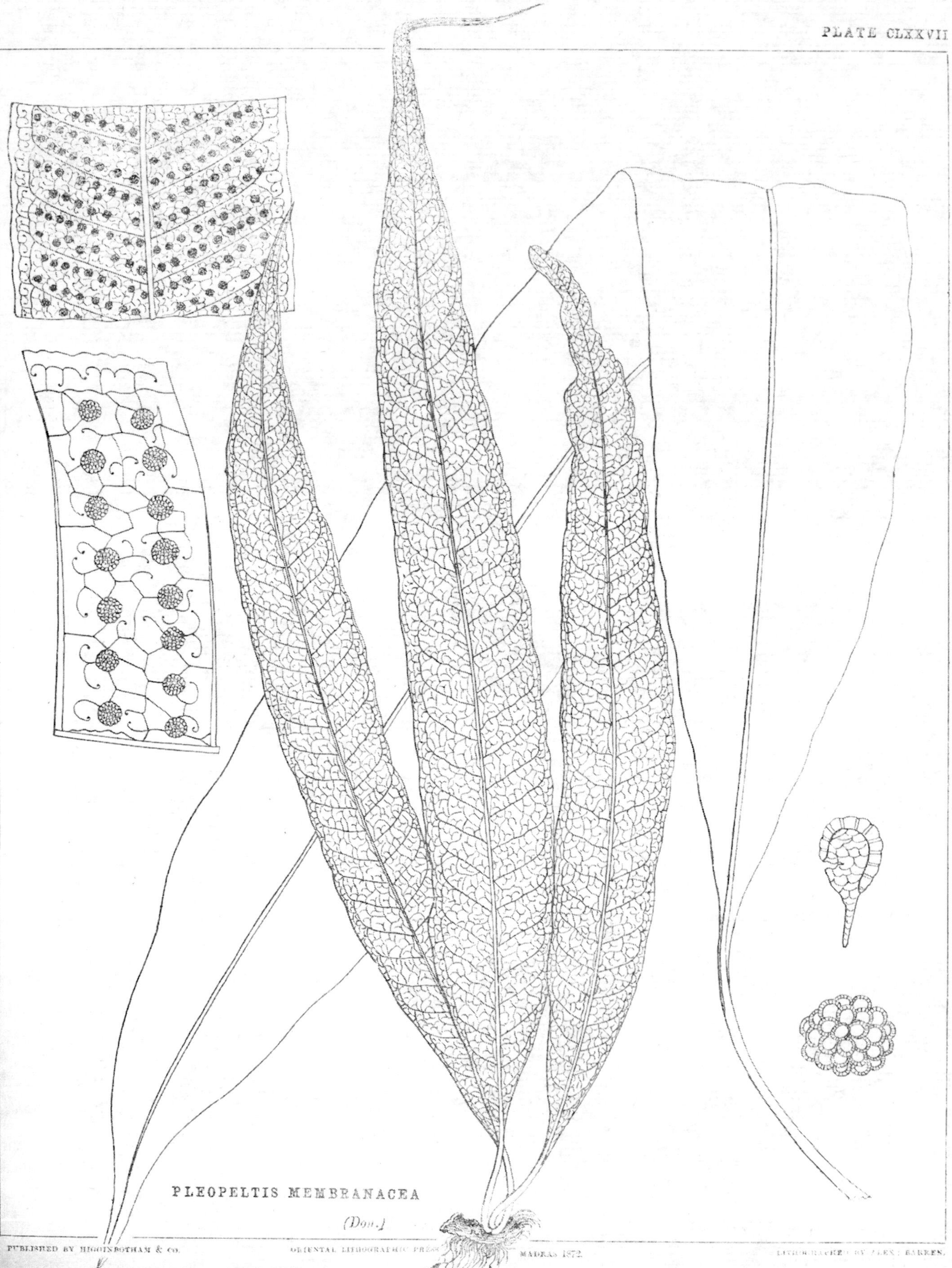

PLEOPELTIS MEMBRANACEA

(Don.)

PUBLISHED BY HIGGINBOTHAM & CO. ORIENTAL LITHOGRAPHIC PRESS MADRAS 1872. LITHOGRAPHED BY ALEX: BARREN.

PLEOPELTIS IRIOIDES *(Poir.)*

PUBLISHED BY HIGGINBOTHAM & CO. ORIENTAL LITHOGRAPHIC PRESS MADRAS 1872. LITHOGRAPHED BY ALEX: BARREN

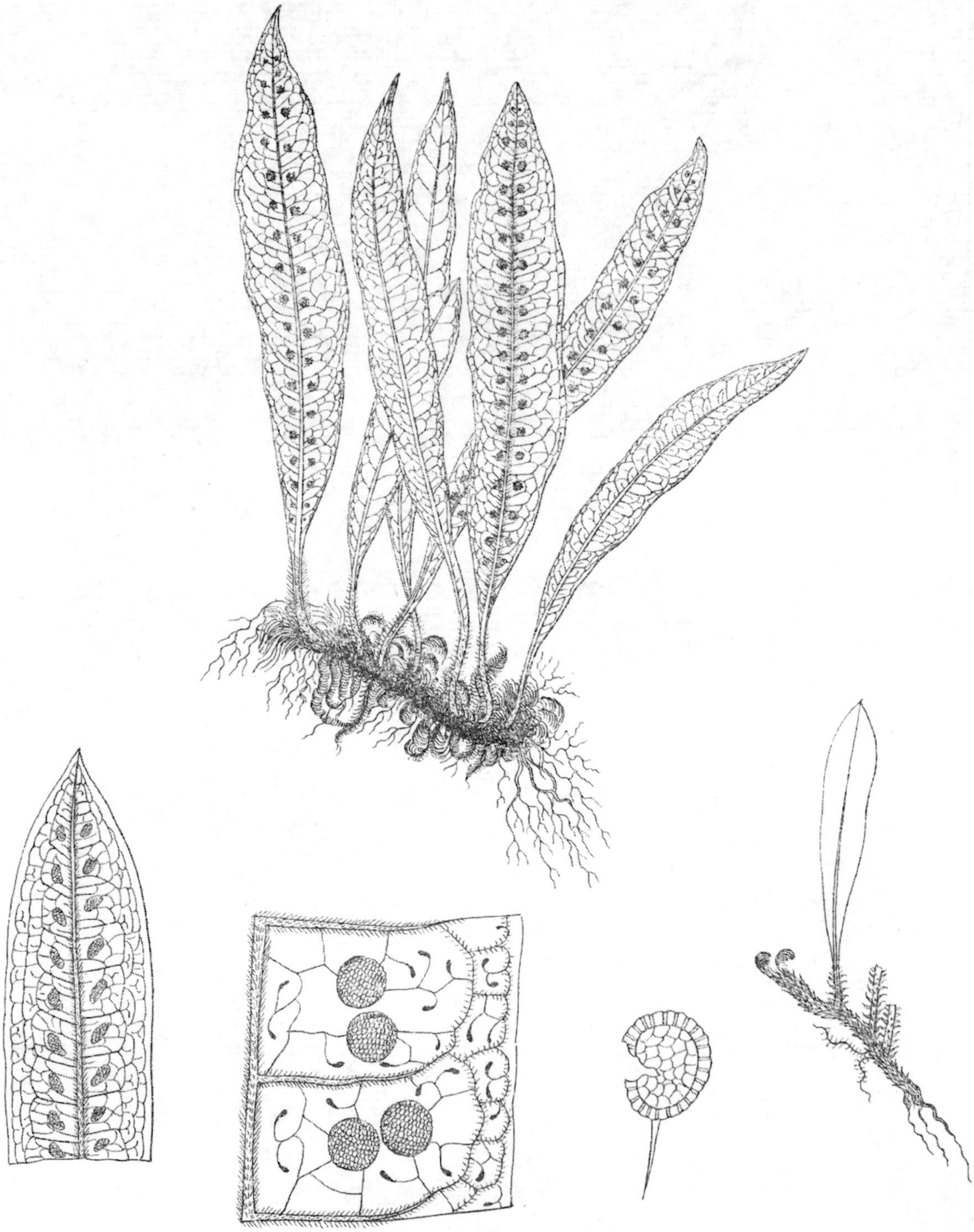

POLEOPELTIS TRIDACTYLA *(Wallich.)*

PUBLISHED BY HIGGINBOTHAM & Co.
ORIENTAL LITHOGRAPHIC PRESS MADRAS 1872

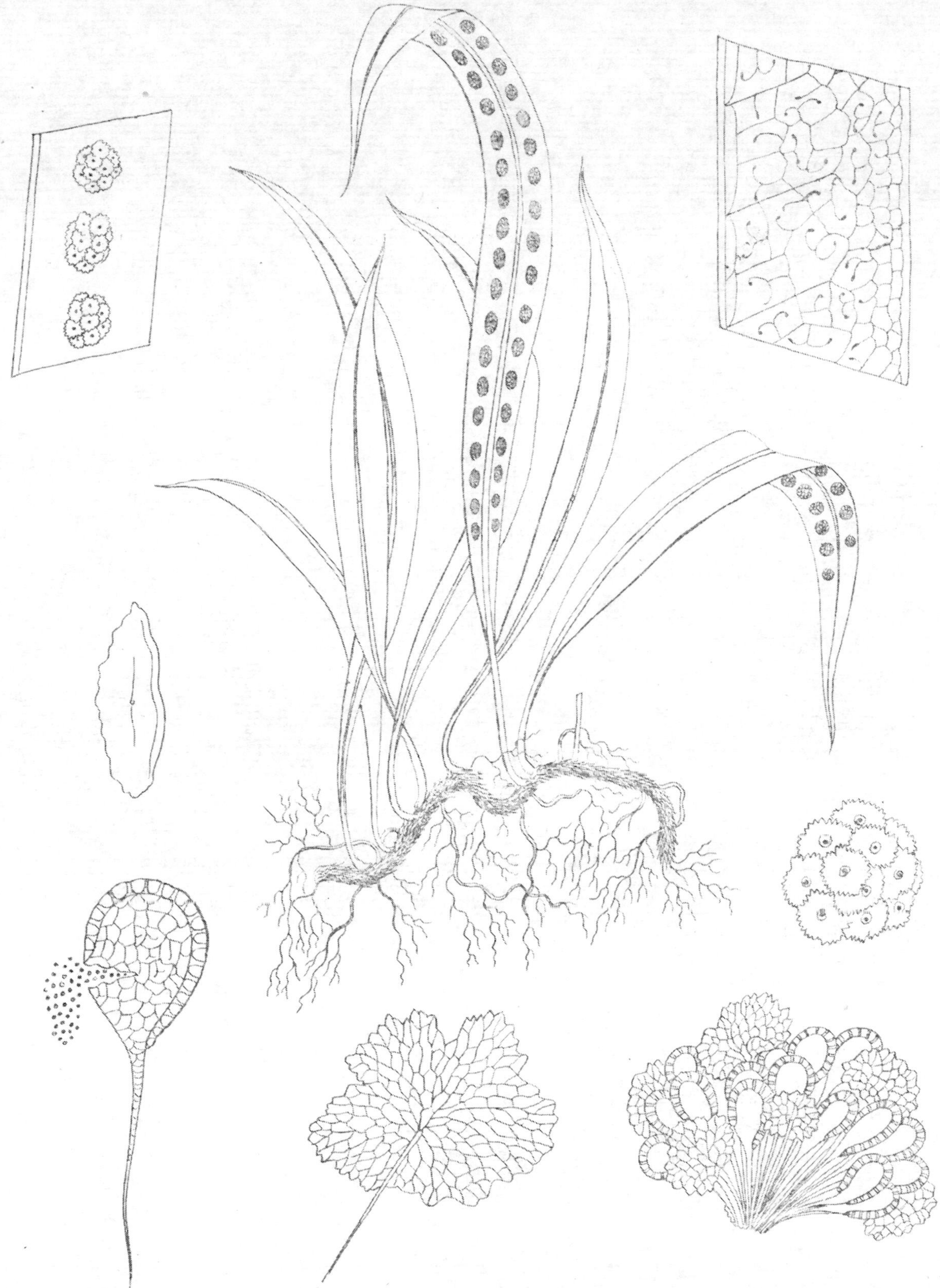

PLEOPELTIS WIGHTIANA (*Wallich.*)

PUBLISHED BY HIGGINBOTHAM & CO. ORIENTAL LITHOGRAPHIC PRESS MADRAS 1872. LITHOGRAPHED BY ALEX: BARREN.

PLEOPELTIS LEPIDOTA *(Willd.)*

PUBLISHED BY HIGGINBOTHAM & CO. ORIENTAL LITHOGRAPHIC PRESS MADRAS 1872. LITHOGRAPHED BY ALEX: FARRAN.

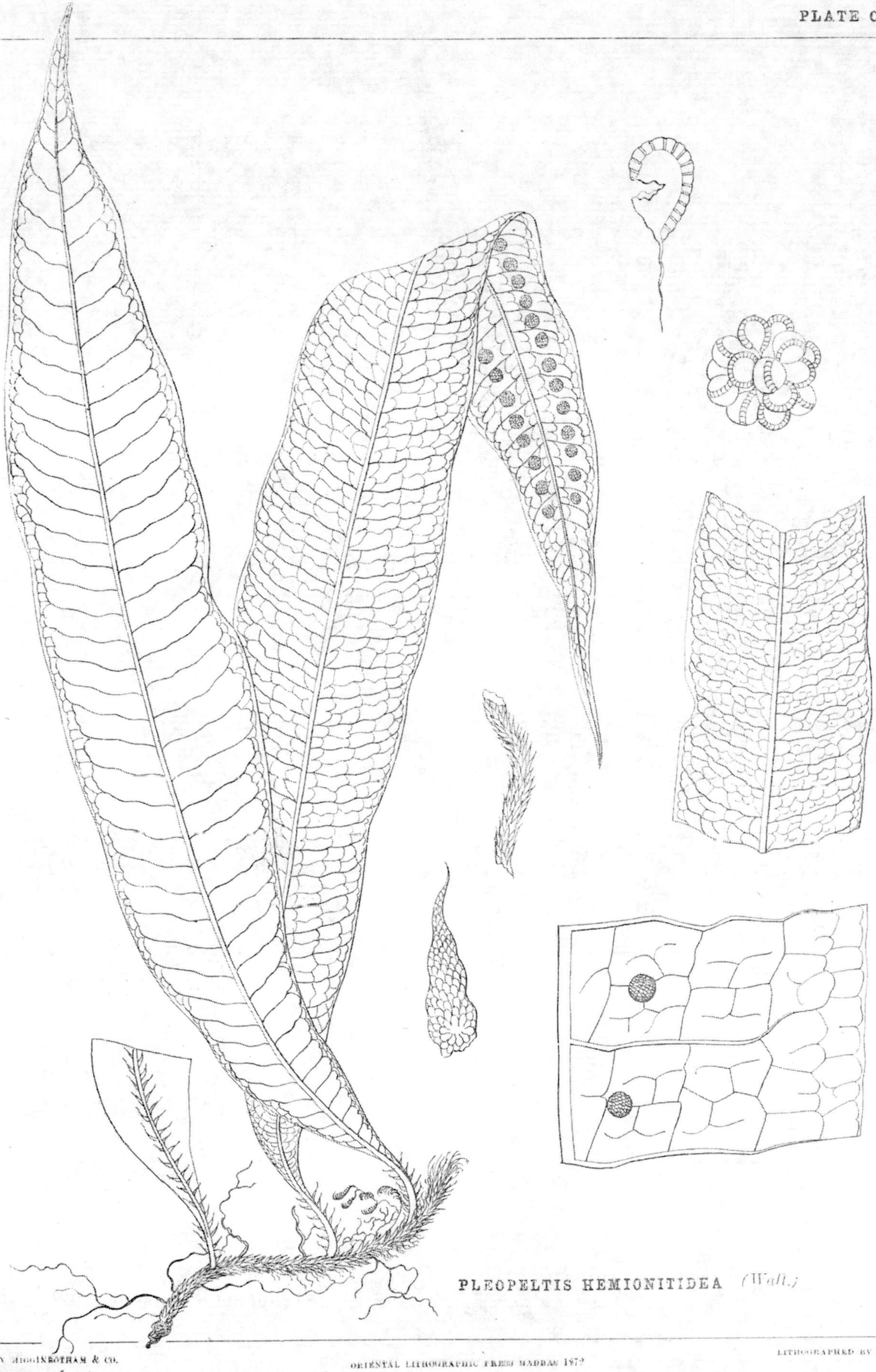

PLEOPELTIS HEMIONITIDEA (Wall.)

PUBLISHED BY HIGGINBOTHAM & CO.

ORIENTAL LITHOGRAPHIC PRESS MADRAS 1872

LITHOGRAPHED BY ALEX: BARREN.

NIPHOBOLUS POROSUS (Wall.)

PUBLISHED BY HIGGINBOTHAM & CO
ORIENTAL LITHOGRAPHIC PRESS MADRAS 1872
LITHOGRAPHED BY ALEX: BARREN.

PLATE CLXXXIV

NIPHOBOLUS ADNASCENS (Sw.)

PUBLISHED BY HIGGINBOTHAM & Co.   ORIENTAL LITHOGRAPHIC PRESS MADRAS 1872   LITHOGRAPHED BY ALEX: BARREN.

NIPHOBOLUS ANGUSTATUS (Sw.)

PUBLISHED BY HIGGINBOTHAM & CO. ORIENTAL LITHOGRAPHIC PRESS MADRAS 1872. LITHOGRAPHED BY ALEX: BARREN,

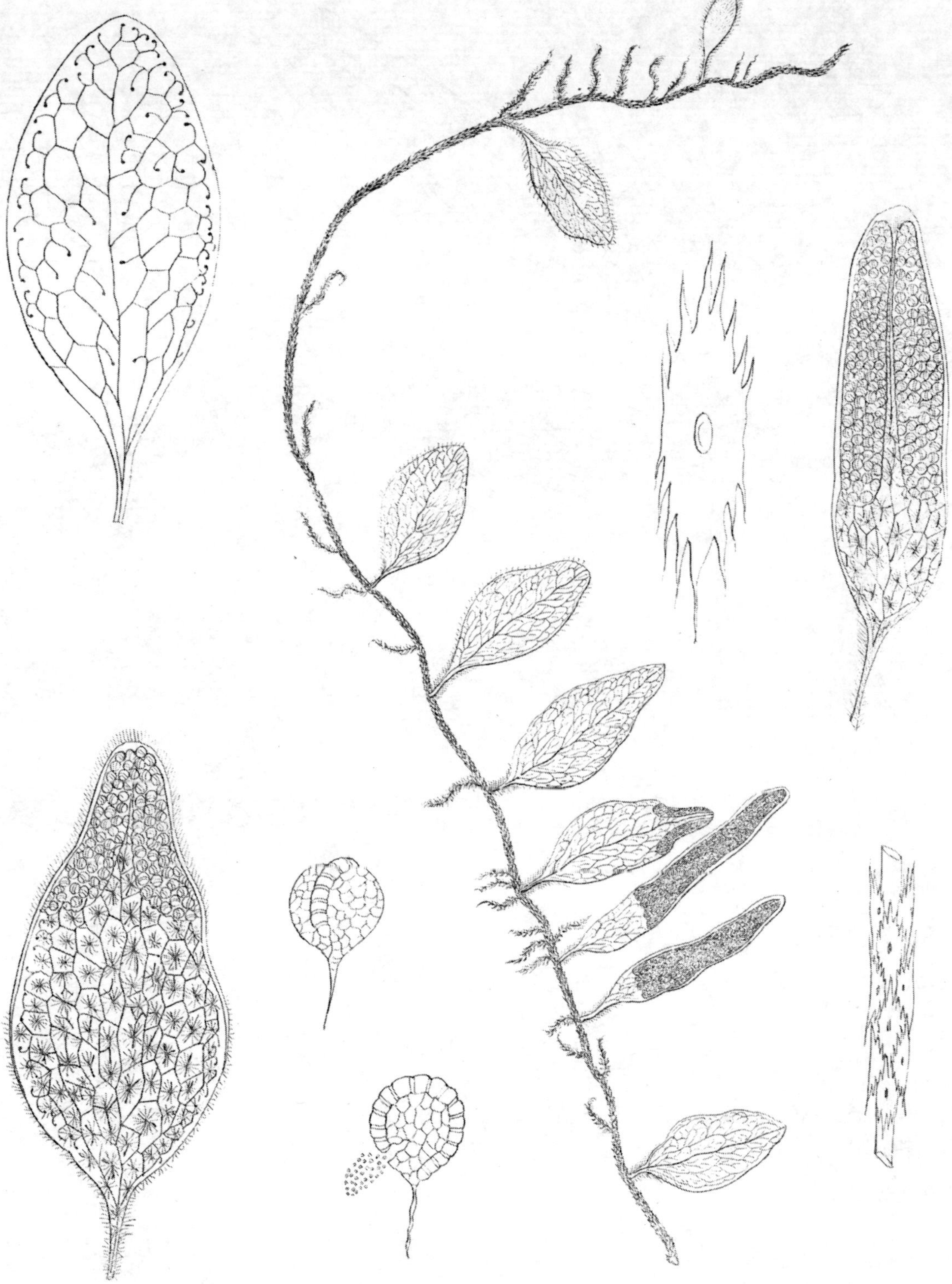

NIPHOBOLUS NUMMULARIFOLIUS (Metten.)

PUBLISHED BY HIGGINBOTHAM & CO. ORIENTAL LITHOGRAPHIC PRESS MADRAS 187[illegible] LITHOGRAPHED BY ALEX. BARREN.

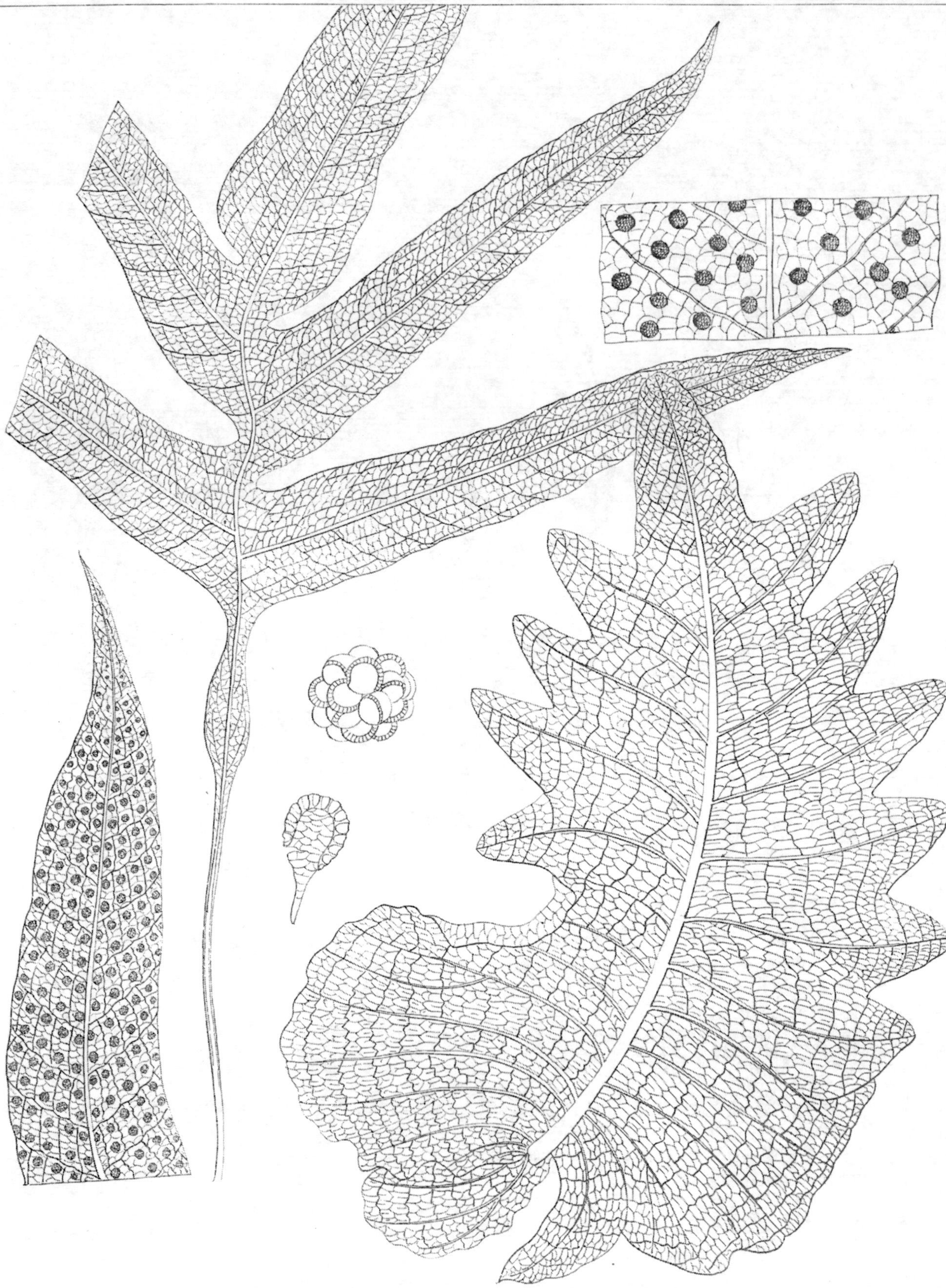

DRYNARIA QUERCIFOLIA (L.)

PUBLISHED BY HIGGINBOTHAM & CO ORIENTAL LITHOGRAPHIC PRESS MADRAS 1872. LITHOGRAPHED BY ALEX. BARREN,

CHEILANTHES TENUIFOLIA (Sw.)

PUBLISHED BY HIGGINBOTHAM & CO. ORIENTAL LITHOGRAPHIC PRESS MADRAS 1872. LITHOGRAPHED BY ALEX. BARREN,

CHEILANTHES VARIANS (*Hooker.*)

PUBLISHED BY HIGGINBOTHAM & CO. ORIENTAL LITHOGRAPHIC PRESS MADRAS 1872 LITHOGRAPHED BY ALEX: BARREN.

CHEILANTHES MYSORENSIS (Wallich.)

PUBLISHED BY HIGGINBOTHAM & CO. ORIENTAL LITHOGRAPHIC PRESS MADRAS 1872. LITHOGRAPHED BY ALEX. BARREN.

CHEILANTHES FARINOSA *(Kaulf.)*

PUBLISHED BY HIGGINBOTHAM & CO. ORIENTAL LITHOGRAPHIC PRESS MADRAS 1872 LITHOGRAPHED BY ALEX. [illegible]

CHEILANTHES BULLOSA *(Kunze.)*

PUBLISHED BY HIGGINBOTHAM & CO. ORIENTAL LITHOGRAPHIC PRESS MADRAS 1872. LITHOGRAPHED BY ALEX: BARREN,

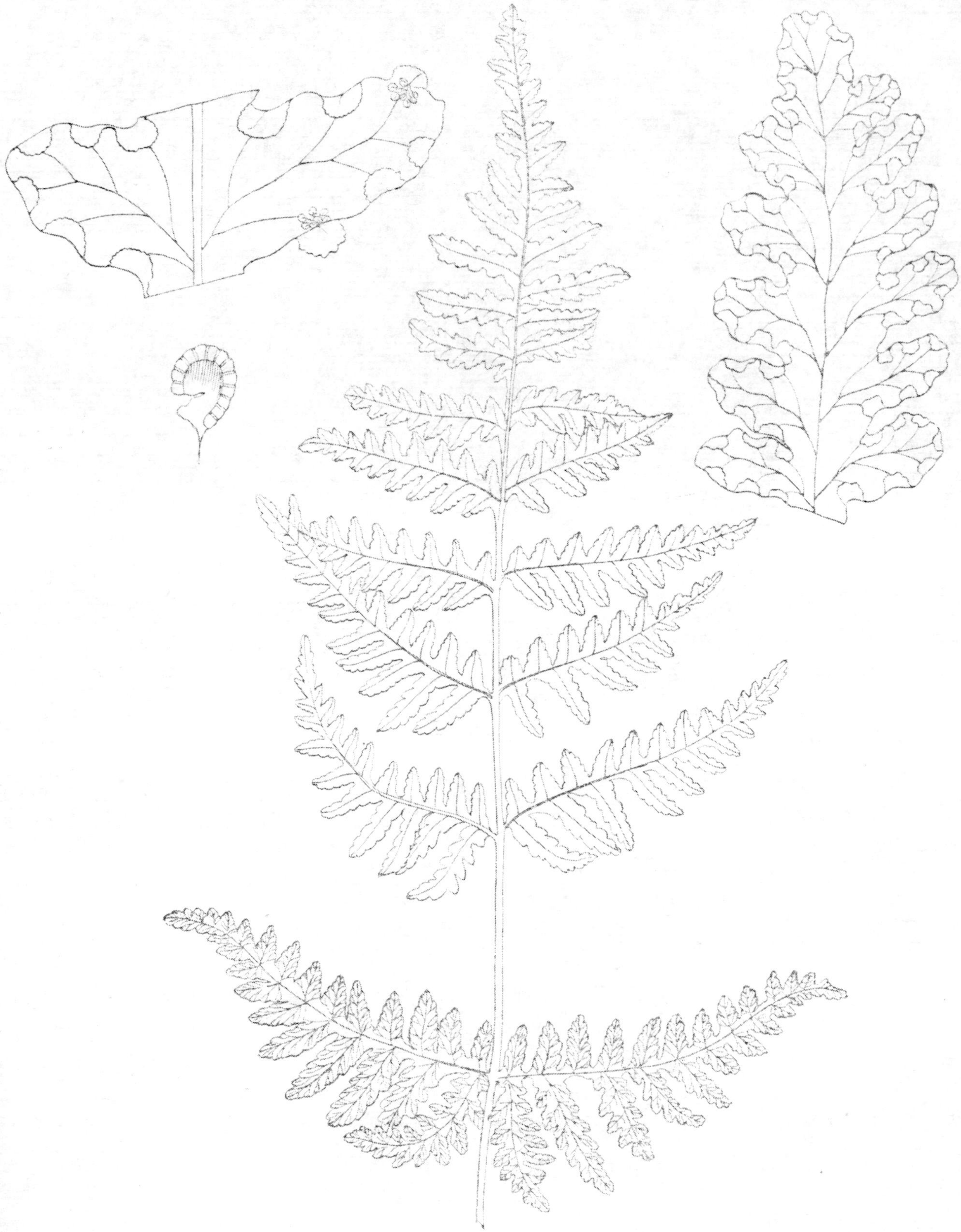

CHEILANTHES DALHOUSIÆ (*Hooker.*)

PUBLISHED BY HIGGINBOTHAM & CO. ORIENTAL LITHOGRAPHIC PRESS MADRAS 1872 LITHOGRAPHED BY ALEX: BARREN.

PLATE CXCIV

POLYBOTRYA APPENDICULATA (*J. Smith.*)

PUBLISHED BY HIGGINBOTHAM & CO. ORIENTAL LITHOGRAPHIC PRESS MADRAS 1872. LITHOGRAPHED BY ALEX: BARREN.

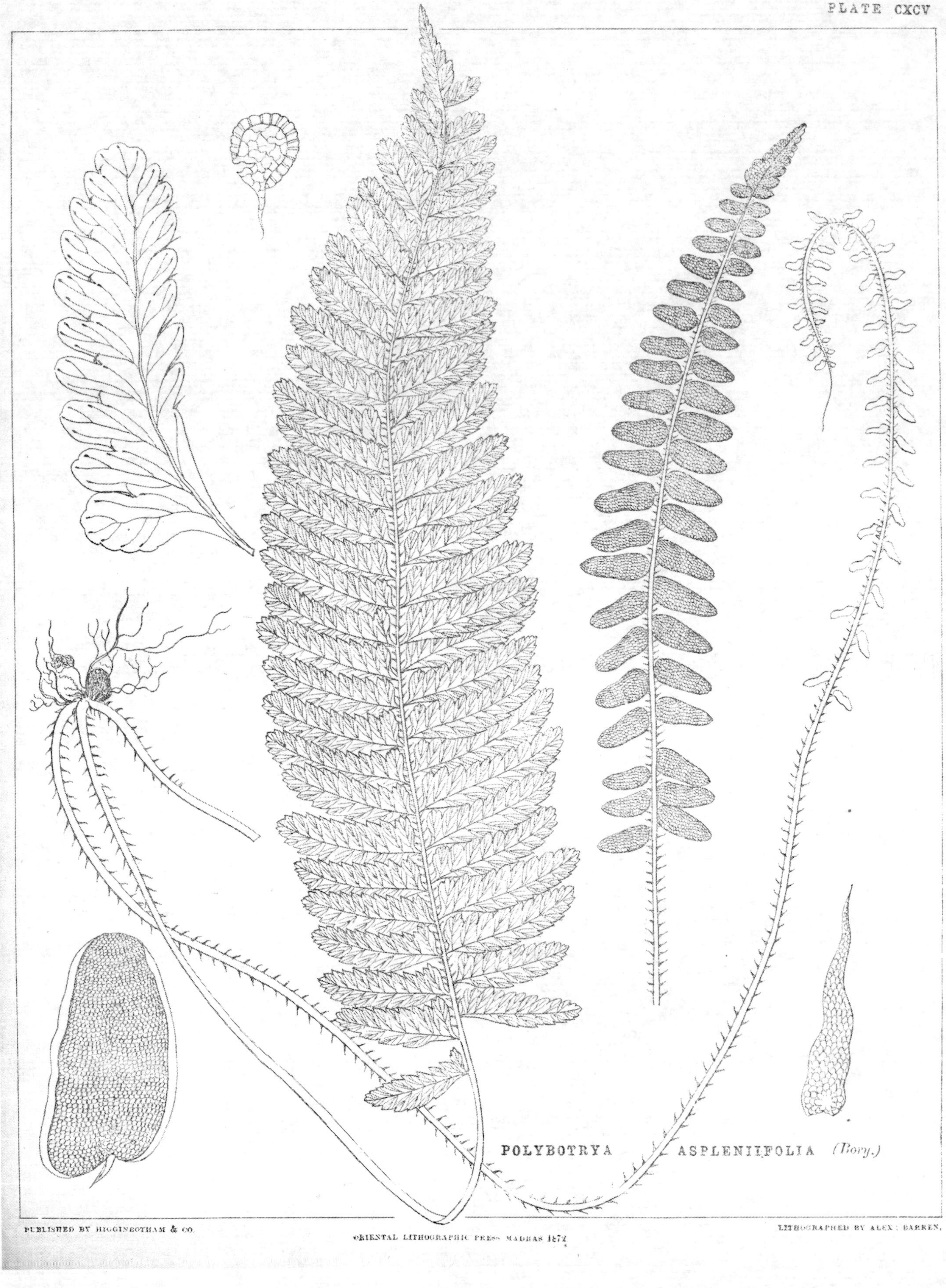

POLYBOTRYA ASPLENIIFOLIA (*Bory.*)

PUBLISHED BY HIGGINBOTHAM & CO.

ORIENTAL LITHOGRAPHIC PRESS MADRAS 1872

LITHOGRAPHED BY ALEX: BARREN.

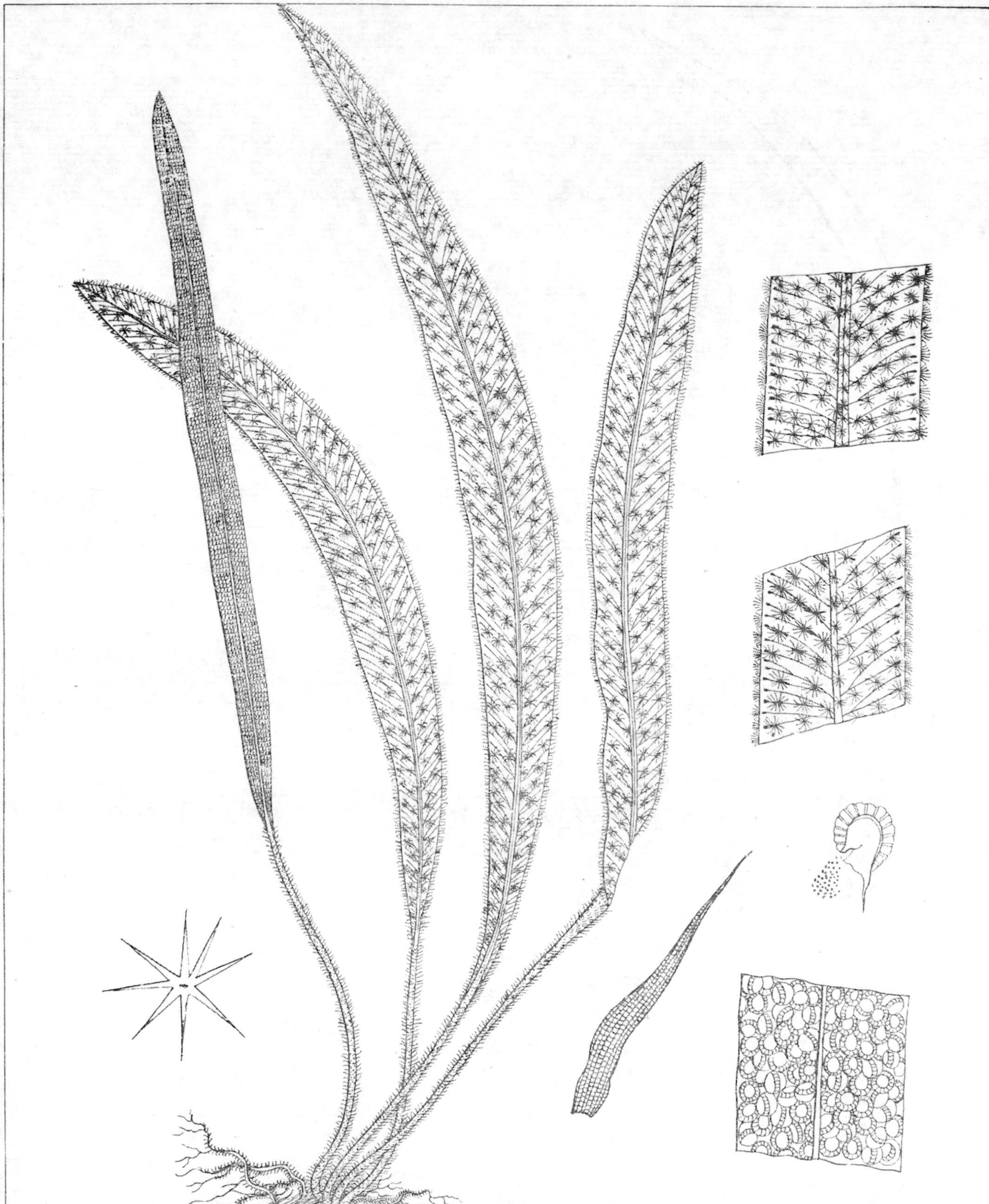

ELAPHOGLOSSUM VISCOSUM (*Schott.*)

PUBLISHED BY HIGGINBOTHAM & CO. ORIENTAL LITHOGRAPHIC PRESS MADRAS 1877. LITHOGRAPHED BY ALEX: BARREN,

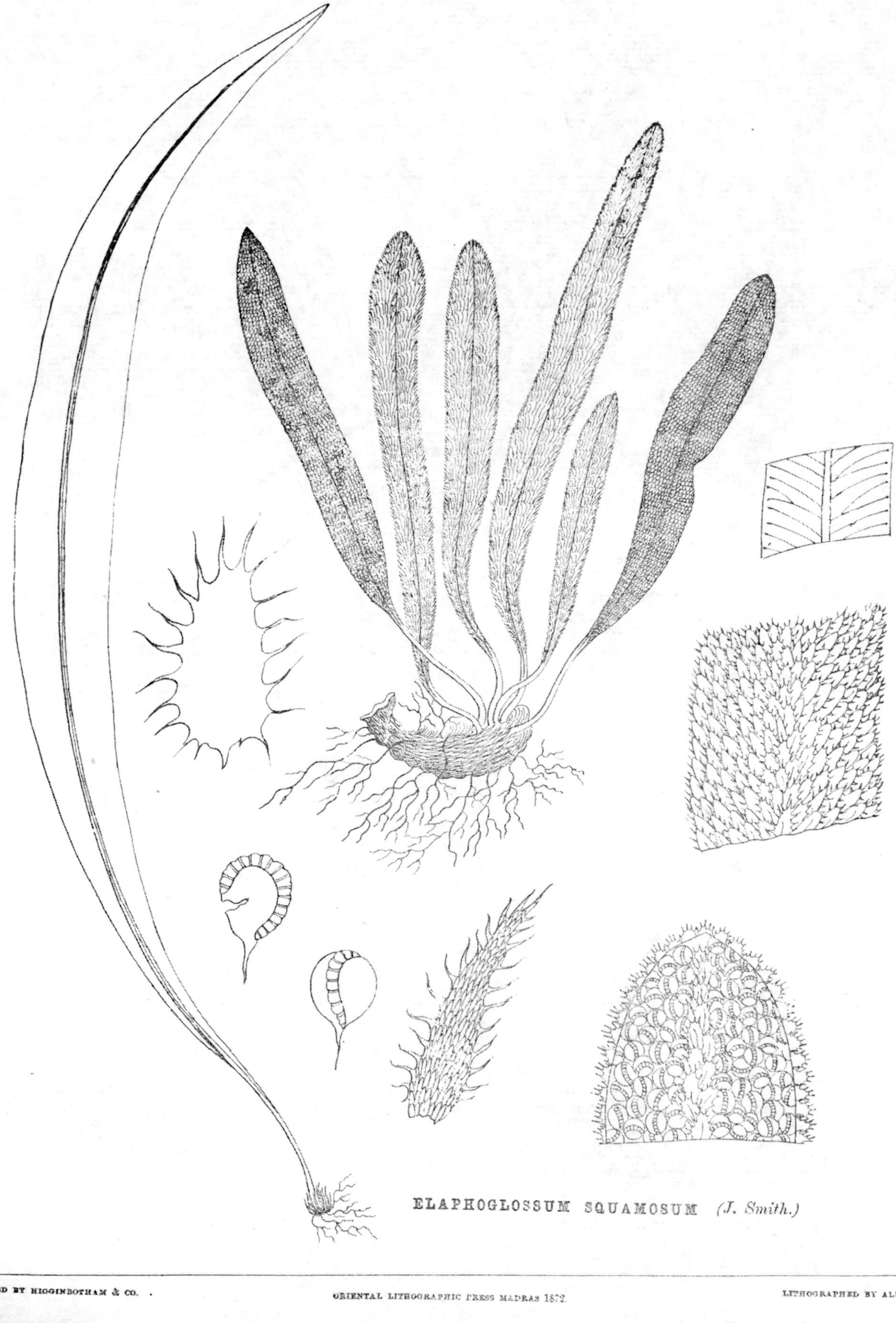

ELAPHOGLOSSUM SQUAMOSUM *(J. Smith.)*

PUBLISHED BY HIGGINBOTHAM & CO. · ORIENTAL LITHOGRAPHIC PRESS MADRAS 1872. · LITHOGRAPHED BY ALEX: BARREN.

PLATE CXCVIII

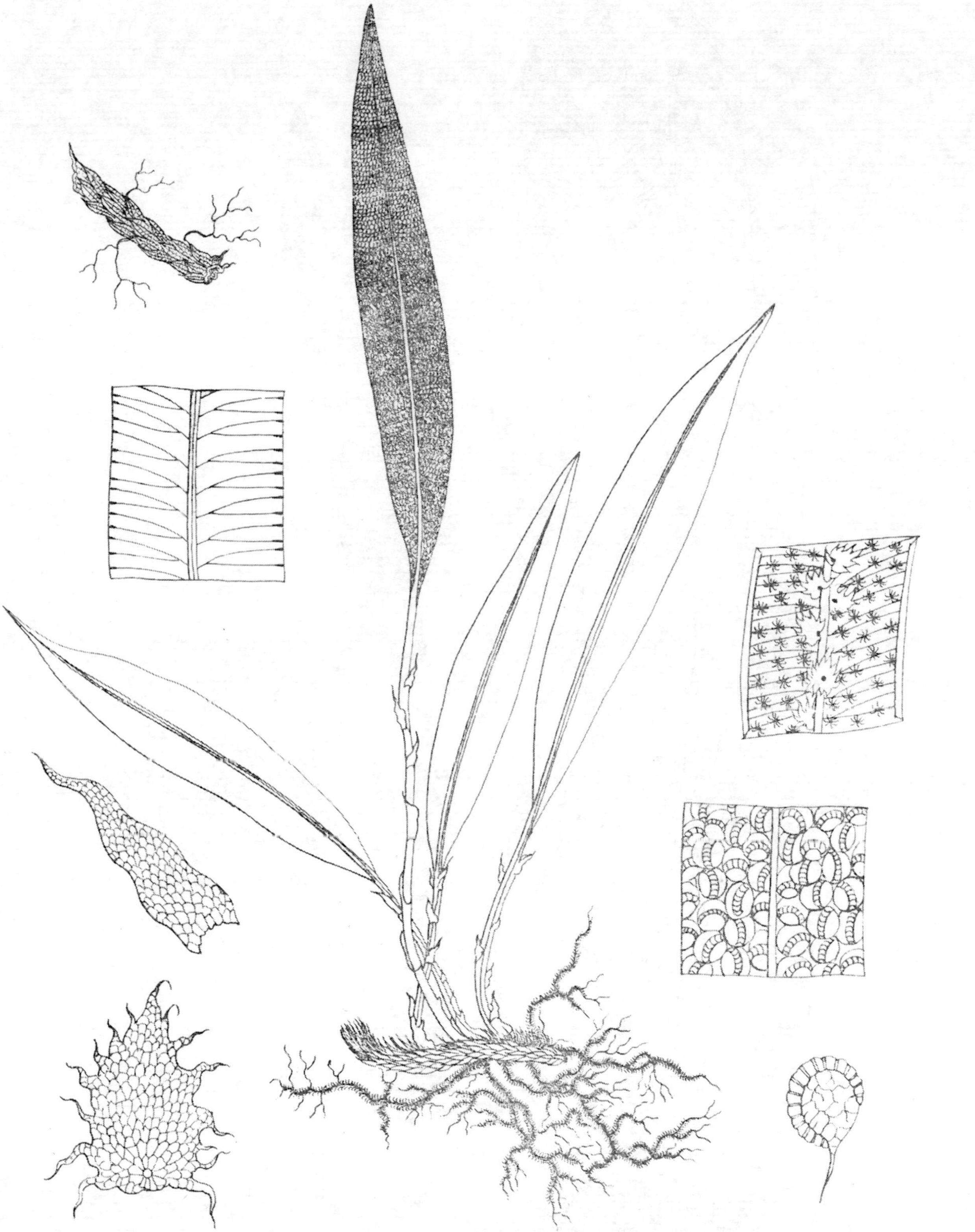

ELAPHOGLOSSUM CONFORME *(Schott.)*

PUBLISHED BY HIGGINBOTHAM & CO.

ORIENTAL LITHOGRAPHIC PRESS MADRAS 1872.

LITHOGRAPHED BY ALEX: BARREN.

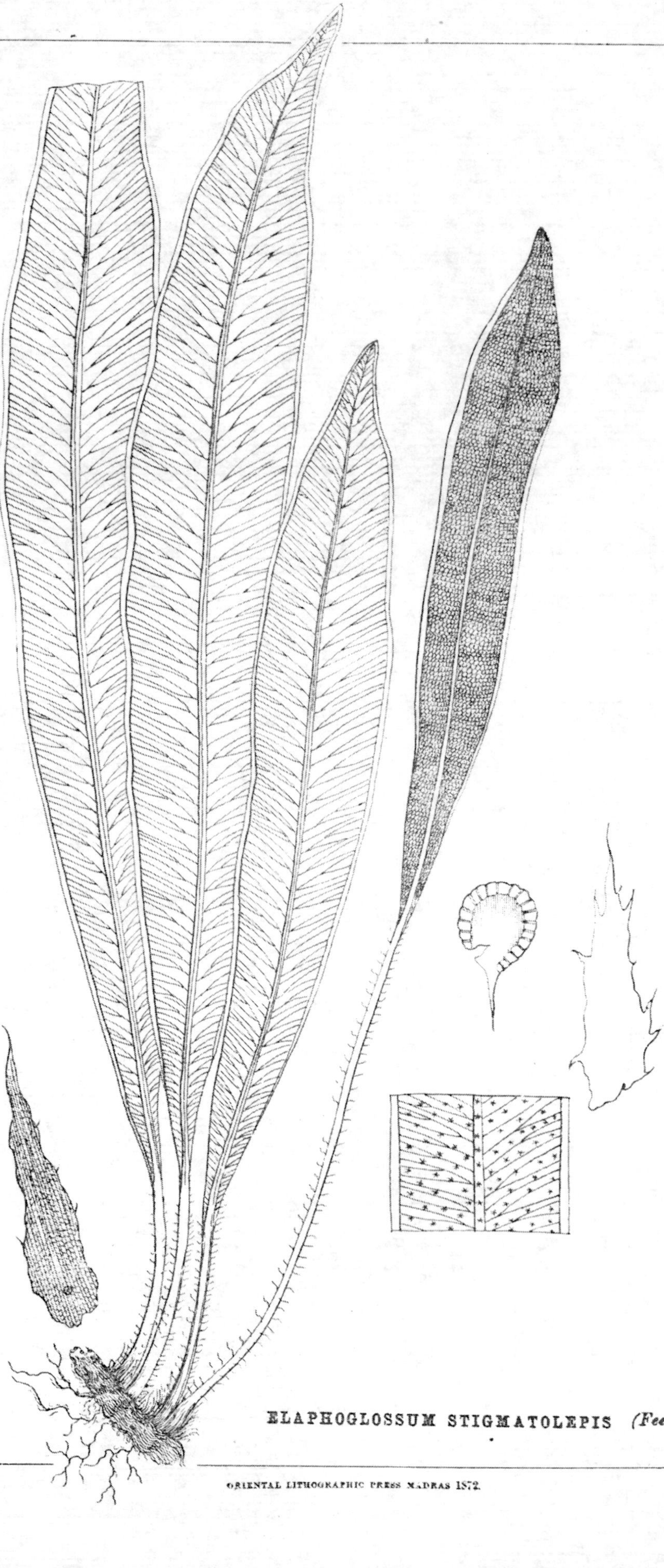

ELAPHOGLOSSUM STIGMATOLEPIS *(Fee.)*

PUBLISHED BY HIGGINBOTHAM & CO. ORIENTAL LITHOGRAPHIC PRESS MADRAS 1872. LITHOGRAPHED BY ALEX: BARREN.

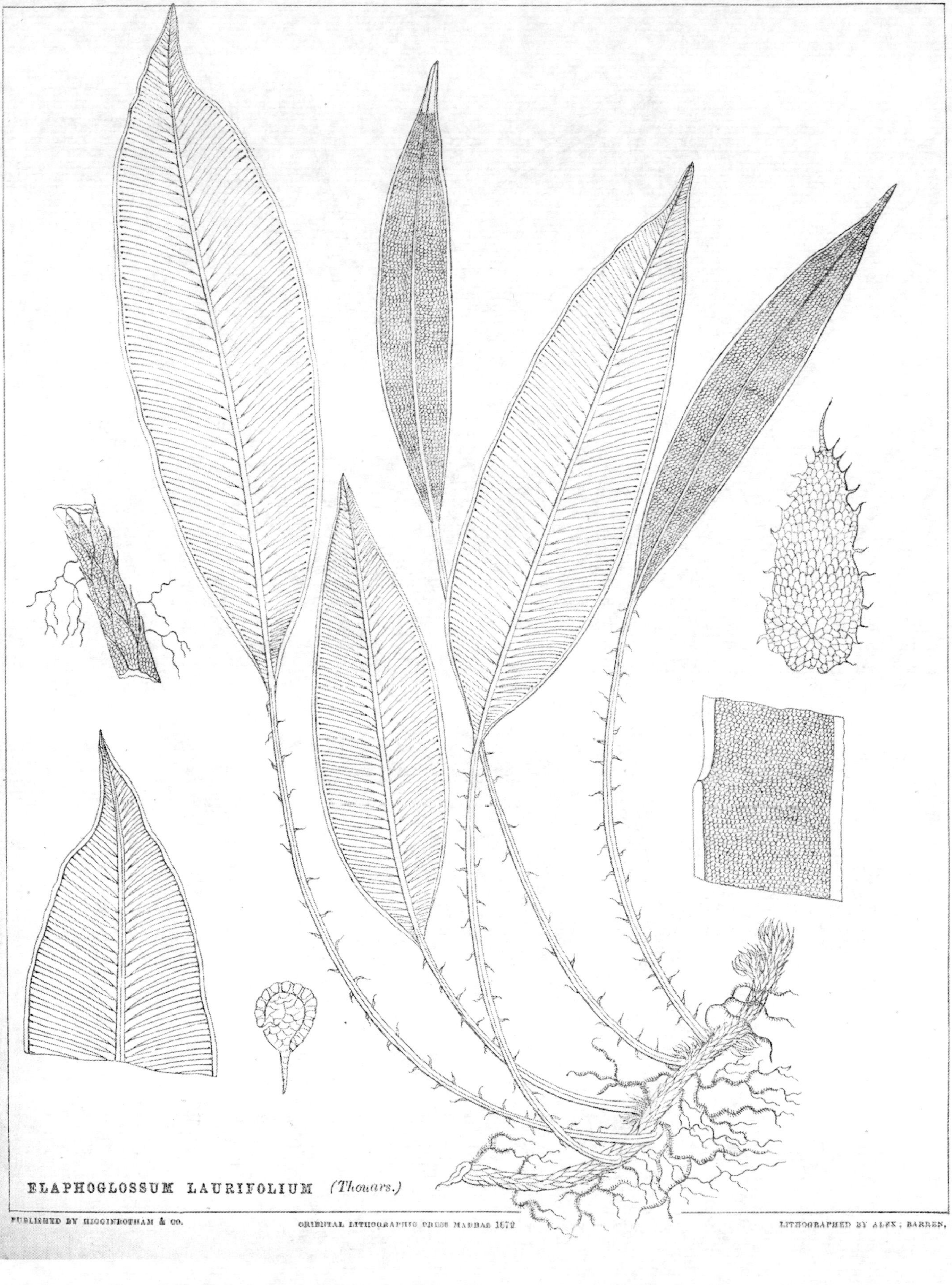

ELAPHOGLOSSUM LAURIFOLIUM *(Thouars.)*

PUBLISHED BY HIGGINBOTHAM & CO. ORIENTAL LITHOGRAPHIC PRESS MADRAS 1872 LITHOGRAPHED BY ALEX; BARREN,

STENOCHLŒNA SCANDENS (*J. Smith*)

PUBLISHED BY HIGGINBOTHAM & CO. ORIENTAL LITHOGRAPHIC PRESS MADRAS 1872. LITHOGRAPHED BY ALEX: BARREN,

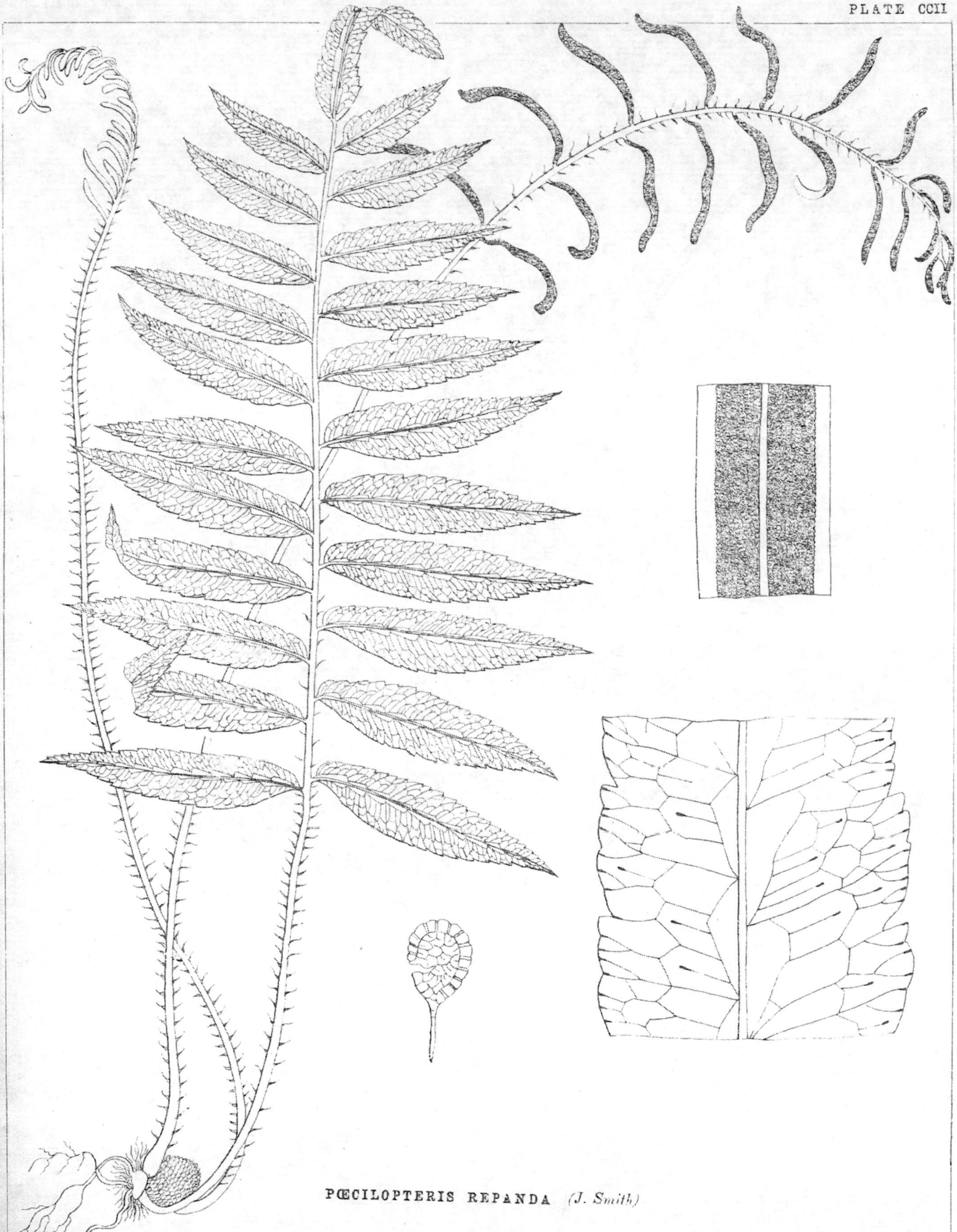

PŒCILOPTERIS REPANDA *(J. Smith)*

PLATE CCIII

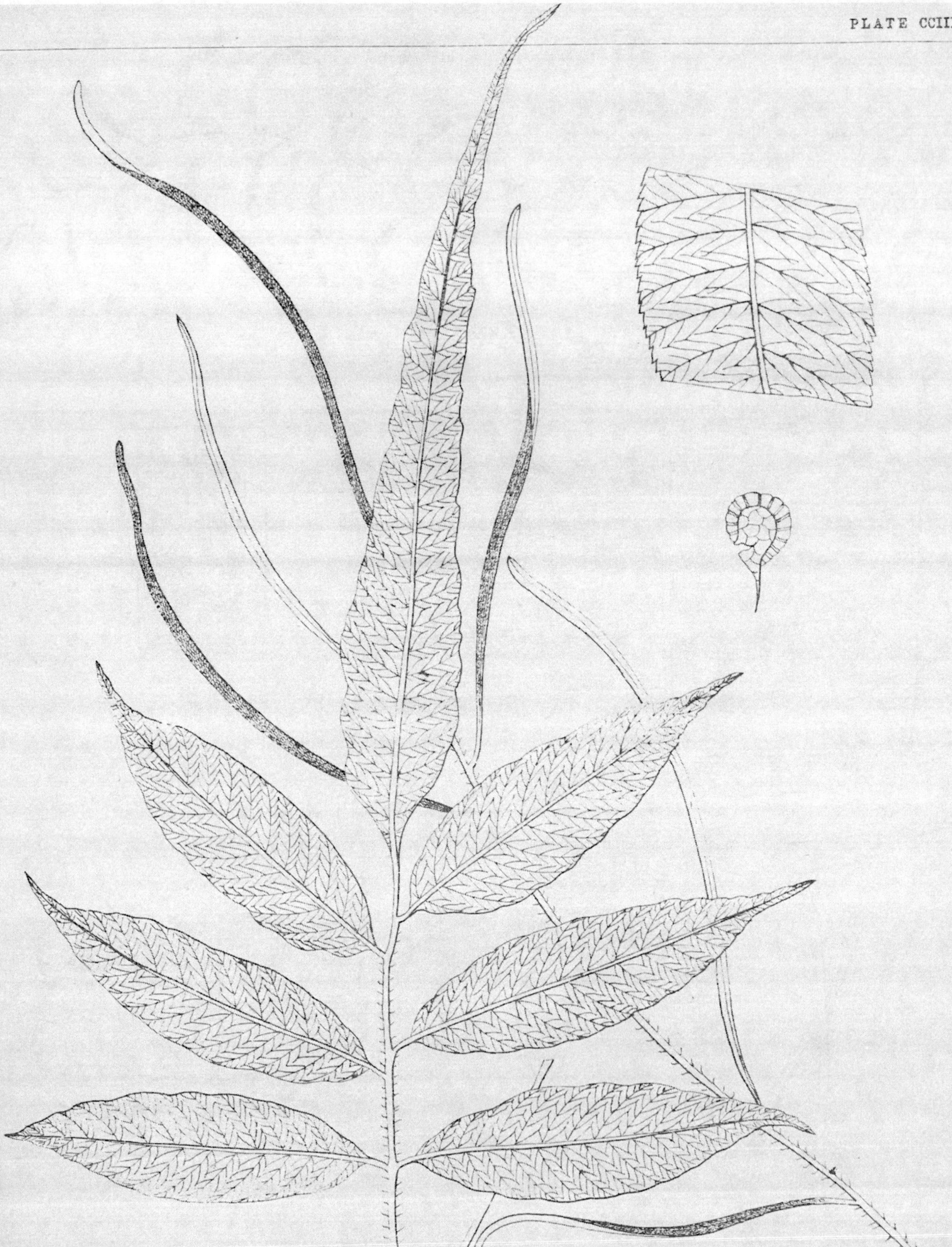

PŒCILOPTERIS TERMINANS (Wallich)

[illegible]BLISHED BY HIGGINBOTHAM & Co

LITHO[illegible] BY ALEX. [illegible]

ORIENTAL LITHOGRAPHIC PRESS MADRAS [illegible]

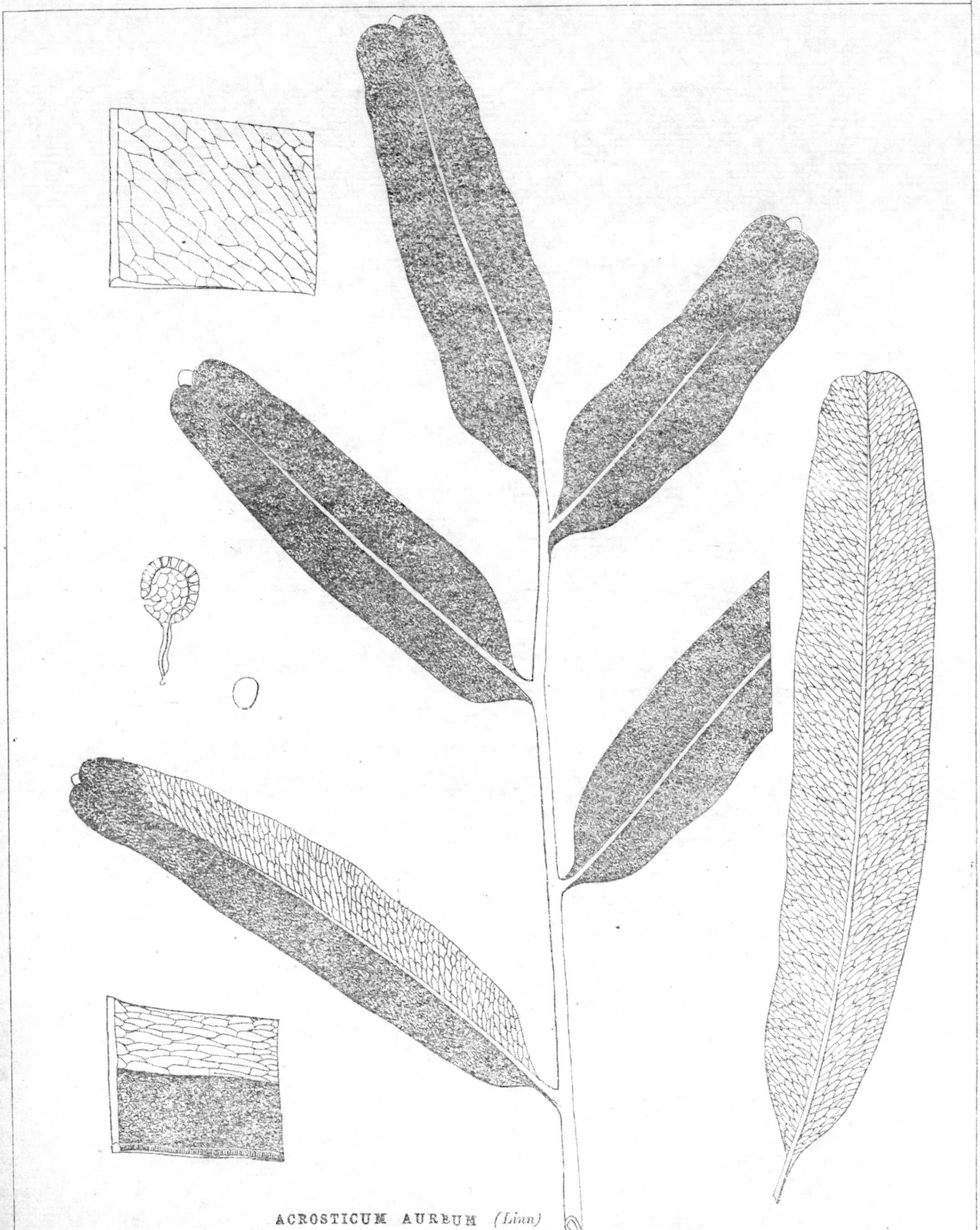

ACROSTICUM AUREUM *(Linn)*

PUBLISHED BY HIGGINBOTHAM & CO. ORIENTAL LITHOGRAPHIC PRESS MADRAS 1872 LITHOGRAPHED BY ALEX: BARREN,

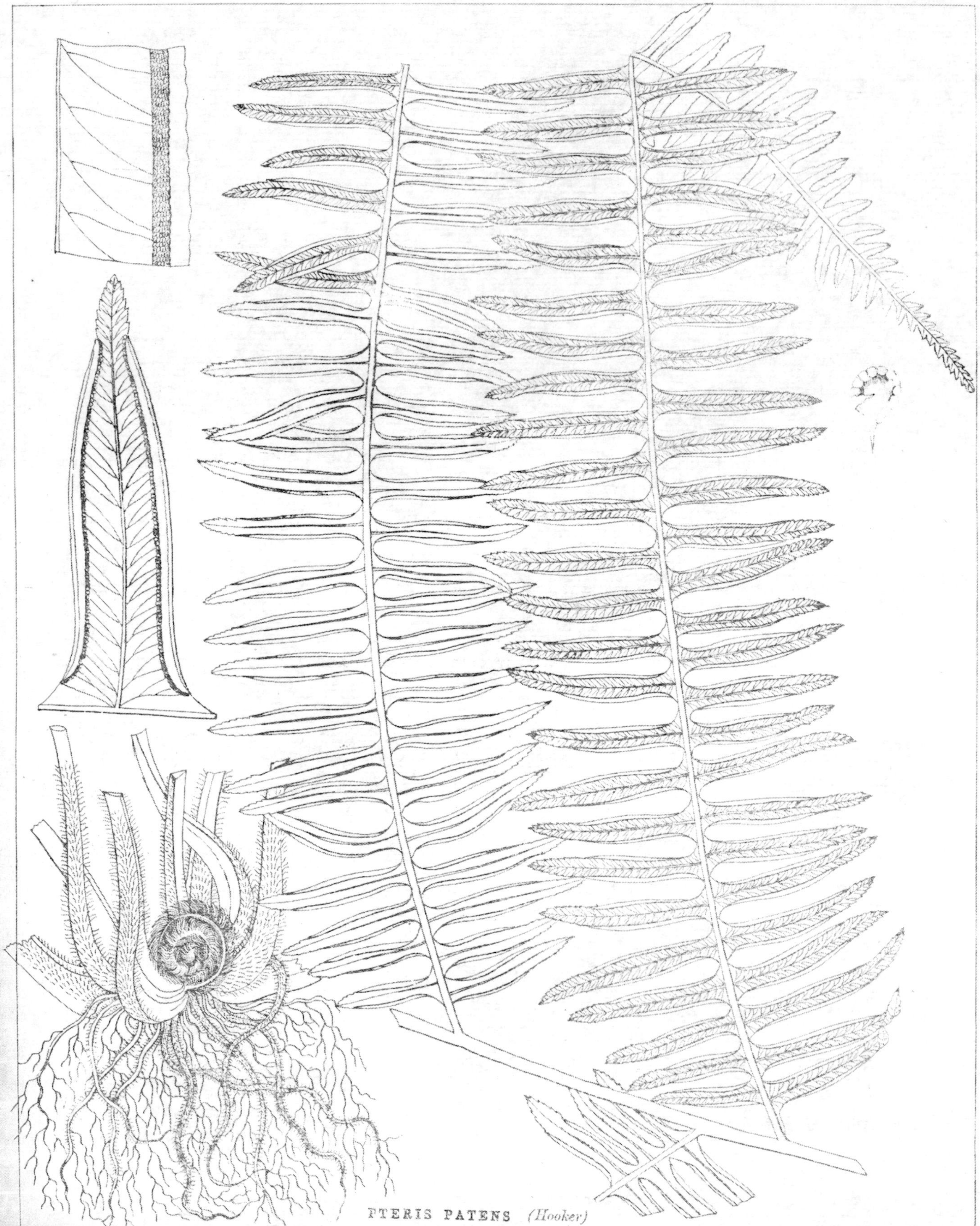

PTERIS PATENS (*Hooker*)

PUBLISHED BY HIGGINBOTHAM & Co. ORIENTAL LITHOGRAPHIC PRESS MADRAS 1877. LITHOGRAPHED BY ALEX: BARREN.

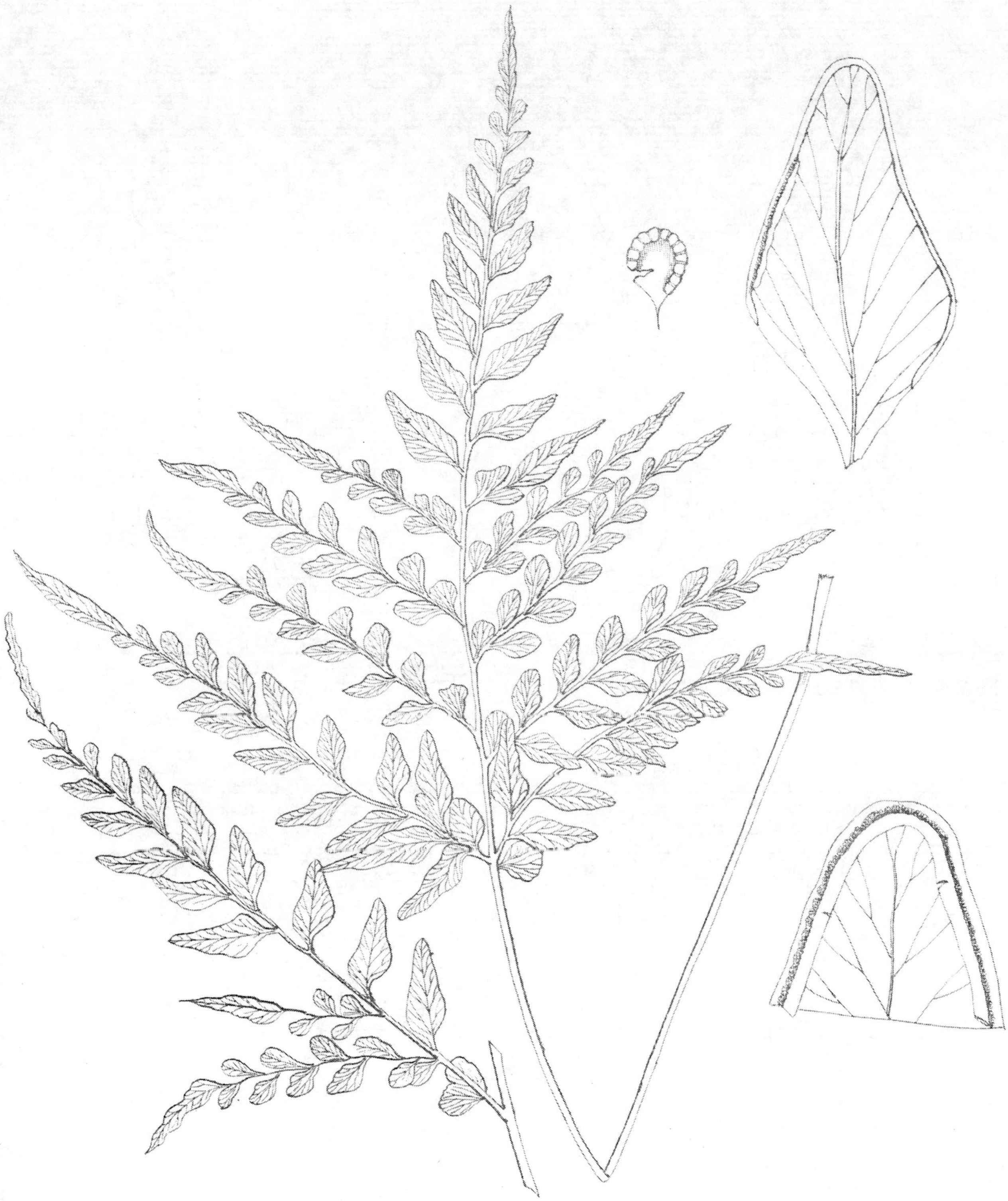

LINDSŒA HETEROPHYLLA (*Bedd*)

PUBLISHED BY HIGGINBOTHAM & CO   ORIENTAL LITHOGRAPHIC PRESS MADRAS 1872   LITHOGRAPHED BY ALEXR BARREN,

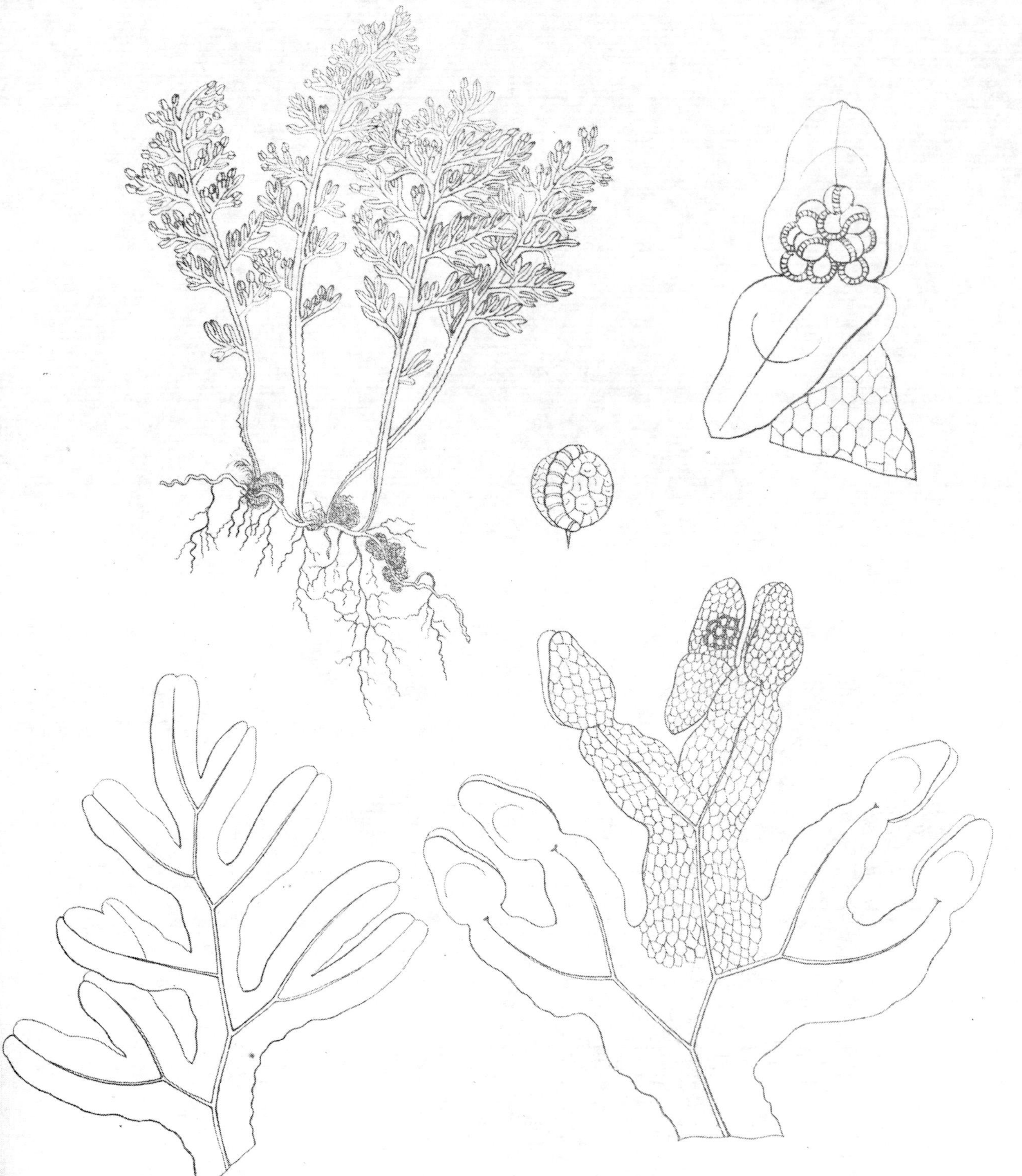

HYMENOPHYLLUM CRISPATUM *(Wall)*

PUBLISHED BY HIGGINBOTHAM & CO. ORIENTAL LITHOGRAPHIC PRESS MADRAS 1872. LITHOGRAPHED BY ALEX. BARREN,

TRICHOMANES INTRAMARGINALE *(Hooker et Grev)*

PUBLISHED BY HIGGINBOTHAM & CO. ORIENTAL LITHOGRAPHIC PRESS MADRAS 1872. LITHOGRAPHED BY ALEX: BARREN,

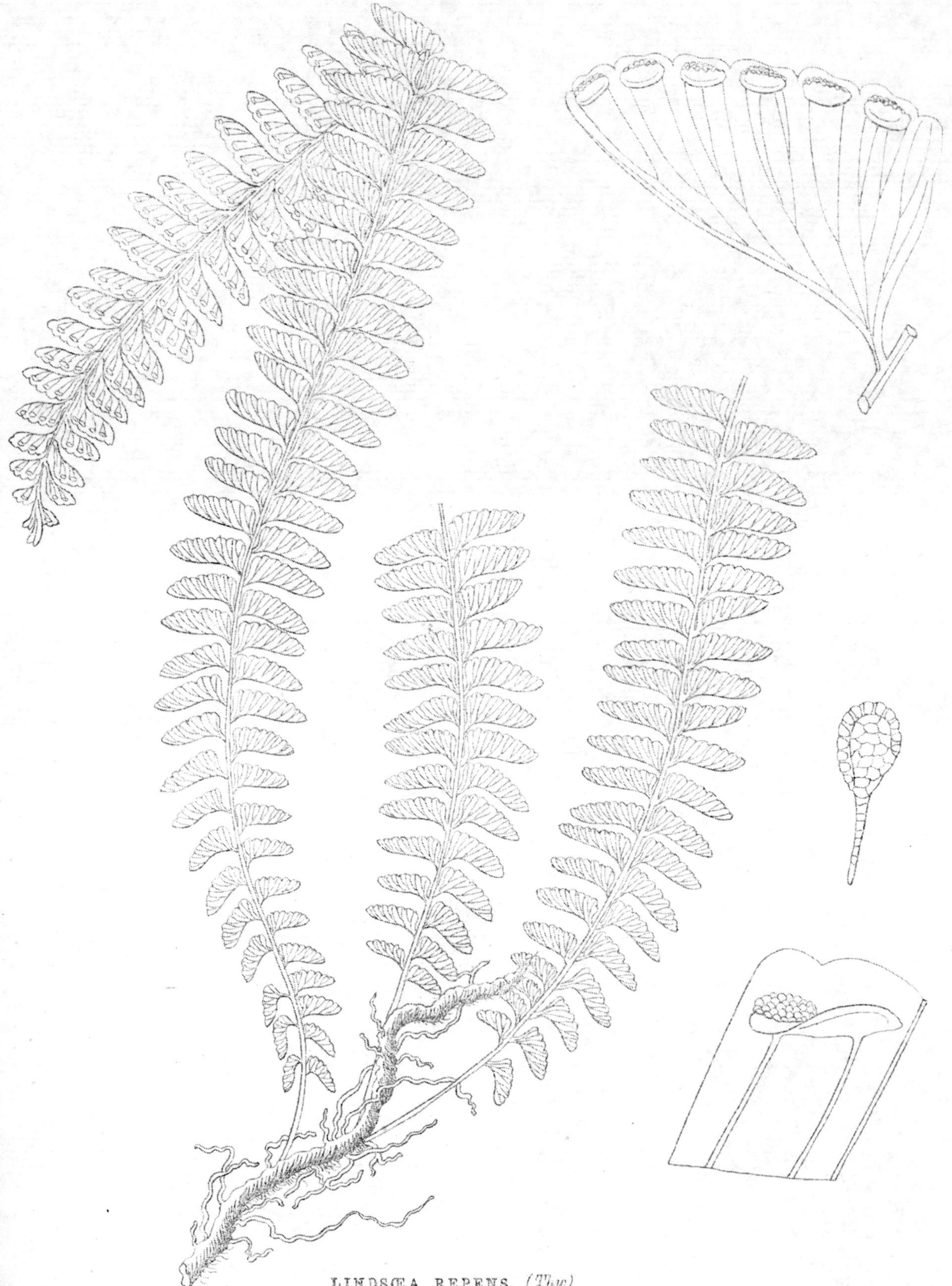

LINDSŒA REPENS *(Thw)*

PUBLISHED BY HIGGINBOTHAM & CO. ORIENTAL LITHOGRAPHIC PRESS MADRAS 1872. LITHOGRAPHED BY ALEX: BARREN,

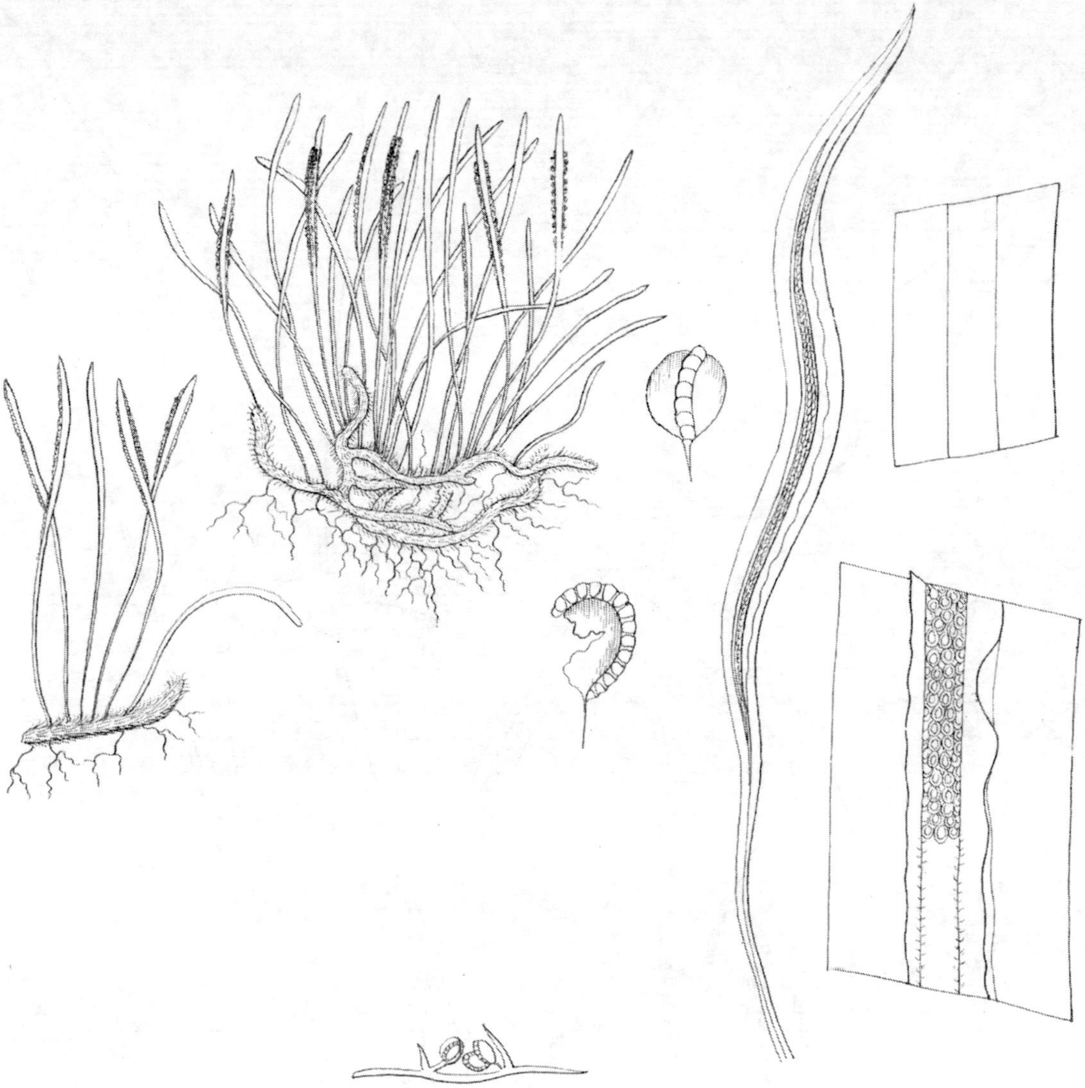

MONOGRAMMA IUNGHUHNII *(Hooker)*

PUBLISHED BY HIGGINBOTHAM & CO. ORIENTAL LITHOGRAPHIC PRESS MADRAS 1872. LITHOGRAPHED BY ALEX: BARREN.

GYMNOPTERIS FEEI VAR PINNATIFIDA *(Moore)*

PUBLISHED BY HIGGINBOTHAM & CO. ORIENTAL LITHOGRAPHIC PRESS MADRAS 187[illegible] LITHOGRAPHED BY ALEX: BARREN.

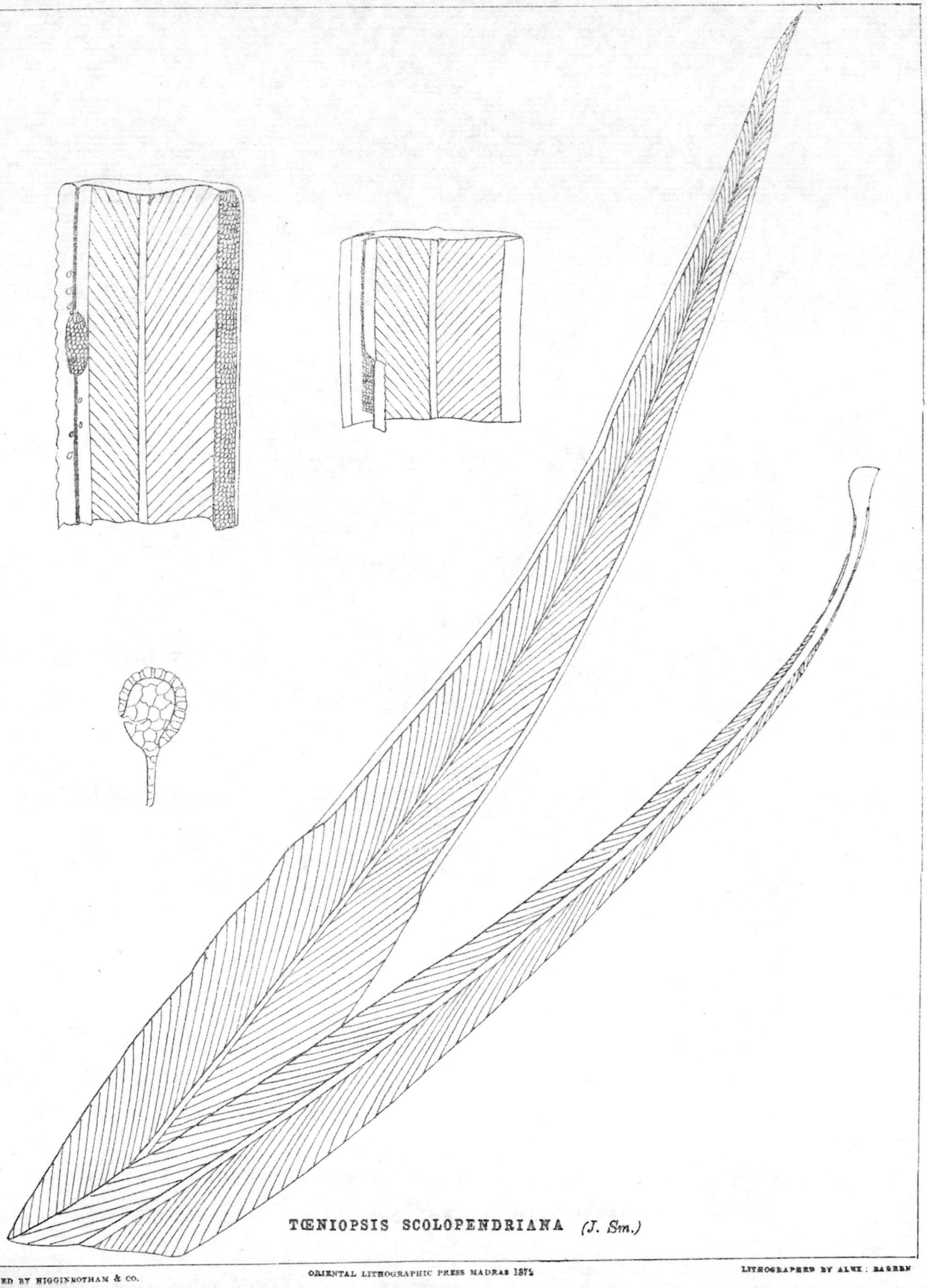

TŒNIOPSIS SCOLOPENDRIANA (J. Sm.)

PUBLISHED BY HIGGINBOTHAM & CO. ORIENTAL LITHOGRAPHIC PRESS MADRAS 1874 LITHOGRAPHED BY ALEX: BARREN

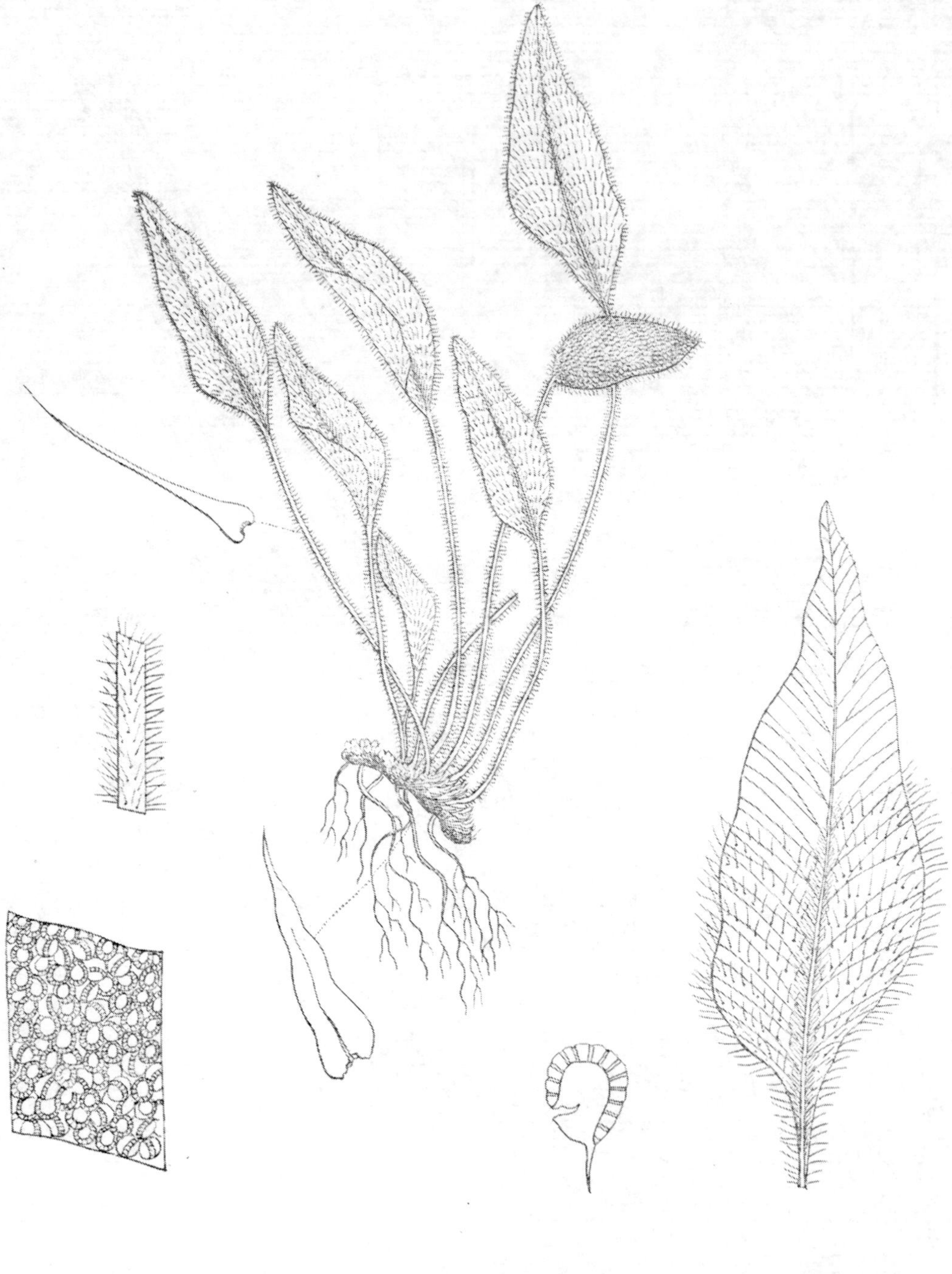

ELAPHOGLOSSUM SPATHULATUM *(Sw.)*

PUBLISHED BY HIGGINBOTHAM & CO. ORIENTAL LITHOGRAPHIC PRESS MADRAS 1872 LITHOGRAPHED BY ALEX: BARREN,

PLATE CCXIV

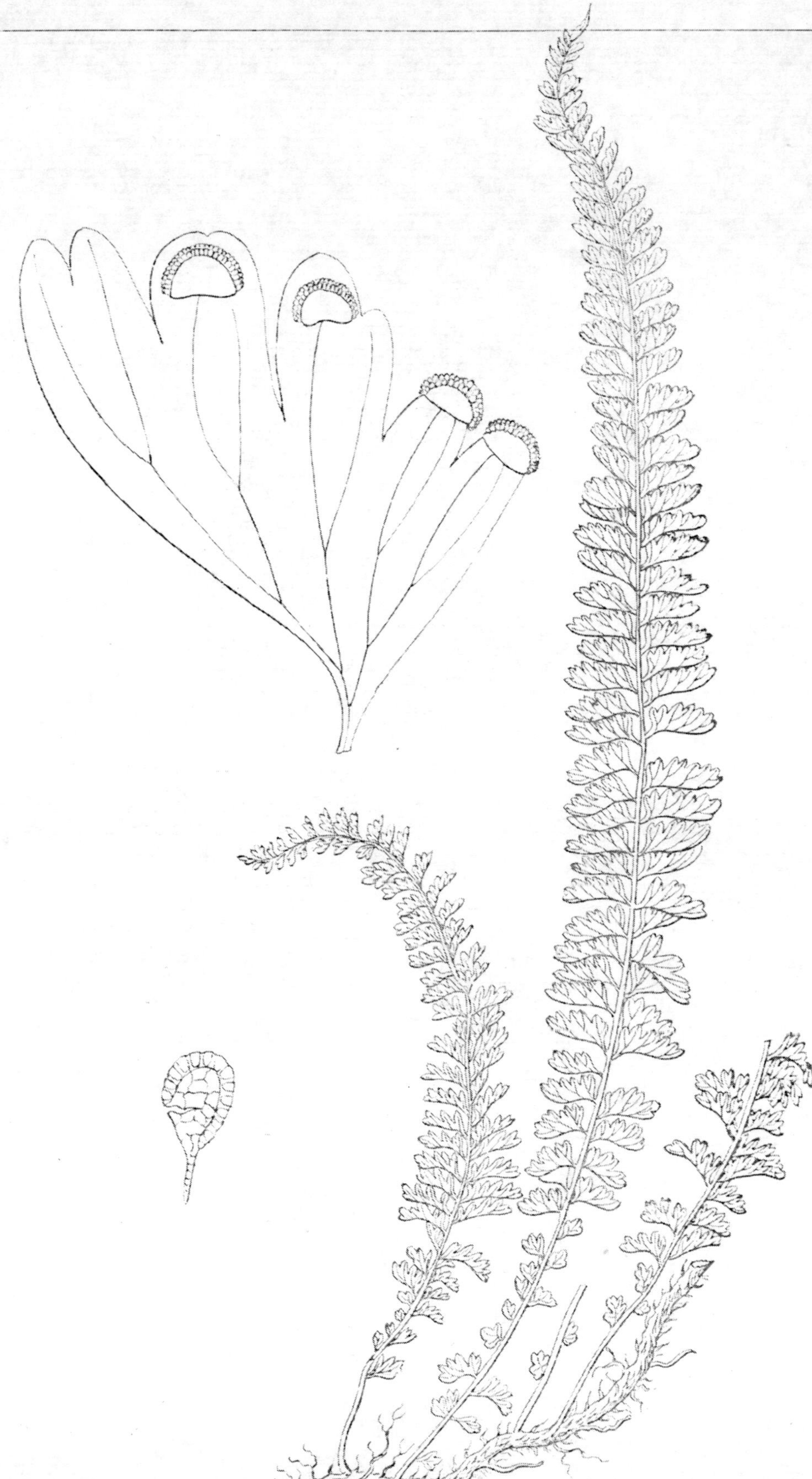

LINDSŒA REPENS VAR MINOR *(Thw.)*

PUBLISHED BY HIGGINBOTHAM & CO. ORIENTAL LITHOGRAPHIC PRESS MADRAS 1872 LITHOGRAPHED BY ALEXR WARREN.

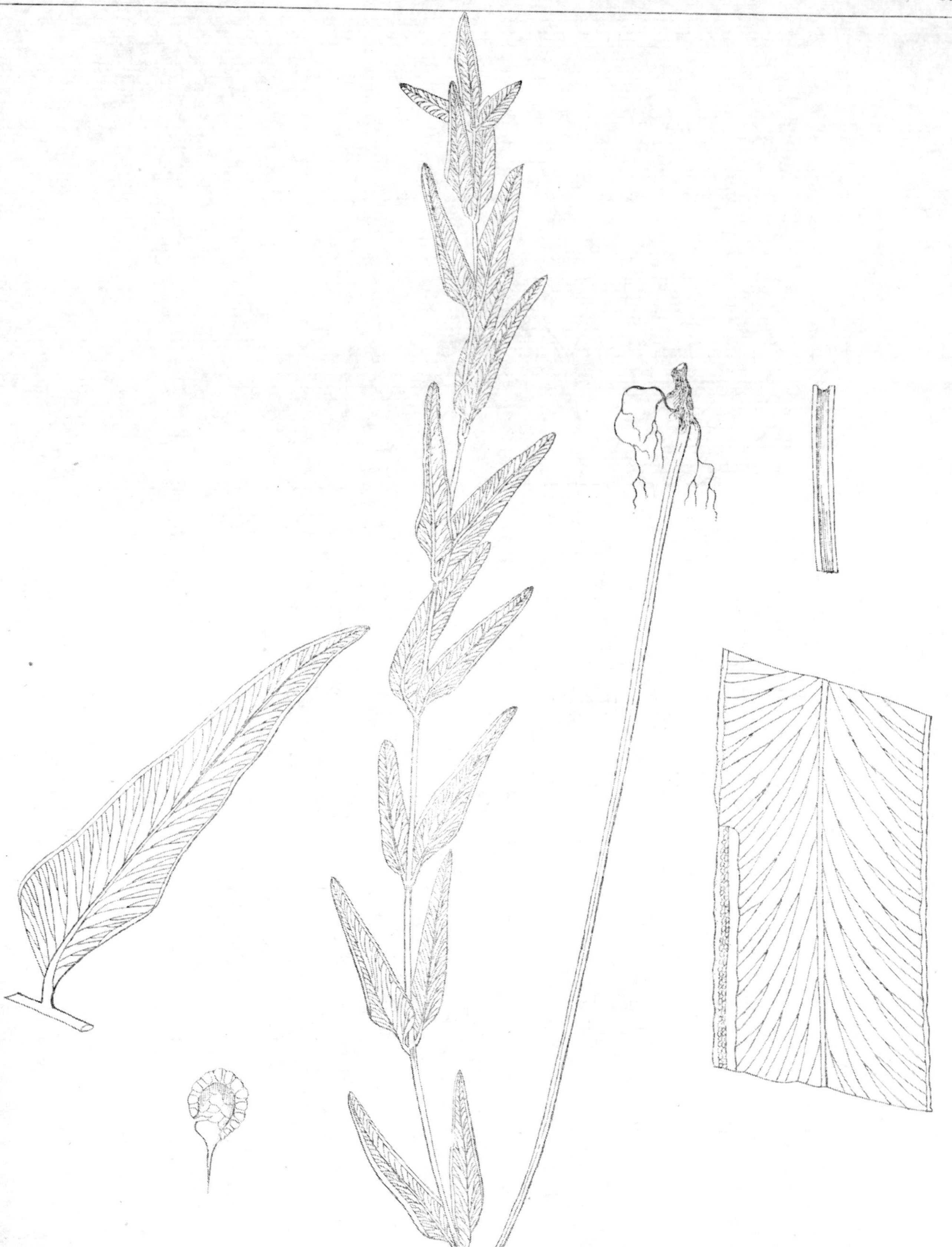

LINDSŒA WALKERŒ *(Hooker)*

PUBLISHED BY HIGGINBOTHAM & CO. ORIENTAL LITHOGRAPHIC PRESS MADRAS 1872. LITHOGRAPHED BY ALEX. BARREN,

LINDSŒA FLABELLULATA *(Dryand)*

PUBLISHED BY HIGGINBOTHAM & CO   ORIENTAL LITHOGRAPHIC PRESS MADRAS 1872   LITHOGRAPHED BY ALEX: BARREN.

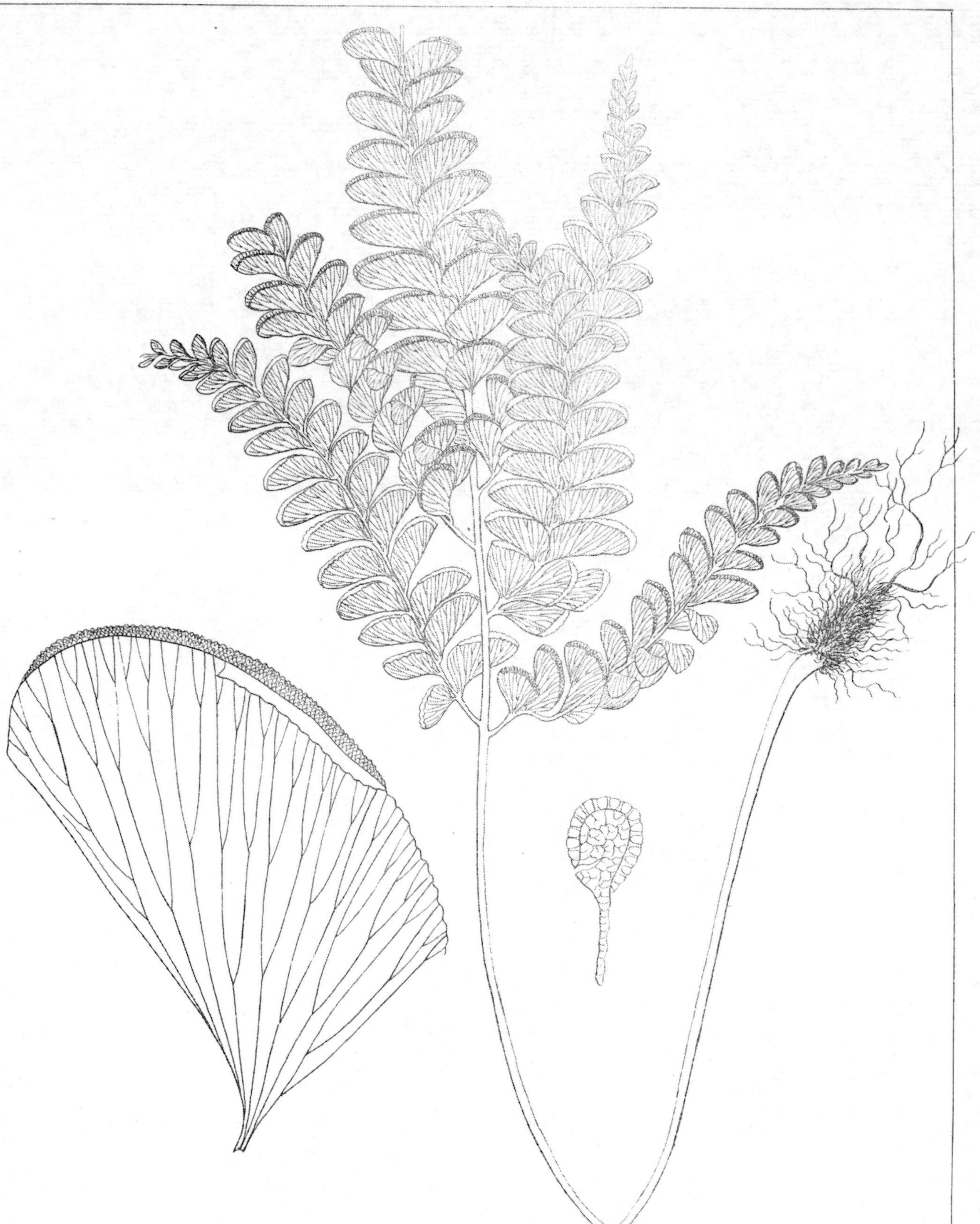

LINDSŒA CAUDATA (*Hooker*)

PUBLISHED BY HIGGINBOTHAM & CO. ORIENTAL LITHOGRAPHIC PRESS MADRAS 1872. LITHOGRAPHED BY ALEX: BARREN.

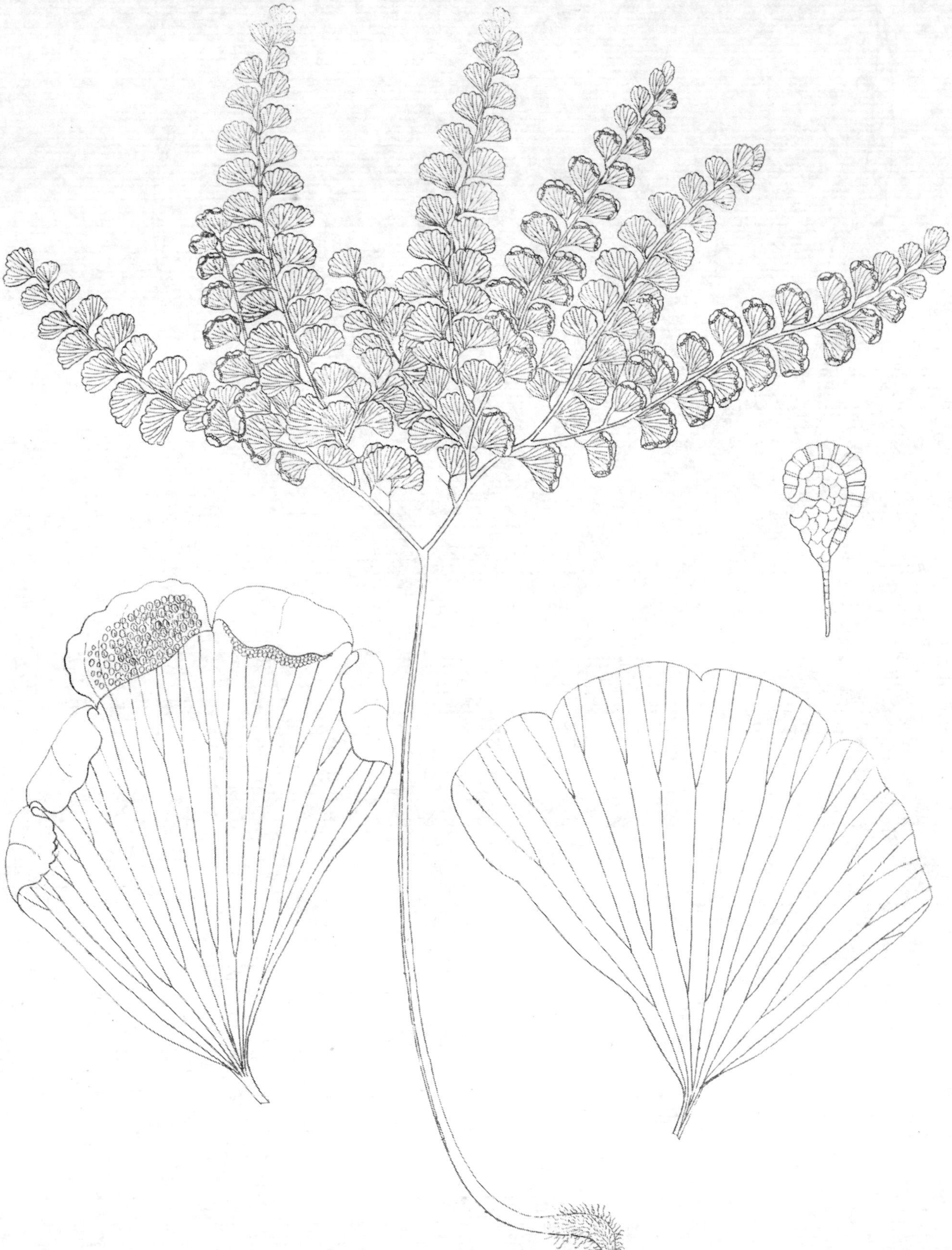

ADIANTUM FLABELLULATUM (Lin)

PUBLISHED BY HIGGINBOTHAM & CO ORIENTAL LITHOGRAPHIC PRESS MADRAS 1872 LITHOGRAPHED BY ALEX: BARREN,

PTERIS OTARIA ?

VAR. *(Bedd)*

PUBLISHED BY HIGGINBOTHAM & CO. ORIENTAL LITHOGRAPHIC PRESS MADRAS 1872. LITHOGRAPHED BY ALEX. BARREN,

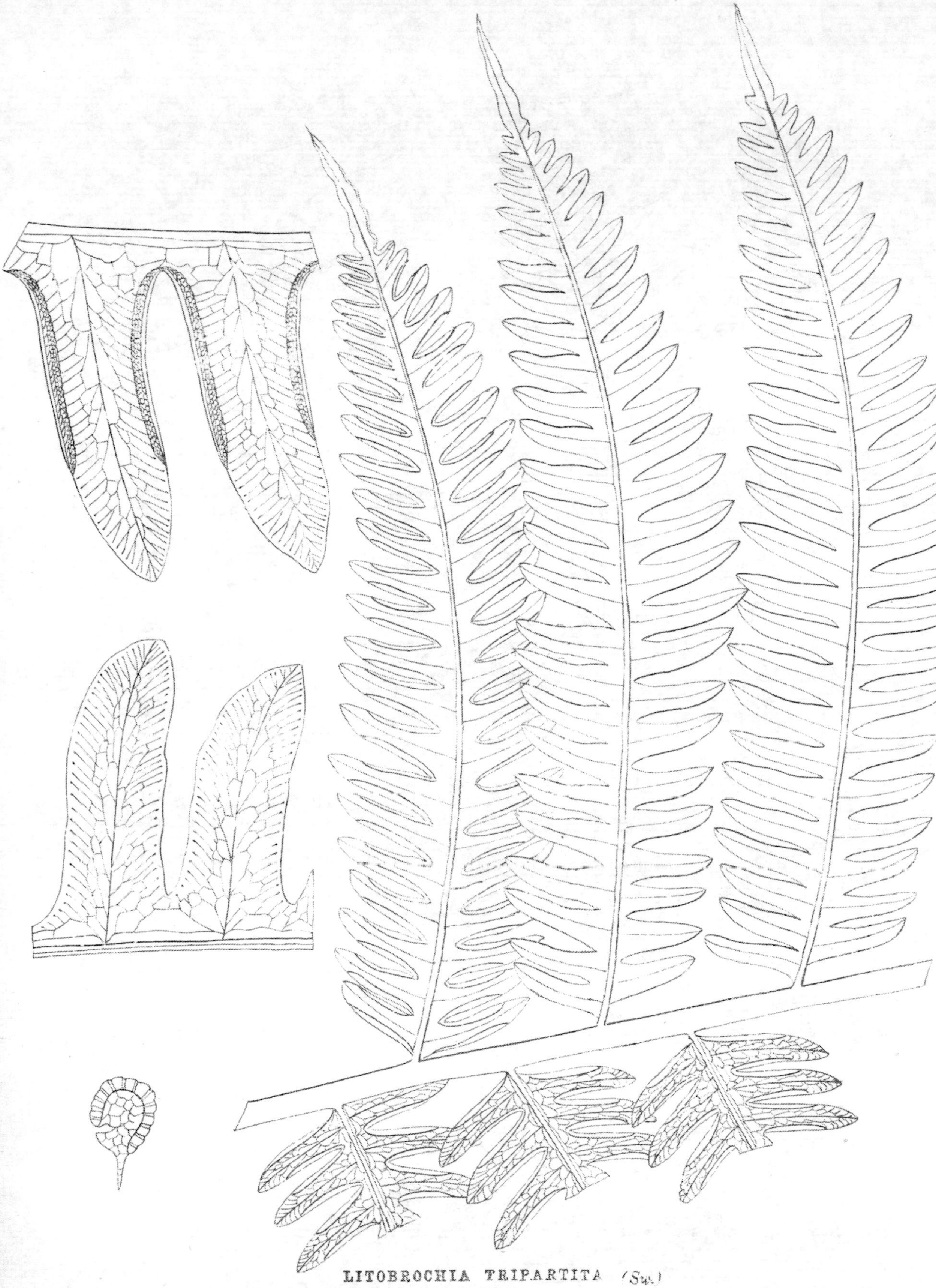

LITOBROCHIA TRIPARTITA (Sw.)

PUBLISHED BY HIGGINBOTHAM & CO ORIENTAL LITHOGRAPHIC PRESS MADRAS 1872. LITHOGRAPHED BY ALEX BARREN

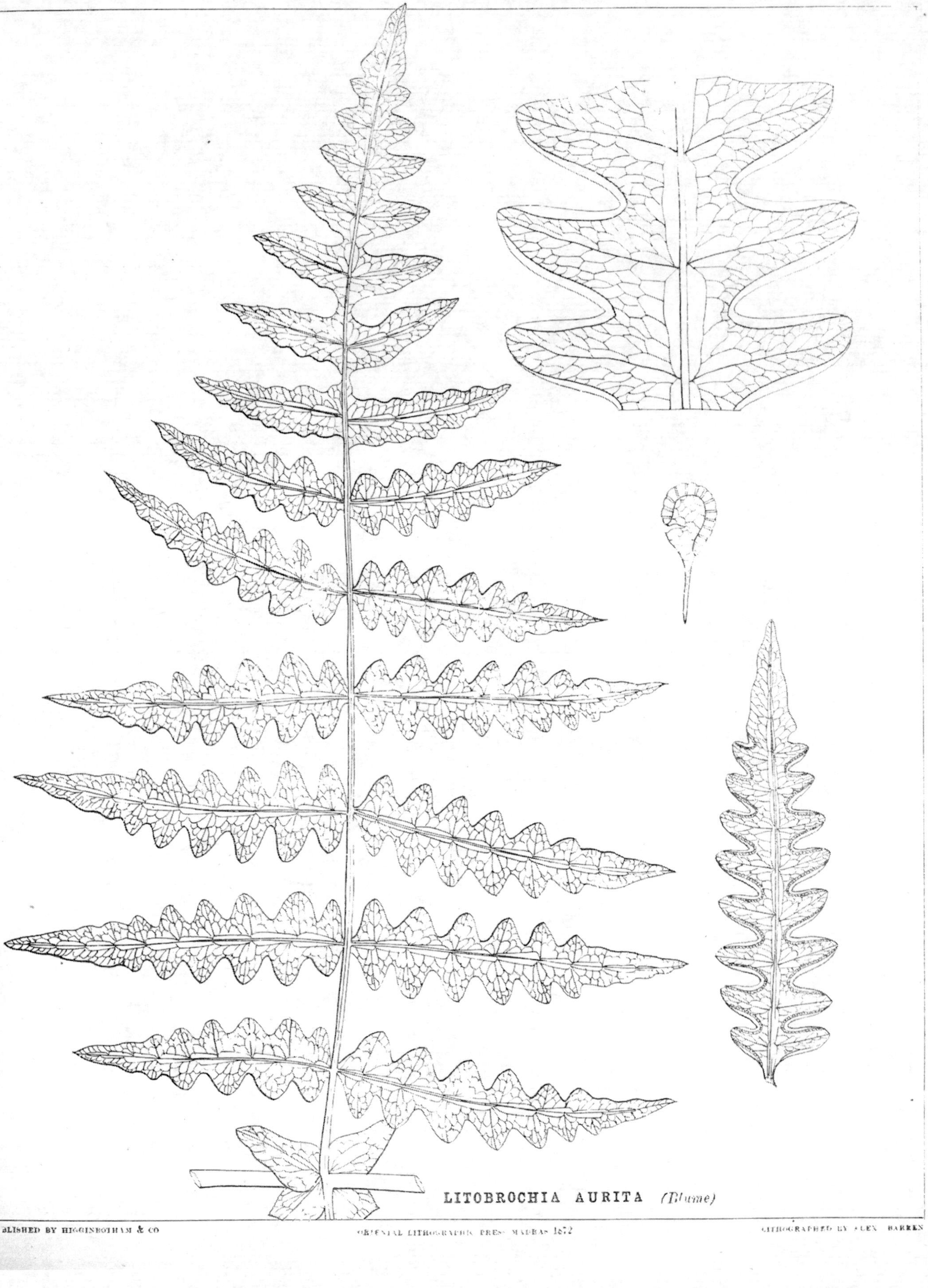

LITOBROCHIA AURITA *(Blume)*

PUBLISHED BY HIGGINBOTHAM & CO ORIENTAL LITHOGRAPHIC PRESS MADRAS 1872 LITHOGRAPHED BY ALEX BARREN

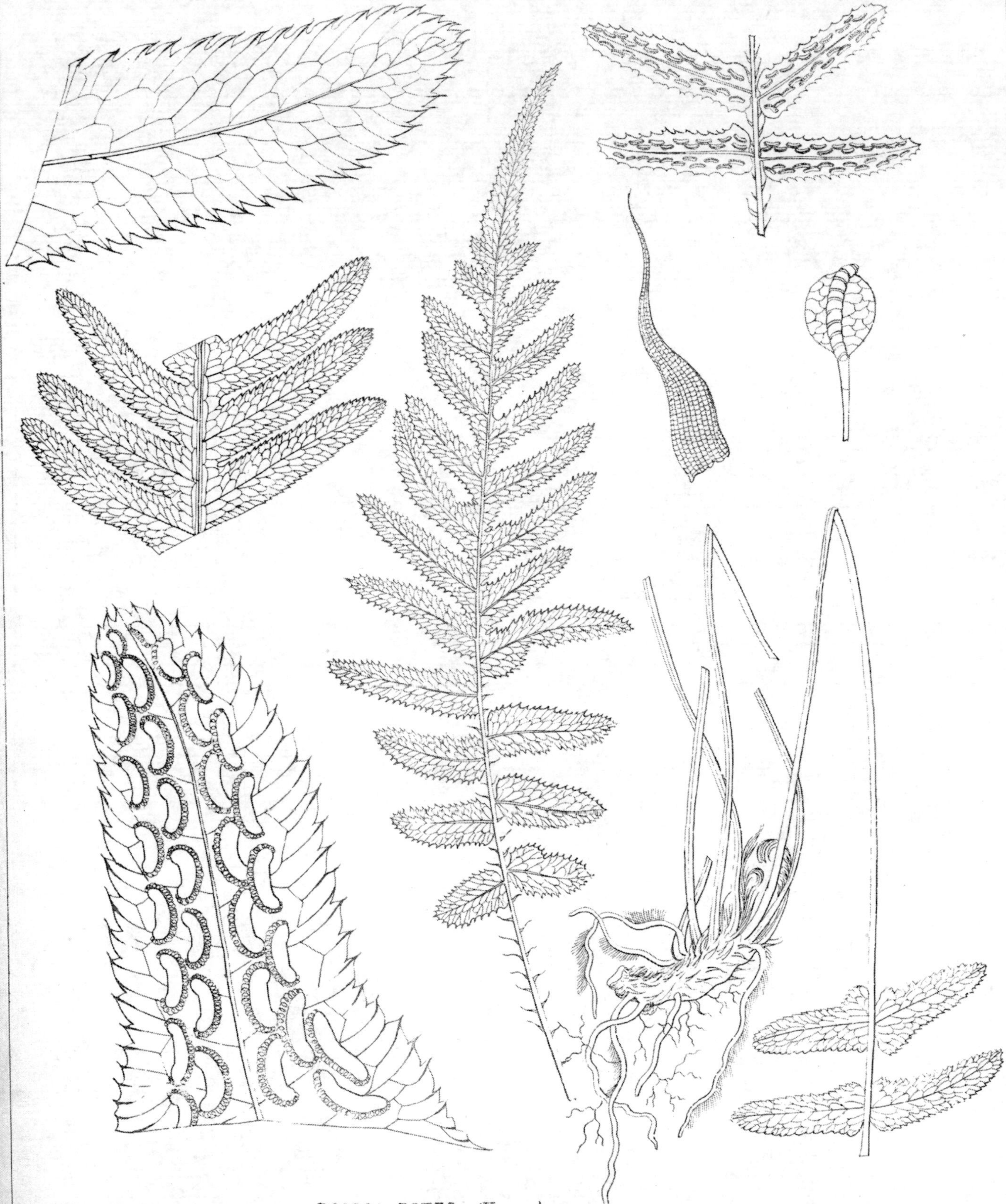

DOODIA DIVES *(Kaunze)*

PUBLISHED BY HIGGINBOTHAM & CO. ORIENTAL LITHOGRAPHIC PRESS MADRAS 1872. LITHOGRAPHED BY ALEX. BARREN,

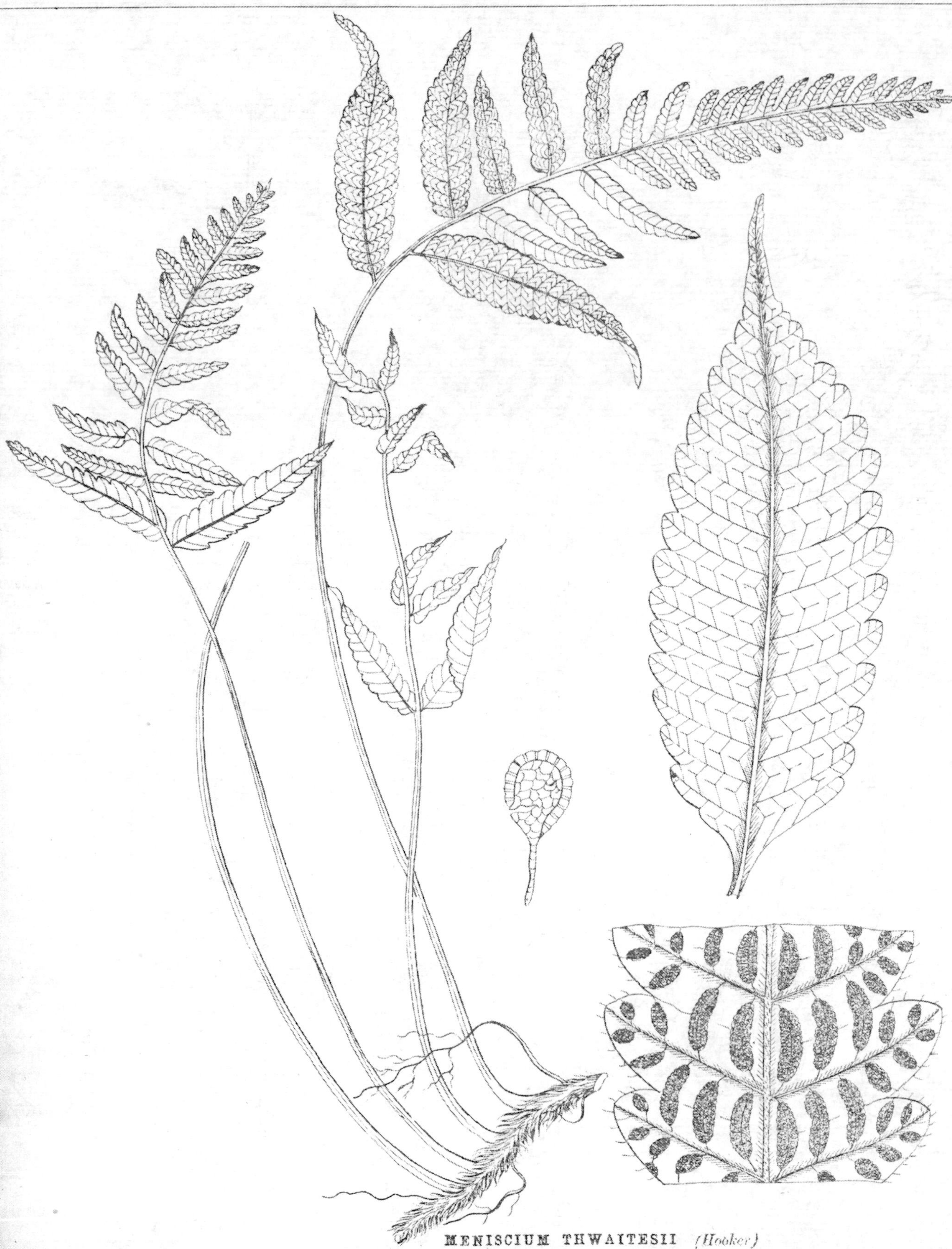

MENISCIUM THWAITESII (*Hooker*)

PUBLISHED BY HIGGINBOTHAM & CO. ORIENTAL LITHOGRAPHIC PRESS MADRAS 1872 LITHOGRAPHED BY ALEXR BARREN.

ASPLENIUM ELONGATUM (*Sw.*)

PUBLISHED BY HIGGINBOTHAM & Co. ORIENTAL LITHOGRAPHIC PRESS MADRAS 1872 LITHOGRAPHED BY ALEX: BARREN.

ASPLENIUM LASERPITIIFOLIUM (*Lam*)

PUBLISHED BY HIGGINBOTHAM & CO. ORIENTAL LITHOGRAPHIC PRESS MADRAS 1872. LITHOGRAPHED BY ALEX : BARREN,

ASPLENIUM SPATHULINUM (*J. Sm.*)

PUBLISHED BY HIGGINBOTHAM & CO. ORIENTAL LITHOGRAPHIC PRESS MADRAS 1872. LITHOGRAPHED BY ALEX : BARREN,

PLATE CCXXVII

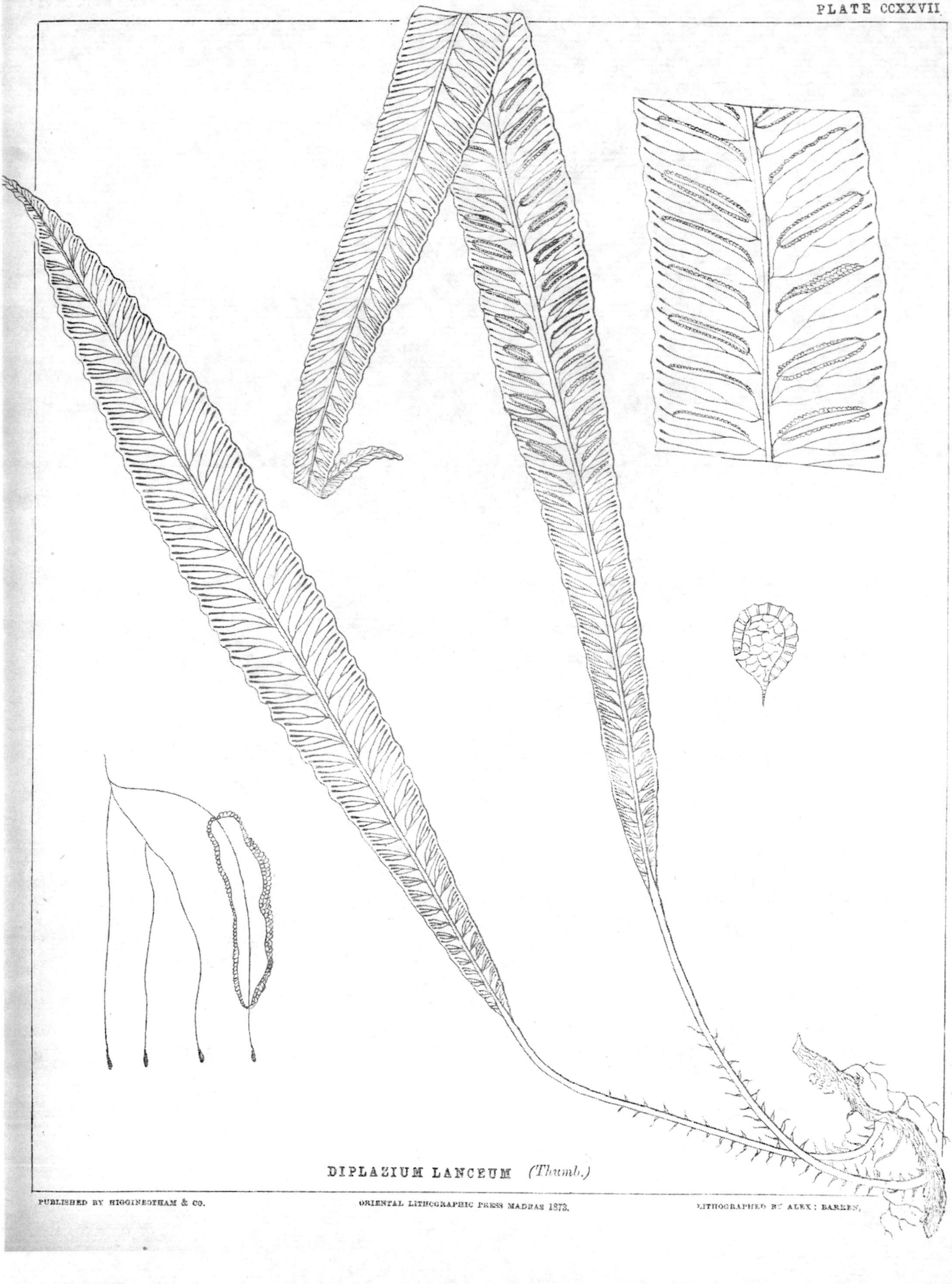

DIPLAZIUM LANCEUM (*Thumb.*)

PUBLISHED BY HIGGINBOTHAM & CO. ORIENTAL LITHOGRAPHIC PRESS MADRAS 1873. LITHOGRAPHED BY ALEX: BARREN,

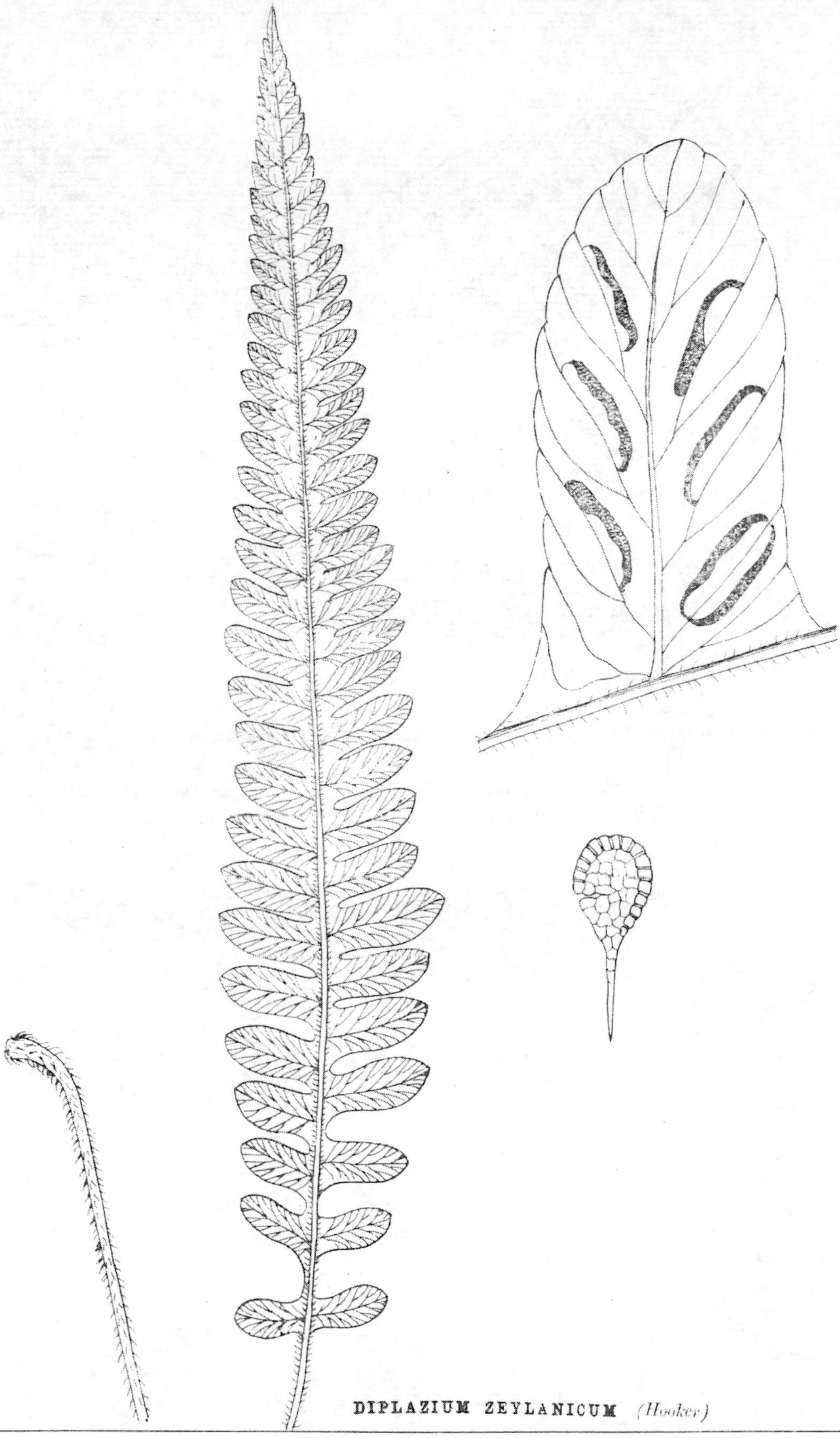

DIPLAZIUM ZEYLANICUM (*Hooker*)

PUBLISHED BY HIGGINBOTHAM & CO. ORIENTAL LITHOGRAPHIC PRESS MADRAS 1872. LITHOGRAPHED BY ALEX: BARREN,

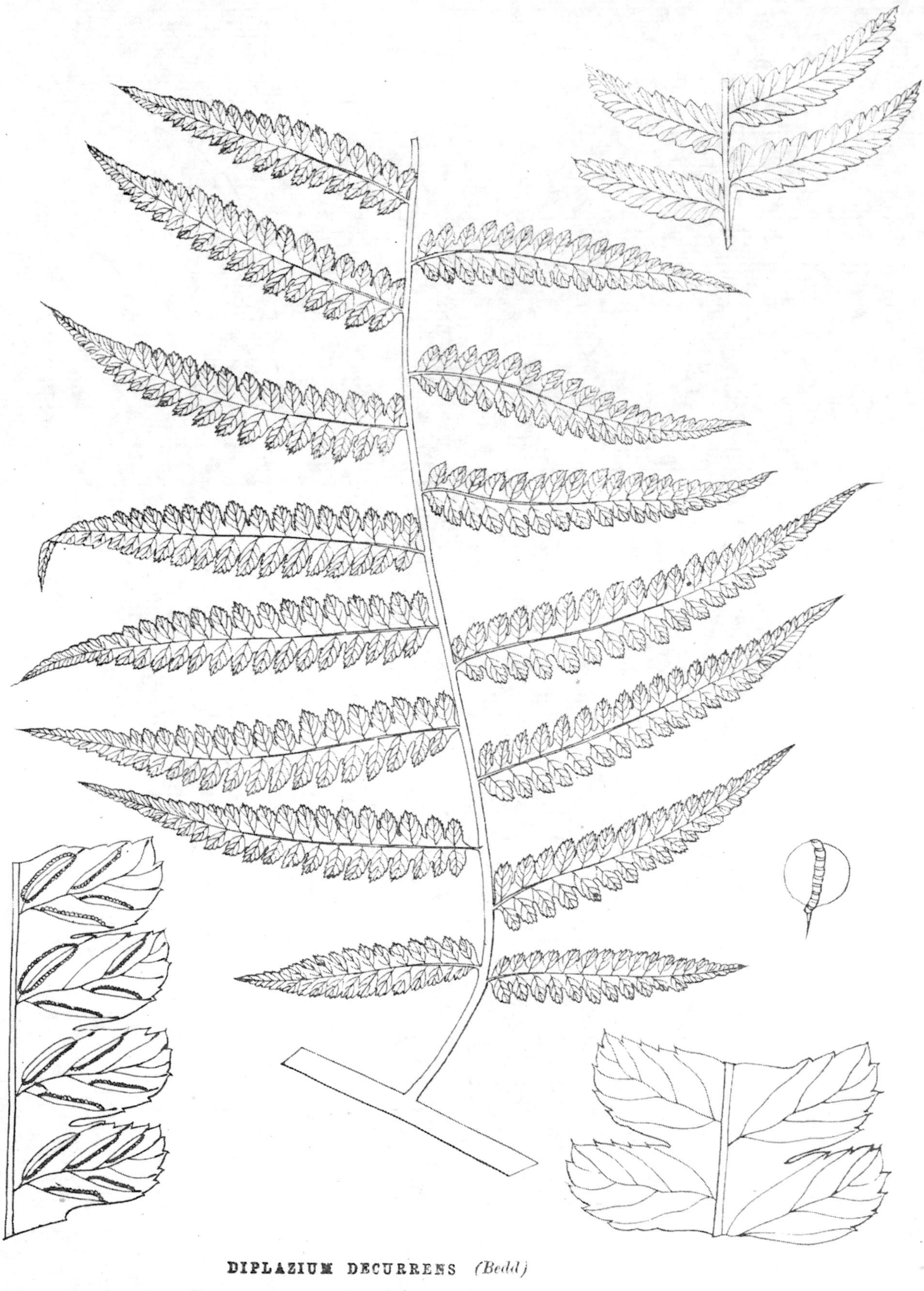

DIPLAZIUM DECURRENS *(Bedd)*

PUBLISHED BY HIGGINBOTHAM & Co. ORIENTAL LITHOGRAPHIC PRESS MADRAS 1872. LITHOGRAPHED BY ALEX: BARREN.

DIPLAZIUM SCHKUHRII *(Mett)*

PUBLISHED BY HIGGINBOTHAM & CO. ORIENTAL LITHOGRAPHIC PRESS MADRAS 1872. LITHOGRAPHED BY ALEX : BARREN.

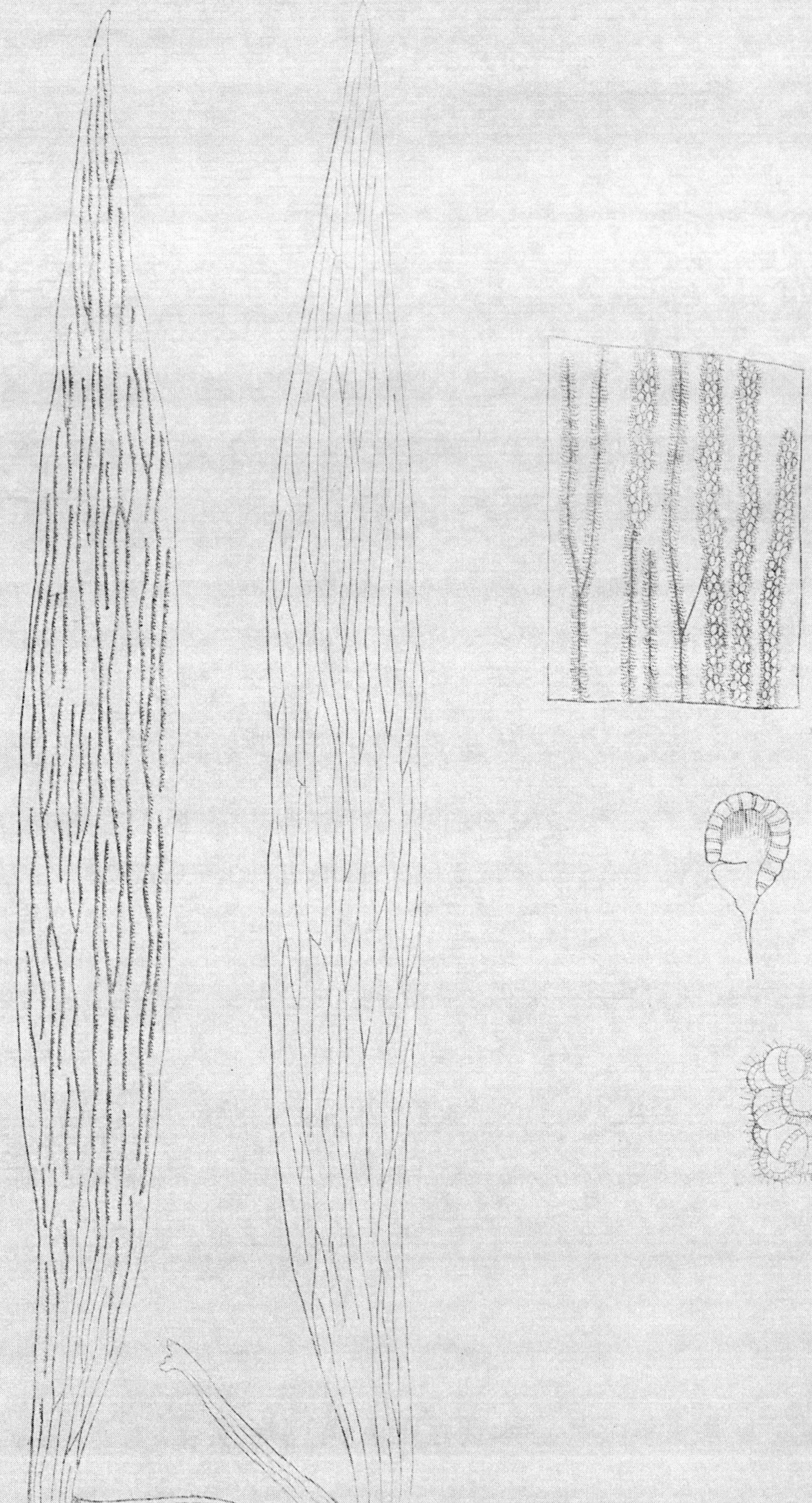

ANTROPHYUM RETICULATUM (Kaulf).

PUBLISHED BY HIGGINBOTHAM & CO. ORIENTAL LITHOGRAPHIC PRESS MADRAS 1872 LITHOGRAPHED BY ALEX: BARREN,

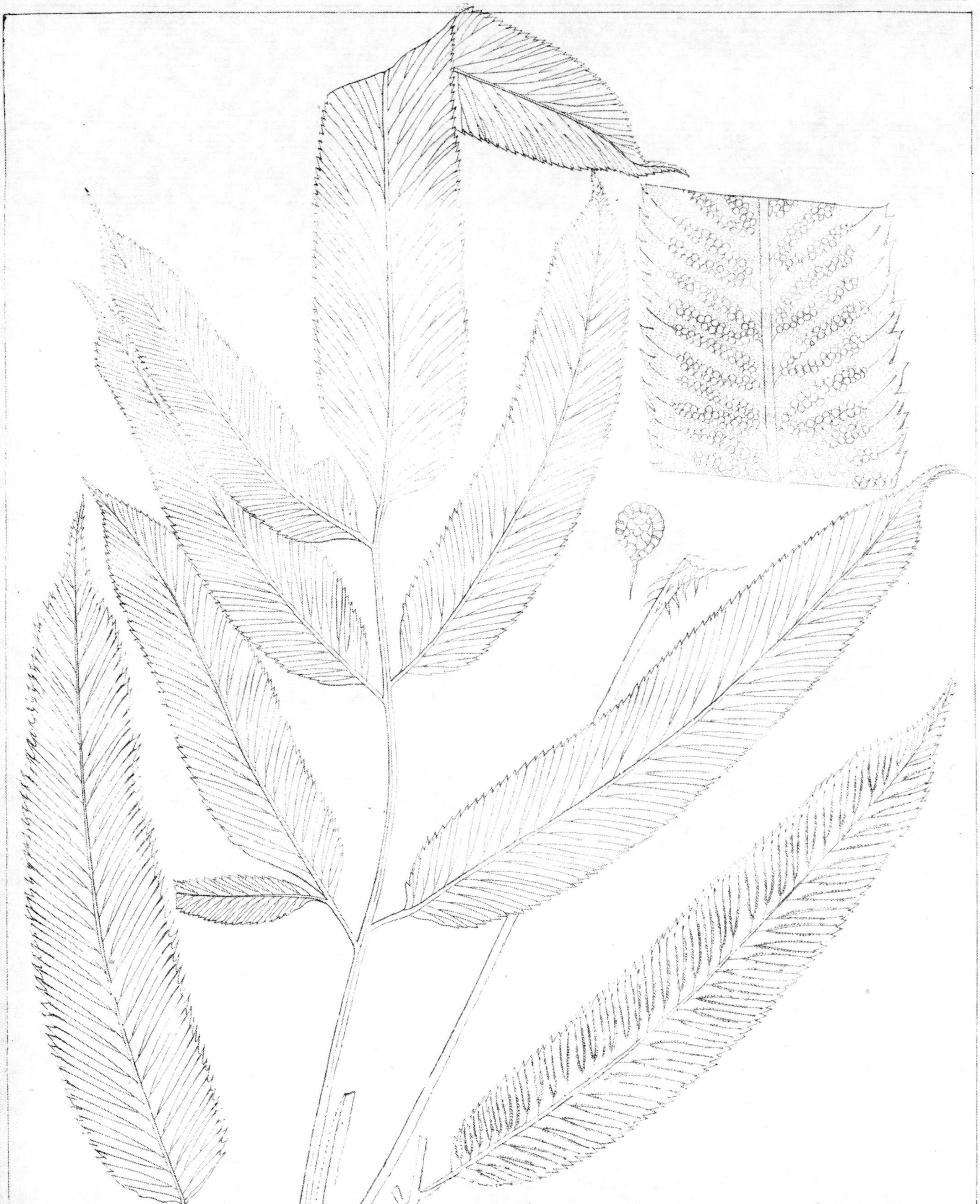

GYMNOGRAMMA JAVONICA *(Bl.)*

PUBLISHED BY HIGGINBOTHAM & CO. ORIENTAL LITHOGRAPHIC PRESS MADRAS 1872. LITHOGRAPHED BY ALEX. J. GARDEN,

CALYMMODON CUCULLATUS (*Presl.*)

PUBLISHED BY HIGGINBOTHAM & CO. ORIENTAL LITHOGRAPHIC PRESS MADRAS 1872. LITHOGRAPHED BY ALEX : BARREN,

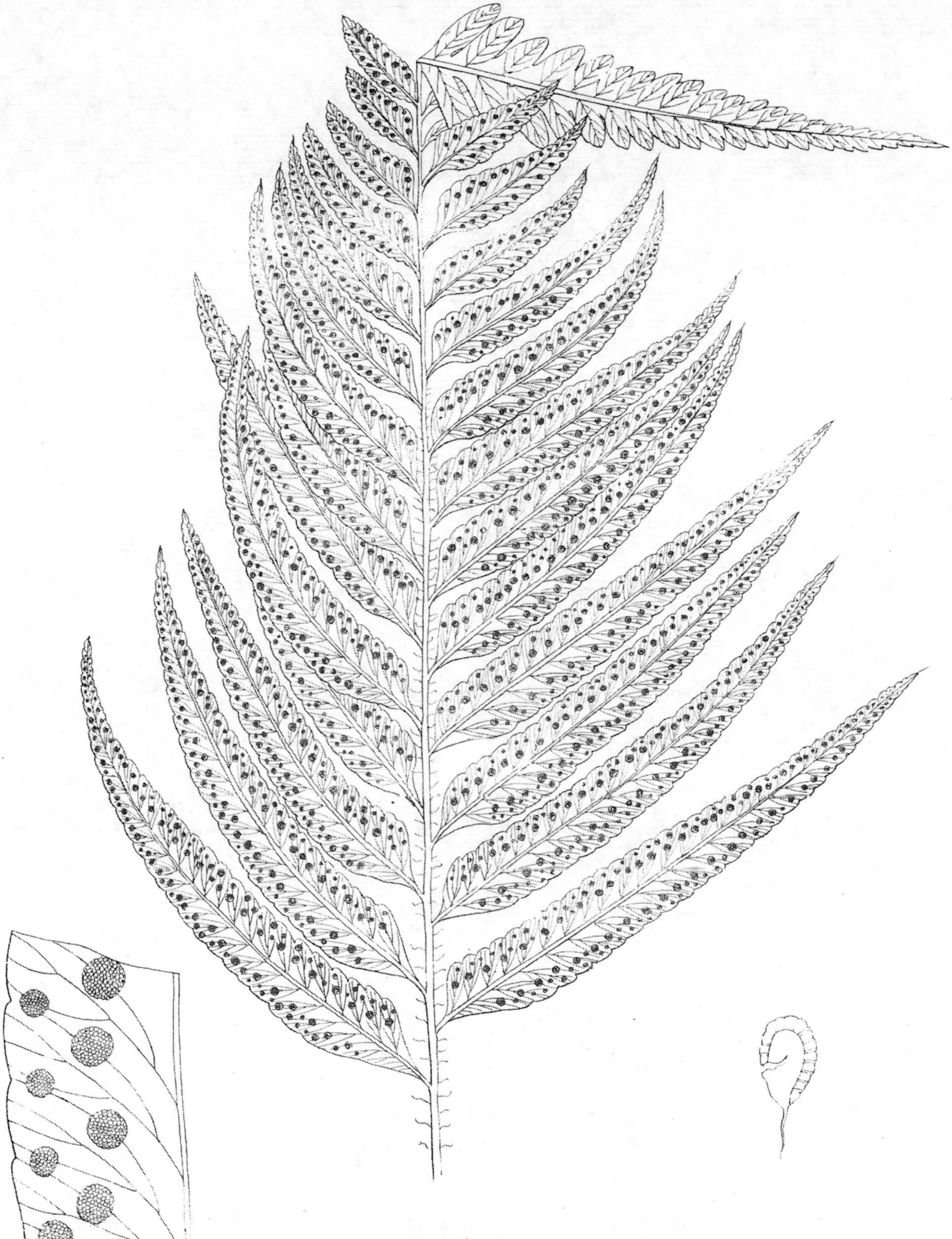

POLYPODIUM WALKERÆ (*Hooker.*)

PUBLISHED BY HIGGINBOTHAM & CO. ORIENTAL LITHOGRAPHIC PRESS MADRAS 1872. LITHOGRAPHED BY ALEX : BARREN,

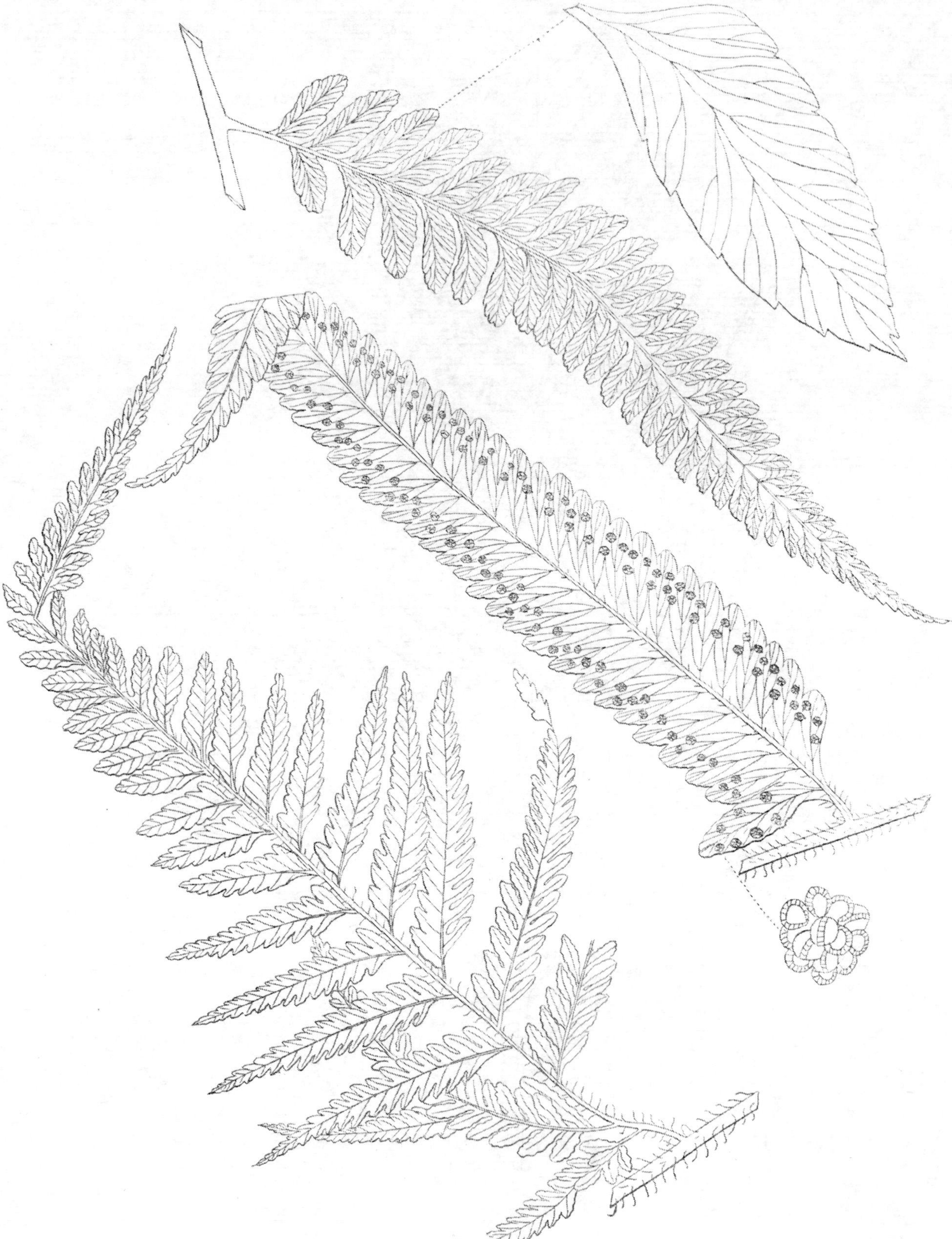

POLYPODIUM WALKERÆ VARIETIES B, Y & D (Wall.)

PUBLISHED BY HIGGINBOTHAM & CO. ORIENTAL LITHOGRAPHIC PRESS MADRAS 1873. LITHOGRAPHED BY ALEX: BARREN,

PLATE CCXXXVI

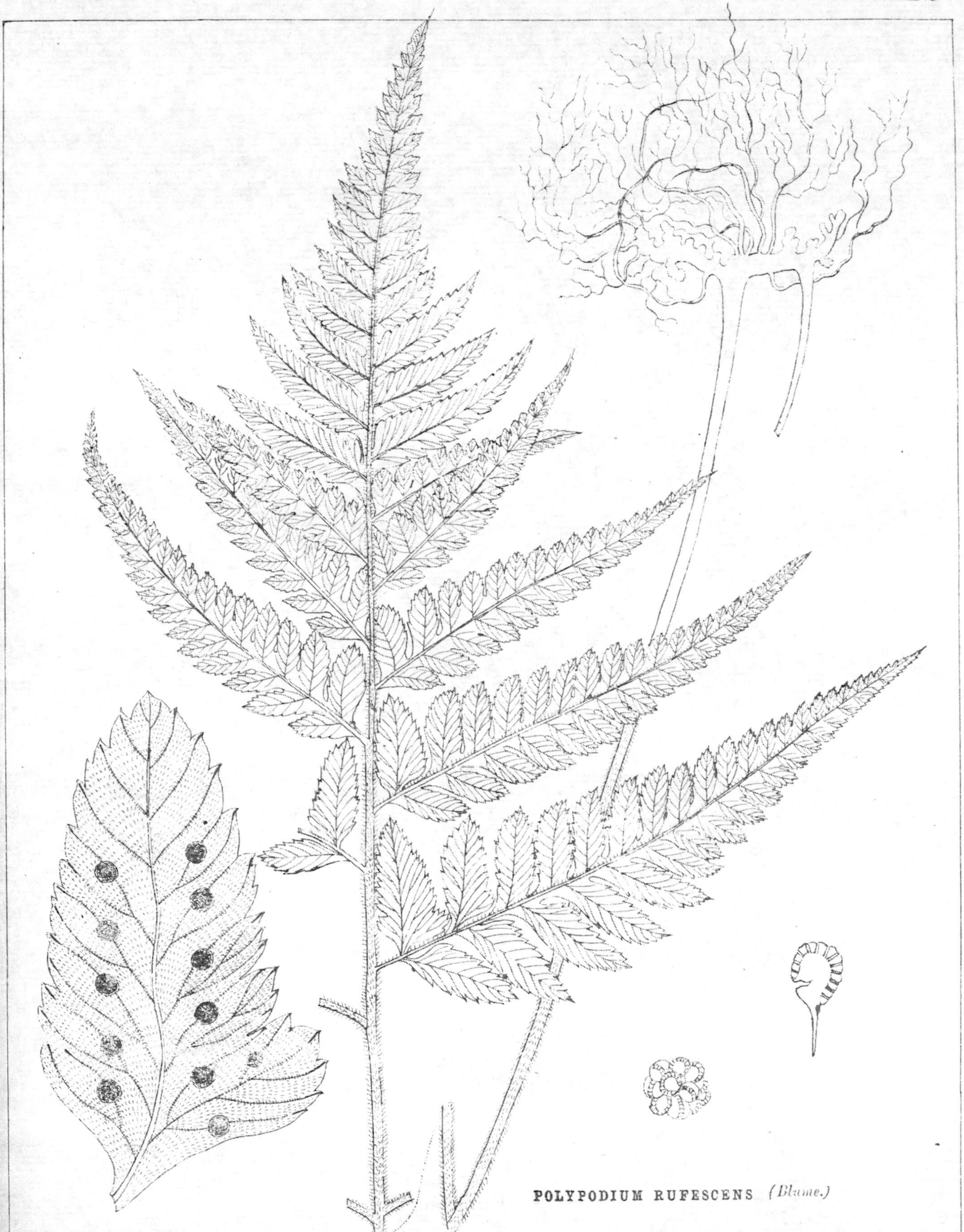

POLYPODIUM RUFESCENS *(Blume.)*

PUBLISHED BY HIGGINBOTHAM & CO.

ORIENTAL LITHOGRAPHIC PRESS MADRAS 1872.

LITHOGRAPHED BY ALEX : BARREN,

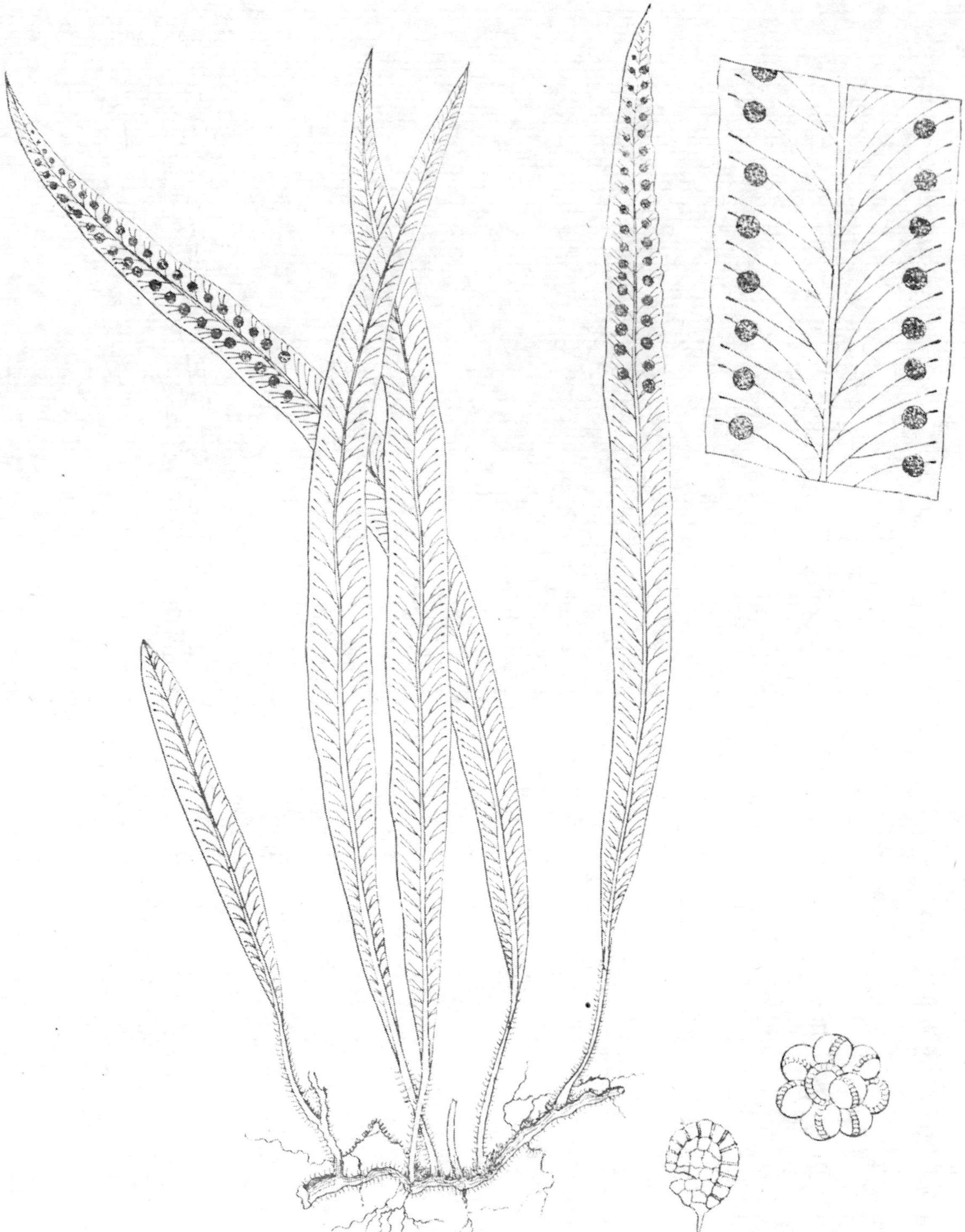

POLYPODIUM ZEYLANICUM (*Metten.*)

PUBLISHED BY HIGGINBOTHAM & CO. ORIENTAL LITHOGRAPHIC PRESS MADRAS 1872. LITHOGRAPHED BY ALEX: BARREN,

POLYPODIUM GLANDULOSUM (Hook.)

PLATE CCXXXIX

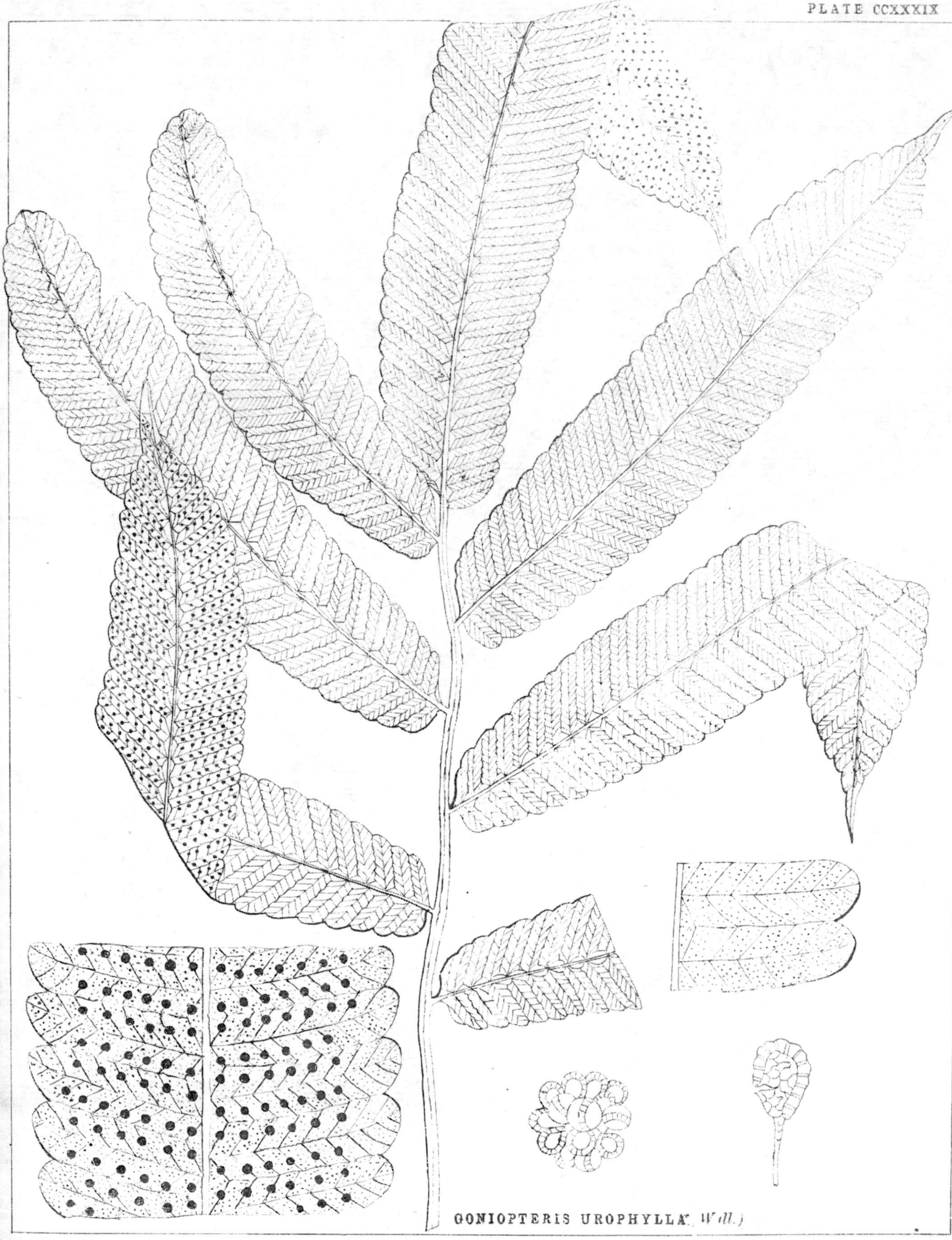

GONIOPTERIS UROPHYLLA (Wall.)

NIPHOBOLUS LINGUA (*Sw.*)

PUBLISHED BY HIGGINBOTHAM & CO. ORIENTAL LITHOGRAPHIC PRESS MADRAS 1873. LITHOGRAPHED BY ALEX : BARREN,

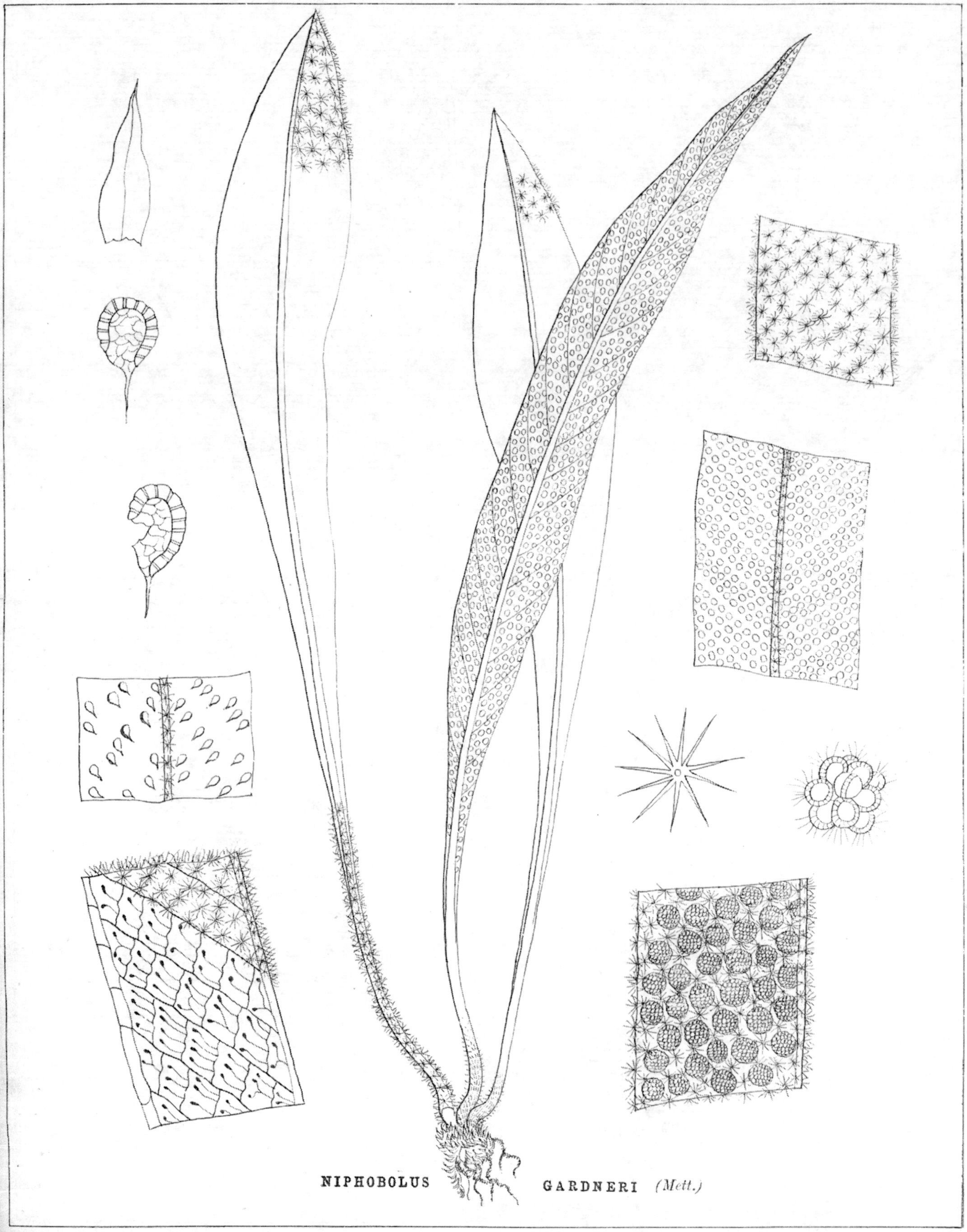

NIPHOBOLUS GARDNERI *(Mett.)*

PUBLISHED BY HIGGINBOTHAM & CO. ORIENTAL LITHOGRAPHIC PRESS MADRAS 1872. LITHOGRAPHED BY ALEX : BARREN,

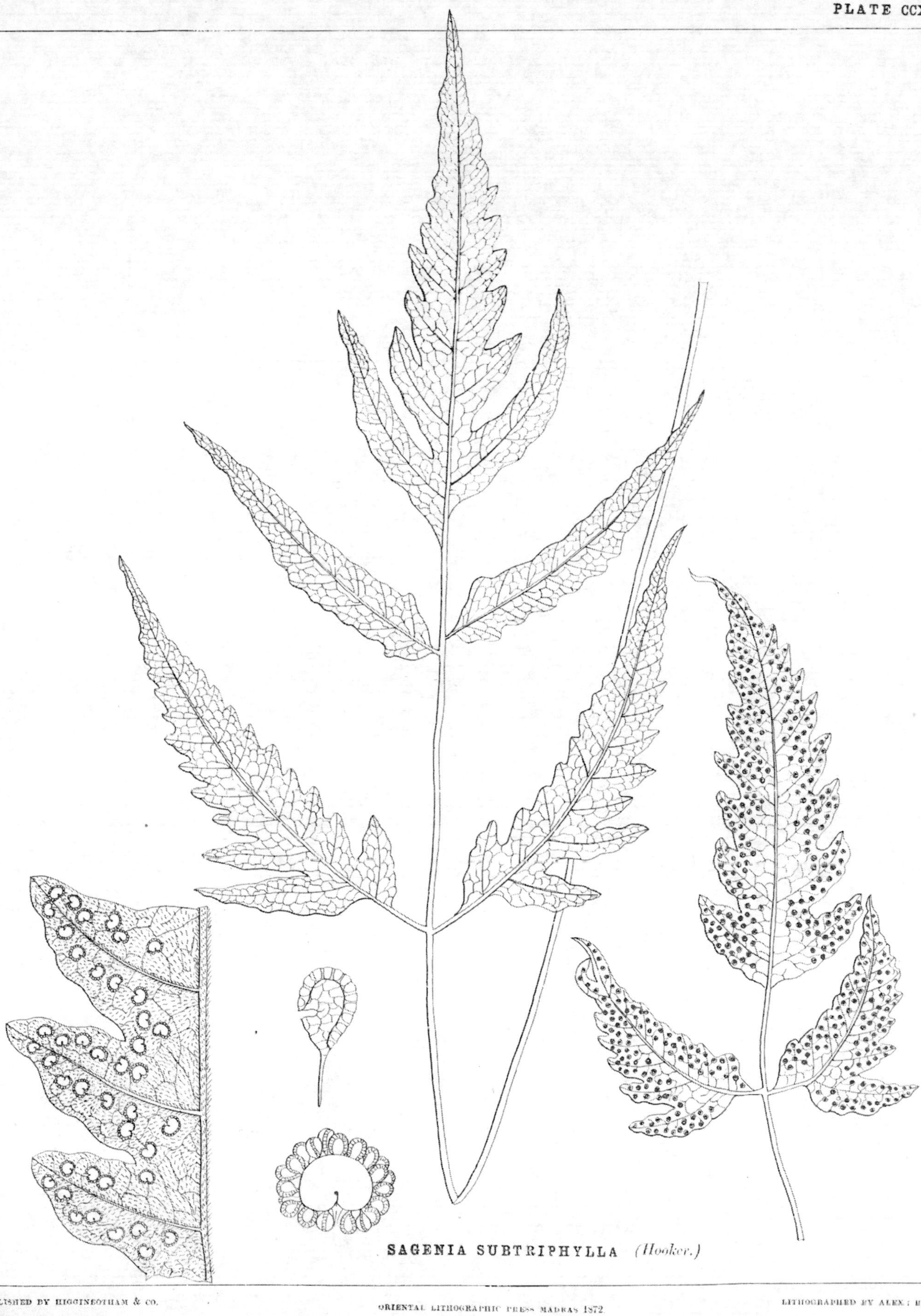

SAGENIA SUBTRIPHYLLA *(Hooker.)*

PUBLISHED BY HIGGINBOTHAM & CO. ORIENTAL LITHOGRAPHIC PRESS MADRAS 1872 LITHOGRAPHED BY ALEXr BARREN,

PLATE CCXLIII

SAGENIA GIGANTEA VAR MINOR (*Bl.*)

PUBLISHED BY HIGGINBOTHAM & CO.

ORIENTAL LITHOGRAPHIC PRESS

LITHOGRAPHED BY ALEX: BARREN MADRAS 1872.

SAGENIA THWAITESII (Be d.)

PUBLISHED BY HIGGINBOTHAM & CO. LITHOGRAPHED BY ALEX: BARREN MADRAS 1872.

SAGENIA PTEROPUS-MINOR (Bedd.)

LASTREA CALCARATA *(Bedd.)*

PUBLISHED BY HIGGINBOTHAM & CO.

ORIENTAL LITHOGRAPHIC PRESS

LITHOGRAPHED BY ALEX: BARREN MADRAS 1872.

LASTREA CONCINNA (*Thw.*)

PUBLISHED BY HIGGINBOTHAM & CO. ORIENTAL LITHOGRAPHIC PRESS MADRAS 1872. LITHOGRAPHED BY ALEX: FARREN,

LASTREA DELTOIDEA *(Bedd.)*

PUBLISHED BY HIGGINBOTHAM & CO. ORIENTAL LITHOGRAPHIC PRESS LITHOGRAPHED BY ALEX: BARREN MADRAS 1872.

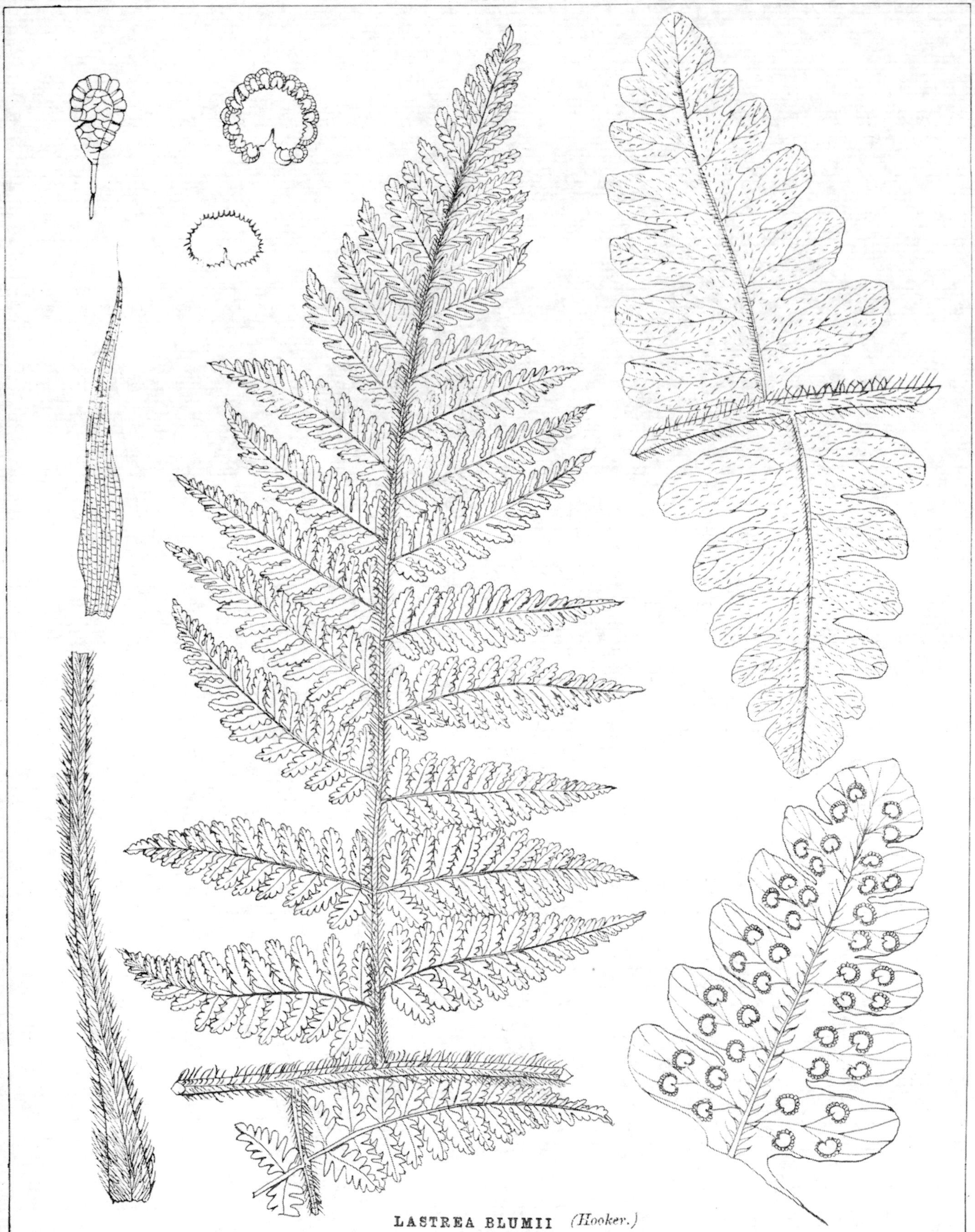

LASTREA BLUMII (*Hooker.*)

PUBLISHED BY HIGGINBOTHAM & CO. ORIENTAL LITHOGRAPHIC PRESS MADRAS 1872 LITHOGRAPHED BY ALEX: BARREN.

LASTREA FLACCIDA (*Hooker.*)

PUBLISHED BY HIGGINBOTHAM & CO. ORIENTAL LITHOGRAPHIC PRESS LITHOGRAPHED BY ALEX: BARREN MADRAS 1872.

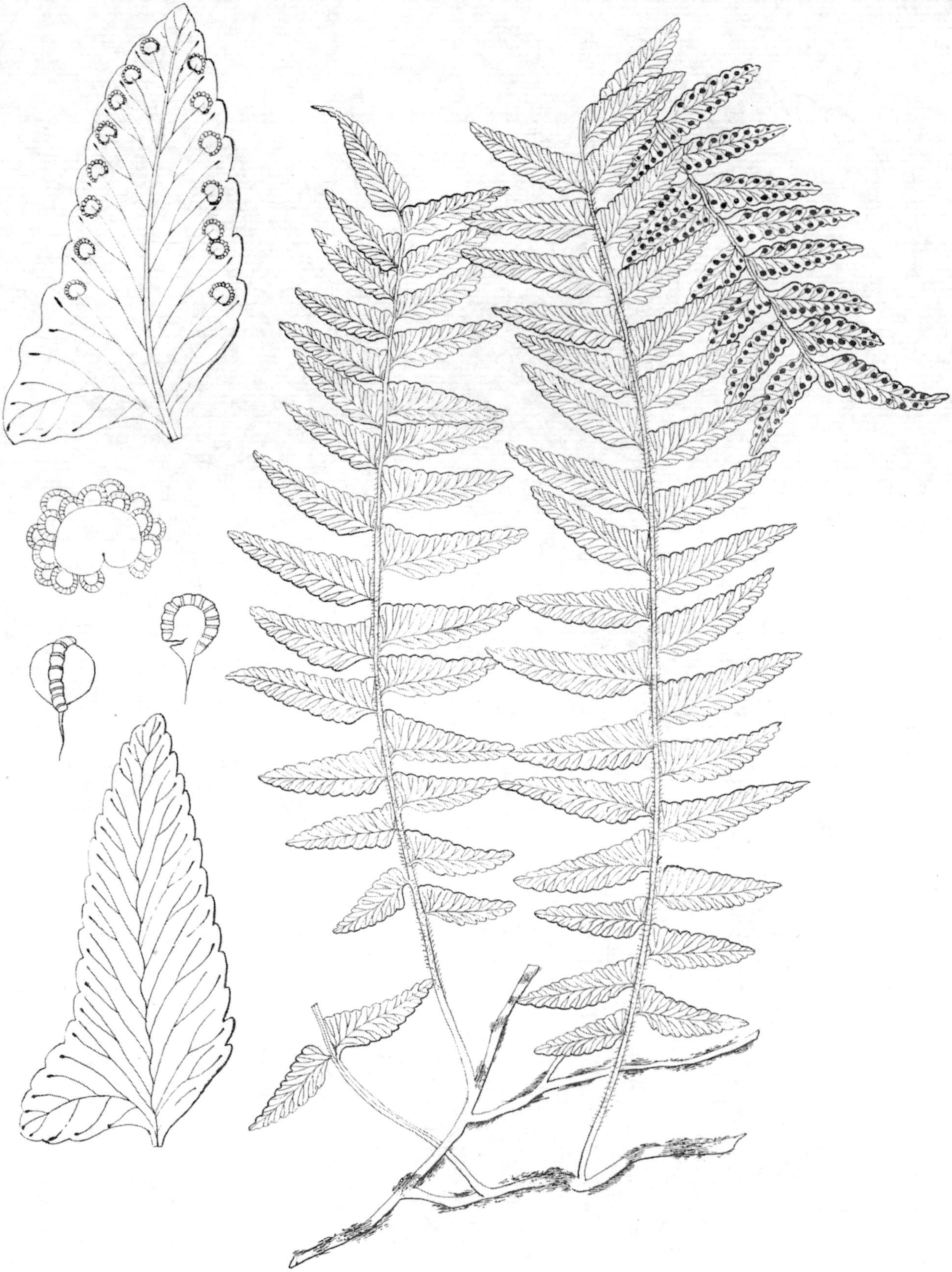

NEPHROLEPIS OBLITERATA (*Hooker.*)

PUBLISHED BY HIGGINBOTHAM & CO. ORIENTAL LITHOGRAPHIC PRESS LITHOGRAPHED BY ALEX: BARREN MADRAS 1872.

ACROPHORUS AFFINIS *(Moore.)*

PUBLISHED BY HIGGINBOTHAM & CO. ORIENTAL LITHOGRAPHIC PRESS LITHOGRAPHED BY ALEX: BARREN MADRAS 1872.

HUMATA VESTITA *(Blume.)*

PUBLISHED BY HIGGINBOTHAM & CO. ORIENTAL LITHOGRAPHIC PRESS LITHOGRAPHED BY ALEX: BARREN MADRAS 1872.

MICROLEPIA PROXIMA (*Blume.*)

PUBLISHED BY HIGGINBOTHAM & CO. ORIENTAL LITHOGRAPHIC PRESS MADRAS 1872. LITHOGRAPHED BY ALEX: BARREN,

MICROLEPIA STRIGOSA (*Moore.*)

PUBLISHED BY HIGGINBOTHAM & CO. ORIENTAL LITHOGRAPHIC PRESS MADRAS 187? LITHOGRAPHED BY ALEX : BARREN.

MICROLEPIA HIRTA *(Kaulf.)*

PUBLISHED BY HIGGINBOTHAM & CO. ORIENTAL LITHOGRAPHIC PRESS MADRAS 1872. LITHOGRAPHED BY ALEX: BARREN,

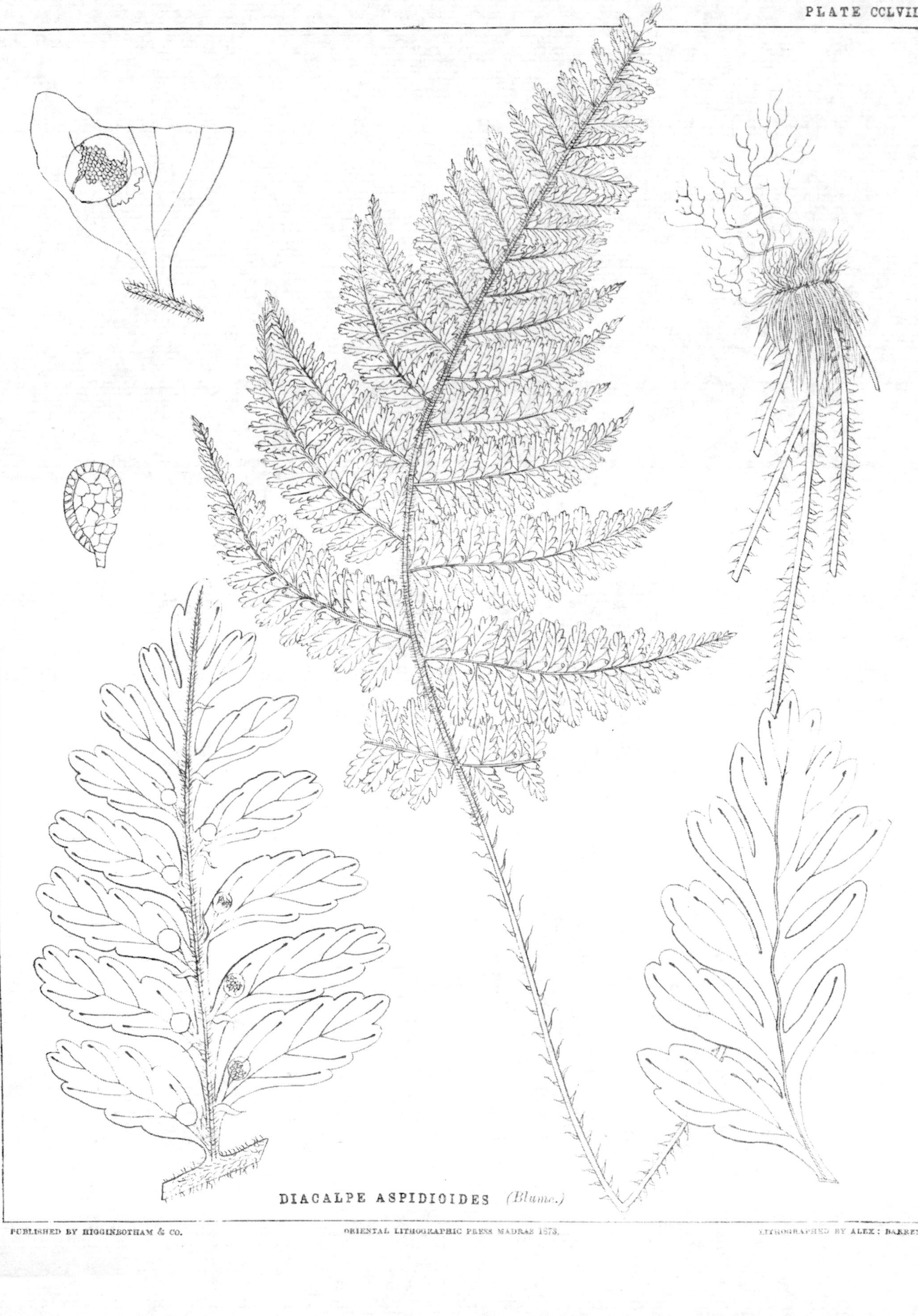

DIACALPE ASPIDIOIDES (*Blume.*)

PUBLISHED BY HIGGINBOTHAM & CO. ORIENTAL LITHOGRAPHIC PRESS MADRAS 1873. LITHOGRAPHED BY ALEX: BARREN.

PLATE CCLVIII

DENNSTŒDTIA DELTOIDEA (*Moore.*)

PUBLISHED BY HIGGINBOTHAM & CO.

ORIENTAL LITHOGRAPHIC PRESS MADRAS 1872.

LITHOGRAPHED BY ALEX : BARREN,

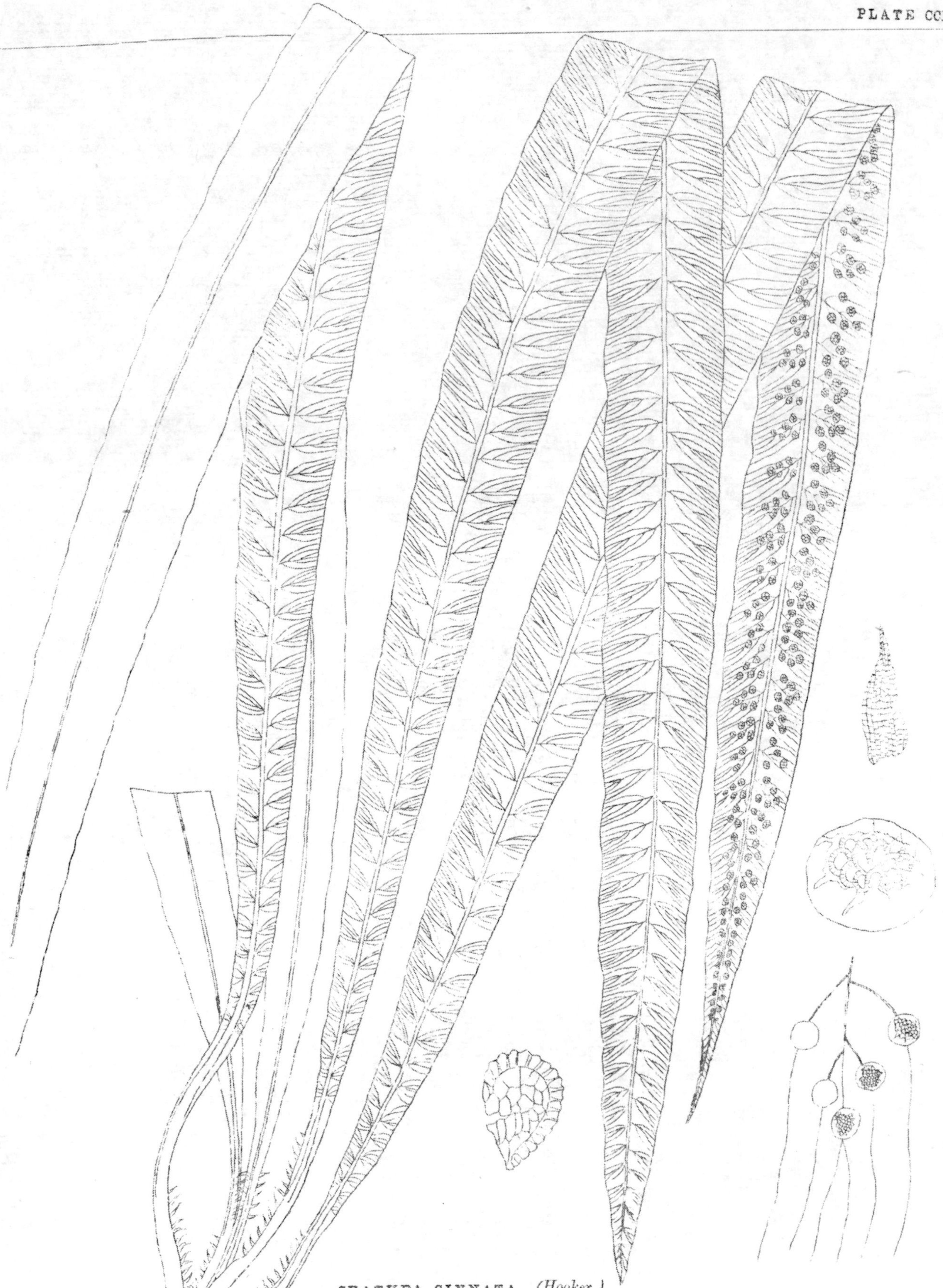

CYATHEA SINNATA (*Hooker.*)

PUBLISHED BY HIGGINBOTHAM & CO. ORIENTAL LITHOGRAPHIC PRESS MADRAS 1872. LITHOGRAPHED BY ALEX. BARREN,

CYATHEA HOOKERI *(Thwaites.)*

PUBLISHED BY HIGGINBOTHAM & CO. ORIENTAL LITHOGRAPHIC PRESS MADRAS 1872. LITHOGRAPHED BY ALEX : BARREN.

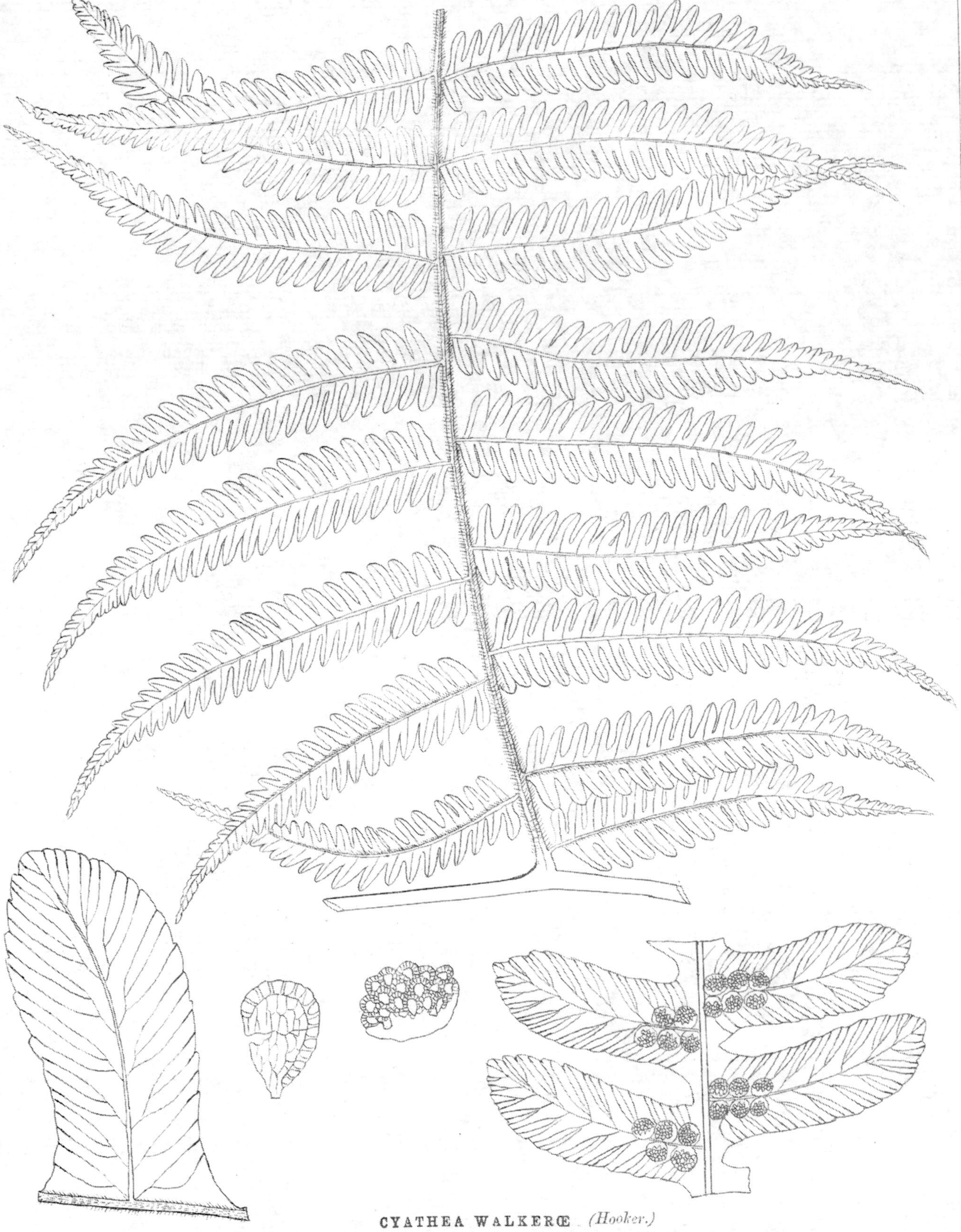

CYATHEA WALKERŒ. (*Hooker.*)

PUBLISHED BY HIGGINBOTHAM & CO. ORIENTAL LITHOGRAPHIC PRESS MADRAS 1872. LITHOGRAPHED BY ALEX: BARREN,

PLATE CCLXII

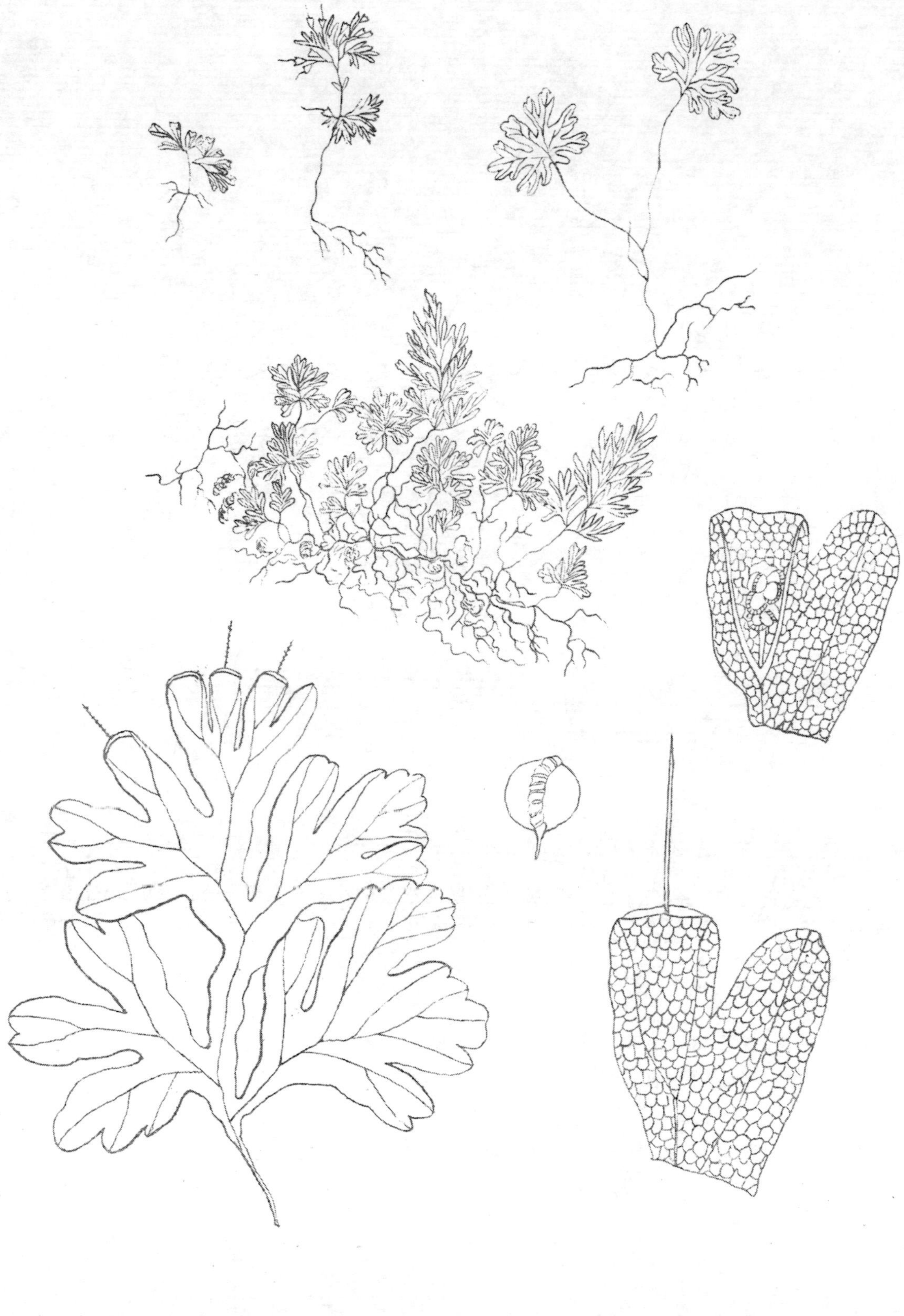

TRICHOMANES PROLIFERUM (*Blume*)

PUBLISHED BY HIGGINBOTHAM & CO. ORIENTAL LITHOGRAPHIC PRESS MADRAS 1873 LITHOGRAPHED BY ALEX: BARREN,

TRICHOMANES GLAUCO-FUSCUM (*Hooker.*)

PUBLISHED BY HIGGINBOTHAM & CO. ORIENTAL LITHOGRAPHIC PRESS MADRAS 1873. LITHOGRAPHED BY ALEX: BARREN,

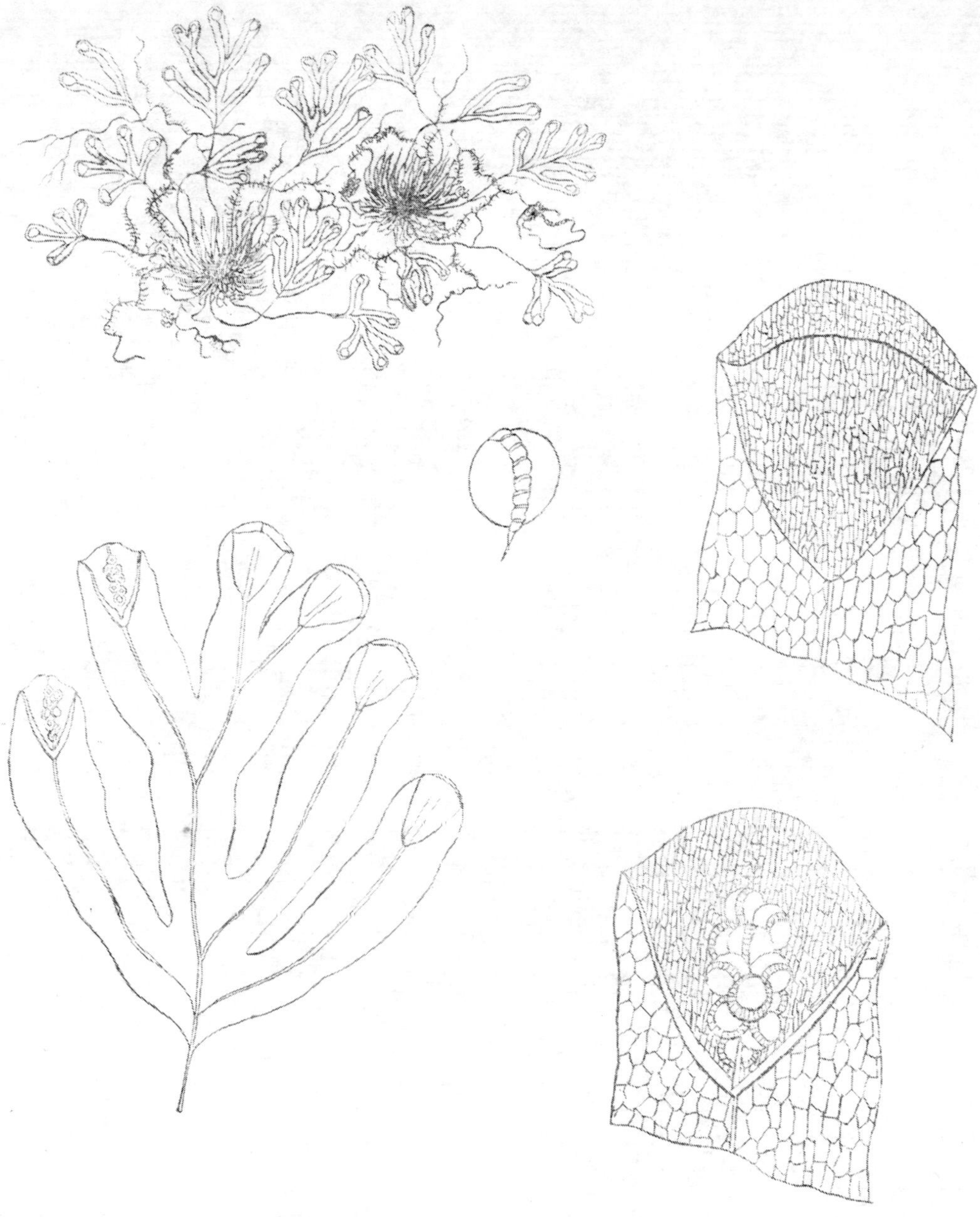

TRICHOMANES CORTICOLA *(Hooker.)*

PUBLISHED BY HIGGINBOTHAM & CO. ORIENTAL LITHOGRAPHIC PRESS MADRAS 1873. LITHOGRAPHED BY ALEX: BARREN.

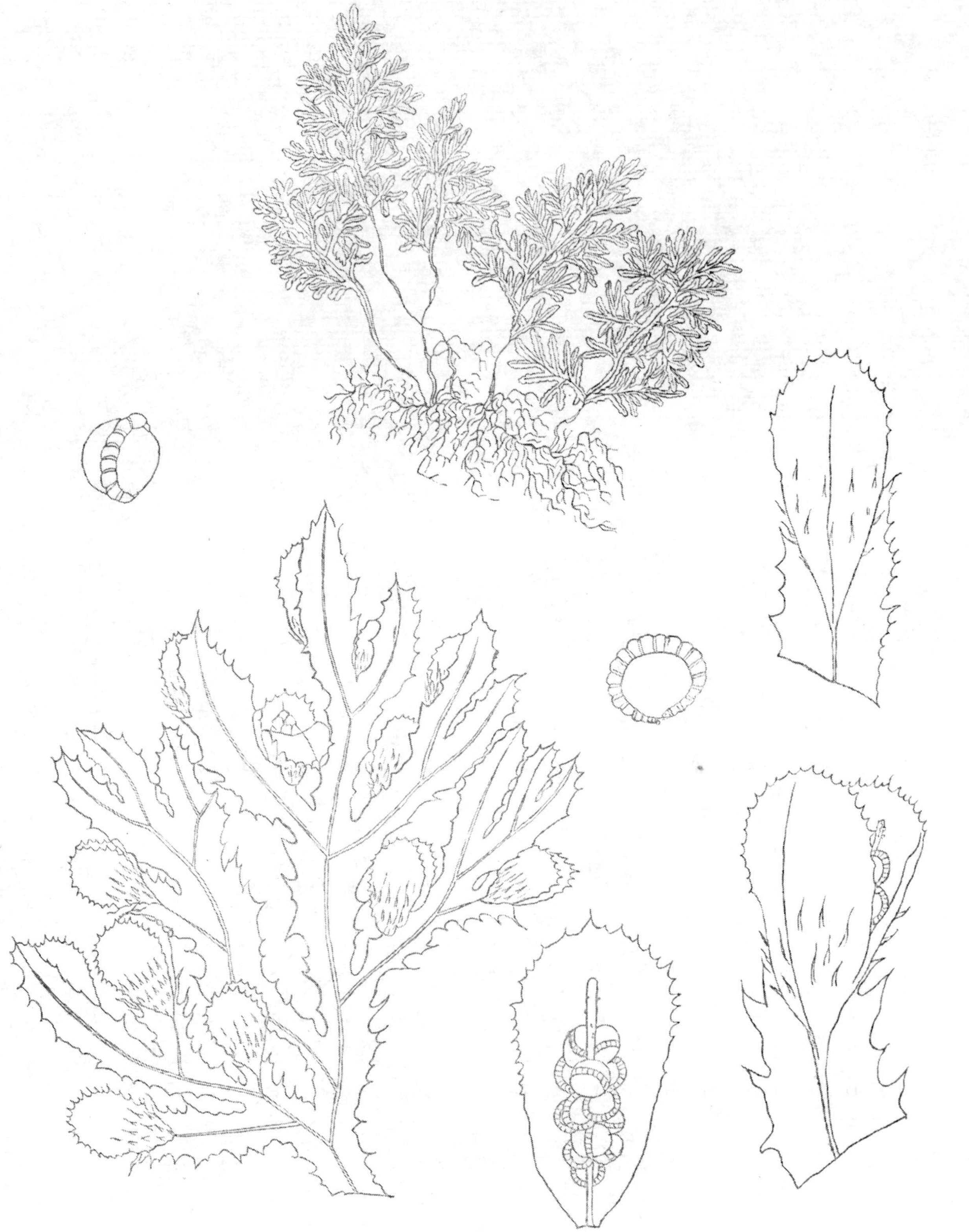

HYMENOPHYLLUM TUNBRIDGENSE (Sw.)

PUBLISHED BY HIGGINBOTHAM & CO. ORIENTAL LITHOGRAPHIC PRESS MADRAS 1873. LITHOGRAPHED BY ALEX: BARREN,

HYMENOPHYLLUM BLUMEANUM (*Spr.*)

PUBLISHED BY HIGGINBOTHAM & CO. ORIENTAL LITHOGRAPHIC PRESS MADRAS 1873. LITHOGRAPHED BY ALEX: BARREN,

HYMENOPHYLLUM POLYANTHOS (*Sw.*)

PUBLISHED BY HIGGINBOTHAM & CO. ORIENTAL LITHOGRAPHIC PRESS MADRAS 1872. LITHOGRAPHED BY ALEX: BARREN,

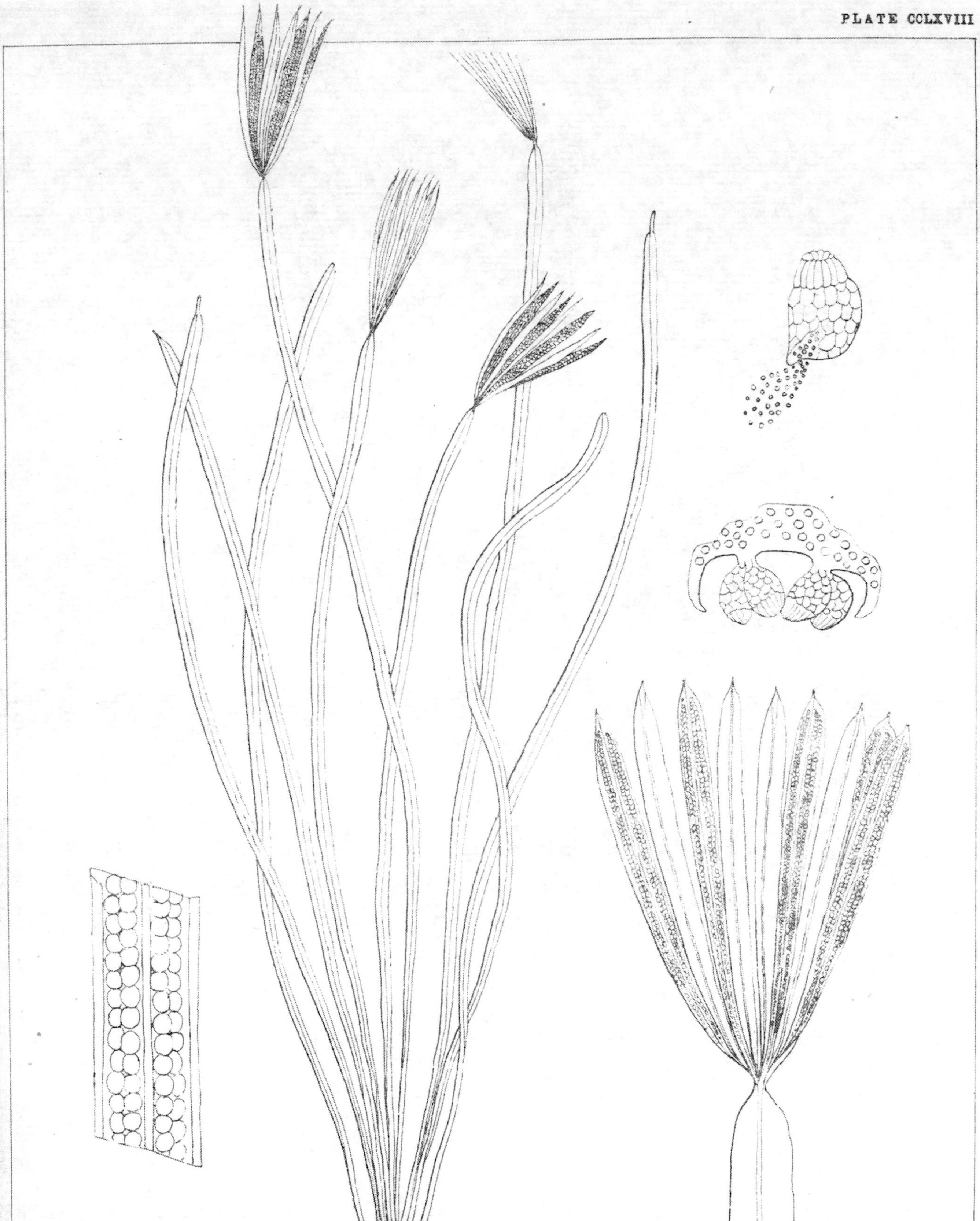

SCHIZŒA DIGITATA (*Sw.*)

PUBLISHED BY HIGGINBOTHAM & CO. ORIENTAL LITHOGRAPHIC PRESS MADRAS 1872. LITHOGRAPHED BY ALEX: BARREN,

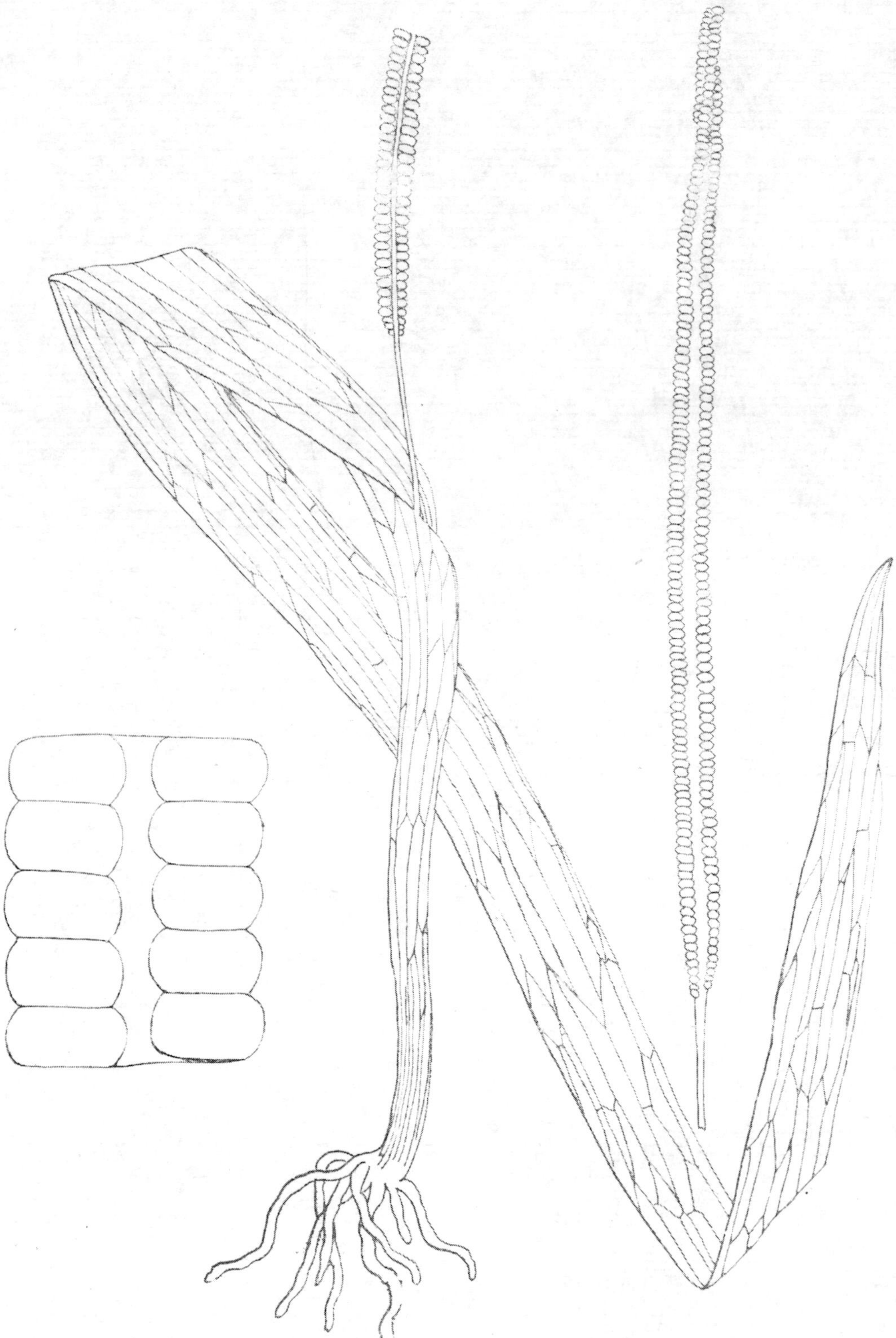

OPHIOGLOSSUM PENDULUM (*Linn.*)

PUBLISHED BY HIGGINBOTHAM & CO. ORIENTAL LITHOGRAPHIC PRESS MADRAS 1872. LITHOGRAPHED BY ALEX : BARREN.

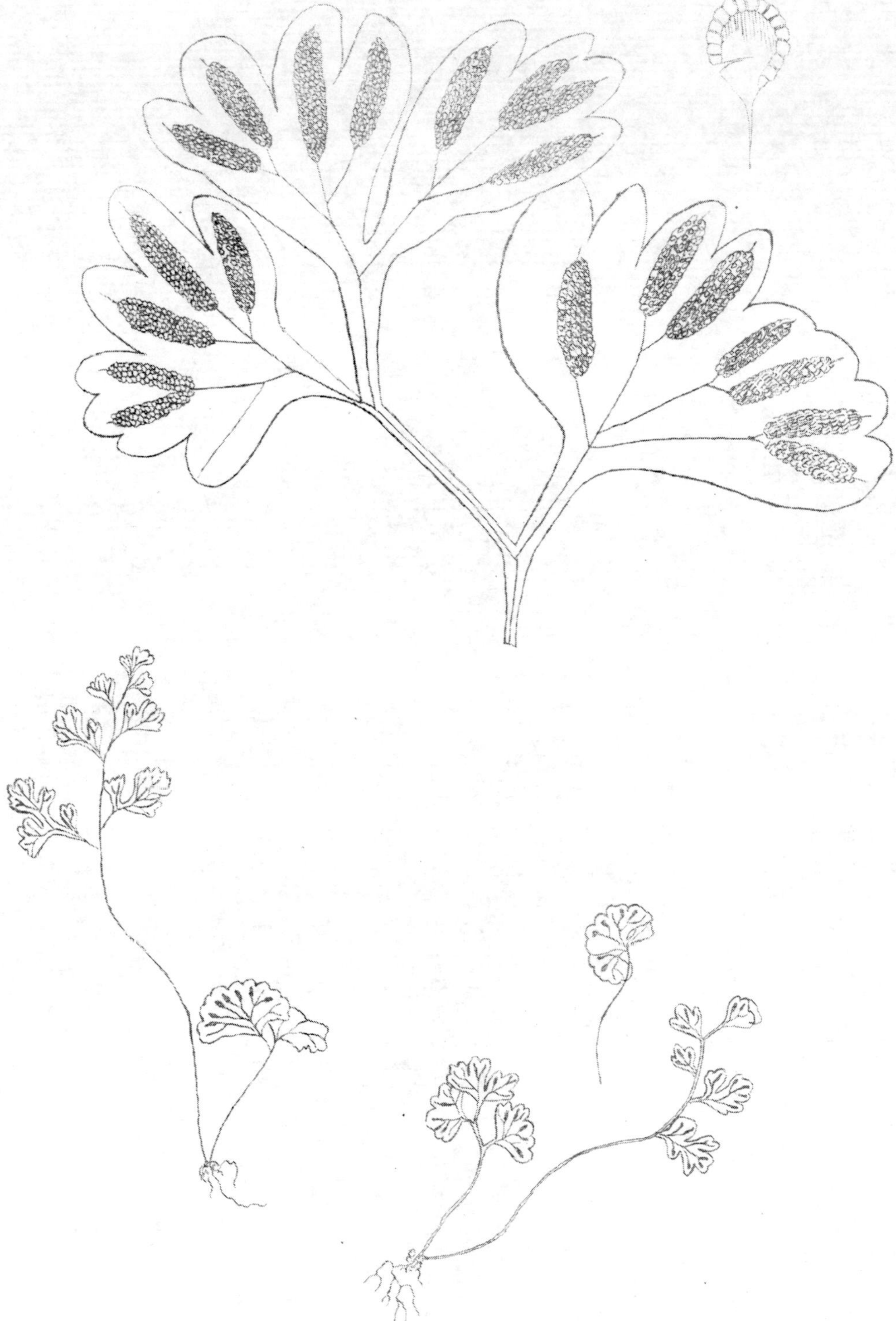

GYMNOGRAMMA LEPTOPHYLLA (Desv.)

PUBLISHED BY HIGGINBOTHAM & CO. ORIENTAL LITHOGRAPHIC PRESS MADRAS 1873. LITHOGRAPHED BY ALEX : BARREN,

PLATE CCLXXI

LASTREA UNDULATA *(Thwaites)*

PUBLISHED BY HIGGINBOTHAM & CO.

ORIENTAL LITHOGRAPHIC PRESS MADRAS 1873.

LITHOGRAPHED BY ALEX: BARREN,

CORRECTIONS

IN THE

NOMENCLATURE OF FERNS OF SOUTHERN INDIA.

Ferns of Southern India Plate.	*For.*			*Read.*	
7.	Trichomanes Filicula	... Linn.	=	Trichomanes pyxidiferum	...L.
27.	Schizoloma recurvatum	...Moore.	=	Schizoloma nitens	...Bl.
52.	Antrophyum reticulatum	... Kaulf.	=	Antrophyum plantagineum	...Cav.
68.	Botrychium subcarnosum	... Wall.	=	Botrychium daucifolium	...Wall.
71.	Ophioglossum parvifolium	... L.	=	Ophioglossum nudicaule	...L. fil.
73.	Peranema cyatheoides	... Don.	=	Sphæropteris barbata	...Wall.
86.	Nephrodium abruptum	... Presl.	=	Nephrodium pennigerum	...Hook.
90.	Nephrodium terminans	...J. Sm.	=	Nephrodium pteroides	...J. Sm.
91.	Oleandra neriiformis	... Cav.	=	Oleandra musæfolia	...Kze.
92.	Nephrolepis tuberosa	... Presl.	=	Nephrolepis cordifolia	...L.
95.	Lastrea eriocarpa	... Don.	=	Lastrea odorata	...Bory.
97.	Lastrea divisa	... Hook.	=	Lastrea Boryana	...Willd.
99.	Lastrea flaccida	... Hook.	=	Lastrea setigera	...Bl.
107.	Lastrea ochthodes—β tylodes	... Kze.	=	Lastrea tylodes	...Kze.
108.	Lastrea spectabilis	...J. Sm.	=	Lastrea syrmatica	...Willd.
110.	Lastrea gracilescens	... Hook.	=	Lastrea Beddomii	...Baker.
113.	Lastrea intermedia	... Bedd.	=	Lastrea elongata—vary montana	...Bedd.
133.	Asplenium multijugum	... Wall.	=	Asplenium normale	...Wall.
151.	Athyrium falcatum	... Bedd.	=	Athyrium grammitoides	...Hook.
155.	Athyrium pectinatum	... Wall.	=	Athyrium aspidioides	...Schl.
163.	Diplazium polypodioides	... Bl.	=	Diplazium asperum	...Bl.
166.	Polypodium parvulum	... Bory.	=	Polypodium repandulum	...Mett.
169.	Polypodium nigrocarpum	... Bedd.	=	Lastrea scabrosa	...Kze.
175.	Pleopeltis oxyloba	... Wall.	=	Pleopeltis trifida	...Don.
179.	Pleopeltis tridactyla	... Wall.	=	Pleopeltis pteropus—var. minor	...Bl.
180.	Pleopeltis Wightiana	... Wall.	=	Pleopeltis linearis	...Thunb.
181.	Pleopeltis lepidota	... Willd.	=	Pleopeltis lanceolata	...Linn.
183.	Niphobolus porosus	... Wall.	=	Niphobolus fissus	...Bl.
186.	Niphobolus nummularifolius	... Mett.	=	Drymoglossum piloselloides—vary.	...Mett.
202.	Pæcilopteris repanda	...J. Sm.	=	Pæcilopteris contaminans	...Wall.
226.	Asplenium spathulinum	...J. Sm.	=	Asplenium affine	...Sw.
234. } 235. }	Polypodium Walkeræ	... Hook.	=	Lastrea Walkeræ	...Hook.
243.	Sagenia gigantea minor	... Hook.	=	Sagenia membranacea	...Hook.
247.	Lastrea concinna	... Thw.	=	Lastrea Thwaitesii	...Baker.
249.	Lastrea Blumei	... Hook.	=	Lastrea intermedia	...Bl.
251.	Nephrolepis obliterata	... Hook.	=	Nephrolepis ramosa	...Beauv.
254.	Microlepia proxima	... Bl.	=	Microlepia Thwaitesii	...Baker.
263.	Trichomanes glauco-fuscum	... Hook.	=	Trichomanes pallidum	...Bl.
267.	Hymenophyllum polyanthos	... Sw.	=	Hymenophyllum emersum	...Baker.

INDEX OF ALL THE SPECIES FIGURED IN "THE FERNS OF SOUTHERN INDIA" AND IN "THE FERNS OF BRITISH INDIA."

Genus	Species	Authority	Ferns of Southern India		Ferns of British India	
Diplazium	Sorzogonense	Presl.	...	...	11	246
"	speciosum	Bl.	...	...	11	290
"	subserratum	Bl.	...	...	11	289
"	sylvaticum	Presl.	1	161		
"	thelypteroides	Presl.	...	...	11	68
"	Thwaitesii	Hook.	...	...	11	291
"	tomentosum	Mett.	...	...	11	195
"	Zeylanicum	Hook.	1	228		
Callipteris	esculenta	Houlst et Moore.	1	164		
"	prolifera	Bory.	...	...	11	70
"	Smithiana	Baker.	...	...	11	332
Anisogonium	cordifolium	Mett.	...	...	11	331
"	heterophlebium	Mett.	...	...	11	329
"	lineolatum	Mett.	...	...	11	330
	§ 14. DIDYMOCHLÆNEÆ.					
Didymochlæna	lunulata	Desv.	...	...	11	15
Mesochlæna	Javanica	R. Br.	...	...	11	344
	§ 15. HEMIONITIDEÆ.					
Antrophyum	latifolium	Bl.	...	...	11	176
"	plantagineum	Cav.	1	52		
"	parvulum	Hook.	...	...	11	267
"	reticulatum	Kaulf.	1	231		
Hemionitis	cordata	Roxb.	1	53		
Dictyocline	Griffithii	H. f. et. T.	...	...	11	155
Syngramma	alismæfolia	Hook.	...	...	11	240
"	vestita	Moore.	...	...	11	154
"	Wallichii	Hook.	...	...	11	153
	§ 16. GYMNOGRAMMEÆ.					
Gymnogramma	Andersonii	Bedd.	...	...	11	190
"	Javanica	Bl.	...	...	11	57
"	leptophylia	Desv.	1	270		
"	opaca	Spr.	...	...	11	238
"	serrulata	Bl.	1	232		
Grammitis	aurita	Hook.	...	...	11	152
"	microphylla	Hook.	...	...	11	148
"	totta	Presl.	1	49		
Calymmodon	cucullatus	Presl.	1	233		
Stegnogramma	aspidioides	Bl.	...	...	11	149
Loxogramma	avenia	Baker.	...	...	11	266
"	lanceolata	Presl.	1	51		
"	involuta	Presl.	1	50		
Selliguea	caudiformis. Hook. description only					
"	*decurrens, Hook. see S. elliptica.*					
"	elliptica	Thunb.	...	...	11	150
"	Feei	Bory.	...	...	11	151
"	Hamiltoniana	Wall.	...	...	11	239
	§ 17. PLATYLOMEÆ.					
Platyloma	falcatum vary. β setosum	J. Sm.	1	22		
Plagiogyria	adnata	Bl.	...	...	11	51
"	euphlebia	Kze.	...	...	11	165
"	glauca	Bl.	...	...	11	90
"	pycnophylla	Kze.	...	...	11	52
Cryptogramma	Brunoniana	Wall.	...	...	11	164
	§ 18. POLYPODIEÆ.					
Allosorus	Stelleri	Rupr.	...	...	11	73
Struthiopteris	orientalis	Hook.	...	...	11	171
Nothochlæna	Marantæ	Br.	...	...	11	1
Polypodium	auriculatum	Wall.	...	...	11	203
"	appendiculatum	Wall.	...	...	11	256
"	dareæforme	Hook.	...	...	11	174
"	decorum	Brack.	1	238		
Polypodium	distans	Don.	1	168	& 11	39
"	Dryopteris	L.	...	...	11	74
"	*elongatum, Wall. see Lastrea cuspidata.*					
"	erubescens	Wall.	...	...	11	213
"	fuscatum	Bl.	...	...	11	324
"	glandulosum	Hook.	1	239		
"	hirtellum	Bl.	...	...	11	172 & 212
"	Khasyanum	Hook.	...	...	11	173
"	*lasiosorum, see P. hirtellum.*					
"	*nigrocarpum, Bedd. see Lastrea scabrosa.*					
"	obliquatum	Bl.	1	167		
"	*obscurum, Hook. see Lastrea sagenioides.*					
"	ornatum	Wall.	1	171		
"	parasiticum	Mett.	1	165		
"	*parvulum, Bory. see Poylp. repandulum.*					
"	repandulum	Mett.	1	166	& 11	189
"	rufescens	Bl.	1	236		
"	rugulosum	Labil.	1	170		
"	Scottii	Bedd.	...	...	11	345
"	sessilifolium	Hook.	...	...	11	119
"	subdigitatum	Bl.	...	...	11	229
"	subevenosum	Baker.	...	...	11	323
"	subfalcatum	Bl.	...	...	11	76
"	Thwaitesii	Bedd.	...	...	11	188
"	trichomanoides	Sw.	...	...	11	2
"	*Walkeræ, see Lastrea Walkeræ.*		...	...		
"	Zeylanicum	Mett.	1	237		
Goniopteris	*lineata, Coleb. see Nephrodium Moulmeinense.*					
"	multilineata	Wall.	...	...	11	231
"	*Penangiana, Hook. see Nephrodium Moulmeinense.*					
"	prolifera	Presl.	1	172		
"	urophylla	Wall.	1	239		
Dictyopteris	Barberi	Hook.	...	...	11	322
"	difforme	Bl.	1	118	& 11	77
"	*irregularis, Persl. see D. difforme.*					
"	tenerifrons	Hook.	...	...	11	4
Goniophlebium	amænum	Wall.	...	...	11	5
"	argutum	Wall.	...	...	11	6
"	*cuspidatum, Don. see G. persicæfolium.*					
"	lachnopus	Wall.	...	...	11	163
"	molle	Bedd.	...	...	11	206
"	persicæfolium	Desv.	...	...	11	79
"	subauriculatum	Bl.	...	...	11	78
"	verrucosum	Wall.	...	...	11	257
Niphobolus	acrostichoides	Sw.	...	...	11	81
"	adnascens.	Sw.	1	184		
"	*angustatus, Sw. see Pleopeltis angustatus.*					
"	Boothii	Hook.	...	...	11	258
"	*costatus, see Niphob. stigmosus.*					
"	*detergibilis, see Niphob. flocculosus.*					
"	fissus	Bl.	1	183		
"	floccigerus, Mett. description only					
"	flocculosus	Don.	...	...	11	162
"	Gardneri	Mett.	1	241		
"	Lingua	Sw.	1	240		
"	lævis	J. Sm.	...	...	11	161
"	nummularifolius		...	...	11	320
"	Penangianus	Hook.	...	...	11	121
"	*porosus, see N. fissus.*					
"	*sphærocephalus, see Pleopeltis angustatus.*					
"	stigmosus	Sw.	...	...	11	120
"	subfurfuraceus	Hook.	...	...	11	259
Pleopeltis	accedens	Bl.	...	...	11	215

INDEX.

A

B

C

D

M

N

O

P

R

S

T

U

V

W

X